STANTON

Lincoln's War Secretary

WALTER STAHR

SIMON & SCHUSTER

New York London Toronto Sydney New Delhi

Simon & Schuster
1230 Avenue of the Americas
New York, NY 10020

First Simon & Schuster hardcover edition August 2017

SIMON & SCHUSTER and colophon are registered trademarks
of Simon & Schuster, Inc.

For information about special discounts for bulk purchases,
please contact Simon & Schuster Special Sales at 1-866-506-1949
or business@simonandschuster.com.

The Simon & Schuster Speakers Bureau can bring authors to
your live event. For more information or to book an event
contact the Simon & Schuster Speakers Bureau at 1-866-248-3049
or visit our website at www.simonspeakers.com.

Interior design by Lewelin Polanco

Manufactured in the United States of America

1 3 5 7 9 10 8 6 4 2

Library of Congress Cataloging-in-Publication Data

Names: Stahr, Walter, author.
Title: Stanton : Lincoln's war secretary / Walter Stahr.
Description: New York : Simon & Schuster, 2017. | Includes bibliographical references
and index.
Identifiers: LCCN 2017022628 (print) | LCCN 2017024010 (ebook) | ISBN 9781476739328
(ebook) | ISBN 9781476739304 (hardback) | ISBN 9781476739311 (trade paperback)
Subjects: LCSH: Stanton, Edwin M. (Edwin McMasters), 1814–1869. | Cabinet officers—
United States—Biography. | United States. War Department—Biography. | Statesmen—United
States—Biography. | United States—History—Civil War, 1861–1865—Biography. |
Reconstruction (U.S. history, 1865–1877)—Biography. | United States—Politics
and government—1861–1865. | United States—Politics and government—1865-1869. |
Lincoln, Abraham, 1809-1865—Friends and associates. | BISAC: BIOGRAPHY &
AUTOBIOGRAPHY / Political. | HISTORY / United States / 19th Century.
| HISTORY / United States / Civil War Period (1850–1877).
Classification: LCC E467.1.S8 (ebook) | LCC E467.1.S8 S73 2017 (print) |
DDC 973.7092 [B] —dc23
LC record available at https://lccn.loc.gov/2017022628

ISBN 978-1-4767-3930-4
ISBN 978-1-4767-3932-8 (ebook)

For my wife, Masami Miyauchi Stahr

Contents

Cast of Characters

Joseph Barnes (1817–1883). Barnes served as a military doctor during the Mexican War and in various army posts thereafter before Stanton made him head of the Medical Department and surgeon general in 1863. Stanton and Barnes became close friends, and Barnes tended Stanton in his last illness.

Edward Bates (1793–1869). A respected Missouri lawyer and judge, Bates was an outside candidate for the Republican presidential nomination in 1860. After the election Lincoln made Bates his attorney general; he resigned and retired in late 1864.

Henry Ward Beecher (1813–1887). Son of the preacher Lyman Beecher, brother of the author Harriet Beecher Stowe, Beecher became a famous preacher and speaker in his own right. Stanton arranged for him to speak on April 14, 1865, at the ceremony to raise the Union flag again at Fort Sumter.

John Bingham (1815–1900). An Ohio lawyer and Whig political leader, Bingham debated Stanton in the election of 1840. Bingham represented Ohio in Congress from 1855 through 1863, worked with Stanton as a judge advocate in the War Department, then returned to Congress, where he was one of the principal authors of the Fourteenth Amendment.

Jeremiah Black (1810–1883). Black became Stanton's friend and patron when Black was attorney general for Buchanan, sending Stanton to California to handle the major land cases there. In late 1860, when Black was promoted to secretary of state, he persuaded Buchanan to bring Stanton into the administration as attorney general.

Montgomery Blair (1813–1883). Member of a powerful political family, Blair practiced law in Missouri and Maryland, then served as postmaster general for Lincoln. He hated Stanton.

Orville Hickman Browning (1806–1881). An Illinois lawyer and political leader, Browning was appointed in 1861 to fill the Senate seat vacated by the death of Stephen Douglas. From 1863 through 1866 Browning was a Washington lawyer, then served Johnson from 1866 through 1869 as interior secretary.

James Buchanan (1791–1868). On paper Buchanan was the best qualified president of the nineteenth century, having been a representative, senator, secretary of state, and minister to Great Britain. After his disastrous single term, he retired to his Pennsylvania farm, writing frequent letters to Stanton, until Stanton switched sides to join the Lincoln cabinet.

Benjamin Butler (1818–1893). Originally from New Hampshire, Butler practiced law and politics in Massachusetts and was one of Lincoln's many political generals. He coined the term "contraband" and became infamous for his military occupation of New Orleans. After the Civil War he was a member of the House and a manager in the Johnson impeachment.

Simon Cameron (1799–1889). An "amiable scoundrel" from Pennsylvania, Cameron lasted less than a year as Lincoln's first secretary of war. After the war he created a political machine in Pennsylvania, serving in the Senate from 1867 through 1877, when he was succeeded by his son James Cameron.

Zachariah Chandler (1813–1879). Chandler was a four-term senator from Michigan, one of the leaders of the Joint Committee on the Conduct of the War, and then a leading Radical during Reconstruction.

Salmon P. Chase (1808–1873). Born in New Hampshire, Chase moved to Ohio as a young man, practiced law, and entered politics. He and Stanton were very close in the late 1840s, although Chase was a Free Soiler and Stanton a Democrat. Chase was elected senator in 1849, elected governor in 1855, and appointed secretary of the treasury in 1861. He and Stanton were again close in later years, when Chase was chief justice.

Charles Dana (1819–1897). A journalist before and after the Civil War, Dana served as Stanton's most trusted assistant secretary during the war, spending many months with Grant at his headquarters and sending detailed reports to Stanton.

Henry Winter Davis (1817–1865). A Maryland lawyer and member of Congress, Davis was a leading Radical Republican in the latter phases of the Civil War. When he died in December 1865, Stanton was one of the pallbearers at his funeral.

John Adams Dix (1798–1879). Dix became friends with Stanton during the weeks they served together in the Buchanan cabinet. Dix was a political general, serving most of the war in New York City, where he received Stanton's frequent messages for the press.

Thomas Eckert (1825–1910). A telegraph engineer before the war, Eckert was in charge of telegraph operations for McClellan in 1862, then served as head of Stanton's telegraph office until 1867. After the war he rose to be president of the nation's largest telegraph company, Western Union.

Charles Ellet Jr. (1810–1862). A brilliant engineer, Ellet built the Wheeling Bridge and stymied Stanton's efforts to have the bridge raised or removed. During the war Ellet worked closely with Stanton to create a fleet of reinforced naval rams, commanded them in the Battle of Memphis, and was mortally wounded.

William Pitt Fessenden (1806–1869). Stanton persuaded Fessenden, a longtime senator from Maine, to serve as Lincoln's second secretary of the treasury. Fessenden soon returned to the Senate, where he provided one of the key votes against the removal of Johnson.

Ulysses S. Grant (1822–1885). Grant graduated from West Point, served in the Mexican War, then struggled in civilian life. He rejoined the army in early 1861, achieved success and rapid promotion, and worked closely with Stanton as commanding general of the Union Army. When Johnson suspended Stanton in 1867, Grant served as interim secretary of war, yielding the office back to Stanton in early 1868. Stanton campaigned for Grant in the 1868 election, and Grant eventually rewarded him with an appointment to the Supreme Court.

Henry Halleck (1815–1872). Scholar, lawyer, and army officer, Halleck first met Stanton in California, where Stanton sued him in a land case. Lincoln brought Halleck to Washington in 1862 as general in chief, but he functioned more as a "first-rate clerk" to Lincoln, Stanton, and Grant.

John Hay (1838–1905). Hay was one of Lincoln's three private secretaries, living in the White House during the Civil War. Later in his life Hay was secretary of state under Presidents McKinley and Roosevelt.

Ethan Allen Hitchcock (1798–1870). Hitchcock was a career army officer who retired in 1855 to pursue religious and philosophical studies. Summoned back to Washington by Stanton in early 1862, he was an important military adviser to the secretary.

Joseph Holt (1807–1894). Stanton met Holt when they worked together in the Buchanan administration. Stanton appointed Holt as the nation's senior military lawyer, the judge advocate general, in late 1862. They worked closely on many legal cases, notably the Lincoln assassination trial.

Samuel Hooper (1808–1875). A Massachusetts merchant and member of Congress, Hooper was one of Stanton's closest friends in the later years of Stanton's life.

Andrew Johnson (1808–1875). A tailor by trade, Johnson worked his way up in Tennessee politics, eventually representing that state in the Senate. From 1862 through early 1865, Johnson was the military governor of Tennessee, reporting to Stanton as the secretary of war. Johnson then became vice president and, with the death of Lincoln in April 1865, president. Disagreements between Johnson and Stanton about reconstruction policy led to the impeachment and near-removal of the president.

Francis Lieber (1798–1872). Born in Berlin, Lieber fought in the Waterloo campaign and for Greek independence. He moved to the United States, studied and taught in Massachusetts, South Carolina, and New York City, and became the nation's leading expert on the law of war. Lieber was a firm friend of Stanton, whom he favored for president in 1868.

Abraham Lincoln (1809–1865). Stanton first met Lincoln in Cincinnati in 1855, when they were co-counsel on a patent case. Although Stanton was a Democrat, with limited administrative experience, Lincoln turned to him when Cameron failed as secretary of war and relied on and trusted Stanton until his assassination.

George Brinton McClellan (1826–1885). McClellan and Stanton became friends in the summer of 1861, when the "Young Napoleon" came to Washington to lead the Army of the Potomac. When Stanton became secretary of war, he joined Lincoln in pressing McClellan to attack. McClellan soon hated Stanton and blamed him for his defeats.

George Wythe McCook (1821–1877). McCook studied law with Stanton in Steubenville, becoming his friend and partner. He fought in both the Mexican War and the Civil War, one of the "fighting McCooks," a family that contributed a dozen senior officers to the Union cause.

George Gordon Meade (1815–1872). A career army officer, Meade was appointed to head the Army of the Potomac on the eve of Gettysburg. He retained command of this army until the end of the war, although Grant made many of the tactical decisions starting in early 1864.

Montgomery Meigs (1816–1892). An army engineer before the war, Meigs was appointed quartermaster general in 1861 and worked closely with Stanton to ensure that the Union Army was properly supplied.

John Pope (1822–1892). Stanton supported General Pope against General McClellan in 1862, but after the disastrous Second Battle of Bull Run, Pope was transferred to the West to fight Indians.

William Rosecrans (1819–1898). Another West Point graduate, Rosecrans commanded mainly in the West. It was to shore up Rosecrans in Chattanooga that Stanton transferred 20,000 troops westward by rail in late 1863.

Thomas Scott (1823–1881). Stanton inherited Scott as an assistant secretary from Cameron and used him in early 1862 to solve railroad and recruiting issues. Scott resigned but returned to federal service to help with the 1863 rail movement.

William Henry Seward (1801–1872). A governor of New York, then a federal senator, Seward worked closely with Stanton in the secession crisis. Lincoln appointed Seward secretary of state, and he retained that post under Johnson, so that he and Stanton were cabinet colleagues from 1862 through 1868. Seward was Stanton's closest friend in the cabinet.

William Tecumseh Sherman (1820–1891). Stanton and Sherman quarreled over Sherman's policies toward blacks and then over Sherman's peace terms with General Johnston. Yet Sherman and Stanton cooperated in many ways, and Stanton provided Sherman's army the support it needed to make its famous marches through Georgia and the Carolinas.

Bessie Barnes Stanton (1863–1939). Stanton's youngest child, born in the midst of the Civil War, Bessie lived until the eve of World War II. She married an Episcopal priest, Henry Habersham, and had four children.

Edwin Lamson Stanton (1842–1877). The only surviving child of Stanton's first marriage, Eddie studied at Kenyon College, worked in the War Department, studied law with his father, then practiced law in Washington. Just before his death, friends committed him to the Washington insane asylum.

Eleanor Adams Stanton (1857–1910). "Ellie," the first child of Stanton's second marriage, married Col. James Bush and had two surviving children.

Ellen Hutchison Stanton (1830–1873). Stanton met his second wife through mutual friends in Pittsburgh in the early 1850s. He wooed her for several years, and they married in the summer of 1856. They moved to Washington later that year and lived there the rest of Stanton's life.

Lewis Hutchison Stanton (1860–1938). The second child of Stanton and his second wife, Lewis attended Princeton University and married Adele Townsend of New Orleans, where he worked as a broker. He was survived by four children, including the artist Gideon Townsend Stanton.

Mary Lamson Stanton (1818–1844). Stanton met his first wife at the Episcopal Church in Columbus, Ohio, where they married in 1836. They had two children, one of whom died young. Mary died in 1844.

Charles Sumner (1811–1874). Stanton met Sumner in the early 1850s, when he was a young antislavery senator from Massachusetts. The scholarly, serious Sumner was Stanton's closest friend among the senators during and after the Civil War.

Benjamin Tappan (1773–1857). Judge Tappan was Stanton's friend, mentor, and law partner. When Tappan served in the Senate, from 1839 through 1845, Stanton was his political deputy in Ohio.

Lorenzo Thomas (1804–1875). Thomas was the adjutant general, the officer responsible for personnel paperwork, when Stanton became secretary of war. Although Stanton disliked Thomas personally, he recognized his strengths and used him to recruit black soldiers. In early 1868,

President Johnson attempted to replace Stanton with Thomas, an attempt that led to the impeachment and near-removal of Johnson.

Benjamin Wade (1800–1875). Wade was a Radical Republican senator from Ohio and a political friend and ally of Stanton. Because Johnson had no vice president, Wade, as president pro tem of the Senate, would have become president if the Senate had convicted and removed Johnson.

Gideon Welles (1802–1878). A lawyer and journalist from Connecticut, Welles was secretary of the navy for both Lincoln and Johnson. He kept a detailed diary, filled with criticism of Stanton.

Henry Wilson (1812–1875). Wilson was a Republican senator from Massachusetts, head of the Senate Military Affairs Committee, and thus in daily contact with Stanton during and after the Civil War.

Pamphila Stanton Wolcott (1827–1899). Stanton's youngest sister, and the only one of his siblings to outlive him, Pamphila married Christopher Wolcott, who served as one of Stanton's assistant secretaries and died during the Civil War. Late in her life she wrote a biography, never published, of her brother.

Horatio Woodman (1829–1875). A Boston intellectual and editor, friend of Louis Agassiz, Richard Henry Dana Jr., and other eminent men, Woodman became a strong supporter of Stanton during the Civil War.

Oella Stanton Tappan Wright (1822–1862). Oella, Stanton's sister, married Dr. Benjamin Tappan Jr.; the marriage ended in a bitter divorce, then she remarried. She died in the midst of the Civil War.

Chronology

December 19, 1814: Stanton born in Steubenville, Ohio.

December 30, 1827: Father, David Stanton, dies.

Spring 1831–Fall 1832: Stanton attends Kenyon College.

Fall 1832–Fall 1833: Stanton works in Columbus bookstore; meets Mary Lamson.

Fall 1833–Fall 1836: Stanton studies law in Steubenville.

December 31, 1836: Stanton marries Mary Lamson.

Spring 1837–Fall 1839: Stanton practices law in Cadiz, Ohio; returns to Steubenville.

March 11, 1840: Daughter Lucy Lamson Stanton born.

August 24, 1841: Lucy Lamson Stanton dies.

August 12, 1842: Son Edwin Lamson Stanton born.

March 13, 1844: Mary Lamson Stanton dies.

September 23, 1846: Brother, Darwin Stanton, commits suicide.

Fall 1847: Stanton moves to Pittsburgh.

February 28, 1850: Stanton argues the Wheeling Bridge case in the Supreme Court, his first case in the high court.

June 25, 1856: Stanton marries Ellen Hutchison; moves that fall to Washington.

March 1857: Buchanan becomes president; Stanton starts doing federal legal work.

February 1858: Stanton departs for California to work on land cases.

January 1859: Stanton returns from California to Washington.

April 1859: Stanton defends Daniel Sickles on murder charges in Washington.

November 6, 1860: Lincoln wins the presidential election; Southern states start to secede.

December 20, 1860: Stanton becomes Buchanan's attorney general.

March 5, 1861: Lincoln becomes president; Stanton returns to private practice.

January 13, 1862: Lincoln nominates Stanton as secretary of war.

January 20, 1862: Stanton starts work as secretary of war.

June 28, 1862: McClellan sends "midnight message" accusing Stanton of sacrificing his army.

December 1862: Battle of Fredericksburg and Lincoln's cabinet crisis.

July 1863: Battle of Gettysburg; surrender of Vicksburg; Stanton's victory speech.

September 2, 1864: News arrives that Sherman has captured Atlanta; Stanton relays the news to the press.

November 8, 1864: Lincoln wins his second presidential term.

January 12, 1865: Stanton and Sherman meet with black leaders in Savannah, Georgia.

April 3, 1865: News arrives that Grant has captured Richmond; Stanton relays the news to the press.

April 9, 1865: News arrives that Lee has surrendered; Stanton relays the news to the press.

April 15, 1865: Lincoln dies; Johnson becomes president; Stanton informs nation.

April 21, 1865: News arrives of Sherman-Johnston peace terms; Johnson rejects the terms.

May 24, 1865: Grand Review in Washington; Sherman refuses to shake Stanton's hand.

February 19, 1866: Johnson vetoes the Freedmen's Bureau bill; Stanton protests.

July 31, 1866: Stanton receives the first reports of New Orleans riot.

August 12, 1867: Johnson suspends Stanton; appoints Grant the interim secretary of war.

January 13, 1868: Senate overturns Stanton's suspension; he returns to office the next day.

February 21, 1868: Johnson attempts to remove Stanton, who refuses to leave the War Department.

February 24, 1868: House impeaches Johnson on basis of attempted removal of Stanton.

May 26, 1868: Senate fails to convict and remove Johnson; Stanton leaves office.

Fall 1868: Stanton campaigns for Grant for president.

December 20, 1869: Grant nominates and Senate confirms Stanton as Supreme Court justice.

December 24, 1869: Stanton dies in Washington.

Introduction

Not long after eleven o'clock on the night of April 14, 1865, a short, burly, bearded man pushed his way through the crowd on Tenth Street, up the curved front steps of a three-story brick boardinghouse, and into the small back bedroom where Abraham Lincoln was stretched on a bed, bleeding and dying. Secretary of War Edwin Stanton soon learned that an assassin had shot the president in the back of the head from point-blank range. The president was not conscious and would not live for more than another few hours. Stanton did not linger. He went into the adjoining parlor, sat down at a small table, and went to work. He launched an investigation to determine who had shot Lincoln at Ford's Theatre and who (at almost the same time but about ten blocks away) had stabbed and nearly killed Secretary of State William Henry Seward. Stanton ordered a massive manhunt to find and catch the assassins and those who had assisted them. He assumed that the attacks on Lincoln and Seward were part of a Confederate plot against the Union leadership, perhaps against Washington itself, so he issued orders to protect the leaders and the city. By a series of messages to the press, Stanton informed the nation about the attacks and the president's condition. He did not announce that he was taking charge: he simply was in charge.

The first telegram Stanton sent, at about midnight, was to Gen. Ulysses S. Grant, the commander of the Union armies, who had left

Washington earlier in the evening, bound by train for a few days with his family in New Jersey. Stanton informed Grant that Lincoln had been shot and would not live. Seward and his son Frederick, the assistant secretary of state, had also been attacked and were "in a dangerous condition." Stanton ordered Grant to "return to Washington immediately." A few minutes later one of Stanton's assistants sent a follow-up message, urging Grant to beware of attacks against himself. Stanton's next message was to the commander of the defenses of Washington. "The Secretary desires," an aide wrote for him, "that the troops turn out; the guards be doubled; the forts be alert; guns manned; special vigilance and guard about the Capitol Prison." Stanton soon sent more specific orders to army officers in the region and beyond: close the bridges out of Washington, question those arriving from Washington, arrest any suspicious persons.[1]

As an experienced lawyer, Stanton knew the value of interviewing witnesses while their memories were fresh. Through his aides he summoned some of those who had seen the attack on Lincoln to the small back parlor at the Petersen House. Stanton himself, aided by the local district judge, posed the questions. When it proved impracticable to make notes in longhand, Stanton had his staff find him someone who could take notes in shorthand. James Tanner, a clerk who lived nearby, was soon seated next to Stanton, scribbling in shorthand. Those whom Stanton questioned that night were certain that Lincoln's assassin was the famous actor John Wilkes Booth. Tanner wrote that after fifteen minutes of this question and answer session, Stanton had enough evidence to convict Booth of Lincoln's murder.[2]

In the midst of the Civil War, Stanton had developed a system for informing the nation of key military events: telegrams nominally sent to John Dix, the general in charge in New York City, were in practice sent directly to the Associated Press. Although the term "press release" would not be used for fifty years, Stanton's messages to Dix were in effect government press releases. His first message on this night, sent about one in the morning, started, "Last evening, about 10.30 p.m., at Ford's Theatre, the President, while sitting in his private box with Mrs. Lincoln, Miss Harris, and Major Rathbone, was shot by an assassin, who suddenly entered the box and approached behind the President." This detailed and remarkably accurate message, composed only a few hours after the attacks upon Lincoln and the Sewards, was followed with three other messages. In one of these Stanton informed the press that investigators had found a letter among Booth's papers referring to the need to consult with Richmond. Stanton's messages were how the nation first learned of the assassinations and of the suspected role of the Confederate leaders.[3]

Charles Dana, one of Stanton's assistant secretaries, later recalled how Stanton dictated and scribbled order after order in Petersen's parlor. "It seemed as if Mr. Stanton thought of everything, and there was a great deal to be thought of that night. The extent of the conspiracy was, of course, unknown, and the horrible beginning which had been made naturally led us to suspect the worst. The safety of Washington must be looked after. Commanders all over the country had to be ordered to take extra precautions. The people must be notified of the tragedy. The assassins must be captured. The coolness and clear-headedness of Mr. Stanton under these circumstances were most remarkable." Charles Leale, one of the doctors attending Lincoln, described Stanton during those hours as being "in reality the acting president of the United States."[4]

Others have taken a far darker view of Stanton. Otto Eisenschiml even suggested that Stanton himself organized the assassination of Lincoln. Eisenschiml argued his case against Stanton mainly through questions: Why was there not a better guard for Lincoln at Ford's Theatre? Why did Stanton not mention Booth in his first message to the press? Why did Stanton not close the bridge by which Booth left Washington and fled into rural Maryland? Why, when federal soldiers finally located and surrounded Booth, was he killed rather than captured and questioned? Bill O'Reilly, in his recent best-selling book on Lincoln's death, has raised these questions again: "Did [Stanton] have any part in the assassination of Abraham Lincoln? To this day there are those who believe he did. But nothing has ever been proved." No serious scholar believes that Stanton helped Booth to kill Lincoln. But historians have accused Stanton of many other errors and crimes, ranging from misrepresentations to "some of the more shameful injustices in American history."[5]

Who was Edwin McMasters Stanton? How did this lifelong Democrat become the secretary of war for the first Republican president? Why was Stanton so controversial, both in his life and after his death?

Born on the banks of the Ohio River, in Steubenville, Ohio, Stanton attended Kenyon College for two years, then studied law with a Steubenville lawyer. He practiced law with increasing success, first in Ohio, then in Pittsburgh, and then in Washington, D.C. By the eve of the Civil War, Stanton was one of the nation's leading lawyers, famed both for his trial work, including the successful defense of a congressman accused of murder, and for his work in the Supreme Court, especially the high-profile challenge to the erection of a bridge at Wheeling, Virginia. Especially during his Ohio years, from roughly 1837 through 1847, Stanton was active in Democratic politics. In private letters he opposed slavery, but he took no public stand on the issue, perhaps because of family connections with the South, perhaps because the Democratic Party was dominated by slave-owning Southern Democrats. When Stanton moved to Washington in 1857, he worked closely with the Democratic attorney general Jeremiah Black, representing the federal government both in California and in the Supreme Court. In late 1860 and early 1861, as the Southern states seceded and formed their Confederacy, Stanton served four months as the attorney general in the cabinet of Democratic president James Buchanan. Stanton claimed then and later that he served Buchanan only to save the Union, but it is hard to confirm just what Stanton said to Buchanan or what effect he had on Buchanan's actions.

When Lincoln became president in early 1861, Stanton returned to his Washington law practice and criticized Lincoln in private letters to Buchanan and others. Stanton also, however, started to do important legal work for members of the Lincoln administration, and in early 1862, when Lincoln needed a secretary of war to replace Simon Cameron, he chose Stanton. For the next three years and three months Stanton worked night and day, raising, arming, feeding, clothing, transporting, and supervising an army of a million men. He dealt with issues great and small and with men and women ranging from the president and governors to generals and private citizens. Stanton was also responsible for the system of military arrests of civilians accused of aiding and abetting the rebellion, some of them rebel spies, some of them merely opponents of the Lincoln administration. Although Stanton's appointment as secretary was praised by almost all the papers, some were soon attacking him and insisting on his resignation. The *Boston Advertiser* demanded as early as the summer of 1862 that Stanton "vacate a department which he has proved himself incompetent to fill." The *New York World* declared in 1863, "When we see any order with Stanton's name at the bottom we are sure that if anything can by any possibility be done wrong, reasoned badly, or unfittingly expressed, we shall surely find it." The *New York Times*, on the other hand, near the end of the war, lauded Stanton's "indomitable industry, inflexible integrity, high courage, and devoted patriotism." Lincoln's private secretary John Hay, writing Stanton not long after Lincoln's death, said that Lincoln "loved" and "trusted" Stanton: "How vain were all efforts to shake that trust and confidence, not lightly given & never withdrawn."[6]

Stanton remained the secretary of war under Lincoln's controversial successor, Andrew Johnson. Stanton, who was now a Radical Republican, and Johnson, who remained a Democrat at heart, soon disagreed about reconstruction. Johnson wanted to turn the Southern states over to the Southern white leadership; Stanton insisted that the federal government and the Union Army should protect Southern blacks and Northern sympathizers. Johnson and Stanton quarreled, first in private and then in public, and their quarrel became part of the larger political war between Johnson and the Republicans. In early 1868, finally fed up, Johnson attempted to remove Stanton and appoint Lorenzo Thomas as secretary of war. For a while the nation had two secretaries of war: Thomas, attending Johnson's cabinet meetings, and Stanton, holed up in the War Department but without access to the White House. It was Johnson's attempt to remove Stanton, which Republicans viewed as utterly illegal, that led to the impeachment and near removal of Johnson. After the Senate declined to convict Johnson, by only one vote, Stanton resigned and returned to private life. So Stanton was a critical figure not just in the Civil War but also in Reconstruction. One simply cannot understand the first impeachment of an American president without understanding Edwin Stanton.

When Stanton left the War Department in the spring of 1868, his health was failing and he had only a few months to live. He devoted much of the fall of that year to Grant's political campaign, both because he favored Grant for president and because he hoped for a suitable appointment in the Grant administration. Grant eventually did appoint Stanton, but too late. In December 1869 Grant nominated and the Senate confirmed Stanton to a seat on the Supreme Court, set to open in February of the following year. Stanton never took the oath of office. He died at the age of fifty-five, of congestive heart failure, a few days after his confirmation.

Stanton's name is familiar, but there is much about him that Americans, even those well versed in the Civil War, do not know. The aim of this book is to tell the whole life story of this important, interesting, contradictory, controversial man.

Chapter 1

"Dreams of Future Greatness"

— 1814–1836 —

E dwin McMasters Stanton was born on December 19, 1814, in Steubenville, Ohio. A few days after his birth, in distant Belgium, British and American negotiators signed the Treaty of Ghent that ended the War of 1812. It would take almost two months for news of the treaty to reach the United States, and in the meantime, on January 8, 1815, Gen. Andrew Jackson would fight and defeat the British forces at the Battle of New Orleans. Jackson's great victory would make him a national hero and propel him to the White House, where he served as president from 1829 through 1837, the years of Stanton's boyhood and youth. The Democratic Party would celebrate Jackson every year on January 8 well into the twentieth century, with speeches and dinners and conventions. So although he was not aware of it, Stanton was born at an interesting moment in American history.[1]

He was also born in an interesting place, on the banks of the Ohio River. The western roads were generally impassable, so rivers served as the main transit routes. According to guide books published at this time, Steubenville was the largest town along the Ohio River between Pittsburgh (with about six thousand people and seventy-five miles upstream) and Wheeling (about fifteen hundred people and twenty-five miles downstream). Steubenville already had about two thousand people and more than four hundred dwellings. As the seat of Jefferson County, the town had a "spacious brick court-house" as well as many local lawyers. Stanton would become a lawyer himself and try many cases in the Steubenville Courthouse; indeed his statue stands outside the current county courthouse. The guide books of his time reported that there were schools and churches, fifty different stores, a weekly newspaper, an iron foundry, and mills to make flour, glass, and cloth. Travel along the rivers at the time of Stanton's birth was by keelboat, but the age of steam was coming. One of the guides, in 1814, reported excitedly on the first western steamboats and predicted that they would soon be "running up and down our numerous rivers."[2]

The Ohio River was not just a highway; it was a boundary between freedom and slavery. Ohio was a free state because of the Northwest Ordinance, which prohibited slavery in all the states formed out of the Northwest Territory. Virginia, just across the Ohio River from Steubenville, was a slave state, with more than 400,000 slaves. The western part of Virginia, the part that bordered Ohio, had fewer slaves than the eastern part of the state, but there were slaves and slave owners within view of the house where Stanton was born. Alexis de Tocqueville, whose journey across America took him down the Ohio River during Stanton's youth, commented on the dramatic difference between the two sides of the river: "On the right bank of the Ohio," that is, in Ohio, "everything is activity, industry; labor is honored; there are no slaves. Cross to the left bank," to the states of Virginia and Kentucky, "and the scene changes so suddenly that you think yourself on the other side of the world; the enterprising spirit is gone. There, work is not only painful: it's shameful, and you degrade yourself in submitting to it."[3] Like many Americans, Stanton had roots on both sides of this stark divide.

Edwin's grandfather Benjamin Stanton was a Quaker from Beaufort, North Carolina, and his grandmother Abigail Macy was a Quaker originally from Nantucket, Massachusetts, a descendant of one of the first white settlers of that island. Benjamin Stanton wanted to free his slaves, as did many Southern Quakers, but was prevented from doing so by North Carolina laws restricting manumission. So in his will he directed his widow to free their remaining slaves as soon as the state law allowed. Rather than wait for the law to change, Abigail and her family made the long hard trip from North Carolina to Ohio, to the Quaker community of Mount Pleasant, so that her slaves could be free and she could raise her own children in freedom. Abigail was a strong woman, a major figure in the life of her grandson Edwin, who told a group of Quakers during the Civil War that he would never "neglect his duty to the slave" as long as he could remember his grandmother "toiling from a slave state with her children about her, that they might have the vigor from the freedom of the North."[4]

Stanton's maternal grandfather, Thomas Norman, was a wealthy farmer and slave owner in Culpeper County, Virginia. At the time of his death, in 1838, he owned more than thirty slaves. Over the course of a long life, he had three wives; the first two died young, including Stanton's grandmother Mildred Tutt. So Stanton did not know this grandmother, but he knew Thomas Norman, visiting him in Virginia twice, once as a young boy and once as a young man not long after his marriage. When it was useful to do so, Stanton could claim these Southern as well as Northern ties. For example, in the late 1850s, in a courtroom in slave-owning Washington, when accused of making an antislavery speech, Stanton replied that he was "proud to say that his father was a North Carolinian and his mother a Virginian."[5]

We do not know why Stanton's mother, Lucy Norman, left her father's house in about 1810, moving to Mount Pleasant, Ohio, where she lived in the household of David McMasters, a Methodist minister. She married David Stanton in February 1814, with McMasters officiating. Because he married outside the Quaker community, David Stanton was expelled from the Quaker meeting, and perhaps for this reason the young couple moved to nearby Steubenville, where they worshipped with the Methodists. It is not clear how David made his living at first—one source says he was a tailor—but not long after Edwin was born his father started to study medicine, preparing to become a doctor. Another son, Darwin, was born to the Stantons in 1816. The next summer the Stantons visited Thomas Norman in Virginia, and Lucy's sister Elizabeth returned to live with them in Steubenville. The family credited Lucy with teaching Edwin to read when he was only three years old. In 1818, after David received his medical license, he purchased a small house on Third Street in Steubenville, perhaps with financial assistance from his father-in-law.[6]

Edwin continued his education at the small schools in Steubenville;

one of those who studied with him remembered him as "delicate phys-
ically, grave and studious." His physical delicacy may have been due to
the asthma that plagued him all his life. Another contemporary recalled
that as a boy Edwin was "somewhat imperious, but never combative or
abusive." Edwin's religious education took place in the Methodist church.
Methodism in the 1820s was not sedate or settled; it was a religion of powerful preachers, dramatic camp meetings, and weeping conversions. The
sect was doubling in size every decade: there were about 64,000 American
Methodists in 1800 and more than 500,000 by 1830. Stanton became a provisional member and then (just after his thirteenth birthday) a full member
of the Calvary Methodist Church in Steubenville, a committed Christian.[7]

Stanton would need his faith, for death was a constant part of his life.
In the summer of 1820, when he was just five, his two-year old sister
Lucretia died. Another sister was born the next spring but (as her father reported in a letter) "in a state of suspended animation." After a few
hours the infant "began to show signs of compression of the brain that
soon assumed the appearance of a perfect apoplexy." The poor girl died
the next morning. A son was born to the Stantons in 1824 but died the
same day. Grandmother Abigail Stanton passed away the next year. And
then, in late December 1827, when Edwin was only thirteen, his father
suddenly died.[8]

Stanton's sister Pamphila would later write, "After an evening passed
in the society of friends who had called, my mother was awakened by
father's violent trembling, and on trying to rouse him, found him unconscious." Dr. Stanton had suffered a stroke; he never regained consciousness, and on December 30 he died. Two days later church bells
summoned the residents of Steubenville of all denominations to his
funeral. The mourners marched behind the coffin on that cold winter
day to see the doctor to his grave. One of the obituaries noted that "as a
neighbor he was strictly honest and upright; hospitable to the stranger;
kind and benevolent to the poor and needy." Another wrote that his
"human feeling," which led him to "sacrifice [his] own comfort to alle-
viate the woes of others," had gained him "the love and affection of his
fellow citizens."[9]

David Stanton left behind a widow, four young children, and few assets. Lucy Stanton received funds from her father and started a short-lived

store in the family home, but the boys also had to work. In the spring of 1828 she removed Edwin from school and apprenticed him to a Steubenville bookseller for a term of three years. A friend remembered that Edwin was "just high enough to get his chin above the counter, selling books for James Turnbull at six dollars a month, and contributing that six dollars a month to the support of his widowed mother." Turnbull's one complaint about Stanton was that "when customers came into the store he was often so absorbed in his book that he did not attend to them very promptly." A girl who lived in the town at the time wrote that Edwin "loved books better than either parties or girls. His habits were excellent—studious, ambitious, industrious, sober."[10]

─────────

As his three-year term with Turnbull ended, Edwin persuaded Daniel Collier, the executor of his father's will and the children's guardian, to loan him the funds necessary to start college. In April 1831, not yet seventeen, Edwin traveled two hundred miles west by stagecoach to enroll in Kenyon College. The college was new and remote, but this was by design, for its founder, Philander Chase, the Episcopal bishop of Ohio, wanted his school far from "temptations to dissipation and folly." Chase had purchased eight thousand acres in the central part of the state, hired workers, cleared the land, planted much of it in corn and other crops, and completed one impressive building with "massive stone walls, four feet thick, and four stories in height." He ran the college like a monastery, requiring the sixty male students to rise before dawn for prayer, study, farm work, and classes. Kenyon was different from other schools, Chase wrote, because it was a "patriarchal institution," under the control of a benevolent patriarch, himself. Chase wanted to train ministers and teachers, and many of the students had enrolled for these purposes, but an early visitor found that most of the students were aiming at "more lucrative employment."[11]

Stanton arrived at a critical moment in Kenyon's history, when conflict between Chase and the trustees and teachers led the founder to resign. For more than a year, the college operated without a president, but it would appear that the bishop's rigorous rules remained intact. Writing home to a friend Stanton complained, "Our faculty, through fear of cholera, have prohibited bathing, and almost everything else but studying—would to God they prohibit that shortly." By the end of Stanton's first term, he owed the college store more than $14 for books (including a Latin grammar and an algebra text), pens, paper, candles, combs, and other items. There was an eight-week recess between the terms, which Stanton presumably spent in Steubenville, before returning to start his sophomore year in November.[12]

Kenyon College, in remote Gambier, Ohio, had only one substantial building, still under construction, when Stanton arrived there in 1831.

Student life at American colleges in the early nineteenth century was dominated by literary societies, where students gathered to socialize and to debate. In February 1832 Stanton joined the main student organization at Kenyon at the time, the Philomathesian Society. He soon presented the Society with a fine leather-bound book with his name in gold letters, in which to record its minutes. Stanton also gave four books to the library of the Society, including Hale's *History of the United States*, again with his name as the donor. For a student on a tight budget, these were generous gifts.[13] The Philomathesians gathered every Friday evening for debates.

One evening in July, Stanton argued that the life of "an agriculturist" was more satisfying than that of a lawyer; his friend Andrew McClintock argued the other side. On another night Stanton argued that the revolutionaries were right to execute King Louis XVI, while David Davis, who would become Abraham Lincoln's friend and campaign manager, defended the king's side. A few weeks later Stanton and Davis were on the same side, arguing together that the Church had harmed rather than helped literature in the Middle Ages.[14]

In an interesting college essay, sounding more like his Quaker ancestors than his future martial self, Stanton asked why "an injury committed by a private individual on an enemy is punished, yet when done by a general is termed a noble deed and worthy of all praise." His answer was that "a halo is spread around the actions of the [general] which, together with the extensive theatre on which he acts, conceals the enormity of his deeds and covers them with a false splendor." Wars among nations might sometimes be necessary, Stanton conceded, but "how much better might they accomplish their ends by some other means?" He continued, "If generals are useful so are butchers and who will say that because a butcher is useful he should be honored? Indeed, both should be considered rather as persons who by their own inclination cater to the depraved appetites of their fellow beings than as noble or honorable men."[15]

In another essay, Stanton discussed the "duty of a good soldier on the eve of battle." He argued that the key was for the soldier to know "the rightness of his cause," and he quoted Shakespeare: "Thrice is he armed whose cause is just." Strength in battle depended upon unity among the warriors; division among those on the same side was "the rock upon which the best split." Stanton apparently wrote this at the time of an election, for he praised the way men had "laid aside sword and bayonet for the more peaceful and powerful ballot."[16]

Stanton worked hard, but he also enjoyed himself, writing to a friend, "I am in chase of a petticoat, what success I may have God only knows." He had passed an evening in the young woman's company so pleasantly that he "took no note of the time" and lost his way in the woods after midnight on his return. He reached his room at about four in the morning, "cold, wet, and tired," and suffered a fever for a few days. "So much for love," he concluded, "rather expensive, don't you think so?" In this same letter he described the Fourth of July celebration at nearby Mount Vernon: there were "no less than three orations," and "every man, woman and child was drunk as a fiddler's bitch."[17]

In August 1832, as his third term at Kenyon neared its end, Stanton wrote to his guardian, Daniel Collier, asking for funds to travel home to Steubenville and also to confirm whether the family's finances would allow him to return for the fall term. Collier apparently replied that, at least for a while, Stanton would have to earn money rather than spend it on his education. Stanton returned to Steubenville determined to find a way to continue his studies. He arranged for a loan to enable him to pay for another term or two of college, but Collier would not hear of the young man taking on debt. Instead Collier arranged for him to manage a new bookstore for his former employer Turnbull in the state capital, Columbus. After some debate, Stanton reluctantly agreed, writing his college friend McClintock that all his "dreams of future greatness" were "dispersed, vanished." He claimed that he would "henceforth be regardless of life, fortune, character, everything, and shall continue to live on, from day to day, objectless, hopeless. . . . I shall go on cursing and being cursed."[18]

———

Columbus did not rank among even the ninety largest cities in the United States in the 1830 census. The largest city in Ohio and sixth largest in the nation was Cincinnati, with 24,831 people, and even Steubenville was on the list, with 2,937 people. But Columbus was growing rapidly; it would double in size by 1840 and triple in size by 1850. The central business district already had several blocks of two-story brick buildings. As in any state capital, there were more than the usual number of newspapers and lawyers. The National Road, a major east-west turnpike, would reach Columbus a year after Stanton's arrival, and soon thereafter the city would have a water route to the north, the Ohio & Erie Canal. There was culture as well, with the Historical and Philosophical Society of Ohio, chartered the year before Stanton arrived. The bookstore in which Stanton worked, according to Turnbull's advertisements, sold a wide variety of books, from theology texts to the latest novels by James Fenimore Cooper.[19]

The capitol building and nearby structures in Columbus, Ohio, as they looked in 1846. The capitol (with the steeple) was already built when Stanton arrived in 1832.

Stanton reconciled himself to life in Columbus, writing his friend McClintock that he was making "acquaintances among the great men of the day" and learning "the proper method of doing business; learning how to cheat, and avoid being cheated." He found the other young men to be "impudent, ignorant, self-sufficient counter-jumpers," but the young women were "modest, sensible and well-informed." He was boarding with Horton Howard, a leading Quaker, and his wife and daughters. "The old folks," Stanton wrote, "are intelligent, hospitable, kind and in short just such folks as you would like. Their daughters—they have four—though not handsome are very agreeable." The morning after attending a party Stanton found that his worn trousers had ripped through, so that he was "showing [his] arse in more ways than one." He closed his letter by assuring McClintock that he would visit Kenyon soon.[20]

Although Stanton did not mention her in this letter, he may have already met the woman who would become his wife, Mary Lamson. He had met her brother-in-law, William Preston, a Kenyon trustee and the rector of Trinity Episcopal Church in Columbus, during his coach trip from Steubenville to Columbus. Stanton, who smoked cigars because he believed they helped his asthma, offered the minister a cigar, which was at first refused but finally accepted. Stanton impressed Preston, who praised him to Mary and her sister, who were staying with Preston and his wife after the recent death of their father. The next Sunday morning, at Trinity Church, Edwin spied Mary and was instantly smitten. Her hair, he later wrote, "was soft and brown; her eyes dark; her brow and forehead beautiful." He went on, "Her teeth, white and regular, were the finest I ever beheld . . . and a full red lip gave to her mouth, especially when she smiled, surpassing sweetness." Mary also saw Edwin, somehow sensing that this was the young man of whom Preston had spoken. The two met that morning and (in the words of Stanton's sister), "the friendship between Mary and Edwin soon became a more tender feeling." This may well have been the point at which Stanton shifted from the Methodist to the Episcopal church, in which he would remain the rest of his life.[21]

Stanton worked at the bookstore and courted Mary for the next few months. In the summer of 1833, cholera returned to Ohio, killing almost a hundred people in Columbus. Cholera was a terrible disease: within hours of the first symptoms a victim could die from vomiting, diarrhea, and dehydration. In August cholera killed six people in the Howard family, with whom Stanton was living: first a young daughter, Ann, then her father and mother, along with a son-in-law and two grandchildren. A family friend, Ebenezer Thomas, had the grim task of writing several letters to another son-in-law to report these deaths.[22]

The story was told in Columbus, and written down years later, that Stanton could not believe that Ann Howard, who seemed healthy when he saw her at noon, had died and was buried by evening. Enlisting a few friends, he supposedly opened her grave that night to confirm she had not been buried alive. The story is almost certainly false. Thomas, the family friend, in his four letters of August 1833, including one written on the day of Ann's death, made no mention of Stanton digging up her grave. Nor did Stanton himself mention the alleged incident in two talkative letters that he wrote in September. In one of these he wrote Collier that he had "sat up" with the Howards one night in August, presumably during the illness or after the death of one of the family members, and that the next day he had an "attack of malignant fever" that "commenced with diarrhea, which continued with cramps of feet, legs and hands, for about six hours." Surely one of these letters or the obituaries would have said so if Stanton had disinterred Ann's body.[23]

The fall of 1833 was a difficult time for Stanton, for he was pulled in different directions. In early September he went to Kenyon to attend the commencement; he longed to return there for at least a year of further study, but he also wanted to remain in Columbus, for he was now engaged to Mary and "desperately in love with her," as he wrote to McClintock. At the same time, he was worried about his family in Steubenville; the last major asset of his father's estate, the family house, was sold at auction in August, and in September he did not know where his mother and siblings were living. He was annoyed with his employer, believing he was working harder and making less than his counterpart in Steubenville. Stanton wrote Collier that he hoped to become a lawyer but was willing to continue with the bookstore if Turnbull would "make anything like an equitable bargain." He assured Collier, "You are in all these things the best judge and to your opinion I shall of course gladly submit." But he admitted to two college friends that he was taking "measures for acting independently of [his] much loved guardian" by discussing with the federal judge for the district of Ohio, John Campbell, the possibility of studying law with him in Columbus. There were a few law schools in the United States at this time, including the relatively new schools at Harvard and Yale, but almost all lawyers trained by apprenticing themselves to more senior lawyers, including judges, so that Stanton's plan to start his legal training in the office of a federal judge was not as odd as it might seem today.[24]

Within a few weeks Stanton's plan to read law with Campbell was "entirely disconcerted" by the death of the judge, yet another victim of the cholera epidemic. But then President Jackson did Stanton an inadvertent favor, making a recess appointment of Benjamin Tappan of Steubenville as the federal district judge for Ohio. Stanton had known Tappan for most of his life; he was the leading lawyer of Steubenville and the father of a friend and classmate of Stanton. Stanton assumed that Tappan would have to open an office in Columbus, the state's judicial center, and hoped he could work for Tappan there. So when his agreement with Turnbull came to an end at the end of October, Stanton went home to Steubenville to talk with Tappan and Collier face-to-face, as well as to check on his family.[25]

Events did not work out as Stanton planned. Stanton could not persuade Tappan to hire him as a law clerk, perhaps because Tappan was unsure whether the Senate would confirm his appointment. Stanton could not speak with Collier, because he was out of town. In late December, Stanton decided that he would return to Columbus, determined to find work there. But his sisters, Oella and Pamphila, begged him to stay, and he relented. Collier finally returned and persuaded Stanton to read law with him, in Steubenville, rather than go to Columbus. Defending his decision in a letter to McClintock, Stanton said that although the lawyers in Columbus were more "eminent" than those of Steubenville, they "would have little time or attention to bestow on their students." In Steubenville, on the other hand, there were several other young men reading law, so that "a regular system of instruction has been adopted." There were other opportunities as well: one of the town's lawyers had "the best library west of the mountains," and on Monday evenings there were debates in the local athenaeum. Stanton could live at home with his mother and siblings and thus save the money that he would have to spend on room and board in Columbus. He did not mention it to McClintock, in fact he may not have realized it himself, but Collier probably hired Stanton because he saw him as a promising protégé.[26]

Stanton spent most of 1834 and 1835 in Steubenville, reading law, working for Collier, and writing frequent letters to Mary Lamson. In one of her letters to him she wrote that she liked arithmetic. "As females often have the character given to them, perhaps justly, of being irresolute and unsettled in purpose, mathematical studies should be of the highest importance." A few months later she wrote asking for advice about what books she should read. Stanton replied, "In my own studies I have so missed the track, that I could not presume to direct you, whose interest I have so much at heart." But then he did direct her, saying that she was wasting her time reading a biography of Lord Byron. "Instances of vice and immorality . . . are too common in life to seek them in books." He was pleased at the thought that on Sundays they were "engaged in the same work," teaching Sunday school, for he had met her at church.[27]

Steubenville, Stanton's hometown, as seen from the Ohio River, at the time of the early steamboats. The trees in the foreground were on the Virginia side of the river.

Stanton's sister Pamphila recalled these two years as pleasant ones. Edwin rented a house for the family, with a flower and vegetable garden, in which he soon started to spend time. His brother, Darwin, was working at a drugstore and hoping to become a doctor. The two brothers were "never overbearing or dictatorial" toward their younger sisters, Oella and Pamphila. Edwin read the newspapers carefully and would often discuss political issues with his mother or his sisters. His sister Pamphila recalled that Edwin was never "satisfied with the simple answer a question might require, but was so well informed through his extensive reading that he made every subject doubly interesting." He also argued cases in moot court with other young law students and debated public issues at the local athenaeum.[28]

Although we do not have records of these Steubenville debates, it seems likely that Stanton discussed slavery. Years later Theodore Weld, an antislavery activist, would recall that when he came to Steubenville, young Stanton agreed with him that it was "the duty of the people of the slave states to abolish slavery at once." Stanton's friend Allyn Wolcott, however, did not remember the incident quite this way; he claimed that Stanton had not endorsed Weld's views, that they simply had a pleasant private conversation with Weld after his lecture. The Cadiz Anti-Slavery Society invited Stanton to speak a year later, but it is not clear whether he spoke or what he said. In short, we do not know Stanton's views on slavery in the 1830s.[29]

Stanton passed the Ohio bar examination in the summer of 1835. He was not admitted to the bar until December of that year, when he turned twenty-one, but even before this, his mentor Collier allowed him to argue some cases under his supervision. A Steubenville resident recalled that one day Stanton was arguing a case in the local court when the opposing lawyer rose to move that Stanton should be disqualified because he was not yet of age. Collier, in the back of the courtroom, rose and said that although Stanton was not quite twenty-one he was "as well qualified to practice law as [Collier himself] or any other attorney of this bar." Stanton remained standing while Collier made this little speech, then he "pitched right in again" without waiting for the judge to rule on the motion.[30]

In early 1836, after he was officially admitted to the Ohio bar, Stanton moved thirty miles west, to Cadiz, the seat of Harrison County, and joined Chauncey Dewey in his law practice there. It is not clear why Stanton moved to Cadiz—whether he thought there were too many lawyers in Steubenville, whether there was tension with Collier or perhaps some connection with his new Cadiz partner. Dewey was a scholar, a graduate of Union College, and a Democratic politician, having served in the state senate, but a local historian wrote that he "did not care for the excitement of the trial-table," and he soon turned most of the office's trial work over to Stanton. Stanton "was a fighter" and reveled in courtroom struggles. He "would be in the court-room all day and if necessary spend the following night, in or out of his office, in preparation for the next day." By one count, Stanton handled hundreds of small cases, most involving less than a hundred dollars, in the Harrison County courts in his first four years of practice.[31]

Stanton's legal success allowed him to persuade Mary that they should marry at the end of 1836. They were both somewhat young: he would be twenty-two in December and she about eighteen (we do not have a firm date for her birth). Another young lawyer who married at about this time, Abraham Lincoln, was thirty-three on his wedding day, and his bride, Mary Todd, was twenty-three. There is some disagreement among demographers, but it seems that in the early nineteenth century the average age at first marriage was about twenty-four for men and about twenty-one for women. Stanton was always impatient, however, and he wanted Mary with him in Cadiz, not in distant Columbus. In October she wrote to him that she prayed that "our Father in Heaven" would "make us know and do our duty, and to be kind and affectionate to each other." In December Stanton traveled by stagecoach to Columbus, but when he reached there, he fell ill. After a week he recovered, and on the last day of the year, in the parlor of Reverend Preston's home, in the company of a few friends and family members, Edwin Stanton and Mary Lamson exchanged their vows. The newlyweds traveled from Columbus to Steubenville over the snow by sleigh, "the brightest sweetest journey of my life," as Stanton later described it. Benjamin Tappan Jr. wrote to his friend Stanton from Paris, where he was studying medicine, "You have taken a ticket in that lottery in which the blanks are at least as numerous as the prizes." Stanton agreed that he had drawn a great prize in the lottery of life—although he would not have long to enjoy her company.[32]

Chapter 2

"Obstinate Democrat"

—— 1837–1847 ——

Stanton did not come from a political family, and his early letters have few political comments, other than a joke that a local election "went off altogether too quietly," without even "a fight or quarrel—a curse upon such tameness of the sovereign people!" But starting in about 1837, he became intensely political: writing letters, giving speeches, attending conventions, and running for office. One impetus for this change was his friend and mentor Judge Benjamin Tappan. Though Tappan was forty years older than Stanton, there was a close connection between the two men, dating back to when Stanton went to grammar school with Tappan's son and namesake. Stanton's sister Pamphila recalled that Tappan's house "was like a second home to Edwin." Just after their wedding, Edwin and Mary lived for several weeks with the Tappans, and later in the spring of 1837 the two men announced that they would work together as law partners. Tappan was a lifelong Democrat, known as "Judge Tappan" because of his service as a state and (for a few months) federal judge. At one point, after a period of silence, a friend asked Tappan what had happened to that "most incorrigible, persevering, uncompromising, unyielding, and obstinate Democrat." Stanton was soon just such an "obstinate Democrat" himself.[1]

Judge Benjamin Tappan, Stanton's friend, partner, and political patron. While Tappan served as senator in Washington, Stanton served as his deputy in Ohio.

Another reason Stanton became more interested in politics was that the United States was in the midst of its first great depression. We call it the Panic of 1837, but this is misleading, for this was no mere Wall Street panic but a deep and widespread depression, and it did not last for just one year but for more than five. The economic crisis led many men to take politics more seriously. About 80 percent of all eligible voters turned out for the presidential election of 1840 and again in 1844. These were the highest turnout percentages in American history up to this point—and among the highest figures to this day. The population was also growing, and the laws were changing to make more men eligible to vote, so the absolute numbers were even more dramatic: about 1.5 million men voted in the presidential election of 1836, more than 2.4 million voted in 1840, and more than 2.7 million voted in 1844. So Stanton was not alone in entering politics when he did; thousands of Americans became more political, more active in politics, in the late 1830s and early 1840s.[2]

After the brief Era of Good Feelings in the 1820s, there were two major political parties from the late 1830s through the early 1850s: the Democrats and the Whigs. The Democrats were the party of Presidents Andrew Jackson and Martin Van Buren, the party that claimed to represent the common people against the wealthy bankers. Democrats derided their opponents as aristocrats and "bank men." The Whigs were the party of Senators Henry Clay, Daniel Webster, and William Henry Seward, committed to internal improvements and national development. Whigs claimed they were the true representatives of the people, against the entrenched political power of the Democrats. Whigs mocked the Democrats as "Loco Focos," a name some Democrats embraced. Almost every newspaper was committed to one party or faction, and almost every edition included articles mocking, attacking, and denigrating the other party. With spring elections for local offices and fall elections for the state legislature, there was no break from politics. In Ohio the struggle between the Whigs and the Democrats was a hard-fought back-and-forth affair. Governors were elected every two years: a Whig in the fall of 1836, a Democrat in 1838, a Whig in 1840, a Democrat in 1842. The Ohio results were often quite close: in 1848 only about 300 votes out of more than 300,000 votes cast in the race for governor separated the winning Whig from the losing Democrat.[3]

Stanton's legal and political work were often related, as in his defense of his friend Daniel McCook, the clerk in nearby Carroll County, Ohio. In the October election of 1836, in which his brother was running for Congress as a Democrat, McCook as county clerk divided the votes of the Whig candidate between "Andrew W. Loomis" and "Andrew Loomis." McCook claimed that his action was perfectly proper because different ballots had used different names, and in any case Loomis won the election, so it should not have mattered. But angry Whigs impeached McCook for filing a false election return. Both McCook's action, splitting hairs over the spelling of the name, and the Whig response, filing impeachment charges despite winning the election, were typical of the "no holds barred" politics of the period. McCook turned to Stanton for his legal defense. After months of delay, the case was dismissed without a decision. McCook and his wife named their sixth son, born in March 1837, Edwin Stanton McCook.[4]

In May of that same year, Stanton took a trip south and east to retrieve his mother and two sisters, who had been staying for a few months with his grandfather Thomas Norman in Culpeper County, Virginia. Pamphila, who was ten at the time, later recalled that they returned by way of Fredericksburg, Virginia, where they stayed with a kind and gracious aunt. From there they went to Washington, D.C., where they toured the major sights, and Frederick, Maryland, where they rode the rails for the first time, on an early section of the Baltimore & Ohio Railroad. Sadly we do not have Stanton's own account of this trip, his impressions of Southern slavery or Washington politics.[5]

When the Stantons returned to Ohio, Edwin installed the whole family (mother, wife, two sisters) in a brick house about a mile from the center of Cadiz. At this time he was working with Dewey on cases in Cadiz and with Tappan on cases in Steubenville, an arrangement he later extended to other lawyers in other towns. Pamphila remembered this Cadiz home as a pleasant place, with a garden and orchard outside and a furnace in the basement, installed by her brother himself. When he returned from his day's legal work, Stanton would often read. He was interested in history, working his way through Napier's dense *History of the War in the Peninsula* and tracing on maps the lines of Napoleon's marches. He loved the novels of Charles Dickens, whose *Pickwick Papers* appeared in serial form at this time. He read the newspapers, often aloud, and discussed events in Washington and Columbus with his mother and sisters. He read and recited poetry, calling "Thanatopsis," William Cullen Bryant's meditation on "the silent halls of death," the "finest piece of poetry he had seen."[6]

Only two of Stanton's letters from 1837 survive, both mainly about legal work. In July he wrote from Cadiz to Tappan in Steubenville about several cases on which they were collaborating. Tappan was under consideration for a seat in the state senate, and Stanton reported that the Masons were working against Tappan both among Democrats and with the Whigs. (The Masons presumably opposed Tappan because of his open atheism.) Stanton sent his love to Tappan's wife, Mary, and said that his own Mary "would like to beat [Tappan] at a game of dungeons," apparently a board game. In the second letter, Stanton wrote to the lawyer on the other side in one of his cases, suggesting a way to eliminate one of the issues: "The case is one that has produced much ill blood between the parties, although it is in its nature one that had better have been mutually accommodated."[7]

Stanton himself was a candidate for office that summer and fall, running as the Democratic nominee for prosecutor for Harrison County, of which Cadiz was the principal town. We cannot say how active he was in this campaign because there are so few surviving newspapers, but we know that he prevailed by a margin of 127 votes. Tappan lost his campaign to become a state senator, however, and the Whigs secured control of the state legislature. For the next two years Stanton would serve as the Harrison County prosecutor, representing the state in the full range of criminal cases, from murder and rape down to petty crimes. This was not a full-time job; Stanton continued his private law practice as well, working with both Tappan and Dewey. And he continued to be active in politics as part of the Democratic Central Committee for Harrison County, responsible for selecting candidates and encouraging Democrats.[8]

Stanton's family went through several changes in these years. In the summer of 1838, Stanton's sister Oella, only sixteen at the time, married Judge Tappan's son and namesake, Dr. Benjamin Tappan Jr., and the couple settled in Steubenville. In the spring of the next year, Pamphila, age twelve, appeared in the Steubenville courthouse and declared that she wanted her older brother as her legal guardian; Judge Tappan agreed to serve as security. A few weeks later, on the Fourth of July, Stanton's brother, Darwin, after completing medical studies at Harvard and the University of Pennsylvania, married Nancy Hooker. Darwin and Nancy settled in Brooke County, Virginia, just across the river from Steubenville. Edwin and his wife, mother, and younger sister moved back to Steubenville, although Edwin continued to work in Cadiz as well.[9]

In the fall election of 1838, Stanton and other Ohio Democrats managed to reverse the results of the prior year, electing Wilson Shannon as governor and securing control of both houses of the state legislature. One of the first acts of the new legislature was to select Judge Tappan to represent Ohio in the U.S. Senate. Tappan started work in Washington in March 1839, and for the next few years Stanton would serve not only as his law partner in Steubenville but as his political eyes and ears in Ohio.[10]

The Ohio state constitution provided that the legislature appoint judges of the state supreme court. In early 1840 Judge Reuben Wood was coming to the end of his first seven-year term and seeking a second term. Since Wood was a Democrat, and since the new legislature was controlled by Democrats, his reappointment might seem obvious. Not to Edwin Stanton. He drafted and published in the state's leading Democratic paper, the *Ohio Statesman*, edited by his friend Samuel Medary, an attack on Wood as false "to the Democratic cause." Using the pseudonym Buckeye, Stanton criticized the judge for joining a court opinion declaring a bank's charter to be "a contract, irrevocable, unalterable." Even one of the Whig judges, he wrote, refused to go that far. Tappan wrote Stanton from Washington to praise his Buckeye article, saying, "We all think here that you must have killed Wood." But Stanton had not killed Wood: the legislature renewed his appointment for another seven years. One of the legislators even attacked Stanton for trying to impose extreme Democratic views on the state's supreme court. "Verily, into what hands has our state fallen, if our judges are to be trammeled by the dictates of heated partisans?"[11]

A few days later another article by Buckeye appeared in the same paper, probably also penned by Stanton. In this article Stanton praised Governor Shannon for his strict approach to bank regulation. Some Whigs now claimed that they favored this approach, but Stanton saw this as mere Whig dishonesty: "The thought that there is penetration enough to detect, and independence enough among the people to oppose principles at variance with the spirit of our free institutions, never seems to have entered their [Whig] minds." For Stanton, the Democrats were always on the side of the people, the Whigs on the side of the banks, and politics was to be played without many rules. "Delicacy and forbearance," Stanton wrote, were "not to be expected from our adversaries."[12]

———

Ohio Democrats gathered every other year in Columbus for their state convention, almost always opening the proceedings on January 8, Jackson Day. Stanton attended several of these conventions, starting in January 1840, when the convention endorsed Van Buren for president and Shannon for another term as governor. Stanton thought the economic conditions would favor the Whigs, the party out of power. He wrote Tappan, "If the Whigs had a thimble full of sense or honesty they would carry the state next fall." His implication was that, because the Whigs lacked sense and honesty, Van Buren and the Democrats might eke out a win in Ohio. He did not need to mention one factor that would hinder Ohio Democrats: the strong ties between the state and the Whig presidential candidate, Gen. William Henry Harrison. Harrison had lived and farmed near North Bend, Ohio, for nearly thirty years, and he had served Ohio as both representative and senator in Washington. Van Buren, from upstate New York, had lived much of his life in Washington, and Whigs were soon attacking his lavish lifestyle in the "presidential palace." Stanton also had doubts about whether Shannon was the right man for governor, doubts Tappan quelled with the comment "As he is nominated he must be supported." In Ohio's political system, Tappan wrote, the governor "was of very little consequence, and Shannon [was] as good as average."[13]

Although many letters are missing, those between Stanton and Tappan that survive show how close they were at this time. For example, in February 1840, Tappan introduced a bill in the Senate to impose strict regulations on banks in the District of Columbia and, in particular, to impose personal liability on bank directors for the debts of their banks. The next day Tappan wrote to Stanton to alert him to the bill, to ask him to have it "printed in all the Democratic papers" to "bring public attention to the pure democracy of its provisions." Stanton promptly drafted an editorial supporting Tappan's bill, saying the measure would "prevent fraud and deception" and ensure "a safe and sound currency." A few weeks later, after Stanton mocked some of his Democratic colleagues, Tappan reminded his protégé that it was his "duty to lead and instruct those [in the party] not as well informed as" he and not just to laugh "at their childish follies." Tappan closed, "Give my love to Mary," who had just given birth to the couple's first child, a daughter, Lucy.[14]

Not long after Lucy was born she was "attacked with scarlet fever." Pamphila wrote that Mary was "not very strong" at this time, so the burden of caring for the sick child fell on Edwin. He walked back and forth, carrying the baby on a pillow on his shoulder, to sooth her restlessness. The few remaining Stanton letters from this period are almost all political, not personal, but there is no reason to doubt that he loved his first child, that she filled him with joy when he returned from his legal and political work.[15]

Many Ohio newspapers are also missing from the archives, making it hard to say how often Stanton spoke during the 1840 campaign. A Whig newspaper printed letters between Stanton and the Whig leader John Bingham about a proposed debate between the two men, but the letters ended without agreement. Many years later, after Stanton and Bingham had become friends and colleagues in Washington, Bingham wrote that he had debated Stanton twice during the 1840 campaign, first at Wintersville, "before an immense crowd." There Bingham charged Van Buren with violating the Constitution and backed his claim by reading "from a pocket edition [he] carried." Stanton quoted the Constitution as well, using "a ponderous volume of state papers" and "denouncing [Bingham's reading] as spurious." Stanton's attack on Bingham's reading of the Constitution was during his half-hour closing argument, to which Bingham had no right of reply, but Bingham recalled, "I got on a chair and charged him with skipping the line and challenged him to another debate." After some back and forth a second debate was agreed upon, to be held in Bloomfield, "before another large crowd." Bingham may not have remembered every detail, but surely he captured the intense, all-out politics of the period: one speaker so angry that he stood on a chair to charge the other with omitting a line in quoting the Constitution.[16]

There were many issues in the 1840 campaign, but the key was the deep economic depression. Ohioans blamed the party in power, the Democrats, and in October elected the Whig candidate, Thomas Corwin, as their governor and a substantial Whig majority for their legislature. A month later, in the presidential election, General Harrison carried Ohio handily, with 148,157 votes, while President Van Buren managed only 124,782. Harrison prevailed in the 1840 presidential election in nineteen of the twenty-six states, including even Van Buren's own New York. Although Tappan, Stanton, and other Democrats were dismayed by the results, they did not lose hope, knowing that elections would follow year after year, and that there could be similar dramatic swings in their favor.[17]

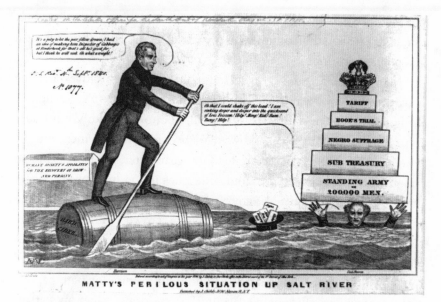

MATTY'S PERILOUS SITUATION UP SALT RIVER

"Matty's Perilous Situation Up Salt River." An 1840 Whig cartoon mocks Van Buren, sinking under the weight of the tariff and other issues, while Harrison navigates his barrel of hard cider to victory.

In early 1841, President-elect Harrison traveled by steamboat up the Ohio on his way to Washington. A committee of Steubenville Whigs was formed to persuade the general to spend a few hours in their town, but Harrison declined, perhaps because he did not want to answer questions from the twenty or thirty men hoping to become the town's next postmaster. When the boat paused at Steubenville, according to a letter from Stanton to Tappan, Harrison was inside, where some were drinking, some were gambling, and a "group round the fire with the old man in their midst were singing 'Van Van is a used up man.'" (This was the 1840 campaign song with the immortal refrain "Tippecanoe and Tyler too.") Harrison, according to Stanton, was "regarded even by his own party as an old imbecile." As to the post office, Stanton had his own plan, suggesting to Tappan that Van Buren should appoint a moderate Whig, disappointing the other candidates, to "breed a deadly strife in the Whig ranks." Tappan rejected the plan as absurd, forcing Stanton to apologize: "Nothing was further from my intention than to give offense to you in the post office matter or to place you in an unpleasant position."[18]

Harrison reached Washington, delivered his inaugural address in early March, then died of pneumonia a month later. His vice president, John Tyler of Virginia, a former Democrat and former governor, was now the president. It did not take long for Washington to discover that, although elected as a Whig, Tyler's ideas were far closer to those of the Democrats. Tappan wrote Stanton that Tyler had assured him in a private conversation that he would work "in all things upon Mr. Jefferson's principles." Stanton was pleased, writing back that he had feared Senator Henry Clay, leader of the congressional Whigs, would become a "dictator absolute and unlimited as any that ever existed at Athens or Rome." Stanton had been traveling for much of the spring, doing legal work but also talking politics, and he reported to Tappan that the Ohio Democrats were "firm and looking forward with confidence to the contest in the fall."[19]

Stanton's legal and political life came to a halt for a few weeks in August 1841, when his daughter Lucy sickened and died. Pamphila remembered that during the weeks of illness that preceded the little girl's death Edwin "was constant in his attendance and devotion to her, scarcely leaving the house save for the most imperative business." After Lucy's death, her father was so distraught that one of his law clerks, Christopher Wolcott, had to write some of his letters to Senator Tappan. Another law clerk, William Buchanan, recalled that about a year after Lucy's death Stanton had her remains removed from the grave and placed in a sealed brass box in the house. If Stanton did this—and there is no evidence other than Buchanan's recollection—he may have done so because he was concerned about a planned relocation of the cemetery, in which Lucy's remains were later reburied.[20]

Stanton was in Columbus again in January 1842 for the biennial Democratic state convention, serving on the Resolutions Committee. Afterward he wrote to Tappan that there was a "division of opinion" on how best to deal with Democrats who were starting to favor more lenient regulation of banks. Some were in favor of avoiding attacks on these "bank Democrats," but Stanton wanted to take a harder line, "exposing them to the people, denouncing them openly as unworthy of confidence," and even "cutting them off from the Democratic Party." We do not have Tappan's response, but it seems likely that he counseled peace. A few weeks later, the Ohio legislature, dominated by Democrats, appointed Stanton to serve as the next court reporter of the state supreme court's decisions. The task of the court reporter was to transform the decisions of the court, often handwritten documents with errors and omissions, into proper printed volumes. The reporter was not just a printer; he was to some extent an editor, working with the judges to prepare a final, polished opinion. The benefits of this patronage position to Stanton were not only the salary of $300 per year but also the opportunity to spend time in Columbus with state leaders and to issue volumes that would make his name known to every lawyer in the state.[21]

In April 1842 the voters of Brooke County, Virginia, just across the river from Steubenville, elected Darwin Stanton to represent them in the state legislature. Many authors have asserted that Edwin helped his brother to secure the nomination and win the election even though Darwin was a Whig. Benjamin Thomas and Harold Hyman, for example, write, "Stanton's zeal for the Democratic party did not overcome his sense of family responsibility." The Virginia newspapers, however, show that Darwin was in fact a Democrat. One paper reported that he was nominated just three days before the election, to replace a candidate who withdrew, but "the Democrats stirred themselves so actively" that they prevailed. Edwin did spend some time that spring in Brooke County, lamenting to Tappan that the Democrats were so disorganized the county was "in great danger of becoming Whiggish." He wrote this *before* his brother was nominated, suggesting but not proving that he had a role in that process. Tappan wrote back that he was "very much pleased that Darwin [was] elected" and was part of a statewide Democratic "revolution" in Virginia.[22]

Economic conditions were hard in Ohio in 1842. Stanton reported to Tappan in May that "factories have stopped and business is dull." Many of the court cases in the spring term were actions to collect, for banks and other lenders were, in Stanton's words, "putting the screws to their debtors very tightly." According to a Cincinnati paper, "The working men are becoming almost desperate for want of work. There is nothing for them to do—they are actually offering to work for their board along the river streets." Democrats declared that the Whigs were to blame. The *Ohio Democrat* noted that the Whigs had promised high prices and a strong economy, but after eighteen months with the Whigs in political control, "the Sheriff is selling wagons for $5.50, hogs at six-pence a head, cows a dollar, and horses which cost 40 or 50 dollars, are knocked off at 2 and 3 dollars each!" Were "prices as low, wages as low, or money so worthless, while the Democrats were in power?"[23]

Not all of Stanton's cases that spring were financial. He represented a Miss McKinley, who sued Dr. Benjamin Mairs for a few dollars owed for board. "In order to scare and cheat her out of the claim," Stanton wrote to Tappan, Mairs countersued for $10 that he claimed she owed him for an abortion. Stanton responded with a suit for slander and libel against Mairs, seeking $5,000 in damages. The key witness for Mairs was "an Irishman he had picked up in some gutter in Pittsburg." He was "dressed in the doctor's own clothes," and when he admitted that he was living with and working for the doctor, there was "great excitement" and a verdict for McKinley on the debt. Fearing he would also lose the libel case, the doctor settled for $900.[24]

Because of the hard times and the anticipated reaction against the Whigs, Stanton believed the Democrats would prevail in the fall. "We can beat them this fall easy," he wrote. On the Fourth of July 1842 he was the main speaker at a Democratic rally in Harrison County. "It was the largest meeting I ever saw," he wrote with pride, "and we greatly outnumbered our adversaries. The Democrats are full of hope and confidence—the Whigs are divided and dismayed." In the October election, Democrat Wilson Shannon received 119,774 votes, the Whig incumbent Thomas Corwin 117,902, and the abolitionist candidate 5,134 votes. A Democratic paper mocked Corwin's campaign: "He begged, appealed, exhorted and 'cracked the whip' over the heads and backs of his followers—he denounced, ridiculed, misrepresented and fairly cursed the democracy of this state, but all to no effect."[25]

Stanton went to Columbus in December to take his oath as court reporter, to start work on his first volume of case reports, and to observe events in the capital. After a tour of the state asylums for the blind, deaf, and mute, he wrote to Pamphila that he was cheered to see the "many ways in which happiness is derived by those who are deeply afflicted." His visits reminded him "of the duties" of those "who have sight and hearing and the gift of speech. How diligent we ought to be, yet how negligent we are." A few days later he described for Tappan a "glorious battle" against a bill to extend certain bank charters, waged by a Democratic state representative named Caleb McNulty. At one point McNulty raised a point of order, which the speaker decided incorrectly; then McNulty "sprang motion after motion—question after question—appeal after appeal, until [the speaker] got bewildered, and could not tell whether he was on his head or his feet."[26]

At this time Stanton's favorite author, Charles Dickens, had a new book out, *American Notes*, critical of Americans, many of whom were in turn critical of the author. Mary wrote her husband, "We owe no thanks to that portion of our people, who disgrace us by receiving Dickens as they did, and will again disgrace us by receiving this book in language abusive of its author." Stanton wrote back on their wedding anniversary to tell her how proud he was of her and their new son, Edwin Lamson Stanton. "I loved you first for your beauty, the grace and loveliness of your person. I love you now for the richness and surpassing excellence of your mind." Then, perhaps realizing this suggested that he thought his wife was no longer beautiful, he added, "One love has not taken the place of the other, but both stand side by side."[27]

In early 1843 Democrats were already starting to debate among themselves whom they should nominate for president. Most, including Tappan and Stanton, favored former president Van Buren. Other Democrats, and not just Southerners, favored former senator John Calhoun of South Carolina. Northerners who supported Calhoun saw him as the best antibank, antibusiness, strict construction candidate. Still others supported Lewis Cass, the former territorial governor and secretary of war, who had recently returned from service as America's minister to France. Tappan thought Cass could never rally the party, writing Stanton that he was "too cold, he has not a warm friend in the world." Tappan and Stanton also suspected that Cass was soft on banks and soft on slavery. When

Cass arrived in Columbus in early 1843, Governor Shannon attempted to convert Stanton to the Cass cause. Stanton reported to Tappan that Shannon and others reasoned that Calhoun and Van Buren would cripple each other. "A bitter animosity is growing up between their respective partisans, which will become irreconcilable, and then Cass will come in sweepstakes." Stanton met with Cass and conversed politely, but he was not converted.[28]

When Stanton's first volume of case reports appeared, Democratic papers praised the book and its author: "Stanton is one of the most promising young lawyers in Ohio—industrious faithful and indefatigable in his exertions—and the state will be greatly benefited, and members of the bar highly accommodated, by his appointment as reporter." Stanton was busy with legal work and politics, writing a friend in July, "The Democrats in this and the neighboring counties have made their nominations and are in fine spirits." In the fall he and his wife set out for Pittsburgh, to consult with a doctor there about her health (some letters suggest she had been ill for some time) and also to visit William Wilkins at his estate on the eastern outskirts of the city. Wilkins was a major figure in Pittsburgh and indeed the nation, a former judge, former senator, and now a candidate for Congress. Stanton hoped to cultivate him as another Washington mentor, but when they reached Pittsburgh Mary was too ill for visiting. Stanton apologized in a letter to Wilkins and then, a few weeks later, when Wilkins prevailed in the congressional election, wrote to congratulate him and to hope that he would become the speaker of the House.[29]

Stanton spent the last few weeks of 1843 in Columbus working with the printers on his next volume of Ohio case reports. In a letter to his wife he quoted from a dense article in the *Edinburgh Review* about the history of the early Jesuits. Mary responded that she would like to read the whole article, for she was "determined upon being somewhat capable of taking part in educating and managing the education of my children. Woman's proper sphere is a high one, and her destiny, if she would but fulfill it, a great one." On the last day of the year, the seventh anniversary of their wedding, Stanton sent Mary, "a prayer that each New Year that may be added to our score, may find us increasing in knowledge, usefulness and love."[30]

Stanton remained in Columbus to attend the January 1844 state convention, where one observer described him as a "tower of strength" for those who favored Van Buren for president and David Tod for governor. "The Cass men," as Stanton described them to Tappan, were "ready to carry out their views against the wishes of the people." But Stanton and the other Van Buren men secured the convention's support: "We have had a hard contest and it is crowned with a brilliant victory." The resolutions, which Stanton had helped to draft, demanded that the United States obtain all of Oregon (which at the time was jointly owned with Great Britain) but were silent on the subject of Texas (an independent nation that many Americans wanted to see become part of the United States). Silence on Texas was probably due to division within the state party, with some favoring and others opposing annexation. Annexing Texas would create another slave state, and would perhaps lead to war with Mexico, which viewed Texas as a rebellious province.[31]

Stanton was en route from Columbus to Steubenville in mid-February when he received an alarming message: his wife was sick with "bilious fever." It seems likely that he was not completely surprised by this news, that Mary had been declining for some time, possibly with tuberculosis, the dreaded disease that killed so many in the nineteenth century. In any case Stanton hastened home and remained at his wife's bedside for the next few weeks. She died in his arms on the morning of March 13, 1844. For a few days Stanton was near madness; Pamphila recalled that at night he "searched the house over . . . and with sobs and tears streaming from his eyes he repeated again and again: 'where is Mary?' " One of his law clerks wrote that Stanton "could not work and could not be consoled. He walked the floor incessantly, crying and moaning."[32]

A week after Mary's death, Stanton wrote to Lewis Tappan, brother of the judge and a leader of the antislavery movement, asking for advice about a marble tombstone, and perhaps indirectly seeking spiritual advice. "This calamity has overwhelmed me," Stanton wrote. "I know not where to look or whither to turn." He and his wife were "young & happy in each other, looking forward to a long life of joy & happiness. By incessant toil & industry we were gathering around us all that we thought would promote our comfort & enjoyment and this spring had in our thoughts attained these. A few days ago I laid her in the grave, and to me they are now ashes, ashes."[33]

———

To support his mother, sister, and son, Stanton was soon back at work. The local paper reported that he prosecuted a murder case "very ably." And he was back in politics, writing to Tappan that he was worried about efforts to deprive Van Buren of the presidential nomination: "The country is flooded with letters from Washington & elsewhere urging the necessity of withdrawing Mr. Van Buren to take some other man. But if our friends remain firm & undaunted we are still safe. Their word should be Van Buren and *no other*." He wrote this letter a few days before a long letter from Van Buren appeared in the newspapers, opposing annexation of Texas because it would "in all human probability" lead to war with Mexico. Van Buren's letter aroused the South against him. Stanton told a friend that if Southerners defeated the Van Buren nomination "the true policy of the Democrats of the Free States would be to support [the Liberty Party candidate James] Birney, and cut loose forever from Southern slavery and Southern dictation."[34]

The Whigs, as expected, nominated their great leader Henry Clay for president in early May. When the Democrats gathered in Baltimore in late May, Van Buren won a majority of the delegates on the first ballot, twice as many as Lewis Cass, but the delegates had adopted a rule requiring that the nominee have a two-thirds majority. Cass gained ground over several ballots, but it became apparent that he too would not be able to secure the required majority. The leaders gathered late at night in their hotel rooms, and the next morning a dark horse emerged and prevailed: the former governor of Tennessee James K. Polk. ("Who is James K. Polk?" Whig editors asked derisively.) Democrats adopted a platform that advocated both the annexation of Texas and the acquisition of all of Oregon, so they seemed to be advocating not just the extension of Southern slavery but the expansion of free Northern territory as well. Stanton probably shared the views of the *Steubenville American Union*, which had previously supported Van Buren, but now pledged to support Polk, calling him "a Democrat of the Jeffersonian and Jackson school" who would "do honor to the distinguished post."[35]

Stanton was a key figure in the 1844 campaign in his part of Ohio. In June the *Cadiz Sentinel* noted that his new legal partner, George Wythe Mc-Cook, had addressed a political meeting and that Stanton himself would address another in a few days. The law offices of Stanton & McCook were in the space once occupied by the defunct Bank of Steubenville. When Samuel Stokely, the Whig candidate for Congress and the former president of the bank, headed a Whig parade past the office, he was greeted by a tombstone, erected by Stanton and McCook, "on which was described the birth, age and death of the poor" Whig bank. The *Cadiz Sentinel* chuckled that Stanton was like the ghost of Hamlet's father, confronting the wrongdoer. In September the *Steubenville American Union* reported that Stanton spoke to a "tremendous and enthusiastic meeting" of Democrats and "skinned the coons and Algerines of Rhode Island handsomely." (Democrats mocked the Whigs for using the raccoon as their symbol and likened the Whig imprisonment of former Rhode Island governor Thomas Dorr to the way American innocents were imprisoned in Algiers.) In early October, on the eve of the state election, Tappan and Stanton addressed yet another mass meeting, this time in Mount Pleasant, Jefferson County.[36]

It was not quite enough. In the October state elections, the Whig candidate for governor prevailed over the Democrat David Tod by about a thousand votes. Stanton himself had ninety-three write-in votes in Jefferson County, votes he probably wished had gone to Tod. The Whigs also gained control of the Ohio legislature, so they would now be able to elect a Whig to replace Stanton's friend and patron Tappan, whose six-year Senate term was ending. In the November presidential election, Clay carried Ohio, but Polk eked out a national victory. It was incredibly close: a swing of a few thousand votes in New York, or in a few other states, would have made Clay the president. The *Steubenville American Union*, trying to look on the bright side, declared that with Polk as president the nation would be "safe" under "the protecting influence of Democracy."[37]

Even before all the votes were counted Democrats began to struggle among themselves over federal appointments. Stanton wrote Tappan from Columbus, "It seems as if almost every man in the state wanted & must have something." Some papers predicted that Cass would be secretary of state, leading men in Ohio to what Stanton derided as "truckling and yielding to the Cass influence to get its recommendations for office."

Stanton asked Tappan whether it was possible that Cass would "be the ruling influence in the administration?" (He would not: Polk ruled his own administration.) There was some talk about making Stanton the federal district attorney for Ohio, but he assured Tappan, "I am not a candidate and *would not accept* if appointed. I would not practice in Leavitt's court while I can make my bread elsewhere." Humphrey Leavitt, the federal district judge, although a Democrat, was a personal enemy of Tappan; he would later become a personal friend of Stanton, but only after Stanton ceased to be a "Tappan Democrat." Although pretending to be disgusted by the scramble for offices, Stanton recommended several men to Tappan, including a candidate for Steubenville postmaster. Stanton favored a man whose family had "for the last three years been the most active and efficient Democrats in town," reasoning that leaders should show their followers that "zeal and industry *before* and *at* the election is the road to office, instead of a hungry appetite after the battle."[38]

In January 1845, Stanton and others were shocked to read that Caleb McNulty, whose stand against banks in the Ohio legislature Stanton had so praised, and who was now clerk of the House of Representatives in Washington, had misappropriated tens of thousands of dollars. Some papers hinted that McNulty was leading a "dissipated" life and involved with "degraded prostitutes." Tappan and other leading Ohio Democrats were named in the reports as McNulty's sureties, meaning they might be liable for the money. Tappan must have assured Stanton that his liability was limited, for Stanton wrote back that he had been "deeply apprehensive on your account and am now greatly relieved by your letter. Your Whig friends have been deeply sympathizing in what they fancied or hoped was your loss." Stanton "advised them to spare their grief, and bottle their tears." When McNulty promised an explanation to the House and then failed to appear, the House removed him from office and recommended prosecution. Even Democratic papers did not attempt to defend him; one wrote that Democrats felt nothing but "astonishment and mortification."[39]

We do not know what if anything Stanton said about Texas during the 1844 campaign, but a letter from early 1845 shows that he still had doubts about annexation. Jacob Brinkerhoff, a member of Congress from Ohio, gave a speech arguing that annexation would benefit only the South. Texas, as slave territory, would not attract Northern immigrants, for they "would not go and plough, and dig, and chop, and grub by the side of the negroes of the South." Stanton wrote Brinkerhoff to praise the speech, saying, "There is too much inclination among Northern men to submit in silence to the insolent demands of the South." Stanton and Brinkerhoff were outnumbered, however; on the eve of Polk's inauguration Congress passed legislation to annex Texas.[40]

As the Polk administration pressed ahead with annexation, and war with Mexico seemed more likely, Stanton started to think about military issues for the first time since his college years. He met John Sanders, a West Point graduate and career army officer stationed in Pittsburgh, and the author of an essay about how the steamboats of the Ohio River could be used in warfare in the Gulf of Mexico. Stanton arranged for the Sanders essay to be published in the *Ohio Statesman*, along with a short article of his own on the same theme.[41]

Stanton's three-year term as state court reporter came to an end in the summer of 1845, as did his legal partnership with Tappan, who retired from legal work when he retired from the Senate. Stanton was still busy as a lawyer, in partnership with George McCook in Steubenville and with others in nearby counties. He was famous for his thorough preparation; for his "pork case," involving a failed pork partnership, a friend recalled that Stanton "travelled all over the country, east and west, for evidence." The case lasted four days, and the jury deliberated all night, during which Stanton walked the streets with his friend because he was "so excited he could not sleep." Finally, at dawn, the jury returned with a verdict in favor of Stanton's client.[42]

In November the *Ohio Statesman* ran an anonymous article arguing that the January Democratic convention should nominate Edwin Stanton for governor: "Mr. Stanton is a man of vigorous intellect—of calm, collected, and energetic demeanor—possesses a warm, lofty, and generous soul." Moreover, and more important to the author, Stanton's political principles were those "of the republican school, as laid down in the Constitution of our country, not only in spirit, but as it is *written*." (There was no Republican Party yet, but Democrats often called themselves and their leaders "republican," in contrast with the elitist Whigs.) A few other Ohio papers referred to the letter, but Stanton was probably not yet well enough known to be the party's candidate for governor.[43]

Stanton was, however, more than able to serve as one of the two defense lawyers for McNulty in his widely watched criminal trial in Washington in December 1845. There were five similar indictments against McNulty, and on the first day of the trial, the federal prosecutor, Philip Fendall, surprised the defense by bringing up the fifth rather than the first indictment. Stanton asked for and received a day's delay, saying that "he had had only a few hours to examine the indictment." On the next day, as the government started to present its witnesses, Stanton went to work, cross-examining them point by point. After Stanton's questions had reduced a government witness to confusion and incoherence, the reporter for the *Baltimore Sun* called Stanton's cross "the severest [he] ever listened to." Stanton also objected, often and with some success, to the government's evidence. At one point, according to the *New York Herald*, he "made an eloquent appeal in defense of the rights of the American citizens, against all the interests and power of the government, and objected to this evidence as an illegal infringement upon the rights of the accused before the jury."[44]

After the prosecution rested, the defense presented a set of Ohio leaders as character witnesses: senators, congressmen, governors, and judges. Since Stanton's defense colleague was a Washington lawyer without Ohio connections, it was probably Stanton who persuaded these men to testify. Interestingly, and impressively, two of these defense witnesses, former governor Joseph Vance and former governor and current senator Thomas Corwin, were Whigs. Darwin Stanton, living and working in Washington as an assistant clerk of the House, described these witnesses in a letter to Pamphila, now living in Akron, Ohio, as the wife of Christopher Wolcott, a former clerk in Edwin's office in Steubenville. The witnesses, according to Darwin, "testified to McNulty's former good character in the clearest and most decided manner, evidently with the greatest effect upon the jury." Pamphila was no doubt proud to hear that their brother was "a great favorite with the crowd."[45]

During closing arguments, Stanton spoke to the jury for three hours. His key point was that the statute in question applied only to funds entrusted to a federal official "by law"; clerks handled funds only by "custom and usage." He argued, "The attempt to convict McNulty upon this law is a case not only of circumstantial evidence, but one of circumstantial law." Stanton also appealed to the jury's emotions, describing McNulty's family circumstances, including his young wife and children. When the jury returned on Christmas Eve with the verdict "not guilty," the spectators "gave a hearty and spontaneous burst of applause." Press reaction divided along partisan lines: the *Ohio Statesman* called Stanton's closing speech "a fine specimen of forensic eloquence"; Whig papers thought Stanton had used a "legal quibble" to save McNulty from prison.[46]

While in Washington, Stanton met with his state's leading Democrats, including Senator William Allen. He almost certainly talked with them about both Oregon, still under discussion with the British, and Texas, to which Polk had sent federal troops. In February 1846, when Senator Allen gave a bellicose speech on Oregon, promising that the United States would fight Britain if necessary to secure the territory, Stanton wrote Allen to praise his stance. In the event, however, there was no war with Britain over Oregon, but there was a war with Mexico over Texas. Stanton, like most Americans, learned of the war through the newspapers; this was the first American war in which there was detailed if delayed press coverage. In early May the papers reported that Mexican troops had attacked American troops on the north bank of the Rio Grande River. Almost all the papers described this as American territory, although it was in fact disputed as to whether it was part of Mexico or part of Texas. The papers also carried Polk's message, not asking Congress to declare war but rather asking Congress to recognize that a state of war *already existed,* and to authorize him to call volunteers into service. Almost immediately, and almost unanimously, Congress passed the requested resolutions. The people supported the war with equal enthusiasm, with thousands rushing to volunteer.[47]

Stanton had no further doubts about Texas. On May 27 he addressed what the local papers described as an immense crowd in the Steubenville town square, declaring, "War on our part is *necessary and just* and no American citizen can oppose it, or withhold his support from it, without sacrificing his duty to his country." He praised those who had already volunteered, including his friend and law partner George McCook, and encouraged others to join the ranks. A few days later, on June 4, thousands turned out to see the Steubenville Greys, under the tall and handsome Captain McCook, march through the town. There were speeches and bands and cannon; men and women cheered and wept. Then the volunteers boarded their steamship and headed down the Ohio River, off to war.[48]

Stanton remained behind in Steubenville, working on his legal cases, writing letters to McCook in Mexico. Stanton's letters have not survived, only notes in McCook's diary, including one saying that Stanton's letters were "the best I ever received for they spoke of her. To rest at a late hour, thinking only of her." McCook was dreaming of Margaret Beatty, an intelligent, beautiful Steubenville schoolteacher. Stanton was also writing to Miss Beatty. In one long letter he thanked her for a poem about love and death: "To mourn or be mourned is a lot which everyone must endure. . . . I have passed through much that you have yet to feel; and much that I trust you may never be called on to endure. . . . On that night when George first told you of his love, there was in your heart a peace tranquility and fullness of joy which no sign, token or speech can express; and none but a heart that has felt it can understand." In another letter he wrote that he was eager "to see her and talk to" her for it filled his "mind with noble fantasies." It seems, although Stanton recognized and approved of the love between Margaret and George, that he was more than a little in love with her himself.[49]

Darwin returned from Washington to his Virginia home with his wife, Nancy, and their three young children. About a week later he sickened with a "brain fever," and on September 23, 1846, he killed himself. Nancy's sister reported to her brother that Darwin had used his razor to "cut himself on his throat and down on his groin where a large artery lays." Stanton rushed across the river, but his brother was already dead. According to later accounts, Stanton "wandered off into the woods without a hat or coat," and the doctor, "fearing a second suicide," sent two men to find him, bring him back, and "watch him every moment." Stanton recovered enough to write a brief obituary of his brother that appeared in the newspaper the next day. He brought Nancy and the children to his home in Steubenville, insisting that "she must make that her home and he [would] help her raise the children as his own."[50]

Stanton alluded to Darwin's death in a long letter to a new friend, Salmon Portland Chase. The two men had similar life stories. After his father died when he was young, Chase was adopted and taught by his uncle, Bishop Philander Chase, the first head of Kenyon College. Like

Stanton, Chase had lost a wife; indeed two of Chase's wives had died young. Chase was a Cincinnati lawyer, passionate about politics, although not a Democrat, having started life as a Whig and now a leader of the Liberty Party. Chase tried to persuade Stanton to join him in arguing before the Supreme Court the case of John Van Zandt, an abolitionist accused of aiding an escaped slave, but Stanton declined: "Events of the past summer have broken my spirits, crushed my hopes, and without energy or purpose in life, I feel indifferent to the present, careless of the future—in a state of bewilderment the end of which is hidden." He claimed to be disenchanted with the Democrats because, in the recent state campaign, their slogan was "Vote for Tod and the black laws." Ohio did not have slavery, but like many Northern states it had black laws limiting the rights of black residents, in particular a provision requiring blacks moving to the state to prove they were not slaves. The Ohio black laws were a campaign issue this year because William Bebb, the Whig candidate for governor, favored the repeal of all laws that discriminated on the basis of race. David Tod, the Democrat, took no position, but this did not prevent some Democratic editors from using the issue against the Whigs. If the black laws were repealed, one Democratic paper argued, nothing would prevent "complete inundation by the useless, toil-worn slaves of the masters of Virginia."[51]

Salmon P. Chase, Stanton's close friend and later cabinet colleague. Chase was a senator, governor, secretary of the treasury, and finally chief justice of the United States.

Stanton was soon writing to Chase often, on law, politics, religion, and literature. A former congressman from Ohio, Thomas Hamer, had recently died in Mexico, where he had hoped to win military glory. "The game he played was a bold one," Stanton wrote, "but death has won it." Stanton suggested that Chase should give Hamer's eulogy: "It seems to me his career, as a politician & warrior, affords a deep lesson that might profit us all, but to which you alone could do full justice." Stanton claimed that he would be guided by Chase in the coming presidential election: "I go by faith more than by knowledge, and have faith in your principles, confidence in your judgment. My feelings are un-enlisted, and I am willing to go for him who will do most for the right." In March 1847 Stanton more or less admitted to Chase that he had been depressed: "Work on the circuit will soon commence, and shake off the torpor of mind & body that has been increasing and overcoming me for months back, so that winter has passed without any memorial of useful labor like yours, for me to boast of." When the Supreme Court, in an opinion by Justice Levi Woodbury of New Hampshire, decided the Van Zandt case against Chase, Stanton consoled his friend: "The dirty work of the South has always found Northern hands to perform it; and I can well imagine the deep scorn & contempt swelling in the bosoms of the Southern judges, as they beheld Levi on his belly crawling through that opinion."[52]

George McCook, now a colonel, and the Steubenville volunteers who had survived their year in Mexico returned in July 1847. When they departed, the local paper had filled column after column with their praises; now, on their return, there was just a brief, tepid report. Many Americans now opposed the Mexican war, and Stanton may have been among them, for he wrote to Sanders, "The laurels in Mexico have all been gathered, and those who remain, are more likely to suffer chagrin, mortification, and disaster than to win glory." Within days of his return, Colonel McCook persuaded Margaret Beatty to elope to Pittsburgh rather than wait for a formal wedding in Steubenville. When she agreed, Stanton escorted her on the steamboat and served as best man at their wedding. He may have used this as a scouting trip for his own Pittsburgh plans. He did not want to move his family, nor abandon his work with McCook in the local courts, but he had mastered the challenges of legal work in his corner of

Ohio. He was bored. He explained to Chase, "My nature requires activity and constant employment, which is not afforded by a country practice in the long vacations." Steubenville was in the country; Pittsburgh was a major city only a few hours away by steamboat. Could he perhaps work in Pittsburgh and travel home to Steubenville from time to time? Stanton decided to try the experiment.[53]

Chapter 3

"The Blackest Place"

—— 1847–1856 ——

Pittsburgh was dark and dirty, brash and booming during the decade Stanton lived there. The population increased from 21,000 in 1840 to more than 46,000 in 1850, with another 21,000 just across the river in Allegheny City. Most of these thousands worked in factories, using the local coal and iron to make cast iron and steel and all manner of steel and iron products. There were glass factories, cotton mills, wharves and warehouses, merchants and lawyers. As Dickens observed when he visited, the city was "beautifully situated" where the Allegheny and Monongahela rivers joined to form the Ohio. The shores were crowded with steamboats heading up and down the rivers with goods and passengers. The city's main feature was what another Briton described as "the smoke and soot with which the whole atmosphere is impregnated." Anthony Trollope, yet another British visitor, wrote, "Pittsburgh is without exception, the blackest place which I ever saw."[1]

Stanton made his move to Pittsburgh gradually. In late October 1847 the *Pittsburgh Daily Post* announced that "one of the ablest lawyers Ohio ever produced" would be moving to and practicing law in Pittsburgh. The next day, on the motion of Charles Shaler, a leading lawyer and former judge, Stanton was admitted to practice law in Pennsylvania. The *Ohio Statesman* urged Stanton to remain in Ohio, saying that his work as court reporter showed him to be "not only one of the first lawyers, but

Pittsburgh as it looked when Stanton lived there in the 1850s. Note the dozens of steamboats along the river's edge.

the first minds in the country." In early December, writing from Steubenville, Stanton told Chase that the reports of his arrival in Pittsburgh were premature. But a week later the *Pittsburgh Daily Post* carried an advertisement for the new law firm of Shaler & Stanton, practicing from an office in the city center.[2]

Stanton still had a home in Steubenville, and his Democratic friends there selected him as delegate to the January 1848 state party convention. He assured Chase they would meet there. When the time arrived, however, Stanton was absent. "Why—why are you not here?" Chase wrote from Columbus. "I came almost solely in the hope of meeting you." Chase was not a delegate, not even a Democrat, but he had hoped through Stanton and others to persuade the convention to speak out against slavery. The convention did almost the opposite, resolving that each state could decide for itself whether to maintain slavery, supporting the soft-on-slavery Lewis Cass for president and taking no position on the Wilmot Proviso, the proposal to prohibit slavery in the territory acquired through the Mexican War. Chase chastised Stanton for his absence: "You have great gifts of God, energy, enthusiasm, talent, utterance. And now a great cause demands you." Stanton responded that he was "busily engaged in a new field of labor," indeed that his legal duties in Pittsburgh "could not be postponed nor on any account abandoned."[3]

After working hard in the 1840 and 1844 presidential campaigns, Stanton did nothing, or at least nothing that remains in the records, in the 1848 campaign. In part this was because he was busy with legal work. Lecky Harper, an ardent Democratic newspaper editor, recalled that Stanton was not much of a Democrat during his Pittsburgh years: "Law, law, law was his god, his mistress, and there he never ceased to worship." Stanton was also torn in 1848 between two parties: the Democrats, the party for which he had worked for so many years, and the Free Soil Party, a new coalition among some Whigs and Democrats and Liberty men, of which Chase was a national leader. Democrats still viewed Stanton as one of their own. In March, when Ohio Whigs passed a controversial law to divide Hamilton County into two electoral districts, a leading Democrat pleaded with Stanton to speak out against the law. In June another Ohio Democrat, Clement Vallandigham, wrote to Stanton, "Politically, the skies were never brighter. Ohio is sure for [the Democratic nominees]. Will you not be in this part of the state [Dayton] sometime during the campaign? You will meet with a hearty welcome." Chase viewed Stanton as a Free Soil sympathizer, writing in June to John Van Buren, son of the former president, "One of the best and ablest democrats in the state, I mean Edwin M. Stanton—said to me today that if John Van Buren should be the nominee of the [Free Soil] Convention he would roll up his sleeves & go to work till the election for the ticket." Stanton seems to have been something of a chameleon, speaking like a Democrat with Democrats and a Free Soil man with Chase and others opposed to slavery.[4]

There were three major candidates for president in 1848: Lewis Cass for the Democrats, the Mexican War hero Zachary Taylor for the Whigs, and former president Martin Van Buren for the Free Soil Party. For a third party candidate Van Buren did well, securing more than 10 percent of the national popular vote. Taylor and Cass each carried fifteen states, but Taylor prevailed because he carried the most populous states, notably New York and Pennsylvania. As the returns were being counted, Stanton wrote to Pamphila, who along with her husband supported the Free Soil Party, saying that he did not regret the "overthrow of Cass," whom he had never liked. He added, "It is to be hoped that the friends of liberty will keep up an organization, and, by preserving an armed neutrality, hold as they may the balance of power in the Free States, until one or the other party, by falling in line, secure our principles." Stanton certainly sounded like he supported the Free Soil Party. And yet within a month he was putting pen to paper to help the Democrats.[5]

There was a struggle over control of the Ohio legislature; indeed for a time there were two rival legislatures, one Whig and one Democrat. The problem was with Hamilton County, where the Democrats claimed that the legislators were two Democrats, elected on a countywide basis, and the Whigs insisted that the rightful legislators were the Whigs, elected in the two districts into which the recent law had divided the county. The *Pittsburgh Daily Post* asked Stanton for his legal opinion. Stanton responded with a long and careful letter, summarizing the facts and quoting the state constitution, which provided for apportionment "among the several counties" and for elections to be held in each county. Because of these provisions, Stanton reasoned, the law dividing the county into two districts was unconstitutional, only the Democrats were validly elected, and the Whig claimants had "no more right to sit in the legislative body, and exercise the law-making power, than any other two citizens of the State." The *Post* printed Stanton's letter with a preface describing him as a leading member of the Ohio bar. The *Washington Daily Union*, in reprinting the letter, called Stanton "one of the most distinguished lawyers in the country."[6]

It is unclear whether Stanton knew, as he wrote this legal opinion, that Chase's political fate would turn on these legislators. Chase hoped the legislature would name him the next senator from Ohio, and it was not a vain hope, for although the Free Soil Party controlled only eleven seats, the party held the balance of power between the two major parties, neither of which had a majority. After weeks of maneuvers, including a backroom deal between Chase and leading Democrats, the legislature in late February 1849 selected him senator. Stanton exulted, writing to Chase, "Thank God the day of small things in Ohio is over!" In May, after a visit from former senator William Allen, the Democrat whom Chase had replaced, Stanton wrote again: "How different were now, my own feelings in reference to [Allen] from the burning zeal with which six years before I had panted for his election."[7]

California, in the midst of its gold rush, applied in 1849 to become a state of the Union. Stanton did not know that he would soon spend a year in California, but like most Northerners he favored its immediate admission as a new state. Southerners insisted that California come into the Union as part of a compromise that would include measures to benefit the South, such as a stronger fugitive slave law. Senator Henry Clay proposed a compromise, and the great senators of the day, including John Calhoun, Daniel Webster, William Henry Seward, and Stephen Douglas, debated the measure for months. In private letters Stanton supported Chase, writing that he had "a calm and strong assurance that truth and right will prevail over the bloody hand and the iron heel." As to California, perhaps "a new republic shall spring up on the Pacific unfettered to the dead carcass of Southern Slavery." If I were a Californian, Stanton added, "I would not court a union that would claim me forever as the partner and ally of slavery, make my state a public agent for slave catchers, and allow them to set their pens and snares throughout her borders." Slavery, he concluded, should be "circumscribed and held within its present limits, within which the system might fester and rot in God's own appointed time."[8]

Stanton did not, however, speak out against the Compromise of 1850 as it passed through Congress. "For Heaven's sake," Chase urged Stanton in March of that year, "get up a rousing meeting forthwith," a meeting to "declare not only the right but the sacred duty of Congress to prohibit slavery in the territories." Two months later Chase teased Stanton for "gathering gold dust, not in the wet but in the dry—aye, dry as parchments & law books can be." Stanton wrote back that Pittsburgh Democrats had no interest in opposing the South on slavery; they supported men such as Cass (now a senator from Michigan) and James Buchanan (former representative, senator, and secretary of state). Chase did not give up on Stanton, suggesting to an Ohio Democrat that the legislature should name Stanton the next federal senator since he was "decidedly and thoroughly antislavery." And Stanton was not so busy with his legal work that he ignored politics; he joined the letter welcoming Robert Walker, a leading national Democrat, when he visited Pittsburgh in the summer of 1850.[9]

Ohio was preparing at this time to revise its constitution, unchanged since the formation of the state, to create a more balanced and modern system. Stanton expected to be a delegate to the Ohio Constitutional

Convention and wrote to his military friend John Sanders that he would "be expected to take some considerable share" of the work. Stanton asked Sanders to advise him about how to reform the state militia system, confessing that he was "ignorant" on the subject "both as respects general principles and details." Sanders responded with a militia proposal that Stanton did not like at all; his handwritten note on the letter describes it as "too complicated, too extensive, too expensive." Stanton would deal with militia issues extensively as secretary of war, but not in the constitutional convention, for he was not a delegate.[10]

In the summer of 1851 some Ohio Democrats wanted to nominate Stanton for a seat on the state supreme court. Stanton wrote to his old friend Tappan that he was not inclined to leave his work in Pittsburgh, but he was willing (in deference to Tappan) to allow his friends to present his name to the convention. They did, and Stanton received sixty-three votes on the first ballot, a respectable showing but not enough to be one of the five nominees for the vacant seats. He was not displeased, writing to Chase that he had consented only "with a view of defeating one to whom I was much opposed and to let it be known that I still hailed from Ohio." The Democratic ticket was "a good one," and he had no doubt that it would be elected.[11]

The following year, 1852, was another presidential year in which Stanton played almost no part. In February he wrote to Tappan from Washington, "The late fight in Philadelphia between the friends of Cass & Buchanan seems to have convinced every one that neither of them can hope to carry the state." He then commented on some of the other candidates but did not mention the name that eventually emerged on the forty-ninth ballot of the national convention: the almost unknown Franklin Pierce of New Hampshire. Stanton was in Washington when the Democrats convened in Baltimore. He could easily have visited but wrote his mother, "I have not been there and shall not go." In the fall he wrote her about the Free Soil candidate John Hale, whom he called "your candidate," suggesting that he himself supported the Democrats that year. Pierce and the Democrats prevailed.[12]

There was some talk among Ohio Democrats in early 1855 about naming Stanton senator. In February the *Steubenville True American* reported, "Edwin M. Stanton on the 4th instant wrote a note to the *Pittsburgh*

Dispatch, denying in the most explicit terms that he either is, or will be in any event, a candidate for the United States Senate. Mr. Stanton has but few if any superiors in the United States, for original power of mind, and for high statesmanship qualifications." William Corry, an Ohio Democrat, also supported Stanton for president, writing to Joseph Holt of Kentucky, "I have been trying for some time to induce Edwin M. Stanton of Pittsburg, another great friend of mine, and lawyer to run for the Presidency with you for Vice P[resident.]" This was an odd suggestion, for Stanton had nowhere near enough political experience to be a serious candidate for president.[13]

At some point in the early 1850s, during one of Stanton's visits to Washington, he met Charles Sumner, the antislavery senator from Massachusetts. Sumner later recalled that he and Stanton did not meet often in those years, but whenever they did it was "as friends." Stanton may have been in Washington in May 1856, when a Southern member of Congress, outraged by a Sumner speech, attacked Sumner on the Senate floor with a cane, beating him almost to death. The attack on Sumner, and almost simultaneous attacks on antislavery settlers in Kansas, made that territory, and slavery in the territories generally, the key issue in the 1856 presidential contest. When the Democrats gathered for their convention in Cincinnati in June, several of Stanton's friends were there, including his partner George McCook and the editor Samuel Medary. The Democrats were divided among themselves on slavery, and only after a bitter fight nominated James Buchanan, who had the advantages of a thick résumé and a thin record on slavery. The Whig Party by 1856 was essentially dead, killed by the division over slavery and the emergence of other parties, including the anti-immigrant Know Nothings and the Republicans. The Republican Party was committed to preventing slavery from spreading into the new western territories. When the party gathered in Philadelphia for its first national convention, some of Stanton's friends were there, including his brother-in-law Christopher Wolcott. Passing over Stanton's friend Chase and future cabinet colleague Seward, this convention nominated the Californian John Frémont for president. Years later Pamphila wrote that her brother had "no confidence" in the "nominee of the Free Soil party in 1856" and, because her brother "certainly would not vote for Buchanan, he changed his residence to Washington city, and did not vote at all." Pamphila was wrong: Stanton was not yet a resident of Washington (whose residents did not vote) in late 1856, and there was no Free Soil nominee that year since the party had dissolved. Stanton probably favored Buchanan for the reasons that many Northern Democrats did: they feared that the election of a Republican president would lead to secession and civil war.[14]

When Stanton moved to Pittsburgh in late 1847, his wife had been dead for more than three years, but he still grieved. "Whatever of good there may be in me is owing to my wife," he wrote to Chase, "whatever evil tendencies there may be, are less restrained since God took her from me." He denied rumors, which had apparently reached Chase, that he was moving to the city for romantic reasons. "I wish it were so. To love, and to be loved, is a necessary condition to my happiness." Similarly, in a letter to Sanders in the summer of 1849, Stanton denied that he was engaged in any "matrimonial pursuit" in Pittsburgh. "If Providence should in due time send a wife the blessing will be thankfully received, but I have not yet hunted one."[15]

Stanton's closest female friend in his early years in Pittsburgh lived in Columbus. Maria Kelley Bates was the daughter of Alfred Kelley, one of the leading Whigs of his generation in Ohio, and the wife of James Lawrence Bates, a Columbus lawyer, later a judge. Edwin and Mary Stanton had met James and Maria Bates at Trinity Episcopal Church in Columbus, where they all worshipped in the late 1830s. Mary and Maria were close friends, and after Mary's death, Edwin wrote long letters to Maria, often about religion. In one he wrote, "The Acts and Epistles of St. Paul have hitherto been my favorite portions of the New Testament," but he feared that he had been "overlooking the merits of the Great Teacher, Christ, and dwelling on those below him." In another letter he wrote, "I have been sensible all my life of the influence of others over myself. There is none now on earth more potent than is exercised by you." It seems that Maria's husband was aware of this correspondence, for at one point Stanton urged that the Bateses visit Pittsburgh so he could show them the sights. When one of Maria's children died, Stanton remembered the death of Lucy: "The child that dies being pure and innocent goes straight to God—but the parent that survived, sin-stained, how shall he become pure?" After a visit to Columbus, to the church where he had first met Mary years ago, Stanton described her to Maria as "a young pure and beautiful maiden in form, but in reality a spirit from the throne of God, whose earthly form was sent to kindle my love, [and] was given to me for a season that her spirit might guide me."[16]

Stanton did not have many friends in Pittsburgh, but he impressed some of those whom he met through his work. Andrew Carnegie, not yet the famous industrialist but a mere telegraph boy, recalled delivering messages to Stanton and being proud to receive his "nod of recognition." Carnegie found Stanton a "vigorous, energetic and concentrated man, always intent upon the subject . . . ever deeply serious." Jane Swisshelm, one of the nation's first female journalists, remembered the determined way Stanton walked: "As we watched him leave the office, in his firm measured tread—feet set down square on the centre—steps apparently of [an] exact length . . . our reflection was 'Ah, Mr. Stanton, you have started with the distinct intention of going someplace, on a bee line, and those who live to see it will find you there.'" Stanton devoted himself to his work and, if he had an hour to spare, to reading. Among the books he read in this period were *Jane Eyre* and *David Copperfield*. "No writer has given me more enjoyment than Dickens," he wrote.[17]

Stanton and his son Edwin Lamson Stanton, about 1850.

Spending most of his time in a hotel in Pittsburgh, rarely seeing his mother and son in Steubenville, Stanton missed them, especially his son. He once reported to Chase that he had "not been able to spend even a day with my family except during the Steubenville court." The first photograph we have of Stanton shows him with his son, Eddie, about six years old. A family servant remembered that Stanton "loved his son passionately. Often have I seen them walking about the yard . . . clasped arm in arm like two school girls." Stanton also remained close with his sisters, Oella and Pamphila. When Oella had difficulties with her husband, Benjamin Tappan Jr., and eventually took the unusual step of seeking a divorce, Stanton advised and supported her and her children.[18]

In November 1849, while working in Pittsburgh, Stanton fell and broke his kneecap. Pamphila wrote that her brother, arriving back in Pittsburgh late at night, "had to cross the deck of another boat to reach the wharf. The hatch had been carelessly left open and he fell into the hold, striking his knee and breaking the knee-cap." An early biographer wrote that "while interviewing pilots at the Pittsburg wharves, he fell into the hold of the *Isaac Newton*, and suffered a compound fracture of the knee, an injury which compelled him to walk with a hitch during the remainder of his life." Stanton went home by steamboat to recover, tended by his mother and sister. He was still in Steubenville in January 1850, when he wrote to Maria Bates that his injury had at least allowed him, "longer than ever before, at any one time, to enjoy the society of the dearest objects of [his] love and contribute to their happiness."[19]

The first hint of a new romance is a letter from late 1851, in which Stanton wrote, "The young lady referred to is still in Pittsburg amiable and attractive as ever, with many admirers, among whom a young officer in the army seems to be the most highly favored. For myself, I have been too much occupied with other engagements to think of what would probably much more contribute to my happiness." The "young lady" may well have been Ellen Hutchison, whom Stanton would eventually marry. Her father, Lewis Hutchison, originally from Kentucky, was now a leading merchant in Pittsburgh. When asked by the census officer in 1850, Hutchison declared that he owned real estate worth at least $200,000, which would make him one of the wealthier men in Pittsburgh. There were four Hutchison children listed as being at home in this census report, including Ellen, age nineteen, and four servants. Hutchison family letters reveal that Ellen and her sisters had attended schools back East, that they had many beaux in Pittsburgh, and that they traveled from time to time to see relatives in Kentucky, where they were surely served by slaves. Ellen was not much of an intellectual. In one letter she confessed to her sister that she had tried to learn how to play chess but was "too stupid ever to learn anything that requires too much thought." Her older brother, James, had married Catherine Wilkins, daughter of William Wilkins, and Ellen addressed Catherine as her "sister" and stayed often at the Wilkins estate. Some have speculated that Edwin met Ellen through a new Episcopal congregation, formed in 1852, but it seems likely, given his own connection with Wilkins, that Edwin met Ellen through Wilkins not long after arriving in Pittsburgh.[20]

Ellen Hutchison, Stanton's second wife, at about the time of their marriage in 1856.

At the time of the 1850 census, Stanton was thirty-five years old and owned real estate worth $17,000. (Even among the lawyers of Pittsburgh, the most common answer to this census question was "zero"; perhaps Stanton was just more willing to admit his wealth to the census officer.)

When his young cousin William Stanton wrote to him asking whether he should study law, however, Stanton's reply was lukewarm. "Success in [the law] depends upon many contingencies that cannot be foreseen; and even successful practice brings much smaller remuneration than is supposed by outsiders, and is subject to evils and annoyances greater than any one can imagine." Still, he did not absolutely advise against a legal career. "I would not dissuade anyone who feels a clear call to the profession in preference to any other mode of life. The question therefore is one that you must decide for yourself. No one can determine it wisely or safely for you."[21]

Stanton spent most of his time in Pittsburgh, but he was also often in Washington, preparing for and arguing cases in the Supreme Court. He did not much like Washington. In early 1852, for example, he wrote to Tappan, "Besides the presidential agitation there is nothing of any interest in Washington. There is no one in either branch of Congress that a person wishes to hear speak; neither is there any question of importance under discussion." (This was a Congress that included the great orators Clay, Douglas, and Seward.) "There are not many pretty faces on the avenue to look at—handsome women are very scarce here. Stupid lectures are delivered at the Smithsonian—so that Lola Montez is the only object at Washington at present of any interest." Montez, the former mistress of King Ludwig of Bavaria, was indeed of interest, dancing each night at the National Theater, but surely there were other sights worth seeing. In late 1854, Stanton described for Ellen Hutchison a Washington dinner party: "While ladies are present the conversation is usually upon general or interesting topics but after their departure wine and cigars, drinking, eating and political topics neither elevating or refining in their tendency ensue. I would never attend such assemblages if it could be avoided."[22]

By the summer of 1854, if not earlier, Stanton was writing warm letters to Ellen, including one describing a picnic in the woods near Steubenville. He encouraged her to read more seriously, writing that she should use the "rare gifts of intellect that Providence has endowed you with." He asked her to share a poem with their mutual friend Judge Jeremiah Black, who would later play a key role in Stanton's career. By now Stanton was in love with Ellen, but she was cool toward him. "What can I say to interest you," he wrote, "since the feelings most strongly pervading my heart find no echo in your bosom?"[23]

It seems that Ellen waited until Valentine's Day of 1855 to say that she cared for him. "I felt last evening not only that I love but am beloved," he wrote her the next day. "May such feelings towards each other continue to dwell in our hearts, growing with our growth, strengthening with our strength." The course of true love never did run smooth, and at some point he angered her with a display of temper. She wrote to chide him for having "a heart careless and indifferent to the feelings of all but those who may contribute to a selfish gratification, and even they must sometimes feel its want of charity." He wrote back to apologize, at length, for his temper. "If the last few years of my life had been different, if I had been blessed with the companionship of a woman whose love would have pointed and kindly corrected my errors, I would have escaped the fault you condemn." It was perhaps because of such tensions that they entered a solemn agreement: "If any difference or misunderstanding should hereafter occur between us, whatever it may be, we will not separate without a kiss of forgiveness and reconciliation."[24]

When Stanton was away from Ellen on legal business, he wrote to her almost daily. From Philadelphia in January 1856 he thanked her for a letter: "It is sweet to know that we live in the thoughts of those whom we love—and, however certain the conviction may be, it is pleasant to receive assurance of what our hearts wish." From Washington he wrote in February that he would probably have to remain there for at least a week to argue a case in the Supreme Court: "The Court has been taken up for two days with long-winded speeches by Reverdy Johnson and other counsel in a slave case that ought not to have occupied more than a couple of hours." Thus did Stanton dismiss the most momentous case of the decade, *Dred Scott v. Sandford*, in which the Supreme Court was considering whether slaves could become citizens. Stanton was back in Washington again in May, thinking of and writing to Ellen: "My spirit has all day been dwelling upon you, longing to be with you, and chafing impatiently at the necessity that keeps me from you."[25]

On June 25, 1856, Stanton wrote to Ellen, "On this morning of our marriage day, I salute you with assurances of deep and devoted love, that this evening will be attested by solemn vow before the world and in the presence of God." They were married at the Hutchison family home by Reverend Edward Van Deusen of St. Peter's Episcopal Church. Ellen's brother, James, in a letter to his daughter, described the wedding as "small, not more than forty persons present, no groomsmen or brides-maids. Aunt Ellen's dress was very handsome, white satin, very heavy, I think it would stand alone." George Harding, a prominent Philadelphia lawyer with whom Stanton had worked, was among the wedding guests; he gave the bride a handsome silver cross. James Hutchison wrote his daughter that the couple planned to travel to "Niagara, Montreal, Quebec, White Mountains, who knows." Ellen and Stanton were gone for weeks; indeed, they may not have returned to Pittsburgh until after the November election.[26]

Stanton's most important case in his Pittsburgh years was *Pennsylvania v. Wheeling & Belmont Bridge Company*, known simply as the Wheeling Bridge case. The dispute originated in 1847, when the Virginia legislature granted a charter to the Wheeling & Belmont Bridge Company to build a bridge across the Ohio River at Wheeling, Virginia, about a hundred miles downstream from Pittsburgh. The company hired a brilliant young engineer, Charles Ellet Jr., who started working on the towers for what would be the world's longest suspension bridge. Tall steamboats passed the Wheeling construction site every day on their way between Cincinnati and Pittsburgh, but for some reason the Steel City's leaders were not worried. That changed in June 1849, as the bridge neared completion, when Stanton's partner Shaler called a public meeting. Shaler and others pointed out that the new bridge, especially at high water, would prevent tall steamboats from reaching Pittsburgh and thus cut off the city's vital river link to Cincinnati and New Orleans. In time Wheeling might even take Pittsburgh's place as the region's major port and communication point. Ellet would later accuse Shaler and Stanton of rousing Pittsburgh to fight against his bridge; he had a point, for it was only after this meeting that work started on the long litigation.[27]

Charles Ellet Jr., the engineer who
built the Wheeling Bridge, then
built the ram fleet for Stanton
during the Civil War.

Stanton and Shaler made several key decisions right away. First, they persuaded Pennsylvania's attorney general Cornelius Darragh that the state itself should file suit against the bridge company. Having the state as plaintiff meant the case could be filed in the U.S. Supreme Court, under the provision of the Constitution giving the Court original jurisdiction of claims by one state against citizens of another state. Second, Stanton would not wait until December, when the entire Supreme Court gathered in Washington. No, he would proceed immediately, seeking a preliminary injunction from Robert Grier, the justice responsible for the circuit that included Pittsburgh. Grier had served for fifteen years as a state court judge in Pittsburgh, and Stanton probably reasoned that no judge would be more sympathetic. Stanton sent a telegram from Pittsburgh to Grier in Philadelphia, asking whether he would hear oral argument on the request for an injunction in mid-August. Soon thereafter Stanton and Darragh traveled to Philadelphia, armed with a revised complaint and a sheaf of supporting affidavits.[28]

The first of Stanton's many oral arguments in the Bridge case took place in August 1849 in the federal courthouse in Philadelphia before Justice Grier. The first question, in a sense, was whether the Supreme Court had jurisdiction at all. John Cadwalader, a leading Philadelphia lawyer, argued for the bridge company that the Court had no jurisdiction because Pennsylvania was not suing as a sovereign: it was representing the merchants of Pittsburgh, who could, if they wished, sue for themselves. Stanton responded by saying that Pennsylvania itself had been hurt because the state had spent millions of dollars on public works that relied on river access to Pittsburgh. The Wheeling Bridge was in legal terms a nuisance that would hinder and obstruct the passage of steamboats along the Ohio River, prevent the passage of goods and passengers, reduce the state's toll revenues, and thus injure the state and its citizens. To prove that the bridge would obstruct river traffic, Stanton presented evidence on the height of the river at flood tide, the height of steamboat stacks, and related points. He demanded that the bridge company "abate the nuisance," in other words, that the company remove or (if this was even possible) raise the bridge so high that it would not affect the steamboats. Cadwalader touted the benefits of the Wheeling Bridge to those traveling by road between Ohio and Virginia and argued that the bridge would not in fact impede steamboat travel up and down the river. He also insisted that Pennsylvania had unfairly delayed, waiting to file its case until the bridge was almost complete.[29]

The Wheeling Bridge, longest suspension bridge in the world at the time it was built, was to Stanton an unlawful threat to commerce on the Ohio River.

After the argument Stanton waited in Philadelphia, thinking Grier might have further questions. In late August he wrote from there to

Sanders to predict that Grier would not issue an injunction because he was "afraid of being overruled and will go off on a question of jurisdiction." It seems Stanton may have had at least a hint from Grier about the imminent decision. Grier ruled in Stanton's favor on the jurisdictional question, finding that the case was proper for the Supreme Court, but he declined to issue an injunction, saying it was too important a question to be resolved by a single justice. Grier sided with Pennsylvania on several key issues, finding that the bridge in its current configuration would prevent passage of "a large class of steamboats down the usual channel of the river in the highest flood." The Wheeling Bridge encroached upon the right to navigate the river; it was a public nuisance; and it didn't matter that it was "but a *small* encroachment or a *little* nuisance."[30]

Stanton was quite pleased, telling Sanders in a second letter that Grier's opinion was "entirely satisfactory—for although he postpones the injunction until December on the ground that there is no immediate impending danger and the question new—yet every point is sustained so far as his opinion goes." Indeed Stanton thought that Grier's "very great caution & forbearance" would give his opinion "more weight than it might otherwise have had." Stanton's one fear was that, rather than fight the case in the Supreme Court, the bridge company might just "raise the bridge without further proceeding. But this I do not desire. Having my hand in I am disposed to push it to the girth." He hoped, in other words, to argue and win the case in the Supreme Court.[31]

The Wheeling Bridge opened for business in October 1849, but Stanton was not troubled; he was "busy taking testimony in the bridge case." In total, he and his colleagues obtained depositions from fifty-two witnesses: they explored the details of how steamboats were designed and constructed, why tall chimneys were preferred, why it was difficult and dangerous to lower or cut the chimneys in order to pass under the bridge at high water. Stanton was no doubt pleased when, in November, several steamboats were stopped at the bridge; one of them had to lower its chimneys in order to pass underneath; another simply unloaded its passengers and goods and returned the way it came. The Wheeling newspapers alleged that it was because of Stanton that the Pittsburgh steamboats claimed the bridge obstructed their way, that the boats would have passed without incident but for Pittsburgh's "diabolical counselor" Stanton.[32]

It was in the course of this work, while crossing a steamboat deck at night, that Stanton injured his knee. He went to Steubenville to recuperate and continued to work from bed. In late November he wrote Robert Walker, former secretary of the treasury, now a Washington lawyer, "Two days before the accident that laid me up with a broken limb I had received authority from the committee having charge of the Wheeling Bridge case to employ such assistant counsel as I might prefer." Stanton had intended to go to Washington in early December to meet with Walker in person, but that would have to wait; in the meantime, he asked Walker to start reading the record. The *Pittsburgh Daily Post* reported that "some of the citizens of Wheeling were particularly pleased when they heard of the accident that happened to Mr. Stanton, and they even boasted that the case in the Supreme Court would have to be abandoned." The *Post* was sure, however, that Wheeling would obtain "no undue advantage over Pittsburg on account of the unfortunate accident that befell the senior counsel in the case."[33]

Stanton's knee was probably still quite painful when he went to Washington two months later. On February 25, 1850, he was admitted to the bar of the U.S. Supreme Court and argued the Bridge case before the full Court. Stanton described the courtroom in a letter as an impressive room on the ground floor of the Capitol Building, "the floor handsomely carpeted, the furniture of the best kind, with sofas on each side for ladies & other visitors." During his two-hour argument, he focused on the facts: the Ohio River at Wheeling was only about a thousand feet wide, but "through this strait, fifty millions in value of property, and over three hundred thousand passengers, are accustomed to pass safely and without impediment, in steamboats to and from Pittsburgh." The Wheeling Bridge would block the passage of large steamboats, the boats that carried most of this trade. The bridge would also hinder progress in steamboat design; it "forbids all advance or improvement in the size and dimensions of vessels." Pennsylvania had suffered and would suffer serious injuries, including loss of toll revenue on state toll roads and canals, loss of trade and construction work at Pittsburgh. Other states, similarly situated, might threaten secession, but Pennsylvania "ma[de] no appeal to force." Instead Pennsylvania asked the Court for an injunction requiring that the Wheeling Bridge be either raised or removed.[34]

The *Pittsburgh Gazette* reported that Stanton was "listened to through-out, with unflagging attention by the court." A friend who was in the audience later recalled that Stanton "had a slight lisp, but not enough to detract in the least from the effectiveness of his speaking. He was dig-nified in manner, and very forcible in his delivery. He would hardly be called an orator, but he was listened to with great interest by the court and by the lawyers." After making his argument, Stanton remained in Washington for a few days to hear the arguments of his colleagues and opponents. Then he returned to Pittsburgh to await the Court's decision. Stanton was not idle, writing to Walker in March that he had arranged for more depositions, to show that during the spring flood the bridge had blocked several more steamboats.[35]

In late May the Supreme Court issued its decision, a one-page order, agreeing with Stanton that the case came within the Court's original ju-risdiction and appointing Reuben Walworth, the learned former chan-cellor of New York, as commissioner to resolve the factual disputes. Although the Supreme Court has original jurisdiction in certain cases, it almost never hears testimony or receives other evidence; it appoints "commissioners" or, in modern terms, "special masters." The Court asked Walworth to focus on two key issues: whether the bridge ob-structed the navigation of the Ohio River, and, if so, whether and how the bridge could be changed so that it would not impede traffic on the river. Stanton told Sanders that he was satisfied with the decision because it ruled in the state's favor on the "only point for which I felt any personal responsibility—the question of jurisdiction & regularity of proceeding." But Stanton was not as pleased as he suggested. He had hoped that the Court would issue the injunction, and now he faced the task of present-ing the evidence again, this time to Walworth, and of persuading Wal-worth to side with Pennsylvania.[36]

Walworth started work in Wheeling in July 1850. Over the course of the next few months, at hearings in Wheeling, Cincinnati, Pittsburgh, and elsewhere, the parties presented evidence from more than eighty witnesses, including boat pilots, passengers, engineers, professors, and state officials. Stanton prepared and presented the witnesses for Penn-sylvania; he also cross-examined the witnesses for the bridge company. He stressed that the bridge blocked not only some current steamboats but would block the even larger steamboats of the future. He presented detailed evidence from engineers to show that, in order to permit passage of steamboats, the bridge should be raised to a height of at least 130 feet above the river. And Stanton cultivated Walworth, both face-to-face when they were together and through letters when they were apart.[37]

Walworth finished hearing from witnesses in the middle of December 1850 and started to write his report. Stanton hoped that Walworth would submit the report in January so the Court could decide the case before its members dispersed, which usually happened in March. Stanton was working on a separate brief to address a few points, but he decided against filing the brief, telling Walworth that he feared the bridge company would use it as an excuse for further delay. Walworth submitted his 700-page report in February 1851, concluding that the bridge obstructed the navigation of the river and recommending that it be raised at least twenty-eight feet to permit the passage of steamboats. Stanton disagreed with some details, but generally Walworth sided with him, and when Stanton went to Washington in February, he hoped for an injunction along the lines Walworth suggested. The bridge company, however, persuaded the Court to delay the case until December to allow time for the parties to prepare and file exceptions to Walworth's report. Stanton remained in Washington for a few weeks to work on another case, and while there he tried to interest a Philadelphia publisher in a book about the Wheeling Bridge case. The case involved "points of practice never before raised," Stanton wrote, as well as general legal questions "of vast importance." The printed evidence to date was about fourteen hundred pages, which Stanton thought he could condense "into the size of one convenient volume," a volume that would be "much sought after by the legal profession." The publisher's response is lost, but no volume appeared.[38]

Stanton returned to Washington in December 1851 to argue the Bridge case again, this time with George Harding of Philadelphia at his side. Stanton and Harding now faced an uphill battle because public opinion about the Wheeling Bridge had shifted. The *American Telegraph*, a Washington paper, praised the bridge as both beautiful and useful, carrying more than 270,000 people by foot and 160,000 wagons each year. The *Ohio State Journal* admitted, "At times of very high water, the boats with very high pipes are compelled to lay by or lower the pipes—what then? Is it necessary for the public commerce that these skyscraping pipes should be erected? We think not." Railroads, which needed bridges, not steamboats, represented the future. "All the power of steam—all the concentrated heat that can be made by pipes sweeping the very clouds, cannot be applied to propel boats so rapidly as the iron horse . . . and the man of business, to whom time is an object, will very soon desert the river, and take to the railroad." The *Philadelphia Ledger* argued that the Wheeling Bridge would serve as a precedent for a second bridge, a railroad bridge, to carry a direct rail route from Philadelphia westward to Cincinnati and beyond.[39]

Stanton's December 1851 argument was again rich with facts, based on his thorough research on the western rivers. Responding to the suggestion that steamboats could if necessary simply lower their smokestacks, he explained that the boats usually approached the Wheeling Bridge at night. "When, therefore, their chimneys are to be lowered, supposing it even possible . . . the task is to be accomplished under the most formidable dangers. Upon a slippery deck, over boilers of steam and fiery furnace, contending with wind and current, the boat must be guided through a narrow space of 100 feet in width, while huge chimneys, three tons in weight, are to be lowered to the deck." Stanton also argued the law: the Ohio River was a national highway, protected by the Commerce Clause of the Constitution; the bridge company was merely a private company, a few men trying to make a profit, claiming they acted under a state charter. Stanton was appealing here to what we would call the "dormant Commerce Clause," the doctrine that a state statute or practice that unduly burdens interstate commerce may be unconstitutional even if it is not in direct conflict with any federal statute. He urged the Supreme Court either to invalidate the Virginia law authorizing the bridge or to construe the law so tightly that the bridge would have to be raised or removed.[40]

The Supreme Court announced its decision in February 1852. The majority opinion, written by Justice John McLean of Ohio, agreed with Stanton that there was jurisdiction for the Supreme Court to hear and decide the case, and agreed that the Wheeling Bridge in its current configuration interfered with interstate commerce along the Ohio River. The Court did not invalidate the Virginia statute, finding instead that the bridge company had exceeded the terms of the statute, but the effect was

similar, for the Court prohibited what it viewed as state or local interference with interstate commerce. After some behind-the-scenes horse
trading among the justices, about which Stanton may well have learned
from his friend Grier, the Court required the company to raise the bridge
by twenty-eight feet or to make some other change so that navigation
would not be obstructed. If the bridge company did not make such
changes within a year, the company would have to remove the bridge
altogether. Stanton had won, or so it seemed.[41]

Even before the Court issued its decision, Ellet and his lawyers were
working on another approach: a draw, a section of the bridge that could
be raised or lowered, allowing boats to pass when raised. The bridge company's lead lawyer, former attorney general Reverdy Johnson, promptly
filed papers to ask that the Court revise its decree to allow for a draw.
Stanton and Johnson argued the issue before the Court in late February.
Ellet, in letters home, said Stanton made a "flaming speech" because he
was angered by the way in which Ellet had countered him "in the flush
of victory, by the suggestion of a draw, dovetailing in most beautifully
with an expression of opinion by the Court." The Court referred the
matter to another commissioner and then amended its order to allow for
a draw.[42]

The bridge company's main focus in 1852, however, was not on the
Supreme Court but on the Congress. The company sought federal legislation to approve the bridge in its current form and to declare the road
across the bridge a national post road. Ellet wrote pamphlets in favor of
the bridge, and Stanton helped to write at least one response, presented
as a pamphlet by his friend William Wilkins. On a Saturday evening in
August, at the end of a long congressional session, the Senate debated a
Wheeling Bridge amendment to the post office appropriation bill. Senator Richard Brodhead of Pennsylvania opposed the amendment, arguing
that it would be an improper attempt by Congress to review and overturn
the decision of the Supreme Court. Senator George Badger of North
Carolina, principal proponent of the amendment, denied this "utterly
and absolutely," saying it was perfectly appropriate for Congress to balance the competing interests of railroads and steamboats. Senator Chase,
probably using arguments provided by his friend Stanton, declared, "This
whole case has been very carefully considered by the Supreme Court

and they have come to a decision that the bridge, in its present position, is a nuisance, and seriously obstructs the navigation of the river." Chase claimed that even Ellet believed the bridge could be raised at a cost of only about $40,000 or $50,000. Chase urged Congress to wait "a few months, until the matter can be settled by experience." But Brodhead and Chase did not have the votes; the Senate adopted the amendment at midnight by a vote of 33 to 10. The House followed suit just before Congress adjourned, and the president signed the measure into law. The *Wheeling Intelligencer* rejoiced that "the question is settled not only for the present, but for all time to come."[43]

Stanton returned to Washington in February 1853, to argue that the bridge company should be held in contempt for not raising the bridge as required by the Court's opinion and order. The Court postponed the question, setting a hearing for the second Monday in December. When that date arrived, for some reason neither Stanton nor any other lawyer for Pennsylvania showed up to argue the case. Stanton himself was in Pittsburgh on that day, arguing a different case in federal court, but surely he had not forgotten the Bridge case. It seems more likely that his client, the new state attorney general, decided there was no point in fighting the federal statute. An Ohio newspaper cheered that Pennsylvania had finally yielded "to the sentiments of the nation" and that "the Wheeling bridge [would] stand." An Indiana paper agreed, predicting that this would "probably be the last of this foolish proceeding."[44]

Not quite. In May 1854, in a strong spring thunderstorm, the cables snapped and the Wheeling Bridge fell into the Ohio River. The *Wheeling Intelligencer* announced the news with "unutterable sorrow" but declared that the community would rebuild as soon as possible. Stanton notified the bridge company that Pennsylvania would apply for an injunction against a new bridge at any height lower than that specified in the 1852 decision. In late June, Stanton appeared before Justice Grier, again seeking an injunction, and this time he obtained one because the bridge company failed to appear. Ellet, however, continued work on the bridge without regard to Stanton or Grier. A temporary bridge opened in July, and Stanton moved for sanctions for violation of the Grier injunction, including the arrest of Ellet and an attachment of the company's assets.[45]

Stanton was back in Washington in December 1854 to argue this phase of the case. The bridge company's lawyer insisted that the federal statute legalized the bridge at its present height. Stanton responded that Congress had no authority to overturn the decision of the Supreme Court. Quoting veto messages by Presidents Madison, Monroe, and Jackson, he argued for a narrow, limited reading of the congressional power to establish post roads, so that Congress did not have authority to protect the bridge by that method. In early 1856 the Court decided this new version of the bridge case against Stanton. The majority ruled that with the statute, Congress had blessed the bridge in its present form. Justice McLean dissented, seeing the bridge as improper discrimination against the port of Pittsburgh. The full Court dissolved Grier's injunction and dismissed the case. "*The Bridge stands,*" a Wheeling paper rejoiced, "in spite of Pittsburgh and Mr. Justice Grier."[46]

The Wheeling Bridge still stands today, a national historical landmark, in spite of Pittsburgh, Grier, and Stanton. Yet from other perspectives Stanton did not fail. Pittsburgh remained a major river port, served by steamboats, for decades to come. Wheeling did not supplant Pittsburgh as the major center of the region. At the end of the nineteenth century, when Pittsburgh's population exceeded 300,000, Wheeling had only 38,000 residents. And from a personal perspective Stanton had established himself not just as a Pittsburgh lawyer, not just as an Ohio lawyer, but as a national lawyer, able to handle the hardest cases in the highest court.[47]

———

Before moving to Pittsburgh, Stanton sometimes sounded like Thomas Jefferson, a radical revolutionary. "Most of our histories have been written by aristocrats," he wrote to Chase, "and are mere lying apologies for aristocracy, its wicked frauds and bloody crimes in all governments and in every age." The echo is not surprising. Jefferson was the patron saint of the Democrats and, as a diehard and well-read Democrat, Stanton almost certainly owned the four volumes of Jefferson speeches and letters published in 1830. But after moving to Pittsburgh, Stanton sometimes worked as a lawyer for the elites, the owners of the factories and the railroads. A prime example is the cotton factory riot case.[48]

Under a new state law, set to take effect on the first day of July 1848, the workday was limited to ten hours, unless individual employees agreed to a longer day. To pressure their workers to sign twelve-hour contracts, the owners of the large cotton factories in Allegheny City closed their doors on July 1. After a standoff of several weeks, one factory persuaded about fifty workers, mostly women, to sign new twelve-hour contracts. When these women showed up at the factory on the morning of July 31, a hostile crowd of their former coworkers jeered at them as "white slaves." By late morning the crowd outside the factory gates had grown to about a thousand, shouting and cursing the owner, Robert Kennedy, the women who were working, and the out-of-town police defending them. Kennedy thought he might disperse the crowd with a blast of the factory's steam whistle. It was a mistake: the escaping steam scalded one girl and spattered many others with hot mud. The outraged crowd now attacked with axes, sticks, rocks, and other weapons and broke through the gates and into the factory itself. Although nobody was killed, many were injured and much equipment destroyed.[49]

The factory owners were determined to prosecute those involved, and they hired Shaler and Stanton as special prosecutors. The grand jury indicted sixteen people, including five young women, for their roles in the riot. The newspaper coverage of the case divided on partisan lines, with Whig papers supporting the owners and Democratic papers siding with the workers. The *Pittsburgh Daily Post* argued that the owners had "violated the social rights of the operatives." It would be unjust to punish a few individuals, the *Post* continued; the answer was political reform to assure that workers had their rights. Shaler and Stanton, both Democrats, found themselves on the Whig side in this case, arguing for law and order.[50]

The trial lasted a week in January 1849, in a packed courtroom. As in any trial there were surprises and setbacks. Stanton called as the first state witness Joseph Scott, one of the deputies. Scott related the details of the riot, but then on cross admitted there probably would not have been much fighting but for the blast of steam. The defense tried to paint the defendants as innocents, men and women of fine character who were just in the wrong place at the wrong time. When a defense lawyer asked one of his witnesses, a young girl, whether she belonged to a church, Stanton objected to the improper character evidence, saying he was "surprised

that so good a lawyer should put such a question." Judge Benjamin Patton agreed and sustained Stanton's objection. In their closing arguments,
Shaler and Stanton stressed that the issue was not the proper length of the
workday but whether the state would be ruled by law or by riotous mobs.
Patton echoed these arguments in his charge, saying that the rioters were
trying to replace the rule of law with "a bloody code."[51]

After deliberating for several hours, the jury convicted thirteen of the
defendants. Some papers criticized the result. One Philadelphia paper
claimed that the state had prosecuted and imprisoned girls as young as ten
years old just because they refused to work twelve hours a day, and called
on the governor to pardon and release the girls: "Do not let them rot in
prison." But it seems that a pardon was not necessary because the defendants left town before the jury rendered a verdict. One paper reported
that the defendants had "taken to themselves wings" and did not intend
to "appear to hear the eloquent sentence of the Court."[52]

In the spring of 1849, Stanton and Shaler were hired to defend "a young
man of good family" accused of shooting and killing a black porter along
the riverside. They argued that the defendant had acted in self-defense
in response to an attack. The *Pittsburgh Dispatch* criticized Stanton for
an overly broad definition of self-defense: "Any killing of a fellow creature would be justifiable, provided the killer *believed* himself in danger.
It would leave to every man to decide whether he should consult his
passion and pride by killing a despised assailant." The jury, however,
agreed with Stanton, finding the defendant not guilty. A few days later
Stanton was on the other side, prosecuting several doctors accused of
disinterring and dissecting human bodies. The government's witnesses
described finding parts of corpses in barrels in one of the doctor's barns.
The *Dispatch* again criticized Stanton, this time for boring the court "with
a long sermonizing speech in the resurrection case." The *Pittsburgh Post*
disagreed, asserting that the audience had expected a great speech from
Stanton and were not disappointed. The *Pittsburgh Gazette* also sprang
to Stanton's side: "Things have come to a pretty pass, indeed, when
such a paper [as the *Dispatch*] speaks thus of a lawyer of the eminence of

Mr. Stanton." The *Dispatch* responded that it had a right to its opinion about Stanton's "verbose" speech and criticized his "rudeness" during the riverside murder trial, "in speaking of our fellow colored citizens as niggers." If Stanton indeed used this term, it would not have been unusual in the place and time; he used it on at least one other occasion, in a political letter in 1861.[53]

Many of Stanton's cases were political, such as his work for former federal senator David Yulee. Yulee was a remarkable man: born a Jew on a Caribbean island, he moved to Florida, studied law, prospered in business, and was elected in 1845 as one of Florida's initial federal senators. Not long thereafter Yulee changed his name, married the daughter of a former postmaster general, and converted to Christianity, raising his children as Episcopalians. Stanton met Yulee in 1847 on a western steamboat and remarked, "[He] impressed me favorably." They talked about slavery, with Yulee arguing that slave owners had the right to take their slaves into the territories. A few months later Yulee sent Stanton a pamphlet version of the argument, noting that when they discussed the issue Stanton "did not seem at that time convinced." Still Stanton must have impressed Yulee as well, for he turned to Stanton to serve as his lawyer in the contest over his Senate seat.[54]

As Yulee's first senate term was ending, the Florida legislature met to select his successor. On the first ballot, there were twenty-nine votes for Yulee and twenty-nine votes for "blank." The speaker announced that there was "no election." Two days later, on a second ballot, a majority of thirty-one voted for Stephen Mallory. Both Yulee and Mallory were Democrats, but Mallory was seen as more moderate, Yulee as more extreme. The Senate seated Mallory in December 1851, but also formed a special committee to consider Yulee's claim. Stanton argued Yulee's case before this committee twice: first in March and then in June 1852. The March argument is not recorded, but Stanton arranged for the June argument to be printed as a pamphlet of forty dense pages.[55]

Stanton contended that Yulee was properly elected in the first round of voting because there was a quorum of both houses of the Florida legislature present and all the votes, of those who voted for any person, were for Yulee. Those who had voted for "blank" had not voted, Stanton insisted, and to prove his point he quoted from British court cases and from Madison's reports of the constitutional convention. The purported election of Mallory on the second ballot, according to Stanton, was meaningless, because the legislature could not deprive Yulee of his Senate seat. The special committee, however, ruled in favor of Mallory, relying on a Florida rule that required a majority of the whole legislature, thirty votes, to elect a man to the Senate. In late August, at almost the same time as the Senate voted against Stanton on the Wheeling Bridge issue, the Senate voted against him in the Yulee election dispute.[56]

Stanton was involved in a wide variety of cases, none more odd and interesting than his work for Joshua Nachtrieb against the Harmony Society, one of the most successful of the many small utopian communities in early nineteenth-century America. The founder of Harmony was George Rapp, a prophetic and forceful minister who had been born in Germany. Members turned over all their property to the Society, living and working in celibacy, combining ancient religious piety with modern business methods. In 1846, after twenty-seven years as a dutiful member, during which he became a skilled hatmaker, Nachtrieb offended Rapp by visiting a nearby town and talking with some former members. Rapp summoned Nachtrieb to a meeting the next day and accused him of trying "to raise a mob." Nachtrieb denied it, saying, "If I had thought it was wrong to go there, I would not have done it." Rapp insisted that Nachtrieb "must *go right off* and leave the town." Two days later, after evening religious services, in front of the whole community, Rapp pronounced that Nachtrieb "must now leave the society; we cannot have such men." As he departed, the abject Nachtrieb signed a receipt prepared by one of Rapp's deputies: "Today I have withdrawn myself from the Harmony Society, and ceased to be a member thereof. I have also received from George Rapp, two hundred dollars as a donation, agreeably to the contract."[57]

Three years later, in 1849, after marrying and moving to Ohio, Nachtrieb approached Stanton, who agreed to represent him in federal court. In his complaint, Stanton claimed that Nachtrieb was "wrongfully excluded from said association, turned out of its possessions, and deprived of all share and participation in its property . . . by the frauds . . . of the said George Rapp and his associates." Stanton alleged that Nachtrieb, through his skilled work, had contributed about $2,000 a year to the income of the Society, and that all he received in return was his room and board and simple clothing, worth perhaps $50 a year. Although Stanton did not use the word, in essence Stanton was arguing that Rapp treated Nachtrieb as a slave. Stanton requested an accounting—a detailed examination of the finances of the Society—so that Nachtrieb could receive "the share he was justly entitled to in the property and estates of said association, and the profits accrued during his membership."[58]

The Society responded that Nachtrieb was not entitled to anything. Its lawyers relied heavily on the receipt Nachtrieb had signed; they also quoted at length from a contract he and others had signed, in which they declared that departing members would not have any right to a share of the property, that departing members would receive only as much as Rapp gave them "as a donation." Stanton summoned witnesses who testified about how Rapp had expelled Nachtrieb, and presented this evidence in Pittsburgh to a federal circuit court composed of Justice Grier and District Judge Thomas Irwin. Although they differed somewhat in their reasons, Grier and Irwin agreed in their 1852 opinions that the receipt and contract did not preclude Nachtrieb's claim. "When we consider the nature and extent of the authority exercised by George Rapp over his followers," Grier wrote, "their reverence and fear of him and their unbounded submission to his command, it must be very evident that the signature of such a receipt as the above would be but slender evidence that the complainant acted voluntarily in withdrawing himself from the Society." Grier and Irwin were not quite sure, at first, how best to estimate what the Society owed Nachtrieb, so they appointed a commissioner to take evidence on the financial issues, including the net worth of the Society as of the date Nachtrieb departed.[59]

Over the course of the summer of 1852, dozens of witnesses appeared before the commissioner and were cross-examined by Stanton and his colleague about the finances of the Society. The printed record of this

phase of the case runs to 158 pages. Eventually the commissioner concluded that there were 321 members of the Society at the time Nachtrieb
departed, that the value of the property as of that date was $901,723, and
that Nachtrieb should have his pro rata share of this amount. Stanton
now argued the case a second time before Grier and Irwin, who rejected
the Society's argument that Nachtrieb's only remedy was to rejoin the
Society. "Such a decree would compel him, perhaps, to forsake his wife
and children, for the small hope of the survivorship in the tontine. This,
we think, would be rendering very scant justice or recompense to a man
for half his life's labor." Grier and Irwin awarded Nachtrieb his share of
the net worth on the date of his departure, plus interest, less the amount
he had received, for a total of about $3,890.[60]

The Society appealed to the Supreme Court, probably because it
feared the circuit court decision would lead other members to depart
from the Society. In December 1856, the same month in which the
Court would hear a second round of arguments in the fateful case of
Dred Scott, Stanton presented Nachtrieb's case in Washington. His argument for Nachtrieb was similar to the opinion of Grier: that Rapp
was effectively the dictator of the Society and that (whatever the receipt
said) he had effectively expelled Nachtrieb from the Society. The Supreme Court was not persuaded: it ruled that the receipt was a contract
between the Society and Nachtrieb, binding on both parties. The case
was not a complete loss for Stanton, for he arranged for his argument
to be printed in pamphlet form, another chance to show his legal skill.
As for the Harmony Society, it would continue until the early twentieth century, leaving behind some beautiful buildings as well as strong
socialist ideals.[61]

———————

Another interesting and very different case was the reaper patent case, through which Stanton met Lincoln. The plaintiff was Cyrus
McCormick, already famous as the inventor of the McCormick reaper,
and the defendant was John Manny, inventor of a competing reaper,
which McCormick claimed infringed his patents. Manny hired a first-
rate legal team, headed by George Harding, with whom Stanton had

worked closely on the Wheeling Bridge case, and Peter Watson, a leading Washington patent lawyer. Harding and Watson hired Stanton as part of their team, and also Abraham Lincoln, a former member of Congress from Springfield, Illinois, because the case was originally to be tried in that state. When the case was transferred to Cincinnati, it seems that nobody on the defense team informed Lincoln that his services were no longer required.[62]

Abraham Lincoln in the 1850s, at the time he met Stanton.

Stanton and the other defense lawyers arrived in Cincinnati in late September 1855 and stayed at the Burnet House, at the time the largest and finest hotel in Ohio, perhaps in the whole Northwest. Stanton wrote to Ellen from there, "Last evening I was very anxious for Mr. Harding had been unwell several days and I was apprehensive he would not be able to be in court so that the scientific part of the case to which I had given no attention would also fall upon me. Accordingly by sitting up all night I got ready for it. This morning, however, he was much better and acquitted himself so admirably that a great burthen is taken from me." Stanton boasted this was the "most important patent cause that has ever been tried, and more time, labor, money and brains have been expended in getting it ready for argument, than any other patent case has ever had bestowed upon it." On the next day he wrote her, "Day by day I think we are making advances upon the enemy, and already have them nearly surrounded. Harding is marking out and opening the trenches and arranging the batteries, and it will be left for me to make the assault for which I am all ready." Stanton was indeed ready for the assault, speaking for a whole day, at one point mocking McCormick by saying that his medals and prizes had blinded him.[63]

One of the "facts" that many people "know" about Stanton is that he insulted Lincoln when the two men first met in Cincinnati. David Donald, in his biography of Lincoln, quoted Harding. "We were all at the same hotel. Neither of us [Harding and Stanton] ever conferred with him [Lincoln], ever had him at our table or sat with him, or asked him to our room, or walked to or from the court with him, or in fact had any intercourse with him." Doris Kearns Goodwin, in her book on Lincoln and his cabinet, wrote that Stanton asked Harding, "Why did you bring that damned long-armed ape here . . . he does not know any thing and can do you no good." Lincoln supposedly told a friend that he was so impressed by Stanton's closing argument (he had never "seen anything so finished and elaborated") that he intended to go home to Illinois "to study law." The problem with these quotes is that none of them was recorded at the time; they are all based on recollections shared years later, and in some cases are second- and third-hand recollections. It does seem likely that Stanton was rude to Lincoln in Cincinnati, for Stanton was often rude. But it is improbable that Stanton called Lincoln a "damned long-armed ape." That quote, from an 1887 letter by Lincoln's law partner William Herndon, sounds suspiciously like George McClellan's memoir, published a few weeks before Herndon's letter, in which the general claimed that Stanton, not long before joining Lincoln's cabinet, had called the president a "gorilla."[64]

The trial court decided the case in Manny's favor in early 1856, but McCormick appealed to the Supreme Court. Stanton worked with Harding on this appeal, in which they prevailed, and on other related reaper cases in the Supreme Court.[65]

We do not know why Stanton decided to move to Washington in late 1856; perhaps he expected to focus more on Supreme Court cases; perhaps he hoped for work from the new Buchanan administration; perhaps he and his wife just wanted to get out of the smoke of Pittsburgh.

Whatever the reason, Stanton moved with Ellen, who was expecting their first child in April or May. They rented a house at 365 C Street Northwest, just a few blocks from the Capitol Building. Stanton would reside in Washington for the rest of his life.[66]

Washington, D.C., as it looked when Stanton and his wife Ellen moved there. The artist imagines a viewpoint over the Capitol, looking down Pennsylvania Avenue toward the White House.

Chapter 4

"Untiring Industry"

—— 1857–1860 ——

S tanton wrote in early March 1857 that his son and nephew were "enjoying themselves with the ceremonies & shows of the inauguration." Stanton may well have been in the audience to hear Buchanan's inaugural address. Buchanan alluded to the pending *Dred Scott* case, saying that, like all good Americans, he would "cheerfully submit" to whatever the Supreme Court decided. We now know that Buchanan was willing to abide by the ruling because he knew, from potentially unethical conversations with members of the Court, how they would decide the case. Two days after the inauguration, in an opinion by Chief Justice Roger Taney, the Court held that Scott could not sue in federal court because, as a black slave, he was not and never could become a citizen of the United States. The Court also invalidated the Missouri Compromise, ruling that Congress could not exclude slavery from the federal territories. Republican papers attacked the decision, but some Democratic papers praised it; one hoped the opinion would "exert a mighty influence in diffusing sound opinions and restoring harmony and fraternal concord throughout the country."[1]

If Stanton disagreed with the *Dred Scott* decision, he kept his views to himself, for he was seeking at least an informal role in the Buchanan administration through his friend Jeremiah Black, Buchanan's choice as attorney general. Stanton and Black had known each other since about 1851, when

Black became a member of the Pennsylvania state supreme court, although there are no surviving letters between them from before 1857. As soon as Black arrived in Washington, a few days after the inauguration, he had a letter from Stanton saying that he had tried to find him at both his office and his hotel. Quoting a recent Dickens novel, Stanton assured Black that he would "always find a knife a spoon and an apartment" with the Stantons. Black explained that he had been very busy and added, "My desire to have a confidential friend of the highest professional ability, just to talk with, is not a whit diminished." Stanton replied that he would "come to see you at any time, at any place, you may designate by note, sign, or message."[2]

Jeremiah Black. As U.S. attorney general he hired Stanton to litigate the California land cases, then persuaded Buchanan to appoint Stanton as the attorney general.

Stanton was not seeking an appointment in the Justice Department for there was no such department yet. But the very absence of a department might allow Stanton to serve as an important informal adviser to Black. Stanton also hoped that Black would hire him to represent the federal government in cases in the Supreme Court, for it was common at the time for the attorney general to rely on private lawyers to argue federal cases.[3]

In October 1857 Black offered Stanton a rather different assignment: to represent the federal government in land cases in California. Black was especially concerned about the claims of José Limantour, a Frenchman now living in Mexico, who claimed thousands of square miles of land under eight Mexican land grants. The federal land board, established by Congress to review and decide Mexican land claims, had approved two of Limantour's claims: one that covered much of San Francisco and another that covered certain key islands, including Alcatraz in the harbor. If affirmed, the board's decision would cost both the federal government and the state's residents millions of dollars in rent to Limantour. Black was worried that Limantour, who was described as having deep pockets and few scruples, would prevail in California district court. The government could appeal to the Supreme Court, but at that point it would be too late for new evidence. "The fabricated titles have been skillfully made," Black wrote, "and the false oaths are perilously bold, so much so that some of the worst cases have found favor in the eyes of the local courts." The new federal district attorney, Peter Della Torre, pleaded from San Francisco with Black for help, and Black in turn asked his friend Stanton.[4]

Stanton told Black that he could not start on the monthlong trip to San Francisco just yet, for he had important cases pending in Pittsburgh and Washington, including another reaper argument before the Supreme Court. Moreover Stanton thought that "much work" should be done in Washington before going to California: reading the Limantour record, already a thousand pages, and reviewing the other California land claim cases pending in the Supreme Court. As Black knew, Stanton was involved in at least one of these cases, as the fourth lawyer out of four on the claimant's brief in *United States v. Fossat*, a dispute about a boundary at the New Almaden mine. Stanton wrote Black that a review of all the California cases, including *Fossat*, would provide "a clear view and accurate knowledge of *every grant* that has been made. After this preparation here, counsel should go to California and *stay there* until every thing be done, and see personally that it is done properly." Black and Stanton apparently agreed that Stanton would go to California but would not leave at once. In the interim, Black started to rely on Stanton to answer legal questions about California cases.[5]

Stanton and Black were focused on California, but the nation was focused on Kansas. There were two rival governments in Kansas: the free-state government of Northerners and the slave state government, known as the Lecompton government because that is where its constitution was drafted. The Lecompton constitutional convention suggested a questionable form of ratification, asking voters to approve the constitution "with slavery" or "without slavery," but not giving them the option to disapprove the document altogether. In his annual message in December, Buchanan supported both the Lecompton constitution as drafted and the proposed form of ratification. The next day, in a three-hour speech, Illinois senator Stephen Douglas denounced the Lecompton constitution and especially the proposed referendum: "If this constitution is to be forced down our throats, in violation of the fundamental principles of free government, under a mode of submission that is a mockery and insult, I will resist it to the last." The Democratic Party was divided from this day forward into the Buchanan wing and the Douglas wing. In spite of this division, Buchanan pushed through Congress a bill to allow Kansas immediate admission into the Union if the state would accept the Lecompton constitution as drafted. The Kansas voters, however, rejected the offer of statehood on these terms.[6]

After Stanton's death, Black claimed that Stanton supported Buchanan on Kansas, that Stanton "was always sound on the Kansas question and faithful among the faithless on the Lecompton constitution." Probably Stanton did, as Black recalled, tell Black that he opposed "the knavish trick of the abolitionists in preventing a vote on slavery" in Kansas. But Stanton also sent a friendly letter to Douglas after his speech, saying that he was pleased "the day has not yet come when an American senator may not boldly speak what he truly believes." Stanton was fortunate that Douglas did not publish this letter, which could easily be read as supporting Douglas on Kansas, for this would have doomed Stanton's chances of working for Black and Buchanan.[7]

In February 1858, as soon as Stanton finished his Supreme Court argument in the reaper case, he and Black agreed on the terms of the California assignment. Stanton would proceed west immediately and work primarily on the Limantour case. Black also authorized Stanton to work on other land cases and urged him to report often. For all this work Stanton would receive a legal fee of $25,000, plus expenses (about $500,000 today). Stanton met on the eve of his departure not only with Black but also with Buchanan, who handed him $250 in cash to cover the travel expenses of his nephew, who would join Stanton as one of his aides.[8]

Stanton made this trip with three other men: his son, Eddie Lamson Stanton, now fifteen; James Buchanan II, about twenty-four; and Horace Harrison, an aging navy lieutenant whom Stanton had defended in a recent court of inquiry. A severe snowstorm delayed them for a day in New York City, allowing Stanton to write a few last-minute letters. The four then embarked on the *Star of the West*, a large steamship bound for Panama. Stanton's first onboard letter to his wife described the four men huddled together in his stateroom, struggling to stay warm. He did not mention to her, but admitted to his friend Peter Watson, that the cold weather "brought on a sharp attack of asthma—the worst I have ever had."[9]

Stanton wrote his wife almost every day, describing the ship, the sea, the sights. They reached Kingston, Jamaica, early on a Sunday and attended services at the Episcopal church, where Stanton described the mixed black and white congregation as "one of the most fashionably dressed, well-behaved, devout-looking assemblages I ever saw." A few days later they reached Panama, where they boarded the new railroad, allowing them to cross the isthmus in only about four hours rather than the three or four dangerous days required during the gold rush. On the Pacific coast, while waiting to board their ship, they visited Panama City, known for its "strong fortifications, the splendor of its churches, and the wealth, luxury and vices of its inhabitants." Stanton, however, saw mainly "dilapidation and decay."[10]

The Stanton party now boarded the *Sonora*, an even larger steamship, with about eight hundred passengers, bound for San Francisco. The ship proceeded far too slowly for the impatient Stanton. When they stopped at Acapulco, he found the Mexicans "ignorant, degraded, lazy and worthless"—yet said the women made "beautiful specimens of shell work & other ornamental trifles." Back on board he spent time studying a Spanish grammar. Finally, on March 19, the *Sonora* reached San Francisco. Stanton and his colleagues went to the International Hotel, an elegant new five-story structure, where they would reside.[11]

The next day, a Saturday, Stanton met the district attorney Della Torre and reviewed the status of the Limantour case. Limantour's lawyers had presented an impressive array of documents and witnesses to District Judge Ogden Hoffman to support the two pending claims. The documents for the San Francisco claim included a letter from the Mexican governor Manuel Micheltorena, offering Limantour land in return for funds the governor needed; a petition from Limantour to the governor asking for the specific tract; a grant signed by the governor for the land in question; and a letter dated later in the year from the Mexican foreign minister, confirming the land grant. Similar documents supported the islands claim. All the witnesses agreed that the signature was that of Micheltorena, and the documents appeared to be on the proper paper and to bear the proper seals.[12]

One of the key witnesses for Limantour was Manuel Castañares, a Mexican government official who had traveled to San Francisco with the permission of the Mexican government and at the request of the French government. Castañares had testified that he himself had printed the official paper used for the Limantour grants, in Monterey in November 1842, and that he had sent about a thousand pages of this official paper to the governor, who was at the time in Los Angeles. Della Torre probably told Stanton more or less what Hoffman would later write about Castañares: that the "official position and the intelligence of this witness" made him most persuasive. Based on this testimony and other evidence, many people believed that the Limantour grants were genuine.[13]

The Limantour case was proceeding slowly; weeks would often pass between one witness and the next. This was good news for Stanton, for he had a plan: to review all the grants and letters for this period, making himself the master of the Mexican procedures. He started at once. In early April 1858 he wrote to Watson that he was spending "almost ten hours every day in examining and arranging Spanish documents, letters, records, etc., in the archives office." He may have been working even more than ten hours a day, for he wrote his wife, "My daily life is to rise at seven, breakfast at eight, go to the office at nine, remain there until five or six in the evenings, dine at six and spend the evenings in my room. Eddie insists that I shall not work later than ten or eleven, and I generally yield to him." One of his assistants recalled that Stanton was soon able "to substantially translate any ordinary Spanish document." Stanton reported to Black that he had "six book binders at work, two clerks & Mr. Harrison, Mr. Buchanan, Eddie & myself from eight in the morning to six in the evening." Stanton and his team worked their way through the archive in San Francisco and then searched for relevant documents elsewhere. Stanton went to Benicia, the former military headquarters, where he found four boxes of old records. He sent young Buchanan to Los Angeles, a difficult and dangerous journey but one that yielded important documents.[14]

Although he worked them hard, Stanton's helpers praised him. Harrison wrote to Black in early June, "Mr. Stanton has had the stables of Augeas to clean, but he brought to the task the powers of a Hercules. I have never seen a man of such untiring industry, indomitable perseverance and well-directed energy." The president's nephew wrote that Stanton was "a kind-hearted and companionable man" and "disposed to give every one a chance—a great merit in young people's eyes." Stanton also received praise from Black and Buchanan in Washington. In late April, Black wrote Stanton that the "progress you make in the Limantour case is just what I expected of your energy and talents." Buchanan "was delighted in his own sagacity in selecting so able and faithful a man for this important business." A few weeks later Black wrote that Buchanan had "expressed great pleasure at learning what an immense amount of work you were doing and had done. When I came to the part of it in which I mentioned the number of volumes you had collected he broke out 'God bless me, what a task.'"[15]

Stanton could not know it at the time, but his work in California was good preparation for the work he would later do in the War Department. In both instances, he had to create order out of chaos: the binders of land records he gathered and organized in California were the predecessors of the binders of telegraph messages he would assemble during the Civil War. His California assignment required him to recruit and manage a staff, something his prior work as a private lawyer had not really required. And in both cases he was working as a *federal* lawyer, having to consider the political as well as legal aspects of his work, dealing with federal financial constraints. If Lincoln needed proof in early 1862 that Stanton could manage the War Department, the way Stanton handled the papers, people, and issues in the California land cases would have been sufficient.[16]

Day by day, document by document, Stanton built his case against Limantour. In the boxes from Benicia he found original letters from the governor, complaining at the time of the purported Limantour deeds that he did not have official paper. Through an expert, Stanton determined that there were only two seals on ten thousand documents from this period: the actual official seal and the fake Limantour seal, appearing on only a handful of documents. At considerable cost he hired photographers to take pictures of some of the key documents. These pictures, Stanton wrote Black, "will afford you and the several departments of the government the means of knowing what the archives are, the forgeries that have been committed, the means of detecting them, and will protect about two thousand square leagues of land." He added, "In the face of these all Mexico may perjure herself at leisure. A lie can't be made the truth, as these photographs will prove."[17]

At some point in the summer Stanton decided that he would start work on a second major land case, involving the New Almaden quicksilver mine. There were several competing claims, including the Fossat claim, on which Stanton had briefly worked in Washington, and the Castillero claim, whose owners were in current control of the mine, reportedly worth $25 million. Rather than work on the pending Castillero case in the district court, Stanton decided to start a new case, in circuit court, seeking an injunction against further operation of the mine. He probably reasoned that an injunction would place intense, immediate pressure on the Castillero claimants, more pressure than any decision by the district court, which would have no effect during an appeal to the Supreme Court.[18]

Stanton worked on the Castillero case with two colleagues, Della Torre and Edmund Randolph, son of the Virginian of the same name who had served as attorney general under President Washington. The three federal lawyers filed a thirty-page complaint against six individual defendants. Among them was Henry Halleck, a lawyer working as the mine's local superintendent, later a general with whom Stanton would work closely during the war. Castillero, the complaint alleged, had never completed the proper procedures under Mexican law to acquire mining rights, so the land belonged to the United States as part of the public domain. All the Castillero title documents on which the defendants relied were "false, forged, ante-dated, and fraudulent against the United States." The defendants were mere trespassers, extracting illegal profits of a million dollars a year. Since the individual defendants could never pay such amounts from their own pockets, the court should use its equitable powers to enjoin them from operating the mine and should appoint a receiver to operate the mine and hold the profits.[19]

Stanton and his colleagues attached to the Castillero complaint forty pages of an extraordinary correspondence among those interested in the claim about how to obtain backdated Mexican documents. One of the letters, headed "very private" and dated May 1849, listed "the documents which Don Andres Castillero will have to procure in Mexico." This correspondence was already in the record in the district court, but by putting it front and center in the new circuit court case, Stanton focused on the credibility of the Castillero claimants. Judge Matthew McAllister at once ordered the defendants to "show cause" in ten days why the circuit court should not issue an injunction and appoint a receiver.[20]

Meanwhile, in the Limantour case, Stanton and Della Torre were pressing to close evidence and to schedule final arguments. Limantour's lawyers sought to delay the case and then, in September, Limantour's main law firm resigned, giving his one remaining lawyer an excuse for further delay. It thus happened that Stanton gave his daylong argument in the Castillero case first, on October 8, in a courtroom crowded with lawyers and others. A week later, on October 15 and 16, he presented his final arguments in the Limantour case. Limantour's lawyer did not bother to reply.[21]

On October 29, as Stanton and his colleagues had requested, the circuit court issued an injunction closing the New Almaden mine. There were two opinions by the two judges of the court: McAllister focused on the legal issues and Hoffman on the facts, especially the Mexican correspondence. The *Daily Alta California* rejoiced, saying that the people of the state were under "lasting obligations" to Stanton and Randolph for bringing the Castillero claim "to a thorough legal test." The paper added that Stanton had accomplished an "immense amount of work since his arrival."[22]

Three weeks later, on November 19, Stanton won another victory when the district court decided the Limantour case. Hoffman's opinion, which covered more than sixty printed pages, reviewed the case point by point, and on almost every point he ruled for the government. The paper on which the Limantour grants were printed was fraudulent, as proved by the letters that Stanton had found at Benicia. The seals on the Limantour grants were fraudulent, as proved by the careful comparison of the genuine seals with the Limantour seal. There was no debt owed by the governor to Limantour, to be "paid for" with land, for Stanton had found and presented other documents showing that the Mexican governor had paid Limantour in full for the amounts he had advanced. Most damning of all were the "blank grants" that the government had introduced into evidence, pages with the Mexican governor's signature but no text. Hoffman wrote, "It is not easy to confine within the limits of judicial moderation the expression of our indignation at the fraud which has been attempted to be perpetrated." The *Daily Alta California* rejoiced again, saying that Hoffman had "utterly demolished" Limantour and predicting, "San Francisco has seen the last of him and his claim." The editors were right; Limantour never returned to San Francisco, nor did he appeal to the Supreme Court.[23]

In his first letter to his wife from San Francisco, Stanton wrote that "everything here is strange and wonderful." Forgetting what he had said to Black—that the lawyer sent to California should "stay there" until the work was done—he told her he might be able to start for home in May. Letters took about a month to travel between San Francisco and Washington, so it was probably because of this letter that Black wrote a stern letter to Stanton about rumors that he would soon return. Black urged:

[Stay] as long as there remains anything in the world you can do for this great cause you are engaged in. There is no other man living on the round earth for whom I would have assumed the responsibility I have taken with you. You must succeed or be able to prove that success was utterly impossible. . . . Your interest in success is like my own exactly—I mean equal to my own in magnitude. The Squire

[President Buchanan] and those who frequent his house . . . must continue to think that the smartest thing they ever did in their born days was to get you to look after the affairs of the parish.

We do not have Stanton's specific response to this letter, but we know that he stayed, just as Black insisted.[24]

San Francisco as it looked when Stanton lived there. This substantial city, one of the fifteen largest in the United States, was a sleepy village only ten years earlier.

San Francisco was indeed "strange and wonderful" in 1858, a city of fifty thousand people that had grown from almost nothing in the gold rush decade. As Stanton noted in a letter to a friend, the city was still overwhelmingly male: "The number of families is too limited and recent to form an established female society, such as exists in other cities of the same size." Because of this, gentlemen formed clubs: "And club life here is very pleasant." He visited one of these clubs and found, "The rooms [are] spacious and well-furnished, and the air of a fashionable assembly of gentlemen prevails." He also reported "a deep, bitter, and revengeful feeling between the Vigilantes and the Law and Order parties." Less than two years before Stanton's arrival, some leading citizens, upset with what they viewed as slow and uncertain local courts, had formed a vigilance committee, hastily tried and hanged four men on murder charges, and forcibly deported others whom they deemed undesirable. After a few months the vigilantes declared victory and dissolved their organization—although a few leaders continued to meet in secret. None of the vigilantes was indicted or tried for their crimes, which the law-and-order men viewed as mere murder. Stanton may well have met one of the leading law-and-order men, William Tecumseh Sherman, originally from Ohio, during the weeks they overlapped in San Francisco, before Sherman boarded a boat to return to the East.[25]

Stanton wrote often about life in California, which he loved. "The climate is very pleasant," he wrote his wife in April, "the forenoon is delightful." The warm weather meant that, even this early in the year, they were eating "strawberries, green peas, cucumbers, and asparagus." After a brief outing into the countryside south of San Francisco, near what is today the San Francisco airport, Stanton wrote, "The earth [was] covered as far as the eye can reach with a rich carpet of flowers of every color and form." Those who lived in California "seem to be hardly conscious of the beauty that spreads around them in rank luxuriance." He teased Black, who was still in Washington in August, "While you have been melting with heat, we have had the freshness of a spring or autumn morning all the while. Every evening I wear an overcoat, and sleep under blankets. Nothing can be conceived more genial than the mornings and forenoons—and the evening breeze is fresh and invigorating beyond description."[26]

Stanton's asthma improved markedly in the California weather. He even claimed in one letter to his wife that the only reason he had traveled west was for his health: "Was it ambition that brought me here dear love? Is it ambition that has detained me here? No dear love, no, no. I came here because I thought your happiness would be promoted by an improvement in my health. I have remained that the improvement might if possible be perfected. All else has been secondary to these objects." In other letters, however, he admitted his ambition, writing near the end of his stay that he had prevailed in "the two most important suits that were ever tried in the world, and gaining them against the expectations of anyone."[27]

There were other, less pleasant aspects to life in California, such as the tendency of the residents to fight and kill one another in duels. Stanton wrote to Watson in May about a rumored duel arising out of a dispute over a fugitive slave. "If it takes place, it will no doubt be a bloody affair." The proposed duel was between George Pen Johnston, the federal commissioner who had released the fugitive slave, and S. H. Brooks, who, according to a newspaper, insulted Johnston by telling him that he had "robbed" the owner "of his nigger." This duel did not take place, but Johnston was involved in another political duel later in the summer, shooting and killing a state senator. "With all its advantages of climate, soil, and minerals," Stanton wrote, "California is heavily cursed with the bad passions of bad men and I would not like to make my permanent abode upon its soil." He returned to this theme in August, writing to Black that when "California becomes settled with a new race of people, and all the thieves, forgers, perjurers, and murderers that have invested it beyond any spot on earth shall be driven off, the coast will breed a race of men that have had no equal for physical & intellectual capacity in the history of recorded time." California was a wonderful place—the only problem was the people.[28]

Stanton was especially negative about Mexicans. The Spaniards, who had controlled California until 1821, he praised, saying in a letter to Watson, "The old Spaniards were a grand race, and their wonderful administrative talent has nothing like it at the present day." Mexicans he dismissed. Traveling with a friend around the bay, they met an Irishwoman, from whom they purchased buttermilk. "The old woman made a good deal of fun for us with a *greaser* or native Californian who had come that afternoon to ask the old woman's Indian girl to marry him." Stanton was simply echoing here the views of most Americans. One of the leading books about California declared that the Mexicans were "generally indolent, and addicted to many vices, caring little for the welfare of their children, who like themselves grow up to be unworthy members of society."[29]

Stanton remained a political person, even in California, writing Black just after the October 1858 elections that he should congratulate

Buchanan on his "most triumphant and glorious victory." The principal parties in California were the Buchanan Democrats, also known as the Lecompton Democrats because they favored the president and the Lecompton constitution, and the Broderick or Free Soil Democrats, antislavery supporters of Senator David Broderick. Buchanan and Broderick were bitter enemies. Broderick had declared in the Senate in March that he hoped historians would "ascribe the attempt of the executive to force this [Lecompton] constitution on an unwilling [Kansas] people to the fading intellect, the petulant passion, and trembling dotage of an old man on the verge of the grave." (Ironically it was Broderick who would soon be in the grave, felled in a duel with the chief justice of the state supreme court.) One of the arguments Buchanan Democrats used in the 1858 California campaign was that the Broderick Democrats were effectively Republicans, at the time a small and unpopular group in the state. As the votes were counted Stanton wrote Black, "From the hour that Broderick reached this shore, until the last moment, his energies were devoted to the contest, and his overthrow is signal and ignominious. You say to the President that his own great name achieved the triumph—to that victory is due."[30]

After Judge Hoffman's November decision in the Limantour case, Stanton was ready to return home, but his departure was delayed because Eddie had a high fever and could not travel. Stanton had hoped to leave on the steamer departing on November 20 but could not, writing to his wife that if "with God's blessing" Eddie improved, they could perhaps leave on December 5 or 20. Those dates passed, however, without the Stantons leaving San Francisco. It was not until January 5 that they boarded the steamship *Golden Gate*, bound for Panama, reaching Washington about a month later.[31]

———

On Sunday, February 27, 1859, at about two in the afternoon, on a city sidewalk just north of the White House, Daniel Sickles, a member of Congress and protégé of the president, shot and killed Philip Barton Key, a federal district attorney and the son of Francis Scott Key. According to the *New York Times*, Sickles told those who gathered around the body, "This man has dishonored my bed." He then walked arm-in-arm with his friend Samuel Butterworth to the home of Attorney General Black "and delivered himself into custody." The news raced through Washington, and Stanton soon heard. Indeed it seems that on that same day Sickles (perhaps through Black) hired Stanton as one of his defense lawyers; Stanton was listed as one of those who visited Sickles in his jail cell that evening.[32]

Daniel Sickles murders Philip Barton Key, in broad daylight, on the streets of Washington.

The *Washington Evening Star* reported on Monday that Key was in the habit of signaling Teresa Sickles by waving a handkerchief from the public square, which she could see from the window of the Sickles townhouse; that the two of them would then go to an "assignation house" in a black section of town; that Sickles had obtained a written confession from his wife of her "criminal conversation" with Key. Teresa Bagioli Sickles, daughter of an Italian music teacher in New York City, "married when not more than sixteen, under circumstances which were subsequently commented upon invidiously by the press." (Their first child was born seven months later.) "Shortly after their marriage Mr. Sickles was appointed secretary of the American legation at London, in the household of Mr. Buchanan, and his beautiful bride won universal admiration abroad." After two years in London, Sickles returned to the United States and was elected to Congress. When the Sickles family moved to Washington in early 1857, they became friends with Key. The *New York Times* reported, "For months past the social world of Washington . . . has been busy with the names of Mrs. Sickles and of Mr. Key," that the handsome young Key was a frequent visitor at the Sickles house but that Sickles had not suspected his wife. Then, on the Friday before the Sunday shooting, Sickles received an anonymous letter stating "that Mr. Key had rented a house on Fifteenth street, above K street, from a negro woman, and that he was in the habit of meeting Mrs. Sickles there two or three times a week, or oftener." Sickles and a friend went to the rented house and confirmed these details. On Saturday evening Sickles confronted his wife and "she admitted her guilt, and besought mercy and pardon." In the presence of two maids she signed a written confession. On the Sunday afternoon Sickles had seen Key in the square waving a handkerchief to signal Teresa to join him. All this and more Stanton would have learned by late on Sunday, either from his client or from other sources.[33]

The first question facing the defense lawyers was whether to apply for bail, which several papers predicted likely. Indeed so strong was the sympathy for Sickles, the aggrieved and outraged husband, that some papers predicted there would be no indictment and no trial. But Stanton and Sickles, himself a lawyer, decided they would not apply for bail because it "would involve a long investigation of the distressing circumstances" and "might procrastinate the period of getting the case before a jury." Stanton and President Buchanan met at least once in the week after the killing, and it seems probable that they discussed the Sickles case, for Buchanan was intensely interested in his former secretary's fate.[34]

The scandalous case was irresistible to newspapers. Many supported the husband. The *New York Herald* wrote that Sickles "admitted Mr. Key to his fireside and his table, to the society of his wife and children . . . [and] this peaceful and happy existence was deliberately invaded, and then desecrated, by the seducer." *Harper's Weekly* agreed: "Assuming Mr. Sickles was well founded in his assumption that a guilty intrigue had taken place between his wife and Mr. Key—a fact of which it appears that there can be no doubt—the public of the United States will justify him in killing the man who had dishonored his bed." Other papers, however, questioned Sickles's own morals. The *Albany Evening Statesman* in New

York alleged that Sickles had a "reputation for everything but integrity, honor, morality, and manhood." The *Washington Evening Star* even suggested that he might have played a role in the relationship: "Married at the child's age of sixteen to an experienced man of the world, who knew well all the dangers to which the virtue of a young and intensely fashionable wife might be subjected in an ill-ordered household, we cannot acquit the husband of all blame for her ruin." His friend Butterworth published a statement suggesting that Sickles had acted in self-defense when Key approached him, grabbed him, and tried to strike him with something in his right hand. But this was not part of Butterworth's initial statement at the coroner's inquest, when he testified that he had been with Sickles in his house just before the shooting, that he had left the house alone and engaged Key in conversation in the square until Sickles approached them and accosted Key. Based on this testimony, the *Baltimore Exchange* urged the authorities to arrest and prosecute Butterworth for aiding and abetting in the murder of Key.[35]

Sickles hired yet more lawyers, including James Brady and John Graham of New York, experienced criminal defense lawyers, and Philip Phillips, originally from the South, now working in Washington. On Tuesday, March 22, prosecutor Robert Ould delivered the indictment, charging that Sickles "feloniously, willfully, and of his malice aforethought, did kill and murder" Key. Stanton demanded that the trial start on the next Monday, reasoning that Sickles had been in jail for almost a month and was entitled to a speedy trial. Ould objected: he said he needed at least an additional week to prepare for trial. Judge Thomas Crawford fixed April 4 for the trial date.[36]

On the appointed morning, Stanton and six other lawyers represented Sickles; the prosecution team was only two, Ould and James Carlisle, hired by friends of Key. The courtroom was "crowded to excess" with lawyers, reporters, and members of the public. The first day proved dull, as juror after juror was dismissed because they already had an opinion on the case or (in a few cases) because they did not meet the property qualification. The second day was much like the first. Near the end of the third day Stanton and Ould debated whether it was proper to disqualify jurors whose net worth was less than $800. Stanton admitted that there was an ancient Maryland statute imposing such a property requirement and that District of Columbia courts generally followed Maryland precedents, but he insisted that this particular statute was rarely cited and not consistent with current customs. Ould admitted that he himself had not insisted on the property requirement in prior cases, explaining, "I was not aware of the existence of the law." Stanton instantly pounced on this admission: Ould was an experienced lawyer, the federal district attorney, yet he did not know of the supposed requirement. Judge Crawford sided with Ould, ruling that the government could, if it wished, insist on the property requirement in this case.[37]

On April 7, with the jury of twelve at last seated, Ould opened for the government. This was not a case of mere manslaughter, he said; the evidence would show that Sickles planned to kill Key, that Sickles left his house armed with a revolver and a Derringer concealed beneath "a convenient overcoat on an inconveniently warm day." Over the next two days, Ould presented about two dozen witnesses who testified to the details of the shooting and killing. Brady did most of the cross-examination for the defense.[38]

Graham then opened for the defense. He quoted the Bible and Shakespeare to prove that Sickles, in killing the man who was sleeping with his wife, acted in accordance with God's law and human nature. Graham argued that Sickles was not in his right mind, that he was "at the time of the homicide, such a mere creature of instinct, of impulse, that he could not resist, but was carried forward, like a mere machine." This was the first time temporary insanity was used in an American murder trial. The defense team then put on its witnesses, including Robert Walker, Stanton's colleague in the Wheeling Bridge case, who testified about the anguish of Sickles on the fatal afternoon. Listening to this testimony Sickles became "seized with violent convulsions and fainted in the box." Stanton asked for a recess, which Crawford granted. Sickles was "carried out by several men in the midst of the utmost excitement," with several jury members "affected to tears as were a great many of the spectators." Later in the day, Brady tried to introduce Teresa's signed confession, arguing that it would help explain her husband's temporary insanity. The prosecution objected, and the judge agreed, but on the next day the statement was printed in the newspapers, and since the jurors were not instructed to avoid the papers, it seems likely they read the confession. The document detailed when and how the two lovers met at the rented house, how they went upstairs and undressed, and how she then "did what is usual for a wicked woman to do."[39]

The courtroom for the Sickles trial, showing Stanton as one of the lawyers at the defense table.

The newspapers filled column after column with detailed reports of the testimony. They also commented on the counsel. The *Washington Evening Star* called Stanton "a fine specimen of vigorous manhood," with a "bulging forehead" and a "wealth of beard." Stanton's "weapon in attack is rather the sledgehammer than the rapier." *Harper's Weekly* contrasted Brady, who was "studiously polite," with Stanton: "There is no ceremoniousness about him. He comes up to the point with a sledge hammer earnestness."[40]

There was a long debate on April 14 about whether a witness should be allowed to testify about his conversation with Sickles regarding his wife's infidelity. Again the defense argued that the evidence would show the defendant's state of mind. Stanton cited a North Carolina case in which similar evidence had been admitted in a slave's defense, saying he wanted for Sickles only "the same right . . . accorded to a North Carolina slave." He accused the prosecution, in its "thirst for blood," of ignoring

basic rules of evidence. Ould responded that the different defense lawyers seemed to have different roles, with Stanton playing the part "of the
bully and the bruiser." (At this, there was a "sensation in court.") Stanton,
in the course of his reply, said of Ould, "I have not the honor of his acquaintance, and after the language just uttered, do not desire it." (There
was "stamping of many feet.") Carlisle now stood up and tried to return
to the legal question: How would the proposed testimony help the jury
decide whether Sickles was insane? Carlisle chided Stanton for bringing
the issue of slavery into the case, saying that the evidentiary rules did not
turn on whether the defendant was a slave.[41]

Stanton asserted that "as the relations of counsel to slavery had been
referred to, he would state here that he had the blood of slaveholding parents in his veins: his father had been a North Carolinian and his mother
a Virginian." Carlisle responded with mock politeness: "That is an interesting fact, which I hope will be chronicled like all other things that take
place here, so that when the gentleman comes to have his biography written, that fact may be mentioned in connection with the doctrines which
he has expressed and maintained in this case." One newspaper reported
that Stanton then declared that the "doctrines which he has maintained
here in defense of homes and families will be the proudest legacy he will
leave to his children." When Crawford finally called a halt to this debate,
he ruled for the government. Stanton may have lost this round with the
judge, but he won with the jury and the public.[42]

At last, after almost three weeks, it was time for closing arguments.
There were two closings for the defense: one by Stanton, focused on the
family, and one by Brady, focused on insanity. Stanton reviewed the disastrous effects of adultery on any family: on the relation between husband
and wife, between father and children, between siblings of perhaps different parents. It thus made sense that God prohibited adultery, that the Bible
prescribed death as the punishment for adultery. (It was the Saturday before
Easter.) Stanton described again how Sickles invited Key into his home and
his family; how Key abused this trust and "debauched his house"; how Key
even persuaded Teresa to ignore her child "in order that he might gratify
his lusts." Then Stanton asked, "Who, seeing this thing, would not exclaim
to the unhappy husband, hasten, hasten, hasten to save the mother of your
child. Although she be lost as a wife, rescue her from the horrid adulterer,

and may the Lord, who watches over the home and the family, guide the bullet and direct the stroke." (At this there was "an unrestrainable burst of applause.") Killing an adulterer was like killing in self-defense: a wife was part of her husband; the adulterer attacked the husband by attacking the wife; so a man could defend himself against an adulterer just as he could defend himself against an assailant. Stanton ended by asking the judge to "plant on the best and surest foundations the principles of law which secure the peace of the home, the security of the family, and the relations of husband and wife, which have been in the most horrid manner violated in this case." As Stanton sat down there was another burst of applause.[43]

After Brady's even longer closing argument, Ould responded for the government, arguing that Sickles shot Key in cold blood. Judge Crawford, in his instructions to the jury, largely accepted the defense's temporary insanity argument, instructing the jurors that they should acquit if they had any reasonable doubt either as to whether the killing was murder or whether the prisoner was sane at the time of the killing. The jury deliberated for only an hour and then declared Sickles not guilty. At this there was "a deafening shout, which for several minutes the utmost exertions of the marshal and his assistants were unable to suppress." In the midst of the chaos Stanton's "stentorian voice" was heard, asking the judge to release Sickles from custody. "Unable to repress the emotions of his big heart," one paper reported, Stanton "almost rivaled David when he danced before the ark of the tabernacle." Eventually Sickles, Stanton, and the others left the courtroom, in triumph.[44]

———

Stanton had been hard at work for many months, first in California, then in Washington on the Sickles trial. He needed a rest, and left town in late April 1859 to stay with the Hutchison family in Pittsburgh. Being Stanton, he could not rest long. In the middle of May he represented a German merchant firm suing the city of Pittsburgh for defaulting on its municipal bonds. Young William Stanton was in Pittsburgh, hoping to get advice from his famous cousin about his legal career, but Edwin did not have much time for him, writing that he had been "unceasingly occupied in court." When he returned to Washington in late June, Stanton went back to work, advising Black on several cases in the Supreme Court.[45]

Eddie Stanton enrolled in Kenyon College in the fall, and his father visited him there soon thereafter, "delighted" to see that one of his son's roommates was the eldest son of his friend Maria Kelley Bates. Stanton wrote to Eddie one of those stern letters that parents write to children away at school: he should study hard, write to his grandmother often, and read history. "Historical reading is the most important to which you can devote your attention. . . . One who is ignorant of history cannot be regarded as a well-informed person."[46]

At about this time, Stanton purchased a lot on the north side of what is now Franklin Square, a short walk from the White House. He wrote to his father-in-law, Lewis Hutchison, who was dying, that Ellen was sending him the plans for the new house and wished that he was well enough to come to Washington to help with the process. The Stanton home would ultimately be a three-story structure, built of stone and brick, facing south toward the square. Ellen gave birth there to the couple's second child, Lewis Hutchison Stanton, on January 12, 1860, named for his Southern grandfather, who passed away in Pittsburgh two months later. Stanton, as the lawyer in the family, was soon dealing with the details of his late father-in-law's estate.[47]

The Stanton home in Washington, on the north side of what is now Franklin Square. The Stantons lived in this house from its completion in 1860 through Stanton's death in 1869.

Stanton was very busy in late 1859 and early 1860 preparing and arguing more than twenty California land cases in the Supreme Court. He and Black worked together on these cases, representing the federal government, often arguing that the purported Mexican land grants were forged. Each case was different, requiring its own careful preparation, and Stanton sometimes had to argue more than one case on a single day.[48] In addition he briefed and argued half a dozen private cases during this term of the Supreme Court. Some of these were California cases; for example, he defended the owners of a ferry between Oakland and San Francisco against charges that they were violating the exclusive rights of a competing ferry. Other cases had nothing to do with California. Together with Judah Benjamin, the future Confederate cabinet officer, Stanton represented a shareholder against the Cleveland, Columbus & Cincinnati Railroad.[49] But Stanton was not too busy to take on yet one more case. He responded to a letter from a prospective client that he would be happy to represent him in the Supreme Court and that his usual fee was $500, "unless it is a case of greater importance and difficulty than yours appears to be."[50]

Stanton was also busy in early 1860 with political work for Buchanan and Black. Isaac Cook, the postmaster at Chicago, was charged with seeking and accepting bribes. The new postmaster general, Joseph Holt, insisted that Cook must go. Buchanan and Black asked Stanton to review the Cook file. Stanton concluded that Cook should resign and advised Buchanan to demand his resignation. But Cook had faithfully supported the Buchanan side of the Democratic Party, against the local supporters of Stephen Douglas, so Buchanan did not act on Stanton's advice. Republicans saw Cook as just one of many corrupt men under Buchanan. In early March the House of Representatives formed a committee to investigate charges against Buchanan and his administration. The Covode Committee, chaired by John Covode of Pennsylvania, questioned dozens of witnesses, many of them disaffected Democrats. One of the key witnesses was Cornelius Wendell, formerly the House printer, who claimed that, with Buchanan's blessing, he had paid bribes to secure passage of the Kansas legislation. Another key witness, the newspaper editor John Forney, testified that Black had offered him printing contracts worth thousands if he would reverse his paper's opposition to Lecompton.[51]

Stanton worked for Buchanan to counter the Covode Committee. At some point in the spring, he drafted a set of questions for the Committee's Democrats to use against Wendell, to point out the inconsistencies in his statements. Buchanan wanted Stanton to meet with Warren Winslow, the senior Democrat on the Committee, to prepare him to question Forney. On the Sunday afternoon before the Monday on which Forney would appear, Stanton wrote Buchanan that he had not been able to connect with Winslow. Later that Sunday, Buchanan wrote to tell Stanton that Winslow had to meet that evening with the Committee; could Stanton meet with him Monday morning at seven? These few pages that have survived are probably the tip of the iceberg of the legal and political work Stanton did for Buchanan—work that did little to stay the anti-Buchanan political tide.[52]

While Stanton was thus engaged, delegates gathered in Charleston, South Carolina, for the national Democratic convention. After a long and bitter debate, the Democrats deadlocked; Douglas had a majority of delegates but not the required two-thirds majority, and Southerners threatened to name their own candidate if Northerners named Douglas. The convention at last adjourned, agreeing to meet in Baltimore in six weeks. Stanton commented to his wife, "I am wearied and harassed and want to get away from here [Washington] as speedily as possible. There is nothing but political confusion, turmoil & anxiety." He apparently did escape, for in early June he wrote to his friend Samuel Medary, the Ohio editor, that he had been away from Washington for three weeks. On his return he found the Democrats still at a stalemate. "The friends of Douglas are confident & uncompromising. The Southern men seem equally decided against him. No solution of the problem has been suggested. Disaster & overthrow impends upon the Democracy & no power seems able to avert a danger that can only be overcome by union & confidence." Two weeks later the Baltimore convention split in two, with the Northern Democrats nominating Douglas and Southerners and a few others quitting the convention and nominating Buchanan's vice president, John Breckinridge of Kentucky, as their candidate. In the interim between the two Democratic conventions, Republicans had nominated Lincoln. After the Democratic division, Stanton wrote to his Republican sister Pamphila, "I suppose you all look forward to Lincoln's election and expect to come here to the inauguration. The election of Lincoln is as certain as any future event can be. The Democratic party are hopelessly shivered and will not reunite for many years, if ever." He wrote to his Pittsburgh partner, Shaler, "The Democrats are so entirely divided that none of their candidates can win, in my opinion. The Western railsplitter will be technically elected, and we shall see great dissension."[53]

In none of these letters did Stanton quite state whom he favored in the four-way campaign for president. But he was now almost a member of the Buchanan administration, and Buchanan supported Breckinridge. Black later recalled that Stanton favored Breckinridge in 1860, that he "regarded the salvation of the country as hanging on the forlorn hope of his election." Stanton viewed the Republicans as the allies of the Abolitionists, the "avowed enemies of the Constitution and the Union." Black, who remained a Democrat while Stanton became an ardent Republican, is not the most reliable source on this point, but he is far from the only source. A local man remembered that, when Stanton's son visited Steubenville in the fall of 1860, he said that Stanton favored Breckinridge. Senator John Sherman, for many years a friend and neighbor of Stanton in Washington, said late in his life that he had known Stanton since his days as "a Breckinridge Democrat." The one dissenting voice was that of Pamphila Wolcott, who wrote in her memoir that if she "had thought for a moment that it was possible for him to support Breckinridge or Douglas, it would have been a matter of great surprise and pain." Perhaps Stanton tactfully hid his views from his sister, or perhaps she did not remember this election years later, for it seems certain that he favored Breckinridge.[54]

Chapter 5

"Surrounded by Secessionists"

— 1860–1861 —

On November 6, 1860, more than four and a half million Americans voted in the presidential election. Stanton was not among them, for as a resident of the District of Columbia he was not entitled to vote in a presidential election. Although the popular vote was split among the four leading candidates, so that Lincoln received less than 40 percent, it was soon clear that he would win the Electoral College vote because the Republicans had carried almost every Northern state. In reporting that Lincoln would be the next president, however, the papers also reported that some Southern states would secede. South Carolina was the first: within days of the election the state's legislature fixed a date for a secession convention. Soon there were similar reports of other Southern states setting secession votes, talking about a Southern confederacy, strengthening their state military forces.[1]

Buchanan spent the month of November watching developments in the South and preparing his annual message to Congress, due in early December. As part of this process he asked Black for his legal opinion on whether and how the president could enforce federal laws in states such as South Carolina, where all the federal judges and officers had resigned. Judge Black's opinion was not a call to arms; rather the reverse. "Troops would certainly be out of place, and their use wholly illegal," Black wrote, for "if [troops] are sent to aid the courts and marshals, there must be courts and marshals to be aided." He doubted whether even Congress could authorize federal warfare against a rebellious state. "There was undoubtedly a strong and universal conviction among the men who framed and ratified the Constitution, that military force would not only be useless, but pernicious, as a means of holding the States together." Buchanan echoed Black in this section of his message, arguing that neither he nor Congress had any right to use force to compel states to remain in the Union. Northern newspapers condemned the message and the messenger. The *New York Times*, for example, lamented, "The country has to struggle through three months more of this disgraceful imbecility and disloyalty to the Constitution."[2]

There is a conflict in the sources, the first of many such conflicts, over Stanton's reaction to Black's opinion and Buchanan's message. In 1870, not long after Stanton died, his friend Henry Wilson, a senator from Massachusetts, published an article in which he said that Stanton had advised Buchanan "to incorporate into his message the doctrine that the federal government had the power, and that it was its duty, to coerce seceding states." Black responded to Wilson with two long articles, insisting that Stanton had approved Black's legal opinion "with extravagant and undeserved laudation" and "gave his adhesion to the annual message in many ways." Stanton himself claimed, in an 1869 interview with the Boston lawyer John Ropes, that Buchanan had asked him for advice before the election about what he should do if Lincoln was elected and the Southern states followed through on their threats to secede. Southern secession, Stanton told Buchanan, would be "a grand opportunity for you to show the country a grand example of the teachings of the Jackson School in which we were educated." (During the nullification crisis, President Jackson had declared that armed secession was treason.) Buchanan "expressed himself very determined to carry on the government and keep up the principles of Andrew Jackson, and said he wanted [Stanton] to draw up for him a brief setting forth the arguments against the right of secession and nullification." Stanton recalled giving Buchanan the requested legal brief, of which there is no copy either in the Buchanan or the Stanton papers. According to Stanton, he was dismayed by the Buchanan message, in which the president declared that he would not use any force against a seceding state. "I felt," Stanton told Ropes, "that we were no longer as one in our political views."[3]

How to resolve this conflict between the sources? In this case we cannot really resolve it, for we do not have anything from Stanton from the time of Black's opinion or Buchanan's message. Black was surely right on some points. Buchanan did not often confer with outsiders, and Stanton was not yet a member of his cabinet and never a member of his inner circle. As Black pointed out, neither he nor Buchanan would have invited Stanton into the cabinet if they believed that he disagreed with them on the central issues facing the nation. Yet by the time he published these articles, Black hated Stanton, whom he viewed as false to Buchanan and false to Democratic principles. And Black wanted to defend himself and Buchanan, already viewed as one of the nation's worst presidents. Stanton too was biased by the time he talked with Ropes: he wanted to distance himself from Buchanan, to claim that he had pushed Buchanan in the right direction. But it seems unlikely that Stanton counseled Buchanan on secession before the election, as he later claimed to Ropes.

Even before Buchanan delivered his annual message his cabinet was falling apart. There were press reports in early December that Treasury Secretary Howell Cobb would resign to return to Georgia and that Interior Secretary Jacob Thompson would return to Mississippi. Their families were reportedly packing up to leave Washington. On December 8, Cobb gave Buchanan his resignation letter, explaining that he believed he had to speak out on the secession question. The same papers that carried Cobb's resignation letter carried his open letter to the people of Georgia, claiming that Lincoln intended to abolish slavery throughout the South and urging Georgia to secede without delay. Buchanan accepted Cobb's resignation on December 10 and appointed Philip Thomas, a former governor of Maryland, as his successor. On December 14, the *Washington Evening Star* reported that Secretary of State Lewis Cass would resign because he disagreed with Buchanan about reinforcing the federal troops in Charleston, South Carolina. It soon emerged that Maj. Robert Anderson, in command of the small federal garrison in Charleston, had requested reinforcements. During the cabinet discussion of Anderson's request, Secretary of War John Floyd, a former governor of Virginia, had opposed reinforcement, but Cass had insisted that Buchanan should support Anderson. When Buchanan said that he would not risk angering South Carolina by attempting to strengthen Anderson, the papers reported, Cass resigned. The *National Republican* demanded that Buchanan reinforce Anderson: "There is not a moment to be lost unless Buchanan wishes to go down with a name linked with that of Benedict Arnold."[4]

The *Evening Star* reported on December 15 that Buchanan would nominate Black to replace Cass as secretary of state and that "Mr. Edwin M. Stanton, formerly of Ohio, well known of late years from his connection with the law business of the Government, in California particularly, will be tendered the Attorney Generalship in Judge Black's stead." The editors added, "No two better appointments could be made—no two more likely to command public confidence everywhere, or to accord to the President more substantial assistance in this hour of the country's travail." Other papers were not so sure: some predicted that Buchanan would nominate Daniel Dickinson, a former senator from New York, to become secretary of state, which would leave Black in his current position as attorney general.[5]

If he had been in Washington, Stanton would have learned about these developments by reading the newspapers or speaking with Black. But he was not in Washington from December 10 through December 20; he was in Cincinnati to try another reaper patent case, in the courtroom of Judge Humphrey Leavitt. So Stanton would have learned the news through Ohio papers or telegrams. Buchanan nominated and the Senate confirmed Black as secretary of state on December 17. Several papers now predicted that Stanton would be the next attorney general. The *New York Herald* and *New York Tribune* reported from Washington that Buchanan sent a telegram to Stanton in Ohio asking whether he would serve. The *Cincinnati Daily Press* reported on the morning of December 19 that Stanton would conclude his oral argument in the pending patent suit by the end of the day. "Some of the ablest attorneys in the country have been employed, among whom is Mr. Stanton, who, it is believed, has received the appointment of Attorney-General in place of Mr. Black." The *Cadiz Sentinel* bragged of the nomination of its former resident, calling Stanton "without doubt the ablest lawyer in the Union."

Buchanan sent the Stanton nomination to the Senate on December 19, and it was confirmed the next day. All of these articles about Stanton joining the Buchanan cabinet were short; the papers were mainly concerned with the secession crisis, not with what seemed a minor change in the cabinet.[6]

Five years later, when Buchanan was generally viewed as a disastrous president and Stanton was being criticized for serving him, Leavitt prepared for Stanton a summary of these events. According to Leavitt, Stanton had asked him after court one day whether he should accept Buchanan's offer to become his attorney general. Leavitt recalled responding that "if after an interview with Mr. Buchanan he ascertained it was his purpose to retain the traitorous members of his cabinet, and yield to the atrocious demands of South Carolina and the other cotton states, he should avoid any connection with the administration, as there would be no hope in accepting the place, that he would be able to effect anything beneficial to the country, while his reputation might be seriously injured by the connection." On the other hand, "if he had reason to believe his taking a place in the cabinet could by possibility induce a change in the policy of Mr. Buchanan's administration, and lead to a decisive stand for the Union and against the rebellion, it was his duty from considerations of patriotism, however undesirable in itself, to take the proffered position." Stanton assured Leavitt that he would adopt this approach. Leavitt thus believed that Stanton "went into Mr. Buchanan's cabinet from the sole and patriotic motive of saving the country from the machinations of treason."[7]

In his interview with Ropes, Stanton gave a similar version of these events: that he had face-to-face conversations with Buchanan and Black before agreeing to join the administration. This seems unlikely. It seems far more likely that Buchanan telegraphed Stanton in Ohio, as the newspapers reported, and that Stanton responded favorably, also by telegraph. With all the difficulties he was having with his cabinet, Buchanan could not afford to nominate a man who would reject the offer. And on December 21, just after returning to Washington, Stanton wrote a friend that he had not "had any interview with any one of the officers of the Government and [was] therefore quite ignorant of the real state of affairs." In other words, on the very day he started work as attorney general, he had not yet talked at length with Buchanan or Black.[8]

***

Stanton arrived back in Washington and joined the Buchanan administration at a critical moment in the secession winter. While he was away, thirty Southern leaders, including Senator Jefferson Davis of Mississippi, published a letter declaring that the Southern states should no longer look to Washington for their protection: "All hope of relief through the agency of committees, congressional legislation, or constitutional amendments, is extinguished." As if in response, Senator John Crittenden of Kentucky proposed a series of constitutional amendments to protect slavery south of the Missouri Compromise line, including any territory "hereafter acquired" south of that line. Ellis Lewis, former chief justice of Pennsylvania, writing Stanton to congratulate him on his appointment, suggested that the Northern states would have to accept something like the Crittenden compromise. Stanton seemed to agree: "By God's help every effort of mine will be directed to the firm and faithful discharge of such duties as may devolve upon me, and with the aid of counsel from wise men like yourself, and the Divine helping, I still feel strong hope that the impending dangers may be passed in peace and safety." Stanton probably wrote this just after news arrived in Washington that South Carolina had formally seceded from the Union. That state's secession was not a surprise, but it was worrisome that the news of secession was greeted with what one paper called "immense enthusiasm" in Alabama, Florida, and Georgia.[9]

On December 22 Stanton was summoned to deal with a crisis at the Interior Department: $870,000 in government bonds were missing from the department's safe. Secretary Jacob Thompson, recently returned from the South, claimed that he knew nothing about the missing bonds. The senior clerk, Goddard Bailey, when cross-examined by Black and Stanton, admitted that he had removed the bonds from the safe but insisted that he was acting not out of self-interest but only to protect his patron, Secretary of War Floyd, and a military firm closely associated with Floyd called Russell, Majors & Waddell. The Russell firm had been issuing promissory notes, which Floyd had been endorsing and which, with this endorsement, were being treated as guaranteed by the government. The bonds were needed, Bailey explained, to pay note holders who were insisting on cash. Buchanan asked Stanton for a legal opinion as to whether any federal law had authorized Floyd to endorse the Russell notes. Stanton's response is not in the file, but it was almost certainly no. Black reportedly told Buchanan that the president would have to demand that Floyd resign.[10]

Jacob Thompson. Originally from North Carolina, Thompson was Stanton's colleague in the Buchanan cabinet, then the senior Confederate representative to Canada.

This corruption investigation was still in progress—Buchanan had taken no action—when Stanton learned on December 24 of a second crisis: that the War Department had ordered the arsenal in Pittsburgh to send more than a hundred large cannons to federal forts in the South. The *New York Tribune* reported from Pittsburgh that the residents were outraged by what they viewed as an attempt "to strip the Allegheny Arsenal and place the guns where the secessionists could get at them." The *Tribune* added that "leading Democrats telegraphed to Washington to have the orders countermanded, saying that the people would not allow the guns to be removed." It seems likely that Stanton received one or more such telegrams from Pittsburgh, perhaps from his former legal partner, Judge Shaler, perhaps from another local leader with whom he was in touch, Gen. William Robinson. And it seems likely that Stanton discussed the issue with Buchanan, warning that he would face rebellion in Pittsburgh as well as Charleston if the War Department attempted to send the arms south. In any case it was Stanton, early in the new year, who sent a telegram to the mayor of Pittsburgh, informing him that the secretary of war had rescinded the orders to move the guns, news that was received with the "liveliest satisfaction" in Pittsburgh.[11]

These crises were soon overshadowed by events in and about Charleston. As soon as South Carolina declared itself an independent nation, it appointed three commissioners, ambassadors really, to negotiate with the United States. The papers predicted that these commissioners, who arrived in Washington on December 26, would demand that the United States turn over the Charleston harbor forts to South Carolina. There was a precedent for the demand: after the United States declared itself independent of the British Empire, the Americans demanded and ultimately obtained the British forts on American territory. Many expected Buchanan to yield the forts. The *National Republican* quoted from the enthusiastic description of Fort Sumter in the *Charleston Mercury* and noted bitterly that the *Mercury* assumed that "South Carolina [would] soon be in possession of [Fort Sumter] and thus enabled to defy hostile fleets." The *Green Mountain Freeman*, a Republican paper in Vermont, declared that Buchanan's surrender of the Southern forts would be like Benedict Arnold's betraying the fort at West Point: "It has been reserved for James Buchanan . . . after having sounded every other depth of infamy in the service of his slave masters, to shock the world by this treason, beside whose gigantic proportions the crime of Arnold is dwarfed into comparative insignificance."[12]

These articles appeared *before* the news arrived in Washington on December 27 that Major Anderson had moved his small federal force, about a hundred men, including eight musicians, from the indefensible Fort Moultrie to the "impregnable" Fort Sumter. The first news reached Washington from an unsigned telegram to the *Baltimore American*: "The government forces have abandoned Fort Moultrie, spiked their guns, and gone to Fort Sumter, commanding the harbor. War has begun." As further reports arrived from Charleston, Southerners in Washington reacted with outrage: they viewed Anderson's move as federal aggression against South Carolina. Southerners believed that Buchanan had promised them he would maintain the "status quo" in Charleston harbor and that Anderson's move broke that promise. Southern senators, including Stanton's former client David Yulee, hastened to the White House to press Buchanan to order Anderson out of Fort Sumter. But Northerners rejoiced; the *Philadelphia Public Ledger* reported that "the conduct of Major Anderson is universally commended by northern men of all parties, and by all Union men from the border states."[13]

Stanton was at the Supreme Court on the morning of December 27 to move the admission to the bar of his brother-in-law Christopher Wolcott. Awaiting him when he returned to his office was a summons to the White House to attend a cabinet meeting, the first of several over several days. The *New York Herald* reported that Washington was "shaken to its extremities by the news from the Carolina forts. Despatches came in as early as half-past ten a.m., and from that hour till late in the evening nothing else was talked of." Buchanan "held a cabinet council, which was attended by every member of the administration, and whose session was protracted beyond the customary dinner hour at the Executive mansion." The *Washington Evening Star* confirmed that the cabinet was "in session until a late hour . . . probably over the news of the course pursued by Major Anderson in quitting the weak post in Charleston harbor and throwing his force into another that gives him the entire command of the Harbor and is practically impregnable." Secretary Floyd could not believe the news and sent a telegram to Anderson for an explanation. Anderson responded, "I abandoned Fort Moultrie because I was certain that, if attacked, my men must have been sacrificed, and command of the harbor lost. I spiked the guns and destroyed the carriages to keep the guns from being used against us." Floyd insisted to Buchanan and his cabinet colleagues that the only way to "vindicate [their] honor and prevent civil war" was "to withdraw the garrison from the harbor of Charleston altogether." Indeed he declared that if Buchanan would not give the necessary orders, he would issue the orders on his own authority as secretary of war.[14]

The *New York Tribune* reported from Washington late on December 28, "The cabinet continued in session nearly six hours, and it is certain that it adjourned until to-morrow without coming to a conclusion on the affairs of South Carolina before them." The reporter added, "I am sorry to have to announce that the President's courage seems to be failing him, and he is said to be in favor of withdrawing the United States troops from Fort Sumter." The impression that Buchanan would yield was reinforced by reports that he met for two hours that day with the three Carolina commissioners. Stanton wrote to Robinson two days later that he was "dumbfounded" by Buchanan's meeting with the Carolinians for it seemed to admit that "South Carolina [was] an independent nation."[15]

"South Carolina's 'Ultimatum.'" South Carolina governor Francis Pickens threatens to fire a cannon (aimed at himself) if Buchanan does not surrender Fort Sumter. Buchanan begs him, "Don't fire! till I get out of office."

The cabinet debate continued on Saturday, December 29. The *New York Tribune* reported that the cabinet was in session "for the third time" on the question of whether to sustain or withdraw Anderson: "The

President exhibits his usual imbecility, being influenced by the last pressure of opinion. Stanton, Black, and Holt have manfully resisted the withdrawal of the troops. Floyd and Thompson insist upon it, as imperatively demanded by southern sentiment, while [Navy Secretary Isaac] Toucey and [Treasury Secretary Philip] Thomas have thus far halted between extreme opinions, and advocate some compromise or other." In a second report, the *Tribune* said the question "was decided by a formal vote," with Black, Stanton, Holt, and Toucey voting to sustain Anderson in his present position, and Floyd, Thomas, and Thompson voting to withdraw the federal troops from Charleston. At that point, "Mr. Floyd addressed a letter of resignation to the president, couched in offensive terms." According to the *National Republican*, "This city has never been so excited as it was during Friday and Saturday, by the pendency of the question in the Cabinet, of recalling Major Anderson. It involved the larger question, of abandoning, or sustaining, national power in the harbor of Charleston. Everybody felt it to be so. The nullifiers worked with frantic energy, and on the other side, in addition to remonstrances from friends here, the President received despatches from Pennsylvania of a most energetic character, against yielding further to the treason of South Carolina." The *Republican* described the cabinet as evenly divided at first, with Toucey undecided, but that he tipped the balance on Saturday by voting against withdrawing Anderson.[16]

The cabinet debated not just whether to withdraw Anderson but also the related question of how to respond to the Carolina commissioners. Buchanan drafted a response, which we do not have, and presented it to the cabinet on Saturday. After thinking about the issue overnight, Black informed Buchanan that he would resign if the letter went out in its current form. Buchanan pleaded with Black to stay and help him rewrite the letter. As Black put it in a note to Holt, "[The president gave me] the paper he had written and requested me to make such changes as I desired; I shall propose a radical alteration of the whole document; and have some reason to believe that my view of the subject may be adopted." Black found Stanton, and together the two men prepared a point-by-point critique of Buchanan's draft.[17]

This memorandum, mainly in Stanton's handwriting, is our best evidence of his views in the midst of this cabinet crisis. The president should strike out "every word and sentence" in his draft letter to the commissioners suggesting that South Carolina was an independent nation with diplomatic rights. "Above all things it is objectionable to intimate a willingness to negotiate with the State of South Carolina about the possession of a military post which belongs to the United States." Major Anderson was not, as Southerners argued, a villain but a hero. "He has done everything that mortal man can do to repair the *fatal error which the administration has committed in not sending down troops enough to hold the forts.*" Buchanan should reject the Southern claim that Anderson, by moving his troops from Fort Moultrie to Fort Sumter, had somehow wronged South Carolina. It would be strange indeed "to say that the United States troops must remain in the weakest position they can find in the harbor." Buchanan should not only revise his letter, Stanton and Black wrote; he should send two armed naval vessels, the *Brooklyn* and the *Macedonian*, to Charleston harbor and should inform Anderson "that his government will not desert him." Black delivered this document to Buchanan on December 30. Stanton, writing Robinson the same day, was not sure how Buchanan would react. He was hopeful that Black, who "exercise[d] a great deal of influence over" Buchanan, would prevail with the president. If the president insisted on sending his letter to the commissioners in its original form, however, Stanton, along with Black and Holt, would resign.[18]

After receiving the memorandum from Stanton and Black, and after the cabinet voted in favor of sustaining Anderson, Buchanan revised his letter to the Carolina commissioners, making it much stiffer. He declared that he would not yield up Fort Sumter, even that he had never had "such an idea." To fill the seat opened by Floyd's resignation, Stanton urged Buchanan to appoint Holt as secretary of war. Stanton later told Lincoln's biographers that he went to "Holt's residence near midnight to urge upon him the acceptance of the post, to impress upon him the grave nature of the exigency, and the need of a man in that place whose sentiments they knew." The *New York Tribune* commented on January 1 that Holt and Stanton deserved "great credit" for their work in the past few days: "Whatever their political predilections may be, all parties will thank them for their timely services." The *Tribune* described Stanton as "a thorough out-spoken Union man [who] . . . labored assiduously to induce the President to stand by the Union."[19]

Joseph Holt. A member of the Buchanan administration, and then Stanton's right hand in military justice in the Lincoln and Johnson administrations, Holt was the lead prosecutor in the conspiracy trial against the Lincoln assassins.

In the months and years thereafter, Stanton often related to Republicans how he had worked in late December to stiffen Buchanan's spine. He started this narrative almost at once, in letters and conversations with his Republican brother-in-law, Christopher Wolcott. On December 29 he wrote to Wolcott, "I hold my present position only to defend this government from its enemies—when it becomes apparent that defense will be unavailing I shall do like Anderson, spike my guns and retire to a stronger position and keep the flag of my country still flying." Wolcott wrote to his wife in early January that he believed Buchanan's newfound firmness was "mainly due to Edwin's influence. Judging from my conversation with him at Washington, he will insist that Anderson shall be backed up with the whole power of the government. He is sound to the core on the great question of vindicating the supremacy of the government, and since the news of Floyd's resignation, I am more hopeful that South Carolina will be promptly dealt with."

Stanton wrote Wolcott later in January that, at the first cabinet meeting about South Carolina, he "found treason with bold and brazen front demanding the surrender of Fort Sumter. The contest continued until dark, when dispute ran so high that we adjourned until eight o'clock in the evening."[20]

About a year later, when Stanton joined the Republican cabinet of Lincoln, a longer account of the December 1860 meetings appeared in the papers, apparently provided by him:

The next meeting was a long and stormy one, Mr. Holt, feebly seconded by the President, urging the immediate reinforcement of Sumter, while Thompson, Floyd and Thomas contended that a quasi-treaty had been made by the officers of the Government with the leaders of the rebellion, to offer no resistance to their violations of law and seizures of Government property. Floyd especially blazed with indignation at what he termed the "violation of honor." At last Mr. Thompson formally moved that an imperative order be issued to Major Anderson to retire from Sumter to Fort Moultrie—abandoning Sumter to the enemy and proceeding to a post where he must at once surrender. Stanton could sit still no longer, and rising, he said, with all the earnestness that could be expressed in his bold and resolute features: "Mr. President, it is my duty, as your legal adviser, to say that you have no right to give up the property of the Government, or abandon the soldiers of the United States to its enemies; and the course proposed by the Secretary of the Interior, if followed, is *treason*." Such language had never before been heard in Buchanan's Cabinet, and the men who had so long ruled and bullied the President, were surprised and enraged to be thus rebuked. Floyd and Thompson sprang to their feet with fierce, menacing gestures, seeming about to assault Stanton. Mr. Holt took a step forward to the side of the Attorney General. The imbecile President implored them piteously to take their seats. After a few more bitter words the meeting broke up. That was the last cabinet meeting on that exciting question in which Floyd participated.[21]

Stanton also described those meetings to the Lincoln cabinet in a conversation recorded by John Nicolay, the president's senior private secretary:

The last I saw of Floyd was in this room [the cabinet room], lying on the sofa which then stood between the windows yonder. I remember it well—it was on the night of the 19th [*sic*] of last December—we had had high words, almost come to blows in our discussion over Fort Sumter. Thompson was here—Thompson was a plausible talker, and as a last resort, having been driven from every other argument, advocated the evacuation of the Fort on the plea of generosity. South Carolina was but a small state with a sparse white population—we were a great and powerful people, and a strong and vigorous government—we could afford to say to S.C.—"See we will withdraw our garrison as evidence that we mean you no harm." I said to him, "Mr. President, the proposal to be generous, implies that the government is strong, and that we as the public servants, have the confidence of the people. I think that is a mistake. No administration has ever suffered the loss of public confidence and support as this has done. Only the other day it was announced that a million of dollars had been stolen from Mr. Thompson's department. The bonds were found to have been taken from the vault where they should have been kept, and the notes of Mr. Floyd were substituted for them. Now all I have to say is that no administration, much less this one, can afford to lose a million of money and a fort in the same week." Floyd lay there and never opened his mouth. The next morning he sent in his resignation and never came into the room again.[22]

Another account of these events appeared in the papers in March 1862, in the form of an open letter from Thurlow Weed, the Republican political leader and close friend of Lincoln's secretary of state, William Henry Seward. In Weed's account, when Buchanan told the cabinet that he would follow Floyd's advice and surrender Fort Sumter, Stanton responded, "That course, Mr. President, ought certainly to be regarded as most liberal towards 'erring brethren'; but while one member of your cabinet [Floyd] has fraudulent acceptances for millions of dollars afloat, and while the confidential clerk of another [Thompson]—himself in Carolina teaching rebellion—has just stolen $900,000 from the Indian Trust Fund, the experiment of ordering Major Anderson back to Fort Moultrie would be dangerous. But if you intend to try it, before it is done, I beg that you will accept my resignation." Black and Holt added that they too would resign if Buchanan ordered Anderson to abandon Fort Sumter. "This of course opened the bleared eyes of the President, and the meeting resulted in the acceptance of Mr. Floyd's resignation."[23]

After Weed's letter appeared in the press, Augustus Schell, a New York Democrat, wrote letters to Black, Stanton, and others, asking them for their comments. Black replied, "Mr. Stanton made no such speech as that put into his mouth by [Weed] nor any other speech inconsistent with the most perfect respect for all his colleagues and for the President. Neither Mr. Stanton nor Mr. Holt ever spoke to the President about resigning, upon any contingency whatever, before the incoming of the new administration." Buchanan wrote a friend that, if any members of his cabinet had "offered [him] the grossest insult," as Stanton claimed, Buchanan would have fired them: "They should not have been in office fifteen minutes." Buchanan also claimed that Stanton "never took much part in cabinet councils, because his office did not require it." And he added, "He was always at my side, and flattered me *ad nauseam*."[24]

In a long letter Stanton drafted but did not send to Schell, he largely agreed with Weed's account. Buchanan had discussed surrendering Fort Sumter with his cabinet members, "some of whom violently advocated it, while others opposed it resolutely as a crime." "After several days' angry debate it was rejected. I asserted then to Mr. Buchanan, and assert now, that the surrender of Fort Sumter by the government would have been, in my opinion, a crime equal to that of Arnold, and that all who participated in the act should be hung like [John] André." (André was the British Army officer, hanged as a spy for his participation in Arnold's plot to surrender the fort at West Point to the British.) Reading this draft letter after Stanton's death, Holt largely agreed with Stanton's version of the meeting, and specifically said that Stanton compared Buchanan with Benedict Arnold. At this, Holt recalled, Buchanan "raised his hands deprecatingly, as if wounded by the intensity of Mr. Stanton's language and manner: 'Oh, no! not so bad as that, my friend!—not so bad as that!' "[25]

Stanton's accounts of these cabinet meetings are quotable and often quoted. Yet most of them are somewhat suspect because they date from a year or years later, when Buchanan was out of office and in disgrace. Stanton, to strengthen his position with Lincoln, with Republicans, and indeed with history, needed to distance himself from Buchanan. But Black's and Buchanan's versions, that Stanton did not play much of a role in these discussions and that he did not threaten to resign, are equally suspect. The newspapers reported on the late December cabinet confrontation in detail, including Stanton's role and his threat to resign. Did Stanton really tell Buchanan that the surrender of Fort Sumter would be like Arnold's betrayal of West Point? This is a more difficult question to confirm, but the answer is probably yes: the Arnold parallel was in the newspapers in late December, and Stanton was not a man to mince words. How much did Stanton and Black influence Buchanan's decision to send troops to reinforce Anderson? This is the most difficult question to answer, for we cannot penetrate the mind of the embattled president. Buchanan himself suggested that he did not decide to send troops until the cabinet meeting of January 2, prompted by the bellicose letter from the Carolina commissioners that he received in the course of that meeting: "Indeed the spirit and tone of the letter left no doubt on my mind that Fort Sumter would be immediately attacked, and hence the necessity of sending reinforcements there without delay." But Gen. Winfield Scott, the aged but still active commander of the army, sent orders on December 31 to place troops and arms on a warship bound for Charleston, orders that Scott would not have sent without Buchanan's blessing. And this Scott order was sent the day *after* Black and Stanton sent their memo to Buchanan recommending that he should not only revise his letter but send troops to Charleston. It seems likely that Black and Stanton at least influenced, and were perhaps the major factor in, Buchanan's decision to attempt to reinforce Anderson.[26]

Gen. Winfield Scott, with whom Stanton worked in the last months of the Buchanan administration on the defense of Washington and plans to reinforce Fort Sumter.

In the midst of these December cabinet meetings, Stanton started to talk with an unlikely ally: Senator William Henry Seward. The senator was not only a Republican but, from a Democratic perspective, an abolitionist. In his most famous speech, given in 1850 but still quoted ten years later, Seward declared that a "higher law than the Constitution" prohibited slavery in the territories. The newspapers in late 1860 were predicting that Lincoln would make Seward his secretary of state, the premier position in the cabinet. In short, Seward was no friend of Buchanan. But at this point Stanton was not especially loyal to Buchanan; he was worried that Buchanan and those around him were disloyal to the Union. So Stanton reached out to Seward, probably as a way of reaching out to President-elect Lincoln. On December 29 Seward wrote to Lincoln of his new relationship: "At length I have gotten a position in which I can see what is going on in the councils of the President. . . . It pains me to learn that things there are even worse than is understood. . . . [Buchanan] is debating day and night on the question of whether he shall not recall Major Anderson and surrender Fort Sumter, and go on arming the South." Two days later an Illinois friend wrote Lincoln with more details about the concerns of Stanton and Seward: "[They feared] the southern plan now is to draw Maryland and Virginia into the revolution before the fourth of March [inauguration day] so as to get possession of the railroad from Baltimore to this place, and the telegraph wires. With these advantages, and these two states swept by the same mania that is now sweeping the South, they hope to prevent your inauguration."[27]

William Henry Seward, with whom Stanton worked quietly in the last weeks of the Buchanan administration, and who was secretary of state under Lincoln and Johnson.

One of the minor mysteries of the secession winter is whether Seward and Stanton spoke face-to-face or only through an intermediary. After the war Weed published an article saying that Stanton and Seward did not meet in person while Stanton was in the Buchanan cabinet, that they communicated only through their mutual friend Peter Watson. Seward confirmed this in a letter he wrote five years later, saying that he and Stanton did not want their respective political friends to know of their conversations. But in January 1861 Weed wrote from Washington to Lincoln in Springfield, "Secretaries Stanton and Holt are doing their duty splendidly. The former is in constant communication with Governor Seward." A month later Seward invited Stanton to join him for dinner with the famed actress Charlotte Cushman, who was in town for a few weeks. And Seward sent Stanton another letter at about this same time, asking him to confirm that he was willing to have his name listed as one of the managers of the Union Inauguration Ball. There is no hint in any of these letters that the relations between Stanton and Seward were secret.[28]

General Scott's original plan was to reinforce Fort Sumter using the *Brooklyn*, an armed naval ship, but he decided on reflection to send a smaller civilian ship with more ability to maneuver in the harbor, the *Star of the West*. In a curious coincidence, this was the same ship on which Stanton had sailed from New York to Panama. The *Star of the West* left New York harbor on the night of January 5 with two hundred soldiers and three months of provisions concealed below decks. Stanton's fears about Southern spies within the government soon proved well founded. Several telegrams were sent from Washington to Charleston to warn of the ship's mission, including one from Stanton's colleague in the cabinet Jacob Thompson. So the Carolinians were well prepared when the *Star of the West* approached Charleston at first light on the morning of January 9. When South Carolina troops fired from Fort Moultrie at the ship, Anderson considered but decided not to fire from Fort Sumter at Fort Moultrie. Though none of the Southern shells hit the *Star of the West*, the civilian captain was not prepared to run the risk, and he turned around and headed home. News of these events soon spread by telegram and in the newspapers. In the North there was a surge of anger, for Southern rebels had fired on the American flag. There was equal anger in the South, because Buchanan, the supposed friend of the South, had sent two hundred armed troops into Charleston harbor. Buchanan, often accused of "doing nothing" during the secession winter, was doing far too much for Southerners, and they pressed for immediate secession. Only one state had seceded in December 1860. Soon after the *Star of the West* incident, five other states followed: Mississippi on January 9, Florida on January 10, Alabama on January 11, Georgia on January 19, and Louisiana on January 26. In spite of the failure of the *Star of the West* mission, in spite of the increasing tide of secession, Stanton and Black did not give up on reinforcing Anderson at Fort Sumter. In the Black papers there is a note from Stanton, covering a note from an anonymous New Yorker, about the best way for a ship to reach and reinforce the fort. And on January 16, Black sent a long note to General Scott, arguing that if a "pirate, or a slaver, or a smuggler" could get into Charleston harbor, the navy could surely do so as well.[29]

On January 8, while the *Star of the West* was still on its way south, Thompson resigned his position as secretary of the interior, claiming that he did not know Buchanan intended to send the ship to Fort Sumter. The *National Republican* reported that with Thompson's resignation there was only one secessionist left in the cabinet, Treasury Secretary Thomas, "but that is one too many." Buchanan accepted Thompson's resignation and sent for John Adams Dix, a New York lawyer and financier, already known as "General Dix" because of his senior position in the state militia. Buchanan may have intended to name Dix to head the Interior Department, but the president was under pressure, both political and financial, to replace Thomas at Treasury. Horatio King, the acting postmaster general, recalled that Stanton tasked him with meeting Dix at the evening train and persuading him to take the more difficult and important treasury assignment. After Dix "heartily agreed to the proposition," King went to inform Stanton at his home: "Having company in the parlor, he met me in the hall, and when I informed him that all was as he desired, he was so filled with delight that he seized me and embraced me in true German style." The next day, January 11, Buchanan nominated and the Senate confirmed Dix as secretary of the treasury. Buchanan did not bother to replace Thompson, letting the assistant secretary serve as acting secretary for the last few months of the administration.[30]

John Adams Dix, a New York lawyer and leader, was a colleague of Stanton in the Buchanan cabinet, then the senior military officer in New York City during the Civil War.

Buchanan sent another message to Congress in early January, again urging compromise and lamenting that the seceding Southern states were seizing federal forts and facilities. Republican William Howard immediately proposed that the House form a special committee to investigate whether Buchanan or anyone else in the administration was "treating or holding communication with any person or persons concerning the surrender of any forts, fortresses, or public property of the United States." Howard specifically demanded an investigation of Buchanan's purported "pledge" to Southern representatives regarding the Charleston forts. There is no draft of the resolutions, in Stanton's hand or any other, but Howard later said that Stanton was the author of the resolutions he proposed: "It would be easier . . . to persuade me that Mr. Jefferson did not write the Declaration of Independence than that Mr. Stanton did not write those resolutions." Stanton and Seward were probably working together in forming and guiding this special committee, which was soon tasked with looking at whether "any secret organization hostile to the Government of the United States exist[ed] in the District of Columbia" and whether federal or city employees were members of such organization. General Scott—with whom Seward had a long and close relationship, having been a principal proponent of Scott for president in 1852—was the committee's star witness. Scott reviewed the military measures he was taking to ensure that there was no violence in Washington on February 13, when the electoral votes were to be counted, or on March 4, when Lincoln was to be inaugurated. The committee also traveled to Baltimore, where they heard that Southern sympathizers were arming themselves to "prevent northern volunteer companies from coming through Baltimore." Through this committee and through their own informal cooperation, Seward, Stanton, and Scott were working to assert Northern control over Washington, to prevent a Southern coup in the secession winter.[31]

Years later, however, some would claim that Stanton encouraged the South during the secession winter. For example, Albert G. Brown, a federal senator from Mississippi at the time of secession, gave a speech in early 1865 in which he alleged that, just as he resigned his Senate seat in early 1861, Stanton supported him. "You are right, said he; go home and urge your friends to stand by what they have done, and all will be well." Montgomery Blair, a colleague of Stanton in the Lincoln cabinet, repeated Brown's charges in an 1865 campaign speech, adding that he heard from a member of the Buchanan cabinet that Stanton had been "most violent in denouncing any attempt to maintain the Union by force." Frank Blair, Montgomery's brother, a Union general and member of Congress, claimed that Stanton "acted with the secessionists" and "favored a division of the Union." Stanton's colleague in the Sickles case, Philip Phillips, a former member of Congress from Alabama, recalled that during the secession winter Stanton was "a stronger sympathizer with the South than [Phillips] was." James Harvey, a journalist originally from South Carolina, wrote to Black after Stanton's death that Stanton was so outspoken in his support of the South during that winter that one friend "wrote him down in his diary as 'a rebel.' "[32]

Despite such reports, there is nothing in the letters we have from Stanton from early 1861 suggesting that he sympathized with secession. On the contrary, Stanton sounded determined to defend the Union. He wrote his brother-in-law James Hutchison in Pittsburgh on January 15, "The government *cannot* be overthrown except by treason and even that could only succeed for a short time. I think the Southern riots will soon exhaust themselves, and that before the 4th of March peace will be restored and business re-established with more activity than ever." He wrote to Robinson that he believed the government could not be overthrown, that "it was ordained of God, and that the powers of hell cannot prevail against it. The city of Washington may be captured, but every effort will be made to prevent that catastrophe, and even if it does happen, the revolutionists will be as far as ever from accomplishing the destruction of the government—but much nearer to their own destruction." A few days later he wrote to Jacob Brinkerhoff, a justice of the Ohio supreme court, "Nothing in my power will be left undone to uphold the honor & the integrity of this Government. I do not believe this Government can be overthrown—it may be *overrun* for a brief period but cannot be destroyed." This is not to say that Stanton was opposed to compromise; indeed like many Democrats he favored the Crittenden compromise. In a letter responding to resolutions adopted in Steubenville supporting compromise he wrote, "If the resolutions of your meeting were sanctioned by the Republican party in Congress, I think that the troubles that now disturb and endanger the country would speedily be removed."[33]

In all these letters, sent in the middle of January, Stanton was not too troubled by the rumors of Southern attacks on Washington. By the end of the month, however, he was not just worried; he was terrified. In a long letter to his friend Salmon Chase, whom the papers were predicting would be in Lincoln's cabinet, Stanton confessed that he feared South- erners would try to seize Washington before March 4, inauguration day, and he now believed this would be a disaster: "The whole question of successful revolution by the South & civil war, in my opinion depends upon *maintaining the Government here*—keeping the forms, archives, and symbols of established government, out of the hands of the revolution- ists." A few days later Senator Sumner wrote to Massachusetts governor John Andrew about a furtive meeting with Stanton. The attorney general took the senator "into his room," an office in the Treasury building, "but there were clerks there." Stanton and Sumner then crossed through "six different rooms" before they found a private corner where Stanton said that he was "surrounded by secessionists, who would report in an hour to the newspapers any interview" with Sumner. He predicted that Virginia and Maryland would soon secede, then mount an attack on Washington. Sumner was at first not persuaded, but two days later, after a meeting with Stanton that ran past midnight, Sumner wrote again to Andrew. "Suffice it to say he *does not think it probable—hardly possible*—that we shall be here on the 4th of March." Stanton feared that the "departments will be seized & occupied as forts," and he asked, through Sumner, whether Massachusetts could send troops to Washington on short notice.[34]

Charles Sumner, the irascible but influential Radical senator from Massachusetts. Sumner and Stan- ton met in the 1850s and become close friends and political allies in the war years and thereafter.

Two Massachusetts lawyers, John Clifford and Stephen Phillips, and two Rhode Island lawyers were in Washington at this time to settle a boundary dispute between the two states. They worked with Stanton for two hours on the proposed compromise order for the Supreme Court, then the five men talked late into the night about the secession situation. Clifford wrote to Andrew the next day that Stanton believed there would be "an attack upon the city of Washington between the 4th and 15th of February, with a view to secure the symbols of government." Phillips wrote that Stanton was especially worried about Virginia, set to vote on secession in a few days. "By fair means or foul," Stanton said, "the convention in Virginia will be made to pronounce in favor of secession," and secessionists in Maryland would follow Virginia's lead. Stanton again urged that New England prepare to rush troops to Washington.[35]

Stanton was fortunate during the secession winter that he did not have much of the traditional work of the attorney general: representing the United States in the Supreme Court and advising the president and department heads on legal issues. He provided only nine brief legal opinions to his cabinet colleagues, none on important questions. He argued only three cases before the Supreme Court as attorney general: one a California land case in which he prevailed; another a state challenge to the federal construction of the Washington aqueduct, in which the Court declined to intervene. Stanton probably helped behind the scenes with another, more important case: Kentucky's lawsuit against the governor of Ohio, in which Wolcott as the state attorney general represented the governor. The case arose out of the escape by a Kentucky slave from his master while they were changing trains in Cincinnati. The governor of Kentucky requested that Ohio extradite a man accused of aiding in the escape, but the governor refused, sending him Wolcott's opinion that the obligation to extradite was limited to common law crimes and acts "which are regarded as crimes by the usages and laws of all civilized nations." Kentucky sued the governor in the Supreme Court, seeking a writ of mandamus to compel him to extradite the accused. Wolcott reported to his wife that he spent the "dullest dreariest Christmas ever" in Stanton's office "examining books in reference to the mandamus sought against the Governor," suggesting that Stanton helped with the research. Chief Justice Taney managed to avoid what could have been a dramatic, divisive opinion, ruling that although there was a moral obligation upon the states to render up those accused by other states, the federal courts could not require rendition.[36]

Beginning on February 4 about a hundred respected national leaders started to meet each day at the Willard Hotel as the "National Peace Convention," a desperate effort to find some compromise between North and South. None of the states that had seceded was represented, however. The seceding states instead sent delegates to Montgomery, Alabama, to start work on a Confederate constitution. Stanton's concerns for Washington's safety had diminished, for he wrote to George McCook, "Scott says he is able to defend the Capitol now. He has three batteries & all the regular force that can be concentrated here without weakening other points that have to be guarded. The stories of disputes & differences between him & the President *are all false.* The understanding between them is not only kind but cordial as *I know.*"[37]

A week later Stanton wrote a similar letter to Clifford in Massachusetts: "The result of the Virginia elections [in which secession was rejected] greatly disheartened the revolutionists in that state and in Maryland, although their prospects are still pushed forward especially in Maryland. The news yesterday from Tennessee [a similar result] also looks favorably towards maintaining that state." He quoted a private letter from Anderson, saying that he was secure at Fort Sumter: "I feel that God has so helped me in all my doings here, that even if attacked, I have no fears of the result." As to the peace convention, Stanton said that he was "unable to form any opinion whether it [would] be for good or evil." What was more important, he thought, was to keep Washington secure. "The determined & vigilant disposition to support the government with requisite volunteer force has produced here a beneficial effect and contributed to the anxiety of the revolutionists for concealing their designs."[38]

The Buchanan cabinet was meeting at the White House on the morning of February 23 when a surprise visitor arrived: Lincoln. Concerned by rumors of a plot to kill him in Baltimore, Lincoln had slipped through there in the middle of the night and arrived in Washington at the crack of dawn, unannounced. Stanton probably heard nothing of this until Seward and Lincoln arrived at the White House and Buchanan introduced the president-elect to the current members of the cabinet. Stanton and Lincoln knew one another from their encounter in Cincinnati in 1855, but they probably did not mention that on this morning. One memoir recalled that Stanton criticized the way Lincoln "crept into Washington." Stanton supposedly said this with a sneer; indeed "every word was a suppressed and very ill-suppressed sneer." When the memoirist told Stanton that he did not know Lincoln well, Stanton "launched out into a downright tirade against him, saying that he 'had met him at the bar, and found him a low, cunning clown.'" The precise words of the memoir may not be accurate, but Stanton's own letters show that he did not like Lincoln at this time.[39]

Stanton sent another letter to Clifford on March 1, reporting that "political affairs" were "still in a state of gloom & uncertainty discouraging to every patriot. The hopes generated by the action of the Peace Convention are rapidly vanishing." Looking forward a few days, he added, "Present indications are that the radical wing will prevail in Mr. Lincoln's cabinet. It seems to me improbable that Mr. Seward and Mr. Chase can harmonize." (Seward and Chase were already viewed as the leaders of the conservative and Radical wings of the likely Lincoln cabinet.) Stanton was also worried that his friend Justice John Campbell, from Georgia and Alabama, would resign; this would "decimate the Conservative branch of the Government and . . . exert a great influence upon the southern mind." Stanton, who was probably at the office working late on the pardons that Buchanan would issue at the end of his term, added that he was "perhaps only expressing the despondency of a hard day's toil and if this letter were written in the morning instead of at near midnight the tone might be more hopeful."[40]

On the morning of March 4, inauguration day, the Buchanan cabinet met at about ten in the president's room in the Capitol building to review the last-minute legislation of the congressional session. Holt showed up late, at about eleven, with an alarming letter from Anderson, reporting that his supplies were limited and that he feared it would require a considerable combined force, perhaps 20,000 troops, to dislodge the Southern forces guarding the entrance of Charleston harbor. Holt said he would share this news "at once" with Lincoln. Buchanan then went to the Willard Hotel to accompany Lincoln from there to the inauguration, while Stanton and the other cabinet members went into the Senate chamber to watch as the new senators and new vice president took their oaths of office. A little before one, Lincoln and Buchanan entered the Senate chamber arm-in-arm, then all the officials processed to the platform on the east side of the Capitol for the inauguration of the president.[41]

Stanton was thus among those on the platform behind Lincoln as he declared, in his first inaugural address, that he would not "interfere with the institution of slavery in the States where it exists." Lincoln also insisted, however, that he would "hold, occupy, and possess the property and places belonging to the government," which Southerners would surely view as an improper attempt to maintain federal forts on their sovereign territory. Lincoln ended his speech with a poetic plea for peace: "We are not enemies, but friends. We must not be enemies. Though passion may have strained, it must not break our bonds of affection. The mystic chords of memory . . . will yet swell the chorus of the Union, when again touched, as surely they will be, by the better angels of our nature." Stanton was not impressed. He wrote that afternoon to Peter Della Torre in California that "the inauguration is over and whether for good or evil Abraham Lincoln is the President of the United States" Lincoln's address would "do no good towards settling difficulties—probably aggravate them. The news from the South is this morning worse than any we have had." (The "news from the South" was almost surely Anderson's letter.) That evening the Buchanan cabinet gathered at the private home where Buchanan was spending his last night in Washington. The former president, Stanton, and the others reviewed and commented on Holt's draft cover letter to Lincoln, forwarding Anderson's letter but also insisting that Anderson had not previously warned Washington about his dire supply situation.[42]

On March 5 Lincoln nominated his cabinet, including Stanton's new friend Seward as secretary of state; his old friend Salmon Chase as secretary of the treasury; Simon Cameron, a Pennsylvania politician, viewed by many as corrupt, as the secretary of war; and Edward Bates of Missouri, a respected former judge, as the attorney general. The Senate confirmed all these nominations on the same day, but Stanton remained the attorney general because Bates had not yet arrived in Washington and not yet taken the oath of office. That afternoon Stanton was one of those who went to the rail station to cheer former president Buchanan as he departed for his home in Pennsylvania.[43]

On the morning of March 6, Seward asked Stanton to come by the State Department, where he handed Stanton a copy of a report by Scott on the situation at Fort Sumter and asked Stanton and Holt (Cameron too had not started work) to stand ready to attend a cabinet meeting that afternoon. Seward also asked Stanton to prepare for Lincoln the papers necessary to nominate Senator John Crittenden for the vacant seat on the Supreme Court. Stanton probably approved of the proposed nomination for the same reason as the *Washington Evening Star:* to name the leading advocate of compromise would be "a practical—tangible—explanation of the purpose of the new administration not to aggress the South, which every southern man would instantly comprehend." In any case Stanton drafted the nomination papers and delivered them to Lincoln. In the afternoon of that same day, in the courtroom he knew so well, Stanton formally presented Bates to the Supreme Court as the next attorney general, then thanked the members of the Court "for the kindness and attention" they had shown him. Perhaps hoping to persuade the Southern justices to remain, he added his "earnest wish for the stability of this tribunal, and for the health and happiness of the judges whose wisdom and learning adorn it." Chief Justice Taney, author of the *Dred Scott* opinion, thanked Stanton and welcomed Bates. Stanton walked out of the courtroom and back to his home, once again a private citizen.[44]

Chapter 6

"Disgrace & Disaster"

—— 1861–1862 ——

L ucius Chittenden, a lawyer from Vermont who first met Stanton
in early 1861, later described him as being

in the very prime of his intellectual and physical life. He was about
five feet eight inches in height, his figure being slightly inclined to
corpulence. His face was dark, and the lower portion of it was completely covered with a long, heavy, dark beard. His eyes were small,
dark, and piercing. His movements were quick. Vigorous alertness
was indicated by every change of his countenance and movement
of his body. His mind was as active as his person. It was original
and mechanical rather than philosophic or thoughtful. Its type was
indicated by his success at the bar, where he had attained an enviable
reputation as an advocate in patent cases, with but little celebrity
in the investigation or discussion of abstract principles. His per-
ceptions were too quick to be always accurate; his ideas seemed to
burst forth from his brain like a torrent from a mountain-side, with
a force of current which swept along with it obstructions of every
description.[1]

Stanton was in his prime, but after leaving the government he did
not have much work to do. As a lifelong Democrat, he was unlikely to

receive many legal assignments from the Lincoln administration, such as he had received from Buchanan's. Nor did it seem likely that many private California claimants would want Stanton, the archenemy of questionable California land claims, to represent them in the Supreme Court. So Stanton faced a lull in his legal practice right as the nation faced secession and civil war.[2]

Stanton spent some of this time writing frequent, long letters to former president Buchanan and former secretary Dix. In the first of his letters to Buchanan, on March 10, he reported that it seemed Lincoln would not nominate Senator John Crittenden to the Supreme Court after all. The "red blacks," Stanton's derisive term for the Republicans, and also some Democrats opposed the nomination. There was a rumor that Stanton's former cabinet colleague Holt, who "appear[ed] now to be the chief favorite of the Republicans," would receive the nomination. Two days later Stanton wrote Buchanan that it was the "universal impression" in Washington that Lincoln would surrender both Fort Sumter, in Charleston harbor, and Fort Pickens, on an island just off Pensacola, Florida. The *New York Herald* reported from Washington that Lincoln had decided to abandon both forts to conciliate the South. Under the headline "Buchanan's Perfidy," the *New York Tribune* quoted Holt as saying that Fort Sumter "could have been re-enforced thirty days ago without serious difficulty, and measures had been taken for that purpose, but Mr. Buchanan positively refused to have them executed." Stanton forwarded this article to Buchanan, saying that James Harvey, the correspondent, was "in daily association with Mr. Holt, but he surely can have no warrant for the assertion in the article."[3]

Buchanan's main concern was not whether Lincoln surrendered Sumter but rather his own reputation in history. He wrote Stanton, "This is the critical moment of my life & I call upon you, in the name of sincere friendship, to devote your whole time and energies to my defense & justification." If Buchanan hoped that Stanton would defend him in print, he was doomed to disappointment, for Stanton would not tie himself in public to the unpopular former president. But Stanton continued to correspond with him, writing on March 16, "I do not think there will be any serious effort to assail your administration in respect to Fort Sumter. That would imply a coercive policy on their part"—that is, on the part of the Lincoln administration—"and hostility to your pacific measures." That day Stanton wrote a long letter to Dix, asking him to sell $5,000 worth of Stanton's securities in the New York markets: "My reason for selling so soon is that every sign here is discouraging. There is no safe principle or line of action—no token of any intelligent understanding by Lincoln, or the crew that groom him, of the state of the country, or the exigencies of the times. Bluster & Bravura alternate with timidity & despair—recklessness and helplessness by times rule the hour. What but disgrace & disaster can happen?"[4]

When Dix sold the stock, Stanton thanked him in another long letter, again critical of Lincoln and his administration:

I *know* that the administration not only have, as yet, no line of policy, but also believe that it *never can have any*, but will drift along, from day to day, without chart or compass. . . . I am inclined to believe that there *never has been a cabinet council*, in the sense in which we understand the term. A member of the cabinet told me yesterday, that he knew nothing of the late appointments to England France etc. until he saw them announced in the papers as having been sent to the Senate. Each Head of Department separately consults the President on the matters relating to it. This is no doubt the plan on which Mr. Lincoln proposes to maintain himself as President, preserving his independence. A very wise man, in quiet times, might get along that way. I doubt its being the best mode now, unless the Cabinet are so hostile that he cannot bring them together without collision.[5]

In early April, as papers predicted war, Stanton wrote Dix, "I do not think peaceful relations will continue much longer. Nor indeed do I think hostilities will be so great an evil as many apprehend. A round or two often serves to restore harmony." Lincoln decided that he would send supplies (not troops or arms) to Major Anderson at Fort Sumter and that he would notify the Confederates of the supply mission. When the Confederate president, Jefferson Davis, learned of the mission, he ordered the general in charge in Charleston to demand that Anderson surrender Fort Sumter. Excited reports arrived by telegraph in Washington late on Friday, April 12: Anderson had refused to surrender; the Confederates had started to shell Fort Sumter; the Civil War had started. Stanton sent a short letter that night to Buchanan: "We have the war upon us. The impression here is held by many: 1st, that the effort to reinforce will be a failure; 2d, that in less than twenty-four hours from this time Anderson will have surrendered; 3d that in less than thirty days Davis will be in possession of Washington."[6]

———

Lincoln conferred with his cabinet over the weekend and prepared a proclamation, calling upon the states to provide the federal government with short-term troops to suppress the rebellion. As in his letter to Buchanan, Stanton predicted in a letter to his brother-in-law James Hutchison that the rebels would soon attempt to capture Washington: "The government will of course strive to protect it but whether successfully or not is perhaps doubtful." Even if Washington was captured, however, Stanton believed the North would continue to fight. "In the end I think the most important & successful operations will have to be by the Mississippi in concert with corresponding movements on the seaboard." Many families were preparing to leave Washington. "I shall remain, and take the chances, feeling a firm faith in the final result in favor of the Government and willing to encounter its risks."[7]

The risks increased in the next few days. Virginia seceded from the Union on April 17, so rebel territory lay just across the river from Washington. The next day a Maryland mob attacked a Massachusetts regiment as it passed through Baltimore; several soldiers and civilians died in the confused struggle. Maryland then severed the railroad and telegraph ties between Washington and the North. The secession of Maryland, and the complete isolation of Washington, seemed imminent. Stanton wrote to Dix on April 23 that matters in the capital were "desperate beyond any conception. If there be any remedy—any shadow of hope to preserve this government from utter and absolute extinction—it must come from New York without delay." After an anxious few days a New York regiment finally arrived in Washington by way of Annapolis, the first of many regiments to arrive in the coming weeks. Stanton wrote to Eddie at Kenyon on May 1, "Last week there was a great panic here. The Virginia and Maryland people stopped everything from coming to market and there seemed to be danger of a famine." He sensed that his son, like many young men, would want to enlist in the army, and he advised against it. Students at college were "remote & secure from all danger and while passions are arming & raging elsewhere their time & thoughts should be diligently devoted to their studies so that when the hour comes for them to enter the busy scenes of life they are well prepared."[8]

Buchanan continued to worry about his reputation, but Stanton counseled him to stay quiet. In early May several papers carried a short letter from Seward's son and assistant Frederick, saying that there was "not a word of truth in the report of an armistice. That sort of business ended on the 4th of March." Buchanan wrote to Stanton that this seemed to be an attack on his negotiations with the South. Stanton replied, "The fling of Mr. F. W. Seward about 'negotiations' would merit a retort if there were an independent press and the state of the times admitted discussion of such matters." Besides, Stanton knew from his conversations with Campbell that the senior Seward would soon face similar criticism. "The negotiations carried on by Mr. Seward with the Confederate Commissioners through Judge Campbell . . . will some day perhaps be brought to light, and if they were as has been represented to me, Mr. Seward and the Lincoln administration will not be in a position to make sneering observations respecting any negotiations during your administration." Indeed within a few days the papers printed a long open letter from Campbell to Seward, accusing him of "systematic duplicity" when he assured the South that Lincoln would surrender Sumter. Stanton now tried to defend Seward to Buchanan: "I have no doubt he *believed* that Sumter would be evacuated as he stated it would be. But the war party overruled him with Lincoln, and he was forced to give up, but could not give up his office. That is a sacrifice no Republican will be apt to make." Stanton also defended Campbell, criticized by some Republican papers. "The Judge has been as anxiously & patriotically earnest to preserve the Government as any man in the United States, and he has sacrificed more than any Southern man rather than yield to the Secessionists." By the time Stanton wrote these words, Campbell had resigned his seat on the Supreme Court and returned to the South, but Stanton sympathized with the *man* if not with the *cause* of secession.[9]

Soon after he issued his first call for volunteers, Lincoln issued a second proclamation, imposing a blockade on the ports of the states in rebellion. Stanton recognized early what would become more apparent with time: that the blockade was one of the North's most effective weapons against the South. He wrote to Chase in June that nothing was more important to the Union war effort "than to maintain the blockade & stimulate capture." He was upset that the new district attorney for the District of Columbia, Edward Carrington, had conceded in two court cases that the defendants did not seem to have any intent to violate the blockade. Stanton insisted to Chase that the government should make no such concessions, that the issues "should be decided by *the court*, and if doubtful or adverse to the government should be delayed *by appeal* so long as possible." Stanton's assessment of Carrington's work was harsh: "Not a single authority was cited, the argument being chiefly prophetic declarations of the policy and intention of the present government, & vituperation of the last one. These are not arguments to the judicial mind, however true the prophecy may be, or just the condemnation." Stanton may have hoped that the federal government would hire him to handle these important and difficult cases. He did not get this assignment, but Stanton would soon have other government work.[10]

As the regiments arrived in Washington, Northern editors pressed Lincoln to attack the Confederates. "We do not want peace now," the *Indianapolis Journal* declared, "nor do we desire a slow or merely defensive war. We want war, swift and overwhelming. The more terrible the war is made, the shorter it will be, and the more humane the policy." Starting in late June the *New York Tribune* demanded daily that the Union Army march "on to Richmond" and capture it before the planned meeting there of the rebel Congress at the end of July. These bellicose editors would soon have their way. Against the advice of General Scott, Lincoln ordered Gen. Irvin McDowell and his army of about 30,000 to advance and attack the Confederates near Manassas, Virginia. McDowell's advance was no secret to the rebels: the papers reported on his march in detail. On July 16 Stanton wrote to Buchanan, "We are expecting a general battle to be commenced at Fairfax to-day." It took a few more days, but the general battle that Stanton anticipated was fought on Sunday, July 21. It was a disastrous defeat for the North. Many of the untrained and inexperienced Union soldiers panicked. Some of them fled on foot all the way to Washington, a distance of about thirty miles.[11]

Writing to his sister a few days later, Stanton reported, "Affairs in

Washington are to some degree recovering from the horrible condition exhibited on Monday and Tuesday—the disorganized rabble of destitute soldiers is being cleared from the streets by slow degrees, the army officers are not swarming so thickly in the hotels and taverns, and are perhaps beginning to join their men." Stanton was surprised that the rebels had not captured Washington. "Why they did not take possession of this city, as they might have done without serious resistance on Monday and Tuesday, is a marvel." He wrote in similar terms to Dix, just appointed to command the federal forces in Maryland: "McDowell is flat. No one vindicates him. The Cabinet also share the general censure." Stanton was even more scathing in a letter to Buchanan: "The dreadful disaster of Sunday can scarcely be mentioned. The imbecility of this administration culminated in that catastrophe; an irretrievable misfortune and national disgrace never to be forgotten are to be added to the ruin of all peaceful pursuits and national bankruptcy as the result of Lincoln's 'running the machine' for five months." (Stanton's word choice is interesting: Republican papers had attacked Buchanan for his "imbecility" and weakness during the secession winter.) "While Lincoln, Scott and the cabinet are disputing who is to blame, the city is unguarded, and the enemy is at hand." Stanton noted that a new general, George McClellan, had "reached here last evening" to take command of the forces in and around Washington. "But if he had the ability of a Caesar, Alexander or Napoleon, what can he accomplish? Will not Scott's jealousy, cabinet intrigues, and Republican interference thwart him at every step?"[12]

George Brinton McClellan, the son of a Philadelphia surgeon, attended first the University of Pennsylvania and then West Point, graduating second in his class. He was an engineer under Winfield Scott in the Mexican War, an official American observer of the Crimean War, and a protégé of Jefferson Davis when he was secretary of war under Franklin Pierce. McClellan resigned his commission in 1856 in order to work for several years as a railroad executive. He was a conservative Democrat, a supporter of Stephen Douglas, a close friend of the New York lawyer and financier S. L. M. Barlow. Just after the secession of South Carolina, he wrote to Barlow from Cincinnati, "Most men here acknowledge that the

South has much to ask that the North ought to & would grant." McClellan rejoined the army not long after the attack on Fort Sumter, winning some minor battles in western Virginia, hailed as major victories in the press. The *New York Herald*, for example, called McClellan "the Napoleon of the Present War" and claimed that, thanks to him, "the backbone of the rebellion is broken." McClellan saw himself in similar terms, writing to his wife just after he arrived in Washington that he was "in a new & strange position here—Presdt, Cabinet, Genl Scott & all deferring to me—by some strange operation of magic I seem to have become the power of the land. I almost think that were I to win some small success now I could become Dictator or anything else that might please me—but nothing of that kind would please me." As Stanton would soon learn, McClellan was not good at working with political leaders, but he was excellent at training an army. As soon as he was placed in charge of the Washington forces he went to work whipping them into shape, drilling and training them, giving them the name by which they are known to history: the Army of the Potomac.[13]

George Brinton McClellan, the Young Napoleon. Stanton was a friend of McClellan at first, then a harsh critic. McClellan would call Stanton the "vilest man I ever knew."

Stanton and McClellan met soon after McClellan arrived in Washington and, sharing Democratic views, they liked one another. In August 1861 they discussed how the army should handle slaves who fled their masters and sought shelter and work in the army camps. At Fort Monroe, the federal stronghold at the tip of the Virginia peninsula formed by the York and James rivers, Gen. Benjamin Butler, a clever Massachusetts lawyer before the war, had likened the escaped slaves to "contraband of war" and welcomed the "contrabands" to his work camps. In a letter to Butler published in the newspapers in early August, Secretary of War Simon Cameron blessed his approach, although he cautioned him to keep careful records so that the slave masters could be compensated after the war. At almost the same time Stanton's friend General Dix wrote a letter to Cameron saying that he would instruct his officers not to allow any slaves into their armed camps; Dix did not want to offend Maryland's slave owners. "Your view of the Negro policy is right," Stanton wrote to Dix. "It accords exactly with General McClellan's view. I had a conversation with him on the subject last Friday & he is gratified to find that you concur with him. He will act on that policy without regard to Cameron's instruction. The letter of Cameron is a prodigious blunder. . . . It will be altogether impracticable as a military policy and will be condemned by the great body of the Democratic party in the Northern States." Stanton was wrong in predicting that Cameron's letter to Butler would cause an outcry—there was little public reaction—but right that the question of slavery would soon become the central national issue.[14]

Simon Cameron, the incompetent and perhaps corrupt political leader from Pennsylvania who lasted less than a year as Lincoln's first secretary of war.

Even as Stanton criticized Cameron in his letter to Dix, Cameron hired Stanton to handle an important court case for the War Department. Lincoln's initial proclamation had called for volunteers to serve for three months; soon thereafter the War Department announced that all volunteers would have to serve for three years or the duration of the war, whichever was shorter. Edward Stevens, a soldier in the First Minnesota Volunteers, filed a federal case, seeking to be released after he completed what he viewed as his obligation, three months. Stanton appeared on behalf of the government on August 23 before Justice James Moore Wayne to argue that, regardless of whether Stevens had signed papers committing to three years, he was bound to serve three years by the army regulations. "These Minnesotans, who begged to get into the service, and kept far better men away and are now keeping them away, now ask you to discharge them. The enemy is at the very gates of the capital—if you discharge the petitioner, you must discharge the whole regiment; if you discharge the regiment you must discharge the whole army; and if you do that, what next? This beautiful edifice must fall into the hands of the rebel foe." Stanton's argument persuaded Wayne, who ordered Stevens to return to his regiment.[15]

Stanton's work on the Stevens case was the first of several government legal assignments drawing Stanton closer to the Lincoln administration even as he continued to criticize the president in private letters. General Scott asked Stanton for advice on how the federal government should respond to the Confederate Sequestration Act, authorizing seizure of Northern property, writing that he was "greatly obliged" for Stanton's detailed legal opinion. Attorney General Edward Bates asked Stanton to write a letter to California seeking information for use in one of the remaining land cases there. In November Stanton drafted and Cameron signed an order stating, "As special counsel of the United States retained by this Department [Stanton] is allowed to occupy the two rooms in the Corcoran building that have heretofore been in his possession as special counsel in the California land cases." In early December Stanton appeared for the United States again in the Supreme Court, arguing two California land cases, in both of which he prevailed. Indeed Stanton was so closely tied to the federal government by this time that, when contacted by a private land company about taking on a new California case against the government, he had to decline the work.[16]

Judge Edward Bates, the venerable Missouri lawyer and leader, was Lincoln's first attorney general.

Almost from the day he arrived in Washington in the summer of 1861, young General McClellan—he was only thirty-four—was in conflict with old General Scott, at seventy-five so obese and infirm that he could not ride a horse. McClellan wanted Scott's position as commanding general of all the armies, as well as his own post at the head of the Army of the Potomac. It was not clear whether McClellan would get his way. As Stanton noted in an October letter to Dix, some newspapers were predicting that when Scott retired, the president would promote Henry Halleck, the mining company lawyer from California, now a senior midwestern general. "There has not for a long time been much harmony between McClellan & Scott," Stanton wrote, "and [Halleck] is said to be an arrangement suggested by Scott and approved by Seward & Lincoln who have not found McClellan as supple or compliant as was desired." In this same letter Stanton reported on a minor battle, Ball's Bluff, that would play a large role in his first months as the secretary of war: "The late disaster near Leesburg is worse than any thing that has occurred during the war. Many think that the loss of life was greater than at Bull Run, but no exact returns have been & perhaps never can be made."[17]

Although Stanton was not aware of it at the time, his friend McClellan bore much of the blame for the "late disaster near Leesburg." McClellan had ordered Gen. George McCall to advance toward Leesburg from the Virginia side of the Potomac River and suggested that Gen. Charles Stone make a "slight demonstration" against Leesburg from the Maryland side. Then McClellan changed his mind and ordered McCall to return to Washington, but he failed to inform Stone. Stone sent about 2,000 federal troops across the river on October 21 under the command of Col. Edward Baker, a member of Congress and friend of Lincoln. As brave as he was foolish, Baker was shot and killed in the futile attack. The federals fled down the bluff and into the river. Rebels standing on the bluff calmly shot and killed many; others drowned while trying to cross the river; still others surrendered. About half the federal troops in the battle were killed, wounded, or captured. At first the Northern press tried to turn this into a sort of victory. The *New York Tribune* on October 24 praised "the splendid behavior of the national troops, who, in the face of an overpowering force, maintained their position till absolutely overrun, and at no moment lost the presence of mind which alone preserved them from total rout." Soon, though, the papers turned much more critical. *Frank Leslie's Illustrated Newspaper* declared that there was "blind, stupid, criminal neglect of the means necessary to insure a successful passage, or a safe retreat."[18]

McClellan was under increasing pressure to do something with the Army of the Potomac he was building in and around Washington. Senator Benjamin Wade of Ohio wrote to Senator Zachariah Chandler of Michigan, "I begin to fear that General McClellan himself has more faith in fasting and prayers to chase these d——s out, than he has in the strength of his regiments." In late October, Senators Wade, Chandler, and Lyman Trumbull met with McClellan and urged him to attack, insisting that even a defeat would be better than continued inaction. McClellan, however, argued that he could not advance because of Scott. He wrote to his wife that the three Republican senators had agreed to persuade Lincoln to retire Scott immediately. "Until that is accomplished I can effect but little good—he is ever in my way & I am sure does not desire effective action."[19]

In his letters home McClellan criticized not only Scott but also Lincoln, Seward, and others. In one particularly quotable letter he wrote that Lincoln was "nothing more than a well-meaning baboon," that Seward was "a meddling, officious, incompetent little puppy," and that Navy Secretary Gideon Welles was "weaker than the most garrulous old woman." In another letter McClellan described Lincoln as an "idiot" and in yet another called him "the original gorilla." After Stanton's death McClellan claimed that Stanton had used similar terms at this time to deride Lincoln: "The most disagreeable thing about [Stanton] was the extreme virulence with which he abused the President, the administration, and the Republican party. He carried this to such an extent that I was often shocked by it. He never spoke of the President in any other way than as the 'original gorilla.'" As the letters quoted in this chapter show, Stanton was quite critical of Lincoln, but there is no source other than McClellan suggesting that Stanton called Lincoln a gorilla.[20]

Stanton and McClellan spent a whole day, October 31, at Stanton's house, working on a long memorandum from McClellan to Cameron. McClellan wrote to his wife that he was "concealed" at Stanton's house "to dodge all enemies in the shape of 'browsing' Presdt etc." He was working with Stanton on a "very important" paper to show that "I have left nothing undone to make this army what it ought to be & that the necessity for delay has not been my fault." The memorandum, the original of which is partly in Stanton's handwriting, insisted that Lincoln had to provide McClellan with additional troops before he could mount a broad attack in northern Virginia. In one of the sentences drafted by Stanton the general told Lincoln that "all the information we have from spies, prisoners &c agrees in showing that the enemy have a force on the Potomac not less than 150,000 strong well drilled & equipped, ably commanded and intrenched." This would not be the last time McClellan overestimated the rebel army and pleaded that he needed more troops before he could attack.[21]

On November 1 Stanton wrote Dix that Scott would soon resign. "He has failed rapidly within a month and as he says is 'dead from the neck downwards.' I think his mental powers have also suffered greatly and that he is wholly unfit for duty." It was on this same day that Lincoln accepted Scott's resignation and appointed McClellan in his place, suggesting that Lincoln made these decisions before he saw the McClellan-Stanton memorandum. That evening Lincoln visited with McClellan and expressed concern about the "vast labor" that would be involved in commanding all the armies as well as the Army of the Potomac. McClellan assured Lincoln, "I can do it all."[22]

Stanton's role as friend and adviser of the Young Napoleon was soon in the papers, some of which described him as a "confidential friend." One issue on which McClellan sought Stanton's advice was the *Trent* affair, started by an American naval captain stopping a British merchant ship, the *Trent*, and seizing from her decks four Confederate diplomats bound for Europe. Like most lawyers, and indeed many nonlawyers, Stanton had views on the legal issues of the case, writing to Dix on November 17, "The ship should have been brought in and condemned for violating neutrality in becoming the carrier of official agents and dispatches at war with the United States." McClellan had what he described to his wife as a "long discussion" about the *Trent* with Stanton, who advised that the American captain was "fully justified by all the rules of International Law & all the decisions in the highest courts which bear upon the case. So it matters but little whether the English Govt & people make a fuss about it or not." Lincoln and Seward, after considering the legal and international issues, especially the risk of war with Britain, would in the end release the four Confederate prisoners to Britain.[23]

Stanton and McClellan also discussed the controversial question of how the army should handle black refugees. As McClellan put it in a letter to his friend Barlow on November 8, he wanted to "dodge the nigger." He insisted that he was "fighting to preserve the integrity of the Union & the power of the Govt—on no other issue." But increasingly it was not possible to "dodge" the question. Col. John Cochrane, a former Democratic member of Congress from New York, gave a speech to his regiment in Washington on November 13. The *National Republican* quoted Cochrane as saying that "this was a war for the preservation of our national existence—a war of self-defense, forced upon us by the South, and that it was our duty to use every means in our power to crush the rebellion." Since Southern slaves were "an important element of their strength and power against us, we should take possession of them, and when necessary *put arms in their hands*, that they might assist in fighting this battle for freedom." Cameron, who was in the audience, then gave what the *Republican* called "a brave and manly little speech" in which he "heartily endorsed every word Col. Cochrane had uttered." On this same day, as it happened, General Dix issued a proclamation to the people of Maryland, assuring them that his army would not "interfere with the condition of any persons held to domestic service" nor "permit any such persons to come within their lines." Stanton wrote to Dix that his proclamation was "highly approved here and *admired*. General McClellan spoke of it yesterday with much commendation without knowing I had seen it."[24]

Interior Secretary Caleb Smith disagreed with Cameron about arming the former slaves, and their disagreement was soon reported by the press. Barlow wrote Stanton that he was glad to learn of the quarrel between Cameron and Smith, although McClellan "must, if possible, keep entirely free" of these issues. Stanton thought the same, writing Barlow, "Cameron, Chase, and Seward are said to agree in the nigger-arming question; Smith, Blair and Lincoln contra. I think the General's true course is to mind his own Department and win a victory. After that all other things will be of easy settlement." Some newspapers reported that Cameron, in his imminent annual report, would advocate arming the former slaves. The *New York Tribune*, for example, said on November 25 that the secretary would provide historical and other arguments for enlisting the former slaves. Other papers denied the rumor. The *New York Herald* predicted on December 2 that Cameron would not "in the remotest degree express himself in favor of arming the slaves," that the secretary's "plan merely amounts to emancipating the slaves of rebels and employing them in military and other works."[25]

Cameron claimed, after Stanton's death, that Stanton helped him to write this annual report, including the paragraph in which he advocated arming the former slaves: "[Stanton] read the report carefully, and after suggesting a few alterations, calculated to make it stronger, he gave it his unequivocal and hearty support." Stanton's first biographer, Frank Flower, asserted that Stanton actually wrote the controversial paragraph. But in light of the intense public interest in the issue and Stanton's own conservative views at this time, it seems more likely that he did not write the section in question. One version of Cameron's report, which appeared in some papers, declared, "It is as clearly the right of the government to arm slaves, when it may become necessary, as it is to use gunpowder taken from the enemy." When Lincoln saw this version he insisted that Cameron change the report, and so another version soon appeared without this language. The press picked up on the change and the reasons behind it. The *Philadelphia Inquirer* stated that Lincoln had told Cameron he must not "dictate to Congress what they should do." The *Chicago Tribune* praised Cameron's original report as "the brightest page in the history of the war" and lamented its "emasculation." It was a political disaster, angering both sides, more Lincoln's fault than Cameron's, for Lincoln should have picked up the signs that Cameron planned to address the issue in his report.[26]

When Congress assembled in early December, some members called for investigations into the defeats at Bull Run and Ball's Bluff; others insisted that these were military issues, that only the military authorities could investigate. Senator William Pitt Fessenden of Maine, a moderate Republican who would become a friend and colleague of Stanton, insisted that Congress had to oversee the army: "While there is agitation in the public mind; while there are so many ideas afloat; so many accusations, unfounded, perhaps, in a very great degree; and no inquiry is made and no step taken to enlighten the public in relation to the matter— that public which carries on this war, and which furnishes the means for carrying it on—shall we, who are the agents of that public, be told that during its progress, be it longer or shorter, we are to ask no questions, make no complaints, no investigations, know nothing, say nothing, and inquire about nothing?" After some debate Congress created the Joint Committee on the Conduct of the War, tasked with investigating not just the two recent battles but *all* aspects of the war. Although there were some Democratic members of the committee, including Senator Andrew Johnson of Tennessee, a state that had seceded but whose senator refused to resign, the committee was dominated by Radical Republicans, notably Senators Wade and Chandler and Representative George Julian of Indiana.[27]

Even as this committee was formed, the newspapers continued to debate who was to blame for Ball's Bluff. The *Cincinnati Commercial*, without quite naming McClellan, declared that the hundreds who lay "drowned at the bottom of the Potomac" were victims of "the senseless orders which precipitated them straight into the jaws of destruction." Other newspapers blamed Stone, reporting that Baker said he would obey Stone's orders even though they would be his "death-warrant." Stone's reputation also suffered because of reports that he was returning fugitive slaves to their masters. Stanton's friend Sumner said in a Senate speech full of sarcasm that Stone was "adding to his achievements" at Ball's Bluff "by engaging ably and actively in the work of surrendering fugitive slaves." Stone responded with a rash letter suggesting that Sumner was a coward because he had failed to fight back when he was attacked with a cane a few years earlier on the Senate floor. Stanton did not comment on these issues, at least as far as his surviving letters show, but they would form some of his first tests as secretary of war.[28]

The Stantons remained in Washington in December and January, in part because the newest member of the family, James Hutchison Stanton, born in October, was near death. A few days after the boy's birth Stanton wrote to Dix that the baby was well even though he arrived "in the dark period of history that will be known & abhorred as Lincoln's administration." By early January, however, Ellen was writing to her sister-in-law Catherine Wilkins Hutchison that the baby was restless, feverish, and had a "dreadful condition of his skin." Jamie's illness, she feared, was the result of his "having been vaccinated before his skin was perfectly clear." One of the family doctors had insisted on inoculating the boy against small pox, "there being so much of it about," and apparently he had contracted the disease from the vaccine. The Stantons had already taken Jamie to see doctors in Baltimore and Philadelphia, but Ellen did not like their recommendations, so Stanton had written to yet another, who sent "eight powders to be given night and morning." A few weeks later the Stantons had Jamie baptized at home by Reverend Charles Hall of Epiphany Episcopal Church, who noted in the parish register that the child was "in extremis."[29]

Stanton wrote to Barlow on January 7 that there had been "no improvement in public affairs, save General McClellan's accession to chief command, but his illness [typhoid fever] has in a great measure prevented the good consequences which might have resulted from that event." Lincoln had announced his decision to release the Confederate diplomats from the *Trent*, but Stanton feared that even this concession would not avoid war with Britain, for his "private advices" from there suggested "a nearly unanimous and almost frantic hostility of the English people to our government." In both Britain and France there was "a bitter contempt for the administration," which Stanton thought had "no consciousness of the dangers, or ability to avoid them." He added, "Seward says 'all's well,' and that is enough for the Republicans."[30]

There is nothing in these January 1862 letters to suggest that Stanton had any hint that he was about to join the Lincoln administration. Nor is there much in the newspapers of late December 1861 or early January 1862 to suggest that Lincoln was about to remove Cameron. True, the Kentucky legislature adopted a resolution demanding that Lincoln, because Cameron advocated arming slaves, should find a new and more moderate secretary of war. A few Democratic papers reprinted this resolution and called for Lincoln to remove Cameron. A few Republican papers defended Cameron. There was hardly a clamor for Cameron's head, however, and none of the major New York or Washington papers predicted that Lincoln was about to make a critical cabinet change. But he was.[31]

Chapter 7

"Put Forth Every Energy"

— January–March 1862 —

P
resident Lincoln spent the morning of January 11 with Secretary of State Seward. Almost certainly they talked about the War Department, about whether to replace Simon Cameron with Edwin Stanton. Even if Cameron was not corrupt—and he was at the least too tolerant of corruption—he was incompetent. As Senator Fessenden put it in a letter home, "The simple truth was that Cameron *could not* manage so large a concern. He had neither the capacity nor strength of will—and there was great mismanagement." Yet naming Stanton to replace Cameron posed political problems for Lincoln. What would be the reaction among Republicans if Lincoln appointed a Democrat to this key position? And in particular how would Pennsylvania Republicans react to Stanton, whose ties to the state were tenuous, in the place of their native son Cameron? As for Stanton's qualifications, Seward probably told Lincoln what he told Chase the next day: that he knew Stanton from their cooperation in the last months of the Buchanan administration, that Stanton had "great force—[was] full of expedients, and thoroughly loyal." Chase met with Stanton on January 11, but Chase's diary suggests they did not talk about the possibility that Stanton would join the cabinet. They spoke instead of McClellan, with whom Chase was displeased, thinking that the general had filled his staff with friends and family and that he did not show proper respect to the president.[1]

The next day, a Sunday, after attending church and dining with his family, Chase went to see Seward. Chase mentioned both Holt and Stanton as possible replacements for Cameron, but said that he was worried that "Holt might embarrass us on the slavery question, and might not prove quite equal to the emergency." Chase had no such concerns about Stanton, whom he described as "a good lawyer and full of energy." As they talked Cameron arrived, angered by a letter from Lincoln saying that he would nominate him as the American minister to Russia. The letter was an insult, Cameron said, a rude dismissal. Chase and Seward calmed Cameron down, persuading him to see Lincoln, urging him to suggest Stanton, a fellow Pennsylvanian, as his successor. Chase wrote in his diary that night that Lincoln "had already mentioned Stanton in a way which indicated that no objection on his part would be made." It seems that Stanton did not know of these weekend discussions among Lincoln, Cameron, Chase, and Seward.[2]

On Monday morning Cameron spoke with Lincoln. The president gave him a revised, backdated letter praising his work as secretary and asking him to take the important Russian assignment. Cameron agreed and urged the president to name Stanton for the War Department. It is possible that Lincoln spoke with Stanton that morning, for a reporter referred to Stanton's being "sent for by the President" just before the nomination was made. If Lincoln *did* speak with Stanton, however, it was not a long conversation, for he sent both the Cameron and Stanton nominations to the Senate around noontime. Lincoln's proposed changes surprised the Senate, indeed "astounded" them, according to Fessenden.[3]

In the nineteenth century, presidents did not announce their nominations in the Rose Garden, so we do not have Lincoln's own explanation for why he selected Stanton. But we do have an explanation by John Hay, the president's protégé and private secretary, who was probably closer to Lincoln than any other man at this time. In one of the anonymous articles he wrote for the *Missouri Republican*, Hay described Stanton as being "personally friendly with every member" of the cabinet and "in entire unity of feeling and thought with the two leading spirits of the Government, Chase and Seward." He was "a Pennsylvanian, and his selection satisfied the jealous State pride that placed General Cameron in the Cabinet." By nominating a Democrat, Lincoln was proving "that former party politics are to be ignored in this great struggle for the National Life." Hay was sure Stanton would fight: "Where he sees the rebellion strong and defiant he will strike blows to stagger it. If it staggers, he will mercilessly strike blows to finish it." He was "an energetic and efficient worker, a man of initiative and decision, an organizer, a man of administrative scope and executive tact—a very good pattern for a Secretary of War."[4]

The nation's newspapers, almost without exception, praised the Stanton nomination. Democratic editors were especially enthused about the prospect of a Democrat in the Lincoln administration. The *New York World* thought Lincoln had removed Cameron because of his Radical position on arming the slaves; the choice of Stanton showed "the firm purpose of the President to adhere to the conservative policy he has repeatedly avowed, and thus far consistently maintained, relative to the object of the war." The *Chicago Times* was even more pointed: "If the appointment of Mr. Stanton signifies all it seems to signify, abolitionism is the victim of a blow from which it will not recover this year, nor the next year, nor the next." Some Republican papers were concerned about just this point; the *Chicago Tribune* feared that Stanton was named in order to "enforce the policy of the Kentucky Unionists, whose efforts for the cause are bottomed on the hope of saving slavery." Other Republican editors were more positive: the *New York Tribune* declared, "Unless we are grievously mistaken in Mr. Stanton, the nation will have ample reason to rejoice over his appointment."[5]

Many of these articles commended Stanton's work in the secession winter. The *New York Herald* commented, "When, in the dark days of the Buchanan administration, he accepted the attorney generalship, it was to save the country. He struck hands with Mr. Holt, the then secretary of war, and they determined that the President should adhere to the Constitution or suffer impeachment." The *Washington Evening Star* argued that "it was, for the most part, through Mr. Stanton's energy, emphasis and clear mind that the temporizing policy of President Buchanan, in the latter part of his administration, was changed to one of vigor against the rebellion." Buchanan could not have been pleased by such reports, but he wrote to his niece that Stanton was a "sound, clear-headed, persevering and practical lawyer, and quite eminent, especially in patent cases."[6]

Stanton himself was to some extent responsible for this favorable newspaper coverage. Malcolm Ives, a Washington correspondent for the *New York Herald*, wrote to his editor, James Gordon Bennett, that it was Stanton who had provided him with information about the Buchanan administration. Stanton also arranged for Ives to have a long interview with McClellan and assured Ives that "the policy of the War Department would fully accord with that of the Commander in Chief & the President." (Stanton was not the only one in those days to refer to McClellan as the commander in chief, the title the general preferred.) A few days later Ives told Bennett that Stanton and McClellan had the same view of the "blundering and abolitionist generals," namely that they would be "dropped."[7]

Dissenting views appeared not in the papers but in private letters. None questioned Stanton's ability; they commented instead on his person and personality. Charles Wainwright, an artillery officer from New York City, wrote on January 19 that he did not like Stanton's looks: "I saw him in the box with President Lincoln the other night at the Opera: a long-haired, fat, oily, politician-looking man." Sam Ward, a Washington lobbyist, wrote to Frederick Seward, "to me he is personally distasteful from the bitterness & injustice with which he persecuted some of my California friends. I thought his motives interested—I am told they were not. But whether he was the tool of Judge Black or the latter an instrument in his hands they certainly did some vile work and endeavored to do more between them." Ward added that he hoped Secretary Seward was on good terms with Stanton, for he heard from a senator that Stanton "was a dangerous foe—a sleuthhound sort of man who never lost his scent or slackened his purpose." Henry Halleck, one of those whom Stanton had "persecuted" in California, now a Union general, wrote to his wife, "Mr. Stanton does not like me, and of course will take the first opportunity he can to injure me. I shall take my precautions accordingly so as not to give him a chance." Stanton, knowing that he would have to work with Halleck, wrote him a short note soon after he became secretary: "You have my perfect confidence and may rely upon the utmost support in your undertakings."[8]

To secure approval from the Senate, Stanton would need support not only from Democrats, who would follow the lead of the *New York*

World, but also from Republicans, who would have questions about the nomination of a Buchanan Democrat. Here Stanton's long friendships with Sumner and Chase proved critical. On the Monday of the nomination, Sumner wrote that Stanton was "a personal friend" and that he was "determined on a vigorous military policy & a positive policy on Slavery." When Fessenden expressed doubts about Stanton, Chase offered to arrange a meeting and sent his carriage for Fessenden. After the meeting Fessenden wrote home that Stanton was "just the man we want. We agree on every point: the duties of the Secretary of War, the conduct of the war, the negro question, and everything else." When Fessenden asked Stanton how the military should deal with fugitive slaves, he responded, "Any officer who employed military force in returning fugitive slaves ought to be court martialed." Fessenden wrote that if Stanton had "the force of character and the will necessary for the place & the occasion, and he is said to have both, we shall soon, I think, see a new face upon public affairs, and God knows we need it." This meeting of Stanton, Fessenden, and Chase took place on the morning of January 15. Later that same day the Senate confirmed Stanton. Thirty-eight senators voted for Stanton; only two senators, Republicans, voted against him.[9]

Republican editors soon warmed to Stanton. The *New York Tribune* reported on January 16 that he was an intimate friend of Sumner and Chase: "Those two names should be sufficient endorsement of the new Secretary, who it may be added is fully acceptable to such men as Senators Wade and Fessenden." The *Tribune* insisted that Democrats who thought Stanton would be an ally "of Slavery, of the Rebels, or of the Border States" would soon be "charmingly disappointed." The *Chicago Tribune* predicted, "The jobbing and corruption that have disgraced the organization of our army will, as fast as [Stanton] can reach the offenders, be brought to an end." The *Tribune*'s editor Joseph Medill followed up with a long private letter to Stanton: "You have a Herculean work before you to penetrate thro' the frauds and swindling that envelop the whole service. You will encounter rottenness and rascality from top to bottom; you will discover scores of lukewarm half secession officers in command who cannot bear to strike a vigorous blow lest it hurts their rebel friends or jeopardizes the precious practice of slavery." Medill then listed several officers who he believed were "lukewarm," including Charles Stone. "The country looks to you with longing heart to infuse vigor, system, honesty, and *fight* into the service. The Army has lost more men in the past four months from inaction and *ennui* than it would have done from ten bloody pitched battles."[10]

Medill's was one of dozens of letters that Stanton received just before and just after he took over the War Department. When the nomination was first announced Justice Grier wrote to be sure that Stanton would accept: "You are young, *strong*, can bear labor, can do great good, and in this crisis your country demands every sacrifice of individual comfort." Samuel Medary telegraphed from Ohio, "Take the War Office for God's sake & the Country." John Dix wrote, "If, as they say, you are Secretary of War, I do not congratulate you, I congratulate the country and the Army cordially." Only a few of Stanton's responses survive. He wrote John Clifford, "I go into the administration as the representative of national feeling and purpose to overcome treason & rebellion and to put forth every energy of the nation to accomplish that end. No pledges were asked, none were given." He told Holt, "The cordial approval you have given to my appointment is known and fully appreciated." (Holt had written to Lincoln that Stanton would be "a friend true as steel & a support, which no pressure from within or without, will ever shake.") Stanton's letter to Holt continued: "Your regard and support strengthen my heart more than I can tell. My feelings toward yourself you already know. We stood together in the beginning of this mighty contest and by God's blessing we will stand together until the end."[11]

What was the role of the secretary of war during the American Civil War? It is a simple question but not an easy one to answer, in part because Stanton was forever changing and expanding his job description. The secretary was of course not the commander in chief. Lincoln filled that role, tentatively at first and then more confidently and successfully. The secretary was also not the general in chief, the post that McClellan occupied when Stanton first took office and that Grant would hold at the war's end. There was not much work for the secretary to do as an intermediary between the president and the general in chief, for the two of them communicated directly, either in person or by telegraph. So what was left for the secretary of war?[12]

One key task was to work with Congress. Secretary Stanton had to persuade Congress to provide the funds needed for the War Department and the Union Army. By the standards of the time, the sums involved were immense. After spending about $23 million in the fiscal year that ended in June 1861, the department would spend $600 million in fiscal year 1863 and more than $1 billion in fiscal year 1865. Stanton not only had to line up reluctant members of Congress to vote for these unprecedented appropriations; he had to work with them on dozens of other military bills: to authorize additional clerks, to establish a draft system, to set the pay and benefits for soldiers and officers. Stanton could not rely on the White House to work with Congress for there was no professional staff there beyond Lincoln's three personal secretaries. Nor did Stanton have a large staff within his own department to deal with Congress; there was nobody like the assistant secretary of defense for legislative affairs, who assists the present secretary of defense. Stanton had to deal directly with senators and representatives, and he did so daily.[13]

Another key task for the secretary was to work with governors. The federal government relied almost entirely on the states to recruit volunteers and form regiments; even when Congress created a dreaded federal draft, it was really a backstop behind the state system. Relying on the states meant that someone in the federal government had to be in close telegraphic touch with the state governors, and that person was generally Stanton, although Lincoln was also actively involved, and Stanton's small staff in the adjutant general's office helped with details. But for messages to governors, it was generally Stanton who picked up his pen and prepared the first draft of the telegram.[14]

Stanton did not pay much attention to the elections during his first year in the War Department, but starting in 1863, and especially in 1864, he was actively involved in politics. He did not go out and give political speeches; he left that to others, including some generals whom he granted leave for this purpose. Instead he worked in Washington: transporting troops home so they could vote, getting ballots to troops entitled to vote in the field, in some cases punishing officers who voted the wrong way. Stanton's election work was not neutral—he favored the Republican candidates—and he disregarded complaints by Democrats about what they viewed as his abuses of his power and position for political purposes.[15]

Stanton recognized, almost from the day he entered office, the importance of the press and popular opinion. As a consequence he cultivated some editors and reporters and started to provide information to the public through messages about military matters. Later, in 1864, he would create an excellent system for providing information to the papers through daily telegrams to Dix, effectively press releases to the Northern newspapers. Stanton also started, almost from day one, to punish and arrest editors and reporters who violated what he viewed as the limits on wartime journalism. This was part of his broader effort to write and enforce rules of military justice, not just within the army but throughout the North. Stanton turned to an outside expert, Francis Lieber, to draft a code to establish rules for the U.S. Army in the field, to summarize centuries of unwritten European laws of war. This code, which still forms the basis of U.S. military law, authorized not only courts-martial to try soldiers who deserted or disregarded their duties but also military commissions to try enemies and civilians. The military commission that would try John Wilkes Booth's colleagues, those accused of conspiring to murder Lincoln, was only one of *thousands* of military commissions organized by Stanton and the War Department during and just after the Civil War.[16]

Stanton also had to coordinate with his colleagues in the cabinet: Secretary of State Seward, Secretary of the Treasury Chase, Secretary of the Navy Welles. In general Stanton's relations with his cabinet colleagues were not good; from their perspective, he was forever treading on their territory. This was especially true with Welles and the navy, for, as Welles noted, Stanton "assumed that the Navy was secondary and subject to the control and direction of the military branch of the government." There were also disagreements about policy; Postmaster General Montgomery Blair, a conservative, soon hated Stanton, whom he believed to be a reckless Radical.[17]

Lincoln and his cabinet. This is a print from the famous painting by Francis Carpenter, showing Lincoln and his cabinet discussing the first draft of the Emancipation Proclamation. Those pictured are (*from left to right*) Edwin Stanton, Salmon Chase, Abraham Lincoln, Gideon Welles, Caleb Smith, William Henry Seward, Montgomery Blair, and Edward Bates.

Stanton supervised several functional offices within the War Department, such as the Ordnance Office, responsible for providing arms and ammunition, and the Quartermaster's Office, responsible for providing all other supplies. These offices dated back to the Revolutionary War, and several of the office heads had served in the army for decades. Stanton realized that two new functions were needed to fight a modern war, to supervise railroads and telegraph lines, so he created new rail and telegraph bureaus. Lincoln and Stanton did not hesitate to use the telegraph to reach out to generals in the field, to obtain information and to give instructions. Such messages might seem to violate the chain of command, but direct communication would prove critical in the chaotic conditions of the Civil War. Especially later in the war, Stanton showed himself a master at using railroads, telegraphs, and logistics in order to move men and materiel. The Union advantage over the Confederacy was not just that it had more *miles* of railroad track and telegraph wire; Stanton and others, both inside and outside the department, also knew how to *use* the rails and the wires to assemble and apply military force.[18]

Stanton's first day as the head of the War Department was Monday, January 20. In those days, the department occupied a rundown four-story building on the corner of Seventeenth Street and Pennsylvania Avenue, about where the north façade of the Eisenhower Executive Office Building stands today. Justice Grier came to the department on the first morning to administer the oath. Stanton pledged that he would "support, protect, and defend the Constitution and Government of the United States against all enemies, whether domestic or foreign" and that he would "bear true faith, allegiance, and loyalty to the same." All the army officers in Washington at the time, perhaps two hundred men in full-dress uniform, were present for the ceremony. One newspaper reported, "As the officers were presented in turn, he had a pleasant word to say to each, especially those whose names are on the record of distinguished services, with which he seemed thoroughly familiar." Stanton then walked up the stairs to the secretary's office on the second floor and started work. That evening he met members of the Joint Committee on the Conduct of the War. One later recalled that Stanton told them that they "must strike hands, and, uniting [their] strength and thought, double the power of the Government to suppress its enemies and restore its integrity." The committee must have expressed impatience with McClellan, for the next day the chairman, Benjamin Wade, wrote to Stanton asking whether there was any such title as that which McClellan used for himself, "commander-in-chief of the army of the United States."[19]

The War Department building as it looked during the Civil War.

Stanton's own impatience was evident as well. On January 22, in response to a Union victory at Mill Springs, Kentucky, he issued a congratulatory message: "The purpose of this war is to attack, pursue and destroy the rebellious enemy, and to deliver the country from the danger menaced by traitors. Alacrity, daring, courageous spirit and patriotic zeal on all occasions and under every circumstance are expected from the army of the United States." Stanton's message was printed in almost every Northern newspaper. Two days later he wrote to Charles Dana, a senior editor at the *New York Tribune*, about "the task that is before us," adding, "I say 'us' because the *Tribune* has its mission as plainly as I have mine, and they tend to the same end." Stanton declared to Dana, "As soon as I can get the machinery of the office going, the rats cleared out, & the rat holes stopped, we shall move. This army has got to fight or run away; and while men are striving nobly in the West, the champagne & oysters on the Potomac must be stopped." On January 27, probably at Stanton's suggestion, Lincoln issued a general order directing that all the Union armies be ready to move by February 22, Washington's birthday. Since the western armies were already moving, this order was directed at McClellan, whose army was in winter quarters in and around Washington, enjoying "champagne & oysters." At least at first, Lincoln and Stanton did not publish this order in the newspapers to allow McClellan time to prepare and move. In another private letter to Dana, Stanton wrote, "Instead of an army stuck in the mud of the Potomac we should have a column of one hundred thousand men thrusting upon Nashville and sweeping rebellion & treason out of Kentucky with fire & sword. But we have had no war, we have not even been playing war. With material for military operations that were never equaled on the globe we seem to have *no* military genius to command our armies."[20]

Why did Stanton shift from being the friend of McClellan to being one of his critics as soon as he became secretary of war? Why did Stanton at once befriend the general's political enemies, Wade and other congressional Radicals? As another senior Washington official observed, eighty years later: "Where you stand depends on where you sit." Stanton was now seated at Lincoln's right hand, and Lincoln was eager to see McClellan in motion. Stanton realized that he would have to work closely with Congress to obtain the legislation and appropriations he needed, and Congress was dominated by Republicans. So Stanton immediately formed ties with key Republicans and soon obtained the first fruits of these ties. By the end of January, Congress had passed three bills requested and in some cases drafted by Stanton: one to give him two more assistant secretaries, a second to add fifty clerks to his staff, a third to give the president broad authority over railroad and telegraph lines. In his new role as secretary, Stanton was painfully aware of the immense expense of raising and maintaining the army and of the congressional and indeed national desire to see this army in action. For all these reasons he joined those pressing McClellan to fight.[21]

For his two new assistant secretaries, Stanton suggested and the Senate quickly confirmed John Tucker, a Pennsylvania railroad executive, and Peter Watson, the Washington patent lawyer through whom Stanton communicated with Seward during the secession winter. During the first part of 1862, however, Stanton's most valuable assistant was Thomas Scott, a former railroad official appointed by Cameron. It was Scott who suggested that Stanton should form separate offices within the War Department to take charge of military telegraphs and military railroads. In early February Stanton sent Scott west to hasten the process of forming troops into regiments. Stanton also instructed Scott to investigate transportation: how many thousand men could be "moved at once from Washington to the Ohio river . . . and also the means of transportation and time required for a movement from the river to the interior of Kentucky and Tennessee."[22]

Thomas Scott, a railroad executive before and after the Civil War, was an invaluable aide to Stanton in the first few months of his tenure in the War Department.

Scott reported to Stanton from Pittsburgh that, if all the rail lines worked together, the United States could move 60,000 men in six days from Washington to Pittsburgh. Scott went to Columbus, Detroit, Indianapolis, and Louisville, meeting with state officials, working to organize regiments, reporting daily to Stanton. Then, out of the blue, Scott received a message from Stanton that started, "You will give no orders to General Halleck, General Buell or any other general in the field." It seems that Scott had annoyed Ohio state officials by dispersing among infantry regiments a cavalry unit that had no horses. Scott responded on February 6, "I have your message of censure. I have not given orders to any general, nor did [I] dream of doing so. In your letter of instructions you direct me to require consolidation of regiments so as to be ready to take the field without delay—this I have done in Ohio and Indiana."[23]

Scott continued to Cairo, Illinois, at the junction of the Ohio and Mississippi rivers, where he found conditions in the quartermaster's office "about as bad as could well be imagined." The quartermasters and their cronies were stealing from the government, for example, by renting boats at $1,800 per month when they could be had for $800. Scott labored tirelessly for months, reporting to Stanton often, with scant thanks from him. In early May, from an army camp in northern Mississippi, Scott sent Stanton his resignation. He explained that he wanted to return to private life, to his work for the Pennsylvania Railroad. Perhaps realizing, as Scott was leaving, that he would be hard to replace, Stanton thanked Scott for his "energy, prudence, and discretion."[24]

Stanton relied not only on his assistant secretaries but also on outside experts. During the course of his first week in office, for example, he had breakfast with Dennis Hart Mahan, the famed West Point professor, and asked for Mahan's views on dividing armies into separate corps and the proper role of a central staff. Mahan responded in writing. Soon thereafter Stanton appointed former New York governor Hamilton Fish and Methodist bishop Edward Raymond Ames to go to Richmond and report on the conditions of the Union prisoners there.[25]

Stanton worked his staff hard and he worked himself hard. Samuel Wilkeson, one of the department's clerks, wrote to former secretary Cameron to complain that Stanton had forced Lorenzo Thomas, the aged adjutant general, to stand at his side for "six hours," so long that poor Thomas's legs were reduced "to pipe-stem proportions." Wilkeson said that he and Thomas longed for that "good old gentleman" from Pennsylvania, who had so "delightfully mingled social courtesies" with the "prompt dispatch of business." On February 10 the overworked Stanton collapsed. The *New York Times* reported that Stanton "was seized with vertigo about noon to-day, and had to retire from his office. He is quite sick this evening, but is not considered in any danger." Thomas wrote to Cameron, "No man can long stand working day by day until ten o'clock at night, and this is his present custom. Today he sunk under it, and for a time was quite unwell—threatened, I think, with a rush of blood to the head." A few days later the *Times* was pleased to report that Stanton was back at his desk. William Stoddard, another of Lincoln's private secretaries, denied the rumors that Stanton's health was failing: "In conversation with a friend, night before last, the Secretary himself referred to this matter, asserting that he never was in better health in his life, his late attack of vertigo being directly traceable to a close room, the gas from a hot coal-stove, and a too long strain at his work."[26]

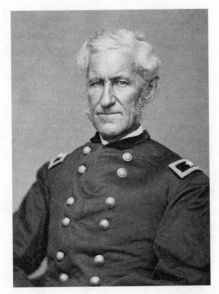

Lorenzo Thomas was in charge of personnel paperwork in the War Department. Stanton did not much like Thomas and sent him west, where he served ably in recruiting black soldiers.

Stanton made many mistakes in his first few months as secretary of war, of which the worst was his arrest and imprisonment of Gen. Charles

Stone. Not long after Stanton started work three members of the Joint Committee on the Conduct of the War visited him and presented their "evidence" against Stone, mainly hearsay reports that Stone was in communication with rebel commanders. It seems likely that Stanton also spoke with Sumner, his closest friend in Congress, and that Sumner shared with Stanton the recent letter in which Stone had essentially called Sumner a coward. Ives wrote to his editor that Stanton condemned Stone but McClellan thought "the case as yet insufficiently investigated." Without waiting for further investigation, however, on January 28 Stanton ordered McClellan to arrest Stone and to "hold him in close custody." McClellan delayed for a few days. Attorney General Bates noted in his diary that the Joint Committee wanted Stanton to remove Stone from command. Bates had not yet heard of Stanton's plan to arrest Stone, but Bates was worried about congressional interference in the choice of commanders, and he wrote Stanton "to put him on his guard." Stanton ignored this advice. When McClellan shared a further report on Stone, Stanton again ordered his arrest, and this time McClellan complied. Army officers arrested Stone on the streets of Washington at about one in the morning on February 9; they transported him to Boston and placed him in a damp solitary cell in Fort Lafayette. Stone sent letter after letter, asking to be informed of the charges against him, demanding that the

Gen. Charles Stone, whom Stanton arrested in February 1862 and kept in prison for six months without charges. Stanton never allowed Stone to resume his military career.

charges be considered by a court-martial. There was no answer. When Stone's brother-in-law, a senior Boston lawyer, asked to confer with the prisoner, Stanton's assistant Watson refused the request.[27]

The same editions of the papers that reported the arrest of Stone also reported the arrest of Malcolm Ives, the *New York Herald* correspondent whom Stanton had so favored in the first few days of his tenure. On February 8 Ives was in the War Department while Stanton was in his office with the door closed, meeting with congressional leaders. When Ives started to open Stanton's door, Watson told him that he must not do so. Ives angrily insisted "that he had a perfect right, as representative of the *New York Herald*, to go into the Secretary of War's apartment at any time he thought proper, no matter who was there." Stanton immediately drafted an order for the arrest of Ives, accusing him of entering government offices "for the purpose of spying and obtaining war news and intelligence" and of threatening that the *New York Herald* would oppose the Lincoln administration unless the paper was "afforded special privileges." Stanton's order was printed in the newspapers, along with the news that Ives was now in prison at Fort McHenry.[28]

The initial press reaction to the arrests of Stone and Ives was positive. Many papers printed what they called the "charges" against Stone: misconduct at the Battle of Ball's Bluff and improper correspondence with the enemy army. The *Cleveland Daily Leader* cheered Stone's imprisonment: "This is the fit disposition of one who has so outrageously violated all honor, patriotism, and official oaths." John Hay, in an anonymous article, wrote that Stanton surely would not have imprisoned the general unless "grave reasons existed for such a course." The *New York World*, after quoting Stanton's order regarding Ives, stated, "Every loyal journal in this city and the country would accept and add emphasis to the opinions of the secretary. He may be sure of their hearty endorsement, not merely of the present act, but of any act necessary to the safe and successful conduct of the war, whatever restrictions it may impose upon them and their employees." The *New York Times* said that Stanton's order for the arrest of Ives "leaves little or no question of the justice or propriety of the proceeding." Views changed as weeks passed and the two men remained in prison; Stanton did not release Ives until late May and Stone until late August.[29]

Lincoln must not have disapproved of these arrests, for on February 14 the president transferred the responsibility for *all* internal arrests from the secretary of state to the secretary of war. In his order, probably drafted by Stanton, Lincoln explained that at the outset of the war "every department of the government was paralyzed by treason," and there were many Northerners "furnishing men, money and materials of war and supplies to the insurgents." In the past few months, however, "a favorable change of public opinion has occurred. The line between loyalty and disloyalty is plainly defined. The whole structure of the Government is firm and stable." Lincoln therefore directed that Stanton should release "political prisoners or state prisoners" if they would pledge not to aid the enemies of the United States. There was a broad exception to this general rule: Stanton could keep in prison "spies in the service of the insurgents, or others whose release at the present moment may be deemed incompatible with the public safety." Stanton started to release some of those arrested while Seward was in charge, appointing his friends Judge Edwards Pierrepont (a senior New York lawyer) and General Dix (also a lawyer by training) to examine the details of each case. Stanton and his aides also continued to arrest and hold those whom they deemed dangerous. In May, for example, on orders from Dix, army officers arrested Judge Richard Carmichael in his Maryland courtroom; he was not released until October.[30]

Back in February, while Scott was still an assistant secretary, he sent Stanton a letter from Cairo, Illinois, on various issues, including the dispute between Gen. Ulysses S. Grant and a quartermaster officer, William Kountz. Kountz's charges suggested that Grant's conduct was not "exactly consistent with our ideas of army rules," Scott wrote. If Stanton read this part of Scott's report, he disregarded it, for it arrived in Washington at the same time as the glorious news that Grant had seized Fort Donelson on the Cumberland River in northern Tennessee and captured more than 10,000 rebel soldiers. With control of the northern sections of the Tennessee and Cumberland rivers, the Union seemed poise to reclaim central Tennessee, and indeed Union troops would enter Nashville unopposed within two weeks. McClellan was apparently the first person in Washington to hear the Donelson news from Grant, for the military telegraph lines still centered on McClellan's headquarters. According to one news report, McClellan himself walked the message through the rain to the War Department, where, after reading the message aloud to the assembled clerks, Stanton "threw up his hat and proposed three cheers, which were given amid the greatest excitement." That same day, February 17, Stanton drafted and Lincoln signed the papers to make Grant a major general, the highest rank in the army at the time. The next day the papers printed Grant's famous reply to his former friend and now adversary, Confederate general Simon Bolivar Buckner, who had suggested a temporary truce: "No terms except an unconditional and immediate surrender can be accepted. I propose to move immediately upon your works."[31]

The newspapers not only reported on Grant's victory; they debated who should get the credit. The *Washington Evening Star* praised the way in which McClellan had used the telegraph to communicate with and instruct the western generals: "Thus it is that the General-in-Chief has been able to carry out so simultaneously, as well as triumphantly, his remarkable military combinations at points so distant from each other." Stanton commented to his friend Dana at the *New York Tribune* on the absurdity of "a certain military hero" claiming credit for a victory by messages sent "six hours after Grant and Smith had taken [Donelson] sword in hand." Dana declared, in the paper, that it was "to Edwin M. Stanton more than to any other individual that these auspicious events are now due."[32]

Stanton liked credit as much as the next man, but this was too much, and he wrote to Dana:

> I cannot suffer undue merit to be ascribed to my official action. The glory of our recent victories belongs to the gallant officers and soldiers that fought the battles. No share of it belongs to me. Much has recently been said of military combinations and organizing victory. I hear such phrases with apprehension. They commenced in infidel France with the Italian campaign and resulted in Waterloo. Who can organize victory? Who can combine the elements of success on the battle-field? We owe our recent victories to the Spirit of the Lord, that moved our soldiers to rush into battle, and filled the hearts of our enemies with terror and dismay. The inspiration that conquered in battle was in the hearts of the soldiers, and from on high; and wherever there is the same inspiration there will be the same results.

Patriotic spirit, with resolute courage in officers and men, is a military combination that never failed. We may well rejoice at the recent victories, for they teach us that battles are to be won now and by us in the same manner and only manner that they were ever won by any people, or in any age, since the days of Joshua, by boldly pursuing and striking the foe. What, under Providence, I conceive to be the true organization of victory and military combination to end this war, was declared in a few words by Gen. Grant's message to Gen. Buckner, "I propose to move immediately upon your works."[33]

Dana printed Stanton's "days of Joshua" letter in the *New York Tribune*, and from there it was printed in dozens of other newspapers. George Templeton Strong, the New York lawyer whose diary is one of the great narratives of the Civil War, wrote, "No high official in my day has written a dozen lines half as weighty and telling. If he is not careful, he will be our next President!" Read today, Stanton's letter seems both perceptive and naïve. He was right to see that the Civil War was a people's war, that it would be won by the enthusiasm of the Northern people, and that he should use the papers to generate and sustain that enthusiasm. He was right to work with Dana and other editors, and he would grow more adept at press relations as time passed. But Stanton was naïve to suggest that nothing had changed since the days of Joshua. The railroad, the telegraph, the steamboats on the western rivers—all of these had changed and were changing warfare. Stanton was only starting to understand and appreciate how the North's technological and organizational advantages could best be used to help subdue the South. And even though Stanton in this letter mocked McClellan's phrase "organizing victory," that is precisely what Stanton would do as the head of the War Department: he and his colleagues would organize the recruiting, training, equipping, moving, feeding, and sustaining of the Union Army so that the North could defeat the South.[34]

Grant's victory at Fort Donelson intensified questions about the Union command structure in the West. For several weeks Halleck, from his headquarters in St. Louis, had been pressing McClellan and Stanton both for additional troops and for *control* over all western troops. Stanton drafted but did not send a long letter to Scott, saying that he hoped to send at least 50,000 troops to the West but that he had not been able to persuade McClellan. On the question of command, Stanton was not especially impressed with either Halleck or his rival general, Don Carlos Buell. Halleck spent his time in St. Louis, and Stanton was "very much inclined to prefer field work rather than office work for successful military operations." Buell was in the field but, Stanton complained, "he communicates nothing to the Department nor even acknowledges communications made to him by me." Halleck was insistent, writing McClellan on February 21, "I must have command of the armies in the West. Hesitation and delay are losing us this golden opportunity." The next day Stanton informed Halleck that Lincoln would make no immediate change in the western command structure. The quarrels among the western generals continued, however. Halleck complained to McClellan on March 2, "I have had no communication with General Grant for more than a week." McClellan responded that Halleck should not hesitate to arrest Grant "if the good of the service requires it." Stanton wrote that he "approved" this message. Grant was able to pacify Halleck, showing him that the problem was due to a telegraph failure rather than neglect, and Halleck reassured Washington that Grant "made the proper explanations." Both Halleck and Grant would remain in their places, for the time being.[35]

———

Stanton may have disliked the phrase "organizing victory," but he was determined to reorganize the War Department. Joshua Speed, a close friend of Lincoln, arrived in Washington in early February seeking artillery for Kentucky. After meeting with Stanton, Speed wrote to Joseph Holt that "instead of that loose shackling way of doing business in the war office" he found "order, regularity, and precision." Speed cited as evidence the way Stanton asked him to write out his precise request, then endorsed upon the document his own order to the head of ordnance. Speed had "accomplished in a few days what heretofore would have taken as many weeks to do," and he was convinced that Stanton would "infuse into the whole army an energy and activity which we have not seen heretofore."[36]

Stanton started work at once on what he termed the "rats" and the "rat holes" within the War Department. Although in theory the quartermaster general and other office heads reported to him as secretary of war, in practice they expected to run their own affairs without much interference from the secretary. Some of the senior officers were excellent, notably Montgomery Meigs, an energetic engineer recently promoted to quartermaster general. Some of the officers in charge were mediocre, however, such as Clement Finley, the surgeon general, whose main qualification was his seniority. One of Stanton's first meetings was a breakfast at his home with the leaders of the Sanitary Commission, a private charitable organization formed to supplement and perhaps supplant the army's weak medical staff. Reverend Henry Bellows, one of the leaders of the commission, wrote his wife that Stanton was "a man of soul, transparent, honest, sturdy, right to the point," and that Ellen Stanton was "a handsome, serious & dignified lady, who was seemingly very interested in the account of the Commission & on whose sympathy I count." George Templeton Strong was also at this breakfast and described Stanton in his diary: "Not handsome, but on the contrary, rather pig-faced. At lowest estimate, worth a wagon-load of Camerons. Intelligent, prompt, clear-headed, fluent without wordiness, and above all, earnest, warm-hearted, and large-hearted. He is the reverse in all things of his cunning, cold-blooded, selfish old predecessor."[37]

Montgomery Meigs, the Union quartermaster general during the Civil War, handled the immense and complex task of making or purchasing all the supplies needed by the Union Army.

To improve communication among the fiefdoms in his department and to educate himself on military matters, Stanton formed a "war board" consisting of the five senior departmental officers. For two weeks he and the board met every day, during which someone took excellent notes, notes that are almost word-for-word transcripts. One day, for example, when the discussion turned to naval issues, Meigs asked whether Welles would remain in the cabinet. "That," Stanton responded, "is a question for the President to consider. He leans to the judgment of [Assistant Navy Secretary Gustavus] Fox, whom he seems to think in possession of the entire amount of knowledge in the naval world." On another day, Lorenzo Thomas asked Stanton about a request from Gen. John Frémont, in New York City, to appoint his personal staff. Stanton insisted that he would not allow Frémont to sit in New York and appoint "quartermasters, paymasters and the like." "I see that they are organizing just such a gang as they had in St. Louis," he continued, for Frémont's command in St. Louis was infamous, "and I intend to prevent it." The conversation turned to Jim Lane, a Kansas senator who had recently received a commission as a brigadier general. Thomas complained that he had not heard from Lane and did not know where he was or whether he intended to accept his commission. "I would not hunt for him or his staff," said Stanton. What about the staff officers, asked Thomas. "I would stop their pay," said Stanton, "strike them from the rolls." But, said Thomas, one of the staff officers was well known to Lincoln. "While I administer this office I will not sanction an abuse of that kind. Discharge them all. If the President doesn't like it, let him so intimate, and I will retire."[38]

To strengthen his central staff, Stanton summoned the aged and eccentric Gen. Ethan Allen Hitchcock from retirement in St. Louis to active duty in Washington. (Hitchcock had been pursuing what he termed "studies of a peculiar nature, not usually supposed to be in harmony with the crash of arms on the battlefield," reading and writing about the works of the obscure Swedish philosopher Emanuel Swedenborg.) On the day Hitchcock arrived in Washington in March, he was disabled by a severe nosebleed, so Stanton visited him in his hotel room, and told him that he and Lincoln wanted him "where they could have the opportunity of consulting with [him]." Within a few days, however, Stanton suggested that Hitchcock should take McClellan's place at the head of the Army of the Potomac. "I was amazed," Hitchcock wrote in his diary, and "told him at once that I could not." Stanton changed tack and asked Hitchcock to remain in Washington as a major general and his personal adviser. Hitchcock counseled Stanton to be cautious in his efforts to remake the army and the War Department. "The Army is something like an organic (living) body; a whole within itself, and yet containing many subordinate organisms, no less whole within their sphere." Stanton was gradually learning the ways of his department, and of the army, gradually starting to impose his own system upon them.[39]

Ethan Allen Hitchcock. Stanton summoned Hitchcock from retirement and brought him to Washington to serve as a military adviser.

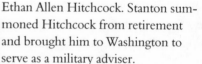

One of Stanton's first legislative successes was a bill that authorized the president "to take possession of any or all the railroad lines in the United States, their rolling-stock, their offices, shops, buildings, and all their offices and appurtenances." The president could "place under military control all the officers, agents, and employees" of the railroads and treat them as "part of the military establishment of the United States." Moreover the transportation of troops and military equipment would "be under the immediate control and supervision of the Secretary of War and such agents as he may appoint." The railroad companies would be entitled to compensation, but only whatever compensation was awarded to them by the government after the war. Lincoln and Stanton could have used this legislation to nationalize all the Northern rail companies, but this was not their plan. Rather, after the bill passed, Stanton summoned the railroad executives to meet with him in Washington and told them they could remain private companies *if* they would follow government instructions and charge the government low rates. Stanton also created a separate military railroad system, mainly formed of railroads captured in the South but also including railroads built by federal railroad teams. By the end of the war, this United States Military Railroad would have more than two thousand miles of track.[40]

In late January, Ives reported to his editor that Stanton was "strongly in favor of the control of the telegraph wires being assumed by the government." The same bill that allowed for federal control of the railroads also provided for federal control of the telegraph lines. As in the case of the rails, Lincoln and Stanton did not nationalize the telegraph companies; they remained private companies, owned by their shareholders, handling private as well as military messages. But Stanton had Lincoln issue an order, dated February 25, in which the president declared that he was taking "military possession of all the telegraph lines in the United States" and that "all telegraphic communication in regard to military operation, not expressly authorized" by the military authorities was "absolutely forbidden." Any newspaper that published such unauthorized military information would lose the right to use the telegraph lines and railroads. Since the papers depended upon the telegraph lines for all their information other than local news, this order was in essence a "death threat" for any paper that published military information the department deemed "unauthorized." Yet the press, at least at first, praised Stanton's order. The *Chicago Tribune*, for example, commented, "The enemy has many times been informed of the purposes and movements of our loyal forces, of the strength of our columns, and of the weaknesses of certain branches of the service, by the injudicious revelations of the New York press."[41]

At about this same time, in late February or early March, Stanton moved the Washington hub of the military telegraph from McClellan's headquarters to the War Department. There Stanton created and staffed a telegraph office in a large library immediately adjacent to his own office so that he could be in constant communication with generals in the field. Lincoln was a frequent visitor, both to read messages as they arrived and to send his own messages. To send a telegraph, Lincoln or Stanton would generally write out the message by hand, then give it to a telegraph clerk to encode and send. Stanton was careful to ensure that his clerks kept a copy of every telegram sent or received. We thus have, for many of the telegrams sent by Stanton during the Civil War, not only a printed version in the *Official Records* but Stanton's own handwritten version in the National Archives. To know what Stanton did in the Civil War, the place to start is in his telegraph office, with the messages he sent from there.[42]

Stanton's military infrastructure consisted of not just rails and telegraphs but also ships. The War Department, not the Navy Department, was responsible for transporting soldiers, whether by land or by sea. In late February, Stanton tasked one of his assistant secretaries, John Tucker, with leasing the ships that would be necessary to transport McClellan's army by sea to some point near Richmond. Tucker arranged for four hundred ships, a fleet that would transport more than 100,000 men and all their horses, mules, artillery, and other equipment over the course of a few weeks. It was an impressive logistical feat, the first of many accomplished by Stanton's department during the Civil War.[43]

Stanton did not cooperate well with Navy Secretary Welles, nor did the War Department vessels always cooperate with the navy. A prime example of this was the Ellet ram fleet. Not long after Stanton became war secretary, he asked Charles Ellet Jr., the engineer who had been his opponent in the Wheeling Bridge case, how best to counter rebel ironclads in the western rivers. Ellet met with Stanton in Washington and suggested reinforcing steamboats so they could be used as rams. Stanton instantly hired Ellet to implement this approach, directing him to go to Pittsburgh and then to Cincinnati to purchase steamboats and turn them into rams. As Ellet headed west, Stanton wrote to Halleck to introduce him: "He is a man of courage and energy, and willing to risk his own life upon his own job." Stanton urged Ellet to select his crews carefully and promised to reward them liberally for "courageous success." Ellet chose as his captains his brothers, nephews, and nineteen-year-old son. Stanton was concerned by press reports that the rebels were building an ironclad at Memphis and wrote Ellet, "Spare nothing to accomplish your object the speediest moment." Almost every day, sometimes several times a day, Stanton wrote messages in his own hand to Ellet and handed them to the telegraph clerks to transmit.[44]

Stanton had known a few of the Northern governors before he became secretary; he would get to know them all through their frequent telegraphic communication. Almost the day he arrived in office, he had a long letter from Governor John Andrew of Massachusetts, with many long enclosures, complaining about the way Gen. Benjamin Butler had been competing with state authorities in raising troops in Massachusetts. Stanton wrote back to assure Andrew that "this department recognizes the right of a governor to commission volunteer officers" and that if Butler presumed to appoint officers he would exceed his authority and he would be *"dealt with* accordingly." When Governor David Tod of Ohio raised questions about recruiting practices, Stanton replied almost humbly, "Your dispatch is received and will receive immediate attention." When Tod complained that Ohio troops were not being paid, Stanton explained that the Treasury Department simply did not have the funds; he assured Tod and other governors with similar complaints that the troops would be paid as soon as possible.[45]

Andrew Johnson reported to Stanton as the federal military governor of Tennessee. Johnson was a logical choice for the post, for he had held almost every political position in that state, ranging from mayor of Greenville to governor. When Tennessee seceded, Johnson remained in the Senate, denouncing secession and supporting the Union. In early March 1862, soon after Union troops captured the state capital of Nashville, Lincoln and Stanton appointed Johnson, giving him broad and vague powers as military governor. Johnson hastened to Nashville, where he started to send frequent messages to Stanton. "For God's sake do not divide East Tennessee into two military departments," the governor wrote the secretary on March 14. A week later Johnson asked Stanton what military forces he could command to keep the state peaceful. Soon Johnson was pressing Stanton to appoint one of his friends to a military command and asking Stanton to what out-of-state prison he could send prisoners. Stanton did not know much about Johnson before his appointment, but he would get to know the future president well through their constant wartime correspondence.[46]

The main question facing Lincoln, Stanton, and McClellan in the first few months of 1862 was how to make use of the Army of the Potomac. This was not only the nation's largest army; its location made it the most visible, the subject of daily reports in the major Northern newspapers. Everyone in the North assumed at this stage that the army's goal should be to attack and conquer Richmond; the only question was how best to accomplish this goal. McClellan wanted to move the army by rail to Annapolis, and then by boat from there to Urbanna, Virginia, a small and lightly defended spot on the Rappahannock River. From Urbanna, Mc-Clellan believed, he could march his force of more than 100,000 men fifty miles west, to Richmond itself. Lincoln and Stanton favored a more direct approach, attacking more or less directly south, along the main roads. Lincoln wrote to McClellan on February 4 to say that he would "gladly yield" to the general's plan if he could answer a few questions, such as whether his plan would take more time and cost more money. Stanton's role in drafting these questions is indicated by the presence of Lincoln's original among the Stanton papers. McClellan did not even bother to answer.[47]

Stanton was dismayed that McClellan did not move against Richmond and that McClellan was allowing the rebels to limit access to Washington in two ways, through artillery batteries along the lower Potomac River and through control of the Baltimore & Ohio Railroad, just beyond Harpers Ferry, Virginia. On February 19, Senators Wade and Johnson (not yet the military governor) visited with Stanton to discuss their concerns, especially the Potomac. According to a memoir, Stanton told Wade and Johnson that "he did not go to bed at night without his cheek burning with shame at this disgrace." McClellan was in the building, and Stanton asked him to come and talk with the senators. When McClellan gave them a long explanation about how he needed to prepare lines of retreat and build bridges across the Potomac, Wade erupted in anger. McClellan had "150,000 of the best troops the world ever saw," men who "could whip the whole Confederacy if they were given the chance." Both the senators and the general noted that Stanton seemed to agree with Wade.[48]

It was not hard to read in the wording of Stanton's Joshua letter that he was tired of what he saw as McClellan's delay. Two similar statements from Stanton appeared in the newspapers at about the same time. The first was a February 17 message to Gen. Frederick Lander, congratulating him for his recent victory in western Virginia: "You have shown how much may be done in the worst weather and worst roads by a spirited officer, at the head of a small force of brave men, unwilling to waste life in camp when the enemies of their country are within reach." The second was a correction to a report regarding Stanton's February 20 conference with the railroad officials. The initial report said that Stanton had praised McClellan, calling the recent victories the result of his "military schemes, gigantic and well-matured." When he read this in the papers, Stanton demanded a correction, and so the papers dutifully reported that Stanton had *not* praised McClellan. In a private letter to Dana, Stanton called the original report an "impertinent effort to puff the general by a false publication of words I never uttered."[49]

On February 26, about midnight, Stanton received a telegram from McClellan, who was in Sandy Hook, Maryland, seeking to regain Union control of the Baltimore & Ohio Railroad at the point where it crossed into northern Virginia at Harpers Ferry. McClellan's engineers had built a temporary bridge across the Potomac; his troops had captured Harpers Ferry; and McClellan reported proudly that they were "in the mood to fight anything." In order to get equipment across the river to support an attack westward, McClellan planned to build a more substantial bridge, using canal boats brought up the Chesapeake & Ohio Canal. But the next day, when his engineers attempted to lower the boats from the canal into the river, they found that the boats were too wide for the locks. McClellan reported this setback to Stanton, saying that he would "probably be obliged to fall back upon the safe and slow plan of merely covering the reconstruction of the Railroad." Stanton brought this message to Lincoln that evening, and when Lincoln asked Stanton what it meant, Stanton replied, "It means it is a damned fizzle. It means that he doesn't intend to do anything." Lincoln summoned McClellan's father-in-law and chief of staff, Gen. Randolph Marcy. "Why in the Nation, General Marcy, couldn't the General have known whether a boat would go through that lock before spending a million dollars getting them there?" According to a reporter, who may have heard the story from Stanton, Lincoln "swore like a Philistine" at Marcy and through him at McClellan.[50]

Leaving a small force behind at Harpers Ferry to continue the slow but steady work on rebuilding the bridge and extending control of the rail lines, McClellan returned to Washington. Stanton continued to complain about him, writing to Holt on March 4, "The enemy is still entrenched at Manassas and a hundred thousand rebels threaten the capital and block up its highway to the sea." Lincoln told McClellan on March 7 that he was worried the general's Richmond plan, by moving essentially the whole army well south of Washington, would expose the nation's capital to rebel attack. Some had suggested, Lincoln said, that McClellan's plan to attack Richmond by way of Urbanna was "conceived with the traitorous intent" of leaving Washington "defenseless." McClellan later recalled that he jumped to his feet and demanded that Lincoln retract the remark. Lincoln assured McClellan that this was not his own view, simply the view of unnamed others, but McClellan was not mollified and said that he would submit his plan to a council of his generals later that morning. The dozen generals, somewhat surprised to be consulted by McClellan, discussed the issue and voted: eight were in favor of McClellan's plan and four opposed. Later that afternoon the dozen generals went to the White House to report to Lincoln and to answer some searching questions from Stanton. Like the president, Stanton was concerned about the safety of Washington; the capture of the capital would have an immense effect not only in the United States but also in Europe, where Britain and France were considering recognizing the Confederacy. Commenting on the eight generals who favored the roundabout water route, and adding McClellan and Marcy to their number, Stanton told Hay, "We saw ten Generals afraid to fight."[51]

The generals returned to the White House the next morning to meet again with Lincoln and Stanton. Lincoln announced that he would support the Urbanna plan, and urged the generals to "go in heartily for this plan." Lincoln also told them that he would be forming corps within the Army of the Potomac, so that instead of having ten generals reporting to him directly, McClellan would have a more manageable structure of five direct reports, each in charge of a corps of about 20,000 men. Four of the five men whom Lincoln named as corps commanders, however, had opposed the Urbanna plan, suggesting that Lincoln was looking not only to simplify the structure but also to reward those willing to stand up to McClellan. The president stressed that his approval for the water plan was contingent upon Washington being left "entirely secure" and that the movement of troops from Annapolis to Urbanna would begin within ten days.[52]

The next day, March 9, the peace of Sunday morning was shattered by a message from Fort Monroe in Virginia. Gen. John Wool reported to Stanton that the rebel ironclad warship, known in the South as the *Virginia* and in the North as the *Merrimack*, had attacked and destroyed several wooden warships in the waters near Newport News. Stanton rushed to the White House; he and Lincoln were soon joined there by Seward, Welles, Hay, and John Nicolay, the president's senior private secretary. Nicolay wrote that Stanton "came in very much excited, and walked up and down like a caged lion." Different people had different fears about the *Merrimack*'s next move: "One thought she would go to New York and levy tribute—another to Phila—a third to Baltimore, or Annapolis where a large flotilla of transport has been gathered—another that she would come up and burn Washington." Hay's diary entry reveals similar thinking: "Stanton was fearfully stampeded. He said they would capture our fleet, take Ft. Monroe, be in Washington before night." Years later Welles wrote, "The most frightened man on that gloomy day, the most so I think of any during the Rebellion, was the Secretary of War." Welles tried to reassure Stanton and the others, telling them that a new Union ironclad, the *Monitor*, was about to leave New York for Fort Monroe, where it would be able to fight the *Merrimack* on its own terms. Stanton was not much calmed by these comments; he sent a message to several Northern governors, warning them of the possibility that the *Merrimack* would attack their principal ports, and he insisted that the government should sink old ships in the Potomac to prevent the ironclad from reaching Washington. Welles resisted this plan, pointing out that Stanton had complained for weeks that rebel batteries were closing the river to commerce, but Lincoln gave Stanton permission to proceed. Stanton himself went out on the river with John Dahlgren, head of the Washington Navy

Yard, giving instructions on blocking the channel and strengthening the shore batteries. By the end of the day better news had arrived from Fort Monroe, for the *Monitor* had arrived there, confronted the *Merrimack*, and forced it to retreat.[53]

Gideon Welles, secretary of the navy under Lincoln and Johnson, a harsh critic of Stanton.

Stanton was not going to rely on the navy to defeat the *Merrimack*. He sent an urgent message to the financier Cornelius Vanderbilt, asking him to name his price to destroy the ship. Vanderbilt came to Washington within a few days, visited with Stanton, and offered his steamship the *Vanderbilt* to protect the troop transports. Stanton thanked him for his "patriotic and generous gift" in a letter and noted that, although Vanderbilt's men would staff the ship, they would be under the command of the War Department. Stanton was soon outraged to learn that Wool had ceded control of the *Vanderbilt* to Commodore Louis Goldsborough, the naval commander in Hampton Roads. "She belongs to the War Department," Stanton wrote Wool, "and is to act exclusively under its orders."[54]

On the same Sunday, March 9, that Stanton learned of the *Merrimack* he learned that the Confederates had left Manassas. McClellan went across the Potomac and reported by telegraph to Stanton that it seemed the rebels were indeed retreating: "I am arranging to move forward to push the retreat of the rebels as far as possible." McClellan asked Stanton for permission to suspend Lincoln's order of the day before, dividing the Army of the Potomac into five separate corps, claiming this suspension was necessary to move the troops more readily. Stanton sent back a stiff refusal: "It is the duty of every officer to obey the President's orders nor can I see any reason why you should not obey them in the present instance." McClellan sent back an equally stiff message at about one o'clock in the morning: if Stanton insisted that the troops move by corps McClellan would have to "countermand all the orders [he had] given for an advance until the formation of the Army is completed." Stanton relented, telling McClellan to move the troops "by divisions or otherwise, according to your own judgment, without stopping to form the corps." At about three o'clock McClellan thanked Stanton and assured him, "The troops are in motion."[55]

On Monday morning most of the army in and around Washington, more than 100,000 men, was on the march toward Manassas and Centerville. When the first of McClellan's troops reached Manassas, however, at about 5:30 in the afternoon, they learned that the rebels had departed late on the prior day and that the Manassas defenses were far less formidable than McClellan had claimed. One reporter wrote, "The fortifications are a damnable humbug and McClellan has been completely fooled." The general did not push the retreat of the rebels as he had promised Stanton he would; he simply occupied Manassas and set up headquarters at Fairfax Court House. On Tuesday, at the regular cabinet meeting, Stanton presented a report on the overall situation, and Attorney General Bates was alarmed to learn that there were almost 700,000 men in the army; in his view this was nothing but "reckless extravagance." Stanton told the cabinet that McClellan "reports nothing" and Bates believed McClellan "has no plans but is fumbling and plunging about in confusion and darkness."[56]

Lincoln and the cabinet decided at this meeting that McClellan, because he was supposed to start soon for Richmond, should no longer have the title and responsibilities of general in chief of all the armies. Stanton drafted the order himself and took it that evening to the White House. When he arrived, Seward, who was chatting with Lincoln, suggested that Stanton should sign the order. Hay noted that Stanton declined, saying that "a row had grown up between him and McC's friends and he feared it would be thought to spring from personal feeling. The President decided to take the responsibility." Lincoln's final order reduced McClellan's responsibilities, appointed Halleck commander of all the western armies, and gave Gen. John Frémont command of a new department, between McClellan in the East and Halleck in the West. The last sentence of the order provided, "All the commanders of departments, after the receipt of this by them respectively, report severally and directly to the Secretary of War, and that prompt, full and frequent reports will be expected of each of them." Suddenly Stanton and his small central staff were responsible for coordinating the many generals in their many different departments, a task Stanton would handle with only moderate success before Halleck's arrival in Washington as general in chief later in the year.[57]

McClellan was of course displeased by this order, but he did not complain directly to Lincoln or Stanton, although word of his private complaints may have reached them indirectly. On March 13 McClellan wrote Stanton to explain that he had changed his Richmond plan. He now proposed to transport his troops by boat from Alexandria to Fort Monroe, on the tip of the peninsula formed by the James and York rivers. He would march the army up the peninsula, past Jamestown and Yorktown, a distance of about eighty miles, to Richmond. Stanton discussed the issue with Lincoln and wired back Lincoln's approval, again emphasizing that McClellan was to "leave Washington entirely secure." In a second message later that same day, Stanton assured McClellan, "All the forces and means of the government will be at your disposal." Part of this force was already in place: the flotilla arranged by Tucker to transport thousands of troops from Alexandria, down the Potomac, out into the Chesapeake, and land them at Fort Monroe.[58]

As his troops prepared to move, McClellan addressed them and ensured that his address was printed in the papers:

> For a long time I have kept you inactive, but not without a purpose: you were to be disciplined, armed and instructed. . . . I have held you back that you might give the death-blow to the rebellion that

has distracted our once happy country. . . . In whatever direction you may move, however strange my actions may appear to you, ever bear in mind that my fate is linked with yours, and that all I do is to bring you, where I know you wish to be—on the decisive battlefield. It is my business to place you there. I am to watch over you as a parent over his children. . . . I shall demand of you great, heroic exertions, rapid and long marches, desperate combats, privations, perhaps. We will share all these together.[59]

Stanton was of course concerned to keep from the Confederates the precise plan for the sea attack on Richmond. When he read a report detailing troop movements in the *Washington Sunday Chronicle*, he immediately drafted an order to arrest the editors and seize all copies of the paper. The *Springfield Republican* in Massachusetts reported that Stanton's order would have been implemented "but for the frank statement of the editor," Lincoln's friend John Forney, "that the publication of army news was the result of carelessness, and that he would not again violate the stringent orders of the department." The *Republican*'s correspondent commented that these were "queer times" in which an "editor has the government down upon him if he chances to make a blunder in the publication of a bit of war news." But other papers supported this instance of Stanton's wartime censorship.[60]

Stanton continued his contradictory comments on McClellan. On March 18, Stanton, Seward, Fox, and John Dahlgren, the naval captain, went by boat to Alexandria; McClellan came down from his headquarters near the seminary to meet them on the wharf and discuss plans. There was some light suggestion that Stanton should promote Gen. Ambrose Burnside, who had just captured New Bern, North Carolina, to lieutenant general, the rank *above* major general. "Oh no," said Stanton, turning to McClellan, "that is for you, when you take Richmond." The next day McClellan's chief engineer met with Stanton and later wrote McClellan that he was "most gratified" by Stanton's assurances that McClellan had "no firmer friend" and that he "ought not to move until he [was] fully ready." At almost the same time, however, Stanton was sharing with Hitchcock "the most astounding facts, all going to show the most astounding incompetency of General McClellan." Speaking with Senator Orville Browning from Illinois, a friend of Lincoln, Stanton expressed his fear that McClellan could not "emancipate himself from the influence of Jeff Davis," with whom he had worked so closely when Davis was secretary of war. Stanton suggested to Browning that Lincoln should appoint Col. Napoleon Bonaparte Buford as a major general, so that Buford could take McClellan's place. Stanton knew almost nothing about Buford; he simply knew that he wanted to be rid of McClellan.[61]

Chapter 8

"The Vilest Man I Ever Knew"

— April–June 1862 —

As Gen. George McClellan left Alexandria in a small steamboat on April 1, 1862, heading south to join his army, he wrote to his wife that he was glad to be leaving Washington, "that sink of iniquity." From the boat McClellan sent Stanton a summary of the troops he was leaving behind: 18,000 in and near Washington and more than 55,000 in Manassas and the Shenandoah Valley. Stanton asked James Wadsworth, the New York general whom Lincoln had just placed in command of the Washington defenses, to review McClellan's numbers. Wadsworth reported to Stanton that McClellan had double-counted some units and that many of the soldiers in and near Washington were so green that they were worthless. Stanton relayed this to Lincoln, who was "indignant" that McClellan had left the nation's capital "defenseless." Lincoln instructed Stanton to keep one corps near Washington. The corps not yet on its way to McClellan was the First Corps, under Gen. Irvin McDowell, and so this corps stayed. From his headquarters near Yorktown, McClellan pleaded with Lincoln to reconsider. "I am now of the opinion that I shall have to fight all the available force of the Rebels not far from here," he wrote. "Do not force me to do so with diminished numbers." If he could not have all of the First Corps, McClellan demanded at least the division under his friend Gen. William Franklin. McClellan soon heard from Franklin that the decision to keep First Corps back "was intended as a blow" at McClellan. "Stanton had said that you intended to work by strategy, and not by fighting, that all of the opponents of the policy of the administration centered around you—in other words that you had political aspirations."[1]

Even as McClellan and other generals were asking for more soldiers, senators were insisting that the army, with about 700,000 men, was too large and too expensive. Senator William Fessenden of Maine offered a resolution to limit the total force to half a million men. Senator Henry Wilson of Massachusetts, chairman of the Committee on Military Affairs, supported Fessenden: "The Senator from Maine the other day proposed to reduce the number of men authorized by law down to five hundred thousand. I agree with him in that. . . . It was suggested also that we ought to stop recruiting. I agree to that. I have over and over again been to the War Office, and urged upon the Department to stop recruiting in every part of the country." Stanton should have resisted this political pressure. He should have explained that the war might not end soon and that the army needed a steady supply of recruits to replace those lost through death, injury, illness, and desertion. But carried away with the widespread hope that the war would end within weeks, when McClellan reached and captured Richmond, Stanton yielded. He issued an order on April 3 to close all the federal recruiting offices. Newspapers at the time praised the order. The *New York Times* declared, "The army of the Union is now complete," and the *New York World* said, "The force now in the field is deemed amply sufficient for the suppression of the rebellion and the speedy termination of the war." Historians have generally and rightly condemned the suspension of recruiting as a mistake, a mistake Stanton would soon have to correct.[2]

Although Stanton's main focus in the spring of 1862 was on McClellan, he was in frequent communications with other generals, including Henry Halleck, in command in Missouri and western Tennessee. The war in Missouri was more violent, more chaotic than anywhere else. Armed bands of Southern sympathizers roamed the state, raiding, burning, raping, and killing. They were countered by armed Northerners, who, in the words of historian James McPherson, "matched the bushwhackers in freebooting tactics." Halleck had issued an order in January explaining that he would use "military commissions," courts composed of at least three officers, to try those who violated the laws of war. Military commissions were not new: George Washington had used one to try John André; Winfield Scott had used them to try both Americans and Mexicans for military offenses in the Mexican War. Now, however, Halleck was using military commissions to try American citizens for what some might call political offenses. In February, for example, a military commission tried and convicted Edmund Ellis, the proprietor and editor of the *Boone County Standard* in Missouri, for publishing "information for the benefit of the enemy and encouraging resistance to the government and laws of the United States." The commission, with Halleck's approval, ordered Ellis to leave the state, threatened him with prison if he returned, and seized and sold his printing press.[3]

Henry Halleck, Union general in Missouri and western Tennessee, who would become general in chief in Washington, essentially Stanton's chief of staff.

Reading about Halleck's military commissions, including the Ellis case, Stanton sent him a note to say that he "heartily approved" of the practice. Stanton also sent a note to John Frémont, in the violent western part of Virginia, urging him to follow Halleck's lead. A few newspapers picked up the Ellis case, especially Stanton's approval of the process, but there was not much interest. The papers did not know, could not know that the Ellis case was an early example of what by the end of the war would be thousands of military commissions used to try civilians for military offenses.[4]

McClellan reported to Stanton on April 7 that his march to Richmond had stalled. A strong rebel line all the way across the Peninsula would require him to use "heavy guns" and "siege operations" to reduce the defenses of Yorktown. From other fronts, on the other hand, there was what Stanton termed "glorious news," including a "complete victory" by Grant at Shiloh, Tennessee, and the capture of Island Number Ten, an important point on the Mississippi River. Hay noted in his diary that there was progress everywhere *except* Virginia: "The little Napoleon sits trembling before the handful of men at Yorktown afraid either to fight or run. Stanton feels devilish about it. He would like to remove him if he thought it would do." In a long letter, Lincoln urged McClellan to "strike a blow." He reminded the general that during their winter discussions he had warned that taking the army by water to the Peninsula rather than fighting near Manassas "was only shifting, and not surmounting, a difficulty." Lincoln predicted that McClellan would "find the same enemy, and the same, or equal, entrenchments, at either place. The country will not fail to note—is now noting—that the present hesitation to move upon an entrenched enemy, is but the story of Manassas repeated." Lincoln closed by insisting, "You must act."[5]

But McClellan would not be hurried. As he constructed his lines and moved his siege guns, he and his allies started a press campaign against Stanton. McClellan's friend and lieutenant, Gen. Fitz-John Porter, worked closely with Manton Marble, editor of the *New York World*. On April 12 the *World* predicted that Stanton's orders cutting off the telegraph privileges of newspapers that published military information would prove "the least creditable portion of [his] brief public career." Stanton's "*ukase* against the press was his first great blunder, and now, in ordering the suppression of all telegraphic messages to the *Philadelphia Inquirer* . . . Stanton has given the most conspicuous example of the evils which may flow from a despotic use of arbitrary power." The *New York Commercial Advertiser* soon joined the fight, arguing that Stanton had failed to provide adequate troop support for McClellan: "The Secretary of War has certainly committed grave errors since he took charge of the department, and we have reason to believe that the President is far from satisfied with the Secretary's treatment of General McClellan. It is even said that after the general commanding went to Yorktown, the President felt it to be his duty peremptorily to interfere for his protection, and sent him troops that Stanton had withheld." The *Advertiser* claimed that Lincoln would not tolerate Stanton's interference with McClellan—the president had "put his foot down" and Stanton would have to "change either his policy or his place."[6]

Stanton also faced at this time his first congressional criticism. Senator James McDougall, a California Democrat, after trying without success to meet with Stanton to discuss the arrest of General Stone, gave a speech about Stone's plight and Stanton's indifference. "Strange times have come upon the land, when the Secretaries of the President deny the right to Senators of official intercourse." A few days later McDougall spoke again, saying Stanton had received "large professional bounties at the hand of the last Administration" and "fought under the banner of Breckinridge in 1860." After the election of Lincoln, however, Stanton changed course and was now "a warm friend of the present Administration." McDougall charged that Stanton was "no Democrat if I know what a Democrat is; he is no Republican if I know what a Republican is. Sir, he *belongs to the party in power*." Senator Wade, for the Republican side, defended Stanton, arguing that he had saved the nation from "utter shipwreck" in the last weeks of the Buchanan administration. But McDougall pressed his point: "Those persons who ignore the Constitution, who deny all law, who assert the existence of a power that cannot be measured by any term, but may at its pleasure by a nod mark its victim; I say that those persons are making war, violent war, upon the integrity of the Union." The *Detroit Free Press* agreed with McDougall about Stanton and Stone: "We care not how honest the Minister may be. His honesty and patriotism are not the safeguards which the people have established for their liberty. The question is, what has the prisoner done? What acts of *his* justify his incarceration?"[7]

━━━━━

Stanton did not respond in public to these editorials and speeches, but two private letters show his mood. In the first, to Robert Bonner, a New York editor and philanthropist, Stanton claimed he did not care about his critics: "In this great struggle for national existence—for republican government in all time—I feel troubled at the thought that any merely personal question should occupy my thoughts for even a moment of that time that can be devoted to duties. For what is any man to the great cause now in judgment before the nations and before God? . . . While holding my solemn official station I wish to be as free from any selfish or self-seeking stain as a priest should be before the altar." He continued, "If the editors and writers who daily put forth their strength in blows against this or that General, or the Secretary of War, could but feel how insignificant the objects of attack are to the great principles at stake, and would unite to uphold the Government—to bind together instead of separating, how speedily would this rebellion be suppressed and peace restored!"[8]

The second, much longer letter was to the prominent Episcopal priest Heman Dyer. Stanton had known Dyer since their days at Kenyon, where Dyer was a friend and teacher. Reverend Dyer wrote to Stanton from New York to ask about reports that he had "intentionally and deliberately thwarted [McClellan's] plans and crippled him in his efforts." Stanton responded with an account of how Lincoln "reluctantly yielded" to McClellan's plan to take the Army of the Potomac south by water, but insisted "that the Army should not be removed without leaving a sufficient force in and around Washington to make the Capitol *perfectly secure* against all danger." After McClellan departed, Stanton had consulted with other generals, who "agreed in opinion that the Capitol *was not safe*." Lincoln then ordered that one corps be kept near Washington. "When this order was communicated to General McClellan, it of course provoked his wrath, and the wrath of his friends was directed upon me because I was the agent of its execution." Lincoln, "anxious that General McClellan should have no cause of complaint," ordered Stanton to ship Franklin's division to McClellan, which he did, although he believed that "the whole force of McDowell should be kept together and sent forward by land on the shortest route to Richmond." In due course the records would show that Stanton had "employed the whole power of the Government unsparingly to support General McClellan's operations" and that he had "not interfered with or thwarted them in any particular."[9]

Turning to the political and personal aspects of the situation, Stanton wrote:

I am not now, never have been, and never will be a candidate for any office. I hold my present position at the request of a President who knew me personally, but to whom I had not spoken from the 4th of March, 1861, until the day he handed me my commission. I knew that everything I cherished and held dear would be sacrificed by accepting office. But I thought I might help to save the country, and for that I was willing to perish. If I wanted to be a politician or a candidate for any office, would I stand between the Treasury and the robbers that are howling around me? Would I provoke and stand against the whole newspaper gang in this country, of every party, who to *sell news*, would imperil a battle? I was never taken for a fool, but there could be no greater madness than for a man to encounter what I do for anything else than motives that overleap time and look forward to eternity. I believe that God Almighty founded this Government, and for my acts in the effort to maintain it I expect to stand before Him in judgment.[10]

The records from early 1862 support Stanton's claim that the War Department provided McClellan and the Army of the Potomac with what they needed. On April 11 McClellan pressed Stanton again to send Franklin and his "indispensable" division. Stanton responded that Franklin and his men were on their way by boat and that Stanton would probably send another division "if the safety of this city will permit." When Franklin's troops arrived, however, McClellan did not even disembark them from their transports for two weeks. Stanton sent John Tucker to McClellan's headquarters to help sort out transportation issues. Tucker wrote to Stanton from there on April 19, "The roads are now in quite good order. The army is abundantly supplied." Stanton also sent General Hitchcock to the Peninsula to see what if anything McClellan needed. Hitchcock reported on his return that McClellan's force was "as large as he can conveniently handle within the Peninsula which he has selected for the scene of his operations."[11]

Stanton's telegrams on a single day, the first of May, show why he was on edge. He sent almost twenty messages that day to ten different senior military officers. Most of them were in Virginia, where, in addition to McClellan's army on the Peninsula near Richmond, there were several other armies under other generals. Stanton wrote to General Frémont in Wheeling, Virginia, asking him to report on his plans and forces. Lincoln through Stanton directed Gen. Nathaniel Banks at New Market, in the Shenandoah Valley, "Fall back with the force under your immediate command to Strasburg or some other convenient point near there." Stanton sent a message to General McDowell at Aquia Creek, between Washington and Richmond, to inform him that he was going to transfer the division under James Shields from Banks to McDowell. Then Stanton sent a message to Shields, asking him to delay his march to McDowell until after Banks had moved his troops, but it would appear that Stanton neglected to send a copy of this to Banks. Stanton wrote to General Wool at Fort Monroe, thanking him for his reports on McClellan's situation. There is no message in the files from Stanton to McClellan on this day, but there is one from Lincoln to McClellan, worried that the general's recent request for more large siege guns suggested "indefinite procrastination." McClellan assured Lincoln and Stanton that the reason he was requesting the siege guns "was to hasten and not procrastinate."[12]

Stanton was also in touch by telegraph on this day with generals and colonels farther afield. He telegraphed to General Halleck, who was at Pittsburg Landing, Tennessee, that the "order stopping recruiting was for the purpose of compelling returns from the respective governors." He claimed that he had now received such reports from the states, so that Halleck could "call upon the governors of the respective states for recruits to fill up the regiments in the field." This was an odd interpretation, to say the least, of Stanton's original order to cease recruiting, and if Halleck "called upon" any governors for troops, few were provided. This was only one of three messages from Stanton to Halleck that day: he also thanked the general for capturing a fort and responded to a request to promote a member of his staff. Stanton congratulated Gen. Ormsby Mitchel, who had recently surprised and captured Huntsville, Alabama, without any casualties. Stanton sent a message to Gen. Edward Canby, in charge of the federal forces in New Mexico, telling him that Gen. Benjamin Butler had recently seized and now controlled New Orleans. Just keeping the many different generals informed of one another's actions took time, and Stanton did yet not have a good central staff.[13]

Stanton also sent messages on May 1 to several civilians. One was a short letter to Count Adam Gurowski, a Polish exile living in Washington, about an officer whose appointment Gurowski had suggested. Gurowski, who would keep one of the great Civil War diaries, was, in the words of another great diarist, Gideon Welles, a "rude, rough Polish bear, who is courted and flattered by a set of extreme partisans." Stanton also wrote to Augustus Bradford, the governor of Maryland, about troops: "Your telegram this moment received and answered affirmatively. Send the men as proposed." To General Dix and Judge Pierrepont, working for Stanton to review the cases of political prisoners, Stanton wrote that when they released a man, they should direct that his personal property be released to him as well. It seemed that no detail was too small for the secretary's personal attention.[14]

Count Adam Gurowski, the eccentric Polish exile and diarist, friend, and supporter of Stanton. The caricature is by Thomas Nast, the leading political cartoonist of the era.

To add to the stress of the war and managing the many generals, Stanton was under stress at home, where his infant son, Jamie, was near death and his wife in despair. Stanton wrote to his sister Oella, "For the last six weeks we have not expected it to live—I have no idea that it can do so. Ellen is up night and day, her strength and health is wasted in taking care of the child. . . . Today she took the baby to Baltimore as a last hope that change of air and change of doctors might do something to save it." There are indeed several notes in the War Department files from this period indicating that Stanton sent telegrams to his wife in care of her brother-in-law, in Baltimore, but the clerks carefully marked the messages "private" and did not retain copies. Stanton wrote to his other brother-in-law, James Hutchison, that the child "still lingers but the doctor tells me there is no probability of it living much longer though Ellen still hopes."[15]

On the morning of May 4 Stanton received a one-sentence message from McClellan: "Yorktown is in our possession." Details arrived over the next few hours: the rebels had abandoned Yorktown during the night, enabling McClellan's army to enter the town without a fight. The rebels, under Gen. Joseph Johnston, were retreating westward toward Richmond, and McClellan promised Stanton by telegram that he would "push the enemy to the wall." The next day the *New York World* blamed Stanton for the easy escape of the rebel army. If only Stanton had provided McClellan with McDowell and his men, the *World* insisted, the rebel retreat would have been impossible. "It is the Secretary of War who is answerable for the escape of Johnston's army—a blunder which has defrauded our brave soldiers of the glory of that valiant and vigorous fighting for which Mr. Stanton professes so much admiration." Late on this same day McClellan wired Stanton that some of his troops were skirmishing with the rebel rear guard near the old colonial capital of Williamsburg.[16]

Stanton did not see this last message for a while because he and Lincoln and Chase were on their way by steamer to see McClellan and the front. The three men, joined by Gen. Egbert Viele, boarded the treasury revenue cutter *Miami* on the evening of May 5. Viele later recalled that, as the *Miami* made its way down the Potomac through the rain and the fog, the four men enjoyed a good supper in the small but comfortable cabin. Stanton fretted aloud that he had made a mistake just before leaving the office in answering a garbled telegram from General Mitchel in Alabama. Mitchel's message (which does not seem to be in the files) required an immediate response, so Stanton had telegraphed, "All right, go ahead." Lincoln told Stanton that what he had probably meant was "that it was all right if it was good for him, and all wrong if it was not." As he so often did, Lincoln then told a brief story. There was a horse for sale near his hometown and a number of prospective buyers. The owner of the horse asked a small boy to ride it back and forth so those interested could see it in motion. One of the men then took the boy aside and asked him in a whisper whether the horse had a splint. The boy was somewhat confused by the question. His answer was "If it's good for him he has got it, but if it isn't good for him he hasn't."[17]

The next morning, as the *Miami* left the Potomac River and entered the Chesapeake Bay, the water became rough. Lincoln did not even attempt to eat lunch, instead stretching out on a locker. The others ate with some difficulty, for, in Chase's words, "the plates slipped this way and that—the glasses tumbled over & slid & rolled abt.—& the whole table seemed as topsy-turvy as if some Spiritualist were operating upon it."[18]

It was after dark, about eight or nine, when the *Miami* reached Fort Monroe. Stanton at once sent a telegram to McClellan, thirty miles away at Williamsburg, saying that Lincoln would be glad to see him for a brief conference the next day. Other generals would have viewed this as an order, but McClellan responded that his work with the army was of such "vast importance" that he could not leave for even a few hours. Stanton also sent word to Wool, and soon the aged general joined the civilian leaders on the *Miami*. Although it was past ten, they decided to call upon the local naval commander, Louis Goldsborough, and they all went by small boat to his flagship, the *Minnesota*. Chase wrote that the "narrow steps up the lofty side" of the *Minnesota* seemed "*very* high & a little fearsome." Etiquette required, however, that Lincoln should be the first up the ladder, and up he went, followed by Chase, then Stanton. The leaders discussed the *Merrimack*, still threatening Union shipping from her base at Norfolk, about twelve miles south of Fort Monroe.[19]

On the morning of May 7, at Stanton's suggestion, Lincoln and the others toured the *Vanderbilt*, whose main feature was a new bow ram, of heavy timber and iron plate, to enable the ship to ram and sink the *Merrimack*. Lincoln, Stanton, and the others also visited the *Monitor*, the small ugly Union ironclad, whose men were pleased that Lincoln "was well acquainted with all the mechanical details." McClellan asked Stanton by telegraph whether Lincoln could direct naval gunboats up the

James River, perhaps even as far as Richmond. If the navy could establish control of the James, then McClellan could use that as an avenue to bypass the Confederate troops blocking him at Williamsburg. That evening Lincoln and Stanton relayed this request to Goldsborough, who hesitated, saying that he would need other gunboats to replace any that he sent. Stanton exploded, Goldsborough recalled, insisting "in the most impatient and imperious manner" that the navy send the boats at once. Stanton drafted and Lincoln signed an order directing Goldsborough to send the *Galena* and two other gunboats up the James River. Stanton also informed McClellan that a naval expedition would head up the James as he had requested. The next morning Stanton telegraphed Peter Watson at the War Department, "Things are moving now."[20]

Stanton suggested and Lincoln ordered that the *Monitor* and five other Union ships bombard the Confederate shore batteries guarding the approaches to Norfolk. Lincoln, Stanton, and Chase watched from a Union fort on a small island. A brief cannonade by the Union warships silenced the rebel guns on Sewell's Point; the Northern ships then turned their guns on a nearby battery. There was a puff of smoke in the distance, near Norfolk, and the leaders said to one another, "There comes the *Merrimack*." Sure enough, a few minutes later the *Merrimack* appeared at the mouth of the Elizabeth River. Most of the Union vessels departed, but the *Monitor* and one other warship "stood their ground." The *Merrimack* approached and threatened the *Monitor*, but then, without a shot being fired, the *Merrimack* "turned back." Chase concluded that the "rebel Monster don't *want to* fight—and *won't* fight if she can help it."[21]

Hearing reports from rebel deserters that the Confederates were dismantling the navy yard and evacuating Norfolk, Lincoln and Stanton decided to capture this important seaport. Lincoln wanted to investigate for himself the possible landing sites, so he and Stanton boarded a small tugboat and Chase and twenty armed soldiers followed them in the *Miami* as they scouted the Virginia shoreline. The boat with Lincoln and Stanton was quite close to the shore when Chase spotted several horsemen, whom he feared were Confederates. Chase asked Lincoln by semaphore whether he should fire upon them, but Lincoln "replied negatively." When they found another good landing spot and returned to Fort Monroe, Lincoln and Stanton ordered Wool to prepare a force to march on Norfolk.[22]

Early on May 10, Lincoln, Stanton, Chase, Wool, and about 5,000 troops embarked and headed for Sewell's Point. Stanton asked Chase to accompany Wool and the troops, perhaps because he did not quite trust Wool. Lincoln and Stanton landed with the troops and watched them march off toward Norfolk; then the two men returned to Fort Monroe. Stanton sent a telegram to Watson from there at noon to report, "Our forces under General Wool are advancing upon Norfolk. The landing was without any accident. Great volumes of smoke in the direction of Norfolk indicate that the rebels are burning the city or the navy yard." Lincoln and Stanton endured a long, anxious wait before Chase and Wool returned at around midnight with the good news that Norfolk had surrendered without a fight. Chase wrote that Stanton "fairly hugged General Wool," and a newspaper reported that Wool had "not yet recovered from the hug which Stanton gave him, nor will he ever recover from the shock given him by seeing so great a man as Stanton, so exalted a man as the president, in his night-shirt." Stanton at once sent a telegram to Watson, which he would release to the Northern newspapers: "Norfolk is ours, and also Portsmouth and the navy yard." Stanton also sent a midnight message to McClellan, telling him that Norfolk was captured, for which McClellan thanked him "from the bottom of my heart."[23]

"Norfolk Is Ours." Stanton, in his night clothes, jumps up to hug General Wool and thank him for the capture of Norfolk.

There was more good news early the next morning: the rebel commander of the *Merrimack*, because he no longer had a base at Norfolk, destroyed the ship. Stanton wired both Watson and McClellan that the rebels set fire to the ship at about three in the morning and it exploded a few minutes before five. Lincoln, Stanton, and Chase now headed for home on the steamship *Baltimore*. Chase wrote to his daughter, "So has ended a brilliant week's campaign of the President, for I think it quite certain that if he had not come down, Norfolk would still have been in possession of the enemy and the *Merrimack* as grim and defiant and as much a terror as ever." A junior officer on the *Monitor* agreed, writing home, "Even the superannuated old fogies begin to show some signs of life and animation." One of the old fogies on the scene, Commodore Goldsborough, wrote to his wife a week later, describing Stanton as a "little man" who was responsible for withholding McDowell's troops from McClellan and thus for the delay in capturing Richmond. Goldsborough added, "Lawyers cannot command armies simply because they can spout before the bar of a court house."[24]

Stanton returned to Washington at about noon on May 12, but he could not go to the War Department that day; he had an "inflamed eye," perhaps an infection. The next morning, as he walked up the steps to his office, he met with Reverend Henry Bellows of the Sanitary Commission. At Stanton's request Bellows followed him to his room, where "a dozen people of greater or lesser magnitude were waiting to see him—while at the door twenty others were glaring in, as at a wild beast on show." Stanton said that he was glad to see Bellows looking so well; Bellows replied that he was sorry to see that Stanton was unwell, with a patch over one eye. Stanton insisted he was "never better," but Bellows thought this "the nervous petulance of a man, who fears that others are fancying him not well and who wants to hide it from himself." Bellows asked if Stanton had read a letter listing those whom the Sanitary Commission wanted to see appointed to the Medical Department. Stanton had not read the letter, and he raged at Bellows, "The government will act when it gets ready!" As Bellows prepared to leave, Stanton apologized but insisted that he could not "allow myself to be interrogated upon matters that belong wholly to the Department." Bellows wrote to a colleague that

Stanton was "a man with a brain in a very dangerous state of irritability," indeed with an "internal temper and cerebral condition which will come to some disagreeable end."[25]

———

Although McClellan now had Franklin's division, he continued to demand more troops. He wrote to Lincoln, "I cannot bring into actual battle against the enemy more than eighty thousand men at the utmost, and with them I must attack in position, probably entrenched, a much larger force, probably double my numbers." In fact, as Lincoln and Stanton sensed, McClellan's army far outnumbered the rebel forces opposing him. After conferring with Lincoln, Stanton wrote to McClellan that they had ordered McDowell to join his forces by marching south from his position near Fredericksburg: "[McDowell was] ordered—keeping himself always in position to save the capital from all possible attack—so to operate as to put his left wing in communication with your right wing, and you are instructed to co-operate, so as to establish this communication as soon as possible, by extending your right wing to the north of Richmond." McClellan was not at all pleased, writing to Lincoln that he feared there was "little hope that [McDowell] can join me overland in time for the coming battle." He was also concerned that McDowell would not be under his command. "I think that my own Department should embrace the entire field of active military operations designed for the capture of [Richmond]." To his wife McClellan was more pointed, writing, "Those hounds in Washington are after me again. Stanton is without exception the vilest man I ever knew or heard of."[26]

McClellan's anger rose not just from what he saw as Stanton's refusal to provide troops but also from reports that Stanton was going to arm blacks. According to the *New York Times*, Stanton was thinking about "using negro soldiery for garrison duty." The *Times* added that the "blacks, thoroughly acclimated, will be saved from the risks of climate; while in the well-defined limits of fortifications they will be restrained from the commission of those revengeful excesses which are the bug-a-boos of the Southern people." McClellan and other Democrats found this outrageous, but for Republicans like David Hunter, the Union general recently appointed to head the department consisting of South Carolina, Georgia, and Florida, it was common sense. In his letter seeking a Southern assignment, Hunter had asked Stanton to let him have his "own way on the subject of slavery," and assured him that the administration "will not be responsible. I alone will bear the blame; you can censure me, arrest me, dismiss me, hang me if you will, but permit me to make my mark in such a way as to be remembered by friend and foe." Once he arrived in the small slice of coastal Carolina under federal control, Hunter requested from Stanton fifty thousand muskets, fifty thousand pairs of scarlet pants, and authority to "arm such loyal men as [he could] find in the country." Hunter did not quite say that he would arm and clothe *black* men, but it would be hard to read his message any other way. Stanton did not send Hunter the requested authority, but he also did not *forbid* Hunter from proceeding as he proposed.[27]

Indeed Stanton sent to Hunter's department another abolitionist general, Rufus Saxton, with instructions to "take possession" of the plantations abandoned by the rebels and to "take charge of the inhabitants remaining thereon." Stanton continued: "By encouraging industry, skill in the cultivation of the necessaries of life and general self-improvement, you will, as far as possible, promote the real well-being of all the people under your charge." His order to Saxton, which was soon in the newspapers, was a first step toward the substantial federal role in helping former slaves. And it seemed that Stanton was thinking not just about helping blacks become self-sufficient but also about using them for military purposes, for Saxton told Chase before leaving Washington that Stanton had "authorized him to procure one or two thousand red flannel suits for blacks, with a view to organization. No arms to be supplied as yet."[28]

Hunter and Saxton were not the only generals with whom Stanton was corresponding about slaves and former slaves. Stanton heard from Gen. Ormsby Mitchel in Alabama that he was receiving valuable information from slaves and believed that, in return, the Union had to protect them in their freedom. Stanton approved, writing back on May 5, "The assistance of slaves is an element of military strength which, under proper regulations, you are fully justified in employing for your security and the success of your operations. It has been freely employed by the enemy, and to abstain from its judicious use when it can be employed to military advantage would be a failure to employ means to suppress the rebellion and restore the authority of the Government." Later in the month Stanton received a letter from Gen. Benjamin Butler, now in charge in New Orleans. Although Butler had welcomed fugitive slaves in Virginia, declaring them contraband and putting them to work, he was concerned in Louisiana that if he offered protection to fleeing slaves, he would be depriving both loyal and rebel masters of their property: "Unless all personal property of all rebels is to be confiscated . . . it is manifestly unjust to make a virtual confiscation of this particular species of property. Indeed, it makes an actual confiscation of all property, both real and personal, of the planter if we take away or allow to run away his negroes as his crop is just growing." Butler's approach was arguably the opposite of Mitchel's, but Stanton again approved, writing Butler that he was "strongly impressed" by his policy and would not "fetter your judgment by any specific instructions." Stanton was more interested in winning the war than in having a single, national policy on how the army dealt with fugitive slaves, and he was hoping to keep the issue quiet and focus on military matters.[29]

General Hunter, however, shattered the quiet by declaring that all the slaves in his department were free. When news of Hunter's decree reached the North, Democrats and moderates urged Lincoln to over-rule Hunter, but abolitionists were pleased and pressed Lincoln to sustain him. The *New York Herald* believed that Stanton rather than Hunter was the author of this controversial proclamation. Lincoln promptly revoked Hunter's order but also hinted that he might issue some form of presidential emancipation proclamation: "I further make known that whether it be competent for me, as Commander-in-Chief of the Army and Navy, to declare the Slaves of any state or states, free, and whether at any time, in any case, it shall have become a necessity indispensable to the maintenance of the government, to exercise such supposed power, are questions which, under my responsibility, I reserve to myself, and which I cannot feel justified in leaving to the decision of commanders in the field." Stanton apparently helped Lincoln in drafting this language, for Lincoln wrote to James Gordon Bennett of the *New York Herald* that he erred in supposing that his secretary of war was behind the Hunter proclamation: "He mixes no politics whatever with his duties;

knew nothing of Gen. Hunter's proclamation; and he and I alone got up the counter-proclamation." Charles Sumner believed that Stanton favored Hunter's goals, if not his proclamation, writing a friend on May 22, "Stanton wished that General Hunter had been allowed to free the slaves without talking about it." Edward Atkinson, another Massachusetts man, quoted Stanton as saying of Hunter's proclamation, "Damn him, why didn't he do it and say nothing about it." And perhaps most telling, Sumner wrote to Governor John Andrew, "Stanton told me this morning that a decree of Emancipation would be issued within two months."[30]

Lincoln might claim that Stanton "mixes no politics" with his duties, but both the president and the secretary knew that whatever Stanton did, or allowed his generals to do, with respect to slaves and former slaves would be politically controversial. Congress was in the midst of an intense debate over whether to authorize the president to confiscate the slaves of former rebels; there was a parallel debate about whether the president, as commander in chief, could or should himself issue some form of emancipation proclamation. In early June, Charles Wickliffe, a Unionist member of Congress from and former governor of Kentucky, secured House approval for a resolution requesting information from Stanton about whether Hunter had organized a regiment of "fugitive slaves" and whether Stanton had authorized him to do so. Stanton responded that he had no "official information" about whether Hunter had organized such a regiment and that he had asked Hunter for a report on the issue. As to Wickliffe's request for the complete correspondence, Stanton asserted what we would call "executive privilege," writing that Lincoln had determined that releasing the information would be "improper and incompatible with the public welfare."[31]

Hunter responded to Wickliffe's resolution with a clever letter in which he said that there were no fugitive slaves in the area under his control, only fugitive masters, who had abandoned their plantations and their slaves. Stanton passed along Hunter's letter to the House without comment, which Wickliffe interpreted as Stanton's approval of Hunter's plan to arm slaves. "I shrink from arming the slave," Wickliffe declared in debate in early July. "I would as soon think of enlisting the Indian, and of arming him with the tomahawk and scalping knife . . . as to arm the negro in this contest." Robert Mallory, another member from Kentucky, agreed with his colleague that blacks should not be soldiers: "One shot of a cannon would disperse thirty thousand of them." Mallory claimed that Stanton agreed with him on this issue, that Stanton had recently told him that he had not only refused a request from an officer for authority to raise a black regiment but had ordered the officer's arrest. Thaddeus Stevens, a Republican from Pennsylvania and perhaps the most Radical member of the House, responded that he feared Lincoln was "misled by the malign influence of Kentucky counselors" on the question of arming slaves. Arming negroes, Stevens argued, was "in exact accordance with the usage of all civilized nations," and he cited the use of black soldiers by both sides in the American Revolution. As to Stanton's views on this issue, Stevens was puzzled. He told the House that he had spoken several times with Stanton about arming the slaves and it seemed that Stanton fully agreed with him. Now, however, after hearing Mallory's comments, Stevens was not so sure. Again it seems that Stanton may have spoken differently with people of different views.[32]

Lincoln and Stanton were frustrated with McClellan, but they were also frustrated with McDowell, near Fredericksburg, and they decided to visit him there, to see if they could prod him toward Richmond. On May 22, without mentioning Lincoln's name, Stanton sent messages to McDowell, asking whether he could meet the next day, and to Capt. John Dahlgren, asking him to have a boat ready to depart that evening. At about nine Stanton and (to Dahlgren's surprise) Lincoln showed up in a carriage at the Navy Yard. There was no food on board, so Dahlgren had to feed the president and the secretary supper at the Yard before they all boarded the boat. Dahlgren later wrote that, as they steamed down the Potomac, Lincoln read aloud to the others from a book of poems; the president had "real dramatic power as a reader, and recited poetic passages with pathos." Lincoln read a long poem about Marco Bozzaris, a Greek general who died fighting for independence from Turkey and who, according to the poet, was "one of the few, the immortal names, that were not born to die." At Aquia Creek the next morning they boarded a common baggage car on a military train, sitting on camp stools. McDowell met them midway and urged them to study a new trestle bridge, built by Herman Haupt, the railroad engineer whom Stanton had appointed head of the Military Railroad Bureau. The bridge was four hundred feet long and as much as a hundred feet high, and in Lincoln's words there was "nothing in it but beanpoles and cornstalks." Although there was "but a single plank for [them] to walk on," Dahlgren recalled that Lincoln said, "Let us walk over," then started himself to cross the precarious bridge. Stanton, Dahlgren, and the others followed, but about halfway across Stanton "said he was dizzy and feared he would fall. So he stopped, unable to proceed." Dahlgren "managed to step by him, and took his hand, thus leading him over, when in fact [his] own head was somewhat confused by the giddy height."[33]

In McDowell's camp at Fredericksburg, Lincoln, Stanton, and Dahlgren found 45,000 men, all in "fine order and spirits." Horses were provided so they could inspect the troops, but Stanton, with his bad knee, could not sit a horse, so he and Dahlgren followed Lincoln in an ambulance. Lincoln also toured the town of Fredericksburg that afternoon; a Washington newspaper reported that many "apostles of secession were unexpectedly afforded a view of their boss." Lincoln, Stanton, and McDowell agreed that within a few days McDowell would march his troops south toward Richmond. After a "plain dinner" at headquarters, Lincoln, Stanton, and Dahlgren boarded first the train and then the boat, heading back to Washington overnight.[34]

When he arrived at the department early on May 24, Stanton found in the telegraph office distressing reports from General Banks. Rebel forces under Gen. Thomas "Stonewall" Jackson had attacked and defeated Banks the prior day at Front Royal, about seventy miles due west from Washington, and Jackson was now attacking Banks again, at Strasburg. Before seven that morning Stanton telegraphed General Dix in Baltimore, "Send all the force you can spare, to re-enforce Banks, speedily as possible." A little before ten, Stanton sent a similar message to General Frémont, reporting that Jackson was "threatening Strasburg and Winchester" and asking him to provide Banks with "any support." At about eleven, Stanton wrote to McDowell, directing that, when he made the planned move south toward Richmond, he should leave behind at least one brigade to assist Banks if necessary. At about three in the afternoon a message arrived from Frémont that showed he had not received Stanton's earlier message. Lincoln now wired Frémont himself, stating, "The exposed condition of General Banks makes his immediate relief a point of paramount importance."[35]

Lincoln and Stanton were not only trying to save Banks and his troops; they were trying to capture Jackson and his forces, as Lincoln explained to McDowell when he directed him to postpone "for the present the movement on Richmond" and instead move 20,000 men as fast as possible "to capture the forces of Jackson and Ewell." Stanton made the same point to Frémont at about the same time, writing, "It is of the last importance that you use every effort to assist Banks and capture Jackson and every one believes you will do it." In the evening a message arrived from Banks, who had retreated to Winchester, claiming he would be able to attack Jackson and recapture Strasburg in the next few days, but Stanton was dubious, asking at ten that night for "more detailed information."[36]

The next day was worse. Jackson attacked Banks again, at Winchester, and Banks retreated again, fleeing for the Potomac River. At ten in the morning Stanton wired to McDowell that Banks was "retreating towards Harpers Ferry." Stanton again asked McDowell to do whatever he could to help Banks and ordered him to send a brigade to Washington immediately. In the early afternoon Stanton wrote that Banks was "in full retreat, hotly pressed, and in great danger." It was at about this time that Stanton sent a telegram to all the Northern governors: "Intelligence from various quarters leaves no doubt that the enemy in great force are advancing on Washington. You will please organize and forward immediately all the volunteer and militia force in your state." In a separate message to three governors, including Andrew in Massachusetts, Stanton was even more specific: "Banks is completely routed. The enemy are in large force advancing upon Harpers Ferry." Andrew, as soon as he received these messages from Stanton, put out his own proclamation, declaring that a "wily and barbarous horde of traitors" was threatening Washington, and calling for the "whole active militia" of the state to assemble in Boston.[37]

Governor John Andrew of Massachusetts, one of Stanton's closest allies among the wartime governors.

By six the next morning, somewhat more calm, Stanton reported to another general that Banks and his troops were safe "without much loss" in Williamsport, Maryland. Stanton spent much of this day dealing with governors on questions raised by his call for volunteers. He wrote to Tod in Ohio that the federal government wanted as many men as would volunteer for three years or "for any other term, not less than three months, according as you can raise them quickest." He wrote in similar terms to Governor Israel Washburn of Maine, saying that he would prefer three-year men, but if these were not available the governor should "enlist them for three months." But this message was followed within hours by a message to all the governors from Adjutant Gen. Lorenzo Thomas: "Enlist no more three-month men." Since Thomas wrote this "by order of the Secretary of War," the governors were understandably upset with Stanton. The anger was especially intense in Boston, where thousands of volunteers had gathered, some of them having marched through the night.[38]

On May 27 the *Boston Advertiser* accused Stanton of causing the defeat of Banks, a former Massachusetts governor, by leaving him with only about 4,000 troops to face more than 15,000 rebels. The editors demanded, "Stanton should vacate a department which he has proved himself incompetent to fill, and should make way for some officer who will not undertake to manage for our generals in the field when sitting in his chair in the War

Office, who will not ruin our campaigns by his interference, and whose vision extends beyond the Department of the Rappahannock." The *Advertiser* editors, when they wrote this, did not yet know that Stanton had reversed course, saying that the army wanted only three-year men and not three-month volunteers. When Andrew announced this to the thousands who had arrived in Boston, there was even more anger against Stanton. The next day the *Advertiser* said that Stanton had sent a pointless request from Washington that led to Andrew's equally pointless proclamation. The *New York World*, under the headline "Secretary Stanton's Panic," castigated Stanton for his alarmed call upon the governors: "We join in the demand of the *Boston Advertiser*—one of the most considerate, discreet, and intelligent public journals in the country—that this impetuous, reckless incapable shall be immediately replaced by a more competent war minister."[39]

Governor Andrew sent a telegram to Samuel Hooper, member of Congress from Boston, saying that the local press "assumes that Sunday's telegram ordering militia was Stanton's personal panic, that President did not approve, and that no justifiable occasion existed." Hooper responded that Stanton's request for volunteers "was made by the president himself upon deliberate consultation with the Secretary of War & other members of the cabinet and military advisers." Hooper claimed that "every intelligent man," including, he believed, Banks himself, "knew well why it became necessary to withdraw a large portion of the forces under Gen. Banks, whose operations at the time were considered subordinate to the present movement on Richmond." Sumner seconded Hooper, writing to Andrew that he knew from conversations with Lincoln, Stanton, and Seward that the *Advertiser*'s article was "absolutely false."[40]

Stanton was not without his defenders, even in Boston. On June 2 a long article appeared in the *Boston Transcript* penned by Horatio Woodman, a young Boston lawyer and friend of Hooper. Claiming that he had official information, Woodman defended Stanton against the charges that he had deprived McClellan and Banks of the troops they needed. Woodman sent a copy of the article to Stanton, under an almost obsequious cover letter, and a few days later Woodman was pleased to learn from Hooper that Stanton had read and approved the article.[41]

Although he was busy with other issues, Stanton continued to watch and encourage Charles Ellet Jr. and the ram fleet, his own private western navy. In late April he informed Ellet that naval commander David Farragut was heading for Memphis: "You should lose no time in starting your fleet to the same point." Ellet soon finished building and staffing his nine rams and went south with them on the Mississippi River. He spent several frustrating days in late May and early June near Fort Pillow, one of the last Confederate forts on the Mississippi north of Memphis, trying to persuade Charles Davis, the local federal naval commander, to mount a joint attack. Stanton sent an angry note on June 5 to Halleck, who had just captured nearby Corinth, Mississippi, complaining that Davis "refuses to join Mr. Ellet or give him the protection of a single gunboat, but also refuses to allow Ellet to attack on his own hook." (Stanton did not complain to Welles, knowing he would insist that naval operations should be under the control of the Navy Department.) By the time Stanton sent this message to Halleck, Ellet had already acted "on his own hook," sending two rams past the fort. Then, when there was no gunfire, Ellet sent his son ashore to confirm that the rebels had, as he suspected, abandoned the fort without a fight.[42]

Ellet and his fleet now steamed south toward Memphis, reaching there at dawn on June 6, just as a battle was about to start between rebel and federal gunboats. Ellet threw himself and his rams immediately into the fray; waving his hat to encourage and direct the others, he steered his ram straight for one of the leading rebel ships, slicing her nearly in two, and suffering a bullet in the knee. Although wounded and prone on the deck, Ellet remained in command, but the battle was over in a few minutes. The federals had disabled, destroyed, or captured the entire rebel fleet. Ellet sent his son ashore with two U.S. flags, one to raise over the customs house and the other over the courthouse. Ellet's proud messages to Stanton were on the front pages of the papers. Stanton congratulated him on his great victory and hoped that his injury would not prevent him from helping to "give the finishing stroke to the enemy at Vicksburg." Ellet's wound, however, became infected, and he died in late June on the deck of one of his rams near Cairo, Illinois. Stanton grieved the loss and appointed Ellet's brother to command the ram fleet.[43]

Stanton's comment to Ellet about "the finishing stroke" at Vicksburg reflected the common Northern assumption at the time, that the Union would soon capture that city, one of the few remaining Confederate strongholds on the Mississippi River. But Stanton did not appreciate, indeed almost no one on the federal side appreciated, how difficult it would be to take Vicksburg, not just a fort with many guns but also a city, perched on a bluff more than two hundred feet above a sharp turn in the Mississippi River. Back in May, when Farragut sent several gunboats up the Mississippi to demand the surrender of Vicksburg, the local military governor responded, "Mississippians don't know, and refuse to learn, how to surrender to an enemy. If Commodore Farragut or Brigadier-General Butler can teach them, let them come and try." Farragut did try, at the end of June and early July, with gunboats and mortar schooners and 3,000 troops provided by Butler. Farragut spent two days lobbing shells into Vicksburg but did little damage. Three thousand troops were nowhere near enough to attack the fortress-city, and Halleck refused Farragut's request for more. It would be many months before Grant and his troops would enter Vicksburg.[44]

Back in the East, McClellan reported from his headquarters near Richmond on June 10 that he was "completely checked by the weather" and would "attack as soon as the weather & ground permit." Stanton by this time did not much believe McClellan. Stanton's brother-in-law Christopher Wolcott, who had just arrived in Washington to start work as an assistant secretary of war, wrote to his wife that "McClellan keeps sending word that he will attack Richmond very soon, but every day brings some new excuse." Stanton, writing McClellan to inform him that another 10,000 troops were on their way, assured him, "There never was a moment when my desire has been otherwise than to aid you with my whole heart, mind and strength since the hour we first met [and] you have never had and never can have any one more truly your friend or more anxious to support you." McClellan by this time did not much believe Stanton, and he did not respond to this excessive claim of friendship. He simply reported that it was raining again and that this would delay his attack.[45]

By now Lincoln and Stanton realized they needed a single general in charge in northern Virginia rather than three generals loosely coordinated through Stanton's office. They also wanted a Republican general; they were tired of Democrats such as McClellan. John Pope was one of the few solid Republicans in the Regular Army, and on June 19 Stanton asked him to come to Washington. Pope later recalled that, when he arrived at the War Department, Stanton's reception room was "uncomfortably full of people, talking or listening to him," so Pope just watched and listened for a few minutes. Stanton "was in no sense an imposing person," for he was "below the medium stature, stout and clumsy," with a "rather red face, well covered with a heavy black beard." The only furniture in the reception room was a high desk, at which Stanton stood impatiently, hearing his visitors one by one, deciding their questions immediately. Everyone in the room could hear everyone else, and "this publicity itself shortened conversations and abbreviated interviews wonderfully." Stanton asked Pope into his small private office and explained that Lincoln wanted him to take charge of the three armies in northern Virginia. Pope was not excited by the offer. He was concerned that the three generals in question all outranked him; that they would resent him, a westerner, coming to take charge of their eastern armies; and that his role in the Richmond campaign would be to "seize and hold the bear by the tail while McClellan beat out its brains." If McClellan succeeded, he would get the credit, but if he failed, Pope would get the blame. Stanton agreed to discuss Pope's concerns with Lincoln, but they were not persuaded. On the next day, June 26, using a draft prepared by Stanton, Lincoln appointed Pope head of the new Army of Virginia, with orders to defend Washington, to attack Stonewall Jackson in the Shenandoah Valley, and to assist McClellan in capturing Richmond.[46]

Lincoln had just returned from a brief visit to West Point, where he conferred with Winfield Scott, now retired and so infirm that he could not travel. Some papers reported (erroneously) that Pope accompanied Lincoln. Other papers speculated that Scott would take Stanton's place or that there would be a change in the generals in charge in Virginia. We do not know what Lincoln and Scott discussed during their five-hour meeting, but we know that Lincoln deflected questions while changing trains in New Jersey on his way back to Washington, insisting that his trip "did not have the importance that has been attached to it." It had nothing to do with "making or unmaking any general." He added that Stanton "holds a pretty tight rein on the Press, so that they shall not tell more than they ought to, and I'm afraid that if I blab too much, he might draw a tight rein on me." This was greeted with "roars of laughter and loud applause, during which the President retired within the car." Lincoln's tone was light, but his point was serious: he supported his secretary of war, including his controversial controls over the press.[47]

Lincoln made these lighthearted remarks on June 25, the first day of what we know as the Seven Days Battles, a week of intense fighting near Richmond between McClellan's Army of the Potomac and the Army of Northern Virginia, now under the command of Gen. Robert E. Lee. Like many Northerners, Stanton believed that this week might decide the war, and he spent much of the week in his telegraph office, waiting for and reading reports. Reverend Dyer, who visited Stanton at this time, described the furniture of his office as "of the simplest kind. There was but little for comfort, and nothing for luxury. The only thing that came anywhere near it was an old, and cheap hair cloth sofa, with at least one half of the hair cloth torn off. Here he spent the nights, sometimes for weeks at a stretch, never undressing, but occasionally lying down and taking such rest as he could find in such circumstances, liable at any moment to be called to receive dispatches from generals in the different armies."[48]

As he paced back and forth, Stanton was frustrated by the lack of detail in McClellan's reports. "Our men are behaving splendidly," McClellan wired on June 25. The next day, though, McClellan lamented that he was facing 200,000 rebel soldiers and threatened that if there was a "disaster" it would be Stanton's fault: "The responsibility cannot be thrown on my shoulders—it must rest where it belongs." Stanton did not respond to this threat but simply told McClellan that he was sending 5,000 more troops, with reinforcements to follow "if needed." But Lincoln did respond, writing, that McClellan's message "pains me very much. I give you all I can, and act on the presumption that you will do the best you can with what you have, while you continue, ungenerously I think, to assume that I could give you more if I would." By the end of the day McClellan was again elated, wiring Stanton, "I almost begin to think we are invincible." But the next noon he reported, "Heavy attack now being made by Jackson and two other divisions," and that evening he sent word that there had been a "terrible contest" in which his army was "attacked by greatly superior numbers in all directions."[49]

At about one in the morning on June 28, McClellan sent another message to Stanton, blaming him for the army's defeat. McClellan claimed that his army was "overwhelmed by vastly superior numbers" in what would prove "the most desperate battle of the war." Without telling Stanton that he had just given orders to retreat to the James River, McClellan insisted, "Had I twenty thousand or even ten thousand fresh troops to use tomorrow, I could take Richmond, but I have not a man in reserve, and shall be glad to cover my retreat and save the material and personnel of the army. . . . I have lost this battle because my force was too small. I again repeat that I am not responsible for this; & I say it with the earnestness of a general who feels in his heart the loss of every brave man who has been needlessly sacrificed today." Stanton must "send me very large re-enforcements, and send them at once." He concluded, "The Govt has not sustained this Army. If you do not do so now the game is lost. If I save this Army now I tell you plainly that I owe no thanks to you or any other person in Washington—you have done your best to sacrifice this Army."[50]

There is a minor mystery as to whether Stanton read the last sentence of McClellan's midnight message when it arrived in Washington. When the telegram was first published, by the Joint Committee on the Conduct of the War in 1863, the message ended with "the game is lost." Soon thereafter, however, in early 1864, Democratic papers printed the full message, often with the last sentence in italics. In 1887 McClellan's friend and executor, William Prime, accused Stanton of omitting the damning sentence from the copy provided the Joint Committee: "The secretary received the accusation in the silence which was the confession of its truth." In his 1905 biography of Stanton, Frank Flower quoted at length from one of Stanton's aides, who recalled that two senior telegraph officers, Edward Sanford and Thomas Eckert, suppressed the last sentence before handing the message to Stanton. Sanford reportedly said that "this was such an outrageous, such an infamous untruth, that he, as telegraphic censor, could not allow" it to reach the secretary. Most authors today accept this version, although it seems doubtful. Eckert was not yet in Washington, and Sanford probably would not have withheld part of a telegram from Stanton.[51]

With or without the scathing sentence, Stanton handed the message to Lincoln, telling him "with much feeling" that everything he had done was "by your authority." Lincoln, describing the incident to his friend Senator Browning, agreed that Stanton had acted on his instructions and called McClellan's message "very harsh." In his response to McClellan, Lincoln urged him, "Save your Army at all events," and assured him that the government would raise and send him more troops, although they would not arrive "today, tomorrow, or next day." Stanton sent instructions to other senior generals that they should send whatever troops they could spare to McClellan in Virginia. There was no word from McClellan on this day—his telegraph line failed just after the midnight message—and the silence of course increased concern in Washington.[52]

Early on June 29 Stanton received a telegram from Charles Fulton, editor of the *Baltimore American*, who had just returned from the Peninsula. Stanton summoned him to Washington so that he could hear his firsthand report on McClellan's situation. The next morning Stanton was outraged to read a message from Fulton to the Associated Press in New York, saying that he was preparing for publication his account of recent events based on "private sources." Stanton immediately ordered the general in Baltimore to arrest Fulton and "confine him closely in Fort McHenry until further order permitting communication with no one." Stanton apparently believed that Fulton was planning to publish what he learned at the War Department, for he accused Fulton of having "obtained facts in confidence in Washington," the publication of which would be a "flagrant and outrageous violation of the confidence with which [he was] treated." When Fulton apologized and promised that he would not publish anything confidential, Stanton relented and released him. Fulton then published an account of his arrest; though he did not name Stanton, he declared that he would "not again voluntarily seek intercourse with those who have thus shown their willingness to play the tyrant."[53]

As soon as they heard from McClellan of his defeat and retreat, Lincoln, Stanton, and Seward acted promptly to raise new troops. Lincoln feared that, if he simply called for additional volunteers, just as the news from McClellan was in the newspapers, there would be a panic. So

Lincoln sent Seward to New York City, to confer there with the Northern governors, to see if they would lend their names to a call for troops. Stanton kept in close telegraphic touch with Seward. Disregarding the defeatist tone of McClellan's messages and focusing instead on signs that McClellan would resume the fight, Stanton urged Seward to make haste. On June 29 he informed Seward that McClellan had removed all his sick and wounded from his former camp at White House: "My inference is that McClellan will probably be in Richmond within two days." The next day Stanton wrote, "If the governors will give us promptly one hundred thousand men the war will be over."[54]

Seward reported to Stanton, however, that the governors did not believe that men would enlist unless immediately paid $25 as an advance on the standard federal bounty of $100. Stanton wired in reply, "Existing law does not authorize the advance of the bounty money and the department ought not to promise it." He would talk with congressional leaders about changing the law, but Seward was adamant, saying, "We can't wait for debate." Stanton for once yielded, wiring Seward, "I will take the responsibility of authorizing the $25" out of an existing appropriation. Using this promised payment, Seward was able to secure, either in person or by telegram, signatures of most of the Northern governors on a letter to Lincoln, urging him to ask for 300,000 volunteers. Most but not all: one of those who did not respond to Seward in time to have his name printed as a signatory was John Andrew. Andrew assured Stanton, "No effort ever has been, or ever will be, spared to meet every wish expressed by your Department." But in a more candid letter to a friend, Andrew wrote, "After all the efforts that I have unceasingly made to have some of those in power treat this as a *war* and not as a *picnic* or a *caucus* . . . I am glad not to have suffered the final humiliation of having my name printed to a document dictated at Washington, but apparently emanating from the governors merely to save appearances."[55]

As planned, Lincoln responded to the letter from the governors with a call for 300,000 volunteers to serve for three years. Both the letter from the governors to Lincoln and Lincoln's response appeared in the Northern newspapers on July 2. Recruiting was under way again, and it would not cease until the end of the war.[56]

Chapter 9

"Hours Are Precious"

—— July–December 1862 ——

T he Northern newspapers were filled in the first few days of July with reports of McClellan's defeat and with editorials against Stanton. The *Detroit Free Press* blamed Stanton for stopping recruiting, thus denying McClellan's army the men it needed, and called upon Lincoln to "dismiss Stanton and put an intelligent and just man in his place." The *New York Herald* reported, "The people are furious against Secretary Stanton. They imperiously and unanimously demand his removal. Throughout this city, on the Fourth of July, there was but a single sentiment, which was heard repeated at every turn by every class and condition of man. It was that if the President trusted McClellan he had no right to harbor Stanton." The *St. Joseph Democrat* of Missouri declared, "A conceited secretary has attempted to manage a campaign, and as a consequence all his armies are beaten in detail." Even the *New York Times* noted that a "very fierce crusade has been opened upon Secretary Stanton," not only by opposition papers but by some papers that usually supported the administration.[1]

Senator Zachariah Chandler was one of the few who defended Stanton in this dark hour. After spending some time with Stanton on July 6, Chandler wrote to his wife that he would "open fire upon the Traitorous Cuss [McClellan] this week in my usually Mild & Conservative way." The next day Chandler proposed a Senate resolution demanding all the correspondence between McClellan and the Executive from February through April. He explained that "the press, the politicians, and the traitors of the country have declared that E. M. Stanton" was responsible for the failure of the Army of the Potomac. Chandler insisted that "Stanton had [nothing] to do with putting the Army of the Potomac in the marshes of the Chickahominy," that Stanton was "merely the clerk of the President of the United States, writes his dispatches, and obeys his orders." There was a criminal, Chandler insisted, but it was not Stanton; it could be only one of two people: Abraham Lincoln or George McClellan. And Chandler left little doubt who was really the "great criminal."[2]

Zachariah Chandler, the Radical Republican senator from Wisconsin, a strong supporter of Stanton both during and after the Civil War.

The Senate debated Chandler's resolution on July 10. Perhaps having heard about McClellan's midnight message, the message accusing Stanton of trying to sacrifice the Army of the Potomac, Senator Henry Rice, a Democrat from Minnesota, suggested that the resolution should request all correspondence between McClellan and Washington through July 1. Chandler readily agreed to this amendment. Senator Joseph Wright, an Indiana Democrat, opposed Chandler's resolution, describing his attack on McClellan as "calculated to divide the friends of the Union and to sow the seeds of dissension." Chandler responded that he only wanted to ensure that the nation had the facts, that the public knew that "Secretary Stanton and the President have sent every man, and every musket . . . to the army on the peninsula that could be possibly spared from the defense of [the] capital." Senator Henry Wilson argued that the question was not whether Chandler's speech was proper; the question was whether the request was appropriate, and for himself, he "should like to see that information." Senator Edgar Cowan, a Pennsylvania Republican, supported the resolution; he believed the record would persuade people that "the Secretary of War is an honest man, trying to do his duty," just as "General McClellan is an honest, brave general, trying to do his duty." The resolution passed, and the next day Chandler wrote to his wife that he would persist. McClellan was "an imbecile if not a traitor," he declared, and he added that Stanton was his "friend & *I will stand by him*."[3]

Stanton agreed that McClellan alone was responsible for his defeat. Christopher Wolcott was almost surely paraphrasing Stanton when he wrote home that McClellan "was simply outgeneraled, and then under the influence of a cowardly fear, retreated instead of retrieving the day by boldly advancing on the enemy." But Stanton used a very different tone with McClellan's father-in-law and chief of staff, Randolph Marcy, when Marcy visited Washington at this time. Years later Marcy recalled that Stanton assured him he was McClellan's "warmest friend" and asserted, "If it would do him any service I would be willing to lay down naked in the gutter and allow him to stand upon my body for hours." Stanton wrote McClellan in similar terms on July 5: "No man had ever a truer friend than I have been to you and shall continue to be. You are seldom absent from my thoughts and I am ready to make any sacrifice to aid you." McClellan was pleased that he and Stanton could resume the "cordial confidence which once characterized [their] intercourse." He urged Stanton to review his "confidential letter" to Lincoln about the political aspects of the current crisis. This was what we know as the "Harrison's Landing letter," in which McClellan lectured Lincoln about how to fight the Civil War. McClellan insisted that the North should target only the Southern armies and that "neither confiscation of property" nor "forcible abolition of slavery should be contemplated for a moment."[4]

Stanton was dealing at this time not only with a national crisis but with a personal crisis: the death of his child. Wolcott wrote to Pamphila on July 5 that Ellen had summoned Stanton to their summer house in the northern hills of the District, where she and the children were staying to escape the heat, because little Jamie "cannot last long." Wolcott noted that, in spite of his son's illness and his wife's distress, Stanton "does not usually go out there more than two or three times a week, but eats and sleeps at the house in town." Jamie Stanton finally breathed his last at about one in the morning on July 10. Stanton was reminded of all the deaths in his life: those of his father, his brother, his first child, his first wife. There was almost no press coverage of the young boy's death, although the *New York World* commented, "While the corpse of his child lay silent in his home, the over-tasked Secretary was toiling in the country's behalf, finding no time to mourn over the little clay." Stanton arranged for an Episcopal funeral service for Sunday morning at their country house. Gideon Welles rode out to the funeral in a carriage with Lincoln and Seward and Seward's daughter Fanny. (Seward's wife, Frances, was at home, in upstate New York, where she remained for most of the war years.) Welles described the Stanton summer house as "a fine old place on the high hills between Tenally Town and the River." Lincoln and almost all the cabinet were at the funeral, along with "some twenty or thirty others, all . . . officers of the Army, or of the War Department." After the funeral service, Stanton and the family went with the coffin to the Oak Hill Cemetery in Georgetown, where they laid the child to rest.[5]

Death dealt a second blow to Stanton three weeks later, on August 1, when his sister Oella died at Urbana, Ohio. Stanton sent a telegram to his brother-in-law, Oella's second husband, saying, "I should start immediately for Urbana but the President declines to release me in the present state of affairs." This was probably not true; Lincoln probably would have urged Stanton to go to Ohio for his sister's funeral. It was probably Stanton, not Lincoln, who believed he could not leave Washington "in the present state of affairs." Stanton and Wolcott sent several messages from the War Department telegraph office so that other family members could travel by train and meet in Urbana in time for the funeral. Of the seven children born to Stanton's parents, three had died as infants or toddlers, two (Darwin and Oella) had died as adults, and only two (Edwin and Pamphila) now remained. Stanton would provide financial support for Oella's children as well as those of Darwin.[6]

On the same Sunday that Stanton buried his son, McClellan was writing to his wife about Stanton, perhaps responding indirectly to Chandler, whom McClellan viewed as speaking for Stanton: "I think that he [Stanton] is the most unmitigated scoundrel I ever knew, heard or read of; I think that (& I do not wish to be irreverent) had he lived in the time of the Savior, Judas Iscariot would have remained a respected member of the fraternity of the Apostles, & that the magnificent treachery & rascality of E. M. Stanton would have caused Judas to have raised his arms in holy horror & unaffected wonder." McClellan added, "I *may* do the man an injustice—God grant that I may be wrong—for I hate to think that humanity *can* sink so low—but my opinion is just as I have told you."[7]

Lincoln and Stanton answered McClellan's Harrison's Landing letter indirectly rather than directly. On July 11 Stanton asked Halleck to come to Washington as soon as possible. The newspapers learned that Halleck was on his way, and some speculated that he would replace Stanton. The *Chicago Times* was "inclined to credit" the rumor that Halleck would become secretary of war, opining, "It is not possible that the President should fail to comprehend the necessity of the removal of Stanton." The *New York Herald* thought Gen. Nathaniel Banks would become secretary of war and Halleck the president's military adviser. Both were mistaken; when Halleck arrived in Washington, Lincoln announced that he had appointed him as general in chief of all the federal armies. Outraged that Halleck had been promoted over his head, that he would now have to report to Halleck, General McClellan wrote to his wife, "I cannot remain permanently in the army after this slight."[8]

Another indication that Lincoln and Stanton intended to fight a "harder war" came from General Pope, who in July proclaimed that he intended to attack; he mocked generals who relied upon defensive works and lines of retreat. Pope followed this pompous proclamation with two general orders, one directing his troops to "subsist upon the country," the other directing them to arrest and deport "all disloyal male citizens within their lines." Decades later, in a memoir, another general claimed that Pope told him the proclamation and orders were "drafted under the dictation" of Stanton to "condemn McClellan's policy of over-caution in military matters." Even if Stanton did not draft Pope's orders—and there is no evidence other than this memoir that he did—Stanton would have approved. They were similar to one of the first orders that Halleck issued as general in chief. "Take up all active sympathizers," he instructed Grant, "and either hold them as prisoners or put them beyond our lines. Handle that class without gloves, and take their property for public use."[9]

John Pope, the commander of the Army of Virginia, and a protégé of Stanton and a rival of McClellan.

McClellan and his friend Gen. Fitz-John Porter did not approve of Pope or his orders. McClellan wrote to his wife, "Stonewall Jackson is after [Pope] & the paltry young man who wanted to teach me the art of war will in less than a week either be in full retreat or badly whipped." Porter wrote from McClellan's headquarters to a friend in Washington, "I regret to see that Gen. Pope has not improved since his youth and has now written himself down, what the military world has long known, an Ass. His address to his troops will make him ridiculous in the eyes of military men abroad as well as at home, and will reflect no credit on Mr. Lincoln, who has just promoted him." The tension between McClellan and Porter, on the one hand, and Stanton and Pope, on the other, would only worsen.[10]

Before ending their session in July and escaping Washington for cooler climes, members of Congress passed two major laws to strengthen the war effort. The Second Confiscation Act created a new crime, engaging in rebellion against the United States, and fixed the punishment at ten years in prison and confiscation of property, including slaves. The act directed the president to use that property "and the proceeds thereof for the support of the army of the United States." Section 9 declared:

> All slaves of persons who shall hereafter be engaged in rebellion against the government of the United States, or who shall in any way give aid or comfort thereto, escaping from such persons and taking refuge within the lines of the army; and all slaves captured from such persons or deserted by them and coming under the control of the government of the United States; and all slaves of such persons found or being within any place occupied by rebel forces and afterwards occupied by forces of the United States, shall be deemed captives of war, and shall be forever free of their servitude, and not again held as slaves.

Perhaps, if Lincoln had never issued the Emancipation Proclamation, this section of the Confiscation Act would have eventually freed most of the slaves in the Confederacy, for in July 1862 most slaves were in places "occupied by rebel forces" that would eventually be "occupied by forces of the United States." There would have been countless questions, however, such as whether a particular slave's master had provided "aid or comfort" to the rebellion. Both proponents and opponents of the Confiscation Act saw it as a major blow against not only Southern but national slavery, and border state politicians pleaded with Lincoln to veto the bill. But after a last-minute amendment to address one of his concerns, Lincoln signed the bill into law. The *Chicago Tribune* rejoiced, thanking "Heaven for the patriotic persistence with which the friends of the Confiscation bill have clung to it through all the opposition that covert treason and unmanly fear excited against it." The new law, if "executed by officers whose hearts are in the work," would be "worth an army of two hundred thousand men."[11]

The Militia Act allowed the president to call state militias into federal service for nine months and, if the states did not provide enough men, allowed the president to draft men to meet the shortfalls. The act also authorized the president to "receive into the service of the United States, for the purpose of constructing entrenchments, or performing camp service, or any other labor, or any military or naval service for which they may be found competent, persons of African descent" and provided that blacks in military service would receive $10 a month, less a $3 clothing allowance. To encourage slaves to flee their rebel masters and work for the Union Army, the Militia Act promised that certain of their relatives would be freed from slavery. The *Brooklyn Evening Star* predicted that, as soon as Southern slaves learned that "service to the Union cause emancipates the wife, the child, and the decrepit old mother," there would "be a movement more dangerous to the rebellion than all the bristling bayonets and ironclad gunboats at the President's command." There were many detailed provisions in the act regarding the army, such as one that "fixed" the problem Seward and Stanton had faced and allowed immediate payment of $25 of federal bounty. These were the kinds of details that Senator Wilson, the main author of the Militia Act, could not have developed without help from Stanton, whom he was seeing almost daily.[12]

Henry Wilson, chairman of the Senate Military Affairs Committee, with whom Stanton spent time almost daily during the war years.

Four days after the Militia Act and the Confiscation Act passed, Lincoln and his cabinet discussed using blacks as laborers and soldiers in the army.

Stanton presented what Chase described as recent letters from General Hunter lamenting that he did not have the troops he needed in his department and requesting authority "to enlist all loyal persons without reference to complexion." The entire cabinet agreed that the army should use and pay blacks as military laborers, but there was a stark division as to whether blacks should also serve as soldiers. Stanton and Chase favored starting the process of enlisting blacks into the army, but Lincoln "was not prepared to decide the question" and "expressed himself as averse to arming negroes."[13]

On the next day, July 22, the cabinet had a far more momentous discussion. After some further talk about arming slaves, Lincoln pulled from his pocket and read to the cabinet a draft proclamation consisting of just three long sentences. The first sentence warned that unless Southerners ceased their rebellion they would suffer the penalties provided in the Confiscation Act. In the second sentence Lincoln said he would continue to urge Congress to pass legislation to compensate any border state that enacted a system for the gradual abolition of slavery. The purpose of such legislation was to restore "the constitutional relation" between the rebellious states and the federal government, which was the sole "object" for which the war was being fought. The third sentence was the key to the whole: "As a fit and necessary military measure for effecting this object, I, as Commander-in-Chief of the Army and Navy of the United States, do order and declare that on the first day of January in the year of Our Lord one thousand, eight hundred and sixty-three, all persons held as slaves within any state or states, wherein the constitutional authority of the United States shall not then be practically recognized, submitted to, and maintained, shall then, thenceforward, and forever, be free."[14]

Our best source on this cabinet discussion is a set of notes that Stanton took, on Executive Mansion note paper, now among the Stanton papers at the Library of Congress:

> The President proposes an order declaring that all slaves in states in rebellion on the——day of——. The Attorney General and Stanton are for its immediate promulgation. Seward against it; argues strongly in favor of cotton and foreign governments. Chase silent. Welles——. Seward argues—that foreign nations will intervene to prevent the abolition of slavery for the sake of cotton—argues in

a long speech against its immediate promulgation—wants to wait for troops—wants Halleck here—wants drum and fife and public spirit—we break up our relations with foreign nations and the production of cotton for sixty years. Chase thinks it a measure of great danger—and would lead to universal emancipation. The measure goes beyond anything I have recommended.

In his own notes, Chase claimed that he said he would give the measure his "cordial support" but advised that emancipation "could be much better and more quietly accomplished by allowing generals to organize and arm the slaves . . . and by directing the Commanders of Departments to proclaim emancipation within their Districts as soon as possible."[15]

Lincoln did not issue the proclamation immediately; he waited until September. Most histories blame Seward for this delay, believing that he persuaded Lincoln it would be better to issue the preliminary proclamation after military success rather than after several military failures. There are contemporary sources, however, that suggest others were involved in the decision to delay. Wolcott wrote home in late July that Lincoln had proposed to his cabinet a proclamation to free the slaves on January 1. "All the cabinet concurred save Seward who opposed, and Chase who doubted, saying 'it was a larger step than he ever contemplated!' We all plied him so vigorously, that he came round the next morning, but Seward had worked so industriously in the meantime that for the present at least, the golden moment has passed away, and Chase must be held responsible for delaying or defeating the greatest act of justice, statesmanship and civilization, of the last four thousand years." Adam Gurowski, by this time a confidante of Stanton, wrote in his diary in early August that

Mr. Lincoln was already raising up his hand to sign a stirring proclamation on the question of emancipation; that Stanton was upholding the President's arm that it might not grow weak in the performance of a sacred duty; that Chase, Bates and Welles joined Stanton; but that Messrs. Seward and Blair so firmly objected that the President's outstretched hand slowly began to fall back; that to precipitate the mortification Thurlow Weed was telegraphed; that Thurlow Weed presented to Mr. Lincoln the medusa-head of Irish riots against the emancipation of slaves in the South; that Mr. Lincoln's mind faltered . . . and that thus once more slavery was saved.[16]

Another document in the Stanton papers, a long letter from Francis Cutting, a New York lawyer and former Democratic member of Congress, summarized Stanton's thinking in 1862 and implicated Weed as the one who persuaded Lincoln to delay the proclamation. According to Cutting's account, when he visited Stanton on the morning of July 22, 1862, the secretary was keen for an immediate emancipation proclamation:

> You insisted that without slavery the Rebellion would not have occurred and as that was the cause of the most atrocious war recorded in history, and of the accompanying horrors, it ought to be finally extirpated and forever extinguished; that the continued existence of the system afforded the most forceful and effective aid to the Rebels; that large numbers of their slaves were used by them on their fortifications and military works, and as teamsters and otherwise, thus affording material relief and assistance to their troops . . . that many of our leading military men instead of striking telling blows against the enemy seemed rather to indulge in acts of complaisance and tolerance towards them such as the restoration to their masters or claimants of slaves who had sought protection within our lines, detaching troops to guard their property and other kindred neighborly acts; that the anti-slavery element had vastly increased in numbers since the attack on Fort Sumter, and we should have mainly to rely on it for future resources of men and money, and that the hopes and demands of this earnest and patriotic portion of the nation could not justly or wisely be ignored; that bold action was indispensable and that the emancipation of the slaves as a war measure, ought to be immediately proclaimed.

Stanton took Cutting to see Lincoln, with whom Cutting used similar arguments and who Cutting thought would issue a proclamation. The next morning, however, when Cutting encountered Weed at the Willard Hotel, he learned that Weed "had undone in the evening what [Cutting] had nearly accomplished in the morning; that after further reflection the President had decided to postpone the proclamation."[17]

Lincoln and Stanton did not wait long to use the power Congress handed them in the Militia Act. On August 4 Stanton issued an order demanding that the states provide to the federal government 300,000 militiamen to serve for nine months. This call for nine-month men was *in addition to* the July 1 call for three-year volunteers, although Stanton issued an order saying that each three-year volunteer would count as four nine-month men. The August 4 order provided that, if the states did not fulfill their quotas by August 15, the federal government would step in and draft to fill the deficiencies. This was an utterly unrealistic deadline, especially since the War Department did not communicate the state-by-state quotas until August 9. Almost every state governor, for one reason or another, asked Stanton for an extension of the deadline, promising that if they had just a little more time, they could raise volunteers and avoid a draft.[18]

There were rallies around the nation to encourage volunteers to step forward, including an immense rally on August 6 on the steps of the Capitol building, still under construction. Benjamin Brown French, the commissioner of public buildings, claimed that he had "never seen more persons assembled in front of the Capitol except at an inauguration, which it very much resembled." Lincoln and several cabinet members were there, but not Stanton, which was perhaps purposeful, for Lincoln used his short speech to discuss the dispute between Stanton and McClellan. Lincoln insisted that, working with both men, he knew that "these two gentlemen are not nearly so deep in the quarrel as some presuming to be their friends." (A voice cried out, "Good.") McClellan wanted to succeed, and Stanton wanted him to succeed, for if "the military commander in the field cannot be successful, not only the Secretary of War, but myself—for the time the master of them both—cannot but be failures." (There was "laughter and applause.") "General McClellan has sometimes asked for things that the Secretary of War did not give him. McClellan is not to blame for asking for what he wanted and needed, and the Secretary of War is not to blame for not giving what he had not to give." (There was more applause.) "[Stanton] withheld nothing from McClellan without my approbation, and I have withheld no one thing at any time in my power to give him." (There was "wild applause" and the call "Give him enough now.") McClellan was "a brave and able man, and I stand here, as justice requires me to do, to take upon myself what has been charged on the Secretary of War, as withholding from him." French was deeply impressed, writing in his diary that Lincoln was "one of the best men God ever created." Chase commented that Lincoln's speech, widely reprinted, "evinces his usual originality and sagacity."[19]

As Stanton worked with the governors to enlist more men, he continued to think about another possible source of volunteers: the black contrabands. In early August, at Halleck's invitation, the nation's foremost expert on military law, Professor Francis Lieber of the Columbia Law School, visited Washington and the War Department. Lieber was not just an academic expert; as a young man he fought in the Waterloo campaign and then in the Greek War of Independence. Stanton met Lieber and asked for his written opinion on several questions, including how best to use the escaped blacks reaching army camps. Lieber soon provided Stanton a long memorandum, arguing that the former slaves (for by reaching and joining the army they became legally free) should be organized into "armed working companies." These black companies should have white officers; they should be armed "and perfectly drilled"; and they should have uniforms "so that they are readily acknowledged as soldiers for whom we will demand the treatment of prisoners of war if captured." This meeting and memo would be the start of a long, productive relationship between Stanton and Lieber.[20]

Francis Lieber, the nation's leading expert on military law and the author of General Orders No. 100, Instructions for the Government of Armies of the United States in the Field, the summary of the laws of war. Lieber would become a friend and supporter of Stanton.

Not long thereafter, on August 25, Stanton issued an order to General Saxton in coastal Carolina: "In view of the small force under your command and the inability of the Government at this time to increase it, in order to guard the plantations and settlements occupied by the United States from invasion and to protect the inhabitants thereof from captivity and murder, you are also authorized to arm, uniform, equip, and receive into the service of the United States such number of volunteers of African descent as you may deem expedient, not exceeding 5,000." Stanton told Saxton that the black volunteers would receive the same pay and benefits as white volunteers. Stanton's order to Saxton is generally viewed as the first solid step toward enlisting blacks into the Union Army, a step he would follow up in many ways in the months to come. Peter Watson, Stanton's friend and assistant, was probably echoing Stanton when he described the Saxton order to a friend as the "one bright spot in the dark pages of the history of these times."[21]

Stanton may have issued his order to Saxton in part because of an Indian uprising in the West. On August 21 he received an urgent and desperate message from Alexander Ramsey, governor of Minnesota: "The Sioux Indians on our western border have risen, and are murdering men, women, and children." The headlines in the *New York Tribune* on August 23 reported "men, women, and children killed" and "their bodies horribly mutilated." Ramsey asked Stanton for permission to delay the draft, and when Stanton refused, Ramsey appealed directly to Lincoln, who equivocated. "Attend to the Indians," Lincoln wrote Ramsey on August 27. "If the draft cannot proceed, of course it will not proceed. Necessity knows no law. The government cannot extend the time." Soon there were similar reports of Indian uprisings from other states, including Nebraska and Kansas, suggesting coordination, perhaps even Southern coordination.[22]

Stanton wanted a senior general in the Northwest, and after Pope's disastrous defeat in late August at Second Bull Run, he had the general to send. On September 6 Lincoln and Stanton created a new Department of the Northwest and appointed Pope its first commander. In his cover letter, Stanton directed Pope to proceed at once to Minnesota and to "take such prompt and vigorous measures as shall quell the hostilities and afford peace, security, and protection to the people against Indian hostilities." Pope took Stanton at his word: one of his first orders when he arrived in Minnesota announced his purpose: "to exterminate the Sioux if I have the power to do so and even if it requires a campaign lasting the whole of next year."[23]

———

Stanton was involved in other campaigns at this time, against draft dodgers and Democratic editors. He had received on August 7 a message from Governor Richard Yates of Illinois reporting, "Large numbers of citizens are leaving this city [Chicago] to escape the draft." Yates asked for authority to declare martial law and to close down the *Chicago Times*, the city's leading Democratic newspaper, for "giving aid and comfort to the enemy." Stanton responded on August 8 with two ill-advised orders. Without citing any legal authority, he ordered that "no citizen liable to be drafted into the militia shall be allowed to go to a foreign country." This was a serious infringement on personal freedom, but the second section of the order was worse, for it declared that "any person liable to the draft who shall absent himself from his county or state before such draft" could be arrested and "placed on military duty for the term of the draft." The third section stated, "The writ of *habeas corpus* is hereby suspended in respect to all persons so arrested and detained, and in respect to all persons arrested for disloyal practices." (This was not the first Civil War suspension of the writ—Lincoln had suspended *habeas corpus* in certain areas in 1861—but as drafted Stanton's order was nationwide.) Perhaps realizing that his order was far too broad, Stanton himself penned an explanation, saying it was intended only to "compel every citizen of the United States subject to military duty to bear his share in supporting the Government." This explanation appeared in the newspapers but without any indication that it was an official interpretation.[24]

Both Republican and Democratic newspapers approved of Stanton's "draft evasion" order. The *Detroit Free Press*, a Democratic paper, reported on the "disgraceful conduct" of young men crossing from Detroit into Canada in order to avoid their military duty. The *Press* insisted that these were not Michigan men: "They are all from other states." The *New York Times*, a Republican paper, said that "all recognize the propriety of the objects to be obtained" by Stanton's order, but that a "literal construction of the second section of the order would put an end to all travel."

George Templeton Strong, a careful lawyer, was far harsher on Stanton's careless drafting. Strong wrote in his diary that the "preposterous order" about travel meant that when he visited Newport, Rhode Island, for the weekend, he "was liable to be arrested, carried to Fort Adams, and kept on military duty for nine months."[25]

George Templeton Strong, the New York lawyer and leader, whose detailed diary is one of the great records of the Civil War.

Stanton's second August 8 order was more important, for it "authorized and directed" both federal marshals and state officials to "arrest and imprison any person or persons who may be engaged, by act, speech, or writing, in discouraging volunteer enlistments, or in any way giving aid and comfort to the enemy, or in any other disloyal practice against the United States." After making such an arrest, the officers were directed to make "an immediate report" to a new War Department official, Judge Advocate Levi Turner, so that "such persons may be tried before a military commission." In other words, Stanton was elevating and generalizing Halleck's approach in Missouri, urging the arrest of any person in any state suspected of "giving aid and comfort to the enemy" or any other "disloyal practice," so that that person could be tried by a military commission composed of military officers.[26]

Stanton's order allowed, indeed encouraged, dozens of arbitrary arrests. Within days the federal marshal in Dubuque, Iowa, arrested Dennis Mahoney, a prominent Irish Catholic Democrat and editor of the outspoken *Dubuque Herald*. Military officers transferred Mahoney to the Old Capitol Prison, where he remained under arrest for weeks. John Hughes, the Catholic archbishop of New York, sent a letter to his friend Secretary of State Seward, saying that he had known Mahoney for thirty years and that "he is not a traitor, though he may have been foolish." To highlight Mahoney's plight, Iowa Democrats nominated him to represent his district in Congress. As best we can tell, Stanton did not comment on Mahoney's arrest or imprisonment, but he also did not order his release until after the election, when Mahoney was finally permitted to return to his home and his newspaper. Mahoney retaliated by writing a book, *The Prisoner of State*, and dedicating it to Stanton.[27]

In Harrisburg, Pennsylvania, the rabidly racist *Harrisburg Patriot and Union* published a fake "recruiting poster" for a black regiment. The purpose of the poster, it seems, was to discourage white volunteers by showing they would serve alongside blacks. Stanton sent his protégé Gen. James Wadsworth to arrest the publishers and editors, and four men were soon prisoners in Fort McHenry. Two weeks passed, and Stanton received an inquiry about when the prisoners would be tried. He prepared the answer himself: "The editors of the *Patriot* will be tried as soon as officers can be spared from the field to organize a military commission." This may have prompted Wadsworth and Turner to summon the four prisoners that same Friday evening; when the prisoners promised not to discourage enlistment, they were released. Upon their return to Harrisburg, the former prisoners were greeted by large crowds, which the *Patriot and Union* claimed proved that the people condemned "a power which assumes the right of dragging men from their homes on the mere information or instigation of irresponsible parties, and denying them the right to trial by jury, or the inestimable benefits of the writ of *habeas corpus*." There would be, the editors predicted, a reaction "expressed at the ballot-box in October."[28]

In late August, Charles Ingersoll, a leading Philadelphia Democrat, gave a fiery speech to a large rally. The Lincoln administration, he declared, had "raised the largest sums of money and applied them to the worst purposes of any government that ever disgraced power." He added that one would have to "go to the older regions of Asia to find as much corruption as exists in the government of Lincoln." The provost marshal promptly arrested Ingersoll under Stanton's order against discouraging enlistments. Ingersoll, represented by some of Philadelphia's leading lawyers, sought release through a *habeas corpus* petition to Federal District Judge John Cadwalader, who promptly issued an order directing those holding Ingersoll to "show cause" why he should not be released. The local federal district attorney sent a telegram to warn Stanton that Cadwalader would probably order Ingersoll's release and that the judge would "not recognize the suspension in your order." Stanton immediately ordered the release of Ingersoll, thereby avoiding a ruling by a respected judge that he had no authority to suspend *habeas corpus*.[29]

Mark Neely, in his study of this period, found that from August 8 through September 8, Stanton's order led to the arrest of at least 354 men and women across the North. In one sense, it is unfair to call these Stanton's arrests because he rarely gave an arrest order himself but instead reacted to arrests by state and local officials. In another sense, the press was right to blame Stanton, for local officials made these arrests because of his August 8 order. Most of those arrested were young men accused of leaving their state or the nation in order to avoid the draft. Some, however, were editors or politicians arrested merely because of what they said rather than anything they did. Neely selected September 8 as the "end point" for this count because on that day Judge Advocate Turner (no doubt with Stanton's approval) ordered that there should be no further arrests without a specific arrest order from Washington or similar specific order by the military commander or governor of a state. Turner's order also ended all restrictions on travel. This was not the end of military arrests of Northern civilians, as we shall see, but it was the end of one phase, a period Neely rightly called "a low tide for liberty" in the United States.[30]

Even as Stanton was dealing with governors and arresting editors, he was also dealing, through Halleck, with McClellan and Pope. When Halleck had first arrived in Washington, on July 23, he spent several hours with Lincoln and Stanton, and for a while they were joined by Generals Pope and Burnside. Lincoln and Stanton told Halleck that their main concern was McClellan, still sitting behind his defensive works on the James River, still claiming that he could capture Richmond if only Washington would send him thousands of reinforcements. Lincoln and Stanton sent Halleck and Burnside by steamboat to confer with McClellan and his officers. When pressed for his plans, McClellan told Halleck that he was thinking about shifting his army to the south side of the James River and attacking Petersburg. Halleck was alarmed; if (as McClellan insisted) Lee really had 200,000 men in his army, then the first priority was to move McClellan's army north so that it could join Pope's army in defending Washington. Halleck was known as "Old Brains" because he was an expert on military strategy and tactics, and McClellan's plan seemed to him to violate the most basic principles, for it divided the Northern force and exposed it to sequential attacks by Lee's larger force. By the end of their discussion, Halleck reported to Stanton, McClellan "largely agreed" that his Petersburg plan was impractical. McClellan insisted, however, that with 30,000 more troops he could attack Richmond on the north side of the James with "a good chance of success." Halleck told him that, at most, Washington could provide him another 20,000, and returned without a resolution. Stanton heard not only from Halleck but also from Burnside, who heard suggestions from McClellan's officers that they were thinking about marching on Washington to take control of the government from the civilians.[31]

After consulting Lincoln and Stanton, Halleck on August 3 ordered McClellan to transfer his entire army as soon as possible to Aquia Creek, where Pope and his army were based. McClellan protested and asked that Lincoln, Stanton, and Halleck reconsider their decision: "I am convinced that to withdraw this Army to Aquia Creek will prove disastrous in the extreme to our cause—I fear it will be a fatal blow." He argued, again, "All points of secondary importance elsewhere should be abandoned & every available man brought here—a decided victory here and the military strength of the rebellion is crushed."[32]

Hoping that Lincoln would change his mind, hoping perhaps that he could mount a small attack toward Richmond, McClellan took his time in moving his troops to the transport ships and then moving them by water to Aquia. Lee, sensing the situation, moved his own army north to attack Pope before he could be strengthened by McClellan. On August 26 Gen. Stonewall Jackson and his rebel army attacked and captured the rail junction at Manassas. Halleck now instructed McClellan to send troops as fast as possible to aid Pope, but McClellan still stalled. On August 29, with Pope under intense attack in the Second Battle of Bull Run, an attack one could hear in Washington, Lincoln asked McClellan what news he heard from the battlefield. McClellan responded from his Alexandria headquarters that his information from Manassas was not reliable. "I am clear," he added airily, "that one of two courses should be adopted: first, to concentrate all our available forces to open communication with Pope; second, to leave Pope to get out of his scrape and at once use all our means to make the capital perfectly safe." Lincoln's response to McClellan was mild, urging him to support Pope. In private, however, with his secretary Hay, Lincoln was outraged, saying that it "really seemed to him that McClellan wanted Pope defeated." Pope was defeated, badly, with more than 14,000 Northerners dead, wounded, or missing, the highest numbers for any eastern battle to date.[33]

Stanton now requested a formal opinion from Halleck: Had McClellan obeyed the August 3 order to send his troops from the Peninsula to Aquia? Halleck responded on August 30, that "the order was not obeyed with the promptness I expected and the national safety, in my opinion, required." With Halleck's letter in hand, Stanton drafted a joint letter from the cabinet to Lincoln, demanding McClellan's removal. "The undersigned feel compelled by a profound sense of duty to the government and the people of the United States, and to yourself as your constitutional advisers, respectfully to recommend the immediate removal of George B. McClellan from any command in the armies of the United States." Stanton continued: "We are unwilling to be accessory to the waste of national resources, the protraction of the war, the destruction of our armies, and the imperiling of the Union and the Government itself which we believe must result from the continuance of George B. McClellan in command." Stanton's wording—"unwilling to be accessory"—strongly suggested that he and others in the cabinet would resign if Lincoln kept McClellan. Stanton signed the document, and Chase and Interior Secretary Caleb Smith signed as well, but Welles refused to sign. He explained (as he related in his diary) that he disliked the way Stanton and Chase were working; there should be a cabinet discussion, not a paper presented seriatim for signature.[34]

Stanton did not have much news on this Saturday from Pope, fighting only thirty miles away at Manassas. But Stanton was worried about the wounded, telling Quartermaster General Meigs, "We have some 8000 patients spread over the field . . . [and a] still greater number of rebels are lying there." He ordered Meigs to send out to the battlefield "all the ambulances in the City & a corps of volunteers from this department." He also sent word to Philadelphia and New York, requesting volunteer surgeons and nurses, a request he soon regretted, for a thousand volunteers arrived, far more than were needed. In the evening he and his wife hosted Lincoln and Hay for dinner. Hay described it as a "pleasant little dinner" with "a pretty wife as white and cold and motionless as marble, whose rare smiles seemed to pain her." Stanton was "unqualifiedly severe upon McClellan" at this dinner, saying that "nothing but foul play could lose us this battle & that it rested with McClellan & his friends." In other words, based on the limited information he had, Stanton believed that Pope was winning or at least drawing the ongoing struggle against Lee.[35]

Later that evening Welles visited the War Department for news, and Stanton talked with him at length about McClellan. Stanton reviewed the whole history of the previous few months: how McClellan had insisted on going to the Peninsula rather than fighting at or near Manassas; how Lincoln had provided McClellan with additional troops over Stanton's objection; how McClellan had stalled and complained about "bad roads, and water, and swamps." More recently, Stanton alleged, McClellan had tried his best to see that Pope was defeated; he no doubt quoted to Welles the "get out of his scrape" message. Welles told Stanton that, while he might agree with all he said about and against McClellan, he considered Stanton's proposed letter "discourteous and disrespectful to the President." At this Stanton nearly exploded. "He knew of no particular obligation he was under to the President who had called him to a difficult position and imposed upon him labors and responsibilities which no man could carry, and which were greatly increased by fastening upon him a commander who was constantly striving to embarrass him. He could not and would not submit to a continuance of this state of things." If Welles captured Stanton's words, Stanton was threatening to resign.[36]

The next morning, a gray Sunday, there was grim news from Pope. As Lincoln told Hay, "We are whipped again, I am afraid." Stanton released to the press both Pope's official report (in which he admitted that he had lost at least 8,000 men but claimed the enemy had lost twice as many) and a short note at day's end, saying, "There has been little if any fighting today." Lincoln conferred with Halleck, but not with Stanton, and decided to ask McClellan to take charge of the defense of Washington. Stanton and his cabinet colleagues, not aware of Lincoln's decision, continued work on their joint letter. Attorney General Bates prepared a new draft, which Stanton, Chase, Smith, and he signed. Welles, however, again declined to sign, insisting that this way "of combining to influence or control the President was not right." Lincoln and McClellan met that night, and Lincoln asked him to take charge of all the armies in and around Washington. McClellan wrote to his wife at midnight, "I have reluctantly consented to take command here & try to save the Capital—I don't know whether I can do it or not, for things are far gone—I hope I shall succeed."[37]

At about eight on Monday morning Stanton and Halleck received a message at the War Department from Pope: "Unless something can be done to restore the tone of this army it will melt away before you know it." Halleck responded, "General McClellan has charge of all the defenses, and you will consider any direction . . . given by him as coming from me." So by early on the morning of September 2, if not earlier, Stanton knew that instead of removing McClellan, Lincoln was putting him in command again.[38]

There are three diary accounts of the cabinet meeting that followed, and they differ in some key respects. According to Welles, the cabinet met at noon, but Lincoln stepped out for a few minutes, during which Stanton told his stunned colleagues that Lincoln had put McClellan in charge of the Washington defenses. When Lincoln returned, he tried to defend his decision: "McClellan knows this whole ground—his specialty is to defend—is a good engineer all admit—there is no better organizer—and he can be trusted to act on the defensive." Welles wrote, "There was a more disturbed and desponding feeling than I have ever witnessed in council and the President was extremely distressed." According to Chase, it was Lincoln and not Stanton who informed the cabinet that he had restored McClellan. Stanton made it clear that he had no role in the order, and Chase protested that giving McClellan command "was the equivalent of giving Washington to the rebels." Lincoln "said it distressed him exceedingly to find himself differing on such a point from the Secretary of War and the Secretary of the Treasury; that he would gladly resign his place, but he could not see who could do the work as well as McClellan." According to Bates, the joint letter was at some point presented to Lincoln, who was "in deep distress." Bates noted that Lincoln was "manifestly alarmed for the safety of the city," saying that "Pope's army was utterly demoralized" and that if the troops fled into the capital "as *a mob*, the City would be overrun by the enemy in 48 hours." Bates believed Lincoln was relying too much on Halleck ("who I think is cowed") and that the army should be able to defend Washington "against all the power of the enemy."[39]

Surely Stanton considered resigning his position just after this contentious cabinet meeting. Why didn't he follow through on his threats? Part of the answer is that Washington was in danger, with the rebel army only a few miles away and the federal army in disarray, so it was not the time for anyone, much less the secretary of war, to resign. Also, whatever Stanton may have said to Welles in a moment of anger, he was in fact loyal to Lincoln. A third point is that Stanton was once again under pressure to resign, and pressure only made him stubborn. Cornelius Agnew, one of Stanton's critics, wrote from Washington on September 2 to Manton Marble, editor of the *New York World*, that this was the moment to force Stanton's resignation. "McClellan can do nothing if Stanton rules in the War Department," Agnew wrote, and unless Stanton was removed "our national life is done." Stanton did not know about Agnew's letter, but he read the newspapers, including the *New York World*. On September 4 the *World* stated that Stanton, "not content with thus wasting the millions of our treasure and watering all the hills of Virginia with the fruitless blood of our bravest and best," was now showing "the bold, audacious cruelty of a despot, and fills the cells of a Bastille with guiltless loyal men." Other papers also reported that Stanton would resign. Such articles helped persuade him to stay.[40]

Many authors have claimed that Stanton was alarmed or even

panicked on this Tuesday, September 2. He reportedly ordered that the arsenal send all guns and supplies to New York, that his department staff gather up papers so they "could be carried by men on foot or on horse-back," and that "a steamer be anchored in the Potomac to whisk away the President and his cabinet." The sources for these secondary accounts, however, are mainly memoirs, most of them by McClellan men. There is nothing in the newspapers or letters of September 1862 about Stan-ton packing up his office or ordering a steamboat to stand ready. Indeed the *National Republican* declared, "No well-informed person here enter-tains the slightest fear for the safety of the capital, or the slightest doubt that this rebel attempt . . . will be a failure." There is a short message from McClellan to Halleck, saying that he heard from the head of the arsenal that Stanton had ordered him "to ship everything to New York." Halleck's response was that fifty or sixty thousand stand of arms, along with most of the artillery, would remain in Washington. There is also a message from McClellan (not Stanton) to Lincoln, suggesting that naval ships should "be ordered to the Potomac to ensure our water commu-nication." Stanton's few surviving messages from September 2 do not sound alarmed; he wrote, for example, to General Butler in New Orleans to forward the complaints of some diplomats there; over the months that Butler was in charge in New Orleans there were many, many complaints about his administration.[41]

Benjamin Butler, one of Lincoln's political generals, would become a member of Congress and an ally of Stanton during the Johnson years.

General Lee did not intend to attack Washington; Stanton and Halleck sensed his intentions as early as September 3, when Halleck wrote to McClellan, "There is every probability that the enemy, baffled in his intended capture of Washington, will cross the Potomac, and make a raid into Maryland or Pennsylvania." Halleck directed McClellan to organize, "immediately," a "moveable army" in order "to meet him again in the field." Stanton, it seems, hoped that Halleck himself would lead such an army, for on this same day he ordered Halleck in Lincoln's name "to organize an army for active operations." But this was never Halleck's concept of his role as general in chief; he viewed himself as a Washington staff officer, not a field general, and so it was McClellan who started to give the orders to counter Lee's anticipated march into Maryland.[42]

On September 5, after consulting with Lincoln, and perhaps with Stanton, Halleck issued orders to remove five generals from their commands: Fitz-John Porter, William Franklin, Charles Griffin, John Pope, and Irvin McDowell. Porter, Franklin, and Griffin were trusted friends of McClellan, but they were to face a court of inquiry to determine whether they had disregarded Pope's orders. Pope was relieved because the armies of the Potomac and Virginia were consolidated under McClellan. Pope protested to Stanton, asking whether he was to lose his army "because of the treachery of McClellan and his tools." But there was nothing Stanton could do for Pope at this point. Indeed a few days later, when McClellan wrote Halleck to insist that he needed Porter, Franklin, and Griffin in their posts in the current campaign, he claimed that Stanton said he would "cheerfully agree to anything of this kind." Because of the crisis, and the power the crisis gave McClellan, the three generals remained in their places, at least for the time being, at McClellan's right hand.[43]

By September 6 McClellan's army was marching out of Washington, heading north and west toward Rockville and the invading rebel forces. Welles noted in his diary that 20,000 or 30,000 men marched by his house on that day, and by the house of McClellan, whom they cheered, but not by the White House. On September 10 McClellan reported that General Lee and his army, which McClellan estimated at more than 120,000 men, were at or near Frederick, Maryland. (In fact Lee had only about 55,000 men.) Stanton was receiving almost daily urgent messages from Andrew Curtin, governor of Pennsylvania, asking for federal troops, asking for state control of the federal troops at Carlisle, asking whether the federal government would provide the equipment if he called all the state militia into immediate service. On September 11 Chase attended a meeting at the War Department to consider Curtin's request. Stanton said that Curtin's proposal was "too large to be entertained" and that "the arms for a general arming could not be furnished." Chase questioned Halleck about Lee's plans. Halleck thought that Lee would "rest, recruit, get supplies, augment force," and then "strike the safest and most effectual blow he can—at Washington, Baltimore, or Philadelphia."[44]

As Lee marched deeper into Maryland, the papers debated whether Lincoln should retain Stanton. The *New York World* called Stanton "mercurial, impatient, vain, pragmatical, officious, meddlesome, incapable of comprehending system or principle, and having no idea of progress." He was "an absolute ignoramus in military science," and his interference in campaigns had resulted in "overwhelming disaster." Stanton then "commenced to play the censor of northern loyalty," and "arbitrary arrests were multiplied until no man felt himself safe." The *National Republican* responded on September 15 by praising Stanton's "wisdom, patriotism, and courage" and declaring that the people would not allow Southern-sympathizing papers "to dictate who shall be Secretary of War." Chase sent this article to Horace Greeley, editor of the *New York Tribune*, with a note saying, "Stanton's voice has ever been on the side of the most vigorous and active employment of all our resources, moral & political, as well as physical." Greeley would have understood that, when Chase said Stanton favored using "all our resources," he meant black as well as white soldiers.[45]

Two of Stanton's cabinet colleagues also believed Lincoln should remove Stanton. Montgomery Blair asked Gideon Welles to help him "get this black terrier out of his kennel." Blair asserted that Stanton was dishonest, indeed that he had taken a bribe. In a long diary entry, Welles wrote that he thought Blair, who hated Stanton blindly, "may fail to allow him qualities he really possesses." He added, "Stanton is no favorite of mine. But he has energy and application." Welles doubted Stanton's sincerity and wrote that he was "impulsive not administrative—has quickness—rashness when he has nothing to fear—is more violent than vigorous—more demonstrative than discriminating—more vain than wise is arrogant and domineering towards those in subordinate positions if they will submit to his insolence—but a sycophant and an intriguer in his conduct and language with those whom he fears." But Welles insisted that he would not join Blair in a "movement against a cabinet colleague."[46]

Montgomery Blair, the postmaster general and a member of the powerful Blair family, hated Stanton and hoped Lincoln would remove him from the cabinet.

The most important person, President Lincoln, wanted to keep Secretary Stanton. August Belmont, the New York publisher and financier, in the course of a long letter to Lincoln, advised him, "New vigor and energy would be infused into our military operations, and the exhausted ranks of our army would be speedily filled, if you would place General Halleck at the head of the Department as Secretary of War, and appoint General McClellan commander-in-chief of the United States forces east of the Allegheny mountains." Stanton somehow heard about Belmont's letter and asked Lincoln about it. Lincoln sent Stanton the relevant passage and offered to let him read the whole Belmont letter. Lincoln signed his note to Stanton "yours as ever." Lincoln knew Stanton had his faults— he would have noticed what Welles noticed—but he also saw Stanton's hard work, and his virtues, and wanted to keep him.[47]

On September 17, 1862, starting at dawn and continuing through dusk, McClellan and the Army of the Potomac fought Lee and the Army of Northern Virginia along Antietam Creek, near Sharpsburg, Maryland. By the end of the day, more than 2,500 Northerners and more than 1,500 Southerners were dead, and more than 15,000 men were wounded. It was the bloodiest single day of the Civil War, indeed of any war in American history. On this day, and for several days thereafter, Stanton knew almost nothing about the battle. A message from McClellan to Halleck arrived in the afternoon, saying, "We are in the midst of the most terrible battle of the war, perhaps of history—thus far it looks well but I have great odds against me. Hurry up all the troops possible. Our loss has been terrific, but we have gained much ground." Stanton apparently sent a brief message to Seward at about this time: "Heavy battle now going on." A message from McClellan's staff arrived in Washington at about ten that night, asking for ammunition. Here at last was something for Stanton and his staff to do; they gathered up the requested ammunition and organized a special train. At midnight Stanton sent a message to the railroad officials, saying that the train must "run through at the fastest possible speed" because McClellan would need the supplies for "the battle to be fought tomorrow."[48]

There was another brief message from McClellan the next morning, reporting, "Our losses very heavy, especially in general officers. The battle will probably be renewed today." A few hours later, there was a message from Harrisburg: "McClellan granted armistice to bury dead." This was correct: neither side attacked on this day, and the "burial details began their grim work." On the morning of September 19 McClellan reported, "Little occurred yesterday except skirmishing, being fully occupied in replenishing ammunition, taking care of the wounded, etc. Last night the enemy abandoned his position, leaving his dead and wounded on the field. We are again in pursuit." But McClellan was not "in pursuit"—he was simply allowing Lee to retreat across the Potomac. At noon McClellan wrote Halleck, "The enemy is driven back into Virginia. Maryland and Pennsylvania are now safe." As McClellan no doubt intended, the department shared his messages with the newspapers, which published them the next day.[49]

McClellan now expected that he could dictate to Lincoln about the

War Department. He wrote to his wife on the morning of September 20, "I have insisted that Stanton shall be removed, & that Halleck shall give way to me as Commander in Chief. I will *not* serve under him—for he is an incompetent fool—in no way fit for the important place he holds." In a second letter, that evening, he was even more pointed: "I have taken the stand that Stanton must leave & that Halleck must restore my old place to me. Unless these two conditions are fulfilled I will leave the service." Lincoln was thinking in quite another way.[50]

On September 22 Lincoln called his cabinet members to a special meeting at noon. He started with a humorous story, reading from a new book by Artemus Ward. Chase noted that the whole cabinet laughed except "of course" for Stanton. Lincoln then turned serious and reminded the men of their July discussion about emancipation. He had decided that the time to issue the preliminary proclamation was now. "When the rebel army was at Frederick, I determined, as soon as it should be driven out of Maryland, to issue a Proclamation of Emancipation such as I thought most likely to be useful. I said nothing to any one; but I made the promise to myself, and (hesitating a little) to my Maker. The rebel army is now driven out, and I am going to fulfill that promise." He did not want to debate *whether* to issue the proclamation but was quite happy to discuss the *wording* of the document. He then read his draft aloud. Seward suggested a few minor changes, which were accepted. Neither Chase nor Welles mentioned in their diaries that Stanton said anything, but Welles would later write that Stanton "made a very emphatic speech sustaining the measure," saying that "the act was so important, and involved consequences so vast, that he hoped each member would give . . . his own individual opinion, whatever that opinion might be." Lincoln issued the proclamation later the same day, declaring that slaves in any states or parts of states still in rebellion on January 1, 1863, would be "forever free." He pledged that the government, "including the military and naval authority thereof, will recognize and maintain the freedom of such persons, and will do no act or acts to repress such persons, or any of them, in any efforts they may make for their actual freedom." And, still hoping to encourage Southern loyalists, he promised that those who "remained loyal" to the United States throughout the rebellion would, at its conclusion, be "compensated for all acts of the United States, including the loss of slaves."[51]

BREAKING THAT "BACKBONE."

"Breaking That Backbone." McClellan and Halleck try to break the backbone of rebellion, but Lincoln tells Stanton that the tool they need is the ax over his shoulder, the Emancipation Proclamation.

The nation was astounded by the preliminary proclamation. The *New York Tribune* declared that this was "the beginning of the end of the rebellion; the beginning of the new life of the nation. God bless Abraham Lincoln!" The *New York Times* said, "There has been no more far reaching document ever issued since the foundation of this Government." The *Albany Evening Journal* of New York went even further, calling the proclamation "the most solemn and momentous declaration the world ever witnessed." Democrats were horrified. The *Harrisburg Patriot & Union*, the paper whose editors and publishers Stanton had arrested, called the Emancipation Proclamation "an outrage upon the humanity and good sense of the country, to say nothing of its gross unconstitutionality." The *Patriot* predicted that Lincoln's proclamation would lead blacks to "massacre white men, women and children till their hands are smeared and their appetites glutted with blood." The *Louisville Journal* called the proclamation "wholly unauthorized and wholly pernicious" and declared, "Kentucky cannot and will not acquiesce in this measure. Never!" Confederates reacted with anger and fear and outrage. A Confederate congressional committee asserted, "This conflict has ceased to be a war as recognized among civilized nations, but on the part of the enemy has become an invasion of an organized horde of murderers and plunderers . . . determined if possible to exterminate the loyal population of these States, to transfer their property to their enemies, and to emancipate their slaves, with the atrocious design of adding servile insurrection and the massacre of families to the calamities of war."[52]

We remember and celebrate the preliminary emancipation proclamation. We tend to forget another proclamation that Lincoln issued just two days later, imposing martial law throughout the nation: "All persons discouraging volunteer enlistments, resisting militia drafts, or guilty of any disloyal practice, affording aid and comfort to the rebels against the authority of the United States, shall be subject to martial law and liable to trial and punishment by Courts Martial or Military Commissions." This proclamation also suspended the writ of *habeas corpus* for anyone arrested or imprisoned by the military authorities. In other words, Lincoln authorized Stanton and other military officials to arrest and imprison anyone whom they believed was "affording aid and comfort to the rebels," and he authorized military rather than civil trials of those so imprisoned. Those accused, arrested, imprisoned, and charged would not have a civilian's constitutional rights, such as the right to a jury trial or the right to confront their accusers; they would be tried in military courts by military officers following military procedures. In one sense, Lincoln's martial law proclamation did not make much difference; arrests and military trials were already in progress under Stanton's August 8 order and indeed under prior orders. In another sense, though, Lincoln's order was momentous, for it confirmed that the military arrests were not just Stanton's policy; they were *Lincoln's policy*.[53]

Lincoln issued these two proclamations during an unusual election. Americans had voted in the midst of wars in 1812 and again in 1846. But never before had Americans gone to the polls during a rebellion, in a campaign in which one party (the Republicans) accused the other party (the Democrats) of aiding and abetting the enemy. Republicans called Democrats "Copperheads," poisonous snakes, and depicted Copperheads attacking Lady Liberty. Democrats responded by wrapping themselves in the Constitution, by denouncing the arbitrary military arrests. The *New*

York World, for example, watched "with dismay and unspeakable shame" the administration's "abuse of its power of arrest" and argued, "There is no such thing as either justifying or extenuating its conduct in this particular. Every principle of American liberty, every regard for the loyal cause, every sentiment of justice, every impulse of manhood, cries out against it." The *Ohio Statesmen*, on the eve of the Ohio election, proclaimed, "Let all men who are in favor of the Union as it was, and the Constitution as it is, vote the Democratic ticket. . . . Let all men who are opposed to the establishment of a military despotism, vote the Democratic ticket. . . . Let all men who are opposed to making slaves of white men for the purpose of making 'freemen' of negroes, vote the Democratic ticket."[54]

Although military arrests by Stanton and the War Department were a central issue in the fall elections, Stanton himself was not much involved in these elections, except through an error in Illinois. On September 18, the day after the battle of Antietam, he received an urgent message from Gen. James Tuttle, in charge at Cairo, Illinois, at the junction of the Ohio and Mississippi rivers. Tuttle reported that General Grant was sending north to Cairo many black refugees, women and children, and Tuttle asked if he could turn the contrabands over to a charitable committee, to move them farther north in Illinois, so they could find work. Stanton agreed and authorized Tuttle "to provide transportation at government expense." Democratic papers soon denounced the "plague" of black refugees, and Stanton's former classmate and Lincoln's former campaign manager, Judge David Davis, wrote to Lincoln, "The spreading of negroes from Cairo, through the central portion of Illinois, will work great harm in the coming election." Even before Lincoln received this letter, Stanton had reversed himself, sending an order to Tuttle on October 13: "You will please send no more contrabands or colored persons to Illinois until further order." Democratic papers now charged that, as soon as the election was over, Stanton would issue new instructions to Tuttle, and "the floodgates reopened the black stream [will] flow over the state." Stanton's order, and the intense reaction, was a key issue in the Illinois election, in which Democrats regained control of the state legislature.[55]

More generally Democrats did well in the 1862 fall elections, capturing several governorships, including the most important one, New York, where former governor Horatio Seymour defeated Stanton's protégé

James Wadsworth. Democrats also increased their share of the House of Representatives by thirty-four representatives. George Templeton Strong, reflecting on these results, thought the voters were sending a message to Washington: "Messrs. Lincoln, Seward, Stanton & Co., you have done your work badly, so far. You are humbugs. My business is stopped, I have got taxes to pay, my wife's third cousin was killed on the Chickahominy, and the war is no nearer an end than it was a year ago. I am disgusted with you and your party and shall vote for the governor or congressman you disapprove, just to spite you."[56]

While voters were heading to the polls, General McClellan and his Army of the Potomac were not heading anywhere. McClellan remained in Maryland, resting and resupplying his army, not recrossing the Potomac into Virginia. Lincoln pleaded with him, and Halleck ordered him, but McClellan would not move. Soon some newspapers had an explanation. The *New York Herald* reported on October 23 that "McClellan is anxious to advance" but was delayed by lack of supplies from Washington. "Stanton should understand that his responsibilities in this business involve the life or death of the nation" and should "see to it that all the necessities of our Army of the Potomac are supplied at once." The *New York Tribune*, probably on information from Stanton, responded the next day that the *Herald*'s report was "utterly without foundation." The *Tribune* reported that Quartermaster General Meigs assured Stanton, "Every requisition from the army under Gen. McClellan has been immediately answered." The issue did not die, and Stanton asked Halleck to review the records. Halleck reported to Stanton that, as best he could determine, the War Department had provided McClellan with the supplies he needed. Indeed Halleck opined, "No armies in the world, while on campaign, have been more promptly or better supplied than ours." Some believed Lincoln wanted to remove McClellan but was waiting until after the elections on November 4 because he did not want to strengthen Democrats. Stanton thought Lincoln should act at once, telling Chase that if Lincoln would just show some firmness by removing McClellan, he would "paralyze the opponents & invigorate the friends of the Administration."[57]

Lincoln waited, issuing the orders on the day after the election to relieve McClellan and appoint Burnside commander of the Army of the Potomac. Stanton was worried that McClellan, or more likely his officers, might resist the orders, so he took the precaution of using a general as his messenger, Catharinus Buckingham. Stanton instructed Buckingham to take Burnside with him to deliver the orders personally to McClellan and to let him (Stanton) know if there was any resistance. There was none: McClellan handed over control to Burnside, issued a grandiose farewell proclamation to the Army of the Potomac, and moved to New York, where he was soon the leading if unofficial Democratic candidate for president.[58]

Gen. Ambrose Burnside was both like and unlike Gen. George McClellan. They were both young, both graduates of West Point (McClellan in 1846 and Burnside in 1847), both veterans of the Mexican-American War, both with civilian as well as military experience. McClellan's neat trim mustache, his rigid posture, his perpetually pressed uniform showed his reserved, cautious character. The exuberant whiskers on the sides of Burnside's face, from which we have the term "sideburns," expressed his warm, gregarious, impulsive nature. Within days of his appointment, Burnside decided to head straight for Richmond, through Fredericksburg. His plans were no secret: the *Brooklyn Daily Eagle* reported on November 18 that Burnside and his army were nearing Fredericksburg and would march from there "on to Richmond again." When he reached Falmouth, however, just across the Rappahannock River from Fredericksburg, Burnside stalled, in part because he did not have the pontoon bridges he expected, in part because he was not the sort of general who could improvise. One of his generals, the irrepressible Joseph Hooker, wrote directly to Stanton on November 19 to say that he had asked Burnside to allow him to take his corps across the Rappahannock ten miles upstream from Fredericksburg. "This movement, made at once, will find the enemy unprepared, for they count on our delay." Burnside rejected Hooker's proposal, and Stanton did not respond to it.[59]

After weeks of delay—weeks that Lee used to gather forces and build defenses—Burnside attacked from Fredericksburg on Saturday, December 13. Thousands of federal soldiers charged across open ground toward entrenched and prepared rebels, who mowed them down from behind a solid stone wall. It was a massacre. The war correspondent of the *Cincinnati Commercial* reported that "we were weakened by the sheer waste of the bravest of the brave. We had, it appeared, made the attack at the strongest point of the enemy's lines, placed ourselves just as they wanted us, made a magnificent display of the devotion and discipline of our soldiers, in a manner that afforded the enemy the entertainment of looking on the display without much danger to themselves, and of slaughtering us without stint." Burnside did not report much or often to Washington on the day of or day after the battle, which was itself worrisome. Senator Fessenden wrote home on Sunday morning, "The best opinion here is that there has been terrible fighting & slaughter, with no decisive results." Burnside wanted to renew the attack on Sunday but was dissuaded by his generals and instead retreated across the Rappahannock. His brief report, that he was now back where he had started in Falmouth, reached the War Department at four in the morning of December 16. Soon the papers were reporting the details and listing the dead and wounded.[60]

Many blamed Stanton for the disaster at Fredericksburg. The *New York Herald* declared on December 16 that Burnside had failed for the same reason as McClellan: the War Department. If the department had provided pontoons in a timely way, Burnside "would have captured Fredericksburg without a struggle," and he "probably would have been in Richmond before now." The *Herald* urged Lincoln, "Lose no time in putting an end to a career of imbecility which is ruining the nation." The *New York World* agreed, calling Fredericksburg the "worst disaster of the war," a "slaughter which was fruitless," and blaming Stanton. The *Chicago Times* demanded, "Stanton must be dismissed and McClellan reinstated, because the Secretary has been always wrong and the General always right." George Templeton Strong described the "universal bitter wrath" against Stanton as "a deeper feeling more intensely uttered than any I ever saw prevailing here. Lincoln comes in for a share of it. Unless Stanton be speedily shelved, something will burst somewhere." Strong added that the "most thorough Republicans, the most loyal Administration men, express it most fiercely and seem to share the personal vindictiveness of men and women whose sons or brothers or friends have been uselessly sacrificed to the vanity of the political schemes of this meddling murderous quack."[61]

Stanton was under attack from another angle as well. John Hoffman, a Democratic judge in New York City, convened a state grand jury to consider charges against Stanton for illegal arrests. The *New York Herald* predicted on December 18 that the grand jury would indict Stanton for "false arrests and the imprisonment of certain citizens in Fort Lafayette." After the indictment, the new Democratic governor, Horatio Seymour, would demand that Lincoln hand over "Stanton to answer the charges against him." The *Herald* rubbed its hands, announcing, "There is a good time coming." Stanton's friend Charles Dana, still in New York but no longer an editor for the *New York Tribune,* warned him that Judge Hoffman was working with Abraham Oakey Hall, the nominally Republican district attorney, and Thurlow Weed, friend and mentor of Secretary Seward. "There is no doubt," Dana wrote, "that Weed & his special friends are going over to the regular Democracy"; that is, that they were going to join the Democratic Party, not the War Democrats who supported the Union Party. According to Dana, Weed had conspired to defeat Stanton's friend Wadsworth in the gubernatorial election and "*Seward was a party to the conspiracy.* They mean now to defeat the emancipation policy & for the sake of slavery they are willing to destroy the government."[62]

Stanton would thus have been worried when he heard that all the Republican senators were meeting behind closed doors to discuss the cabinet. At the first meeting, on December 16, Senator Morton Wilkinson of Minnesota called Seward the "source of all our difficulties and disasters" because he had "never believed in the war." Other senators agreed. Some must have been puzzled that the secretary of state rather than the secretary of war was being blamed for a military defeat, but it seems that none of the senators called for Stanton's removal. At a similar session the next day, Ira Harris of New York offered a resolution: "That in the judgment of the Republican members of the Senate, the public confidence in the present administration would be increased by a reconstruction of the Cabinet." John Sherman of Ohio argued against Harris's wording, which suggested that Lincoln should replace *all* the cabinet members; Sherman insisted that none of the senators wanted to see Chase resign. The senators then adopted a revised resolution, calling for *partial* change in the cabinet, and appointed a committee of nine to meet with Lincoln. At that meeting, on the evening of December 18, the senators argued in favor of "government by cabinet" rather than by the president alone, or by the president in consultation with one or two cabinet members, and they pressed Lincoln to accept the resignation letter Seward had submitted.[63]

Stanton probably learned about much of this as it happened, from his senatorial friends, including Fessenden and Sumner. Indeed Welles wrote in his diary that Blair believed "Stanton had been instrumental in getting up this movement against Seward to screen himself, and turn attention from the management of the War Department." On the morning of December 19, Lincoln summoned his cabinet, except Seward, to discuss the crisis. Welles described Lincoln as "shocked and grieved" by the way the Republican senators had attacked Seward, who had once been their Senate leader. Lincoln told his cabinet members that they had "sustained and consoled" him through the country's crises and that he was not prepared for "a total abandonment of old friends." Lincoln asked the cabinet members to join him that evening in another session with the senators.[64]

The meeting that evening included the president, six members of the cabinet (all except Seward), and eight senators, including Fessenden and Sumner. Lincoln started with a long speech in which he said that the cabinet had generally discussed and agreed on the key questions. Chase followed, admitting that "there had been no want of unity in the cabinet, but a general *acquiescence* in public measures." This surprised the senators, for they had been hearing from Chase that Lincoln did *not* consult his cabinet. Several senators again argued that the "whole cabinet" must "consider and decide great questions." Blair "dissented most decidedly from the idea of a plural executive" and insisted the president alone was "accountable for his administration." Neither Fessenden nor Welles mentioned any comments by Stanton, but the *New York Herald*, in a remarkably accurate report of this closed-door meeting, quoted Stanton as saying that the resolution "was evidently aimed at some one else besides Secretary Seward. If any one supposed he [Stanton] was responsible for the disaster that had occurred, they were mistaken; that all the charges made against him were false; that the President knew that the charge that he was responsible for the movement on Fredericksburg was groundless; that neither he nor Gen. Halleck were responsible." After the cabinet members and some senators left at about midnight, Lincoln told the few who remained that if he accepted Seward's resignation he would likely lose much of his cabinet, for "Chase would seize the occasion to withdraw" and "it had been intimated that Stanton would do the same."[65]

Early the next morning, December 20, Stanton went to see Seward at his home. Welles found the two of them there, with Seward "talking vehemently" and warning "Stanton that he would be the next victim." To support his point, Seward mentioned an article in the *New York Herald* about a meeting in New York City, called by Oakey Hall and others, to discuss the "misconduct of the war." Seward handed a copy of the *Herald* to Welles, but Stanton "seized the paper," concerned about the "Hoffman-Hall-Weed" alliance against him in New York City. Stanton soon left for the War Department, where Fessenden found him. There Stanton told Fessenden that "what the senators had said about the manner of doing business in the Cabinet was true" and that "he was ashamed of Chase, for he knew better." Stanton also said that "Seward had got up the resolution offered by Harris, with a view of producing the impression that the Senate proceedings were aimed at him, Stanton; that he, Stanton, had not tendered his resignation, and did not mean to be driven out of the Cabinet by Seward." Stanton, it seems, saw a link between what was going on in Washington, where Seward's friends amended the Senate resolution in a way that might harm Stanton, and what was going on in New York City, where Seward's friends were supposedly behind the effort to indict Stanton.[66]

Senator William Pitt Fessenden, one of Stanton's close friends in the Senate and the author of the most detailed account of the late 1862 cabinet crisis.

Later in the morning, when Welles went to the White House, he found Stanton and Chase in Lincoln's anteroom. Lincoln invited all three men into his office, where they sat down by the fire. Chase said he was "painfully affected" by the previous night's meeting and that "he had prepared his resignation." "Where is it," asked Lincoln, "his eye lighting up in a moment." As Chase pulled the letter out, Lincoln seized it with his "long arm and fingers." "This," said Lincoln, "with a triumphant laugh," would cut "the Gordian knot." Stanton then solemnly told Lincoln, "I informed you the day before yesterday that I was ready to tender you my resignation. I wish you sir to consider my resignation at this time in your possession." "You may go to your Department," said the President, "I don't want yours. This," holding out Chase's letter, "is all I want—this relieves me—my way is clear—the trouble is ended."[67]

Dismissing Stanton, Welles, and Chase, Lincoln wrote short letters to both Seward and Chase, declining to accept their resignations. Seward eagerly, and Chase reluctantly, agreed to remain. Lincoln had solved his problem, for the senators could not complain about a solution that kept Chase in the cabinet. The New York Herald reported that in all his conversations with the senators Lincoln had "defended Mr. Seward warmly" and "expressed the most unbounded confidence in Secretaries Stanton and Chase." Indeed the Herald's reporter was sure that Lincoln would "not remove any member," that unless one or more cabinet members resigned "and insist upon their resignations being accepted, there will be no change." In this instance the Herald was right: the cabinet crisis was over, with no changes in the membership.[68]

The aftermath of the Fredericksburg disaster was not over, however, for there was still the question of command. Burnside arrived in Washington on this same December 20, and he found Lincoln "greatly depressed by the attacks made upon him for the Fredericksburg affairs." Burnside told Lincoln that he would publish a letter "taking the whole responsibility upon his shoulders." When Burnside saw Stanton the next day, the secretary received him "coldly" and said, "You have not published the letter you promised the president you would publish." Burnside recalled that he had reacted angrily, telling Stanton that "this was a wholly private matter between him and the President—that he should do as he pleased about it." But then, at a second meeting a few hours later, according to Burnside, Stanton "very handsomely apologized for the heat he had shown, and disclaimed any wish to dictate to [Burnside] on the subject." Burnside's letter to Halleck, which was in the newspapers on December 23, was gracious. He praised the "extreme gallantry, courage and endurance" of his officers and soldiers and prayed for the wounded. He declared that Halleck "left the whole movement in [Burnside's] hands" and that he had moved "against the opinion of the President, Secretary of War and [Halleck]" so that he alone was responsible for Fredericksburg. Some suspected that Stanton helped Burnside write this letter, and they may have been right, for there is a copy of it in the Stanton papers at the Library of Congress, with some editing, although the editing does not appear to be in Stanton's hand.[69]

Just as the cabinet crisis ended, Congress passed legislation on December 22 to create a new state, West Virginia, from the loyal western counties of Virginia. Article IV of the Constitution arguably prohibited forming a new state within the borders of an existing state; *at most* the Constitution allowed formation of a new state with the consent of the legislature of the existing state. But this raised another question: Was the consent of the Unionist legislature, meeting in Wheeling, claiming but not exercising authority over all of Virginia, sufficient for these purposes? And there were political questions, such as whether making West Virginia a state would make it harder at the end of the war to persuade Virginia to rejoin the Union. Lincoln asked each member of his cabinet for a written opinion. Stanton knew western Virginia better than any of them; he was born within sight of the bluffs of western Virginia and had worked for years on the Wheeling Bridge case. His opinion was simple, perhaps even simplistic. He asserted that the Constitution "expressly authorizes a new state to be formed within the jurisdiction of another state" and that the consent of the Wheeling legislature was valid. Forming a new state would shift the boundary between slave and free states, which he viewed as a major benefit. Lincoln eventually agreed and signed the measure into law on December 31, the last day of the year.[70]

———

Stanton did not have time to pause and reflect as the year ended, but we should take a moment to consider his first year as secretary of war.

In many cases it seems Stanton was less than truthful. For instance, Fessenden wrote that, on the morning of December 20, Stanton told him he had not tendered his resignation to Lincoln. Yet Welles wrote that, about an hour later, Stanton told Lincoln he "was ready to tender [his] resignation." Perhaps both statements are correct; perhaps Stanton had not tendered his resignation, in the sense of handing a resignation letter to Lincoln, but simply told Lincoln informally that he would resign if Lincoln asked him to do so. But Stanton's listeners heard two rather different things: Fessenden heard that Stanton would not give up his post without a fight, while Lincoln heard that Stanton was quite ready to resign. In another instance, when Representative Mallory informed the House in July that Stanton not only opposed arming former slaves but had threatened to arrest an officer for simply suggesting a black regiment, and Representative Stevens responded that Stanton had told *him* that he favored enlisting black soldiers, one senses that the two men were accurately reporting their private conversations. And when Stanton wrote to McClellan in early July that "no man had ever a truer friend," even as he was pressing Lincoln to replace McClellan with another general, he protested too much.[71]

The real issue is not whether Stanton always told the truth—he did not—but whether his duplicity impaired his work as secretary of war. Even Stanton's enemies would concede that his department was utterly unlike that of his predecessor, Cameron; there was no hint of corruption in the Stanton administration. Stanton and Meigs and their officers managed well the process of recruiting, training, arming, feeding, and moving the troops. As Halleck said, "No armies in the world, while on campaign, have been more promptly or better supplied than ours." To be sure, Stanton made a mistake when he yielded to congressional pressure and suspended recruiting, a mistake he had to correct soon thereafter. McClellan's allies in the press suggested that, if Stanton had not stopped recruiting, if he had given McClellan reinforcements, McClellan would have captured Richmond. This seems unlikely. John Hay later recalled that Stanton said one day with his "natural hyperbole" that if McClellan had an army of "a million men, he would swear the enemy had two millions, and then he would sit down in the mud and yell for three." Stanton perhaps did not say this, but he certainly *believed* that no matter how many soldiers McClellan had in his army, he would always delay and always demand more.[72]

Even if McClellan had attacked the Confederate forces around Richmond, there is little reason to believe that he would have *captured* the city. Stanton was expressing a common but mistaken view when he wrote in February 1862 that battles would be won by the tactics that had worked "in the days of Joshua, by boldly pursuing and striking the foe." If McClellan had attacked the entrenched Confederates around Richmond in the summer, there is every reason to think that his troops would have been killed, and defeated, as Burnside's troops were killed by entrenched defenders at Fredericksburg in December. In the unlikely scenario in which McClellan captured Richmond in 1862, there is little reason to believe that this would have ended the Civil War. Stanton and others who assumed in 1862 that the war might be over in a matter of months were simply wrong. The British Army captured the "rebel capital" of Philadelphia in 1777, but that did not end the armed rebellion we know as the American Revolution. George Washington and his army survived, and with an army and popular support the rebellion continued and eventually prevailed. Unless McClellan had captured or destroyed Lee's army in 1862, and the Union achieved similar success in the West, the Confederacy would have survived and continued the war. Lincoln appreciated this truth sooner than Stanton, sooner than almost anyone else, and he would express it well in 1863, when he told McClellan's successor, "Lee's Army, and not Richmond, is your true objective point."[73]

Stanton's worst errors in his first year as secretary were his arbitrary arrests. He arrested Gen. Charles Stone in February 1862 on slight pretexts and kept him in military prison until August, without charges or a court-martial. Indeed Stanton would probably have kept Stone in prison longer but for legislation passed by Congress requiring that imprisoned army officers receive charges within a month. Stanton may not have personally ordered the arrest of Dennis Mahoney, the Iowa editor, but it was his general August 8 order that provided the basis for the arrest, and Stanton did nothing for many weeks to release Mahoney. Many other civilians suffered, like Mahoney, for exercising their constitutional right to speak against the Lincoln administration. There is no doubt that Stanton sincerely believed such arrests were necessary to support the Union war effort. In his first annual report, submitted to Congress in December 1862, he wrote, "Reflecting minds will perceive that no greater encouragement can be given to the enemy, no more dangerous act of hostility can be perpetrated in this war, than efforts to prevent recruiting and enlisting for the armies, upon whose strength the national existence depends." But Stanton's sincerity in his arrest policy, and Lincoln's support of Stanton's policy, do not absolve Stanton of blame for arresting officers and civilians and holding them without charges.[74]

It would be a mistake, however, to conclude this preliminary assessment of Stanton's work as secretary of war on such a negative note. George Templeton Strong, after meeting Stanton for the first time, had it right: Stanton was "worth a wagon-load of Camerons."[75]

Chapter 10

"Indomitable Energy"

— January–June 1863 —

arly on the first day of the new year, before any of the elegant receptions, Lincoln and Stanton met with Halleck and Burnside. Burnside was outraged that several of his generals had gone behind his back to meet with Lincoln and question his leadership. He offered his resignation and said that Stanton and Halleck should also resign because neither the military nor the public had confidence in them. Lincoln did not accept Burnside's resignation, nor would he comment on Burnside's remarks about Stanton and Halleck. When Burnside demanded to know the names of the generals who had denounced him, Lincoln refused to reveal his sources. Burnside turned to Stanton and Halleck and asked whether they approved his plans for another attack at Fredericksburg. Neither would answer the question, saying only that they favored some form of forward movement. It was an unpleasant, unsatisfactory meeting.[1]

Annoyed not only with Burnside but also with Halleck, Lincoln wrote at once to Halleck, asking him to go to Falmouth to study the ground, to talk with the generals, and to approve or disapprove Burnside's plan. "If in such a difficulty as this you do not help, you fail me precisely in the point for which I sought your assistance." Halleck, who saw his role as a Washington staff officer, not as a field officer, responded with his own resignation letter. Lincoln had to back down, noting on his copy of the letter to Halleck that it was "withdrawn because considered harsh by General Halleck."[2]

By tradition, both the president and the cabinet members hosted receptions on New Year's Day. The first hour of the president's reception was reserved for senior officials—cabinet members, senators, representatives, diplomats—and their families. Stanton and his wife were at the White House, then hastened home to prepare for their own reception. The weather, according to Noah Brooks, a young reporter who had recently arrived in Washington, was "soft and spring-like." Brooks and a few friends went to the receptions at the homes of Seward, Chase, and Stanton. "At Secretary Stanton's we were met by the wife of that war-like gentleman, and found her a ladylike looking woman of Pittsburg extraction and a pleasant demeanor." Stanton himself greeted the visitors in the dining room. "Oysters, salads, game pasties, fruits, cake, wines and various other fixings were arranged with a most gorgeous display of china, glass and silver, two silent and attentive colored men serving the guests, who were numerous." Brooks later recalled that Stanton could not hide "the worry that must have distressed him on that anxious, unfestive day."[3]

We think of January 1, 1863, as a great and festive day, the day upon which Lincoln issued the Emancipation Proclamation, declaring millions of slaves free and promising to enlist free blacks in the Union Army. But for Stanton the proclamation was old news; he never doubted that Lincoln would keep the promise he had made in the preliminary proclamation. Stanton was anxious, and not especially festive, because of Burnside, Halleck, and various other generals. Grant had failed in his attempt to march south and capture Vicksburg, the rebel citadel over the Mississippi River. Sherman and his troops, who were supposed to attack Vicksburg in tandem with Grant in late December, were instead thrashed at the Battle of Chickasaw Bayou.[4]

Stanton was also worried about Gen. William Rosecrans and his Army of the Cumberland. Like Grant and Sherman, Rosecrans was originally from the Midwest. He attended West Point, graduating near the top of the class of 1842, then worked as a West Point instructor, an army engineer, and a mining engineer. When Stanton and Rosecrans first met, in the spring of 1862, they liked one another. Rosecrans wrote home to his wife that Stanton assured him their meeting was "the beginning of good luck" for Rosecrans. On the first few days of 1863, Stanton knew that Rosecrans and his army were fighting against his Confederate counterpart, Braxton Bragg, near Nashville, Tennessee—but that was about all Stanton knew. It was not until January 5 that Stanton received a telegram from Rosecrans that started, "God has crowned our arms with victory. The enemy are badly beaten and in full retreat." Rosecrans and his army were so stunned and bloodied after this "victory" that they would not move for many months.[5]

William Rosecrans, the western general whom Stanton supported with a great troop transfer in late 1863.

Grant caused problems for Stanton and Lincoln at almost this same time with an ill-advised order, issued in the middle of December, expelling Jews "as a class" from his military department. Lincoln and Stanton learned of this order not from the general but from the newspapers, and then from angry letters and telegrams from Jewish leaders. On or about January 5, no doubt after consulting with Lincoln and Stanton, Halleck sent a telegram to Grant: if he had issued any such order against Jews he should rescind it at once.[6]

On January 3, probably the same day he learned of Grant's expulsion order, Stanton received an angry telegram from Gen. John McClernand, complaining that he had been deprived of the command promised him by Lincoln and Stanton. McClernand, a senior Illinois politician and general, had arrived in Washington in the fall, asking for orders to raise troops in the Midwest for an expedition down the Mississippi to capture Vicksburg and to open the river all the way to New Orleans. Stanton's confidential October orders authorized McClernand to raise troops, directed him to send the regiments to Memphis, and then added, "When a sufficient force not required by the operations of General Grant's command shall be raised, an expedition may be organized under General McClernand's command against Vicksburg and to clear the Mississippi." Stanton knew, though McClernand did not, that Grant was even at that time demanding more troops. McClernand went to Illinois and raised thousands of troops, keeping in close telegraphic touch with Stanton. In early December, Senator Browning wrote to McClernand from Washington that Lincoln and Stanton were "very anxious for you to have command of the expedition, and intend to stand by you." But when McClernand arrived at Memphis at the end of December, expecting to find his troops, they were gone, taken by Sherman under Grant's orders. McClernand's role would be to command just a corps under Grant. McClernand may not have been a great general—indeed he would prove to be a poor one—but Lincoln and Stanton mistreated him, leading him to believe he would have command of an independent expedition and then using him mainly as a glorified recruiting agent.[7]

Another angry general, Benjamin Butler, arrived in Washington on January 5 to meet in person with Lincoln and Stanton. Back in December, Lincoln had removed Butler from his command in New Orleans and placed Banks in the post. Many papers speculated that Butler would replace Stanton as secretary of war. Soon after Butler arrived in Washington, Sumner wrote him that if Stanton had "known your real position with regard to the Proclamation, he would have cut off his right hand before he would have allowed anybody else to take your place. That his fixed purpose was that on first January a General should be in command in New Orleans to whom the Proclamation would be a living letter, and that in this respect it was natural, after the recent elections in Pa. and N.Y., that he should look to a Republican rather than to an old Democrat." Indeed the concerns Butler had expressed to Stanton about loyal white masters, and the quarrels between Butler and abolitionist officers in his department, provided Lincoln and Stanton with good reason to question how committed Butler was to the emancipation of the slaves. At the end of the month, however, Lincoln wrote Stanton that he would like to see Butler back in charge in New Orleans. Stanton dutifully drafted the orders, and Chase urged Butler to take up the task, but Butler declined, explaining in a long letter to Chase that he would not have enough troops or enough authority.[8]

The most troublesome general of all, George McClellan, was in New York City in early 1863, working on his voluminous report about the Peninsula Campaign, renewing his friendships with Democratic leaders, starting his informal campaign to become the next president. Stanton's friend Pierrepont visited Washington in February and then wrote a remarkable letter to Horatio Seymour, the Democratic governor of New York: "It is quite clear to me that you can receive the Democratic nomination for President within about a year and that you can be elected." Pierrepont promised Seymour that, if he was interested, he could "secure the entire force and zeal and vast energy of the War Department in your favor," which would be especially useful in the Midwest and West. "Great efforts will be made to bring forward McClellan for the presidency not on the ground that he is a military man, but a martyr." Thurlow Weed wrote in his memoir that Lincoln told him at about this time that he would support Seymour as his successor. What seems far more likely is that Lincoln and Stanton were hoping that someone other than Mc-Clellan, someone like Seymour, would be the Democratic nominee but would lose in the general election to Lincoln. There is nothing to suggest that Seymour accepted Stanton's offer through Pierrepont, and when the time came, Stanton would prove central in Lincoln's 1864 campaign.[9]

Civil War armies generally did not attempt to march or fight in the winter, and Burnside's "Mud March" of late January 1863 shows why. Desperate to prove himself after the disaster of December, Burnside decided to march the Army of the Potomac upstream, cross the Rappahannock at lightly guarded fords, then descend upon Fredericksburg from the west. But a strong winter storm defeated his plans before the rebels fired a shot. "It is solemnly true," one Union general wrote to his daughter, "that we lost mules in the middle of the road, sinking out of sight in the mud-holes." General Hooker "denounced the commanding general [Burnside] as incompetent, and the President and Government at Washington as imbecile." What the nation needed, Hooker said, was "a dictator, and the sooner the better." Burnside heard of Hooker's comments and went straight to Washington. He presented Lincoln and Stanton with a simple choice: either they would dismiss Hooker and the other dissidents in the Army of the Potomac, or Burnside himself would resign. Lincoln, apparently without consulting Stanton, decided to relieve Burnside and appoint Hooker to lead the Army of the Potomac.[10]

"Fighting Joe" Hooker, whom Lincoln appointed to head the Army of the Potomac but also warned against political intrigues.

Even as he appointed Hooker, Lincoln warned him, "During Gen. Burnside's command of the Army, you have taken counsel of your ambition, and thwarted him as much as you could, in which you did a great wrong to the country, and to a most meritorious and honorable brother officer." Lincoln had also heard that Hooker believed "both the Army and the Government needed a Dictator. Of course it was not *for* this, but in spite of it, that I have given you the command. Only those generals who gain successes, can set up dictators. What I now ask of you is military success, and I will risk the dictatorship." When Stanton learned that Lincoln had appointed Hooker, an aide recalled, his "first conclusion was that he should resign; his second, that duty to his chief and the public forbade his doing so; his third, that Hooker must be loyally supported so long as there was the least chance of his doing anything with the army placed in his keeping." Hooker went south to join the Army of the Potomac, to start work on what would become the Chancellorsville Campaign.[11]

Encouraged by the 1862 fall elections, Democrats were more aggressive in Congress in the first few months of 1863. The most vocal Copperhead was Stanton's former friend Clement Vallandigham, now a member of Congress from Ohio. In a widely reported speech, Vallandigham denounced the war and the Lincoln administration. It was not possible, he declared, for the North to conquer the South, any more than it had been possible for Britain to conquer America. The North should abandon the pointless attempt, its abolitionist war to free the slaves, and reach a peace agreement as soon as possible. "[If I am] discouraging enlistments," Vallandigham added, "then first arrest Lincoln, Stanton, and Halleck, and some of your other generals," for they were the men responsible for the "blood poured out like water."[12]

Stanton was more worried about legislation than speeches, and especially focused on military measures. In his annual report in December, he had written that there were "serious defects in the militia law" and promised to work with the "appropriate committees of Congress" on legislation. He cooperated closely with his friend Henry Wilson, chairman of the Military Affairs Committee, on the revolutionary conscription bill that Wilson introduced in early February. (Welles complained in his diary that the bill "was got up in the war department" and all the secretaries other than Stanton "were ignorant of its extraordinary provisions.") The first section of Wilson's bill declared that "all able-bodied male citizens of the United States, between the ages of eighteen and forty-five years" would become "the national forces" of the United States. There were a few exemptions, mainly based on family circumstances; for example, "the only son of aged or infirm parents dependent upon him for support" would be exempt. Every congressional district would become a federal draft district, for which a federal provost marshal would be appointed, answerable to the provost marshal general and ultimately to the secretary of war.[13]

Under the bill, each provost marshal would "enroll" all the men in his district eligible for the draft, that is, would prepare a complete and accurate list of all such men. If a district failed to provide its assigned number of volunteers, provost marshals could draft men from the list in order to fill the quota. Provost marshals were also required to arrest deserters and to "inquire into and report to the provost marshal general all treasonable practices." The bill did not define "treasonable practices," nor did it define "aid or counsel" when it created a new crime, aiding or counseling any person to avoid or resist the draft. Those drafted could avoid service in two ways: they could find a substitute, someone who would serve in their place, or they could pay a commutation fee of $300. The commutation provision was instantly controversial, and Stanton would later claim that he had opposed it, but Senate leaders viewed the clause as a way of ensuring that the market price of arranging a substitute did not increase to *more* than $300.[14]

The Senate passed Wilson's enrollment bill with only a few changes, such as one that made recent immigrants who had "declared on oath their intention to become citizens" subject to the draft, but there was intense opposition in the House. Vallandigham attacked not only the bill but also Stanton: "Treasonable practices! Disloyalty! Who imported these precious phrases, and gave them a legal settlement here? Your Secretary of War. He it was who . . . authorized every marshal, every sheriff, every township constable . . . to fix, in his own imagination, what he might choose to call a treasonable or disloyal practice, and then to arrest any citizen at his discretion, without due process or any process of law." Vallandigham argued that the bill would allow Stanton to continue and expand his arrests. "Men, women, and children are to be haled to prison for free speech. Whoever shall denounce or oppose this Administration; whoever may affirm that war will not restore the Union, and teach men the gospel of peace, may be reported and arrested . . . and imprisoned as guilty of a treasonable practice."[15]

Clement Vallandigham, a Copperhead member of Congress and a merciless critic of Lincoln and Stanton.

Vallandigham and the Democrats did not have the votes in the House of Representatives to defeat the enrollment bill, but they could delay the bill until it was too late to pass in the congressional session, which would end on March 4. From Stanton's perspective this would be a disaster, for the next Congress would not convene until December, meaning many months without the threat of a draft to encourage volunteers. Stanton probably spoke with House Republicans before they amended the bill in late February to remove the most controversial provisions, for example, the reference to "treasonable practices." With these changes the bill passed, and Lincoln signed the Enrollment Act into law on March 3.[16]

On this same day, Lincoln signed into law another bill in which Stanton had an intense interest, what is now known as the Habeas Corpus Suspension Act of 1863. One purpose of the bill was to remove questions about whether Lincoln, as president, had the authority he had already exercised when he had suspended the right to petition for release by *habeas corpus*. But another key purpose, from Stanton's perspective, was to protect from state lawsuits the federal officials involved in arresting and imprisoning those accused of aiding the rebellion. Later in the war Stanton told Welles that, if federal officials were liable in state court for supposedly false arrests, he "would be imprisoned a thousand years at least."[17]

The House and Senate passed different versions of this bill, and a conference committee was formed to resolve the differences. Stanton knew well at least two members of this committee: Representatives Thaddeus Stevens of Pennsylvania and John Bingham of Ohio. The conference committee reported its compromise to both houses at the tail end of the session, on March 2. Democrats in both houses objected to the measure, and in the Senate there was an all-out filibuster, lasting most of the night. Senate Democrats decried Stanton's arbitrary arrests and claimed that this bill would immunize him and others from any liability for such arrests, even arrests made without any basis or arrests for purely personal purposes. Finally, at about five in the morning, Senator Samuel Pomeroy of Kansas, a Republican, announced from the president's chair, "The ayes have it. It is a vote. The report is concurred in." Democrats, perhaps asleep, did not notice for a few moments, and then objected to no avail, for Pomeroy declared that the bill had passed. "By that kind of jockeying?" asked one bitter Senate Democrat.[18]

Stanton probably did not much like Section 2 of the Habeas Corpus Suspension Act, which required that the War Department prepare lists of all persons who were imprisoned in "any fort, arsenal, or other place, as state or political prisoners, or otherwise than as prisoners of war." Congress required the department to provide these prisoner lists to the federal district courts and to *release* any prisoners who were not indicted and tried soon after being named on such a list. But Stanton surely approved and appreciated Section 4 of the Act, which provided that "any order of the President, or under his authority, made at any time during the existence of the present rebellion shall be a defense in all courts to any action or prosecution, civil or criminal, pending or to be commenced, for any search, seizure, arrest, or imprisonment . . . under and by virtue of such order." This provision of federal law would govern not only in federal but also in state courts, under the Supremacy Clause, giving Stanton and others a solid defense against claims that they had violated state laws in arresting and imprisoning civilians.[19]

Even as Congress was finishing up its work, Stanton started to focus on the spring elections in New England. First on the calendar was New Hampshire on March 10. There were three candidates for governor: Joseph Gilmore, the Republican; Ira Eastman, a Peace Democrat; and Col. Walter Harriman, a former Democrat running as the Union candidate while still serving in the Union Army. The *Detroit Free Press* reported that Stanton had promised Harriman promotion to brigadier general in return for accepting the Union nomination. The *Press* alleged that the Union Party was not really a party at all—it was a front set up in Washington, by Republican leaders, so "that by a political trick they may cheat the people out of their choice for Governor."[20]

In this case, the Democratic allegations have some support in Republican documents. Representative Edward Rollins of New Hampshire wrote to Lincoln a few months after the election to remind him that they had talked "just prior to our election, when our state was in great peril, and you authorized us to make certain promises to Col. Harriman concerning a brigadiership. We found it absolutely necessary to have the Col. run as a Union candidate for Gov., to save us from overwhelming defeat."

If Lincoln and Stanton made any such promises, they did not view them as binding, for Harriman had to wait two years for his promotion.[21]

Stanton's main role in this election was getting troops home to New Hampshire to vote. Almost all states at this time required that men vote in person, although some states were reconsidering and others had already changed these laws. Many Republicans believed they had lost the fall elections because their most ardent supporters were away in the Union Army and thus could not vote. Most New Hampshire soldiers now supported Lincoln and the Republicans. The Fourteenth New Hampshire Regiment, in a widely reprinted address, declared that it would be "better far that the unbridled license of the press be held in check; better that individual liberty be abridged; better that all the property of rebels be confiscated; better that the shackles be stricken from every slave, and the freed man arrayed against his oppressor; better that the whole Southern domain be made a howling wilderness, than that this infamous conspiracy [the Southern rebellion] against the rights of man succeed, and our once noble country made the reproach of nations."[22]

Stanton sent the Fourteenth Regiment, and several other New Hampshire regiments, home on furlough so that they could vote in early March. The Democrat Eastman received 32,833 votes, the Republican Gilmore 29,035, and the Union candidate Harriman 4,372. Because Eastman did not have a majority of the votes, state law required the election be decided by the Assembly. Republicans dominated the Assembly, so it was certain they would select Gilmore. Democrats cried foul, insisting that Eastman would have been elected but for the interloper Harriman. Democrats cried foul again when, just after the election, Stanton dismissed Andrew Jackson Edgerly, a Democratic officer with the Fourth New Hampshire Regiment. The official order described Edgerly's offense as "circulating Copperhead tickets and doing all in his power to promote the success of the rebel cause in his state."[23]

The next election on the calendar was that of Connecticut, set for April 6. The incumbent Republican governor, William Buckingham, faced a stiff challenge from a Peace Democrat, Thomas Seymour, a cousin of the New York governor. Stanton sent a telegram to Buckingham on March 21: "If I can do anything to assist you in the coming election, let me know and it will be done." Although we do not have Buckingham's response, he almost certainly asked Stanton to furlough soldiers so they could return to the state to vote. The *New York Express*, a Democratic paper, reported that one of Buckingham's aides visited Stanton in Washington, telling him that "Connecticut would be sure to go for Seymour unless the soldiers could go home and vote." Stanton said he would grant the furloughs. When the state official fretted that the furlough paperwork would take at least three days, Stanton supposedly told him, "Give their names *to me*, and I will put them through in *three hours*."[24]

Again the result was quite close: Buckingham received 44,458 votes and Seymour 43,917. The soldier vote, almost all Republican, probably made the difference. Stanton was one of the first to send a telegram congratulating Buckingham, who responded, "Copperheads have sunk into their holes & hiding places & I only hope that whenever they make their appearance again they will receive the indignation & contempt which treason merits." A few weeks later Stanton wrote that he rejoiced in the Connecticut victory, believing it "the most important election held since the war commenced."[25]

One striking feature of the Connecticut campaign was that one of the principal political speakers was a woman, Anna Dickinson. Democratic papers sneered that Buckingham was so desperate he was relying on a woman, but Republican papers praised her. The *Hartford Press* described one of her speeches as a "masterly sketch of the war in its inception, continuance, and prospective end, exhibiting a knowledge and careful estimate of men and measures which continually astonished her listeners." Soon after the election, Isabella Beecher Hooker, part of the famous Beecher family, wrote to Stanton about Dickinson's speeches. Stanton responded that he was "very desirous to hear and see Miss Dickinson" and that her "eloquence is spoken of by everyone in high terms." If Hooker sensed from Stanton's letter that he was favorable toward the nascent women's movement (in which both Dickinson and Hooker would become leaders), she was not alone in this perception. Jane Swisshelm, who first met Stanton in Pittsburgh, met him again in Washington in early 1863, where she was now the Washington correspondent for Minnesota's *St. Cloud Democrat*. Stanton greeted her warmly, and she described to her readers how, when she first knew him, he had approved the "radical idea of a married woman's right to own property." Swisshelm was pleased to learn that Stanton was "particularly cordial, now, in recognizing the many efforts of ladies to aid our soldiers." Stanton would soon provide Swisshelm with a job in Washington as a clerk in the Quartermaster's Office, one of the very few women working for the federal government during the Civil War.[26]

Stanton was also involved in Indiana politics in the spring of 1863. The Democratic legislature, elected in the fall, refused even to receive the annual address from Oliver Morton, the Republican governor. Morton warned Stanton that Democrats in Indiana and nearby states might try to form an alliance with the Confederacy against New England, whose "fanatical crusade against Slavery" northwestern Copperheads viewed as the cause of a war in which they wanted no part. Morton sent Robert Dale Owen, a former member of Congress from Indiana, to Washington to talk with Stanton. Owen reported back that Stanton agreed there was probably a conspiracy to reconstruct the Union without New England, but he thought the plot would not succeed. Democrats adjourned the state legislature without passing any appropriations, confident that this would force Morton to give them control over the state's military machinery. Morton decided to disregard the legislature, and state law, and to fund the government from other sources, including private loans. He visited Washington and talked with Stanton. The War Department had an appropriation available for "raising troops," and Stanton decided he could use these funds to support Morton's government—after all, the federal government could not raise troops in Indiana without a state government with which to work. Soon after Stanton's death, while Morton and others involved were still alive, Wilson published an account of Morton's conversation with Stanton: "A quarter of a million of dollars were needed, and Mr. Stanton took upon himself the responsibility, and drew his warrant upon the treasury for that amount, to be paid from an unexpended appropriation made, nearly two years before, for raising troops in States in insurrection." As Stanton handed the warrant to Morton, the governor said, "If the cause fails, you and I will be covered with prosecutions, and probably imprisoned or driven from the country." Stanton replied, "If the cause fails, I do not wish to live."[27]

Governor Oliver Morton of Indiana.
When the state legislature, dominated by
antiwar Democrats, refused to provide
funds for the state government, Stanton
provided federal funds to Morton
to keep the state in operation.

One of Stanton's major efforts in the first half of 1863 was to strengthen and systematize military justice, work he had started the prior year. A provision of the Militia Act of July 1862 created within the War Department the Office of Judge Advocate General and tasked this officer with overseeing all courts-martial and military commissions. The Act also authorized the department to hire judge advocates to work under the judge advocate general, both as legal advisers to generals in the field and prosecutors in military trials. Stanton persuaded his friend and colleague, the brilliant and abrasive Joseph Holt, to become the first judge advocate general under this new law. Holt in turn recruited bright, able lawyers to work under him as judge advocates. Many of these men were or would become famous, such as John Bingham, a former and future member of Congress, and John Chipman Gray, a future Harvard law professor and founder of Boston's leading law firm.[28]

Both the War Department in Washington and generals in the field were encountering difficult legal questions almost every day: What duties did a victorious army owe to the prisoners of war it captured? What were the proper procedures for a captured soldier to "give his parole" and the procedures for the exchange of paroled soldiers? To what extent could an army seize or destroy the property of civilians in the war zone? Was it legitimate, as the North contended and the South denied, to use former slaves as soldiers? To help answer these questions, Stanton and Halleck summoned Francis Lieber to Washington.[29]

Stanton and Halleck asked Lieber in December 1862 to draft "a code of regulations for the government of armies in the field, as authorized by the laws and usages of war." Although Lieber was nominally part of a commission of five, including Gen. Ethan Allen Hitchcock, he drafted most of the code himself. What Stanton and Halleck had in mind was a "plain English" document that generals could use in the field. Lieber succeeded brilliantly, writing rules that form the basis not only of American but of international military law. With respect to prisoners of war, for example, the Lieber code provided that they could be imprisoned but "subjected to no other intentional suffering or indignity." Prisoners should "be fed upon plain and wholesome food, whenever practicable, and treated with humanity."[30]

While Lieber was still working on his draft, Joseph Holt handled the most controversial court-martial of the war, the trial of Gen. Fitz-John Porter, accused of disobeying orders issued by Gen. John Pope during the Second Battle of Bull Run. The Porter court-martial was seen, then and now, as an indirect attack by Stanton on McClellan, Porter's best friend and sponsor. Not only was Stanton's friend Holt the chief prosecutor in the case; several of the judges on the court, including David Hunter and Ethan Allen Hitchcock, were close to Stanton. But Porter had able defense counsel, Senator Reverdy Johnson, whom one of the other military judges, the future president James Garfield, described as asking questions with such "direct searching fierceness" that they would "make a witness suspect himself to be a villain and fear that he is lying." And the trial was open to the public, so that reporters could and did provide daily accounts of the witnesses and their evidence.[31]

Stanton did not much like Porter. And he would have liked him even less if he could have seen his private letters to Manton Marble, editor of the *New York World*. Back in April, in the early phases of the Peninsula Campaign, Porter had written to Marble that the nation needed "a military head to direct affairs at Washington," adding, "Such an ass as Stanton would ruin any cause but ours in such good hands as it is here." In June, as McClellan demanded yet more troops from Washington, Porter wrote to Marble that Lincoln and Stanton "ignore all calls for aid." Porter suggested that the *New York World* should "put the question—does the President (controlled by an incompetent secretary) design to cause defeat here for the purpose of prolonging the war?" Stanton may well have had Porter in mind when he wrote to Lincoln that generals who "indulge in the sport" of politics "must risk being gored. They cannot, having exposed themselves, claim the procedural protections and immunities of the military profession."[32]

On January 6 Stanton prodded Gen. David Hunter, president of the Porter court-martial, to finish the trial promptly so that the various officers could return to other duties. The trial was almost over, hearing the last few rebuttal witnesses, and Hunter gave Porter's lawyers a few days to prepare their closing argument. For some reason, Holt did not present a closing argument. The judges concluded that Porter was guilty on several serious charges and recommended that he be dismissed from the army. Lincoln, whose approval was necessary, asked Holt to review and summarize the record. Holt's review was not impartial; he pressed Lincoln to approve the decision and the sentence, and Lincoln did just that on January 21. When the decision was announced, the press divided on partisan lines, with the Republican papers praising and Democratic papers denouncing it. One paper in Illinois rejoiced that "this tool of McClellan and minion of slavery" had been dismissed. Porter described the case as a "political persecution" and claimed, "The court [was] packed against me, selected by Halleck & Stanton." He promised to fight his case "to the bitter end," and he did—for decades to come.[33]

Lieber finished a draft of his code in February. Halleck edited the draft somewhat, focusing especially on military commissions. Although there does not appear to be a draft with Stanton's editing, he certainly reviewed and perhaps edited the code. Lincoln approved and issued the code on April 23 as General Orders No. 100, Instructions for the Government of Armies of the United States in the Field. The War Department printed thousands of copies in small pamphlets so that officers could carry the code in their pockets.[34]

Several sections of the code covered courts-martial and military commissions. Courts-martial deal with "military offenses under statute law," while military commissions address offenses not covered by statutes using "the common law of war." The code outlined and defined some of the offenses that could be tried and punished by military commissions, such as spying, providing information to the enemy, and fighting without uniforms or orders. Under Article 84, those who "steal within the lines of the hostile army for the purpose of robbing, killing, or of destroying bridges, roads, or canals . . . are not entitled to the privileges of the prisoner of war." By its nature, a "common law of war" is flexible and expansive, and the code did not attempt to provide an exhaustive list of all the offenses that could be tried by military commission.[35]

The ink was barely dry on the code when news arrived in Washington that General Burnside, now in charge of the Department of the Ohio, had arrested Clement Vallandigham, a former member of Congress, sometimes mentioned as a possible presidential candidate, for giving an anti-administration speech. The speech, at a Democratic rally on May 1 in Mount Vernon, Ohio, was nothing new for Vallandigham. He argued against the war, which he called "a war for the freedom of the blacks and enslavement of the whites" and "a war for the purpose of crushing out liberty and erecting a despotism." There was no national press coverage of the speech. But without consulting Washington, Burnside sent a squad of soldiers to Dayton, Ohio, where they arrested Vallandigham, breaking down the door of his house after midnight on May 5. This armed military arrest of a major political figure was reported in all the newspapers and of course denounced by Democrats. But Stanton backed Burnside, sending him a telegram on May 8: "In your determination to support the authority of the Government and suppress treason in your department you may count on the firm support of the President."[36]

Burnside promptly organized a military commission, which tried and convicted Vallandigham and sentenced him to spend the rest of the war in a military prison. The prisoner's friends filed a *habeas corpus* petition in the federal district court in Ohio, where it was assigned to Stanton's friend Judge Humphrey Leavitt. Stanton, worried that Leavitt might grant the petition and release Vallandigham, drafted a special order for Lincoln to suspend the writ of *habeas corpus* in the Vallandigham case. After consulting with Chase and Seward, however, Lincoln decided that there was no need to issue Stanton's proposed order. Leavitt denied Vallandigham's petition in an opinion that one Republican paper called "eminently sound and patriotic."[37]

Lincoln still had a problem, for some Republican papers were joining Democratic papers in denouncing the arrest, trial, and imprisonment. The *New York Tribune*, for example, wrote that the "federal and state constitutions do not recognize perverse opinions, nor unpatriotic speeches" as grounds for arresting and imprisoning a political leader. Lincoln and Stanton also had a problem with Burnside, who was not keeping them informed. Stanton himself penned a telegram to Burnside on May 18: "The President desires to know what you have done with Vallandigham—and if sent away by what route and where to." Later on this same day Lincoln commuted the punishment for Vallandigham from imprisonment to exile. Lincoln did not disapprove of the arrest and trial by military commission, and other military commanders may well have noticed this aspect of Lincoln's decision more than the change of sentence. In a letter to a friend in Steubenville, Stanton wrote that "the president thought it would be better to send him away among his friends than to have the trouble of keeping him." His wording suggests that, if left to his own devices, Stanton would have kept Vallandigham behind bars.[38]

In early June, again without consulting Washington, Burnside seized the offices and closed down the presses of an anti-administration paper, the *Chicago Times*. Lincoln and Stanton apparently learned of Burnside's actions through telegrams, including one that arrived late on the evening of June 3 from Isaac Arnold, a Republican member of Congress from Chicago, and Lyman Trumbull, a Republican senator from Illinois. Arnold and Trumbull forwarded to Lincoln a resolution, signed by two dozen Chicago leaders, asking him to overturn Burnside's order. The next morning Lincoln sent a note to Stanton saying, "We should revoke or suspend the order suspending the *Chicago Times*, and if you concur in opinion, please have it done." Stanton, through his aide Edward Townsend, immediately instructed Burnside to revoke the order. Soon thereafter Stanton sent a second message to Burnside: "The President directs me to say that if you have not acted upon the telegram from Adjutant General Townsend of this date you need not do so but may let the matter stand as it is until you received a letter by mail forwarded yesterday." Burnside, no doubt confused, wrote back to Stanton to say that he had already allowed the *Chicago Times* to resume operation. Stanton's letter, when it arrived, probably confused Burnside yet more. In it Lincoln suggested that Burnside should "take an early occasion to revoke" the order closing down the *Chicago Times*. "The irritation produced by such acts is in his opinion likely to do more harm than the publication will do." Stanton again assured Burnside, "The Government approves of your motives and desires to give you a cordial and efficient support," but he emphasized, "Upon administrative questions such as the arrest of civilians and the suppression of newspapers not requiring immediate action the President desires to be previously consulted."[39]

Lincoln did not make many speeches or public statements during the Civil War, but in June 1863 he decided to write two long public letters defending the military arrest and trial of Vallandigham. In the first letter, to Erastus Corning and other New York Democrats, Lincoln claimed that the army arrested Vallandigham because he was working "to prevent the raising of troops, to encourage desertions from the army, and to leave the rebellion without an adequate military force to suppress it. He was not arrested because he was damaging the political prospects of the administration, or the personal interests of the commanding general; but because he was damaging the army, upon the existence, and vigor of which, the life of the nation depends. He was warring upon the military; and this gave the military constitutional jurisdiction to lay hands upon him." Then, using the plain but powerful language of which he was master, Lincoln asked, "Must I shoot a simple-minded soldier boy who deserts, while I must not touch a hair of a wily agitator who induces him to desert?"[40]

The second letter was to Matthew Birchard and other Ohio Democrats who had just nominated Vallandigham for governor of their state, even though he was in exile in Canada. Here Lincoln claimed, "The military arrests and detentions, which have been made, including those of Mr. V. . . have been for *prevention*, and not for *punishment*—as injunctions to stay injury, as proceedings to keep the peace—and hence, like proceedings in such cases, and for like reasons, they have not been accompanied with indictments, or trials by juries, nor, in a single case by any punishment whatever, beyond what is purely incidental to the prevention."

Those who had been arrested and imprisoned probably would have disagreed with Lincoln's argument that they had not been punished. But Stanton would have agreed with every word of Lincoln's two letters.[41]

The Lieber code and the Lincoln letters marked a turning point in military arrests and trials of Northern civilians. For example, in the first half of 1863, there were only a handful of military commissions in the Department of the Cumberland, in eastern Tennessee. In the second half of the year, there were many more, involving at least thirty-five defendants. In the Middle Department, covering Delaware and Maryland, there were no military commissions in the first part of the year, but near the end of the year fifteen civilian defendants faced military commissions. Gideon Hart has described and documented a "national explosion" of military commissions in the latter part of 1863. Those arrested and tried were charged with a wide array of crimes: spying for the rebels, robbing and killing, forging medical certificates to avoid the draft, cheating the government on military contracts, and "using disloyal language."[42]

Section 2 of the Habeas Corpus Suspension Act could have seriously impeded the War Department's ability to make military arrests and use military trials by requiring that the department list all its prisoners and *release* any who were not indicted in a timely way by the civilian courts. But Holt interpreted this section narrowly, writing Stanton in June that he did not believe that Congress, when it required lists of "state or political prisoners," intended to reach "guerillas or bushwhackers," defendants whose cases "are clearly triable by court-martial or military commission and which are being every day thus tried." So the lists Holt provided to the district courts were very short, and not many prisoners were released. Lincoln, Stanton, and Holt would use military commissions to try thousands of Northern civilians during the course of the war.[43]

———

By the end of 1862 and beginning of 1863 thousands of black refugees were living in contraband camps near army encampments. There were camps in Virginia near Hampton and Norfolk, down in coastal South Carolina, and along the Mississippi River, such as the large camps at Cairo, Illinois, from which Stanton had allowed Tuttle to send some contrabands north. Many of the men in these contraband camps worked for the army, often lifting and loading for the quartermaster's office, and many of the women worked more informally, cooking or washing for the soldiers. So Stanton was responsible not just for an army of a million men, not just for tens of thousands of civilian employees working in armories and factories owned and operated by the department, but also to some extent for these tens of thousands of black refugees.[44]

In November 1862 Stanton asked LeBaron Russell, a Boston physician and philanthropist, to go to Fort Monroe to investigate the condition of the contrabands in that region. Russell reported back in December that there were more than 7,500 black refugees in six large camps in the Hampton Roads area. Conditions varied from camp to camp: in some places the refugees were living in buildings constructed by the government; in others in "small wooden houses which they have built for themselves"; in yet others "among the ruins of the old town." At some camps the men working for the quartermaster's office were earning $2 a month, although the government had not paid them for many months. Elsewhere the men supported themselves by "oystering and fishing." Russell especially noted and commended "the interest taken by the negroes in religious services and their devotion to the churches with which they are connected."[45]

Russell's report was useful, but it looked only at one region and did not address how best to make *military* use of the former slaves. Stanton discussed this issue with his friend Sumner and, in March 1863, Stanton formed the American Freedmen's Inquiry Commission. The commission was composed of three leading intellectuals and reformers: Samuel Gridley Howe, James McKaye, and Robert Dale Owen. Conscious that he had no explicit congressional authority for any such commission, Stanton explained in his order forming the commission that it was important for the War Department to have "the most authentic and accurate information" about the "great and constantly increasing colored population thrown upon the care of this Department in the progress of the war." He directed the commission to investigate and report on those recently freed from slavery, both their "protection and improvement" and how they could best help in "the suppression of the rebellion." The commissioners would each receive $8 per day for their work, plus their travel expenses, plus a secretary, selected by Stanton. The commissioners went right to work, visiting camps in person and gathering information by correspondence.[46]

Stanton probably had Russell's report in hand when he told Sumner in late December 1862 that he hoped to "have 200,000 negroes under arms before June—holding the Mississippi River & garrisoning the forts, so that our white soldiers can go elsewhere." In relating this news to a friend, Sumner added, "The President accepts this idea. Let the music sound and the day be celebrated." Lincoln did indeed now accept the idea of black soldiers, although, like Stanton, he seemed to view them in defensive rather than offensive terms. The final Emancipation Proclamation, which Lincoln issued on January 1, 1863, announced that free blacks would be "received into the armed service of the United States to garrison forts, positions, stations, and other places, and to man vessels of all sorts in said service."[47]

Stanton's professed goal of 200,000 black troops would require rapid work, for at the start of the year there were only about 3,000 black troops, including three regiments of Louisiana Native Guards, drawn largely from the free blacks in and around New Orleans, and a regiment in South Carolina organized by Saxton under Stanton's August orders. But in the first few months of the year Stanton did not apply all his famed energy and skill to the task of raising and training black regiments. It was not until the end of January that he authorized Governor Andrew to start work on raising black regiments in Massachusetts, regiments that would become the famed Fifty-fourth and Fifty-fifth Massachusetts Volunteers. It was March when Stanton sent the man who would prove his most effective recruiter, Adjt. Gen. Lorenzo Thomas, to enlist white officers and black volunteers in the Mississippi Valley. Two more months passed before Stanton established the Bureau of Colored Troops within the War Department. Henceforth, with very few exceptions, black regiments would have national designations, such as the Thirty-ninth U.S. Colored Troops, rather than state designations, which were in any case misleading because so many soldiers were from "out-of-state." One historian called the War Department's initial efforts at black recruiting "slow, uncertain, halting, and timid."[48]

Lorenzo Thomas was a curious choice for the important task of raising black regiments, for Stanton did not much like him. Moreover, unlike others involved in black recruiting, Thomas was from a slave state, Delaware, and not an abolitionist. Indeed, he insisted in a letter to a friend that he did not have "nigger on the brain."[49] But from the moment Thomas arrived in the West, and visited a contraband camp at Cairo, finding hundreds living and dying in miserable conditions, he sympathized with the former slaves. He worked not only to raise black regiments but to establish farms on abandoned plantations so that blacks could be working rather than living as refugees. Thomas wrote that he hoped to establish "a system of culture for all blacks who do not enter the military service; to transfer the burden of their support from the government to themselves, and to demonstrate that the freed negro can be paid fair wages and yield a handsome profit to his employer." The *New York Evening Post*, describing and praising the work of Thomas, said it would be hard to "over-estimate the important consequences that are destined to flow from the institution, by the government, of this negro labor system."[50]

To raise black regiments, Thomas traveled from place to place, giving speeches to thousands of white troops, with black workers often on the margins of the crowd. On April 6 he reported to Stanton that he had addressed 7,000 soldiers at Helena, Arkansas; on April 9, in two separate speeches, he reached more than 10,000 men at Lake Providence, Louisiana. In his speeches Thomas declared that it was now the Lincoln administration's policy to raise and arm black regiments; that some of the white soldiers and officers could, if they wished, become officers in such black regiments; that black regiments would help win the war. Thomas would then invite the Union generals on the platform with him to give their own speeches, and most of them supported the president's policy. Most, but not all. Gen. William Tecumseh Sherman, when Thomas spoke to his troops near Vicksburg, said that he hoped that if the government raised black regiments "they would be used for some side purpose & not be brigaded with white men." In private Sherman was even more opposed to the idea of black soldiers, writing, "I won't trust niggers to fight yet."[51]

Many white officers and soldiers found the prospect of promotion through service in a black regiment attractive. Encouraged by Thomas and others, they would seek and find blacks to serve as soldiers both in the contraband camps, near their army encampments, and farther afield. Thomas wrote to Stanton in April from Grant's headquarters near

Vicksburg, "The west bank of the Mississippi being under our control, General Grant will send forage parties to the east bank to collect the blacks, mules, &c, for military and agricultural purposes. We shall obtain all that we require. I shall find no difficulty in organizing negro troops to the extent of 20,000, if necessary." Thomas informed Stanton in May that he had one complete regiment at Helena, another in formation there, five regiments in formation in Louisiana, and two in formation in Mississippi. Stanton praised Thomas for his hard work and urged him to continue.[52]

The questions Stanton and others had about whether black troops would fight were largely answered by two battles in May and June. On May 27, 1863, General Banks ordered an attack on Port Hudson, looming over the Mississippi River about twenty miles north of Baton Rouge. Two black regiments, the First and Third Louisiana Native Guards, played prominent roles in this attack, suffered severe casualties, and by almost all accounts displayed great courage. In his official report to Halleck, Banks said the black regiments "answered every expectation." They "made three charges upon the batteries of the enemy, suffering very heavy losses and holding their position at nightfall." Banks concluded that the "severe test to which they were subjected, and the determined manner in which they encountered the enemy, leaves upon my mind no doubt of their ultimate success. They require only good officers, commands of limited numbers, and careful discipline, to make them excellent soldiers." As soon as this report arrived in Washington, Stanton passed it to the press. The *New York Times* commented, "This official testimony settles the question that the negro race can fight with great prowess. These black soldiers had never before been in any severe engagement. They were comparatively raw troops, and were yet subjected to the most awful ordeal that ever veterans have to experience—the charging upon fortifications through the crash of belching batteries. . . . It is no longer possible to doubt the bravery and steadiness of the colored race, when rightly led."[53]

On June 7, 1863, three new black regiments, organized under orders from Thomas, fought in the short, sharp battle at Milliken's Bend, Louisiana. These troops were very new; some had received their rifles only the day before the battle. According to a report in the *Cleveland Daily Leader*, "The fight was carried on with energy and desperation by our forces. . . . The negroes have fought better than their white officers, many of whom it is said skulked away." *Harper's Weekly* printed a report of the hand-to-hand combat and, perhaps more persuasive, a print showing black and white soldiers using bayonets and clubbed rifles. Stanton heard from an officer at Grant's headquarters that "the sentiment of this army with regard to the employment of negro troops has been revolutionized by the bravery of the blacks in the recent battle of Milliken's Bend. Prominent officers, who used in private to sneer at the idea, are now heartily in favor of it." Stanton also learned that the Confederates had hanged several prisoners, "black and white," captured at the battle.[54]

This raised an issue that had troubled Stanton and others for many months: that the Confederates would not treat black soldiers or their white officers as legitimate warriors, that they would murder them even if they surrendered or would enslave captured black soldiers rather than treat them as prisoners of war. In fact Jefferson Davis had announced that "all negro slaves captured in arms" and their white officers would be tried under the laws of the Southern states, which usually meant blacks and whites would suffer the death penalty for "inciting servile insurrection." The Confederate Congress agreed, declaring that any white officer recruiting or leading black soldiers would "be deemed as inciting servile insurrection, and shall if captured be put to death or be otherwise punished at the discretion of the court." The reports from early battles, however, suggest that Confederate soldiers were not observing any such procedures; they were simply killing black soldiers who tried to surrender.[55]

Stanton and Halleck wanted Lieber to deal with the question of black soldiers, and he did: Article 57 of the code specified, "No belligerent has a right to declare that enemies of a certain class, color, or condition, when properly organized as soldiers, will not be treated by him as public enemies." In other words, the Confederacy was violating the laws of war when it treated black soldiers differently from white. Article 58 amplified on the point: "The laws of nations know no distinctions of color. . . . If an enemy of the United States should enslave and sell any captured persons of their army, it would be a case for severest retaliation." And Article 62 addressed the "no quarter" approach, killing rather than taking prisoners: "All troops of the enemy known or discovered to give no quarter in general, or to any portion of the army, receive none." In other words, if a Confederate army gave no quarter to black Union soldiers, and killed them as they were trying to surrender, the U.S. army would be "within its rights" to give no quarter to soldiers from that Confederate army.[56]

But the code was less than clear, because it was not *possible* to be clear, on what would happen if the Confederacy murdered blacks rather than taking them prisoners, or if the Confederacy failed to treat captured blacks or their white officers as prisoners of war. "Retaliation," such as killing an innocent prisoner of war to protest the other side's violation of the laws of war, was the method by which belligerents had traditionally "enforced" the laws of war. But, as Lieber wrote in the code, retaliation was "the sternest feature of war" and therefore should "never be resorted to as a measure of mere revenge, but only as a means of protective retribution, and moreover, cautiously and unavoidably." Would the United States be willing to kill innocent Southern soldiers, selected at random, as a way of protesting and punishing Southern treatment of black soldiers?[57]

The grim knowledge that, if they tried to surrender, they might be murdered, and if captured, they might be enslaved, of course reduced the number of blacks willing to join the Union Army. But another issue that impeded black recruiting was unequal pay. Indeed, because it was so immediate and so painful, unequal pay was probably a more serious issue than the risk of rebel violence. When he first asked General Saxton to raise a few black regiments in South Carolina, Stanton had promised that they would receive the same pay as white regiments. Congress, however, in the Militia Act, provided a separate, lower pay scale for black soldiers, $10 per month, less a $3 clothing allowance, so effectively only $7 a month. Stanton asked the solicitor of the War Department, William Whiting, to review the issue, and Whiting concluded that the $7 a month would stand. If he had wanted to do so, Stanton could have reviewed this legal issue himself; he was, after all, a leading Supreme Court lawyer. With a little legal creativity he could have reached a different conclusion, perhaps relying upon Lincoln's general constitutional war powers, perhaps relying upon statutes other than the Militia Act. But Stanton did not do so; instead he issued Whiting's opinion as a general order in June 1863. When Governor Tod complained, Stanton responded that black soldiers would have to "trust to state contributions and the justice of Congress in the next session." The next session would not start until December, and even then it would take months before Congress acted.[58]

Stanton did not reach, in 1863 or indeed ever, his goal of having 200,000 black troops. But by the end of the Civil War, a total of 178,975 black soldiers had served at one time or another in the Union Army, about 10 percent of all the soldiers who served the Union in the Civil War. Many people deserved credit for this, ranging from Lincoln to the thousands upon thousands of brave black volunteers. But Stanton surely deserves much credit for starting and persisting in the process of recruiting blacks into the army.[59]

Yet another member of Stanton's family died this spring: his brother-in-law and assistant secretary Christopher Wolcott died of tuberculosis at his home in Akron, Ohio. The telegram arrived on the first Saturday in April, just as Lincoln left Washington, heading south to see the Army of the Potomac, so Stanton responded that he would "attend the funeral if the President returns in time for me to leave here." On Tuesday morning he sent a telegram to Lincoln, still with the army: "With your permission I would be glad to attend the funeral of my brother-in-law Mr. Wolcott tomorrow." Without waiting for Lincoln's response—there was none— Stanton and his son boarded a special express train, arranged by Stanton's friends on the Baltimore & Ohio Railroad, and headed for Steubenville, where Wolcott was buried on Wednesday. Wolcott's death must have reminded Stanton of his own father's death: another young man leaving behind a widow and young children. Stanton returned to Washington on Sunday, April 10, by another special B&O train, and went immediately to the War Department, reviewing and sending messages. One telegram was to his mother, in Steubenville: "Arrived here safely this morning. All well. Will write you today."[60]

Not long after he returned to Washington, Stanton probably saw a letter to Chase from Murat Halstead, editor of the *Cincinnati Commercial*, urging Chase to talk with Lincoln and Stanton about Grant, whom Halstead called "a poor drunken imbecile. He is a poor stick sober, and he is most of the time more than half drunk, and much of the time idiotically drunk." Stanton had seen similar reports before and had recently acted upon them, sending Charles Dana, the former *New York Tribune* editor, now an assistant secretary of war, to Grant's headquarters near

Vicksburg. Grant, who might have resented Dana as Stanton's spy, instead welcomed him, seeing him as a useful back channel to Washington. Dana's reports to Stanton were filled with details, captured with his reporter's eye, such as the way McClernand's corps was delayed because the general was loading his wife and her baggage onto the boat. Dana supported Grant, which helped bring Stanton around. Not long after Dana arrived at Grant's headquarters Stanton told him that Grant could deal as he wished with McClernand: "General Grant has full and absolute authority to enforce his own commands and to remove any person who by ignorance, inaction or any cause interferes with or delays his operations."[61]

Charles Anderson Dana, the assistant secretary of war upon whom Stanton relied for detailed reports from the headquarters of Grant and Rosecrans. The photo shows Dana in the field at Grant's headquarters.

On April 19 Lincoln, Stanton, and Halleck boarded a government steamship "before daylight" and headed to Aquia Creek for a one-day meeting there with General Hooker. The reporter Noah Brooks, who had accompanied Lincoln on a similar trip two weeks before, described "the Creek" for his readers as "a point of considerable importance, as a vast amount of supplies pass through the little *entrepot* daily, for the use of the army." Stanton must have surveyed this bustling port with pride, for this was all the work of his department. John Sedgwick, one of the generals under Hooker, noted in a letter home that Hooker had gone to see Lincoln and Stanton at Aquia, but that nobody other than those involved knew what they discussed. It seems likely, however, that Hooker talked with Lincoln and Stanton his plans to attack Lee by moving around him, north and west, as soon as the roads were dry and hard. Henry Bellows, the New York minister, who visited Hooker at about this same time, wrote, "He means to have no uncertain or equivocal result; that he would either whip the enemy terribly or be terribly whipped by them." Bellows added that Hooker "spoke slightingly of the Sec of War—and said that the President is not much of a soldier."[62]

On his return to Washington, Bellows met with both Stanton and Seward. When he asked Stanton why he was so hostile to the Sanitary Commission, Stanton replied that he resented how the Commission had effectively appointed one of his direct subordinates, Surgeon General William Hammond, over his objection. "I am not used to being beaten," Stanton explained, "and I don't like it, and therefore I am hostile to the Commission." George Templeton Strong, a friend and colleague of Bellows, noted in his diary that Stanton had at least admitted what the Sanitary Commission long suspected. Strong believed the Commission and its influential friends could, if they tried, force Stanton's resignation, but he thought they should "make no assault on him," should not at this time do anything that would "weaken any one man's faith in the national government." Bellows complained to Seward about Stanton, but Seward would not listen. He told Bellows that Stanton was "full of energy, ability & labor" and worked so hard and so long that he "settled twenty questions a day to his own one." Seward conceded that Stanton was "irritable, capricious, uncomfortable" and "there was not a person in the Govt from the President down to the porter, whom Stanton had not treated rudely." But Stanton was also "good-hearted, devoted, patriotic."[63]

Noah Brooks, in a sketch for his newspaper of the members of the cabinet, more or less agreed with Seward. "Stanton is what is popularly known as a 'bull-head'; that is to say, he is opinionated, implacable, intent, and not easily turned from any purpose. He is stout, spectacled, black as to hair and eyes, and Hebraic as to nose and complexion. He has a little, aristocratic wife, lives in handsome style, consuming much of his large fortune, probably, in his ample and somewhat gorgeous way of living." Stanton "works like a trooper and spends day and night at his office when under strong pressure. He does not appear to have the maggot of the next Presidency in his brain, but plugs right on, unmindful of what anybody says or thinks concerning him." Brooks added, with his characteristic wit, that Stanton "wears good clothes, goes to an Episcopal church—if at all—and would be much more popular if he were not so domineering and so in love with the beauties of military law."[64]

Edwin McMasters Stanton, as he looked during the war years. Lucius Chittenden recalled that "his face was dark, and the lower portion of it was completely covered with a long, heavy, dark beard. His eyes were small, dark, and piercing."

Stanton was aware of his reputation. When he did a favor for Isabella Beecher Hooker, he wrote to her, "In my official station I have tried hard to do my duty as I shall answer to God at the great day, but it is the misfortune of that station—a misfortune that no one else can comprehend . . .— that most of my duties are harsh and painful to someone, so that I rejoice at the opportunity, however rare, of combining duty with kindly offices." Writing to her sister Harriet Beecher Stowe, the author of *Uncle Tom's Cabin*, Stanton said, "It will always give me pleasure to render any service to you or yours." In social settings Stanton could be pleasant. Seward's teenage daughter, Fanny, meeting Stanton for the first time, described him as having "a cheery look, and a merry twinkle of the eye" and admitted, "I like him very much—his manners are warm and hearty." Dana recalled Stanton as a "man who was devoted to his friends, and he had a good many with whom he liked to sit down and talk. In conversation he was witty and satirical; he told a story well, and was very companionable." As for characterizations of his "impatience and violence," Dana thought they were "exaggerated." The secretary "could speak in a very peremptory tone, but I never heard him say anything that could be called vituperative." The problem was that Stanton "was a man of the quickest intelligence, and understood a thing before half of it was told him. His judgment was just as swift, and when he got hold of a man who did not understand, who did not state his case clearly, he was very impatient."[65]

Dana, the man who had received and published Stanton's letter about "the days of Joshua," was struck by his "deep religious feeling and his familiarity with the Bible." He thought Stanton "must have studied the Bible a great deal when he was a boy." Stanton's religion "was the straightforward expression of what he believed and lived, and was as simple and genuine and real to him as the principles of his business." He was also "a serious student of history. He had read many books on the subject—more than on any other, I should say—and he was fond of discussing historical characters with his associates." He liked to discuss legal questions as well "and would listen with eagerness to the statement of cases in which his friends had been interested."[66]

———

In late April, General Hooker led his army north and west, crossed the Rappahannock, and attacked Lee's army. During the first few days of May, Stanton knew that Hooker was fighting Lee near Chancellorsville, but almost nothing about the battle. Visiting the telegraph office on May 4, Welles found Lincoln, who said he had a "feverish anxiety to get facts—was constantly up and down for nothing reliable came from the front." Then, at about three in the afternoon on May 6, a message arrived from Hooker's chief of staff, reporting that Hooker had recrossed the river, in other words, that Lee had once again defeated the Army of the Potomac and forced it to retreat. Noah Brooks recalled that when Lincoln heard this news, he was struck as if by a thunderbolt. "Clasping his hands behind his back, he walked up and down the room, saying 'My God! my God! What will the country say!'" Welles heard the news from Sumner, rushed to the War Department, and asked Stanton where Hooker was. When Stanton did not know, Welles "looked at him sharply, and . . . with some incredulity, for he, after a moment's pause, said he is on this side of the river but I know not where." William Stoddard, the third of Lincoln's private secretaries, wrote that Stanton called this "the darkest day of the war." Lincoln and Halleck immediately headed south by steamboat to see the situation in person.[67]

Stanton tried, as best he could, to calm both generals and governors. He sent a message to Hooker telling him, "The result does not seem to have produced panic. Gold has only risen by 6 per cent in New York." When Lincoln returned that evening, Stanton sent a midnight message to all the Northern governors assuring them that there had "been no serious disaster" and the "Army of the Potomac will speedily resume its offensive operations." Some Northern papers renewed the call for Lincoln to replace Stanton. It was not surprising to see such attacks in the *New York Herald*, but it was interesting to see Brooks, generally supportive of Lincoln and his administration, join the critics: "Stanton, by his mismanagement, his arbitrary measures, his stupidly blundering regulations of public affairs and interference with private matters, and by his willful wrongheadedness, has succeeded in alienating himself from every public and private interest and seems to have scarcely a friend left in the ranks of the army or in civil life, except so far as self-interest induces men to be his friends and sycophants. Were the President to dismiss him and replace him with Banks or Butler, it would undoubtedly be one of the most popular measures of this Administration."[68]

Robert E. Lee did not wait for Hooker to "resume offensive operations." In the middle of May, Lee started to move the Army of Northern Virginia north, aiming to invade Maryland and Pennsylvania. Hooker, learning that Lee was heading north, proposed to Lincoln that he take his army south in order to capture Richmond. Lincoln responded on June 10, "*Lee's army*, and not *Richmond*, is your true objective point. If he comes towards the Upper Potomac, follow on his flank, and on the inside track, shortening your lines, whilst he lengthens his. Fight him when opportunity offers." Stanton on this same day sent Gen. Darius Couch, a senior general who had chafed under Hooker's command, to Harrisburg to take charge of the defenses there. Stanton also sent a note on June 10 to Thomas Scott, his former assistant secretary, now a senior railroad officer in Philadelphia: "No time should be lost in organizing for defense."[69]

Stanton himself certainly lost no time. He was at the War Department almost around the clock in the middle of June. When Scott arrived in Washington at 1:00 a.m. on June 15, he found Stanton, Seward, and

Whiting working. The four men reviewed and revised a draft proclamation by Lincoln, calling upon the states to provide 100,000 militiamen to serve for six months. At about 2:00 a.m. Stanton scribbled out and handed to the telegraph clerks a message to Governor David Tod in Ohio: "Reports received yesterday & last night have rendered it certain that Lee's army is advancing in force with his whole army." When Lincoln issued the formal call for militia, around noon on this day, he received almost immediately a message from Simon Cameron in Harrisburg, who said he did not believe that Pennsylvanians would volunteer to serve for as long six months: "If you authorize Gen. Couch to accept them for the emergency a very large force will be on hand immediately." Stanton (no doubt annoyed) replied to Cameron, "The law has fixed the period for which the troops shall be called. If the emergency is over before that time, they can be discharged." On this same day, Governor Horatio Seymour of New York promised Stanton that his state would provide 20,000 militiamen, the first of whom would be on their way within twenty-four hours. Stanton thanked Seymour, and thanked him more fulsomely a few days later, when the New York troops arrived in Harrisburg: "I cannot forbear expressing to you the deep obligation I feel for the prompt and candid support you have given the Government in the present emergency. The energy, activity and patriotism you have exhibited, I personally and officially acknowledge." Of course these were merely militia troops, civilians with little training and no experience. "Five thousand regulars could whip them in the open field," Couch warned Stanton.[70]

As he moved his veterans north to fight Lee, Hooker visited Washington on June 23 and met with Lincoln and Stanton. The general almost certainly renewed his request for more authority, for he commanded only the Army of the Potomac, not all the troops in Virginia, Maryland, and Pennsylvania. Stanton recalled for the Boston lawyer and military historian John Ropes that the three men also discussed Maryland Heights, the high ground overlooking Harpers Ferry. The Heights "had been fortified and provisioned at vast expense, and it was agreed that they should not be given up, General Hooker concurring without objection." A few days later, however, Stanton and Halleck were surprised to learn that Hooker had ordered William French, in charge at Harpers Ferry, to abandon the

Heights so that the troops at Harpers Ferry could form part of Hooker's army. Thinking there was some misunderstanding, Halleck ordered French to disregard Hooker's order. This was the last straw for Hooker, who sent Halleck his resignation.[71]

When he received Hooker's message, Stanton asked Lincoln to come to the War Department. According to postwar memoirs, as Lincoln read the message his face "became like lead." Stanton asked him, "What shall be done?" and Lincoln replied, "Accept his resignation." Lincoln and Stanton then "canvassed the merits of various officers and decided to place [Gen. George] Meade in command." Stanton sent one of his aides, Assistant Adjt. Gen. James Hardie, to wake Meade at three in the morning to tell him that he was now in charge of the Army of the Potomac. At around ten, when the cabinet met, Lincoln explained that he had "observed in Hooker the same failings that were witnessed in McClellan after the Battle of Antietam. Want of alacrity to obey, and a greedy call for more troops which could not, and ought not to be taken from other points." There was some discussion among the cabinet about which general would be the best successor, before Lincoln "finally remarked" that he had already issued the orders to appoint Meade. Welles was annoyed that Lincoln was consulting the cabinet after the "matter had already been settled."[72]

George Gordon Meade, whom Lincoln and Stanton placed in command of the Army of the Potomac just before the Battle of Gettysburg.

Lincoln and Stanton were focused on Lee and Hooker and Meade, but they did not lose sight of Grant and Rosecrans. With Grant, Stanton had the advantage of Dana, who sent him reports almost daily, although they would take a week or more to arrive in Washington because they had to travel by boat upriver to Cairo first. By early June, Grant had surrounded and besieged Vicksburg and seemed likely to capture the city any day. On June 14 Dana reported to Stanton, "All indications point to a speedy surrender of this place," and asked him where he should go and what he should do when Vicksburg was in Grant's hands. On June 29 Dana informed Stanton that the half-starved Southern deserters told the Union soldiers that Vicksburg would surrender on July 4, "if, indeed, it can hold on so long as that."[73]

Communications between Washington and Rosecrans were more difficult, not because of the telegraph lines, which were good, but because of the general himself. For many months in early 1863, Rosecrans and his Army of the Cumberland remained at Murfreesboro, Tennessee, resting and replenishing. Stanton and Halleck sent him increasingly pointed messages, prodding him to move. On June 16, for example, Halleck wired to ask Rosecrans, "Is it your intention to make an immediate movement forward? A definite answer, yes or no, is required." Rosecrans hedged: "If immediate means tonight or tomorrow, no. If it means as soon as all things are ready, say five days, yes." Another eight days would pass, however, before Rosecrans at last informed Halleck that his army of about 80,000 men was on the march, heading south and east, toward Chattanooga, Tennessee.[74]

Stanton sent a note on June 30 to Lincoln: "Will you be so kind as to call at the department as soon as convenient. A dispatch is coming in from the West." Welles complained in his diary on this same day that Lincoln canceled the cabinet meeting because he was with Stanton in the telegraph office. There was no telegraph equipment in the White House, so Lincoln was often in the War Department, in the telegraph office, as was Stanton; this was why he set up the telegraph office right next to his own office. One of the telegraph clerks recalled that Lincoln "visited the War Department telegraph office morning, afternoon, and evening, to receive the latest news from the armies at the front. His tall, homely form could be seen crossing the well-shaded lawn between the White House and the War Department day after day with unvaried regularity." In the winter Lincoln would wear "a gray plaid shawl thrown over his shoulders in careless fashion, and, upon entering the telegraph office, he would always hang this shawl over the top of the high, screen door opening into Secretary Stanton's room, adjoining. This door was nearly always open. He seldom failed to come over late in the evening before retiring, and sometimes he would stay all night in the War Department."[75]

Lincoln spent more social time with Seward, but he spent more working time with Stanton than with any of his other cabinet members, mainly time in the telegraph office. Lincoln's presence in the telegraph office is proved not only by memoirs but by the many telegrams in his hand in the department's files. On June 24, for example, Lincoln sent a telegram to General Couch in Harrisburg: "Have you any reports of the enemy moving into Pennsylvania? And if any, what?" Couch responded that deserters reported that Gen. Richard S. Ewell, with 30,000 men, was at Greencastle; Lee's headquarters was reportedly at Millwood. Lincoln wrote on the copy of Couch's message, "Please forward this to Gen. Hooker," and Stanton's telegraph clerks did so. A telegram arrived from Simon Cameron on June 27, pleading with Lincoln to provide federal uniforms for the Pennsylvania militia. Lincoln wrote on the copy of Cameron's message, "I think the Secretary of War better let them have the clothes." Lincoln often used this light tone with Stanton. When General Dix wrote to Lincoln from Fort Monroe about conflict there between the army and the navy, Lincoln scrawled on the envelope, "Submitted to Mars & Neptune."[76]

The men who worked in the telegraph office remembered the "esteem and affection" between Lincoln and Stanton. Stanton's private secretary A. E. H. Johnson wrote, "No two men were ever more utterly and irreconcilably unlike. The secretiveness which Lincoln wholly lacked, Stanton had in marked degree; the charity which Stanton could not feel, coursed from every pore in Lincoln." In times of crisis, "Lincoln was as calm and unruffled as the summer sea," while "Stanton would lash himself into a fury over the same condition of things. Stanton would take hardships with a groan; Lincoln would find a funny story to fit them."

And yet, for all their differences, "no two men ever did or could work better in harness. They supplemented each other's nature, and they fully recognized the fact that they were necessary to each other."[77]

Lincoln and Stanton would need all their patience over the first few days of July. General Couch sent a message from Harrisburg on June 30, reporting rumors that Lee's army was heading for Gettysburg, "saying they expected to fight a great battle there." Over the next few days Stanton received reports not just from Meade at Gettysburg but also from Couch at Harrisburg and Herman Haupt, whom he had sent to Baltimore to arrange rail transport. The reports were never fast enough or detailed enough for Lincoln and Stanton. At one point Haupt refused a request by Stanton that he run trains every three hours from Baltimore toward Gettysburg, explaining that to send such frequent trains down the single track would delay supplies.[78]

A message from Meade, received on the morning of July 3, reported that "after one of the severest contests of the war" the enemies were "repulsed at all points." Meade added, "We have suffered considerably in killed and wounded." Later that day and night messages arrived in Washington reporting that fighting had commenced again: "The enemy thus far have made no impression upon my position." Finally, at about six o'clock on the morning of July 4, a message arrived that Meade had sent the prior evening: "[Lee] assaulted my left center twice, being on both occasions handsomely repulsed." Stanton informed Burnside at eight that morning that Meade now had "the prospect of complete victory." Lincoln was somewhat more cautious in a message for the press, saying that the reports from Gettysburg "promise a great success to the cause of the Union." By five that afternoon Stanton could send good news to Dix: "Advices just received represent Meade's victory as complete and that Lee commenced retreating towards Chambersburg at three o'clock this morning."[79]

The North celebrated once, and then a second time, when news arrived in Washington on July 7 that Vicksburg had surrendered to Grant. Not only did Grant have the city and its guns, clearing the Mississippi River; he had captured 30,000 rebel soldiers, whom he would parole so they could not fight again against the United States. That evening a large crowd, accompanied by a regimental band, visited first the White

House and then the War Department. Stanton emerged onto the steps and, when the crowd quieted, he spoke. He said they were "celebrating a victory achieved by General Grant," the general who had first become famous for "those noble words we love to remember: 'I shall move immediately against your works.'" Ever since then, ever since the spring of 1862, Grant and his men had been moving "against their works, and the result is—Vicksburg." The crowd cheered. Stanton predicted, "The same strategy, the same bravery, the same indomitable energy, which has driven the enemy from the banks of the Susquehanna and Mississippi will ere long drive every rebel from the field and every Copperhead to his hole." He even expressed the hope that before year's end he would be able to "announce to them the clearing of the rebels from every battle-field." When Stanton closed, declaring that the people of the United States would never forget the great work of the armies of the Potomac and Mississippi, there was "vociferous cheering."[80]

Chapter 11

"Too Serious for Jokes"

—— July–December 1863 ——

A s soon as they knew that Lee and his army were retreating from Gettysburg, Stanton and Halleck pressed Meade to pursue him, to attack him and his army before they could cross the Potomac and reach the relative safety of Virginia. Halleck also sent a message to Gen. Benjamin Franklin Kelley at Clarksburg, Virginia, instructing him to hasten toward Williamsport, Maryland, where Lee and his army would probably attempt to cross the river. When Kelley answered that it would take a day or two to gather his forces, Stanton exploded: "I have seen your dispatch . . . and regret to hear you talk about 'some days' to concentrate when minutes are precious." Why, Stanton asked, was Kelley still at Clarksburg rather than on the march? On the evening of July 6, Lincoln sent a message to Halleck. "I left the telegraph office a good deal dissatisfied," he wrote after reading several recent messages. One was a report from Gen. William French at Frederick, Maryland, "saying the enemy is crossing his wounded over the river in flats, without saying why he does not stop it, or even intimating that it ought to be stopped." Another was a message from Meade that his main army would not "move until it is ascertained that the rebels intend to evacuate the Cumberland Valley." All of this looked to Lincoln rather like Meade intended "to get the enemy across the river again without a further collision" but did *not* intend "to prevent his crossing and to destroy him."[1]

Halleck wired Meade on July 7 that he should "push forward and fight Lee before he can cross the Potomac." Meade responded testily that his army was making "forced marches." This was only part of the story, however. Meade had not started his army from Gettysburg immediately, and (although he was making a few cavalry attacks) his infantry and artillery were following rather than attacking Lee. Meade wrote to Halleck on July 10 that he would "advance cautiously on the same line tomorrow until I can develop more fully the enemy's force and position." Two days later he promised Halleck that he would attack Lee and his army the next day at Williamsport "unless something intervenes to prevent it." What intervened was a council of war that Meade held that evening, at which he secured the approval of his corps commanders for what he wanted: to probe the enemy's defenses around Williamsport rather than make an all-out assault. When Stanton and Halleck saw Meade's report of this council and realized that he had let another day pass without an attack, they were outraged. Halleck sent a message to Meade on the evening of July 13: "Call no council of war. It is proverbial that councils of war never fight." Meade must not "let the enemy escape."[2]

By the time Halleck sent this message, he and Stanton were facing a second crisis: the New York draft riots. As required by the Enrollment Act, federal provost marshals were making detailed lists of all the men in their districts eligible for the draft. In many places there was resistance and in a few places violence. At midday on July 13, Stanton received an alarming report from Edward Sanford, his senior telegraph officer in New York: "A serious riot is now taking place on Third Avenue, at the provost marshal's office. The office is said to have been burned, and the adjoining block to be on fire." A few hours later Sanford informed Stanton that the riot was "entirely beyond the control of the police." A third message from Sanford, which arrived in Washington about midnight, reported that the rioters were chasing, beating, and killing blacks. "The situation is not improved since dark. The program is diversified by small mobs chasing isolated negroes as hounds would chase a fox." The mob had attacked and "partially sacked" the offices of the *New York Tribune* and "the telegraph is especially sought for destruction." Stanton responded at one in the morning, posing several questions, such as what measures the local police and federal forces (under Gen. John Wool) had taken "to quell the riot."[3]

There was more bad news about noon on July 14: a telegram from Meade to Halleck reporting that Lee and his army had crossed the Potomac River into northern Virginia. Hay noted in his diary that Lincoln was "deeply grieved" by this news. "We had them within our grasp," Lincoln sighed. "We had only to stretch forth our hands & they were ours. And nothing I could say or do could make the army move." It was "a dreadful reminiscence of McClellan." At the cabinet meeting soon thereafter, Stanton asked Lincoln to step out for a few minutes. When the two men returned, Welles thought they looked worried. One of the cabinet members asked about the rumors that Lee had crossed the Potomac. Stanton claimed "he knew nothing of Lee's crossing." Lincoln, with what Welles described as a "look of painful rebuke to Stanton," announced, "If he [Lee] has not got all of his men across—he soon will." A couple of hours later, when Welles visited the War Department for the latest news, he found Lincoln stretched out "upon a sofa, completely absorbed, overwhelmed with the news." Stanton shared with Welles one of Dana's recent messages, describing the men and materiel that Grant had captured at Vicksburg. Lincoln, Stanton, and Welles all had the same view: if only Meade had achieved a "Vicksburg victory" in the East, the South might be near surrender. As Stanton put it a few weeks later in a letter to a friend, "Since the world began, no man ever missed so great an opportunity of serving his country, as [Meade] lost by neglecting to strike his adversary at Williamsport."[4]

On this day, July 14, however, Stanton had no time to lament; he was far too busy dealing with the draft riots. He sent a message to the mayor of New York City, asking what the federal government could do to help restore order. When the mayor answered that "the military force at command is altogether inadequate," Stanton replied, "Five regiments are under orders to return to New York." He sent a note to Gen. Robert Schenck in Baltimore to ensure that there was no delay when a regiment changed trains on its way from Frederick, Maryland, back to New York City. There were worrisome reports of riots not only in New York but in Boston, Philadelphia, and elsewhere. "The government will be able to stand the test," Stanton insisted to Sanford, "even if there should be a riot and mob in every ward of every city." John Jay, the grandson and namesake of the founding father, wrote to Stanton that what New York needed was a proper leader: neither "an octogenarian general" (Wool was seventy-nine years old) nor "a politician like Gov. Seymour but a general who will be ruthless in enforcing law & thus save in the end thousands of lives. If you have no better man pray send us Dix." That was just what Stanton had in mind; he sent a telegram this same day to General Dix at Fort Monroe, directing him to come as soon as possible to Washington, and then head to New York City. Dix rather than Wool would command the Eastern Department, including New England as well as New York, and under him Gen. Edward Canby would command the federal forces in New York. Stanton assured David Dudley Field, a leading lawyer in New York, that the government would provide Dix and Canby with "whatever force" they needed "to execute the law of the United States."[5]

The papers described in detail the "Copperhead riots" in New York City. Republican editors blamed the Democrats, with their anti-administration, anti-conscription rhetoric, for the riots. So did Stanton. Count Gurowski noted in his diary that Stanton was "in rage and despair" for it seemed there were "riots everywhere." The riots "coincide with the invasion by the rebels. At the best, these riots are generated by the Fourth of July Seymourite speeches and by the long uninterrupted series of articles in New York papers, like *World* etc." The speech to which Gurowski alluded was one in which Seymour denounced the draft and threatened, "The bloody and treasonable and revolutionary doctrine of public necessity can be proclaimed by a mob as well as by a government." After the riots started, Seymour addressed a crowd of rioters as "my friends" and promised them he would seek to have "this draft suspended and stopped."[6]

As federal troops arrived, they restored order in New York City, although not before at least a hundred people, and perhaps five hundred, were dead. Stanton was adamant that the draft would proceed in New York, writing on July 17, "The law will be executed in New York, and having conquered the rebel armies in the field, their rebel aiders and abettors in our northern cities will share the same fate." Seymour wanted Lincoln to delay the draft in New York until the courts could rule on the constitutionality of the Enrollment Act, but Lincoln and Stanton rejected this idea. As Stanton put it in a letter to his friend James Brady, if "the national Executive must negotiate with state executives in relation to the execution of an act of Congress, then the problem which the rebellion desired to solve is already determined." The United States was a national government, Stanton insisted, not a mere confederation. The president would not negotiate national law with state governors.[7]

After a brief delay to ensure that sufficient troops were on the ground, the draft resumed in New York City in the middle of August. Stanton took the precaution of sending Dix documents authorizing him, if necessary, to proclaim martial law and to call upon Seymour for militia. In his cover letter Stanton told Dix that the government had the "utmost confidence" in his "energy courage and discretion." With more than 15,000 federal troops in the city, and with close coordination between Dix and the provost marshals, the draft proceeded peacefully. The *New York Times* reported that there was "neither insurrection, riot, row, nor shindy; not even so much as a quarrel or a tiff." The paper praised Lincoln for "his firmness in the execution of the enrollment law in this city of New York." Not only was Lincoln obtaining thousands of needed troops to replenish the federal armies; he was showing one and all, North and South, "that the government of the United States is a government to be obeyed."[8]

Even as Stanton was dealing with the short-term crisis of the draft riots, he was dealing with long-term issues such as black refugees and black soldiers. He received the preliminary report of his freedmen's commission on June 30, the very eve of the three days of Gettysburg. The commissioners shared Stanton's view that young black men should be encouraged to enlist in the army. "The negro must fight for emancipation if he is to be emancipated. . . . [The nation must] give the negro an opportunity of working out, on those battle-fields that are to decide our own national destiny, his destiny, whether as slave or freedman, at the same time." But if thousands of black men joined the army, who would care for their wives and children? The commissioners recommended that the War Department extend and expand its system of support, creating a separate staff devoted to the problems of the freedmen, headed by a brigadier general as the "superintendent-general of freedmen." As might be expected, given its composition, the commission was especially keen for "these uneducated people" to receive "enlightened instruction, educational and religious." Private charities were doing good work, but the commission believed the federal government would soon have to help with the education of the black refugee children. Stanton approved the commission's report and he published it in August. But, somewhat to the dismay of the three commissioners, he did not implement at once their recommendation of a separate freedmen's staff. Stanton probably believed he could not do this without legislation and that he had already stretched a bit to form the commission in the first place.[9]

In letters he sent in August, Stanton summarized the department's progress and plans for black recruiting. There were about 20,000 black troops in regiments, and another fifty regiments were in formation. So far the commissioned officers were white, but "it is the design of the Department to promote such of the colored troops as may evince capacity and fitness for command." Stanton did not expect to recruit many blacks in the North: "I have never supposed that a very large force of colored troops could be raised in the free states, because the colored population in those states is comparatively small, and the wages which they can command are such as to render it unnecessary for them to enter the military service." He hoped and expected, however, to enlist tens of thousands of blacks "along the line of the Mississippi and in all of the Cotton States." Lorenzo Thomas had been in the East for a few weeks, recovering from an illness and helping in the Gettysburg crisis, but Stanton was about to send him back to the West to continue his recruiting work. Stanton also sent George Stearns, a Massachusetts merchant and abolitionist, to Tennessee, with orders to raise black regiments there and with letters to commanders to support Stearns in this work. Almost immediately Stanton received protests about Stearns from the military governor, Andrew Johnson, and had to caution Stearns to work within the limits imposed by Johnson: "All dissension is to be avoided." Stearns found a way to work with Johnson and was soon reporting good progress in Tennessee.[10]

Frederick Douglass, the nation's foremost black leader, wrote a public letter in early August saying, "I must for the present leave to others the task of persuading colored men to join the Union Army." Lincoln and Stanton, Douglass explained, were silent about Southern atrocities against black soldiers. "[There is no] word of retaliation when a black man is slain by a rebel in cold blood. No word was said when free men from Massachusetts were caught and sold into slavery in Texas." This letter from Douglass "crossed in the mail" with a proclamation by Lincoln, drafted by the War Department, issued at the end of July, which promised just such retaliation. The proclamation declared that the government would "give the same protection to all its soldiers," black and white. "And if the enemy shall sell or enslave anyone because of his color, the offense shall be punished by retaliation upon the enemy's prisoners in our possession."[11]

Frederick Douglass, the nation's foremost black leader, whom Stanton tried to entice to join the War Department.

Douglass visited Washington and met Lincoln and Stanton on August 10, 1863. He reported in a letter to Stearns that Stanton met with him in his office for about half an hour, "which must be considered a special privilege in view of the many pressing demands upon his time and attention." Douglass started his conversation with Stanton with some comments about blacks in general, saying that some were "brave and others cowardly," some were "ambitious and aspiring and another part quite otherwise." Stanton "instantly inquired" in what way his department's recruiting practices "conflicted with the views I had expressed." Douglass pointed out the unequal pay and that blacks could not, under present practices, aspire to be commissioned officers. Stanton responded with "an interesting history of the subject" and claimed that he had drafted a bill providing equal pay for black troops but that it failed in Congress. Stanton still favored equal pay for black soldiers and was ready "to grant commissions to any reported to him by their superior officers for their capacity or bravery." He urged Douglass to go to Mississippi and recruit there with Thomas. Douglass reminded him that he was already working to recruit in the East, but Stanton was "very imperative" and said that he "would send me sufficient papers immediately." Douglass believed Stanton was offering him a senior commission in the army.[12]

A few days later Douglass received a letter from one of Stanton's aides, asking him to report to Thomas. Douglass then wrote to Stanton himself, asking for the details of his new assignment: What would be his rank, his pay, his duties? Writing to a friend, Douglass complained that Stanton "keeps me in the dark on all essential points. He only commands me to go." A few days later, Douglass received a second letter from Stanton's aide. There was no commission, just a further request: "Aid General Thomas in any way that your influence with the colored race can be made available." There was not even a promise of a federal salary. Here the correspondence ceased, probably because both men realized this arrangement would not work. Stanton could not afford to outrage moderates by giving Douglass, not only a black but a Radical, a commission in the army, and Douglass could not afford to lose his independence as the leading voice for black Americans. Years later Douglass would write, "I have no doubt that Mr. Stanton in the moment of our meeting meant all he said, but thinking the matter over he felt that the time had not then come for a step so radical and aggressive."[13]

Stanton devoted several paragraphs in his year-end report to the topic of black soldiers. He noted that there were now 50,000 black soldiers and predicted that that number would "rapidly increase as our armies advance into the rebel states." Many people had believed or "pretended to believe" that "slaves would not make good soldiers; that they would lack courage, and could not be subjected to military discipline." Black soldiers had now proved themselves, Stanton wrote, at Milliken's Bend, at Port Hudson, at Fort Wagner. He urged Congress to end the unfair salary difference, so that the federal government should pay black soldiers the same amount as whites. "Soldiers of the Union, fighting under its banner, and exposing their lives to uphold the Government, colored troops are entitled to enjoy its justness and beneficence."[14]

As to the refugees, Stanton wrote that the war had "brought within our lines a large number of colored women, children, and some aged and infirm persons. Their care, support, and protection rest a solemn trust upon the Government. Their necessities have to some extent been supplied by this Department." Stanton urged Congress "to devise and adopt a general and permanent system for their protection and support." He recognized that this would cost money, but he viewed it as money well spent, for it would deprive the rebels of slaves. "Is it not better that we should feed them than that they should support the rebel master who is in arms against us?" Stanton's recommendation would eventually lead to the formation of the Freedmen's Bureau.[15]

Prisoner exchanges were another major issue for Stanton in 1863. When he first arrived in the War Department, in early 1862, there was no general system of exchange, so each side was holding prisoners of the other. There was already concern about the Southern treatment of Northern prisoners, and one of Stanton's first actions as secretary was to send a commission to Richmond to assess and report on the condition of prisoners there. The South was not interested in having Northern visitors; it wanted a general system of prisoner exchanges and so refused to allow Stanton's commissioners to reach Richmond. Lincoln and Seward were reluctant to enter into such an overall arrangement; they did not want to treat the Confederacy as a "belligerent" under international law, for that would give it certain rights, such as the right to borrow in foreign financial markets. Northern papers, including such pro-Lincoln papers as the *New York Times*, demanded prisoner exchanges, saying that it was pointless to deny that the rebels were belligerents. In June 1862, acting under instructions from Stanton, General Dix was able to reach a broad "army-to-army" agreement on prisoner exchanges, known as the Dix-Hill Cartel because the other signatory was the Confederate general Daniel Hill.[16]

Prisoners were exchanged under the Dix-Hill Cartel for about ten months, and then exchanges ended, mainly because the South refused to treat black soldiers and their white officers as prisoners of war. In the summer of 1863 Lincoln and Stanton determined that they would cease exchanges unless and until the rebels would exchange *black* as well as *white* prisoners. Lincoln's July 30 proclamation, although it did not mention prisoner exchanges, effectively announced this policy. As more and more Northern men suffered in Southern prisons, however, Democratic newspapers attacked what they viewed as a ridiculous refusal to exchange prisoners. The *Detroit Free Press* argued that by stopping exchanges the Lincoln administration was "forcing our men to remain in Richmond and suffer."[17]

General Hitchcock, with Stanton's encouragement and editing, responded with a long letter to the *New York Times*. (There is a note in the files from Stanton to Hitchcock, saying that he would be out of town for a few days and asking Hitchcock to hold the letter until he returned and reviewed it.) Hitchcock quoted Jefferson Davis and others threatening to treat black soldiers and their white officers as criminals. He noted that, to date, there was no instance of a black soldier or white officer in a black regiment being treated properly as a prisoner of war. On the contrary, such soldiers and officers were either executed or enslaved. As an example, Hitchcock described the recent case of a white officer and his twenty black soldiers captured and "hanged within twenty-four hours afterward." He rejected the recent Southern suggestion that all prisoners should be exchanged, because this would release about 13,000 Northern and 40,000 Southern prisoners. What would happen with those 40,000? Based on recent practice, Hitchcock predicted that the South would declare them released from their paroles on some spurious ground and that they would soon be back in battle against the North.[18]

Stanton made similar arguments in his annual report, released a few days later. To allay concerns about the condition of Northern prisoners, he described how the War Department was providing food and other supplies for the Northern prisoners in and around Richmond. To address Southern criticism of the conditions in Northern prisons, he asserted that Southern prisoners had "good quarters, full rations, clothing when needed, and the same hospital treatment received by our own soldiers." A few weeks later, at the very end of the year, Lincoln and Stanton took a boat to Point Lookout, on the peninsula at the confluence of the Potomac and Chesapeake rivers, in order to see for themselves the federal prison camp there. Point Lookout at this time was holding about 10,000 Southern prisoners, housed in tents on the open, windswept, sandy ground. Lincoln and Stanton did not comment on the conditions, at least not in any documents that survive, but news articles reported, "Not less than a thousand, or about a tenth of the whole number, are ready to enter the service of the United States." Stanton issued the necessary orders to release those willing to enter the federal military service and those whose homes lay "safely within our lines."[19]

In early August, Stanton sent his wife and children to Bedford, Pennsylvania, to escape the heat. On August 25 he wrote her that she had missed "ten days of hot, dusty weather, the most disagreeable I have ever known." Stanton and Lincoln "have been arranging to make a trip to Bedford, but something always turns up to keep him or me in Washington. He is so eager for it that I expect we will accomplish it before the season is over." Lincoln, however, could not get away from Washington, so Stanton went alone, relying upon John Garrett, head of the Baltimore & Ohio Railroad, and Thomas Scott, the former assistant secretary who was now head of the Pennsylvania Railroad, to make the rail arrangements. Stanton apparently left Washington late on September 4 and returned late on September 7—a very short visit indeed. It is perhaps just as well that he did not remain in Bedford to read the September 11 edition of the *Bedford Gazette*. In a humorous critique of the administration, the editors asked, "What is a Secretary of War?" Their answer: "A man who arrests people by telegraph."[20]

One reason Stanton was able to get away for a few days was that there was not much happening on the main eastern front. Meade had followed Lee into Virginia and now had his army near its old base, along the Rappahannock River. But Meade did not attack Lee. Stanton would surely have agreed with Lincoln's comment to Welles, that it did not seem Meade "was doing anything, or wanted to do anything." It was "the same old story of the Army of the Potomac. Imbecility, inefficiency—don't want to do—is defending the Capitol." But Stanton and Halleck did not press Meade too hard, for Lincoln had cautioned them that he did not want to force Meade into a rash attack—he did not want another Chancellorsville.[21]

Meade was not the only stationary general; from the perspective of Washington it seemed that Rosecrans was equally immobile. Back on July 7, when the great news from Vicksburg first arrived, Stanton had wired Rosecrans at Tullahoma, Tennessee, "You and your noble army now have the chance to give the finishing blow to the rebellion. Will you neglect this chance?" Rosecrans responded angrily that "this noble army has driven the rebels from Middle Tennessee." Stanton should have quoted to Rosecrans from Lincoln's message to Hooker: the objective was not to conquer *territory* but to capture rebel *armies* and thus to end the rebellion. Two weeks later Halleck wrote to Rosecrans, "The patience of the authorities here has been completely exhausted, and if I had not repeatedly promised to urge you forward, and begged for delay, you would have been removed from the command." Rosecrans answered that he would be happy to be replaced and that Stanton was prejudiced against him. Halleck insisted that Stanton was not biased, just disappointed by the delay. Chase, writing to James Garfield, now an aide to Rosecrans, conveyed the same message: "The Secretary feels most deeply the importance of activity and aggressive movement: and as his temper is not the most patient in the world, he expresses himself very decidedly against dilatoriness." By the time Chase sent this letter, on August 17, Rosecrans at last had his army on the move, pushing Gen. Braxton Bragg back toward Chattanooga.[22]

At the end of August, Stanton informed Rosecrans that he was sending Dana to his army headquarters. Rosecrans must have hated the thought of having Stanton's spy among his officers. Stanton instructed Dana to visit Governor Andrew Johnson and others in Nashville on his way to Rosecrans: "Pay particular attention to the condition of colored persons in the respective armies, and the region of country in which the armies are operating, making yourself acquainted with the wants and necessities of that class of the population, what supplies or assistance are required, [and] what evils or abuses they may suffer." Even before Dana reached Rosecrans, there was great news from that front: Bragg evacuated and Rosecrans occupied Chattanooga on September 9.[23]

Not long thereafter Northern papers reported that the Confederates were sending the division under Gen. James Longstreet from Virginia to reinforce Bragg in Tennessee. Such reports were often erroneous, but in this case they were correct: after a difficult rail journey, Longstreet's forces joined Bragg's near Chattanooga in mid-September. Thus strengthened, Bragg attacked Rosecrans on September 19, along the Chickamauga Creek in northwestern Georgia. Dana kept Stanton informed by frequent telegrams. On September 20 he sent Stanton a message that started, "My report today is of deplorable importance. Chickamauga is as fatal a name in our history as Bull Run. . . . The total of our killed, wounded, and prisoners can hardly be less than 20,000, and may be much more." Rosecrans and the remains of his army retreated into Chattanooga, while Bragg and his army occupied the surrounding heights.[24]

The next day Lincoln sent two messages to General Burnside, with his army near Knoxville, Tennessee, urging him to march his troops the hundred miles south and west to Chattanooga, to reinforce Rosecrans there. There was no immediate response from Burnside, however, for there was no good telegraph line to his headquarters. Halleck had already sent a message to Vicksburg on September 15, asking that "all the troops that can possibly be spared" be "sent without delay to assist General Rosecrans on the Tennessee." This message did not even reach Vicksburg for a week, and the response from Grant would not get to Washington for another week. What *did* reach Washington, on the night of September 22, was a rather desperate message from Rosecrans in Chattanooga: "General Burnside will be too late to help us. We are about 30,000 brave and determined men; but our fate is in the hands of God, in whom I hope."[25]

The next evening three telegrams arrived in the War Department more or less at the same time. One was from Dana to Stanton, saying that although Rosecrans intended to hold Chattanooga, he might not be able to do so: "To render our hold here perfectly safe no time should be lost in pushing 20,000 to 25,000 efficient troops to Bridgeport. If such reinforcements can be got there in season everything is safe, and this place, indispensable alike to the defense of Tennessee and as a base of future operations, will remain ours." A second message was from Garfield to his patron Chase: "[Bragg] no doubt outnumbers us two to one, but we can stand here ten days if help will then arrive." Like Dana, with whom he may well have spoken, Garfield suggested that "twenty-five thousand men should be sent." Last but not least was a message from Rosecrans to Lincoln: "All the reinforcements you can send should be hurried up." Stanton, reading these messages, must have feared that Bragg would achieve a "Vicksburg victory" over Rosecrans, that Bragg would not only beat Rosecrans in a battle but trap his army in Chattanooga, capturing them all. Such a defeat would be disastrous from a military perspective, for Chattanooga was a critical rail hub, a base from which the Union Army could advance south into Alabama and Georgia. And a dramatic defeat would be a political disaster in states such as Ohio, Pennsylvania, and New York, states with imminent elections.[26]

As Stanton was reading these telegrams, John Hay stopped by the telegraph office. Stanton told him that he was about to summon Lincoln from the Soldiers' Home, his summer residence, for a late-night conference about Chattanooga. Stanton sent Hay to retrieve Lincoln, and sent another messenger with a note to Seward. "We have news from Chattanooga which should I think be considered tonight. I have sent for the President General Halleck and Mr. Chase. Will you be so good as to come over to the War Department?" While he was waiting for Lincoln and the others, Stanton sent messages to three senior railroad officials: John Garrett, of the Baltimore & Ohio Railroad; Thomas Scott, of the Pennsylvania Railroad; and Samuel Morse Felton, of the Philadelphia, Wilmington & Baltimore Railroad. The messages were essentially identical: "Please come to Washington as quickly as you can."[27]

Lincoln with his private secretaries, John Nicolay and John Hay. Stanton worked closely with both young men, including in the 1863 rail movement.

Hay noted in his diary that eight other men attended this midnight meeting at the War Department: Lincoln, Seward, Stanton, Chase, Halleck, Watson, James Hardie, and Daniel McCallum, head of the U.S. Military Railroads. According to Chase's diary entry, Stanton started the meeting by saying that he was "thoroughly convinced that something must be done & done immediately to ensure the safety of the army under Rosecrans." Stanton asked Halleck what force Burnside could send from Knoxville to Chattanooga. Perhaps 12,000 men, Halleck responded. How long would it take? Perhaps eight days. Lincoln observed, "After Burnside's men begin to arrive, the pinch will be over." Stanton then asked Halleck how long it would take Sherman's men to reach Chattanooga from Vicksburg. "About ten days," Halleck responded, if they had "already marched from Vicksburg." Had Sherman's men already started from Vicksburg? Stanton asked. Halleck admitted that he had no idea.[28]

After this bit of dialogue, Stanton declared that no timely support would reach Rosecrans: "I do not believe a man will get to him from Burnside or Sherman in time to be of any use in the emergency which is upon us. The Army of the Potomac is doing nothing important; nor is it likely to be more actively employed. I propose, therefore, to send 20,000 men from the Army of the Potomac to Chattanooga, under the command of General Hooker." Lincoln and Halleck objected to Stanton's proposal and insisted that it was impractical. Stanton responded that "he had fully considered the question of practicability & should not have submitted his proposition had he not fully satisfied himself on that head by conference with the ablest railroad men of the country." At this point he may have turned to McCallum, who was indeed one of the nation's railroad experts, and asked him to comment. Lincoln mocked Stanton's plan, saying that he could not get a single corps from northern Virginia into Washington in the one-week time frame in which he claimed he could get two corps all the way to Tennessee. As he often did, Lincoln illustrated his point with a story, at which Stanton, "greatly annoyed," said that "the danger was too imminent & the occasion too serious for jokes." But Stanton added that since "he saw himself overruled he would give up the point," and he "invited us all into the adjoining room where he had caused a light collation to be prepared."[29]

Seward and Chase were not yet prepared to "give up the point." As the men ate and drank, Chase "expressed my entire confidence in [Stanton's] ability to do what he proposed." Seward also "took up the subject & supported Mr. Stanton's proposition with excellent arguments." The "scale was turned," and Lincoln agreed that Halleck should telegraph Meade: if he was not planning an "immediate movement," then two corps, about 20,000 men, would be transferred by rail from Meade to Rosecrans, just as Stanton proposed. The meeting dispersed, and Stanton and Halleck went to work in the telegraph office. Garrett had asked Stanton whether he should come on a midnight train; Stanton responded at about 1:30 a.m., "Morning will be time enough." Halleck sent a message to Meade, asking whether he planned an "immediate movement." When Meade responded that he did not have any such plans, Halleck instructed him to start preparing the Eleventh and Twelfth Corps to move to Washington within twenty-four hours. Stanton sent a message to Dana in Chattanooga at 3:30 a.m. on September 24: "We have made arrangements to send fifteen thousand infantry under General Hooker from here and will have them in Nashville in five or six days from today, with orders to push on immediately wherever General Rosecrans wants them."[30]

───────

One phase of the process was over: Lincoln had authorized Stanton to move up to 20,000 men by rail from northern Virginia to southern Tennessee. The second, much more difficult phase was about to begin: using multiple separate private rail lines to move thousands of soldiers, along with artillery, animals, and associated equipment. Stanton had been thinking about such a rail movement for many months; indeed, in his first month in office he had asked Scott about a possible troop transfer from Washington "to the interior of Kentucky and Tennessee." And in recent days Stanton may well have renewed his thinking and planning. In a message to Stanton at about six in the morning of September 24, Garrett promised to bring with him from Baltimore to Washington "full information regarding engines and cars." This suggests that Stanton and Garrett, or their aides, had already spoken about Stanton's ambitious idea. But it is one thing to consider a possibility; it is quite another to devise and implement a massive, complex plan, involving dozens of government and private railroad officials, officials who could communicate with one another only by telegraph.[31]

Garrett and William Smith of the Baltimore & Ohio arrived at the War Department at about ten o'clock on the morning of September 24, and Scott and Felton arrived around noon. Surrounded by rail maps, the men sketched a fairly direct line west, joining different railroad lines, through Baltimore, Wheeling, Columbus, Cincinnati, Louisville, and Nashville. At about 11:00 a.m. Stanton sent a telegram to Robert Bowler, the president of the Covington & Lexington Railroad, asking, among other questions, about the gauge or width of the rail tracks in the region. Bowler's response, when it arrived at about 2:00 p.m., was worrisome, for his railroad used five-foot gauge, but the Louisville, Frankfort & Lexington line used six-foot gauge. This would mean time-consuming transfers between different equipment. Stanton and his colleagues also considered another alternative: perhaps the troops could travel by rail to Cincinnati, and then by boat down the Ohio River to Louisville? The team in Washington sent another telegram, to the Baltimore & Ohio agent in Cincinnati, asking whether there was enough water in the Ohio River for navigation. The agent responded that the water was somewhat low, but there were "plenty of light draft boats." Knowing well the vagaries of the Ohio River, Stanton decided against this option.[32]

Stanton and his colleagues settled on the final route by about three in the afternoon; it was outlined in messages sent by Garrett from the War Department to the other railroads that would be involved. The first stage would be on McCallum's military railroads, bringing the troops from their camps near Culpeper, Virginia, in to Washington, D.C. The Baltimore & Ohio would take the troops north and east from Washington for fifty miles, to Relay, a rail junction about six miles south and west of Baltimore. At Relay the trains would turn west on the main B&O line, through Harpers Ferry, Martinsburg, Cumberland, Grafton, and finally Benwood, just south of Wheeling, West Virginia. From Benwood the troops would cross the Ohio River by ferries to Bellaire, Ohio, and then board trains on other rail lines that would take them through Columbus and Dayton to Indianapolis. Here the soldiers would change trains, heading south to Jeffersonville, Indiana, and take ferries to cross the Ohio again, to Louisville, Kentucky. The Louisville & Nashville Railroad would carry them to Nashville, then the Nashville & Chattanooga Railroad to Bridgeport, Alabama. The South controlled the last few miles of the N&C tracks to Chattanooga, so the soldiers would probably have to march from Bridgeport to Chattanooga, along the Union supply route on the north side of the Tennessee River.[33]

At about four in the afternoon of September 24, Stanton sent a message to Gen. J. T. Boyle, the military commander in Louisville, informing him, "Colonel Thomas A. Scott, of this Department, will arrive in Louisville Saturday about noon." Scott had resigned his government position in 1862 to return to his railroad company, but somehow Stanton had persuaded him to return to federal service, at least for these few weeks. Stanton asked Boyle to ensure that the managers of the Louisville & Nashville, the Kentucky Central, and the Nashville & Chattanooga Railroads were *all* in Louisville when Scott arrived so that they could consult and coordinate. Questions and problems started almost as soon as the plan was agreed on. McCallum, in Alexandria, informed Stanton that one of the corps was 2,000 men larger than anticipated and that the B&O "would not be able to furnish the cars as promptly as possible." Later that evening Meade sent a question to Halleck: Should the troops leaving in the morning take any more ammunition than the forty rounds in their boxes? Halleck had gone home for the night, so it was Stanton who responded, telling Meade that forty rounds would suffice.[34]

Early on the morning of September 25, just as Stanton had hoped, the first troops boarded the first military trains in northern Virginia. Because the Orange & Alexandria Railroad was a single-track line, McCallum's men spread the trains out so that they could load several at once. From northern Virginia the military trains crossed the Long Bridge into Washington, and using recently laid tracks on the city streets, they rolled all the way to the Baltimore & Ohio station on New Jersey Avenue. Here the soldiers changed trains, boarding the trains that would take them to the Ohio River. Garrett reported proudly on the evening of September 25 that his railroad had managed to get 194 troop cars in place in Washington and that the first two trains of 51 troops cars were already on their way west. Stanton was not satisfied, asking McCallum to "crowd the B&O RR every hour with a fresh telegram."[35]

On September 26 the troops were in motion along hundreds of miles of rails. Some were still boarding military trains in northern Virginia, while the lead three trains, bearing about 2,000 men, had by ten o'clock on that morning reached Martinsburg, West Virginia. Stanton received a report from Baltimore in the early afternoon that more than 7,000 troops had passed Relay and were now heading west. Rebel raiders often cut the Baltimore & Ohio line in the remote region beyond Harpers Ferry, and Halleck sent a telegram to Meade, stressing that his army must protect the tracks at all costs while the troops were moving. Stanton himself worked on the problem of finding more rail cars, sending a telegram to Cairo, Illinois, that he wanted all the spare rail cars there "immediately to be put on the road to Nashville."[36]

First thing the next morning, September 27, Stanton sent a telegram to McCallum in northern Virginia: "Please report the state of the movement. Nothing from you later than ten o'clock last night." McCallum responded that his men had just loaded the First Division of the Twelfth Corps in the military rail cars to move them in to Washington. Smith, in Baltimore, reported to Stanton that the Ohio River at Benwood was too low for the usual system of ferries. The Baltimore & Ohio had taken the initiative to build a temporary "bridge of scows and barges" so that the soldiers could *march* across the river. Smith also reported, with pride, that the first of his Baltimore & Ohio trains had now reached Benwood, "two hours less than our promise of forty-four hours through." McCallum informed Stanton that there were only about 4,000 men, from the Twelfth Corps, who had not yet boarded the trains. Stanton posted a man at the station in Washington and asked him to report by telegraph on each train arriving from Virginia and each train departing for Baltimore. At about ten in the evening, Stanton informed Scott, in Louisville, that the entire Eleventh Corps was already beyond Cumberland and that the Twelfth Corps was on trains close behind them: "The whole force will be moving tonight."[37]

Not all was well, however. In the early afternoon of September 27, Stanton had a message from Smith, reporting that the railroad agent at Grafton had received an order to hold trains there "until General Schurz arrives." (Carl Schurz was the most prominent German American general, a key supporter of Lincoln, now in command of the Third Division of the Eleventh Corps.) Smith told Stanton he had instructed that the trains should keep moving unless the order came from Stanton himself. Stanton wired Smith, "You have done right," and demanded to know who had given the order. At nine that evening, Stanton received a message from Grafton, saying that the hold order was from one of Schurz's staff officers. The agent "had great difficulty" with Schurz himself when the general arrived in Grafton, for Schurz again sent a telegram to delay the trains with his troops, and he tried to commandeer an engine for himself. Stanton exploded. He drafted a message to Schurz, telling him that Hooker had "orders to relieve you from command and put you under arrest." Stanton changed the draft slightly before sending it, writing Schurz that Hooker would "arrest any officer who undertakes to delay or interfere with the orders and regulations of the railroad officers in charge of the transportation of troops." Stanton also sent messages to Smith, approving his course and suggesting that the railroad telegraph operators not send any similar messages from any other generals. The next morning a chastened General Schurz asked the secretary, "Am I to understand from your dispatch that I am relieved from command?" Stanton responded that Hooker had orders to relieve any officer, "whatever his rank may be, who delays or endangers transportation of the troops." It would be up to Hooker, Stanton said, whether to remove Schurz.[38]

Stanton also learned, at some point on September 27, that the *New York Evening Post* had reported that part of Meade's army, under Hooker, was "in motion," heading west by the Baltimore & Ohio Railroad. Stanton knew that the South received copies of Northern newspapers; he knew that some parts of the railroad line were within reach of rebel cavalry raids; he knew that Bragg, if alerted that Hooker was about to arrive with thousands of troops, might hasten to attack Rosecrans at Chattanooga. Stanton had thus tried hard to ensure that there would be no press coverage, sending an army officer to every correspondent in Washington, pleading with them not to report the news that thousands of troops were transferring through Washington and heading west. Stanton "raged like a lion," and Lincoln himself was "very mad," according to Noah Brooks, when they learned that the *New York Evening Post*, usually an "out-and-out Administration paper," had revealed the troop movement in progress. A few papers reprinted the *Post*'s report, but not many, and it seems that the Southern commanders were not aware of the troop transfer for a while longer.[39]

All through the night, Stanton's agent at the Washington train station sent him telegrams as the troop trains arrived and departed. By midday on September 28, McCallum could report from northern Virginia that the last troop train had left from there for Washington. In the early afternoon Stanton asked Smith for a report on how the troops were progressing *beyond* the Ohio River. Smith responded that he did not have timely reports from the railroad officials in Ohio, but he did know that the "first three trains have passed Columbus." At eight that evening, Smith relayed word from Hugh Jewett, head of the Central Ohio Railroad, that more than 5,000 troops were already beyond Columbus. Stanton was not satisfied; he sent a note to Smith at about ten that evening, asking whether he or Garrett could go in person to Indianapolis to "prevent any hitch in the consummation of what has been so ably managed." Smith responded that there was no way he or Garrett could go west; they had too much work still to do in Baltimore. But he assured Stanton they had a first-rate man already in Indianapolis and that if necessary they would send more men to help. Scott, in Louisville, asked Stanton whether he should extend the Louisville & Nashville Railroad down to the Ohio River wharf to speed the process of moving men and materiel through Louisville. Stanton responded that Scott was "authorized to go on with whatever work in your judgment will facilitate the military transportation."[40]

Chase returned to Washington that day from a brief visit to Baltimore and found Stanton "greatly delighted" with the progress so far in moving the troops to the West. The last few trains from northern Virginia were about to reach Washington. "In five days the men who, as the President was ready to bet, could not be got to Washington, would be already past that point on their way to Rosecrans, while their advance had reached the Ohio River." Chase added, "If this whole movement is carried through to the end as well as it has been thus far, it will be an achievement in the transportation of troops unprecedented, I think, in history."[41]

On September 29 Stanton learned from Scott that the first troops had crossed the Ohio River by ferry to Louisville and boarded trains there heading south for Nashville. Stanton sent Scott "a thousand thanks" for his hard work. Smith reported from Baltimore that trains were now reaching Indianapolis regularly and rapidly; from Washington to Indianapolis was a distance of more than six hundred miles, covered in about fifty hours, "upon a track three times redeemed from hostile possession, and three times rebuilt by private enterprise since the present war began." In a message Stanton received about two in the morning on September

30, Scott reported that he expected the first men would soon reach the current end of the rail line, in Bridgeport, Alabama. Twenty-four hours later, at about one in the morning on October 1, Stanton received word that the first four trainloads of troops had reached Bridgeport. General Hooker, thousands more troops, and many tons of critical equipment would arrive to support Rosecrans over the next few days.[42]

Hooker congratulated Stanton on the successful troop movement: "You may justly claim the merit of having saved Chattanooga to us." Hooker may have claimed too much—Chattanooga was not yet saved— but historians agree that Stanton's troop transfer was impressive and important. Allan Nevins wrote that this was "one of the great transportation feats of the war" and that "Stanton might well be proud of his achievement." James McPherson described it as "an extraordinary feat of logistics—the longest and fastest movement of such a large body of troops before the twentieth century."[43]

———

As the second phase of the project, *moving* 20,000 troops, was ending, a third phase was starting: *using* the troops to defend Chattanooga and if possible to attack the Confederate Army. This would depend upon the general in charge, and Stanton had lost faith in Rosecrans. When Dana suggested to Stanton that, after his great work at the Battle of Chickamauga, Gen. George Thomas would be a logical next commander of the Army of the Cumberland, Stanton agreed. He wrote to Dana on September 30, "If Hooker's command get safely through, all that the Army of the Cumberland can need will be a competent commander. The merit of General Thomas and the debt of gratitude the nation owes to his valor and skill are fully appreciated here, and I wish you to tell him so. It was not my fault that he was not in chief command months ago." Lincoln agreed, telling Hay that after Chickamauga Rosecrans was "confused and stunned like a duck hit on the head."[44]

Stanton's doubts about Rosecrans only increased in the first few weeks of October, as he read the reports from Rosecrans, Dana, and Meigs, whom Stanton had also sent to Chattanooga. Dana informed Stanton on October 3 that the Confederates had attacked and destroyed a large Union wagon train bringing ammunition and supplies to Chattanooga.

Rebel raiders were also attacking the Nashville & Chattanooga Railroad, so that Rosecrans had to use Hooker's forces to defend the rail line on which he depended for food and other supplies. Meigs reported to Stanton that Confederate artillery was lobbing shells into Chattanooga from the heights of Lookout Mountain; the Confederates also held Missionary Ridge, right over the town. The supply line was so tenuous that the troops were on reduced rations and the horses were starving. On October 16 Dana warned Stanton, "Nothing can prevent the retreat of the army from this place within a fortnight, and with a vast loss of public property and possibly of life, except the opening of the river. . . . In the midst of all these difficulties General Rosencrans seems to be insensible to the impending danger, and dawdles with trifles in a manner which can scarcely be imagined. . . . All this precious time is lost because our dazed and mazy commander cannot perceive the catastrophe that is close upon us, nor fix his mind upon the means of preventing it." On this same day, Halleck sent a telegram to Grant, instructing him to travel to Louisville "to meet an officer of the War Department with . . . instructions & orders." Stanton sent two messages of his own this evening, one to Scott and one to Meigs, telling them to meet Anson Stager, head of the military telegraph, at the Galt House in Louisville. What neither Stanton nor Halleck said, for security reasons, was that the officer heading west was Stanton himself.[45]

Ulysses S. Grant, whom Stanton first met at the Indianapolis train station on October 18, 1863, to offer him command of all the western forces.

Stanton had never met Grant, but he felt that he knew him, through the frequent, positive reports of Dana. And like others in Washington, Stanton believed, especially after Grant's victory at Vicksburg, that Grant was the right man to take control of all the western armies. The secretary of war left Washington by special train early on the morning of October 17, heading west on the same path that the troop trains had just used. When Grant arrived at the Indianapolis train station at about two o'clock on the afternoon of October 18, he received a request to wait there for Stanton, who was expected soon. This was probably the first notice Grant had that he would be meeting with Stanton. According to a news report, Stanton arrived about ten minutes later and "at once transferred himself to General Grant's train," in which they headed south toward Louisville.[46]

Forty years later one of Grant's aides wrote that Stanton, as he entered their rail car that afternoon, had "somewhat impulsively" greeted the staff surgeon, mistaking him for the general. "Trivial as this incident may seem, Dana and the officers present always believed that it produced an unfavorable impression [on Grant] which lasted till the secretary's death." There is no trace of Stanton's alleged confusion in Grant's own detailed memoir, however, nor in the memoirs of others on Grant's staff. It seems likely that this incident never happened—that it was one of those details that gets added to the story over time, then repeated until it becomes an accepted part of history.[47]

As their train headed south, Stanton and Grant discussed the orders making Grant commander of a new Division of the Mississippi, which would cover the entire region between the Appalachian Mountains and the Mississippi River. The orders gave Grant the option of removing or retaining Rosecrans, and he decided on removal. As Stanton explained in a telegram to Halleck the next day, Grant deemed it "indispensable that Rosecrans should be relieved because he would not obey orders."[48]

Like the troops before them, Stanton, Grant, and their party had to get out of the train at Jeffersonville and wait for the ferry to carry them across the Ohio to Louisville. Grant's wife, Julia, remembered being "greatly troubled that someone of the staff had not telegraphed for a boat to be in readiness, as the weather was bad with rain and sleet, and Mr. Stanton was suffering from a severe cold. But I afterwards learned that this seeming neglect was intentional, as it was not considered safe to telegraph in the portion of the country through which we passed the presence of the Secretary and the General." Eventually they all reached the warmth and comfort of the Galt House, where the staff had had no warning that such important guests were arriving.[49]

Stanton and Grant spent the next morning in conference, and in the afternoon the general "indulged in a ride on horseback about town." According to a news account, the people of Louisville were anxious "to catch a glimpse of the hero of Vicksburg" and somewhat disappointed that Grant was not a taller, bigger man. Grant recalled in his memoir that when he and his wife returned to the hotel later that night, they were met with frantic messengers, saying that Stanton wanted to see him. "I hastened to the room of the Secretary and found him pacing the floor rapidly in his dressing gown." Stanton showed him a worrisome telegram from Dana, and Grant "immediately wrote out an order assuming command of the military division of the Mississippi." It is hard to square this section of Grant's memoir with the telegrams, for there is no message in the files from Dana to Stanton on October 19, and Grant had already taken command the prior day. There is, however, a message from Grant in Louisville to Thomas in Chattanooga, sent at 11:30 p.m. on October 19, instructing him to hold Chattanooga "at all hazards." So perhaps Grant was right in remembering that Stanton was worried that night, although wrong on some details.[50]

Grant left on the morning of October 20, heading south for Chattanooga, but Stanton remained in Louisville for two days, conferring with Garfield, Scott, and others. He informed Watson in Washington that he would leave Louisville on the morning of October 22, adding, "I will not make as quick time on the way home as I did here." Stanton may have made a brief detour on his return trip to visit his aging mother in Steubenville, but he was back at his desk in Washington on October 26. One of the messages awaiting him was from Dana in Chattanooga, reporting the arrival there of Grant, "wet, dirty, and well." Stanton was pleased with the report, pleased with Grant, pleased that he now had the right general in charge in the West.[51]

———

In the summer and fall of 1863, Stanton worked on political as well as military issues. The two were closely related. Although off-year elections nominally involved only state offices, in practice the issues at stake were national. Democrats argued that the war was doomed to failure, that the Abolitionists (as they called them) should be ousted from power so that Conservatives (as they styled themselves) could make peace on reasonable terms with the Southern states. Democrats also continued their merciless criticism of Lincoln and Stanton, especially for what they believed were arbitrary arrests. Republicans (who now called themselves Unionists) denounced the Copperheads for effectively siding with the Confederates. Republicans feared and Democrats hoped that, with strong results in 1863, Democrats could elect a president in 1864, one who would end the war and negotiate peace with the South. So the 1863 fall elections were, in the words of Allan Nevins, "one of the important turning points in the political history of the nation."[52]

The first election on the fall calendar was in Maine, which would elect a new governor on September 14. Fessenden wrote to Stanton from Maine in late July to ask whether it would be possible for the recent recruits to remain in the state until election day. Stanton declined: "I am deeply impressed with the importance of carrying the election in your State, and shall be happy to cooperate, as far as possible, in accomplishing that result. While, however, political emergencies are not to be overlooked, you are aware that military necessities will sometimes require a hazard to be run; and that is precisely the position in which we now stand, in view of the necessity of reinforcing the Army of the Potomac." Stanton helped in the Maine election in other ways. He gave a furlough to Gen. Oliver Otis Howard, now in command of one of the corps in Meade's army, to return home to his native Maine, where Howard gave strong Union speeches. Although Stanton was not willing to slow down the process of recruiting new soldiers into the army, knowing he could not grant such a favor to Maine without other states making similar requests, he was willing to grant short furloughs to a few veteran Maine soldiers, to allow them to go home to vote, and then return immediately to their regiments. And as soon as the news arrived on election day that the Union candidate had prevailed, Stanton sent a congratulatory message: "Nine cheers for Maine!" The *New York Times* credited "the gallant soldiers of the Union army who fought at Gettysburg and Vicksburg" for the victory in Maine. "The vision of the Union restored has become too vivid to the eyes of all true patriots for them to allow any 'flaunting lie,' representing its division, to be hung out anywhere in the North."[53]

An even more important and dramatic election was in Ohio, where the Democrats in June nominated Clement Vallandigham, in exile, as their candidate for governor. The Union Party responded with John Brough, whom Stanton termed one of the ablest and most patriotic men of the state. The Ohio legislature had recently passed a law to allow Ohio soldiers to vote "in the field," but it was unclear whether the statute would survive an anticipated constitutional challenge. Stanton was taking no chances. On October 7 he wrote to the incumbent Union governor to say that he would instruct the general in charge of Camp Chase, the federal training facility outside of Columbus, to send the men there home to vote. "If there be any other action of this Department that will contribute to the defeat of the public enemies let me know," he offered. Stanton sent a similar message to the military commander of the state, instructing him not only to grant leave but to provide government transportation. "You may also adopt any other measures that may enable soldiers and officers in your command to exercise their legal elective franchise."[54]

Stanton's rail cars, moving 20,000 soldiers from Virginia to Tennessee, passed through Ohio near the end of this state election campaign. The troops, almost all of whom hated Vallandigham, made their views known. Some of them decorated the outside of their rail cars with political signs: "Death for Vallandighamers" and "No Peace Makers among Us." Others gave political speeches from rail platforms when their trains stopped at stations. Stanton did not plan the rail transfer for political reasons, but it proved to be sound politics, showing the Midwest the might of the Union Army and the strong Union sentiment among the troops.[55]

Lincoln, Stanton, and others gathered in the War Department telegraph office on the night of October 13, election day in Ohio and Pennsylvania, to read the results as they arrived. When a message came in from Steubenville, reporting that the Union Party had won there, Stanton wrote back, "I am proud of my native town and rejoice that the enemies of our country have been so signally rebuked." A little while later, when Brough himself wired Stanton that he would prevail statewide, Stanton responded "with perfect joy." At about one in the morning, when word arrived from John Forney, in Philadelphia, that Pennsylvania would also support its Union candidate for governor, Stanton wrote, "All honor to the Keystone State! She upheld the federal arch in June and with steel & cannon shot drove rebel invaders from her soil, and now in October she has again rallied for the Union and overwhelmed the foe at the ballot box." When all the votes were counted, Stanton was especially pleased to see the support for Brough among the Ohio soldiers: more than 95 percent voted for him. One Ohio lieutenant reported the results in his regiment as "Brough, 650, the Traitor, 70."[56]

The election season was not over: New York, Maryland, and several other states would vote on November 3. Like the other border states, Maryland was not covered by the Emancipation Proclamation: it was still a slave state. The central question in the fall election was whether Maryland should emancipate the slaves. Those opposing emancipation were led by Montgomery Blair, Stanton's cabinet colleague, and those in favor by Henry Winter Davis, a Kenyon contemporary of Stanton, now running for Congress. Blair gave a speech in September in which he claimed that Radical abolitionists wanted to "make the manumission of the slaves the means of infusing their blood into our system by blending it with 'amalgamation, equality, and fraternity.'" Stanton must have known that Blair, in quiet conversations with other leaders, called Stanton an "unprincipled liar" and a "great scoundrel." So it is not surprising that Stanton sided with his friend Davis over his enemy Blair.[57]

Another key figure in the Maryland election was Robert Schenck, the Union military commander in Baltimore, also a Republican member of Congress from Ohio. On October 21 a delegation of Eastern Shore planters arrived at the White House, complaining about the way Schenck's troops were "frightening the quiet people" and luring or forcing their slaves into the army. When Lincoln asked Schenck to explain, he responded that the only violence was by "rabid secessionists" who had shot and killed one of his officers. Lincoln told Hay that Schenck was "complicating the canvass with an embarrassing element, that of forcible negro enlistments." Lincoln feared that Schenck's method was "to take a squad of soldiers into a neighborhood & carry off into the army all the able-bodied darkies they can find without asking master or slave to consent." Lincoln summoned Schenck to Washington and warned him to stop conscripting the slaves.[58]

On October 27 Schenck caused yet more controversy with an order announcing that he would send federal troops to the state polling places, ostensibly to prevent disruption or violence. By his order Schenck required that every voter swear an oath not only to "support, protect and defend the Constitution and Government of the United States" but also to take no action against the government, including "aiding, abetting or countenancing those in arms against them." When Governor Augustus Bradford learned of the order, he sent an outraged telegram to Lincoln. In response Stanton sent a telegram to Schenck on November 1, informing him that Lincoln wanted to see him as soon as possible, and adding, "Issue no order in respect of the election until you see him." Schenck responded that he would come to Washington but that his order was already out: "If it is revoked we lose this state."[59]

After Lincoln, Stanton, and Schenck discussed the situation, Lincoln sent his response to Bradford, sustaining Schenck in most respects. He told Bradford that he could not risk allowing those disloyal to the Union to cast votes in the imminent election. In a side conversation with Schenck, Stanton urged him to work against the Blairs. At least that is how Henry Winter Davis reported the conversation in a letter to a friend: that Stanton told Schenck, "Take Blair, skin him, turn his hide, pickle it—and stretch it on a barn door to dry!" Davis added, "Such are the happy relations of the Cabinet among themselves—respectful deference & courtesy shine through their rough utterances of honest hate!"[60]

Lincoln, Stanton, and Hay were at the telegraph office again on November 3, awaiting election results. They were cheered to learn that the Union candidates had prevailed in New York. The Maryland election was too close and confused for results that night, but within a few days it was clear that those in favor of emancipation would have a majority in the state legislature. The *New York Times* commented that the Maryland election "was a square fight between the spirit of the Emancipation Proclamation and the spirit of the old Slave Power. And the best thing about the result of the election is that the Emancipation spirit is on its feet, and its foe in the dust." The *Detroit Free Press* believed the election was not "square" at all, that it was tilted by Schenck, supported by Stanton. "There is no better evidence of the degeneracy of these days than the favor in which such men as Schenck are held."[61]

Another campaign was in progress in late 1863: between Lincoln and Chase for the Republican presidential nomination. Newspapers viewed Lincoln as the conservative choice and Chase as the Radical favorite. Since Stanton was now close to several Radicals, and since Stanton and Chase had been friends for almost two decades, one might assume that he would favor Chase. Amid the many cold, official letters between the two men, dealing with departmental disputes, there were still a few warm personal notes. In early 1863, for example, Stanton wrote to Chase in order to return his knife, "which by some means found its way into my pocket." He added, apparently quoting a poem, "If you love me like I love you, no knife can cut our love in two." And at the end of 1863, Stanton sent a note to Chase saying that the Episcopal bishop of Pennsylvania would be baptizing their newest child, Bessie, at their home that day. "Mrs. Stanton very much desires you to stand God Father and dine with us at 6 p.m. Will you gratify her?" Those in the best position to judge, however, believed that Stanton supported Lincoln. Hay, who worried about Chase's candidacy and who saw Lincoln, Stanton, and Chase every day, wrote in his diary that Stanton had no presidential ambitions himself "and is for Lincoln." He was surely right.[62]

In early October Lincoln issued a proclamation, setting the last Thursday of the next month as a day of national thanksgiving, and Stanton decided to return home in late November to Steubenville, where his mother had just marked her seventieth birthday. His sister Pamphila recalled that, during this short visit, Stanton said that even if he died in office, a hundred other men could do his job, that "the cause [would] go on just the same." Watson kept Stanton posted by frequent messages from the War Department, relaying the news that was arriving from Tennessee. Late on November 25 Watson reported that Thomas "took Missionary Ridge by a magnificent charge and Hooker . . . penetrated to the rear of the rebels." Two days later Watson provided Stanton with long quotes from the messages of Grant and Dana, describing how the Union Army had captured the heights around Chattanooga and chased the rebels into Georgia. Stanton was no doubt thankful.[63]

In their annual messages in early December 1863, Lincoln and Stanton reviewed the progress in the war to date. Lincoln announced an amnesty for most rebels if they would take an oath to abide by federal laws and the Emancipation Proclamation. He also announced that, once 10 percent of the prewar electorate in a Southern state took such an oath, they could form a new state government. In his report Stanton rejoiced that the Mississippi River, "that great highway of the continent," was again in Union control. "The rebel territory has been cut in twain; the states west of the Mississippi no longer furnish their ample supplies to the rebels." Stanton did not, in this official document, make any prediction about when the war would end, but he was less guarded on Christmas Day in informal comments with sick and wounded soldiers at the Stanton Hospital in Washington. (Other than this one visit, there is nothing to suggest a special relationship between Stanton and the hospital named after him; Civil War facilities were often named after state and national leaders.) In his remarks, Stanton assured the invalids that, after the war, if they still suffered from their wounds or illnesses, he would see that they "received a proper reward." And he expressed the hope, surely shared by all who heard and read it, that by Christmas of the next year, "this war will be ended, and you will have returned to your homes and your firesides."[64]

Chapter 12

"You Cannot Die Better"

— January–June 1864 —

Stanton faced a congressional crisis in the first few days of 1864. He was working to persuade Union soldiers, many with three-year terms that would soon expire, to reenlist for the remainder of the war. He was also working to recruit at least 300,000 new volunteers. In both of these efforts, federal bounties were one of his key tools: $400 for soldiers who reenlisted and $300 for new men. Congress had passed legislation that would terminate the federal government's ability to pay these bounties after January 5. At Stanton's suggestion, Lincoln pressed Congress to extend the authority for bounties, but many senators were concerned about the cost, and wanted assurances from Chase that the government could afford the bounties. In a long letter to Chase, Stanton emphasized the importance of the veteran soldiers: they were cheaper than new recruits (they did not have to be trained and equipped) and they were far more effective in battle. Chase only reluctantly supported the bounty bill, complaining privately to Stanton, "If you were charged with the responsibilities which oppress me, you would be even more unwilling than I to see new difficulties added." It is not surprising that there was tension at this time between Chase and Stanton. From Chase's perspective, Stanton was spending money like water; from Stanton's perspective, Chase was slow in providing the funds that he needed to pay the troops and win the war. Congress passed the bounty bill on January 13, and the recruiting process resumed.[1]

Recruiting required cooperation between federal and state governments, and Stanton sent messages almost daily to one or more governors. Governor John Andrew of Massachusetts inquired about a woman who claimed that Stanton had ordered her to report to the governor. Stanton explained that he had merely ordered her away from the army, that in his opinion "she ought to be in some asylum," that he hoped state officials could help her. During the few days in which the legal authority to pay the federal bounty lapsed, Governor Oliver Morton of Indiana suggested that the War Department would find a way to pay. No, Stanton said. "It is my duty to obey the law, and I do not mean to violate or sanction its violation." Governor Richard Yates of Illinois demanded answers to questions about the recruiting process. His office was working on answers, Stanton replied testily, but they had "to be carefully considered in connection with information to be gathered at other points." There were two governors of Virginia at this time: the Confederate governor, based in Richmond, and the Union governor, Francis Pierpont, based in Alexandria. Each claimed to govern the whole state, and each denounced the other as illegitimate. Pierpont complained to Stanton that Gen. Benjamin Butler, now in charge in coastal Virginia, was issuing improper orders to banks in Norfolk. Stanton shared the letter with Lincoln, who drafted a response in Stanton's name, reminding the general that the governor was in charge of civilian questions.[2]

Governors in their states and Stanton in Washington often saw issues very differently. Stanton wanted to recruit black soldiers everywhere, including in the slave state of Kentucky, whose governor complained to Lincoln about the anger among whites caused by recruiting among blacks. Stanton, with whom Lincoln shared this letter, responded with a letter that he hoped Lincoln would forward to the governor. Stanton wrote:

> Until lately many wise and patriotic men doubted or denied the capacity of persons of African descent in this country to constitute efficient soldiers. Recent events have removed all doubt upon this question, and have shown that, in many essential particulars, this class of persons constitute soldiers quite as efficient as those of any other race. . . . [At] Milliken's Bend, at Port Hudson, Morris Island, and other battle fields, they have proved themselves among the

bravest of the brave in fighting for the Union, performing deeds of daring and shedding their blood with a heroism unsurpassed by soldiers of any other race. With these facts before us, no one can doubt the wisdom and expediency of a nation, struggling against rebels and traitors for its existence, to employ such aid. For the United States Government to cast away such help in this contest would seem to be suicidal madness, without example in the history of mankind.

Lincoln agreed, but he knew Kentucky better than Stanton, so he did not forward the letter. Stanton sent Lorenzo Thomas to see what could be done in Kentucky. After meeting with the governor and other leaders in Louisville, Thomas advised Stanton to suspend efforts to recruit black soldiers in that state. For the next few months, Stanton and Thomas focused their black recruiting efforts on states other than Kentucky, including Mississippi and Tennessee.[3]

Some of the issues Stanton faced were within his own department, such as what to do with Surgeon General William Hammond. Stanton had never liked Hammond, whom he viewed as foisted upon him by the meddling men of the Sanitary Commission. In the latter part of 1863, Stanton had effectively suspended Hammond, sending him west on "inspection tours" and appointing Dr. Joseph Barnes as the acting head of the Medical Bureau. Stanton also started an informal investigation of Hammond's purchasing practices, to which Hammond responded by demanding that if there were any charges against him, they should be considered by a proper court-martial. Hammond's friends and supporters at the Sanitary Commission, including George Templeton Strong and Reverend Henry Bellows, started work on a circular letter to support him.[4]

One day in early January, Stanton's friend Samuel Hooper, a member of Congress from Boston, brought him a curious document. It was the printed Hammond circular, apparently signed by ten eminent men. What made this copy curious was that the famous Harvard professors Louis Agassiz and Benjamin Peirce had added handwritten notes, stating that although their names appeared on the printed document, they had in fact *not* signed the circular letter. Hooper, in a letter to another of the supposed signatories, Joseph Warren, wrote that Stanton was pleased to learn that Agassiz and Peirce had not signed the letter and would be making inquiries about the other supposed signatories. Sure enough, within a few days, Stanton had a letter from Warren, saying that he too did not sign the document but only wanted a fair hearing for Hammond.[5]

Agassiz and Peirce were in Washington at this time to attend a session of the National Academy of Sciences, and Seward invited Stanton to a dinner at his home in honor of the visiting academics. Stanton, according to Strong's diary, "replied Stantonically 'meet them at dinner! I'd rather send them to Fort Lafayette!'" Strong wrote that when Agassiz and Peirce heard of Stanton's wrath, "their hearts failed them and their knees became as water, because they had given offence to a great mandarin and a Cabinet member, so they declared it was all a forgery and a fabrication. . . . Did the Honorable Secretary suppose they didn't know their place? Of course, they knew their place. Were they not even as dead dogs before our Honorable Secretary?"[6]

Perhaps because Agassiz and Peirce had already disavowed their support for Hammond, or perhaps to please his friend Seward, Stanton went to the dinner. As to Hammond, his time was coming. Stanton arranged for him to be arrested and tried by a court-martial, which, after many months, convicted him of purchasing "supplies of inferior quality" and paying "exorbitant prices" and recommended that he be dismissed from the service. Strong raged in his diary that the court-martial's decision was "a base tyrannical outrage on law and right effected by the vast power of the man at the head of the War Department who hates Hammond, and whose hates are as unscrupulous as they are bitter and dangerous." Historians have tended to agree, siding with Hammond against Stanton, but Lincoln sided with Stanton and confirmed the court-martial sentence.[7]

The new year was a presidential year, and the leading candidate for the Democratic nomination was Gen. George McClellan. Little Mac had been working for almost a year on his long and one-sided report on the Peninsula Campaign, and parts of the report started to appear in the papers in January 1864. McClellan's argument in his report and in his presidential campaign was that he lost on the Peninsula because Lincoln and Stanton denied him the troops he needed to win. One of the documents McClellan released as evidence was his midnight message, in which he accused Stanton of doing his best to sacrifice the Army of the Potomac. Democratic papers gleefully printed and reprinted this message, while some Republican papers printed other correspondence, perhaps provided by Stanton as a way to counteract McClellan's version of these events.[8]

On the Union Party side, the two leading candidates were Chase and Lincoln. Radicals generally supported Chase. They argued that Lincoln and Stanton were mismanaging the war, and they feared Lincoln would compromise over slavery. Radicals now wanted a constitutional amendment to end slavery throughout the United States; Lincoln had expressed no view yet on this question.[9]

Lincoln and Stanton were both in the great hall of the House of Representatives on the evening of January 16 to hear Anna Dickinson, the young orator who had played such a prominent role in the Connecticut election. Twenty-five hundred people packed the hall to hear the first woman to speak from this stage—senators, representatives, and hundreds who purchased tickets, for this was a benefit lecture to raise funds for the care of sick and wounded soldiers. Noah Brooks described Dickinson arriving in the hall to a "splendid burst of applause" on the arm of Speaker of the House Schuyler Colfax. She was "dressed in a black silk dress, with a long train, and lighted up with red velvet. Her figure is graceful and full, of medium height, and her face is open, sunny and bright."[10]

In the first part of her speech, Dickinson sounded like a Radical, like a Chase supporter. She praised the soldiers and their bravery, especially the black soldiers, and argued, "Doing a soldier's duty, the black man should have a soldier's pay. Burdened with a man's responsibility, he should have a man's rights." She urged Congress to pass a constitutional amendment so that there was no question at the end of the war that slavery was dead. There should be no compromise between North and South, she insisted, for no "arm of compromise in all the North [was] long enough to stretch over the sea of blood and the mound of fallen Northern soldiers to shake hands with their murderers on the other side!" But near the end of her speech, Dickinson endorsed Lincoln. There was much to do, she said, to win the war and to establish freedom. "We had the man to complete the grand and glorious work, and that work was left for *his second term in office.*" According to one news report, the crowd responded to this with "tremendous and long-continued applause."[11]

Anna Dickinson, the remarkable young orator, who was invited to speak in the hall of the House of Representatives in January 1864. Stanton was "very desirous to see and hear Miss Dickinson."

Chase continued his not-so-quiet campaign for the nomination. In early February, for example, Welles noted in his diary a conversation with Chase that started with "army and naval operations." Chase lamented to Welles "the want of energy and force of the President, which he said paralyzed everything," adding that Lincoln's "weakness was crushing us." Welles "did not respond to this distinctive feeler and the conversation changed." Chase's campaign came out into the open in late February, with the publication of the Pomeroy circular. Senator Samuel Pomeroy of Kansas and the members of a "National Executive Committee" argued in this circular that the reelection of Lincoln was "practically impossible against the influences which will oppose him." Lincoln was not the right man to lead the nation any longer, for his tendency "towards compromises" meant that "the cause of human liberty will suffer." Pomeroy and his colleagues believed that Chase alone had "all the qualities needed in a President."[12]

Among the Stanton papers from this time period there is a draft letter from Stanton to Benjamin Franklin Loan, the Unionist member of Congress representing St. Joseph, Missouri. The draft, in Stanton's voice but Lincoln's handwriting, notes that at Loan's request the War Department had been using the *St. Joseph Tribune* for advertisements: "I have just been informed that the *Tribune* openly avows its determination that in no event will it support the re-election of the President." Lincoln would not object to editors supporting other candidates, but he would not provide federal dollars to papers "cultivating a sentiment to oppose the election of any when he shall have been fairly nominated by the regular Union National Convention." We do not know if Stanton sent this letter to Loan; we do not know if Stanton cut off advertisements in the *St. Joseph Tribune*; but the draft itself shows Stanton and Lincoln working closely together to head off the Chase campaign. As one of his biographers has concluded, Chase "underrated Lincoln's skill in using patronage to build party support."[13]

The Pomeroy circular led to a flurry of editorials and resolutions in favor of Lincoln. Most damaging to Chase, the Union Party members of the legislature of his home state of Ohio gathered a few days after the release of the circular and endorsed Lincoln for president. In early March, just before a cabinet meeting, from which Chase was absent, Welles observed Seward and Stanton having a "corner chat and laugh about Chase, whose name escaped them, and whom they appeared to think in a dilemma." Chase was indeed in a dilemma: he wanted more than anything to become president, but friends were advising him that he could not run in the face of the Ohio resolution. A few days after this, papers published a letter from Chase, conceding that in light of the action by the Ohio legislators he must "ask that no further consideration be given to my name." Some believed this was not the end of Chase's campaign, that he was still pursuing the nomination, but with stealth. The *New York Herald* advised that "the Salmon is a queer fish; very shy and very wary, often appearing to avoid the bait just before gulping it down." Attorney General Edward Bates agreed, writing in his diary that Chase's letter was "not worth much," that it proved "only that the *present* prospects of Mr. Lincoln are too good to be openly resisted." And Bates, for some reason, thought Stanton was supporting Chase. He wrote that Lincoln should "either control or discharge Mr. Stanton. If I were in his place, I would never submit to have the whole influence of the two most powerful departments, Treasury and War, brought to bear upon the election—against the President and for the aspiring Secretary."[14]

The *New York Herald* had its own candidate: Ulysses Grant. The editors explained that the nation needed a military man as its next president, that Grant would be able to manage the war far better than Lincoln and Stanton. Grant was not interested, writing in response to one inquiry, "I do not know what I have ever done or said which would indicate that I could be a candidate for any office whatever within the gift of the people." Grant's chief of staff, John Rawlins, told Representative Elihu Washburne of Illinois, a friend of Lincoln, that Grant paid no attention to the *New York Herald*: "He is unambitious of the honor and will voluntarily place himself in no position nor permit himself to be placed in one he can prevent that will in the slightest manner embarrass the friends of the government." Lincoln was relieved to learn that Grant would not seek the nomination, that the general was focused on the military task of defeating the Confederates.[15]

Because of the short distance between the two cities—it is only about a hundred miles from Washington to Richmond—leaders in each Civil War capital planned attacks on the other. Back in May 1863, when a federal cavalry raid under Col. Hugh Judson Kilpatrick had reached the outskirts of Richmond, Lincoln wrote that the cavalry "could have safely gone in and burnt every thing & brought us Jeff. Davis." Pressure for a Union attack on Richmond mounted with press reports of the mistreatment of the thousands of federal prisoners in the two major prisons in Richmond. In January 1864, Stanton met with General Butler and approved a plan for a raid to release the prisoners. In describing his goals to another general, Butler said, "If any of the more prominent men can be brought off, a blow will be given to the rebellion from which it will never recover." Butler's raid failed, as did almost all the military maneuvers of that cross-eyed political general. He reported to Stanton that his cavalry had reached a bridge only ten miles from Richmond in the middle of the night, but, faced with an unexpected rebel defense force, the federals had simply turned and retreated. Stanton replied, "While regretting the want of success, I am glad the enterprise has not suffered disaster. Perhaps there will be better luck next time."[16]

Four days later, on February 12, Stanton met at the War Department with Kilpatrick, now a brigadier general, to plan for "next time."

Kilpatrick's new proposed raid would have several purposes, as he put it in a report a few days later: first, to distribute the president's amnesty proclamation in the counties around Richmond; second, "to destroy, as far as practicable, the enemy's communications"; and third, to "attempt the release of our prisoners at Richmond." Stanton and Kilpatrick may have discussed a fourth purpose, not mentioned in Kilpatrick's report: to capture or kill Jefferson Davis. That, at least, was one of the raid's goals as set out in the papers found on the body of Col. Ulric Dahlgren, second in command to Kilpatrick, who was killed in what is now known as the Dahlgren raid.[17]

Ulric Dahlgren was the son of John Dahlgren, the commander of the Washington Navy Yard in the early part of the Civil War, now an admiral. Stanton knew the Dahlgren family well, saw them socially, and had personally promoted young Dahlgren two ranks, to full colonel, explaining, "Your gallant and meritorious service has, I think, entitled you to this distinction, although it is a departure from general usage." At the time of this promotion, the summer of 1863, it was unclear whether Dahlgren would survive; he was so badly wounded at Gettysburg that his right leg had to be amputated. He was still weak in early 1864, and some questioned why he was assigned to lead troops in a cavalry raid; some suspected that he was chosen because of his political connections. It is quite possible that Dahlgren, before leaving Washington on February 22 to join Kilpatrick and the troops, discussed the raid directly with Stanton.[18]

Stanton first learned that the Dahlgren raid had failed on the evening of March 3, when Butler reported that Kilpatrick had returned but Dahlgren had not. A few days later, Stanton learned that Dahlgren was dead, and read in the Richmond press the papers purportedly captured on Dahlgren's body. In one of the documents, Dahlgren reportedly told his men: "You have been selected from brigades and regiments as a picked command to attempt a desperate undertaking—an undertaking which, if successful, will write your names on the hearts of your countrymen in letters that can never be erased." The address described their goals thus: "We hope to release the prisoners from Belle Island first, and having seen them fairly started, we will cross the James River into Richmond, destroying the bridges after us and exhorting the released prisoners to destroy and burn the hateful city; and do not allow the rebel leader Davis and his traitorous crew to escape." Another document found on Dahlgren's body stated, "The men must keep together & well in hand & once in the City it must be destroyed & Jeff. Davis and Cabinet killed."[19]

Southern editorials accused Lincoln and Stanton of violating the laws of war by attempting to kill President Davis and burn Richmond. "Let Lincoln and the others remember," the *Richmond Examiner* warned on March 5, "that they have bidden their subordinates give no quarter to the Confederate chiefs!" Nothing would "prevent a just and stern vengeance from overtaking them for this revolting outrage on civilization and the rules of war!" Northern journals responded by claiming the Dahlgren papers were Southern forgeries. The *New York Times*, for example, declared, "No officer of the American army would ever dream of putting to death civil officers taken captive by such a raid, and no officer in his senses, even if he were barbarous enough to contemplate such a result, would ever put such orders in writing."[20]

We do not know what orders Stanton (and perhaps Lincoln) gave Kilpatrick (and perhaps Dahlgren) regarding their Richmond raid. It is quite possible that Stanton directed Dahlgren to attempt to kill or capture Davis. Some historians have argued not only that Stanton targeted Davis but that in doing so he committed a war crime: "Assassination of civilian leaders was regarded as beyond the pale." But Davis was the military commander of the armed forces opposing the United States; under the laws of war he was a legitimate target for the army. Other questions would be raised if Stanton had, for example, ordered Dahlgren to burn Richmond to the ground. The rules of war, as codified by Lieber and blessed by Stanton and Lincoln, prohibited unnecessary violence against civilians or civilian property. The key point, however, is that after the Dahlgren raid, and the publication of the Dahlgren papers, senior Confederate leaders *believed* that Lincoln and Stanton had authorized an illegal assassination attempt. This may have led the Confederates to contemplate a similar assassination attempt against Lincoln and Stanton; it may have led them to provide financial or other assistance to John Wilkes Booth and his colleagues in their 1865 attempt to capture or assassinate the Northern leaders. We do not know, and will probably never know, whether the Confederate government played any role in the assassination of Lincoln. But *if* the Confederate leaders targeted Lincoln and Stanton, they probably justified their actions by the Dahlgren raid.[21]

———

The Dahlgren raid was a brief flurry of fighting in an otherwise quiet winter in Virginia. Adam Gurowski noted in his diary, "Everyone in the War Department, Stanton, Holt, the young colonels, shudder in disgust at Meade's inactivity." This was the main reason Stanton supported the bill to revive the rank of lieutenant general, previously held only by George Washington and (on a brevet basis) Winfield Scott. The bill was seen as a way to promote Ulysses Grant over all the other Union generals, to put him in real charge of the Union armies rather than leaving Halleck in nominal charge. Senator Fessenden wrote home that he voted for the bill only because Stanton "assured me that if Grant was made Lieut. Genl. the first thing he would do would be to reorganize the Army of the Potomac." Fessenden and Stanton thought that otherwise "the Army of the Potomac will accomplish nothing, for its leading officers lack both ability and skill." Others also saw Stanton's hand behind Grant's promotion. Gurowski wrote to Governor Andrew that "Grant's elevation was forced upon Lincoln by Stanton."[22]

On February 29 Lincoln signed the bill into law and nominated Grant to fill the new position of lieutenant general. Grant was in Nashville at the time, and Stanton asked him by telegram to go to that city's telegraph office so they could have "direct telegraphic communication," the nineteenth-century equivalent of a text message conversation. A few days later, after the Senate confirmed Grant as lieutenant general, Halleck sent Grant orders to come to Washington to accept the promotion. Grant arrived on March 8, checked in at the Willard Hotel, and walked over to the White House, where his presence caused intense excitement among those attending the president's evening reception. After the crowd departed, Lincoln, Stanton, Grant, and a few others met in a small room to discuss the ceremony the next day. Lincoln explained that he would say a few words—he gave the general a draft of his speech—and that the general would be expected to respond. Grant left the White House that evening with Stanton.[23]

At the ceremony the following afternoon, with Stanton and the rest of the cabinet present, Grant said just the right few words: "With the aid of the noble armies that have fought on so many fields for our common country, it will be my earnest endeavor not to disappoint your expectations. I feel the full weight of the responsibilities now devolving on me and know that if they are met it will be due to those armies, and above all to the favor of that Providence which leads both Nations and men." According to a memoir by Mathew Brady, the famous photographer, Stanton saw another side of Grant's character a few days after this. Stanton and Grant arrived late in the afternoon at the studio so that Brady could photograph Grant. To let more light into the room, Brady sent a worker up to the ceiling to pull back a canvas from the skylight. But the worker broke the skylight: "Down came that heavy glass in a shower all around us—pieces as large as your hand, of all triangular shapes, cutting and smashing everything." Stanton became "white as a sheet," but Grant "never moved, not a muscle." Brady recalled that Grant "went through the sitting as if nothing had happened."[24]

Over the days and weeks after Grant's promotion, Lincoln, Stanton, Grant, and Halleck worked out their plans for the spring campaign. Grant would be in charge of all the Union armies, but his headquarters would be in the field, with Meade and the Army of the Potomac. Stanton and Halleck would remain in Washington to raise the troops, to arm and supply them, to coordinate the armies. As soon as the weather and the roads permitted, Grant and Meade would march south, toward Richmond, but their goal would be to destroy Lee's army, not to capture the capital. General Sherman, now in charge of the armies in the western United States, would march his main army south from Chattanooga toward Atlanta defended by Gen. Joseph Johnston. Grant instructed Sherman to "move against Johnston's army, to break it up and to get into the interior of the enemy's country as far as you can, inflicting all the damage you can against their war resources." To the extent possible, Grant and Sherman would apply pressure *at the same time* to prevent the Confederates from shifting their troops from one front to the other. The government had learned the lessons of the prior two years.[25]

Stanton and Grant worked closely together that spring, seeing one another often in person and communicating daily by telegraph. In early April, Julia Grant and Ellen Stanton stopped by the War Department and sent through Stanton a message: "Their compliments to General Grant and hope he is very well today." Grant's aide Adam Badeau responded by telegraph that Grant was out riding "and of course well." When the governors of four states offered to provide 100,000 additional troops, fully furnished, but for only one hundred days, Stanton asked Grant whether the government should accept them. Grant wired back that, this summer, the men "might come at such a crisis as to be of vast importance." In spite of his own strong aversion to short-term troops, Stanton recommended that Lincoln accept the governors' offer. Montgomery Meigs, the quartermaster general, hoped for a chance to command troops in the field. Again Stanton raised the issue with Grant. "It is my wish," Stanton wrote, "to conform to whatever you desire, and to subordinate everything else to the success of your impending military operations." Grant believed that the quartermaster general would be more useful in Washington, so Stanton informed the unhappy Meigs, "The vast expenditures of your department require the supervision of its Chief."[26]

In mid-April, Stanton received reports that Southern soldiers under Gen. Nathan Bedford Forrest had slaughtered at Fort Pillow, Tennessee, about 300 black soldiers *after* they had surrendered. The Fort Pillow massacre was in a sense not a surprise; it was a continuation of the policies that the South had adopted ever since the North started using blacks in its army. But if the initial reports reaching Stanton were correct, Forrest had killed many more blacks at Fort Pillow than any other Confederate officer had killed in any similar attack. Stanton immediately instructed Sherman to investigate "the alleged butchery." By the end of the month it was clear that, in Lincoln's words, "a large number of our colored soldiers, with their officers, were, by the rebel force, massacred after they had surrendered." Lincoln asked each cabinet member for a written opinion on how the government should respond. Stanton recommended designating 300 captive Confederate officers as hostages, to be held until the Confederate government turned over the officers responsible for the Fort Pillow massacre. If the responsible officers were not turned over within a reasonable time, Stanton recommended that the Union should punish the hostages, "as justified by the laws of civilized warfare." Stanton did not use the word "execute," but that is clearly what he had in mind: executing 300 randomly selected Southern officers as retaliation for the deaths of

300 black soldiers. Lincoln in the end took no specific action regarding the massacre, perhaps realizing that the only effective way to punish those responsible was to win the war. Nathan Bedford Forrest, later infamous as a leader of the Ku Klux Klan, was never charged or convicted for his role at Fort Pillow.[27]

The close cooperation between Stanton and Grant did not prevent some newspapers from claiming that they quarreled. On April 21 the *New York Herald* reported, "There is just now considerable difficulty in the councils of the government between General Grant on the one hand and Secretary Stanton and General Halleck on the other." As a result "General Halleck has already tendered his resignation" and "Secretary Stanton is likely to vacate his place in the cabinet." Halleck, in a letter to his friend Sherman, said these rumors were "all bosh. Not a word of truth in them." Grant refuted the rumors in his own way in a letter to Lincoln on May 1, as he prepared to launch his spring attacks: "From my first entrance into the volunteer service of the country, to the present day, I have never had cause of complaint, have never expressed or implied a complaint, against the administration, or the Sec. of War, for throwing any embarrassment in the way of my vigorously prosecuting what appeared to me my duty." He emphasized, "I have been astonished at the readiness with which every thing asked for has been yielded without even an explanation being asked." Lincoln and Stanton did not release this letter immediately, but release it they did, in the fall, in the midst of the election campaign.[28]

———

Washington enjoyed lovely weather in early May 1864, "spring manifested in ideal perfection," in the words of George Templeton Strong, who was in town for a few days. Stanton was spending almost every hour in the telegraph office, following Grant and his army as they headed for Richmond, and Sherman and his army as they headed for Atlanta. At first there was almost no news from Grant. Hitchcock noticed one evening, "In reaching for a piece of paper [Stanton's] fingers showed a nervous tremor, which I had never observed before. Had he received some signs of failure on the part of Grant?" Strong and his colleagues had chosen the wrong moment to press Stanton about the Sanitary Commission. Stanton was annoyed at what he called the Commission's "scurrilous attacks on me and on the Administration." Strong, for his part, dismissed Stanton as "not a first-rate man morally or intellectually. His eye is bad and cold and leaden and snaky, even when he is most excited. His only signs of ability at this conference were remarkable memory and capacity for details."[29]

On the evening of May 6 Stanton learned that there was a message for Dana from Henry Wing, a military reporter for the *New York Tribune*. (Dana was not in the War Department to receive this message because Stanton had just sent him off to Grant's moving headquarters, to provide direct daily reports, as he had from the western campaigns.) Wing, writing from a telegraph office near Manassas, claimed that he had been with Grant as recently as four that morning. Stanton sent a reply, demanding to know precisely where Wing was when he left Grant. Wing answered that he would tell the department all he knew, but only if Stanton would allow him to send a hundred-word message to his newspaper. No, Stanton replied, he would sooner have Wing arrested as a spy. At this point, however, Lincoln arrived and overruled Stanton, telling Wing by telegraph that he could send his message to the *Tribune*. By eleven o'clock that night, Stanton was sending out reports based on Wing's information that there had been a "collision" between the two armies near Chancellorsville. "A general battle is expected today."[30]

On the morning of May 8, Stanton sent a message to General Dix in New York City. Although there were "no official reports from the front," there was a request from Grant's quartermaster for rations and railroad equipment, which Stanton read as an indication of "material success." He added a few words about Sherman, that "skirmishing had taken place" near Dalton, Georgia, "but no real fighting yet." Then Stanton authorized Dix, "Give such publicity as you deem proper to the information transmitted to you. It is designed to give accurate official statements of what is known to the Department in this great crisis and to withhold nothing from the public." Dix shared Stanton's message with the Associated Press, so that it appeared in the nation's papers the next day.[31]

This May 8 message was the first of dozens from Stanton through Dix to the press over the next few months. Almost all of these press messages, in the files of the outgoing telegrams of the secretary of war and his staff, are in Stanton's own distinctive handwriting. He quoted from the messages he received from Grant, Sherman, and other generals, but he quoted *selectively*, he edited, he commented. On May 11 Grant wrote to Stanton, "We have now entered the sixth day of very hard fighting. The result to this time is much in our favor. Our losses have been heavy as well as those of the enemy. I think the loss of the enemy must be greater. We have taken over five thousand prisoners, in battle, while he has taken from us but few except stragglers. I propose to fight it out on this line if it takes all summer." This arrived at the War Department at about eleven that night, along with a more detailed message from Grant to Halleck, estimating Union losses in dead, wounded, and missing at over 20,000 men. Stanton edited these messages somewhat, making no mention of the estimated casualties, and relayed the text to Dix. Grant's message, as edited by Stanton, appeared in the nation's papers over the next few days, often with the last line in capital letters. So although Grant was the author of the famous sentence "I propose to fight it out on this line if it takes all summer," Stanton was the editor and publisher, making it part of the national vocabulary.[32]

Newspapers were soon noticing Stanton's role in providing them with military news. The *New York Times* commended his reports for their relative neutrality: "They have been quite free from exaggeration, swagger or prophecy. . . . Facts without fringe, circumstance without imagery, are what we have been favored with. It is this that has given value to these dispatches; it is upon their verity that their continued value depends." The *Chicago Tribune* said it was "indebted to Secretary Stanton's new and commendable policy of publishing to the country the official news of army operations as soon as it is received by the War Department." Like the *Times* the *Tribune* cautioned that the reports had to be unbiased. "Let the War Department realize, as they have in this campaign, that this is a people's war . . . and that all the people want to know is the truth, whether the tide of battle is with or against them."[33]

On May 18, at about noon, Stanton learned that the *New York World* and the *New York Journal of Commerce* had published a purported proclamation by the president, regretting the failure of Grant's campaign, calling for a national day of fasting and prayer, and demanding that the states provide an additional 400,000 soldiers. The news arrived in the form of a telegram from Dix to Seward, asking whether the president and secretary of state had indeed issued such a proclamation. Seward, probably with Stanton at his shoulder in the telegraph office, sent Dix an immediate message for the public: the supposed proclamation was "an absolute forgery." (The original of this message is in Seward's handwriting but Stanton's files.) A few minutes later Stanton followed up with his own message to Dix: "I have just seen a copy of the spurious proclamation referred to in your telegram. It is a base and treasonable forgery."[34]

Stanton found Lincoln, and they issued several orders. The first, from Lincoln himself, directed Dix to arrest and imprison the "editors, proprietors, and publishers" of the two papers and to seize and hold their offices. As Lincoln knew well, his order would result in the arrest of some prominent people, including Manton Marble, the editor of the *New York World*, and William Prime, editor of the *New York Journal of Commerce*. The second order, from Stanton, directed Dix to close the offices of the Independent Telegraph Company and to "arrest the manager, operators, and superintendent, and hold them in close custody." Stanton sent similar orders to close the offices and arrest the personnel of the Independent Telegraph in Baltimore, Harrisburg, Philadelphia, and Pittsburgh. And in Washington itself, Stanton closed down a small independent news syndicate, run by three reporters: Henry Villard, Adams Hill, and Horace White.[35]

Lincoln and Stanton had been working only the day before on a draft proclamation calling for an additional 300,000 troops. Stanton apparently believed that someone in Washington had leaked this proclamation, sending it by telegraph to New York, where it was published in garbled form in hostile newspapers. The perpetrators could not have used the American Telegraph Line—it was monitored by the War Department—so Stanton reasoned that they must have used the Independent Telegraph. Similarly it did not seem likely that the Associated Press, so closely connected with the War Department, was involved, so suspicion fell on Villard and his small press agency. Indeed the Associated Press itself accused Villard's agency of transmitting the false proclamation.[36]

A few hours after Lincoln and Stanton issued these initial orders, Stanton received a message from Dix, reporting on the results of his investigation in New York City. The bogus proclamation, Dix said, was delivered at about four in the morning in the standard form for messages from the Associated Press. Most of the major newspapers had suspected something and had not published the document. The *New York Herald* had printed the proclamation in some of its first edition papers but then realized its error and suppressed these; the *New York World* had printed the proclamation, but then issued a retraction in later editions. Dix had three copies of the document as it was delivered to the newspapers, and he was confident that he would soon find and arrest its author. He added at the end that he had just received the order to arrest the editors: "I shall execute it, unless the foregoing information shall be deemed sufficient by the President to suspend it until my investigation is concluded."[37]

Stanton and Dix were personal friends as well as former cabinet colleagues. Stanton once signed a letter to Dix, "Not with regard only, but with sincere personal affection." But friendship did not matter now. Stanton wired Dix, "the President's telegram was an order to you which I think it was your duty to execute immediately upon its receipt." Dix persisted, telling Stanton that he would arrest the editors " unless I hear from you before the guards are ready." Stanton was outraged: "A great national crime has been committed. The editors, proprietors, and publishers, responsible and irresponsible, are in law guilty of that crime. You were not directed to make any investigation, but to execute the President's order." A few hours later, somewhat calmer, Stanton wrote Dix again: "The officer in charge of the investigation, respecting the forged proclamation, reports that he is led to believe it originated in this city and that the New York publishers were not privy to it. If your conclusions are the same you may suspend action against them." A relieved Dix responded at ten that night: he would *not* arrest the editors, but he had closed down their newspaper offices, and he had arrested the telegraph personnel, who were on a boat bound for Fort Lafayette.[38]

The next morning Lincoln received a message from the editors of four major New York newspapers, including the *New York Tribune*. The editors argued that the hoax could easily have "succeeded in any daily newspaper establishment in this city" and that the two newspapers that printed the document were "innocent of any knowledge of wrong." The editors pleaded with Lincoln to rescind immediately his order suspending publication of the two newspapers. Most newspapers, Republican and Democratic, agreed. The *New York Evening Post* called the suppression of the two papers a violation of the Constitution. Lincoln and Stanton were not moved, at least not yet. Indeed Stanton arrested one of the Washington reporters, Henry Villard, and personally questioned another of them, Horace White, in his office at the War Department.[39]

On the afternoon of May 20, Dix informed Stanton that he had identified and arrested the author of the bogus proclamation, Joseph Howard Jr. According to Dix, Howard had admitted all the key details, and his testimony was corroborated by that of other witnesses. Nobody at the two closed newspapers nor at the telegraph company was involved in any way in the fraud. Stanton responded that, although Lincoln believed the proprietors and editors were "responsible for what appears in their papers," Lincoln was not inclined to be "vindictive." Dix should therefore restore the newspaper offices to the owners and editors and allow them to resume publication. Stanton sent this message after 9:00 p.m. on a Friday evening. Did he know that it would arrive too late to allow the two newspapers to publish on Saturday morning? And that neither of them published Sunday editions? So that the two papers would not resume publication until Monday, May 23? And was it just a coincidence that, on this same weekend, Stanton's former friend Samuel Medary, editor of the anti-administration paper *The Crisis*, was arrested in Ohio?[40]

Stanton's Friday message to Dix said nothing about the telegraph operators or the telegraph company, nor did he take immediate action to release Villard from prison. The Independent Telegraph did not resume operations until after Stanton worked out an arrangement with its president to connect its lines directly to the War Department—and to subject those messages to the department's supervision and censorship. As to Villard, he was released a few days later. One of Stanton's aides recalled, "Although no apologies were made to him or to his colleagues, some choice scraps of news later found their way to the office of the syndicate." The *Bridgeport Republican Farmer* in Connecticut argued that the arrests of the editors in New York and Ohio were part of a pattern of "administration tyranny and despotism," that Stanton was boasting that he "had now got the telegraph under his control, and he wished that he had the newspapers also."[41]

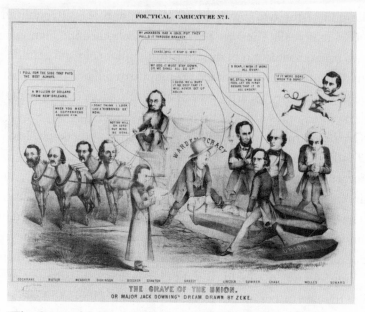

"The Grave of the Union." Stanton drives the hearse as Lincoln
and his cabinet members prepare to bury the corpse of the Constitution. Democrats insisted that Lincoln and Stanton were shred-
ding the Constitution.

Lincoln and Stanton probably did not see this issue of the *Bridgeport Republican Farmer*, but the "arbitrary arrest" argument was by now
a familiar part of the Democratic case against the Lincoln administration. Yet Lincoln and Stanton did not give orders to cease all such arrests,
nor did they cease to use military commissions to try Northern civilians
charged with war crimes. At most they would intervene from time to
time in specific cases to order releases. In early June, Lincoln received a
message from General Rosecrans, now in charge of the Department of
the Missouri and based in St. Louis, who reported that he had "detailed
information" about a "plot to overthrow the government" and that he
wanted to send an aide to Washington with the documents. Lincoln told
Hay that it seemed Rosecrans wanted "to force me into a conflict with
the Secretary of War and overrule him in this matter. This at present I
am not inclined to do." So Lincoln sent Hay to St. Louis instead. Before
Hay even arrived, however, Stanton learned that Rosecrans had arrested
Charles Hunt, a St. Louis lawyer. "The President directs," Stanton wired

to Rosecrans, "that you release Charles Hunt." A few days later Stanton received a message from Grant, complaining that Rosecrans had arrested Grant's friend Dr. James Barrett. "The Doctor is a Copperhead," Grant admitted, "but I have no idea that he has done anything more than that class of people are constantly doing and not so much." Stanton directed Rosecrans to release the prisoner.[42]

Stanton devoted his time not just to newspapers and prisoners but to the task of raising, moving, and supplying the armies. The *New York Times* in late May praised this aspect of his work: "Secretary Stanton has been the best abused man of the war. . . . Without discussing the exact value of his services to the country, it is worthwhile to consider one grand fact which is almost forgotten by the public, and yet which must redound in history to the credit of his administration. We mean the wonderful organization by which our immense armies are kept constantly supplied with food, clothing, ammunition and weapons." For the past three years, the *Times* continued, the War Department had been "equipping, feeding, arming and transporting an army of at least 700,000 men, to different points as widely distant as the Potomac and the Rio Grande. . . . Hundreds of thousands of horses have been supplied; artillery by the hundred pieces; small arms by the hundreds and hundreds of thousands; coats, shoes, hats, haversacks, and all kinds of equipment by the millions."[43]

The War Department acquired this equipment mainly by purchasing it from private companies, but the department itself was also a manufacturer. More than 100,000 men and women worked for the department in various arsenals and other factories, making equipment as diverse as tents, mortars, and shoes. At about two in the afternoon of June 17, 1864, Stanton learned of an explosion at one of these facilities, the Washington Arsenal, where women worked stuffing paper tubes with gunpowder to make cartridges. He immediately directed Halleck to send officers to investigate and was soon on the spot himself to "comfort the unfortunates." One paper reported, "The scene was horrible beyond description. Under the metal roof were seething bodies and limbs, mangled, scorched, and charred beyond the possibility of recognition." Twenty-one women died and dozens more were injured. Stanton directed the head of the Arsenal to pay the expenses of the funerals. "You will not spare any means to express the respect and sympathy of the Government for the deceased and their surviving friends." Stanton himself was among the thousands of mourners at what Noah Brooks described as the "remarkable and imposing funeral pageant."[44]

The mood in Washington was somber in June 1864 not only because of this terrible tragedy but because of the news from Grant. True, Grant was marching south, nearing Richmond, and killing, wounding, and capturing thousands of Confederates. But his army was suffering casualties by the thousands. On June 3 Grant ordered a massive morning attack on the entrenched rebels near Cold Harbor. Within an hour the attack had failed and thousands of federal troops were dying or dead. Grant's report to Washington that afternoon masked the dreadful disaster: "We assaulted at 4:30 am this morning, driving the enemy within his entrenchments at all points, but without gaining any decisive advantage. . . . Our loss was not severe, nor do I suppose the enemy to have lost heavily." Stanton relayed this, word for word, to the press. Only later, as the lists of those killed emerged, did the public realize that the Union loss was severe indeed.[45]

Grant had suffered a terrible defeat at Cold Harbor, but he did not retreat. Instead he decided to march south, to cross the James River, to attack Petersburg, the key rail point twenty miles south of Richmond. Stanton was elated. On the morning of June 15 Stanton shared the news with the nation, summarizing a message from Grant of the prior day: "Our army will commence crossing the James River today. The enemy have shown no signs yet of having brought troops to the south side of Richmond." When he saw this report in the newspapers, Grant was no doubt annoyed, for he would have preferred silence regarding the troop movement. Grant did not write to Stanton about his press releases, but Sherman told Halleck to ask Stanton not to publish his messages: "For they reach Richmond in a day & are telegraphed at once to Atlanta." Sherman counseled, "Absolute silence in military matters is the only safe rule—let our public learn patience & common sense." Stanton may not have agreed, but he released almost nothing about Sherman's army for the next few weeks.[46]

Stanton's messages to Dix often listed officers who were reported killed or wounded. In many cases these were not just names for Stanton but friends. In early May, Grant reported to Halleck that James Wadsworth, the general with whom Stanton had worked so closely in the defense of Washington, was killed at the battle now known as the Wilderness. Stanton urged Meade to make "every effort to recover the remains of the gallant General Wadsworth." Meade wrote to Lee, who arranged for the body to be transferred in a black coffin across the lines, from where it was transported to Wadsworth's home county in New York. A few weeks later, Stanton learned from Sherman that, in the chaotic fighting at Kennesaw Mountain, Col. Daniel McCook was among the mortally wounded. He was the younger brother of Stanton's law partner George Wythe McCook; Stanton knew the whole family well. He immediately sent messages to Alexander and George McCook, notifying them that their brother was wounded, "it is feared mortally." He had been shot in the chest but somehow lived another two weeks, dying at the family home in Steubenville. Stanton wrote to George McCook that he was "deeply grieved" by his brother's death. "Of the many gallant officers that have fallen the earth covers none more worthy of memory. Give to your mother and accept for yourself my sincere condolences."[47]

It was at about this time, in June 1864, that Stanton and Meigs decided to use part of the Lee family estate at Arlington as a national cemetery. The Union Army had already buried a few soldiers on the lower reaches of the property, but Meigs recommended that these bodies be moved up so they were near the mansion. "[The land should] be appropriated as a National Military Cemetery, to be properly enclosed, laid out, and carefully preserved for that purpose." He added, "The grounds about the Mansion are admirably adapted to such use." Stanton agreed, instructing Meigs to set aside not more than two hundred acres for the new national cemetery. "The bodies of all the soldiers dying in the hospitals in the vicinity of Washington and Alexandria will be interred in this Cemetery," Stanton wrote, adding that Meigs should not take land from the freedmen who lived in a small village on another part of the property.[48]

***

If Stanton sometimes annoyed Sherman with his press releases, Sherman sometimes angered Stanton with his opposition to black soldiers. In early June, Sherman issued a special order, prohibiting any recruiting among the blacks working as laborers for his army and threatening to arrest any officers recruiting in violation of this order. Lorenzo Thomas protested to Sherman that the order would "stop altogether recruiting with [Sherman's] army." When Congress passed a law authorizing the state governors to send recruiting agents into the South to recruit black troops, Sherman informed Halleck that he would not allow any such agents in territory he controlled. Stanton regretfully informed one of the Northern governors, "Sherman objects to admitting state recruiting agents within his lines and the field for recruiting is nearly all within his command." It was probably Stanton who suggested that Lincoln write to Sherman, reminding him that this was not merely a policy but a federal law, which neither he nor Sherman could ignore. Lincoln added that he favored recruiting blacks: "Unlike white recruits, [they] help us where they come from, as well as where they go to." Lincoln closed by asking for Sherman's "hearty co-operation." Sherman responded that he had "the highest veneration for the law, and will respect it always, however it conflicts with my opinion of its propriety." He promised Lincoln a fuller explanation after he had "taken Atlanta."[49]

William Tecumseh Sherman, the brash, bold western general, with whom Stanton would often quarrel over black soldiers and other issues.

A week later Sherman wrote a long letter to John Spooner, a Massachusetts recruiting agent: "The negro is in a transition state and is not the equal of the white man." Recruiting among blacks only delayed "the universal draft" in the North, which Sherman thought would be necessary to overcome the South and to "separate the sheep from the goats, and demonstrate what citizens will fight for their country and what will only talk." In Sherman's view the proper military role for blacks was as "pioneers, teamsters, cooks, and servants"; he would only gradually allow a few of them "to experiment in the art of the soldier, beginning with the duties of local garrisons." He added that these were "some of my peculiar notions, but I assure you they are shared by a large proportion of our fighting men."[50]

As Sherman probably intended, his letter to Spooner soon appeared in the Northern newspapers. Democratic papers printed it happily, for Sherman was siding with them on the question of whether blacks could be soldiers or citizens. Sherman claimed in a letter to Halleck that his letter to Spooner was "never designed for publication" and that he hoped it would "not be construed as unfriendly to Mr. Lincoln or Mr. Stanton." Sherman insisted to Halleck that black soldiers could not "improvise roads, bridges, sorties, flank movements &c. like the white man." In a letter to another friend, Sherman was more blunt: "I like niggers well enough as niggers, but when fools and idiots try and make niggers better than ourselves, I have an opinion."[51]

―――――

While Grant was fighting in Virginia and Sherman was fighting in Georgia, delegates from the Northern states gathered in Baltimore for the Union Party's national convention. Stanton reported on June 7 to Dana, who was with Grant at the time, "Mr. Lincoln will be re-nominated without opposition. The chances of [Hannibal] Hamlin and Andy Johnson for Vice President about even." On the next day, equally briefly, Stanton informed Butler, "Lincoln nominated Johnson VP." By this time Stanton knew Johnson well; as a military governor, Johnson reported directly to Stanton and had visited Washington to meet with him and Lincoln several times during the war. Johnson sometimes irritated Stanton with his repeated requests on minor matters, but overall Stanton thought Johnson had done a good job in a difficult situation. But there is nothing to indicate that Stanton *cared* much at the time about whether Johnson or Hamlin or someone else was nominated as vice president, even though the choice of Johnson would prove so momentous for Stanton and for the nation.[52]

Even after Lincoln and Johnson were nominated by the Union Party, there was still talk among Radicals about Chase as president, talk of a second convention to abandon Lincoln. At the end of June, in the midst of a patronage dispute, Chase submitted yet another resignation letter to Lincoln, probably assuming that his threat would force Lincoln to yield on the patronage question. Instead Lincoln surprised Chase by accepting his resignation. "Of all I have said in commendation of your ability and fidelity, I have nothing to unsay; and yet you and I have reached a point of mutual embarrassment in our official relation which it seems cannot be overcome, or longer sustained, consistently with the public service." Chase did not speak with Stanton before he sent Lincoln his resignation, but after the president accepted, Chase wrote Stanton a warm letter: "I felt myself bound yesterday to send my resignation to the President. It would have been grateful to me to be able to consult you: but I feared you might be prompted by your generous sentiments to take some step injurious to the country. Today my resignation has been accepted, and if you have not already been informed of it, it is due to you that I should give you the information, as soon as received by myself."[53]

To replace Chase at the Treasury Department, Lincoln wanted former Ohio governor David Tod, but he declined. Lincoln then asked Fessenden, chairman of the Senate Finance Committee, who wanted to decline but was persuaded by Stanton and others to accept. In a letter home a few days after the events, Fessenden quoted Stanton as saying, "You can no more refuse than your son could have refused to attack Monett's Bluff, and you cannot look him in the face if you do." (Fessenden's son was recently involved in the failed attack at that site.) Fessenden told Stanton that he feared the long hours and hard work as treasury secretary would kill him. "Very well," Stanton replied, according to Fessenden's letter, "you cannot die better than in trying to save your country."[54]

Chapter 13

"Tower of Strength"

— July–November 1864 —

A s Stanton was dealing with the treasury transition, he heard from John Garrett in Baltimore that substantial Confederate forces were moving toward Harpers Ferry. Gen. Franz Sigel sent a similar report from the town itself. Garrett then informed Stanton on July 3 that the rebels were at Martinsburg, West Virginia, apparently heading for Maryland. Stanton was skeptical, writing to Garrett that the "great difficulty" in such cases was to "avoid being misled by stampede and groundless clamor." Two days later, Stanton knew that Garrett was right; a rebel force under Gen. Jubal Early, estimated at 20,000 to 30,000 men, was in Maryland. Grant was reluctant to send troops from his army around Petersburg, but Stanton and Halleck finally insisted because they had no forces on hand to defend Baltimore or Washington. On July 5 Stanton sent telegrams to several governors, including Curtin in Pennsylvania, calling on them to send militia to defeat another invasion. Stanton underlined an order from Halleck to Gen. David Hunter at Parkersburg, West Virginia: "You cannot be too speedy in your movements in this direction with your whole force."[1]

Lincoln, Stanton, and Halleck once again spent day and night in the War Department's telegraph office, sending and receiving messages. Stanton's telegraph office was the predecessor of the White House Situation Room, the point from which the president and the secretary exercise civilian control over military operations. Lincoln and Stanton had to work with far more limited and erratic information than do modern presidents and secretaries. On July 7, for example, Stanton had no direct telegraphic communication with Gen. Lew Wallace, the future author of *Ben Hur*, at Frederick, Maryland, only about forty miles north of Washington and forty miles west of Baltimore. Stanton had to rely upon Garrett, in Baltimore, for this brief report from Wallace: "My troops are engaging the enemy to the west and in the skirts of Frederick. Warm cannonading going on. I will hold the bridge at all hazards. Send on troops as rapidly as possible." Another, even more worrisome message arrived from Wallace through Garrett at about nine that evening: "I think my troops are retiring from Frederick. If so, they have been directed to fall back upon the Baltimore Pike to the crossing of the Monocacy, and to hold the crossing at all hazards." Stanton urged Garrett to forward to Wallace as soon as possible the troops that were arriving by boat in Baltimore.[2]

Stanton and Halleck spent July 8 trying to determine where the Confederates were and to organize and move Union troops to counter them. Halleck's report to Grant at midday gives some sense of the confusion in the War Department: the enemy was "around Maryland Heights, at Hagerstown, Boonsborough, and Middletown, and threatening Frederick." Halleck advised Grant that Hunter's army—supposedly on its way by rail from West Virginia—"moves so slow, and the railroad is so broken up, that I fear he will be too late to give us much aid." There was "considerable alarm in Washington, Baltimore, and Pennsylvania." Gen. Darius Couch, at Harrisburg, told Stanton that in the chaos there it would take too long to organize the militia in regiments. Could he "muster in by companies"? No, Stanton replied, unless and until the militia were "organized in regiments they are of no use whatsoever." Other governors managed somehow. If Curtin's staff was "incompetent he can readily change it, and make it as good as Brough's or Morton's." By ten o'clock that night, Stanton and Halleck had a clearer if bleaker picture of Early's forces and plans. Halleck wired Grant that Early had up to 30,000 men marching south toward Urbana, Maryland. "The militia is not reliable even to hold the fortifications of Washington and Baltimore," Halleck wrote, so that Grant must send "considerable reinforcements" directly and immediately to Washington.[3]

On July 9 General Wallace, with only about 6,000 federals, fought an all-day battle at Monocacy Creek against General Early and his force of about 15,000 rebels. Stanton and others at the War Department had essentially no information on the fighting, so at five in the afternoon, Lincoln sent a message to Garrett, asking what news he had from Monocacy: "We have nothing about it here except what you say." Garrett responded that, according to his agents near the battlefield, "things looked very badly, indeed." At about eleven that night there was a brief message from Wallace through Garrett: "Held the bridge to the last. They overwhelmed me with numbers." A longer message from Wallace arrived about an hour later: "I am retreating with a foot-sore, battered and half-demoralized column. Forces of the enemy at least 20,000. They do not seem to be pursuing. You will have to use every exertion to save Baltimore and Washington. Colonel Seward, son of the Secretary, is wounded, and is a prisoner." Stanton had not been sending any of these messages to Dix for release to the press, but he now drafted and dispatched one, editing Wallace's message severely so that it reported the defeat, but not that the troops were battered and demoralized. Stanton also went in person after midnight to see the Seward family, to tell them the news about their son Col. William Seward. Fortunately this part of Wallace's report proved incorrect: Seward was not captured and his injuries were not severe.[4]

Wallace and his troops retreated to Baltimore, and Early and his troops marched for Washington, reaching the outskirts on the afternoon of July 11. Lincoln went out to watch the skirmishing at Fort Stevens, but it seems that Stanton remained at the War Department, reading and sending messages. Among the many that he sent on July 11 were telegrams to Gen. James Barnes, in charge at Point Lookout, asking what naval force he had available there; to General Wallace, telling him that Gen. Edward Ord now had command of the Eighth Corps; and to John Garrett, asking what news he had from his rail agents. Welles wrote that Stanton showed "none of the alarm and fright I have seen in him on former occasions. It is evident he considers the force not large, or such that cannot be controlled." Years later, however, Albert Johnson, one of Stanton's aides, recalled that the "city was wild with excitement and fear" and that Stanton had him take some of the Stanton family's gold and bonds, stored in the safe in the War Department, to the Stanton home.[5]

As Stanton assured Welles, the rebel force was not strong enough to break through the federal defenses, especially as more federal troops arrived at the wharves and marched up Seventh Avenue. Late on July 12 and early on July 13, Early retreated, heading for the fords across the Potomac River. Once again Washington tried to capture a retreating Confederate force on the north side of the Potomac. Stanton sent a message at four in the afternoon to encourage Gen. H. G. Wright, who was in charge of the pursuit of Early. But Wright was still in Washington, while Early and his men were approaching the Potomac. They crossed into Virginia, but not into safety, for there would be no safety in the Shenandoah Valley for Confederates this summer. Grant sent word to Halleck on July 14 that Union troops should "eat out Virginia clear and clean as far as they go, so that crows flying over it for the balance of the season will have to carry their provender with them." Grant's protégé Gen. Philip Sheridan would implement these harsh instructions in the coming weeks, in a series of battles and raids in the Shenandoah Valley.[6]

While they were in the Washington suburbs, Early and his rebels had burned to the ground Montgomery Blair's mansion in Silver Spring, Maryland. Blair denounced Halleck and the officers involved in the defense of Washington as "poltroons," calling it a "disgrace" that with a "million of men in arms" the government could not protect his home on the northern outskirts of the national capital. Halleck, hearing of this, wrote an angry letter to Stanton, demanding to know whether Lincoln approved of Blair's comments. If Lincoln approved, the army officers involved should be dismissed, but if he disagreed, "the slanderer should be dismissed from the cabinet." Stanton relayed this to Lincoln, who responded in what his secretaries Nicolay and Hay called "his most masterful manner." Lincoln wrote to Stanton that he was not sure whether Blair had really called Halleck a "poltroon," but that in any case he was not inclined to dismiss the postmaster general. "I do not consider what may have been hastily said in a moment of vexation at so severe a loss, is sufficient ground for so grave a step. Besides this, *truth* is generally the best vindication against slander. I propose continuing to be myself the judge as to when a member of the Cabinet shall be dismissed." When Lincoln dismissed Blair a few weeks later, in a compromise with the Radicals, who in exchange abandoned their support for Frémont for president,

Senator Zachariah Chandler celebrated Blair's departure "by having a good drunk." A friend reported to Butler that Stanton "said he would have liked to have known when & where" Chandler was celebrating so "that he might have a hand in it."[7]

Stanton and his family spent some of their time this summer halfway to Silver Spring, on the grounds of the Soldiers' Home, a small army retirement community set on more than two hundred wooded acres, about five miles due north of the Capitol. The Lincoln family spent three summers in what is now known as President Lincoln's Cottage, although several other presidents lived there before and after the Civil War. The Stanton family lived in a nearby house this summer, 1864, and at least once after the war, with Stanton himself sometimes joining his family in the evening and sometimes remaining at the house in town. According to Francis Carpenter, the artist who was living with the Lincolns at this time, one evening this summer the secretary teased the first lady a bit, saying he planned "to have a full-length portrait of you painted, standing on the ramparts of Fort Stevens overlooking the fight!" Mrs. Lincoln responded, "I can assure you of one thing, Mr. Secretary, if I had had a few ladies with me the Rebels would not have been permitted to get away as they did!"[8]

David Bates, a clerk in the War Department's telegraph office, recalled riding out to the cottage one summer evening to deliver messages to Stanton: "I found Stanton reclining on the grass, playing with Lewis, one of his children." Stanton "invited me to a seat on the greensward while he read the telegrams; and the business being finished, we began talking of early times in Steubenville, Ohio, his native town and mine." One of them mentioned "mumble-the-peg," a game requiring one to throw a pocket knife into the ground as close as possible to one's own feet. Stanton "proposed that we should have a game then and there" and the secretary "entered into the spirit of the boyish sport with great zest, and for the moment all the perplexing questions of the terrible war were forgotten. I do not remember who won."[9]

Lewis Stanton remembered that he and Tad Lincoln kept peacocks this summer at the Soldiers' Home. To keep the birds from flying away, some of the soldiers tied blocks of wood to their feet. One evening, when Lincoln and Stanton arrived from Washington, they noticed that the peacocks were in the trees, with their strings and blocks tangled among the branches. "The two men immediately went to work, solemnly going to and fro unwinding the ropes and getting them in straight lines and carefully placing the small pieces of wood where without catching they would slide off when in the morning the birds flew down."[10]

Congress finished its session on July 4, 1864, just as the first rebel troops were splashing across the Potomac and marching into Maryland. Stanton was pleased that Congress finally passed legislation to equalize pay between black and white soldiers, as part of the army appropriation, though the bill did not address all the concerns of the black soldiers. One section provided that all black troops would receive equal pay and other benefits, retroactive to January 1, 1864. Another section provided that blacks who were free on April 19, 1861, and who had enlisted in the army thereafter would receive equal pay and benefits, retroactive to the date of their enlistment. The net effect of these two sections was to discriminate against the black soldiers who were slaves at the outset of the war and who enlisted before 1864, for they could not receive pay all the way back to their date of enlistment. Stanton probably disliked but accepted this congressional compromise.[11]

Another measure close to Stanton's heart was the bill to create a Freedmen's Bureau within the War Department. The bill passed the House of Representatives in March 1864 by a very close vote. To speed the bill along, Senator Charles Sumner tried to persuade the relevant Senate committee to report the bill out in the form in which it had passed the House, but when that failed, he amended the bill as some of his colleagues wished, to place the new bureau within the Treasury Department. Senator Henry Wilson argued that this made no sense whatsoever, because it was the army that provided protection to the freedmen, and it was around army camps that the freedmen gathered. But Wilson's argument failed, and the Senate passed the bill in its "treasury" form at the end of June. There was no time in the busy last days of the session to reconcile the two bills, so Stanton would have to wait on this issue until the next session, beginning in December.[12]

From Lincoln's perspective, the most important measure of this session was the Wade-Davis bill, named after its sponsors, Senator Benjamin

Wade and Representative Henry Winter Davis. Unlike Lincoln's December proclamation, which took a relatively lenient line toward former rebels, allowing new state governments to form when only 10 percent of a state's population promised to obey federal law, the Wade-Davis bill took a far harsher line. Wade and Davis would insist that 50 percent of voters swear an oath of allegiance, and would restrict the right to vote to the handful of Southerners who could take the "ironclad oath" that they had never supported the rebellion. The Wade-Davis bill treated the Southern states as no longer part of the Union and provided that no former state could return to the Union unless its new constitution prohibited slavery.[13]

Henry Winter Davis, Stanton's Radical friend from Maryland and one of the authors of the Wade-Davis reconstruction bill.

Benjamin Wade, Radical senator from Ohio, the other author of the Wade-Davis bill, another member of Congress with whom Stanton worked closely.

Stanton may or may not have been in the president's room in the Capitol building on the last day of the session, when several senators pressed

Lincoln to sign the Wade-Davis bill. Hay noted in his diary Chandler's warning that if Lincoln vetoed the measure, it would damage the party "fearfully in the North West" in the coming elections. "I do not see," Lincoln responded, "how any of us can deny and contradict all we have always said, that Congress has no constitutional power over slavery in the states." Because the session was ending that day, Lincoln did not have to explain his concerns about the bill; he could just "pocket" the measure and prevent it from becoming law. But on July 8, as Stanton was shifting troops to defend Washington and Baltimore, Lincoln issued a message to explain why he had not signed the Wade-Davis bill, pointing out that it would invalidate "the free-state constitutions and governments already adopted and installed in Arkansas and Louisiana." Lincoln also said that he was "fully satisfied with the system for restoration contained in the Bill, as one very proper plan for the loyal people of any State choosing to adopt it"—as if any Southern state would *choose* the harsh language of Wade-Davis over the easier provisions of Lincoln's 10 percent plan.[14]

Wade and Davis themselves did not intend to let Lincoln have the last word. They worked through the month of July on a long letter that appeared in the *New York Tribune* on August 5, 1864. Their bill, unlike Lincoln's approach, would protect the United States against the "great dangers" of a "return to power of the guilty leaders of the rebellion." The governments of Arkansas and Louisiana, which Lincoln recognized, were "mere oligarchies imposed on the people by military orders under the form of elections." Lincoln would probably try to pervert the presidential election, seeking all the Southern electoral votes, by setting up similar spurious governments "in every rebel State where the United States have a camp." Lincoln, they declared, "must understand that our support is of a cause, and not of a man: that the authority of Congress is paramount, and must be respected; that . . . if he wishes our support he must confine himself to his executive duties—to obey and execute, not make the laws; to suppress by arms armed rebellion, and leave political reorganization to Congress."[15]

This Wade-Davis manifesto appeared at a grim moment for Lincoln and Stanton. Grant was stalled near Petersburg and had just lost almost 4,000 men in the disastrous Battle of the Crater, a failed attempt to open a hole in the Confederate lines by exploding a mine. Grant told Halleck the battle was "the saddest affair I have witnessed in the war." Not only had Early threatened Washington; a rebel cavalry raid had just burned to the ground Chambersburg, Pennsylvania. Newspapers complained that Stanton had ceased to provide them with his daily official reports, but Stanton had his eye on the elections, so he could not relay messages such as Grant's "saddest affair" report.[16]

Radicals were determined to have someone other than Lincoln as their candidate for president: perhaps Gen. Benjamin Butler; perhaps Gen. John Frémont, already nominated by a splinter party. One of Butler's friends wrote to him from Washington on August 11 to report on a conversation between Lincoln and Andrew Jackson Hamilton, the military governor of Texas. Lincoln told Hamilton he knew that he would be beaten in the presidential election, "and unless some great change takes place badly beaten." The reason: "People promised themselves when Gen. Grant started out that he would take Richmond in June—he didn't take it, and they blame me." Hamilton responded that people wanted to see a complete change in the cabinet, that "everybody about you here except Fessenden shall be turned away, and men put in their places in whom they can have confidence. You cannot disregard this will & be saved." (It was probably not coincidence that newspapers were reporting that Lincoln was about to replace Stanton with Butler.) According to this letter, Lincoln did not disagree with Hamilton's comment about the cabinet, but he also did not make any changes.[17]

More grim political news arrived in Washington later in August. Henry Raymond, editor of the *New York Times* and head of the National Union Committee, wrote to Lincoln from New York on August 20 to report that he was hearing from every state in the North that "the tide is setting strongly against us." There were two key reasons why Lincoln's chances of winning the presidential election looked so poor: "the want of military success" and the belief that he would insist on the end of slavery as the price for peace. Raymond urged Lincoln to extend an offer of peace "on the sole condition of acknowledging the supremacy of the constitution," with all other questions, including slavery, "to be settled by a convention of the people of all the states." Lincoln was sufficiently concerned, sufficiently persuaded, that he drafted (but did not send) a letter to authorize Raymond to go to Richmond, to meet there with Jefferson Davis, to discuss peace without preconditions other than "restoration of the Union and the national authority." Lincoln also drafted a memorandum to the cabinet: "This morning, as for some days past, it seems exceedingly probable that this Administration will not be re-elected. Then it will be my duty to so co-operate with the President elect, as to save the Union between the election and the inauguration; as he will have secured his election on such ground that he cannot possibly save it afterward." Lincoln folded this message so that the cabinet members could not read it, then asked them all to sign it, his curious way of committing them to try "to save the Union" if McClellan was elected.[18]

After working together so closely in the Buchanan administration, Stanton and Judge Jeremiah Black had not talked in several years, for Black was an inveterate enemy of the Lincoln administration. But one evening in August the two men met, and Black told Stanton he was heading to Niagara Falls, where he hoped to speak about peace prospects with their former cabinet colleague Jacob Thompson, now the leading Confederate agent in Canada. Stanton did not object, and Black may have interpreted this as approval. But Stanton was no doubt annoyed to read in the *New York Herald* on August 19 a report from the Canadian side of the Falls, saying that both Black and Thompson had just arrived there: "This, taken in connection with the facts that have been received within the last twenty-four hours, in reference to the alarm and fear that have taken possession of Old Abe, have given rise to the rumor that Judge Black came with the permission of Secretary Stanton." Stanton was probably even more annoyed to read a further report in the *Herald* on August 22, claiming there was now no doubt that "Judge Black came here on behalf of the administration." The *Herald* believed that Lincoln and Stanton were so worried about Lincoln's election prospects that they sent Black to Canada "to reopen negotiations with the rebel ambassadors." Black wrote a long letter to Stanton on August 24, summarizing his conversations with Thompson, claiming that Stanton had "expressed his approbation" of Black's plan to visit Thompson in Canada. Stanton responded on August 31, denying that he had approved Black's trip and utterly rejecting the idea of an armistice.[19]

The political situation had changed by this time because of the Democratic platform, adopted the prior day at their national convention in Chicago. The second section of the platform, drafted by Stanton's former friend Vallandigham, declared, "After four years of failure to restore the Union by the experiment of war . . . justice, humanity, liberty, and the public welfare demand that immediate efforts be made for a cessation of hostilities." Union Party papers instantly leaped on this peace plank, calling it a "miserable, cowardly, craven, pusillanimous acknowledgment of Southern independence." Many Democrats were dismayed, including the party's nominee for president, McClellan. He worked through six drafts of his acceptance letter, trying both to accept the nomination and insist that he would continue the war for the Union. Administration newspapers gleefully laughed at his difficulties in straddling the two wings of the Democratic Party and accused him and the Democrats of effectively working for the Confederates.[20]

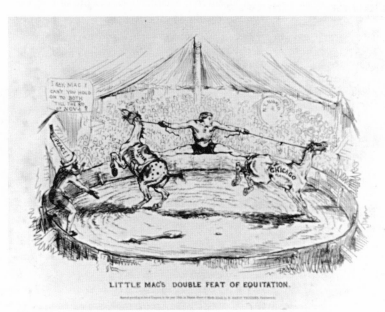

LITTLE MAC'S DOUBLE FEAT OF EQUITATION.

An 1864 political cartoon mocks McClellan's effort to join the antiwar Chicago platform with his own pro-war wing of the Democratic Party.

And then, on the evening of September 2, a message arrived in Stanton's telegraph office from one of Sherman's officers, stating that Sherman's troops had entered Atlanta at about noon that day. Stanton immediately sent one of his press releases through Dix and followed up with a second telegram at about ten that evening, when he had a few more details. George Templeton Strong, reading Stanton's messages in the New York newspapers the next day, wrote in his diary, "Glorious news this morning—Atlanta taken at last!" Strong believed that this news, "coming at this political crisis," was "the greatest event of the war." Stanton relayed to the press, as soon as he had it, an edited version of Sherman's official report: "So Atlanta is ours, and fairly won." Some papers used variants of Sherman's words as their headline.[21]

Official Dispatches from Secretary Stanton.

Atlanta ours and fairly won.

Hood's army cut in Two.

We capture 1,500 Prisoners.

Sherman's army engaged in battle or skirmish since the 5th of May.

Hood blows up the magazine at Atlanta and destroys several locomotives and cars.

OFFICIAL BULLETIN.

War Department, Sept. 4.
To Gen. Dix :
    Sherman's official report of the capture of Atlanta has just been received, dated 26 miles south of Atlanta, yesterday morning. It had been detained by the breaking of the telegraph lines, as already reported.

Stanton's September 1864 message to Dix, reporting that Sherman's troops had entered Atlanta, becomes the front-page headline in the *New York Times* the next day. Stanton often sent such messages late in the evening, knowing they would appear in the morning papers.

Almost every issue Stanton faced in the summer and fall of 1864 was in part political. For example, in July he received what seemed a routine request from Samuel Cony, the governor of Maine, to raise a few hundred troops to defend the coast and border of the state. When Stanton approved, Cony sent another message to say that he assumed the state could count these troops against its quota under the president's recent call for another 500,000 soldiers. No, Stanton responded, that would be unfair to other states. Only troops that were part of the general Union Army could count toward the quota. Cony replied with a long passionate telegram about the danger of rebel invasion along Maine's deserted borders and coastline. "I trust, Mr. Secretary, that you will reconsider your decision, for I should very much regret to be obliged to say to the people of Maine that this pitiful favor had been refused them." Cony did not mention, did not need to mention, that Maine would hold one of the first state elections of the fall season, set for September 13. A Democratic victory in Maine would encourage Democrats everywhere else; conversely a victory for Cony would strengthen the Union Party nationwide. In an era before political polls, the early state election results helped predict and influence the presidential contest. At stake in Maine was not just Cony's election; it was to some extent Lincoln's own election.[22]

So Stanton responded to Cony carefully, with a long telegram that was legal and military and political. Other states were exposed to similar dangers and might make similar demands.

> Our armies in the field are rapidly diminishing from casualties in battle and other incidents of a fierce and extensive war. Strong places captured from the enemy require to be immediately garrisoned to prevent their reconquest. Other points held by the rebel army require operations for their reduction. These are existing, imminent, and indispensable necessities, upon which the national existence depends. They are the purpose for which the troops have been called and to which the law and the President's proclamation require that they should be applied and credited. What you ask is not a "favor" within the power of this Department to bestow. Whether you will "say to the people of Maine that this pitiful favor has been refused them," or whether you will appeal to their patriotism and paramount interest in the national existence to answer the President's call and afford him the means to put an end to the war that has cost them so much blood and so much treasure, is for your own judgment to decide.[23]

A few weeks later, Maine voted as expected, for the Union Party candidates, and the margins were large, a hopeful sign for Lincoln. Cony could not resist including in his victory report to Stanton a request for "a little more time" to solicit volunteers so there would be no need for the dreaded draft in Maine. Many others were also urging Lincoln and Stanton to delay the draft in their states, for fear of a backlash that would cost the Union Party the elections. Stanton answered Cony that the draft must proceed "without an hour's delay" for he had just received "urgent appeals for an immediate draft from Atlanta and Petersburg." The appeals to which Stanton referred were telegrams from Generals Grant and Sherman, both saying they needed more troops, both urging the government to draft them as soon as possible. Grant wrote, "We ought to have the whole number of men called for by the President in the shortest possible time. A draft is soon over, and ceases to hurt after it is made. The agony of suspense is worse upon the public than the measure itself. Prompt action in filling our armies will have more effect upon the enemy than a victory over them." Stanton not only published these messages from Grant and Sherman in the newspapers; he had *sought* the message from Grant. Two days earlier he had sent Grant a telegram saying that he "would be glad if you would send me a telegram for publication urging the necessity of immediately filling up the Army by draft." So Stanton and Grant were working *together* on a press strategy to respond to political pressure to suspend the draft.[24]

Stanton and the generals were also working together to ensure that the Union soldiers could and would vote for Union Party candidates. The situation was different this year because many Northern states, including the most populous states of New York, Pennsylvania, and Ohio, had passed laws to allow soldiers to "vote in the field." For these states, the task this year would be getting the ballots and other materials to the soldiers in their camps and then back to the state authorities to be counted. For the states without voting in the field, including the critical states of Illinois and Indiana, Stanton and the generals would have to consider which troops could be spared for a few days to go home to vote in person. The situation was complicated by the calendar, for Ohio, Pennsylvania, and Indiana would vote on October 11 to select congressmen and state officials, and then all the states would vote on November 8 to choose the president.[25]

Stanton's rumored resignation was one political issue this summer. Several papers reported in August that he was about to resign or had indeed already done so. The *New York Times* hoped these reports were false for few men could fill Stanton's shoes: "To control an army in time of war is always and at best a serious and laborious affair; but to create such armies as are now in the field, to organize, officer and equip them, to

supervise and direct the construction, preparation, purchase and distri-
bution of all the material of war, to watch and direct the actual operations
of this enormous force in the field . . . all these requirements consti-
tute such a combination and accumulation of labor and responsibility as
have seldom devolved upon any one man in any country or in any age."
Lincoln might change his cabinet, but the *Times* urged him not to start
with a change at the War Department. From Henry Wilson, a Steubenville friend, Stanton received a more personal plea: "If, in this crisis, *you*
should leave, *Ohio is gone.* For God's sake, stand to your post. . . . We
hope cheerfully to carry the October elections but I see no hope if you
give up. Your name in Ohio is a tower of strength for Lincoln." We do
not have Stanton's response to Wilson, but in response to a similar letter
from another supporter he wrote that it gave him "infinite satisfaction"
to have the "esteem of sensible and patriotic men" in the midst of all the
"misunderstandings & misrepresentations."[26]

"Running the 'Machine.'" An anti-Lincoln cartoon from 1864. An
aide presents Stanton with a message reporting a "great victory" in the
capture of one prisoner and one gun. Stanton responds, "Ah, well.
Telegraph to General Dix immediately."

In early September, Stanton received a letter signed by Governor Oliver Morton and fifteen other Indiana leaders. Morton and his colleagues had the "gravest doubts" about whether the Union Party could carry Indiana in October unless there was a "delay in the draft until the election has passed" and also "the return, by election day, of fifteen thousand Indiana soldiers." The Indiana leaders stressed that the issue was not only the state election but also the presidential election, for the result in October would "beyond a doubt" determine the November result in their state. They feared that if the "secession element" prevailed they would force Indiana to cease giving any military aid to the Union government. Stanton shared the letter with Lincoln and they both responded. Stanton wrote to Morton that Sherman's army was "jealously watching whether the draft will be suspended or enforced." Stanton quoted Sherman to Morton: "If the President modifies [the draft] to the extent of one man, or wavers in its execution, he is gone. Even the army would vote against him." So the answer to Morton's first request—for a delay in the draft— was no. But the answer to the second request was yes, at least to some extent; there would be furloughs. Lincoln himself wrote to Sherman, explaining the grave risks of losing the Indiana election. "Any thing you can safely do to let her soldiers, or any part of them, go home and vote at the State election, will be greatly in point. They need not remain for the Presidential election, but may return to you at once. This is, in no sense, an order, but is merely intended to impress you with the importance, to the army itself, of your doing all you safely can, yourself being the judge of what you can safely do."[27]

Sherman sent home from Atlanta mainly the sick and wounded Indiana soldiers, but this still amounted to thousands of votes. In early October, when Morton informed Stanton that the quartermaster in Cairo, Illinois, was refusing to provide transportation to the Indiana soldiers heading home, Stanton immediately wired Gen. Robert Allen, the senior quartermaster for the western states, saying that the quartermaster in Cairo "will be required to obey his orders and will not be suffered to evade them by resignation." Allen responded that Morton was misinformed; the officer in question was providing transportation just as Stanton would wish. A few days later Stanton sent an order to Meigs and the other bureau chiefs in Washington, directing them to send home all employees who were residents of Pennsylvania, Ohio, or Indiana "to enable them to exercise the elective franchise at the approaching elections." Every vote would count, and Stanton was trying to get every possible vote.[28]

Stanton was also doing what he could to influence the elections through frequent press releases. After Sherman's victory in Atlanta, there was not much news from Sherman or Grant, but there was exciting news from Gen. Philip Sheridan, fighting against the Confederates in the Shenandoah Valley. On September 20 Sheridan informed Stanton that he had attacked General Early's army near Winchester. "We just sent them whirling through Winchester, and we are after them tomorrow. This army has behaved splendidly." Lincoln's secretary William Stoddard recalled that he was sitting on a sofa with Stanton in the War Department, talking about his recent visit to Arkansas, when this message from Sheridan was handed to the secretary. "Up jumps Stanton," Stoddard wrote, "and out he dashes into the hall. There is a swarm there of generals and other officers, of Senators and Congressmen, and among them the grim Secretary absolutely dances up and down, swinging his dispatch, and shouting the glorious good news." Stanton instructed Stoddard to take the message at once to Lincoln, to run to the White House, and Stoddard remembered doing just that. Stanton also informed the nation, sending a press release to Dix. Indeed there were three separate telegrams from Stanton to Dix on this one day, printed in the newspapers the next day. One headline in the *New York Times* read, "The Enemy Thoroughly Whipped."[29]

———

On the evening of October 11, as the state election returns trickled in by telegraph, Lincoln, Stanton, and a few others were in the War Department telegraph office. John Hay summarized in his diary some of the messages: a report from Ohio that Rutherford Hayes (future president) had been elected as a member of Congress; a report from Indiana that the Union Party candidates in one key county had improved upon last year's majority; a report from Philadelphia that "leading Democrats had given up the state." In the gaps between the messages, Lincoln read aloud to the group from the political satire of Petroleum Vesuvius Nasby. Hay wrote that the Nasby stories were "immensely amusing" and that "Stanton and Dana enjoyed them scarcely less than the President." Dana remembered Stanton's reaction quite differently: "I shall never forget the fire of his indignation at what seemed to him to be mere nonsense. The idea that when the safety of the republic was thus at issue, when the control of an empire was to be determined by a few figures brought in by the telegraph, the leader, the man most deeply concerned, not merely for himself but for his country, could turn aside to read such balderdash and to laugh at such frivolous jests was, to his mind, repugnant, even damnable."[30]

Hay also noted in his diary some of Stanton's comments. When an "enthusiastic" telegram arrived from Indiana predicting that Morton would have a majority of about 30,000, someone asked Stanton about the signatory, "McKim." Stanton explained that he was "a quartermaster of mine" who was "sent there to announce that," adding, "A very healthy sentiment is growing up among the quartermasters. Allen is attending all the Republican meetings, so is Myers. A nephew of Brough that I placed at Louisville & made a Colonel, I reduced to a Captain and ordered him South the other day. He was caught betting against Morton." Hay mentioned to Stanton that Colonel George Dandy, a former McClellan staff member, whose regiment was now "all for McClellan," wanted promotion to brigadier general. "'He will get it,' said the Secretary, puffing a long blue spiral wreath of smoke from his stern lips. Colonel Dandy's dream of stars passed away in that smoke." Hay's prediction of Dandy's fate was wrong, for he would receive his promotion, although not until spring of the next year.[31]

By the early morning hours of October 12, the results were clear: the Union Party would carry all three critical states. In Ohio, seventeen out of nineteen congressional seats would be held by Union Party men. In Indiana, Morton would carry the state by a majority of more than 20,000. In Pennsylvania, the Union Party would have a slight majority, expected to get stronger as the soldiers' votes were counted. Stanton sent a note to a friend in Steubenville, bragging, "The army vote so far heard stands about ten Union to one Copperhead."[32]

As the voters headed to the polls in October, Grant and Sherman were discussing by telegraph what Sherman should do next with his army. Sherman wanted to cut loose from his rail supply line, to head south toward the coast at Savannah. Grant was at first concerned that, if Sherman moved south, the Confederate general John Bell Hood would move north, into Tennessee, as indeed Hood would do. Sherman was not troubled, writing Grant that if necessary he would "make a wreck of the road and the country from Chattanooga to Atlanta, including the latter city," and then "move through Georgia, smashing things to the sea." If allowed to move south, "instead of my being on the defensive, I would be on the offensive; instead of guessing what he means to do, he would have to guess at my plans." Stanton informed Grant that Lincoln was also worried about Sherman's proposed march and hoped that it would be "maturely considered." Lincoln and Stanton were not concerned about Southern civilians; they were worried that Sherman and his army could not be reinforced and might be defeated. Grant now shifted from a skeptic to an advocate of Sherman's plan, assuring Lincoln and Stanton, "Such an army as Sherman has (and with such a commander) is hard to corner or capture." Lincoln and Stanton yielded, and Stanton sent a message to Sherman on October 13, telling him that his bold plan was approved. "Whatever results you have the confidence and support of the Government."[33]

Sherman did have the support of the government, but the government did not have Sherman's support on the question of black troops. In late October, as he was finishing plans for his march, Sherman wrote to Stanton that he was not "adverse to the organization of negro regiments, further than as to its effects on the white race." Sherman hoped that the white race would "rule and determine the future destiny of America; but if they prefer trade and gain, and leave to bought substitutes and negroes the fighting (the actual conflict), of course the question is settled, for those who hold the swords and muskets at the end of this war (which has but fairly begun) will have something to say." He added that he would "much prefer to keep negroes yet for some time to come in a subordinate state, for our prejudices, yours as well as mine, are not yet schooled for absolute equality." He was against bounties and substitutes and black troops: "It is not right to pay $1,000 to some fellow, who will run away, to do his fighting, or to some poor negro, who is thinking of the day of jubilee, but that every young and middle-aged man should be proud of the chance to fight for the stability of his country, without profit and without price." Sherman did not mention it, but Stanton was well aware that there would be no black regiments in his army when it marched out of Atlanta in early November, intending, in Sherman's words, to "make Georgia howl."[34]

_____

When Stanton arrived at the War Department at about seven on the morning of October 13, he learned that Chief Justice Roger Taney had died at his home during the night. Stanton immediately informed two men by telegram: Salmon Chase in Cincinnati and Justice Robert Grier in Philadelphia. Grier responded that he hoped Lincoln would nominate Stanton as chief justice: "I know of no man more competent to fill the place, or who deserves it so much as yourself. You have been wearing out your life in the service of your country, and have fulfilled the duties of your very responsible and laborious office with unexampled ability, and I think the President owes it to you, and that you should be suffered to retire in this honorable position." Grier noted that the newspapers were already naming Chase as Taney's successor; he hoped Lincoln would not "attend to the dictation of the journalocracy." Chase, apparently not aware of Stanton's own candidacy, wrote Stanton that he hoped for the appointment: "I think I should accept it if offered: for I am weary of political life & work. What do you think?"[35]

Ellen Stanton shared Grier's view that her husband was the right man for chief justice. On October 16, while her husband was away in Virginia, Ellen summoned to the Stanton home Senator Orville Browning, a longtime Illinois friend of Lincoln. Browning wrote in his diary that she "expressed to me a great desire to have her husband appointed chief justice, to fill the vacancy occasioned by Judge Taney's death, and wished me to see the President upon the subject." Browning was not keen about Chase and described Stanton as "an able lawyer, learned in his profession, and fond of it, of great application, and capacity of endurance in labor . . . a just man— honest and upright, and incapable of corruption." Browning spoke with Lincoln the next day. "He said nothing in reply to what I urged except to admit Mr. Stanton's ability and fine qualifications." Lincoln intended to keep his own counsel for a while about this coveted appointment.[36]

Stanton himself had left Washington early on October 15, bound by steamship for City Point, Virginia, Grant's headquarters on the James River, near the Petersburg siege lines. Stanton took along with him

Treasury Secretary Fessenden, Quartermaster General Meigs, and several other senior officials. When they arrived the next afternoon, Grant and several aides went with Stanton by boat to General Butler's nearby headquarters. One of these aides, Horace Porter, remembered that Stanton "did most of the talking" and had a habit of removing his spectacles "from time to time when he was talking earnestly, and wiping the glasses with his handkerchief." Stanton said, "In getting away from my desk, and being able to enjoy the outdoor air, I feel like a boy out of school." Porter had heard rumors of disagreements between Lincoln and Stanton, but on this afternoon "the Secretary manifested a genuine personal affection for Mr. Lincoln" and indeed "an admiration for his character which amounted to positive reverence."[37]

The next day, after breakfast with Grant, Stanton and the others headed by train for Meade's headquarters. Theodore Lyman, one of Meade's aides, described the group in a letter to his wife as the "greatest posse of large bugs," arriving just as Meade was hoping to enjoy his solitary morning cigar. After a few words with Meade himself, the aides "carted them all to see Fort Wadsworth." Stanton, "on being informed that there was only a picket line between him and the enemy, pulled out his watch and said they really must be going back! which indeed they did." Lyman wrote that Stanton "looks like his photographs, short, very stout with a big head & beard; a face expressive of large intelligence, but coarse." After this brief tour of the Petersburg lines, Stanton returned to Grant's headquarters, talking with him especially about the situation in the Shenandoah, and then Stanton and his party dined on board a warship near Norfolk. Arriving back at the War Department on the night of October 19, Stanton learned that rebel raiders from Canada had attacked and sacked St. Albans, Vermont, that day. So instead of heading home, he stayed at the office a while, sending messages to Vermont.[38]

———

Stanton's main focus in October and November 1864 was the presidential election. Even after Sherman's victory in September, even after the state victories in October, Lincoln and Stanton believed the presidential election would be close. On October 13, using a sheet of War Department letterhead, Lincoln estimated the electoral college vote. He predicted that McClellan would carry the two largest states, New York and Pennsylvania, and several others, including Illinois, for a total of 114 votes. He believed that he would receive 117, just enough to prevail. A week later, on October 20, William Prime sent McClellan a similar electoral analysis, predicting that McClellan would carry New York, Pennsylvania, Illinois, Connecticut, and other states, winning the election. So Stanton did not believe that he could relax his efforts but had to work to ensure Lincoln would get every possible vote.[39]

The October results were still being counted when Morton sent telegrams from Indianapolis to both Lincoln and Stanton, pressing them to allow the soldiers who had been furloughed to remain another month so they could vote in November. Lincoln was hesitant, noting that he had promised General Sherman his Indiana soldiers would be furloughed *only* for the October election and not for November. But Morton was insistent, pointing out that most of the soldiers in question were sick and wounded, so they would not be of any use at the front. Stanton relented to some extent, allowing the sick and wounded an extension of their leave until early November.[40]

"Behind the Scenes." Lincoln, in blackface, is preparing to play the role of Othello, with the rest of the cast in chaos around him. Stanton, to the right, tells soldiers they are to play in the "farce of the election."

Stanton was not afraid to use his department for political purposes, but sometimes he was blamed or credited for things he did not do. In late October, for example, there was a small item in a few Democratic papers alleging, "Secretary Stanton has dismissed twenty clerks in the Quartermaster Department for sympathizing with the rebellion." The *Springfield Republican* in Massachusetts extended the story, claiming that Stanton had started to weed out Lincoln's political opponents. "Mr. Stanton has dismissed thirty or forty clerks, who spend their evenings in denouncing Abraham Lincoln and their days at the War Department, drawing pay therefor with great regularity. Let the ax decapitate all these cheating knaves!" The *Chicago Tribune* amplified, asserting that one of the dismissed clerks had asked Stanton whether he was "disloyal because he favored the election of Gen. McClellan." Stanton supposedly replied, "When a young man receives his salary from an administration and spends his evenings denouncing it in the most offensive language, he cannot complain if that Administration chooses one of its friends to take his place!" The story has made its way into the history books, but there is nothing other than these partisan reports to suggest that Stanton actually dismissed twenty quartermaster clerks.[41]

Delaware was one of the states that did not allow its soldiers to vote in the field, and the governor went to Washington in late October to plead with Stanton to send as many soldiers home to vote as possible. "Without the vote of our troops in the field it will be utterly impossible to carry our state, and the election of U.S. senator, representative to Congress, and emancipation in Delaware depend upon the result." Stanton sent messages to Grant and other generals asking them to send Delaware troops home on furlough to vote. Grant reluctantly agreed but asked Stanton to keep the furloughs short so that the troops could be back in the field as soon as possible.[42]

Stanton's political work in late October and early November involved almost every Northern state. When he heard from a political leader in Hartford that federal surgeons were refusing to allow furloughs, Stanton demanded details, "What surgeons and in what hospitals refuse to furlough Connecticut soldiers? If you have complaints designate the individuals so that the evil can be corrected—otherwise your complaints are worse than useless." He instructed Gen. George Thomas in

Nashville, and presumably other generals elsewhere, to send home sick and wounded men from Connecticut, Illinois, Indiana, Massachusetts, Michigan, Ohio, Pennsylvania, and Wisconsin. Several of these states allowed for voting in the field, but perhaps Stanton was worried that ballots would not reach troops in hospitals. The *Pittsburgh Daily Post* complained, "Railroads now fairly swarm with soldiers and officers sent home to vote. There would be no objections to this were the administration fair to all the soldiers in its service; which it is not. The McClellan soldiers are kept back and the Lincoln soldiers are sent forward. We have heard of hundreds of cases where, upon one pretext or another, passes were refused to soldiers who would not pledge themselves to vote for Lincoln."[43]

In late October the papers reported that the army had arrested New York State agents in Baltimore and Washington and charged them with forging the signatures of soldiers on Democratic ballots. Stanton himself issued the order appointing Gen. Abner Doubleday to lead a military commission to try the defendants as soon as possible. Union Party papers filled column after column, day after day with evidence from Doubleday's military commission, under such headlines as "Astounding Frauds" and "Forged Votes by the Box Full." Democratic newspapers tried to argue that there was no voting fraud, and that if there were questions, they should be resolved in state courts rather than by a federal military commission. Stanton may not have issued the initial orders to arrest the New York agents, but he certainly approved of the arrests and the military commission. Late on the night of October 28, he sent a message to Harpers Ferry, instructing the general in charge there to be on the lookout for one William Turman of New York, "engaged in the recently discovered frauds against the soldier votes" and supposedly headed from New York to Virginia. "Please watch for and arrest him and report to this department." Two days later Stanton's aide Dana sent a message to Marsena Patrick, a Democrat and the provost marshal in Meade's army: "Reports have reached this Department that you are cooperating with the election agents sent to the army by Governor Seymour to the extent of showing them favor and furnishing them with facilities not warranted by the passes granted them by this Department and not accorded by you to the agents of the Union party. I am instructed by the Secretary of War to notify you that he expects from you careful and exact impartiality toward the representatives of the two parties; and also that as the agents of Governor Seymour here and in Baltimore have been detected in the perpetration of gross frauds & forgeries for the purpose of causing the votes of soldiers to be counted in favor of Democratic candidates when those soldiers intended to vote against such candidates, he expects you to exercise vigilance for the detection of all such crimes within your jurisdiction." Patrick grumbled in his diary that the telegram was "most insolent."[44]

On November 1 Stanton saw a report claiming that New York's Governor Seymour had asked the head of the state militia to post state soldiers at the polling places on election day. Stanton immediately sent a message to Grant, insisting, "No time should be lost in placing at General Dix's command, under loyal, suitable officers, not less than 5,000 or 6,000 troops. Western men should be sent if possible. If General Butler could be spared it would be well to send him." Grant instructed Butler to report at once to Stanton in Washington, and Butler recalled that when he arrived there early the next morning, Stanton showed him papers suggesting that there would be an election riot in November far worse than July's draft riot. Butler arrived in New York City by train the next day, somewhat annoyed to find no troops to command. Dix was also annoyed, writing Stanton that he did not know what Butler and several thousand troops would do in the city, explaining, "This is not the weak point." Stanton tried to calm them both, assuring Dix that sending Butler was "not designed in any way to impair or interfere with your supreme command, but is only a brief temporary assignment."[45]

Butler told Stanton on November 5 that he would like to issue an order directing the state militia to obey federal orders. Stanton shared this with Lincoln, who commented that he would like to set the idea aside for a day: "The tendency of the order, it seems to me, is to bring on a collision with the State authority, which I would rather avoid, at least until the necessity for it is more apparent than it yet is." On the eve of the election, Butler sent Stanton a long description of how he proposed to deploy his troops. "I have done all I could to prevent the secessionists from voting, and think have had some effect." He pressed Stanton again to approve his order, but Stanton declined, explaining that Lincoln did not want to clash with state government. The next day, election day, passed quietly in New York City, although Democratic papers complained that the Union troops discouraged Democrats from voting.[46]

Stanton was not among those in the telegraph office on the night of November 8, as the presidential election results arrived. Noah Brooks reported from Washington that Stanton was "sick abed with chills and fever." He had been sick for a few days; the *New York Tribune* reported in late October that he was "quite ill with chills and fever, supposed to have been contracted from the miasma along the James." But on this historic night Stanton surely arranged to have the election returns brought to him by messenger as they arrived by telegraph at the War Department, so that he knew not long after midnight that Lincoln would win.[47]

We think of the election of 1864 as a landslide for Lincoln, and it is true that McClellan in the end carried just three states: Delaware, Kentucky, and New Jersey. But the results in several states, including the two largest, were very close. Lincoln received only 51.5 percent of the votes in New York and only 51.6 percent in Pennsylvania. Stanton's decision to send Butler to New York may well have been the critical factor in that state. A shift of a few thousand votes in these two states would have put them into McClellan's column, giving him a total of seventy electoral votes. A shift of a few thousand votes in a few other states would have made McClellan president. Scholars still debate what would have happened if McClellan had won. Some believe he would have entered into peace negotiations with the South, that the Confederacy would have survived in some form as a result. Others believe that McClellan would have carried on the war, as he claimed he intended to do. Stephen Sears, the best recent biographer of the general, declares that "it is impossible to imagine his election producing a military outcome different from the actual one." But most agree that McClellan would have been soft on slavery, that slavery would have survived in the South. Indeed this was what one of Sherman's soldiers wrote at the time: that McClellan, if elected president, would compromise with the South "by letting them have their slaves." That would mean that the North would have to fight the South "again in ten years. But let Old Abe settle it, and it is always settled." Stanton could claim substantial credit, or take blame, for securing for Lincoln one of the most momentous elections in our nation's history.[48]

Stanton's work was especially important in encouraging, one might say coercing, soldiers to vote for Lincoln. He was no doubt pleased to receive telegrams from Grant reporting that about three-quarters of the soldiers who voted in Meade's army had voted for Lincoln. (Many soldiers who favored McClellan did not vote, for, as Jonathan White observes, "it took some mettle to be a Democrat in the Army in 1864.") Grant sent a message to Stanton asking him to congratulate Lincoln on the "double victory," for not only had the president prevailed, but the election had "passed off quietly, no bloodshed or riot throughout the land." That was itself a "victory worth more to the country than a battle won." Stanton shared Grant's message with Lincoln as well as the newspapers.[49]

Stanton remained in bed for about two weeks after the election, reading and sending a few messages from there. Even before all the votes were counted the newspapers started to speculate that Lincoln would make changes in his cabinet. The *New York Herald* reported that Stanton would become chief justice and that Butler would head the War Department. The *New York World* did not think Stanton suited for the Supreme Court: "His quick, hot, impetuous temper is inconsistent with that turn for grave and cautious deliberation, that weighty and impressive sobriety of thought . . . which belong to the great office to which he aspires." The *World* reminded readers of Stanton's letter in which he "poured public scorn on all strategy more recent than the days of Joshua," and suggested that Justice Stanton would disregard all laws more recent than the Old Testament. The *Cincinnati Gazette* speculated, "Stanton's unexpected illness—for no one had ever connected the thought of possible sickness with his burly form and bullying ways—may of course compel a change in the War Department sooner than Lincoln had intended." The *New York Tribune* declared that "the physical prostration" of Stanton made it "inevitable" that he would leave his position soon and that Lincoln had just "tendered the position yesterday to Gen. Butler in person." The *New York Times* thought all such reports were in "bad taste" while Stanton was "lying ill from over-work." The *Times* was confident that Stanton would, "if his health permits," remain secretary until "the close of the war."[50]

Stanton read these reports while in his sickbed. He wrote to Chase on November 19 that he was "better now, and again at work, but with feeble and broken strength, that can only be restored by absolute rest and relief from labor and care. This I long for, and hope soon to have." The cause of the Union, he hoped, was now "beyond all danger, and when

Grant goes into Richmond my task is ended. To you and to others it will remain to secure the fruits of victory, and to see that they do not turn to ashes." The many conflicting reports about the cabinet, as Chase knew, were just "lies invented by knaves for fools to feed on." There would probably be some changes in the cabinet, but they would be "made in a time & manner that no one will be looking for." As to the position that Chase and others coveted, that of chief justice: "I am not a candidate for it, do not want it, and this office has not been spoken of between the President & me, except that I have given him a number of recommendations and solicitations for your appointment." Stanton closed by saying that he hoped soon to see his friend in Washington.[51]

Chapter 14

"Gratitude to Almighty God"

—— November 1864–April 1865 ——

Although Stanton assured Chase that he was not a candidate for chief justice, others were not so sure. The *New York Herald* reported that Lincoln was inclined to appoint Stanton, "an excellent lawyer; a man of sterling integrity and immense industry; a practitioner of enlarged experience in the courts of the United States." Stanton's close friend Judge Edwards Pierrepont wrote a long letter to Lincoln, stressing the importance of the appointment and describing Stanton as "able, fearless, honest—a great lawyer and a great man—both quick and accurate, true and brave—devoted to his country, and next to [Lincoln] will stand in the history of this war as the one upon whom a grateful people will bestow its blessings." Pierrepont added that Stanton "tells me that he has no wish for the office and that his name is not among the candidates," but Lincoln probably read this as meaning that Stanton would serve if named.[1]

At this very time, however, late November, Grant arrived in Washington and urged Lincoln to keep Stanton at the War Department. According to the memoirs of his aide Badeau, the general told the president that he "could hardly find a more efficient war minister; certainly none more earnest, or more ready to hold up the hands of the commander of the army." Badeau went on to describe Stanton as "overpowering in will, masterful in passion, bending men and means and circumstances to his own purpose, massive in intellect, sleepless in energy." Badeau also noted that "his friendships were warm, his friends devoted, and in his family he was tenderly loved." When he read this in draft form, Grant wrote to Badeau to confirm his recollection and to praise his description of Stanton.[2]

The Brooklyn preacher Henry Ward Beecher, hearing that Stanton was sick, wrote "to cheer [him] a little." He praised Stanton's "energy, vitalizing industry, and fidelity," and above all his "*moral vision*." He had hoped that Stanton might fill the chair once filled by John Marshall and Roger Taney, but he now saw that Stanton's real work was in the War Department. If Stanton died tomorrow, Beecher wrote, he would have done enough to secure his fame, but Beecher was confident he would live to see the end of the war: "The Lord will fulfill his word: 'As thy day, so shall thy strength be also.'" Stanton replied that he was deeply moved by Beecher's letter: "Your friendly words are a cordial that strengthens me, and your kind sympathy will serve to dispel the gloom and despondency that, as you rightly judge, do sometimes in moments of physical weariness, gather upon my brain and press heavily upon my heart." There were issues he would like to discuss with Beecher, and he hoped Beecher would "visit Washington at an early day."[3]

Reverend Henry Ward Beecher, leading preacher and reformer. Stanton selected Beecher to give the speech at the raising of the flag in Charleston, South Carolina, on April 14, 1865.

Lincoln nominated Chase to be chief justice on December 6, 1864, and the Senate confirmed the nomination on the same day. Stanton's aide Dana, writing to a friend a week later, said, "The appointment was not made by the President with entire willingness. He is a man who keeps a grudge as faithfully as any other living Christian, and consented to Mr. Chase's elevation, only when the pressure became very general, and very urgent." A few days later, when Chase took the oath of office as chief justice, Stanton was almost certainly part of what one paper called the "brilliant assemblage" in the courtroom.[4]

Stanton was more focused this December on Nashville and Savannah than on Washington. As he and Grant had feared, Hood marched northward as Sherman marched southward, and by early December Hood and his army threatened to capture Nashville. Gen. George Thomas had more than twice as many men as Hood, but he would not attack. On December 2 Stanton wrote Grant that Thomas was using "the McClellan & Rosecrans strategy of do nothing and let the rebels raid the country." A few days later Stanton wrote to Grant again, lamenting, "Thomas seems unwilling to attack because it is hazardous, as if all war was anything but hazardous." Grant agreed, promising that if Thomas did not move promptly he would replace him. On December 11 Grant ordered Thomas, "Delay no longer for weather or reinforcements." Thomas responded that he could not move: "The whole country is covered with a perfect sheet of ice & sleet." Finally, a little after eleven o'clock on the night of December 15, a telegram arrived from Thomas reporting that he and his troops had attacked Hood that day, driven the rebels from their trenches, killed or captured thousands. Stanton immediately sent this message to Dix, so that the news was in the papers the next morning. Then Stanton sent a message to Thomas, congratulating him on his victory and urging him to press forward. Thomas would do just that over the next few days, effectively destroying Hood's army.[5]

On December 18 Stanton received a message from Sherman, sent on December 13 from a federal gunboat off the Georgia coast, reporting that his troops were attacking Savannah and that they would capture it within a few days. "The army is in splendid order and equal to anything. Our march was most agreeable, and we were not at all molested by guerillas."

Sherman boasted that his army had "utterly destroyed over 200 miles of rails, and consumed stores and provisions that were essential to Lee's and Hood's armies." As soon as he entered Savannah, his "first duty" would be "to clear the army of surplus negroes, mules and horses."[6]

Grant was in Washington on the day this message arrived, and he, Stanton, and Halleck discussed what Sherman should do next, after resting and resupplying in Savannah. Grant had been thinking about transporting Sherman's army by sea so that Sherman could help him "wipe out Lee" in Virginia. Sherman's message showed that he was thinking about another march, north through the Carolinas. "The whole army is crazy to be turned loose in Carolina," he wrote, "and with the experience of the past thirty days I judge that a month's sojourn in South Carolina would make her less bellicose." Grant was inclined to accept this suggestion, in part because he learned that a transfer by sea would take at least two months. Halleck was enthused, writing Sherman that if he captured Charleston he hoped "that by some accident the place may be destroyed, and if a little salt should be sown upon its site it may prevent the growth of future crops of nullification and secession."[7]

The four men continued to discuss plans over the next few days. In a long message Sherman argued, "We are not only fighting hostile armies, but a hostile people, and must make old and young, rich and poor, feel the hard hand of war, as well as their organized armies. I know that this recent movement of mine through Georgia has had a wonderful effect in this respect. Thousands who had been deceived by their lying newspapers to believe that we were being whipped all the time now realize the truth, and have no appetite for a repetition of the same experience." He had destroyed not only rails but houses and crops in Georgia, and he informed Stanton and Grant that he would use even harsher tactics in South Carolina. "The whole army is burning with an insatiable desire to wreak vengeance upon South Carolina. I almost tremble at her fate, but feel that she deserves all that seems in store for her." Halleck had mentioned Charleston, but Sherman was thinking about the state capital instead. "I look upon Columbia as quite as bad as Charleston and I doubt if we shall spare the public buildings there, as we did at Milledgeville," the wartime capital of Georgia. Grant gave Sherman permission to make his march: "Break up all the rail-roads in

South & North Carolina and join the Armies operating against Richmond as soon as you can."[8]

When Sherman and his army entered Savannah on December 22, he sent a message by sea to Lincoln: "I beg to present you as a Christmas gift the City of Savannah with 150 heavy guns & plenty of ammunition & also about 25,000 bales of cotton." Stanton received and relayed this message to Dix on December 25, and it appeared in the papers in the midst of a chorus of praise for Sherman. The *Cleveland Daily Leader* declared that Sherman's march proved the weakness of the Confederacy and presaged the imminent capture of Augusta and Charleston. The *Chicago Tribune* stated, "As a result of this achievement we now have a strong Union army securely in occupancy of a first class Southern city, a key to its railroad system, and admirably well located for a winter campaign." A newspaper in Warren, Ohio, published a local soldier's account that included some details of destruction: "Many square miles in the heart of Georgia have been desolated, stripped of horses, cattle, negroes and subsistence." As the forces left Milledgeville they "burned the state buildings, exploded quantities of ammunition, and destroyed the depots." But the overall tone was triumphant. Stanton agreed, rejoicing in Sherman's success, not worrying about the hints of random violence.[9]

Savannah was a major Southern port, but Wilmington, North Carolina, was even more important, an avenue through which goods continued to enter the South in spite of the Northern naval blockade. The key to Wilmington was Fort Fisher, a stronghold on a sand spit at the mouth of the Cape Fear River. In late December a joint Union force, under General Butler and Adm. David Porter, attempted once again to capture Fort Fisher. Porter tried and failed to blow up the fort, using a ship packed with explosives, and Butler tried and failed to attack it, turning back when he heard that rebel reinforcements were on their way. Grant reported to Lincoln on December 28 that the Fisher attack was a "gross and culpable failure" and he would try to determine "who is to blame." Two days later Grant informed Stanton that he was assembling troops and transport to make another attempt on Fort Fisher. Stanton "rejoiced" to hear that there would be another attack, and he urged Grant to send "an express" to Porter "to let him know at the earliest possible moment what to expect before he leaves." This message may have been what prompted Grant to write Porter that same day: "Please hold on where you are for a few days and I will endeavor to be back with an increased force and without the former commander." Grant's message made it clear that he intended to remove Butler, but for some reason he did not send a similar message on the same day to Stanton. When he did write to Stanton about Butler, he was tactful but clear: "In my absence Gen. Butler necessarily commands, and there is a lack of confidence felt in his military ability, making him an unsafe commander for a large army." Stanton agreed.[10]

The Northern newspapers in the first few days of January 1865 were filled with reports about the supposed Richmond peace mission of Stanton's former cabinet colleague Montgomery Blair and his father, the senior statesman Francis Preston Blair. The *New York Tribune* announced on January 2 that the two Blairs were on their way "to Richmond to see whether any termination of our national struggle is possible." Although the mission was not official, the *Tribune* suggested it would be "absurd to pretend" that it did not have Lincoln's approval in light of the close personal relations between Lincoln and the Blairs. On January 4, however, the *Tribune* reported that the senior Blair had not been able to reach Richmond because Stanton, "believing no good could be effected by his proposed conference with the Confederate chiefs, saw fit to intimate to Gen. Grant that he did not approve of Mr. Blair's proceeding." If this was true, the *Tribune* continued, "the majority of the American People will regret Mr. Stanton's decision." The *Tribune* was wrong to blame Stanton for Blair's failure to reach Richmond; Blair had a pass from Lincoln, allowing him to go to Richmond, so Stanton's opinion did not matter. But the *Tribune* may well have been right that Stanton did not see any point in a peace process.[11]

———

Stanton was himself planning a trip south, to Savannah, to see Sherman there. One reason for the trip was to persuade Sherman to allow blacks to enlist in his army. Stanton agreed on this issue with Chase, who wrote Sherman on January 2 to express concern that he still opposed recruiting black soldiers and viewed black refugees "as a set of pariahs, almost without rights." The *New York Times*, perhaps based on conversations with Stanton, reported that his visit to Sherman would "result in the inauguration of a new policy in Sherman's command in reference to treatment of negroes who may come into his lines hereafter. Such negroes will be armed and allowed to do effective service in the Union ranks." Stanton also hoped that warmer weather would improve his health. Meigs noted in his diary that Stanton was so sick he had to leave his own New Year's reception. Stanton's aide Edward Townsend later recalled that it was Stanton's doctor, Surgeon General Joseph Barnes, who insisted that Stanton take this Southern trip.[12]

Dr. Joseph Barnes, the surgeon general of the United States and Stanton's personal friend and physician.

On January 5, the day on which he would board the boat heading south, Stanton sent a flurry of last-minute messages. One was to his former assistant secretary John Tucker, in Philadelphia, asking him to ascertain from Stanton's life insurance company whether it would waive the standard "war exclusion" clause in his policy, in other words, whether his wife would be paid if Stanton were killed in Savannah. "Get it in writing," Stanton insisted. Another message was to Grant, asking him to write his friend Sherman about organizing and using black regiments. "He does not seem to appreciate the importance of this measure and appears indifferent if not hostile." Stanton also drafted and released to the press a brief description of his proposed trip, saying that he was leaving for "Fortress Monroe, Hilton Head and Savannah to consult with Generals Grant, Foster and Sherman. The supplies and exchange of prisoners; the organization of colored troops; raising the blockade in Savannah and opening it to free trade; the seizure of rebel property and products, will be among the subjects of his consideration."[13]

Stanton was joined on this trip by Meigs, Barnes, Townsend, and the collector of the port of New York, Simeon Draper. They boarded an army ship at the Navy Yard in the late afternoon, steamed through the night, and arrived the next afternoon at Fort Monroe. Stanton immediately sent a telegram to Grant, who was about eighty miles up the James River, at his headquarters at City Point: "I arrived here an hour ago *en route* for Savannah via Hilton Head and shall remain until tomorrow morning." Stanton hoped that Grant would come to see him, but Grant relied on telegrams instead, suggesting that Stanton persuade Sherman to have black soldiers "garrison the forts and islands." Stanton and his aides remained overnight at Fort Monroe, boarding the steamer *Nevada* the next day, departing for Hilton Head at about noon.[14]

Willard Saxton, an aide to his brother Gen. Rufus Saxton, based in Beaufort, South Carolina, wrote in his diary on January 10, "Wind blew hard in the night, & hard storm has prevailed all day, the rain falling in torrents at times." Stanton must have suffered from the same weather as the *Nevada* approached nearby Hilton Head. On his arrival Stanton met with General Saxton, who had been in the Sea Islands for the past several years, and Gen. Oliver Howard, originally from Maine, recently reaching the Sea Islands after marching with Sherman through Georgia. Saxton and Howard almost certainly urged Stanton to make the Sea Islands a model for the way blacks would live in the postwar South: working as farmers, some growing for themselves on small plots, others planting and harvesting cotton for Northern landowners; both children and adults were studying at schools and attending black churches. Black life there was, if not perfect, far better than in other parts of the South.[15]

On January 11 Stanton met with Sherman in Savannah. Much had changed since the days when Stanton was a lawyer and Sherman a banker in San Francisco. Both men understood that Sherman's military success gave him practical political power—that it would be difficult if not impossible for Stanton to force him to do anything that he did not want to do. On the question of blacks, Sherman no doubt told Stanton more or less what he told Chase and Halleck in letters at this time. "On approaching Savannah," Sherman wrote to Chase, "I had at least 20,000 negroes, clogging my roads, and eating up our substance. Instead of finding abundance here I found nothing and had to depend on my wagons till I opened a way for vessels and even to this day my men have been on short rations and my horses are failing." Sherman seemed to think that blacks, instead of fleeing their masters and following the Union Army, should stay put in slavery. But he denied that he was opposed to black soldiers. "Every negro who is fit for a soldier and is willing I invariably allow to join a negro regiment, but I do oppose and rightfully too, the *forcing* of negroes as soldiers. You cannot know the arts and devices to which base white men resort to secure negro soldiers, not to aid us to fight, but to get bounties for their own pockets." Sherman added, "Stanton is here now and will bear testimony to the truth of what I am saying."[16]

Sherman wrote even more frankly to Halleck, whom he had known since their days at West Point: "But the nigger? Why, in God's name, can't sensible men let him alone? When the people of the South tried to rule us through the negro, and became insolent, we cast them down, and on that question we are strong and unanimous." Halleck had warned Sherman that Radicals were gaining power, to which Sherman replied that Lincoln would have to put the Radicals in their place. "But I fear, if you be right that that power behind the throne is growing, somebody must meet it or we are again involved in war with another class of fanatics. Mr. Lincoln has boldly and well met the one attack, now let him meet the other."[17]

In his memoirs Sherman recalled that Stanton questioned him about news reports that one of his generals, Jeff Davis (not a relative of the Confederate president), had prevented black refugees from crossing Ebenezer Creek, leaving them to be captured or killed by Confederate cavalry. Sherman wrote that Stanton showed him a newspaper article criticizing Davis for the heartless way he had abandoned the black refugees. Sherman and Stanton did discuss this issue, but not because of a newspaper article, for the papers had not yet reported on the incident. Sherman presumably told Stanton more or less what he wrote to Halleck during Stanton's visit: that the claims against Davis were a "cock-and-bull story."

Davis and his army were encumbered by "old men, women and children," and Davis pulled up his pontoon bridge "not because he wanted to leave them, but because he wanted his bridge." Sherman insisted to Halleck that the rebels had not killed *any* of the black refugees left behind by Davis at Ebenezer Creek. Modern scholars disagree; they believe that more than a hundred blacks died there, either drowned in the river or killed by the rebels.[18]

On January 12, at Stanton's request, he and Sherman met with twenty black leaders, mainly ministers. It was a historic meeting, and Stanton made it more so by writing out his questions, getting the answers in detail, and publishing the transcript. Garrison Frazier, a Baptist minister in his late sixties, answered on behalf of the black delegation. One of Stanton's first questions echoed his initial instructions to the American Freedmen's Inquiry Commission: "State in what manner you think you can best take care of yourselves, and how you can best assist the Government in maintaining your freedom." Reverend Frazier responded that the freedmen needed land, to be worked by the women, children, and older men, while "the young men should enlist in the service of the Government, and serve in such manner as they may be wanted." He reiterated, "We want to be placed on land until we are able to buy it and make it our own." Stanton asked, "In what manner . . . would [you] rather live, whether scattered among the whites or in colonies by yourselves?" Frazier responded, for the group, that blacks would "prefer to live by ourselves, for there is a prejudice against us in the South that will take years to get over." When Stanton asked whether freedmen in this region wanted to serve as soldiers, Frazier assured him that "thousands of young men . . . [would] enlist." As a minister, Frazier was somewhat troubled by this eagerness to fight and to kill, and he was also troubled by the questionable recruiting practices sometimes used to lure blacks. A few weeks later Stanton told Chase that Frazier was "truly eloquent."[19]

Near the end of the meeting Stanton asked Sherman to leave the room, and he then asked the black leaders for their views of the general. Frazier said that, even before Sherman arrived, blacks viewed him "as a man, in the providence of God, specially set apart to accomplish this work." Some of the black ministers had visited with Sherman soon after his arrival, and they told Stanton that "he did not meet the Secretary with more courtesy than he met us." Years later Sherman was still angry at Stanton for asking these questions. "It certainly was a strange fact," Sherman wrote in his memoirs, "that the great War Secretary should have catechized negroes concerning the character of a general who had commanded a hundred thousand men in battle, had captured cities, conducted sixty-five thousand men successfully across four hundred miles of hostile territory, and had just brought tens of thousands of freedmen to a place of security."[20]

It might seem that Stanton and Sherman were miles apart on the question of black rights, yet they managed to join forces to help blacks through Sherman's famous Field Order 15. The first sentence of the order declared, "The islands from Charleston south, the abandoned rice-fields along the rivers for thirty miles back from the sea, and the country bordering the Saint John's River, Florida, are reserved and set apart for the settlement of negroes now made free by the acts of war and the proclamation of the President of the United States." The order excluded whites, other than soldiers, from this area, and specified, "The sole and exclusive management of affairs will be left to the freed people themselves," subject only to military authority and congressional legislation. Blacks desiring land in this region could apply to General Saxton or his officers, who would allocate land "so that each family shall have a plot of not more than forty acres." The order did not mention mules, but it was the origin of the phrase "forty acres and a mule" and the widespread hope that the federal government would compensate former slaves with land. Sherman was careful to note in the order that he was merely giving blacks possession of the land, not title to it, but few noticed this legal distinction.[21]

This order, drafted by Sherman and heavily edited by Stanton, served both men's interests. Stanton wanted to confirm and extend the approach that was working in the Sea Islands, to show that blacks could farm for themselves and govern themselves. Sherman wanted to encourage blacks to remain in the Sea Islands rather than follow his army as it headed north. He also wanted to counter critics like Chase and Sumner with a "grand gesture," to show the world that he was not against blacks, just against blacks who impeded his army. When he described Stanton's visit for his wife, he declared that Stanton was "cured of that Negro nonsense." He added, "I am right and won't change."[22]

Sherman and Stanton did not agree about blacks, but they agreed about other issues, such as cotton. Stanton had urged Sherman in December to secure all the cotton in Savannah for the United States. Sherman concurred, writing to Stanton that "half the people in Savannah" had approached him with cotton claims and that his "invariable answer has been that all the cotton in Savannah was prize of war and belonged to the United States." Cotton was "one of the chief causes of this war," and now cotton should "help to pay its expenses." Some of the bales of cotton had labels suggesting that they were owned by British merchants, but Sherman and Stanton agreed that these labels were almost surely false. They also agreed, or at least they did not disagree, about Sherman's harsh tactics toward Southern civilians. In light of what Stanton knew about Sherman's march through Georgia, and what Sherman had said in telegrams about South Carolina, Stanton might well have cautioned him to protect civilians and their property to the extent possible. That is what Lieber's code, which Stanton had helped to devise and promulgate, required. But nothing suggests that Stanton had any such cautionary conversation with Sherman while they were together in Savannah.[23]

On January 14 Stanton and his colleagues stopped at Beaufort, South Carolina, to see the Saxtons. Willard Saxton observed that Stanton was greeted at the wharf by a military band and that a regiment of blacks lined Bay Street to honor the visitors. Stanton walked up from the ship arm-in-arm with Gen. Rufus Saxton, followed by Generals Townsend and Barnes, followed by Draper and a New York merchant, Robert Minturn, whom Saxton had heard was worth "two & a half millions." Mathilda Saxton somehow served dinner to this large group in her small home. The other guests left early, and Stanton spent the night with Rufus and Mathilda Saxton. Years later she remembered that Stanton told them he was not well, that he would retire soon to his room, but then he sat up late beside their fire, reading poetry with them. She read part of "Horatius at the Bridge" by Thomas Macaulay:

> To every man upon this earth
> Death cometh soon or late.
> And how can man die better

Than facing fearful odds
For the ashes of his fathers
And the temples of his gods.

Stanton responded with "Ivry," by the same author, ending with:

For our God hath crushed the tyrant, our God hath raised the slave,
And mocked the counsel of the wise and the valor of the brave.
Then glory to His holy name, from whom all glories are!
And glory to our sovereign lord, King Henry of Navarre.[24]

On the next day, a Sunday, the Saxtons took Stanton on a carriage tour of the island, "where the live-oaks were draped with graceful gray moss, the birds singing and the air was soft and bland." They went to see a school for black children run by young Elizabeth Botume of Boston. She later described Stanton as "genial and unassuming as an old and well-known friend" and added that he "asked many questions about the contrabands and our work with them, in all of which he seemed deeply interested." Botume talked with Stanton eagerly about her work with the children. As he and Saxton rose to leave, Stanton told her, "I have been sick, but I feel sure I could get well here. I pitied you when I came down, but I envy you now." Mathilda Saxton remembered that, during his brief stay with them, Stanton was no longer the "Titan War Secretary" but rather "the genial companion, the man of letters, the lover of nature—the *real* Stanton."[25]

As Stanton and his friends steamed north, they passed close to Fort Fisher and strained their eyes to see which flag it was flying. Townsend recalled their joy "when the Stars and Stripes became distinguishable. The Secretary at once decided to put in, to learn the particulars of the capture and to congratulate the officers." Gen. Alfred Terry reported on the battle, concluded just a few hours earlier, and presented Stanton with the fort's former rebel flag. Stanton directed Townsend to make out brevet promotions for all the officers involved. The next day, from Fort

Monroe, Stanton sent Lincoln a long description of the battle for Fort Fisher and praised the "peace and order at Savannah since its occupation by General Sherman's army." Stanton had hoped to see Grant at Fort Monroe, to talk about "matters that cannot be safely written," but Grant could not get away from his headquarters, so he promised Stanton by telegram that he would "run to Washington to see you in a day or two."[26]

When he returned to Washington late on January 18, Stanton learned that Francis Blair had visited Richmond while Stanton was in Savannah. Blair had now returned to Washington with a letter from Jefferson Davis, saying that he was willing to enter talks "with a view to secure peace to the two countries." Lincoln responded through Blair that he was willing to negotiate "with the view of securing peace to the people of our one common country." Blair left Washington to return to Richmond, bearing Lincoln's letter, on January 20. This was the same day on which Stanton reported to the cabinet that there was "little or no loyalty in Savannah, and the women are frenzied, senseless partisans." On the basis of Stanton's statement and other evidence, Welles feared that it would be many months before the rebels surrendered: "If the fall of Savannah and Wilmington will not bring them to conciliatory measures and friendly relations, the capture of Richmond & Charleston will not effect it. They may submit to what they cannot help, but their enmity will remain."[27]

On the evening of January 29, Stanton received a message from Gen. Edward Ord, whom Lincoln had placed in Butler's stead as the head of the Army of the James. Ord reported that three senior Confederate leaders, including Vice President Alexander Stephens, were in nearby rebel territory and wanted to pass through his lines "on their way to Washington as commissioners." Stanton responded immediately; Ord should not allow the commissioners to proceed until he received the president's instructions. The next day, Lincoln sent Thomas Eckert, head of Stanton's telegraph office, to see the three commissioners. Lincoln instructed Eckert that he should not allow the Confederates to proceed unless they agreed to negotiate on the basis of his letter to Blair, that is, on the basis of "one common country." On the last day of January Lincoln instructed Seward to head to Fort Monroe to represent the United States if there were in fact peace negotiations with the Confederacy.[28]

Thomas Eckert, head of Stanton's telegraph office and his trusted aide and adviser.

Stanton may or may not have known of Seward's planned trip before he himself left the office on the late afternoon of January 31 for Baltimore, to attend a speech there that evening by Henry Ward Beecher. The purpose of the speech was to benefit the Baltimore Association for the Moral and Educational Improvement of the Colored People, and so Beecher talked mainly about the recently freed slaves and their future. According to one news report, he was "in favor of making all emigrants from Europe and all colored people citizens immediately." On the subject of peace, he "repudiated all peace negotiations with traitors with arms in their hands." Another press account said that Beecher opposed any negotiations with the Confederate leaders, for they were "malefactors of the blackest dye, criminals against a nation's life and against humanity, marching to the gibbet." At this someone screamed out "Blair, Blair" and the meeting "became turbulent with protest against the intervention of peace negotiators between the soldiers of the Union and the armies of the Rebellion." Stanton stayed in Baltimore overnight and returned to Washington early the next morning by train with Chase and Beecher.[29]

Lincoln and Stanton heard from Eckert on this first day of February that the rebel commissioners were not prepared to accept Lincoln's "one common country" condition. Lincoln, disappointed, was about to instruct Seward to return from Fort Monroe. But then, at four o'clock on the morning of February 2, a message from Grant to Stanton arrived at the War Department. Grant was "convinced" on the basis of his own informal conversations with the three Confederates "that their intentions are good and their desire sincere to restore peace and union." "I fear now their going back without any expression from any one in authority will have a bad influence," he added. Stanton delivered this message to Lincoln, and the two of them discussed the situation. Lincoln decided that he would go himself to Fort Monroe and departed within an hour or two, taking a special train to Annapolis, then a boat to the fort. Stanton had no way of knowing on February 3 what Lincoln and Seward were discussing on that day with the three Confederate commissioners. But Stanton did know, at some point during the day, that Lincoln and Seward were returning overnight, for he sent a telegram to John Garrett asking him to have a special train waiting at Annapolis at seven o'clock on the morning of February 4.[30]

That morning, just after he returned to Washington, Lincoln stopped by the telegraph office and drafted a message from Stanton to Grant: "The President desires me to repeat that nothing transpired or transpiring with the three gentlemen from Richmond is to cause any change, hindrance, or delay of your military plans or operations." Grant responded that the peace talks had not influenced his military plans at all. He was working slowly (it was, after all, midwinter) to position forces to the west of Petersburg, so that when he attacked that city in the spring, Lee's army would not be able to escape. Lincoln and Seward briefed the whole cabinet at noon on their Fort Monroe discussions. Welles noted in his diary that "no results were obtained," but perhaps Lincoln had achieved something by showing his willingness to talk with the Confederates. The *Washington Evening Star* agreed:

> The President, by his journey to Fortress Monroe, and the patient hearing he has given to the rebel deputation, has afforded to the country the best evidence of his disposition to do all that may be done consistent with the national honor to put a stop to the further effusion of blood. . . . The rebels, or their leaders at least, are not yet prepared to accept the only terms we can offer, i.e., to lay down their arms and return to the Union. It is well that the mask has been thus effectually stripped from the face of these assumed peace commissioners by

President Lincoln and Secretary Seward. All parties here will now recognize that there is to be no peace short of fighting the thing squarely through. While Lee's army remains intact at Richmond there can be no peace worth having. So, push on the column![31]

Sherman was certainly pushing on his columns, marching north from Savannah toward Columbia, South Carolina. Sumner wrote to a British friend that Stanton "thinks that peace can be had only when Lee's army is beaten, captured, or dispersed; & there I agree with him." Sumner reported that Stanton estimated that Lee still had about 65,000 soldiers in his army. (We now know that with deaths and desertions the actual number in Lee's force was closer to 45,000.) "Against him is Grant at Petersburg—a corps now demonstrating at Wilmington—& Sherman marching from Georgia. The latter will not turn aside for Augusta or Charleston, or any fortified place, but will traverse the Carolinas until he is able to co-operate with Grant." This was indeed the plan—and Stanton would have been horrified to know that Sumner had shared it in this way. A few days later Stanton reported to the press that Sherman and his troops had entered Columbia and that the rebel troops had left Charleston. Judge Pierrepont wrote from New York to congratulate Stanton: "I do not think the end is yet but the monster is in your grasp and you will now destroy him. The day is not distant when your valor, your firmness, your vigor, your great abilities and your trusting faith will be appreciated by a grateful people."[32]

Robert E. Lee could see the end as well, and on March 2 he sent a letter to Grant, which Grant at once forwarded to Stanton. Lee wrote that he believed, on the basis of informal comments by one of Grant's subordinates, that it might be possible through a "military convention" to reach some resolution of the "present unhappy difficulties." Lee suggested that he and Grant should meet to explore the possibility of such peace terms. Stanton carried Grant's message to Lincoln, and together the two men drafted the response. "The President directs me to say," Lincoln wrote in Stanton's voice, "that he wishes you to have no conference with General Lee unless it be for the capitulation of Gen. Lee's army, or on some minor, and purely, military matter. He instructs me to say that you are not to decide, discuss, or confer upon any political question. Such questions the President holds in his own hands; and will submit them to no military conferences or conventions. Meantime you are to press to the utmost, your military advantages." Stanton did not want to embarrass Grant, so he did not publicize this exchange in the papers. Nor, it seems, did Grant share the exchange with other generals, notably his friend Sherman.[33]

As the session ended in early March, Congress at last passed the freedmen's bill that Stanton had been pressing for months, writing to Sumner that he hoped that "some measure may speedily be adopted by Congress to discharge the duty which the government owes to the colored people of the South." Sumner's version of the bill had encountered opposition from not only the Democratic Party but also the Union Party. Senator John Hale of New Hampshire, an ardent abolitionist, opposed a provision that would prohibit the government from helping whites. Hale would go as far as "Christianity and humanity require me to go," but he would not vote for "a provision which would actually forbid our officers from extending any relief, even the slightest, to a white refugee, provided there was a colored person who wanted it." A new conference committee was appointed, with Henry Wilson taking Sumner's place, and a new and shorter version of the bill prepared. This version passed both houses and was signed into law by Lincoln late on March 3. Stanton was probably at Lincoln's side, for Welles wrote in his diary that the entire cabinet was with Lincoln at the Capitol that evening.[34]

Andrew Johnson, military governor of Tennessee under Stanton during the Civil War, vice president under Lincoln for a month, and then president after Lincoln's assassination.

The next day, March 4, was inauguration day. Stanton and Halleck were worried that rebels, or rebel sympathizers, would make some kind of attack on Washington, but as Halleck wrote in a letter at day's end to Lieber, "Thanks to abundant preparations we had no disturbance, no fires, no raids or robberies." Stanton was among the officials present in the Senate at noon for the swearing in of the new senators and the new vice president. His friend John Clifford, the former governor of Massachusetts, was also there, and he wrote home afterward that Andrew Johnson was "so drunk he could not know what he said," that it was "the most humiliating & mortifying spectacle ever exhibited in the country." In the course of his long, incoherent speech, Johnson addressed each of the cabinet members by name, "without the official handles to their names." Welles, sitting next to Stanton, whispered that Johnson was "either drunk or crazy," to which Stanton replied that there was "evidently something wrong." When Johnson at last finished, and garbled slightly the oath of office, the officials moved outside for the inauguration of the president. A crowd of almost forty thousand, white and black, civilian and soldier, cheered as Lincoln emerged from the Capitol. Stanton was seated in the front row with the other cabinet members, looking out over the crowd, as Lincoln delivered his immortal address:

> Fondly do we hope—fervently do we pray—that this mighty scourge of war may speedily pass away. Yet, if God wills that it continue, until all the wealth piled by the bond-man's two hundred and fifty years of unrequited toil shall be sunk, and until every drop of blood drawn with the lash, shall be paid by another drawn with the sword, as was said three thousand years ago, so still must it be said "the judgments of the Lord, are true and righteous altogether." With malice toward none; with charity for all; with firmness in the right, as God gives us to see the right, let us strive on to finish the work we are in; to bind up the nation's wounds; to care for him who shall have borne the battle, and for his widow, and his orphan—to do all which may achieve and cherish a just, and a lasting peace, among ourselves, and with all nations.[35]

As Lincoln's first term ended and his second term started there were a few changes in the cabinet. Edward Bates resigned and was replaced as attorney general by Lincoln's Kentucky friend James Speed. As Bates was leaving Washington, Stanton told him that his two sons in the army should write to Stanton directly and "frankly" for "anything that they need, and *I* will do for them anything which they might reasonably expect from *you.*" Bates was touched by the kindness. Stanton's friend Fessenden returned to the Senate, and Hugh McCulloch, the comptroller of the currency, was promoted to head the Treasury Department.[36]

Orville Hickman Browning, a Washington lawyer who would become Stanton's colleague in the Johnson cabinet.

In February 1865, Orville Browning and his wife were among the guests at a small dinner party at the Stanton house. A few weeks later, Browning returned to Stanton's house on a less pleasant mission. Browning had a friend and partner, James Singleton, described by one newspaper as a "semi-secesh Western politician of the Copperhead persuasion." Browning had obtained from Lincoln a pass allowing Singleton to go to Richmond and return "with any Southern products." Singleton had entered agreements in Richmond to purchase millions of dollars' worth of cotton, tobacco, and turpentine. Now Browning was distressed to read press reports that Grant's troops had destroyed several tons of Singleton's tobacco on a rail siding near Fredericksburg. Browning went first to

Lincoln, who was sympathetic, and then to Stanton, who was not. Stanton had no interest in any form of trade between the North and South, believing that such trade would just strengthen the South to fight longer. Browning wrote in his diary that Stanton was "vehemently opposed to the whole system of trade in foreign products as now carried on. Said every man who went through the lines to buy cotton ought to be shot—that it was trading in the blood of our soldiers, and sacrificing the interests of the Country to enable mercenary scoundrels to amass large fortunes &c, and that he had rather every pound of tobacco, and every pound of cotton in Richmond should be burnt, than that we should buy it, and pay for it in greenbacks." Stanton also wrote to Grant, telling him that even if Lincoln granted a pass, Grant was within his rights, as the commander on the scene, to "prohibit trade through your lines, and may seize goods in transit either way."[37]

Stanton went to see Grant in person on March 15, traveling by the *River Queen*. The secretary took a large group with him on this trip, including his wife, his son Eddie, and Grant's wife. Theodore Lyman, a young aide to Meade, was somewhat surprised to find that Stanton was not a tyrant, that he was "mild as drawn butter." Lyman, later a noted naturalist, described Stanton in a letter as "short, dark, very thick set, very big-headed [with] a somewhat goblin air." Julia Grant, in her memoirs, recalled that Stanton was worried about his son, telling her that his son "thinks he is in love and wants to take a wife. He could not pay for his own bread and butter, let alone take care of a wife." (Eddie was twenty-two, working as an assistant in the War Department, so he *could* pay for his bread and butter.) Stanton was even more distressed that his wife was "doing everything in her power to bring it about and encouraging them in every way." Mrs. Grant assured Stanton that the young woman in question was in love with a general, and thus safe from Stanton's son.[38]

The whole party went out to Meade's headquarters, where one of the corps paraded for them. The *New York Tribune* commented that the visit had two purposes: improving Stanton's health and "squelching whatever might remain of contraband trade permits." (Indeed Stanton was not well; another paper reported, "The wear and tear of the last two years have been too much" and that Stanton's health, rather than his temper, was now the explanation for his "paroxysms of passion.") The trip had at least one other purpose: to allow Grant and Stanton to talk at length before Grant started his spring campaign against Lee's army in and around Petersburg.[39]

Edwin Lamson Stanton, the son of Stanton's first marriage, was an aide to Stanton during the war years.

Stanton had been back in Washington only a few days when Lincoln headed south on March 23 to see Grant himself. Lincoln and Stanton were in daily telegraphic contact during Lincoln's trip to Virginia, which would last more than two weeks. Stanton sent his first message a few hours after Lincoln and his party left: "I hope you have reached Point Lookout safely notwithstanding the furious gale that came on soon after you started." The next day he wrote, "Nothing new has transpired here. Your tormentors have taken wing and departed." The weather in Washington was "cold, windy, and disagreeable. I think you went to the sunny South in good time." As Meade's troops attacked Lee's forces west of Petersburg, Lincoln reported to Stanton that he was about "five miles from the scene of this morning's action" and that he had seen the rebel captives, more than 1,500 of them, for himself. Stanton was pleased that the "rebel rooster" could not "hold the fence." He also cautioned Lincoln: "Remember General Harrison's advice to his men at Tippecanoe, that they 'can see as well a little farther off.'" One of Grant's aides remembered that Lincoln laughed aloud when he read this and said, "The serious Stanton is actually becoming facetious."[40]

Stanton outlined for Lincoln his plans for a ceremony to raise over Fort Sumter the same American flag that Anderson had lowered four years earlier. Stanton had lined up Henry Ward Beecher as the principal speaker, and Stanton himself was planning to attend. Lincoln, ever the careful lawyer, noticed an error in Stanton's order. He was "quite confident" that Fort Sumter fell on Saturday, April 13, rather than Sunday, April 14, for it was on that Sunday that he and his cabinet worked on the proclamation calling for troops. Stanton, also a careful lawyer, wrote back at some length, quoting the official report, which showed that the surrender ceremony was on the afternoon of the fourteenth. Lincoln responded that in the end it would "make little difference" on which of the two days Stanton held the ceremony.[41]

On March 27 Stanton received a long message from Sherman, who had left his army in North Carolina and was now at Fort Monroe, on his way to see Grant at City Point. Sherman's engineers had restored the railroads heading inland from New Berne and Wilmington, but they needed locomotives and cars. He wanted to know how many narrow-gauge locomotives and cars were on their way by sea to North Carolina, for the tracks in question were not standard gauge. Stanton responded almost at once, not only providing the numbers Sherman needed but also arranging for his senior railroad officer, Daniel McCallum, to travel to City Point so that he could go with Sherman to sort out the railroad issues in person. Lincoln, Grant, Sherman, and Adm. David Porter conferred on the *River Queen* for a day about how to end the war. Porter recalled in his memoir that Lincoln wanted "the surrender of the Confederate armies and desired that the most liberal terms be granted them." As he prepared to leave City Point to return to North Carolina, Sherman thanked Stanton for "the prompt attention given to [his] wants." Stanton answered, "God speed you; and that he may have you in his keeping, shield you from every danger, and crown you with victory, is my earnest prayer."[42]

After Lincoln had been away from Washington for a week, he wrote to Stanton that he thought he "ought to be at home" soon. Stanton, though, urged him to remain where he was: "I have strong faith that your presence will have great influence in inducing exertions that will bring Richmond; compared to that, no other duty can weigh a feather." So Lincoln remained at City Point, where one of his roles was that of reporter for Stanton, summarizing messages from Grant, who was near the front. Stanton, in turn, summarized these messages for Dix and the press. On April 2, for example, he sent four separate long messages to Dix, ending with one at eleven that night, quoting Lincoln: "All seems well with us, and everything quiet just now."[43]

At about ten o'clock on the morning of April 3, a message from Lincoln to Stanton arrived in the telegraph office: "Grant reports Petersburg evacuated; and he is confident Richmond also is. He is pushing forward to cut off if possible the retreating army. I start to him in a few minutes." Almost immediately there was a second message, from Gen. Godfrey Weitzel, from Richmond, saying that he and his troops were in the city. The *Washington Evening Star* reported that Stanton's announcement to the War Department, that the Union Army had entered Richmond, "caused a general stampede of the employees of that establishment to the street, where their pent-up enthusiasm had a chance for vent in cheers that would assuredly have lifted the roof from that building had they been delivered with such vim inside." The news "caught up and spread by a thousand mouths, caused almost a general suspension of business, and the various newspaper offices, especially, were besieged with excited crowds." One of Stanton's clerks wrote home that "every clerk in the department shut up his book without leave or license and in twenty minutes the guards alone were left to guard." Stanton sent a message to Dix for the press, and sent a caution to Lincoln: "Allow me respectfully to ask you to consider whether you ought to expose the nation to the consequence of any disaster to yourself in the pursuit of a treacherous and dangerous enemy like the rebel army. If it was only a question concerning yourself, I should not presume to say a word. Commanding generals are in the line of their duty in running such risks; but is the political head of the nation in the same condition?"[44]

Soon after the news arrived from Richmond, a crowd gathered at the War Department, filling the park in front of the building and "nearly obstructing the street." The crowd shouted for Stanton, and he emerged on the steps, "so overcome by emotion that he could not speak continuously," Brooks recalled. "Friends and fellow citizens," Stanton began,

> in this great hour of triumph, my heart, as well as yours, is penetrated with gratitude to Almighty God for his deliverance of this nation. Our thanks are due to the President, to the Army and Navy, to the great commanders by sea and land, to the gallant officers and men who have periled their lives upon the battlefield and drenched the soil with their blood. Henceforth our commiseration and our aid should be given to the wounded, the maimed and the suffering, who bear the marks of their great sacrifices in this mighty struggle. Let us humbly offer up our thanks to Divine Providence, for his care over us, and beseech Him that He will guide and govern us in our duties hereafter, as He has carried us forward to victory in the past; that He will teach us how to be humble in the midst of triumph, how to be just in the hour of victory, and that He will enable us to secure the foundations of this Republic, soaked as they have been in blood, so that it shall live forever and ever.[45]

Most of Washington spent the rest of the day in celebration. Brooks reported, "The departments of the government and many stores and private offices were closed for the day, and hosts of hard-worked clerks had their full share of the general holiday." Stanton stayed in his telegraph office, however, sending and receiving messages. He relayed reports that Richmond was on fire and that the federal troops were "endeavoring to put out the conflagration." He sent word to the editor of the *New York Tribune* that two of the paper's reporters would receive passes to go to Richmond. Not long thereafter he received a message from Lincoln at City Point: "Thanks for your caution, but I have already been to Petersburg, stayed with Gen. Grant an hour & a half and returned here. It is certain now that Richmond is in our hands, and I think I will go there to-morrow. I will take care of myself."[46]

Stanton had another message from Lincoln early the following morning, reporting that the region west of Petersburg was "full of stragglers, the line of retreat marked with artillery, ammunition, burned or charred wagons, ambulances, &c." Lincoln did not inform Stanton about his own movements—this was the day on which he would visit Richmond—nor did Stanton have much news from Grant. Perhaps this is why Stanton sent Dana to Richmond, urging him, "Give all the details you can ascertain as quickly as possible." To celebrate the fall of Richmond, Washington was illuminated on this night. Townsend recalled that Stanton ordered not only the War Department building but all the nearby military buildings to be illuminated at once, by soldiers at the windows lighting candles. "So promptly was each match applied, that spectators wondered what mechanical process . . . could have been used in this instance." Stanton himself was in the department until late that night, sending a message to Dix at eleven so it would be received in time for the morning newspapers.[47]

Stanton was busy not just with reports from generals and to the press but with arrangements for the ceremony at Fort Sumter. He invited various leaders to accompany him on the steamship *Arago* bound for Charleston, where they would hear Beecher speak and see Anderson raise the flag that he had been forced to lower four years earlier. Soon Stanton was answering requests for berths on the steamship, such as one from the famous abolitionist editor William Lloyd Garrison. On April 6 Stanton informed Anderson that he had postponed the departure of the *Arago* by two days so that Stanton could join them at Fort Monroe. Two days later, Stanton wrote to Anderson again, regretting that because Lincoln had not returned, and Seward had been injured, Stanton would not be able to go to Charleston after all.[48]

The injury to Seward nearly killed him. "About two hours ago," Stanton reported by telegram to Lincoln, "Mr. Seward was thrown from his carriage, his shoulder bone at the head of the joint broken off, his head and face much bruised and he is in my opinion dangerously injured. I think your presence here is needed." A few hours later Stanton reversed himself, writing that Barnes assured him there was no "dangerous symptom" in Seward's case. "I have also seen and conversed with him and although suffering much pain he is composed and in complete possession of his faculties." By the next morning Stanton could write to Lincoln that he need not return to Washington just yet. Seward's daughter Fanny recorded in her diary Stanton's frequent visits to see her father. Stanton "wiped his lips—spoke gently to him—and was like a woman in the sickroom." At one point Seward tried to thank his friend. "God bless you Stanton—I can never tell you half," he started. Stanton, "much affected," told him not to try to speak. "You have made me cry," Seward said, "for the first time in my life I believe."[49]

Dana was by this time providing Stanton with frequent, detailed, candid reports from Richmond. On April 5, for example, he wrote that Grant had "commanded armies in person since [the] beginning of operations, having got disgusted with General Meade's stickling about his own dignity." John Campbell, former justice of the Supreme Court, and Gustavus Myers, a Richmond lawyer, "had an interview with the President here this morning to consider how Virginia can be brought back into the Union." Dana heard that Lincoln told Campbell "he had the pardoning power, and would save any repentant sinner from hanging." Two days later Dana wrote that there was a meeting of a few Virginia legislators "upon the President's propositions to Judge Campbell." Dana described Lincoln's propositions as an unsigned set of terms, similar to Lincoln's previous peace terms, and an order from Lincoln to General Weitzel authorizing "members of the body claiming to be legislature of Virginia to meet here for purpose of recalling Virginia soldiers from rebel armies, with safe conduct to them, so long as they do and say nothing hostile to the United States." The legislators, as best Dana knew, had not agreed upon anything, and he reported Lincoln jesting that "Sheridan seemed to be getting Virginia soldiers out of the war faster than this legislature could think." Dana also noted that Weitzel had authorized the churches to open on Sunday, "on condition that no disloyal sermons be preached" and that "Episcopal ministers [be] required to read the prayer for the President." Stanton may have been displeased by Lincoln's attempt to deal with the rebel legislators, but he did not overrule Lincoln's order (as Grant later alleged in his memoir). Until Lincoln returned to Washington late on April 9, it seems that Stanton did not comment at all on Lincoln's attempt to work with the legislators.[50]

Lincoln and Grant were providing Stanton with reports, which Stanton was in turn providing the press through Dix. On April 7 he sent a message to Dix that started, "Sheridan attacked and routed Lee's army," and listed four rebel generals captured. On April 8 Stanton's message to Dix declared that Grant was "very confident of receiving the surrender of Lee and what remains of his army." Each of these was of course the headline of the next day's papers. Stanton also *withheld* certain information from the press. For example, he did not relay an April 8 message from Dana, whom he had asked to investigate reports that Weitzel was providing rations to Richmond civilians. Dana explained that, unless there were some system for feeding the civilians, "many persons must die of absolute starvation."[51]

Stanton was a member of Epiphany Episcopal Church, whose rector at the time, Charles Hall, later described him as a "wall of strength to this parish during the darkest days of the war." Stanton rented the pew that had once belonged to Jefferson Davis and worshipped alongside friends such as Joseph Barnes and Montgomery Meigs. Hall differed with Stanton "in many notions, for his was a Western education, and also as a lawyer, he was disposed to use force before persuasion." But Hall also wrote that when he visited Stanton during the war years, he "led me into his private office and invited me to pray—'pray for Mr. Lincoln, pray for the country, pray for our armies and their commanders, and pray for me.'" After services on April 9, Palm Sunday, Stanton went to his office, where there was a message from Grant, sharing his correspondence to date with Lee, suggesting surrender soon. Another message arrived that evening, from Dana in Richmond, reporting that Weitzel had informed the Episcopal priests in Richmond that they need not offer the standard prayer for the president. Stanton dashed off an angry telegram to Weitzel: "As I am unwilling to believe that a general officer of the United States, commanding in Richmond, would consent to such an omission of respect to the President of the United States, you are directed immediately to report by telegraph your action in relation to religious services in Richmond, and the prayer for the President in Episcopal churches." And then, at about nine in the evening, there was another message from Grant: "General Lee surrendered the Army of Northern Virginia this afternoon on terms proposed by myself. The accompanying correspondence will show the conditions fully." It was the simplest, greatest victory message of the war, and Stanton relayed it word for word to the press. Stanton also wrote to Grant, "Thanks be to Almighty God for the great victory with which he has this day crowned you and the gallant armies under your command." This too Stanton shared with the press.[52]

"Most people were sleeping soundly in their beds" on Monday morning, Noah Brooks reported, when "a great boom startled the misty air of Washington, shaking the earth and breaking the windows of the houses about Lafayette Square . . . for that was Secretary Stanton's way of telling the people at daylight that the great rebel army had laid down its arms and surrendered to the invincible prowess of the Union legions." Some people took the day off to celebrate, but Stanton worked. He had messages from both Dana and Weitzel about the prayer issue. Dana reported, "Weitzel's decision not to give a positive order was also in a great measure the result of the President's verbal direction to him, to let them down easy." Lincoln had returned to Washington on Sunday evening, and he and Stanton met on Monday and talked about Virginia. Stanton later testified that he had "several very earnest conversations with Mr. Lincoln upon the subject" and that he "vehemently opposed" Lincoln's approach "of undertaking to restore the government through the medium of rebel organizations." Welles also urged Lincoln not to rely upon the rebel legislators, reminding him that the administration had recognized and worked with the loyal Virginia government of Francis Pierpont.[53]

After Lincoln's death, Stanton recalled that in this brief period—between Lincoln's return from Virginia on April 9 and his assassination on April 14—Stanton tried to resign. In one version, printed in the *New York Independent* in May 1865, Stanton told Lincoln that "his work was done" and that "his duty was to resign." Lincoln, "greatly moved," responded, "You have been a good friend and a faithful public servant, and it is not for you to say when you will no longer be needed around here." In another version, in a letter dated September 1866, Stanton wrote that Lincoln placed his hands on Stanton's shoulders and, with "tears filling his eyes," said, "Stanton, you cannot go. *Re*-construction is more difficult and dangerous than *con*-struction or *de*-struction. You have been our main reliance; you must help us through the final act." Stanton explained that he was not leaving the president without plans, that he had developed plans for the reconstruction of the Southern state governments, that he had worked with Meigs on plans to transfer the railroads from government to private hands. "Stanton," Lincoln supposedly said, "you give the very reason why you should not resign. You admit that you have looked into the future, foreseen troubles there, and tried to prepare in advance for my relief and the benefit of the nation. Your recitation sustains me exactly. You must stay." This second version, at least, does not sound much like Lincoln. But even if Stanton's stories about his last conversations with Lincoln were just that, stories, it seems likely that he talked with Lincoln about resignation. The conversation may well have been part of a conversation about reconstruction, in which Stanton opposed the way Lincoln had tried to work with the rebel Virginia legislators.[54]

Lincoln set out his approach to reconstruction more generally on April 11, in a long evening speech to a crowd on the White House lawn. He focused on Louisiana, where a new government was operating under a new constitution but whose elected representatives were not yet granted their seats by Congress. Lincoln said that twelve thousand men in Louisiana had "sworn allegiance to the Union" and adopted a state constitution "giving the benefit of public schools equally to black and white, and empowering the legislature to confer the elective franchise upon the colored man." This government had already ratified the pending constitutional amendment abolishing slavery. To reject the new state government, in Lincoln's view, was to "reject" and "spurn" the loyal men of Louisiana. He would like to see the state constitution provide the right to vote to blacks, at least for "the very intelligent" and for "those who serve our cause as soldiers." But he argued that the fastest way for Louisiana blacks to get the vote was by moving forward under the existing state constitution rather than by starting over, as the Radicals insisted.[55]

Whether Stanton agreed with Lincoln about Louisiana is hard to say; he did not comment on this speech. But several sources suggest Stanton was concerned about Lincoln's lenient approach to reconstruction. Sumner wrote to Chase on April 12 that Stanton was "very much disconcerted & feeling that we might lose the fruits of our victories." Chase himself, in two letters to Lincoln at this time, urged him to form new state governments composed of "loyal citizens, without regard to complexion." Newspapers, commenting on Lincoln's speech, predicted conflict with the Radicals. The *New York Commercial Advertiser* described the emerging Radical faction as consisting of "Chase, Sumner, Wade, Butler, Winter Davis, Stanton and others" and opined that they would insist that former rebel states adopt new constitutions, granting former slaves the right to vote, before they could be admitted back into the Union.[56]

Early on April 12 Lincoln sent a telegram to Weitzel. On the prayer issue, he wrote that he had "no doubt that you have acted in what appeared to you to be the spirit and temper manifested by me while there." Stanton was probably annoyed by this, for he did not consider the prayer issue a minor point. Lincoln asked Weitzel, "Is there any sign of the rebel legislature coming together on the understanding of my letter to you?" Weitzel responded that permission letters had been sent, to allow the members of the former legislature to pass through Union lines into Richmond, and "it is common talk that they will come together." Later that day, apparently thanks to Dana, Lincoln saw an account by Campbell of his conversations with Lincoln. Lincoln now sent a second, far sterner message to Weitzel, asserting that he had been careful to distinguish between "the legislature" and the "gentlemen who have *acted* as the Legislature of Virginia in support of the rebellion" because he wanted "to exclude the assumption that I was recognizing them as a *rightful* body." Lincoln only "dealt with them as men having power *de facto* to do a specific thing, to wit, to withdraw the Virginia troops." Now, however, since Grant had captured the Virginia troops, and since Campbell was misrepresenting the president's words, Lincoln directed that Weitzel should not allow the legislators to assemble in Richmond. Stanton later testified that he pressed Lincoln to send this message, indeed that he had insisted that Lincoln strengthen his first draft.[57]

There was still one major rebel army in the field, that of Joseph Johnston in North Carolina. There was no telegraph line from Washington to Sherman in North Carolina, but it seemed that Sherman would soon force Johnston to surrender. The rebel government, including Jefferson Davis, had fled Richmond, and there were worrisome rumors that Davis intended to set up a new headquarters, perhaps somewhere in or near Texas. But Stanton felt sufficiently confident that he started the process of reducing the army. Stanton sent word to Grant that he wanted to talk, either in Washington or in Virginia, and when Grant arrived on April 13, the two men spent several hours together. Later that day Stanton sent a message to Dix for the press, promising several steps: first, "to stop all drafting and recruiting in the loyal States"; second, "to curtail purchases for arms, ammunition, quartermaster and commissary supplies, and reduce the expenses of the military establishment in its several branches"; third, "to reduce the number of general and staff officers to the actual necessities of the service"; and fourth, "to remove all military restriction upon trade and commerce so far as may be consistent with public safety." The *New York Times* hailed Stanton's message as "the proclamation, through practical measures, that the era of war, of great military operations and great armies, has closed, and that the era of peace, with its activity and freedom in trade and commerce, has opened."[58]

April 13 was yet another night of celebration and illumination in Washington. The *Washington Evening Star* reported that the War Department, "as upon former occasions, presented a magnificent appearance, the Star Spangled banner being entwined around the columns of the portico on the northern front." Over the main entrance there was a lighted transparency with the single name, "Grant." Stanton also decorated his home with flags, and the "magnificent display of fireworks in front, rendered every flag and color plainly visible from the remotest limit of Franklin Place, where hundreds assembled to honor our brave soldiers." Stanton himself, with a few friends, including Grant, was standing on the steps of his home to listen to the music and watch the fireworks. Witnesses later testified that a man, who seemed to be drunk, had asked after Stanton, even entered the foyer of the house, but it seems Stanton was not aware of him.[59]

Grant remained in Washington overnight and joined the cabinet meeting the next morning, April 14. We have various accounts of this final meeting of the Lincoln cabinet, many of them written much later. As it happens, the first account was by Stanton, part of a message he sent to Dix at about one o'clock the next morning. "At a Cabinet meeting yesterday," he wrote, "at which General Grant was present, the subject of the state of the country and the prospects of speedy peace was discussed. The President was very cheerful and hopeful; spoke very kindly of General

Lee and others of the Confederacy, and the establishment of government in Virginia." In a similar message to Charles Francis Adams, the American minister to Great Britain, also sent on April 15, Stanton wrote, "[Lincoln] was more cheerful and happy than I had ever seen—rejoiced at the near prospect of firm and durable peace at home and abroad, manifested in marked degree the kindness and humanity of his disposition and the tender and forgiving spirit that so eminently distinguished him."[60]

A few days later Welles wrote a diary entry, saying that Stanton had presented at this cabinet meeting a reconstruction plan with two parts: "one for asserting the federal authority in Virginia—the other for establishing a state government there." The second part of Stanton's plan, "seemed to me [Welles] objectionable in several essentials, and especially as in conflict with the principles of self-government which I deem essential." Welles did not even mention North Carolina in his notes. There was not much discussion, he wrote. "The understanding was that we should each be furnished with a copy for criticism and suggestion." Lincoln called the government of the Southern states "the great question now before us," on which "we must soon begin to act." He added that he was "glad Congress was not in session."[61]

In a later conversation with a foreign visitor, Stanton recalled that Lincoln was serious at this meeting. Stanton "noticed, with great surprise, that the President sat with an air of dignity in his chair instead of lolling about it in the most ungainly attitudes, as his invariable custom was; and that instead of telling irrelevant or questionable stories, he was grave and calm." In congressional testimony Stanton said that "the subject of Reconstruction was talked of at considerable length" at this cabinet meeting. He had prepared a "rough draft of a form or mode by which the authority and laws of the United States should be re-established and governments reorganized in the rebel States under the federal authority, without any necessity whatever for the intervention of the rebel organizations or rebel aid." Lincoln mentioned the draft to the cabinet, then "went into his room, brought it out, and asked me to read it, which I did, and explained my ideas in regard to it." Stanton had left one important point in the draft open, the point on which he knew there would be differences: "whether the blacks should have suffrage in the states, or whether it should be confined for the purposes of reorganization to those who had exercised it under the former state laws." Like Welles, Stanton said he was asked "to have a copy printed for each member for subsequent consideration." He also remembered telling Attorney General James Speed, as the two of them left the meeting together, that it was "the most satisfactory cabinet meeting I have attended for many a long day!"[62]

Welles published an article in 1872 in which he described Stanton's draft in much more detail than he had in his 1865 diary entry. Stanton supposedly proposed "establishing a military department to be composed of Virginia and North Carolina, with a military governor." Welles objected to forming a single military department out of two states and to disregarding the existing Virginia government: "We had acknowledged and claimed that Pierpont was the legitimate and rightful Governor." Lincoln, according to Welles, asked Stanton what he proposed to do about the Pierpont government. Stanton replied "that he had no apprehension from Pierpont, but the paper which he had submitted was merely a rough sketch subject to any alteration." Lincoln then instructed Stanton to prepare separate plans for the two states and to circulate them to the cabinet before their next meeting. Welles, as did Stanton, recalled Lincoln's kindness. Commenting on the rebel leaders, Lincoln supposedly said that "none need expect he would take any part in hanging or killing those men, even the worst of them." He hoped to "frighten them out of the country, open the gates, let down the bars, scare them off." Then he shook "his hands as if scaring sheep."[63]

Frederick Seward, the assistant secretary of state, attended this meeting for his injured father and wrote in his memoir that there was a wide-ranging discussion. "There was a loyal governor in Virginia. There were military governors in some of the other states. But the southern legislatures were, for the most part, avowedly treasonable. Whether they should be allowed to continue until they committed some new overt act of hostility; whether the governors should be requested to order new elections; whether such elections should be ordered by the general government—all these questions were raised." Seward recalled that Stanton's plan focused more on the federal than on the state governments. "In substance, it was that the Treasury Department should take possession of the custom-houses, and proceed to collect the revenues; that the War Department should garrison or destroy the forts, take possession of arms and munitions, and maintain the public peace," and the other departments fulfill their various functions. As to state governments, Seward wrote that Lincoln said, "We can't undertake to run state governments in all these southern states. Their people must do that, though I reckon that, at first, they may do it badly."[64]

We do not, in short, know just what happened at this last meeting between Lincoln and his cabinet, and it is perhaps best not to pretend to precision. We do know that, after the meeting, Stanton went back to his office and dealt with a few routine matters, such as a telegram directing the arrest of the former Kentucky governor "for holding intercourse with rebels in arms." After office hours Stanton stopped at Seward's home to brief him on the military situation and the cabinet meeting, and then returned to his own home. Several military officers visited, and Stanton made them a brief speech. He also spoke from his steps with "a colored procession [that] went with shouts and cheers to call on the secretary of war who was considered their special friend." Then he retired to his bedroom for the night. All was normal and peaceful and indeed joyful.[65]

Chapter 15

"The Stain of Innocent Blood"

— April–July 1865 —

At about half past ten on the night of April 14, 1865, two breathless men arrived on foot at the Stanton house on K Street. One of them, Joseph Sterling, a clerk in the War Department, remembered that it was Eddie Stanton who opened the door. Sterling and his companion told Eddie that Lincoln had just been shot. Eddie roused his father, who came downstairs and demanded that the clerks tell him all they knew. Sterling explained that, hearing a commotion in Ford's Theatre, they entered and learned that John Wilkes Booth had shot Lincoln and then fled. Sterling added that, as they raced the few blocks from the theater to the Stanton home, they heard that someone else had assassinated Seward. "Oh that can't be so, that can't be so," Stanton said, and he immediately decided, over his wife's protests, to go by carriage to the Seward house.[1]

Welles wrote in his diary that he and Stanton reached Seward's house "almost simultaneously." The two men parted the crowd in the foyer, where there were many diplomats who, having heard of the "murderous assault," rushed to the house "to ascertain the facts." Stanton and Welles hastily ascended the stairs to the third floor, to the room where Seward was lying in a bed "saturated with blood," his face and neck slashed by the assassin's knife. Fanny Seward described how her father related to Stanton and Welles "in a clear, distinct manner, his recollections of the whole scene—between each word he drew breath, as one dying might speak, & I feared the effort might cost him his remaining life." Stanton and Welles also stopped in the next room to see Frederick Seward, unconscious, his head battered by blows from the assassin's pistol butt. The doctors feared that Frederick was "more dangerously injured than his father." The assassin had escaped, slashing and stabbing three other victims. "There was so much blood everywhere," wrote Fanny.[2]

As they descended the stairs, Welles asked Stanton what he knew that was reliable about the attempt on Lincoln's life. Stanton replied that Lincoln had been shot at Ford's Theatre, that he knew this from someone who was in the theater at the time. Welles suggested they go to the White House, but Stanton said that Lincoln was not there; he was at the theater, on Tenth Street, so they should head there. They found Meigs at the foot of the stairs, and Stanton ordered him to "take charge of the house and to clear out all who did not belong there." Eckert, who arrived on horseback at the Seward house as Stanton and Welles entered their carriage, "protested vehemently against Stanton's going to Tenth Street—said he had just come from there—that there were thousands of people of all sorts there and he considered it very unsafe for the Secretary of War." Welles replied that "I knew not where he would be safe, and the duty of both of us was to attend the President immediately." They drove off, with a few soldiers on horseback alongside. When they reached Tenth Street, the crowd was so dense that Stanton and Welles had to step down from the carriage and make their way on foot to the Petersen House, across the street from Ford's, to which soldiers had recently carried Lincoln.[3]

Stanton and Welles went up the stairs, down the hall, and into the back bedroom, where "the giant sufferer lay extended diagonally across the bed which was not long enough for him." They soon learned from the doctors that Lincoln was "dead to all intents—although he might live three hours or perhaps longer." Stanton decided that he would stay in the house, in the room next to Lincoln's, and work from there. There was no telegraph in the Petersen House, but Stanton had aides who could run messages to the nearby War Department, and he was closer to Lincoln, closer to the witnesses, at the house than he would be at his office. He started at once to work on several related tasks: determining who had killed Lincoln, finding and arresting those involved, protecting senior officials against further attacks, and informing the nation of these dreadful events.[4]

Stanton's initial investigation is reflected in the shorthand notes of James Tanner, a crippled veteran who was now a federal stenographer, and in a detailed letter from Tanner written only days after the assassination. When Tanner arrived at the Petersen House that night he "found Secretary Stanton sitting on one side of the library and Chief Justice [David] Cartter of the Supreme Court of the District at the end. They had started in to take what testimony they could regarding the assassination, having someone write it out in longhand. This had proved unsatisfactory. I took a seat opposite the Secretary and commenced to take down the testimony." Tanner's notes reflect the testimony of six witnesses, most of whom had seen the events in the theater and most of whom were certain the assassin was Booth. Tanner wrote, "In fifteen minutes I had testimony enough down to hang John Wilkes Booth, the assassin, higher than ever Haman hung." (In the biblical book of Esther, Haman was the evil adviser to the Persian king, hanged on a gibbet fifty feet high.) Stanton could not and did not work just on the investigation. Tanner noted, "Our work was often interrupted by reports coming in to Secretary Stanton and more often interrupted by him when he halted the testimony to give orders." For example, at ten minutes after one, Stanton scrawled out a telegram to John Kennedy, chief of police in New York City: "Send here immediately three or four of your best detectives to investigate the facts as to the assassination of the President and Secretary Seward. They are still alive, but the president's case is hopeless, and that of Mr. Seward nearly the same."[5]

Stanton's progress in the first hours of the investigation is detailed in his messages to Dix. In the first such message, marked as sent at 1:30 a.m. on April 15, Stanton described the attack on Lincoln and added, "About the same hour an assassin, whether the same person or not, entered Mr. Seward's apartment, and, under pretense of having a prescription, was shown to the Secretary's sick chamber." Stanton did not name Booth in this first message, perhaps because he started to draft it before he heard the testimony of the six witnesses taken down by Tanner. In his second message to Dix, sent at 3:00 a.m., Stanton specified John Wilkes Booth as the assassin of Lincoln and said that it was still unclear whether Booth was also the assassin of Seward. By the time of his third message, sent at 4:10 a.m., Stanton was sure there were at least two assassins, Booth and "a companion whose name is not known, but whose description is so clear that he can hardly escape." Stanton added that "a letter found in Booth's trunk" at the National Hotel showed "that the murder was planned before the 4th of March, but fell through then because the accomplice backed out until 'Richmond could be heard from.'" Stanton was paraphrasing here from what became known as the "Sam letter" because it was signed by "Sam," later identified as Booth's friend and co-conspirator Samuel Arnold. By the time of this third message to Dix, federal authorities were already looking for Arnold. James McPhail, the alert provost marshal in Baltimore, had sent a telegram to the War Department: "Samuel Arnold and Michael O'Laughlen, two of the intimate associates of J. Wilkes Booth, are said to be in Washington." McPhail was also searching in Baltimore for clues to their whereabouts.[6]

McPhail's message underscores that, in the hours and days after Booth shot Lincoln, there were several separate investigations. Stanton and the War Department were investigating, but so were the Washington Metropolitan Police Department, Provost McPhail and others. Washington detectives learned within hours of Booth's shot that John Surratt was a close friend of Booth and that Booth was often at the boardinghouse run by John's mother, Mary Surratt. When police officers first visited the Surratt House, at about two in the morning on April 15, Mary Surratt told them that John was in Canada, a story confirmed by one of her boarders. So by six in the morning, even before Lincoln's death, Stanton and his co-investigators were looking for several men, including Booth, Surratt, Arnold, O'Laughlen, and the unnamed assassin who had attacked Seward, later identified as Lewis Powell. Stanton and the others involved had made amazing progress in their investigation in just a few short hours.[7]

Stanton probably heard during the course of this long night some version of the report that he himself was a target of the assassins. A correspondent for the *Cincinnati Enquirer*, in a telegram sent from Washington before Lincoln's death, reported that as two government messengers approached Stanton's house "a man jumped from behind a tree-box in front of the house, and ran away." Stanton's custom was to go from his office to his house between nine and midnight, "usually unattended," and the reporter "supposed that the assassin intended to shoot him as he entered the house." The *New York Times* published a similar report, saying that government messengers approaching Stanton's house met just outside "a man muffled in a cloak who, when accosted by them, hastened away." The *Times* continued, "It therefore seems evident that the aim of the plotters was to paralyze the country by at once striking down the head, the heart, and the arm of the country." Stanton ordered that soldiers stand guard not only outside his own residence but outside the residences of each of the cabinet officers, guards that Stanton would keep in place for the next few weeks.[8]

Mary Lincoln spent most of the last night of her husband's life in the front parlor of the Petersen House, in the company of her son Robert and a few friends. From time to time, she would visit the back room, where her husband was suffering and dying. One of the doctors recalled that, at some point in the night, while she was in the back room, she was startled by a change in her husband's breathing pattern, and she "sprang up suddenly with a piercing cry and fell fainting to the floor. Secretary Stanton hearing her cry came in from the adjoining room and with raised arms called out loudly: 'Take that woman out and do not let her in again.' Mrs. Lincoln was helped up kindly and assisted in a fainting condition from the room. Secretary Stanton's order was obeyed and Mrs. Lincoln did not see her husband again before he died."[9]

At about seven o'clock on the morning of April 15, as Lincoln's breathing slowed and faltered, Stanton entered the back room. A reporter for the *New York Herald*, relying apparently upon one or more of those present, wrote, "Even stoical Stanton, whose coolness and self-possession were remarkable, could not keep back the silent monitors of inward sorrow which rolled out from his eyes upon his cheeks." In the *Herald*'s account, Lincoln "died without a struggle, and without even a perceptible motion of a limb. Calmly and silently the great and good man passed away." The *Washington Evening Star* reported that evening, "Immediately on its being ascertained that life was extinct," Lincoln's pastor, Reverend Phineas Gurley, "knelt at the bedside and offered an impressive prayer which was responded to by all present." According to the *Star*, Reverend Gurley then went into the front room and prayed there with Mary and Robert Lincoln and John Hay. Maunsell Field, an assistant secretary of the Treasury, who was among those in the room when Lincoln died, described in a letter published in the *New York Times* on April 17 how the "few persons" in the room at the moment of death were "profoundly affected" by Gurley's prayer. In his letter of April 17, Tanner wrote that in the minutes before Lincoln's death "the utmost silence pervaded, broken only by the sounds of strong men's tears." Just after the president died, Gurley "offered up a very impressive prayer. I grasped for my pencil which was in my pocket, as I wished to secure his words, but I was very much disappointed to find that my pencil had been broken in my pocket. . . . The friends dispersed" and Secretary Stanton "told me to take charge of the testimony I had taken." Welles wrote in his diary a few days after the events that Lincoln's "respiration became suspended at intervals, and at last entirely ceased at 22 minutes past seven. A prayer followed from Dr. Gurley, and the Cabinet, with the exception of Mr. Seward and Mr. McCulloch, immediately thereafter assembled in the back parlor."[10]

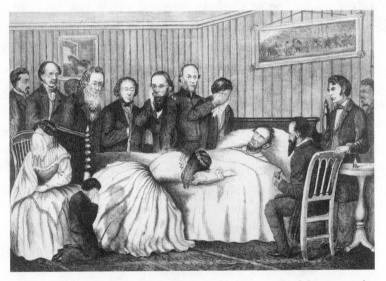

"Lincoln's Death Bed." One of many fanciful images of the scene; the room could not possibly hold all those pictured. Stanton is behind the bed, hand to his chin.

None of these accounts, nor any other account published before 1890, claimed that Stanton said anything in the moments just after

Lincoln's death. It was in that year that John Hay, in an article written with John Nicolay, first published the words we remember about Lincoln's death: "At twenty-two minutes after seven he died. Stanton broke the silence by saying 'Now he belongs to the ages.'" Charles Taft, one of the doctors attending Lincoln, more or less agreed with Hay in an article he published three years later, writing, "When it was announced that the great heart had ceased to beat, Mr. Stanton said in solemn tones, 'He now belongs to the Ages.'" Tanner too agreed with Hay, writing in 1905 that after Gurley's fervent prayer, "Stanton raised his face, the tears streaming down his cheeks, and ejaculated while he looked, oh so lovingly, at the face of his beloved chief: 'He belongs to the ages now.'" Tanner repeated this several times in other articles, but somehow his words were transformed after his death to "belongs to the angels now."[11]

In light of the twenty-five-year lapse between Lincoln's death and Hay's article, the lack of an early source for "angels," and the uncertainty about whether Hay was even *in the room* when Lincoln died, it seems unlikely that Stanton said anything right after Lincoln died—about ages or about angels. The words we can definitely attribute to him were more mundane: a one-line message to Dix informing the nation, "Abraham Lincoln died this morning at twenty-two minutes after seven o'clock." Stanton must have sent this telegram within minutes of Lincoln's death, for it was printed in extra editions of New York newspapers before nine that morning. Stanton also met with his cabinet colleagues right after Lincoln's death, and together they sent a formal notice to Vice President Andrew Johnson, partially drafted by Stanton: "The emergency of the government demands that you should immediately qualify, according to the requirements of the Constitution, and enter upon the duties of the President of the United States."[12]

His colleagues departed after this cabinet meeting, but Stanton stayed with Lincoln's body at the Petersen House for about two hours after his death. At some point in these quiet hours Stanton clipped from Lincoln's head a lock of his hair, placed it in a plain white envelope, signed his name in the corner, and addressed the envelope to Mary Jane Welles, the wife of Gideon Welles. Stanton knew that Welles did not like him, but he also knew that Mary Jane Welles had befriended and supported Mary Lincoln. The Welles family would later frame the lock of hair, and the envelope, and some flowers from Lincoln's funeral.[13]

At about nine in the morning, on Stanton's orders, soldiers wrapped the president's body in an American flag and lifted it into the plain, pine coffin they had brought with them. They carried the coffin down the curved steps to Tenth Street and placed the body of their late president on the back of a wagon to be taken to the White House. Some soldiers, including generals, walked behind the wagon, their heads bared, silent. It was a simple procession for a simple man. Welles wrote, "The colored people especially—and there were at this time more of them [in the streets] perhaps than of whites—were painfully affected."[14]

Stanton was not at Andrew Johnson's hotel when the new president took the oath of office at about eleven. Perhaps Stanton was in his telegraph office, writing messages. In one long message, sent at 11:40 a.m., he informed the American minister in London, Charles Francis Adams, of Lincoln's death. Stanton gave Adams a detailed and accurate summary of the events, reported on the health of his friend Seward, and noted that there was already evidence "that these horrible crimes were committed in execution of a conspiracy deliberately planned and set on foot by rebels, under pretense of avenging the South and aiding the rebel cause." Stanton asked Adams to "communicate these deplorable events to all the ministers and diplomatic agents of the United States with whom you are in communication." In another message, sent at 12:10 p.m., Stanton informed Sherman of Lincoln's death, warning that there was "evidence that an assassin is also on your track, and I beseech you to be more heedful than Mr. Lincoln was of such knowledge." Both Adams and Sherman were out of reach of the telegraph; it would take three days before Sherman and ten days before Adams learned of Lincoln's death.[15]

From his telegraph office Stanton hurried to the Treasury Building, where he joined a noontime cabinet meeting with Johnson. Welles noted in his diary that Johnson "deported himself admirably"—he was no doubt thinking about Johnson's drunken display at the inauguration. Rather than give any kind of address, Johnson said, "His acts would best disclose his policy," that "in all essentials it would be the same as that of the late President." He asked the cabinet members to "go forward with their duties without any interruption." Stanton reported this to the press through an afternoon telegram to Dix, mentioning that Johnson "desired to retain the present Secretaries of Departments as his Cabinet."[16]

At some point in the afternoon, after the body of Lincoln was cleaned and embalmed, Stanton supervised the dressing of Lincoln for the funeral, choosing the Brooks Brothers suit the president had just worn for his second inaugural. General Grant arrived in Washington at about two o'clock on this afternoon and almost at once sent a message to General Ord in Richmond, directing him to arrest the mayor and other local leaders: "Extreme rigor will have to be observed whilst assassination remains the order of the day with the rebels." Ord pleaded with Grant to reconsider, pointing out that there was no evidence that the mayor or others posed any threat. Grant relented; Ord could regard his prior message as a suggestion rather than an order. Stanton worked on finding experienced detectives for his investigation. "I desire your services," he wired Henry Steel Olcott in New York, directing him to "come to Washington at once." Olcott, who had worked for Stanton during the war as a financial investigator, and who would later become a leading American Buddhist, wrote back that he and a few colleagues would be on the midnight train. Stanton sent a similar message to Lafayette Baker, an abrasive detective of dubious reputation, with whom he had worked earlier in the war, before demoting him and sending him to New York: "Come here immediately and see if you can find the murderers of the President." Both Baker and Olcott would arrive the next day and start work.[17]

April 16 was Easter Sunday. Churches across the North were packed, but instead of a joyous mood, the people were grim and mournful and vengeful. Altar guilds had to decorate with white flowers and black cloth. If Stanton attended services on this Sunday morning—and he almost certainly did—he would have heard Reverend Charles Hall at the Church of the Epiphany speak of both grief and hope: "We gather now around an open grave, permitted to be opened on this Easter Day by the awful and wicked tragedy of this last Good Friday." On the day of the president's sudden death, "of all the days of his administration, he was probably most bent on thoughts of mercy." Hall closed with a prayer, not only for the afflicted families but also for the "wretched criminals who have stained their hands, wantonly and stupidly in innocent blood," that they might repent their sins "before they are called upon to meet the just punishment of their atrocities."[18]

Stanton probably rushed from Epiphany to the Treasury Building, for Welles noted in his diary that Stanton was "more than an hour late" for the cabinet meeting that started there at ten o'clock. One topic of discussion was reconstruction. As Lincoln had requested, Stanton now had two separate plans for North Carolina and Virginia, with a new military governor suggested for North Carolina and the Pierpont government extended to cover the whole state of Virginia. There was not much discussion, but Welles wrote that Johnson was "not disposed to treat treason lightly" and insisted that "the chief rebels he would punish with exemplary severity." That of course assumed the federal government could find and capture the chief rebels. For a few days after the fall of Richmond, Jefferson Davis and the Confederate cabinet worked from Danville, Virginia. But as of April 16 the federal government did not know where Davis was.[19]

Grant was now based in Washington, keeping in touch with all the generals in the field, so he and Stanton decided to send Halleck to Richmond. Halleck explained in a letter to his friend Lieber, "The government is not satisfied with the policy adopted by our officers in that city & state towards blatant rebels, and seems to think that my administration in the West will suit that latitude." (Halleck was alluding to his harsh administration in Missouri, implying that this was the sort of administration Stanton now wanted in Virginia.) Halleck also assured Lieber that Johnson would be a good president. Johnson was the only military governor "who gave us no trouble, and who had the good sense to act always right. This speaks volumes for him." Sumner likewise was pleased with the new president, writing after an early interview that he was "charmed by his sympathy, which was entirely different from his predecessor's." Almost everyone at this stage believed the best about Johnson.[20]

On this same Sunday, in the evening, Welles visited the War Department and was chatting with Stanton by his fire when Sumner and a few other members of Congress arrived. Welles described in his diary, and then in more detail in a letter and an article after Stanton's death, how Stanton took from his desk his reconstruction plans for Virginia and North Carolina and read them aloud. Even though it was common for cabinet members to share drafts with key congressional leaders, Welles claimed these were "cabinet documents" that should not be shared before they were approved and issued by the president. Sumner interrupted Stanton's reading to ask "whether any provision was made for enfranchising the colored man," asserting that unless "the black man is given the right to vote, his freedom is mockery." Stanton responded, "There were differences among our friends on that subject, and it would be unwise in his judgment to press it in this stage of the proceedings." Sumner "declared he would not proceed a step unless the black man had his rights. He considered the black man's right to vote the essence—the great essential." Welles was summoned away while Stanton and Sumner were still talking, so he did not know how this meeting ended.[21]

Stanton and his detectives made progress day by day in their investigation of the Booth conspirators. During a search of the Surratt house, a man knocked on the door who, when later confronted by the Seward family witnesses, proved to be Lewis Powell, the attempted assassin of the Sewards. The detectives arrested Powell and Mary Surratt, and for a while the other residents of the house. (John Surratt had fled to Canada. He was not among those captured or tried in 1865; he was arrested abroad in late 1866 and then tried in Maryland in the summer of 1867.) Provost McPhail was able to find Samuel Arnold at Fort Monroe, to arrest him there, and to get a confession that Booth, Arnold, and others had plotted to kidnap Lincoln. McPhail then made what from Stanton's perspective was a terrible mistake, sharing a summary of Arnold's confession with the press. Stanton sent McPhail a blistering message, threatening to remove him from his post, then issued a more general order, directing that those involved in investigating the assassination should not release any information except to the War Department: "All parties violating this order will be looked on as obstructing the prompt arrest of the conspirators."[22]

Stanton received encouraging news on April 17. In a message sent from Raleigh on April 15, Sherman forwarded correspondence indicating that General Johnston was about to surrender his army. Sherman wrote, "I will accept the same terms as General Grant gave General Lee, and be careful not to complicate any points of civil policy." Stanton shared the news with the papers, several of which predicted that Johnston would likely surrender on these terms. The papers were also reporting that

Gen. Edmund Kirby Smith, in command of the rebel forces beyond the Mississippi, intended to surrender his substantial army.[23]

Stanton somehow found time, in these chaotic days, to attend to the arrangements for the funeral train that would transport Lincoln's corpse from Washington to Springfield, Illinois. The route was somewhat circuitous to allow the train to stop at Philadelphia, New York, Buffalo, Cleveland, Chicago, and other major cities. Almost as soon as the route was fixed, Stanton started getting requests from other cities to be included, from his friends in Pittsburgh, for example. He had to reply that the route could not be changed. From New York General Dix wanted to know whether there would be a military escort on the funeral train or whether he should provide one. Both, was Stanton's answer: there would be a small military escort, headed by Townsend, to accompany the funeral train all the way from Washington to Springfield, but Dix should arrange a "larger escort" for the portion of the journey within his department.[24]

Stanton was also involved in arranging Lincoln's funeral services, held at the White House and at the Capitol on April 19. It was no accident that two of Stanton's friends were among the four ministers who participated in the services at the White House: Reverend Charles Hall of Epiphany Church, who read the Episcopal funeral service, and Bishop Matthew Simpson, who gave the opening prayer. The president's pastor, Reverend Phineas Gurley, recalled in his remarks how Lincoln "in this very room" told a group of clergymen that his "hope of success in this great and terrible struggle rest[ed] on that immutable foundation—the justice and goodness of God." Stanton's friend Henry Winter Davis was not impressed, writing that evening, "The prayers & discourses were full of bad eulogy, questionable politics, doubtful prophecy bordering on the boastful. Some religion but no Christianity. This I stood and endured an eternity of two or three hours!" After these private services at the White House, there was a public procession along Pennsylvania Avenue, in which Stanton and thousands of others participated, including black and white troops. One Southern observer described it as a "promiscuous motley procession headed & tailed by Ethiopian Americans." Following the casket, Johnson, Stanton, Grant, and other officials entered the Capitol, where a public service was held, with Gurley reading the burial service in what the *Evening Star* described as "a very impressive manner." Years later men recalled that "no grief was keener" than that of Stanton on this day.[25]

———

Stanton spent part of the next day, April 20, drafting a War Department poster to offer $100,000 for the capture of John Wilkes Booth and his accomplices David Herold and John Surratt. The poster threatened that "persons harboring or secreting" Booth and his colleagues would "be treated as accomplices in the murder of the President" and "subject to trial before a military commission and the punishment of *death*." In calling for help to find and punish the criminals, Stanton echoed the Easter sermon of Reverend Hall: "Let the stain of innocent blood be removed from the land by the arrest and punishment of the murderers." A draft of this famous poster, in Stanton's own hand, is in the archives at the New-York Historical Society.[26]

Stanton's poster offering a reward for the capture of John Wilkes Booth, David Herold, and John Surratt.

The files at the National Archives show that Stanton was himself involved in the assassination investigation. The Archives contain two pages of notes in Stanton's hand from an interview with James Purdom, a Maryland farmer, about another conspirator, George Atzerodt. Purdom related and Stanton recorded that a few days after Booth killed Lincoln, Atzerodt declared, "If the other man had done his duty we would have got Grant too." Atzerodt was arrested on April 20 and charged with being the assassin sent to kill Vice President Johnson. There is also an undated note in Stanton's hand directing his aides to "collate the evidence" regarding the horses used by Booth and Powell; it includes the directive to have Dr. Samuel Mudd, who was reported to have tended to Booth's leg, broken in his fall at Ford's Theatre, "brought here immediately and get his statement & also his household & keep them confined." It is not clear whether it was this Stanton note or other factors that led to the arrest of Dr. Mudd in southern Maryland on April 24.[27]

For ten days after Lincoln's death Stanton did not know where Booth was or where he was heading. There were sightings from every point of the compass, and Stanton had no choice but to respond to every credible report. He received one letter claiming that Booth was in Chicago, in a brothel on Tenth Street, disguised as a woman. One of Stanton's aides promptly sent a telegram to Chicago, asking the military authorities there to investigate and report back. Stanton heard that Booth was heading for West Virginia, so he ordered searches along the Baltimore & Ohio Railroad and into West Virginia. He sent similar orders to New Orleans, reporting that Booth might be heading west for Texas and urging that the Mississippi River crossings be closely watched. The *National Republican* believed that Booth was still in Washington, in hiding with some Southern sympathizer, and urged Stanton to conduct a house-to-house search of the District. A message from Bryantown, Maryland, about forty miles south of Washington, stated that Booth had been sighted there, with a broken leg. Stanton at once sent officers to investigate. This last message would ultimately prove to be accurate.[28]

Stanton also did not know where Jefferson Davis was. A correspondent for the *New York World* reported from Richmond that "those who know him best" believed that Davis would "die fighting or plotting." Davis would join Johnston and his army in North Carolina, or would cross the Mississippi to "prolong the contest" from Texas, or perhaps even "escape to Mexico, and make himself the pertinacious and eternal enemy of the country." Other papers speculated that Davis was heading for Texas to join General Smith and his "powerful, well-organized and finely supplied army of fifty thousand men." Stanton was understandably concerned that Davis and others would continue the Civil War for months or years to come, perhaps fight a guerrilla war of the sort the Spaniards had waged so well against Napoleon.[29]

On April 20, while thousands were passing by Lincoln's body, lying in state in the Capitol building, there was a message at the War Department for Grant. An officer was on his way from Sherman's army, bearing what the officer described as dispatches "from General Sherman, dated Raleigh, 18th instant, containing the conditions of an agreement made that day between General Sherman and the rebel General Johnston." So Stanton knew on this afternoon that Sherman had reached an agreement with Johnston, and he probably assumed that the terms were the "Grant-Lee terms," based on Sherman's prior messages.[30]

Stanton was up early the next day, heading first to the Capitol to oversee the removal of Lincoln's coffin, and then to the Baltimore & Ohio train station to see the funeral train depart. At eight o'clock, as bells tolled and Stanton and others stood silently, Lincoln left Washington for the last time.[31]

Sherman's courier arrived in Washington in the late afternoon of this day, April 21, and delivered his messages to Grant. After reading them, Grant sent a hasty note to Stanton: "I have received, and just completed reading the dispatches brought by special messenger from General Sherman. They are of such importance that I think immediate action should be taken on them, and that it should be done by the President, in council with his whole cabinet. I would respectfully suggest whether the President should not be notified, and all his cabinet, and the meeting take place tonight." Stanton soon found Grant and read Sherman's messages for himself.[32]

Sherman had not, as everyone expected, followed the terms used by Grant when Lee surrendered. Instead, after negotiations with General Johnston and Confederate secretary of war John Breckinridge, Sherman had signed an overall peace treaty, an arrangement Sherman boasted to

Grant would "produce peace from the Potomac to the Rio Grande." The Sherman-Johnston-Breckinridge terms provided that the Confederate armies would disband and deposit their arms at the various Southern state capitals. The federal government would recognize the Southern state governments "on their officers and legislatures taking the oaths prescribed by the Constitution of the United States, and where conflicting state governments have resulted from war the legitimacy of all shall be submitted to the Supreme Court of the United States." The people of the Southern states would be "guaranteed, as far as the Executive can, their political rights and franchises, as well as their rights of person and property, as defined by the Constitution of the United States and of the States, respectively." Sherman and Johnston recognized that they did not have authority to "fulfill these terms," but they pledged to work to "obtain the necessary authority and carry out the above program." In his cover note to Grant, Sherman pressed for Johnson to approve the terms without changes and without delay, since it was "important to get the Confederate armies to their homes as well as our own."[33]

Stanton recognized the fatal flaws in Sherman's agreement. A guarantee of property rights, as defined by the Southern state constitutions, would perpetuate slavery, in contravention of the Emancipation Proclamation. (The Thirteenth Amendment was not yet part of the federal Constitution, so it would not prevent this result.) Recognizing the Southern state governments would mean disbanding, or at least calling into question, the loyal governments in Louisiana and elsewhere. Sherman's terms would allow former rebel leaders, almost immediately, to take charge of the Southern states—and Sherman's "oath" requirement was meaningless for there was no oath prescribed by the federal Constitution for state officials. A general amnesty would mean that none of the rebels would be prosecuted for their war crimes—not Jefferson Davis for his alleged role in the assassination, not Nathan Bedford Forrest for the murder of surrendering soldiers at Fort Pillow.[34]

Stanton agreed with Grant that Johnson and the cabinet should meet at once to consider Sherman's terms. Stanton himself penned some of the messages to summon his cabinet colleagues to meet at eight that evening. He also started work on a set of points to explain why Johnson had to reject Sherman's agreement. Stanton knew that the people were keen for the war to end, that Sherman's peace terms would appeal to many, especially Democrats. Stanton assumed (rightly) that Sherman had already released his peace agreement to the press in an announcement in which he promised "peace from the Potomac to the Rio Grande" if Washington would just approve his terms. So Stanton's points were his effort to *respond* to Sherman's press campaign in favor of his peace agreement—even before Stanton was quite sure that there *was* any such Sherman press campaign.[35]

Stanton's reaction to Sherman's terms was emotional and visceral as well as rational. Less than a week had passed since Booth had killed Lincoln and Powell had attempted to kill Seward. The team of assassins, Stanton believed, had intended to kill him and Grant as well. Stanton was convinced that Booth and his colleagues were not acting alone, that they had support and probably orders from Jefferson Davis. Booth, Davis, and other Southern leaders were still at large, still presumably plotting to kill more Northern leaders and Northern soldiers. Stanton did not want to make a generous peace with the South a week after Lincoln's death. He wanted to fight the war until every Southern leader and every Southern soldier surrendered. Questions of peace and reconstruction were not questions for generals; as Lincoln and Stanton had reminded Grant in their March message, they were questions for political leaders. Above all, Stanton did not want to defer on these issues to Sherman, the general who had proved so fractious on the question of black soldiers, who was now proving fractious on far more important issues.[36]

Stanton had in hand at least some form of his points against Sherman's agreement when he arrived for the eight o'clock cabinet meeting at the private home where Johnson was staying. Welles noted in his diary that Stanton started the meeting by asking Grant to read Sherman's messages. There was not, it seems, much discussion; everyone agreed that Johnson should disapprove Sherman's terms. "Among the cabinet and all present there was but one mind on this subject," Welles wrote. "The plan was rejected, and Sherman's arrangement disapproved. Stanton and Speed were emphatic in their condemnation, although the latter expressed personal friendship for Sherman." Grant agreed, though he carefully "abstained from censure." Stanton "came charged with specified objections, four in number, counting them off on his fingers. Some of his argument was apt and good—some of it not in good taste nor precisely pertinent." Johnson and the cabinet decided that Grant should go to Sherman in Raleigh to explain in person why the terms were disapproved and to take charge of the continuing campaign there, assuming that Johnston would not surrender without conditions.[37]

Stanton returned to his office and resumed work. He prepared and signed stern instructions to Grant, directing him to go to Sherman's headquarters, to tell him that the prior peace terms were disapproved, to order that the fighting be resumed, and to require that any new peace terms conform to Lincoln's March 3 message. Grant left Washington at about midnight, not even telling his wife where he was heading. Stanton sent a telegram to Halleck in Richmond notifying him that Johnson had rejected Sherman's terms and that "Sherman [was] ordered to resume hostilities." But for some reason Stanton did not send a press report that night or the next morning about Sherman's terms or Johnson's rejection of the terms.[38]

The next day, at noontime, Stanton received a message from Halleck that Davis and his cabinet had taken with them substantial amounts in gold and silver bars and coins when they left Richmond. "They hope, it is said, to make terms with General Sherman or some other Southern commander by which they will be permitted with their effects, including this gold plunder, to go to Mexico or Europe." Halleck feared that Johnston's negotiations with Sherman were aimed at helping Davis to escape, a fear that was reinforced for Stanton by a copy of a message from Sherman to Gen. George Stoneman, one of his subordinates, directing Stoneman to withdraw his troops from their advanced positions. Stanton immediately sent another message to Halleck, telling him again that Sherman's terms were disapproved, that Stanton and Grant had ordered Sherman "to resume hostilities immediately, as his order to Stoneman will allow Jeff. Davis to escape with his plunder."[39]

At about ten o'clock that night, April 22, Stanton sent a long message to Dix for the press. He related that Johnson and "every member of the cabinet" had disapproved Sherman's peace terms. After quoting, in full, Lincoln's instructions to Grant about peace terms, he said that Sherman had disregarded these instructions. (Sherman would later insist that he had never seen these instructions.) Stanton added that Sherman's instructions to Stoneman to withdraw to Raleigh would "probably open the way for Davis to escape to Mexico or Europe with his plunder, which is reported to be very large, including not only the plunder of the Richmond banks, but previous accumulations." (Stanton had no way of knowing where Davis was, and thus no way of knowing whether moving Stoneman's forces would facilitate Davis's escape.) Stanton printed Sherman's terms, in full, but he also printed his own points about why Johnson had disapproved the terms, explaining that Sherman "undertook to re-establish the rebel state governments that had been overthrown at the sacrifice of many thousands of loyal lives and immense treasure, and placed the arms and munitions of war in the hands of the rebels at their respective capitals, which might be used as soon as the armies of the United States were disbanded." Stanton also noted that Sherman's agreement, by restoring "the rebel authority in their respective states, would be enabled to re-establish slavery."[40]

Stanton's message to Dix was printed in all the Northern papers, starting with a few on Sunday morning, April 23, and followed by many others on April 24. Welles predicted that the way Stanton had attacked Sherman would "be likely to cause difficulty, or aggravate it, with Sherman, who has behaved badly, but I hope not wickedly." Welles was right—although perhaps a better term than "difficulty" would have been "all-out war." Most newspapers agreed with Stanton that Sherman's truce was utterly unacceptable. The *New York Herald*, for example, wrote that it could not see how Sherman, "after what had occurred in connection with the surrender of Lee's army, could imagine for a moment that the humiliating concessions proposed by him in view of the surrender of Johnston would be listened to at Washington." A few newspapers sympathized with Sherman. The *Brooklyn Daily Eagle*, for example, believed that Sherman would likely be "mortified" by Stanton's harsh disapproval of his terms and asked whether Stanton could have achieved his goals without insulting the great general.[41]

The cabinet at its regular meeting on April 25 continued to discuss Sherman's terms. Welles recorded that Speed had "little doubt that Sherman was designing to put himself at the head of the army. Thought he had been seduced by Breckinridge and was flattering himself that he would be able to control and direct public affairs." Welles conceded that

Sherman had made an error, a serious error, but Welles "had no fears of his misleading the army or seducing them to promote any selfish personal schemes of ambition." Welles believed that Speed was echoing Stanton when he asked what would happen if Sherman arrested Grant when he arrived in Raleigh: "Men will have strange phantoms." Stanton was relieved to receive a message that evening from Grant in Raleigh. Grant had arrived there early Monday morning and spoken with Sherman, who claimed that he was "not surprised" that Johnson had rejected his peace plan. Sherman immediately sent word to the rebel general Johnston that the agreement was disapproved and that he would soon resume fighting if no terms were agreed. Stanton sent this information to the press through Dix late on Tuesday night.[42]

The War Department's search for Booth had continued while Stanton reacted to Sherman's peace terms. At about five o'clock on April 26 two detectives, Lafayette Baker and Everton Conger, arrived at Stanton's house, where they found him in his parlor, resting but not sleeping on a sofa. Baker later recalled that, when he told Stanton they had "got" Booth, Stanton did not react for a moment, then rose and started asking questions. Conger described for Stanton how the troops had located and surrounded Booth and Herold in a barn near Port Royal, Virginia; how, as Herold surrendered, Booth fired upon the troopers; how one of the federals returned fire and hit Booth; how Booth suffered two or three hours and then died on the porch of a farmhouse. Conger spread out several objects they had taken from Booth, including a diary and a compass. Stanton examined them and handed them back. He was not quite ready to rejoice; he wanted to be certain that the body on its way to Washington was in fact that of Booth. And he was somewhat disappointed that Booth was dead, for he had hoped to learn from him that he was acting on Confederate orders and with Confederate support. Stanton directed Baker to intercept the boat with Booth's body and to arrange for the body to be taken to the *Montauk*, the ironclad ship on which several of Booth's colleagues were prisoners.[43]

On the next morning, Stanton informed the press through Dix that Booth was dead and Herold was in prison: "Booth, in making his escape, was shot through the head and killed, lingering about three hours, and Herold was captured. Booth's body and Herold are now here." At Stanton's request various people examined Booth's body on board the *Montauk*, including Surgeon General Joseph Barnes and Booth's own doctor and dentist. They carefully recorded the evidence that the body was Booth's, including the tattoo "JWB" on his hand. Barnes told Stanton, "The cause of death was a gunshot wound in the neck. . . . All the horrors of consciousness of suffering and death must have been present to the assassin during the two hours he lingered." Then, again on Stanton's instructions, Baker, Eckert, and others buried Booth's body within the walls of the Washington Arsenal. Stanton later testified that he instructed that Booth "should be interred in that place, and that the place should be kept under lock and key." He did not want Booth's grave to become a shrine for Southern sympathizers.[44]

Now that Booth was dead and some of his colleagues were in prison, Stanton concentrated on finding Davis and his cabinet. He sent a message on April 27 to Gen. George Thomas at Nashville that Davis was carrying millions of dollars in gold and coins and directed Thomas and his subordinates, "Spare no exertion to stop Davis and his plunder. Push the enemy as hard as you can in every direction." In yet another slap at Sherman he also emphasized, "Pay no attention to any orders but your own or from General Grant." The next day Stanton instructed Dix to find and arrest the former Canadian Confederate leader, Jacob Thompson, who was reported headed for Boston. Late on this day Stanton learned by telegram from Grant that Johnston and his rebel army would surrender to Sherman on the same terms Grant had given to Lee. This was great news—but not yet the end of the war, for other Confederates were still fighting against other Union armies.[45]

Stanton worked on the military trial in Washington of the Booth conspirators. He had already indicated in his reward poster that he would use a military commission rather than a civilian court for this trial. Although his choice was controversial at the time, and remains controversial, this was not a difficult decision for Stanton. There were dozens of other military commissions around the nation considering claims ranging from sabotage on Northern railroad tracks to attempted arson in New

York City. If these cases could be tried by commissions, Stanton believed, surely a military commission could try those who plotted against and killed the head of the nation's military in the nation's capital. Johnson ratified Stanton's decision with a May 1 order authorizing a military commission in Washington to try the eight defendants. Although Johnson's order referred to a legal opinion by the attorney general, Speed had not yet prepared his final legal opinion; he had simply given Johnson a *single sentence* expressing the view that a military commission was appropriate. Stanton was willing to proceed without a full opinion, for he was certain that a military commission was proper, and he was eager to get the commission started on its work. Indeed on the same day that Johnson signed the order forming the commission, orders went out from Stanton's office to various generals summoning them to Washington to serve on the military commission.[46]

Stanton prepared in his own hand the first draft of the procedures for this, the most famous of all American military commissions. The lawyers for the prisoners, for example, had to be men who had "taken the oath of Congress or shall take said oath before being admitted to appear in the case." (This "ironclad oath," requiring that one swear one had never supported the rebellion in any way, would effectively prevent any Southern lawyers from representing the prisoners.) "No reporters but the official reporter shall be admitted in the court room," but Judge Advocate General Joseph Holt could provide a daily summary of the testimony, to the extent that he deemed its publication consistent with "the ends of justice." Aside from the official court reporter, nobody would be permitted in the courtroom other than the judges, the defendants, the witnesses in turn, and the lawyers.[47]

Stanton also chose the prosecutors, starting with his friend and colleague Holt. During the war years, Holt had worked directly with Lincoln, reviewing hundreds of cases in which the president had to approve or disapprove the decisions of military courts. Holt had grown to know and love Lincoln, so Stanton was certain Holt would throw himself wholly into the effort to convict those who had conspired and assisted in killing Lincoln. Holt would be ably assisted by two younger lawyers: John Bingham, a former and future member of Congress from Ohio, and Henry Burnett, another of Holt's military lawyers, also originally from Ohio.[48]

Stanton and Holt selected the nine officers who would form this military commission, including its president, Maj. Gen. David Hunter, who had served the same role in the court-martial of Gen. Fitz-John Porter. Maj. Gen. Lewis Wallace, who had commanded at Monocacy, was a member. Brig. Gen. Cyrus Comstock was among those initially selected, but he wrote in his diary that he wished he did not have to serve, for he believed the defendants should be tried in the civil courts. "This commission is what is yet worse a secret one I believe." The next day Comstock got his wish: he and Horace Porter were replaced with two other officers. The explanation given was that Comstock and Porter were members of Grant's staff and thus might be biased against those who had attempted to assassinate Grant.[49]

Stanton was also involved in framing the charges against the defendants. On May 2 he sent a note to Holt, saying that Johnson wanted that same morning "a list of the persons late in Canada and Richmond against whom there is evidence of complicity" in the murder of Lincoln and the attempted murder of Seward. Holt provided a list, which Stanton turned into a proclamation issued that same day by Johnson, declaring that there was "evidence" in the War Department files that the murder of Lincoln and attempted murder of Seward "were incited, concerted, and procured by and between" Jefferson Davis, Jacob Thompson, Clement Clay, and three other named Confederate leaders. Johnson's proclamation offered rewards for the arrest of each of these men, including $100,000 for the arrest of Davis.[50]

Newspapers were skeptical about the claim that Davis and other rebel leaders were parties to the plot to assassinate Lincoln. The *New York Times*, at this time quite friendly to the Johnson administration, said that it was "extremely desirable that the charges which have been so solemnly made against Jefferson Davis, Jacob Thompson & Co., in the President's proclamation, should be fully borne out on the trial." But the *Times* cautioned Stanton and Holt to avoid "anything like exaggeration" in their case against Davis and his colleagues. The *Cincinnati Enquirer* doubted that Davis was involved in the assassination: "We do not believe that

Mr. Davis is, in any sense, an assassin of the late Chief Magistrate. We do not think that such was the character of the man. The charge, as it stands, looks to us like an excuse for offering a reward for one whose destruction is predetermined." Soon the papers were printing statements by Thompson and other Southern leaders, declaring that they had no role whatsoever in the assassination. So for Stanton and Holt, the imminent military commission would have two purposes: to try the eight Booth defendants for their roles in the murder of Lincoln and attempted murder of Seward, and to present evidence that Davis and other Southern leaders were part of the plot.[51]

Newspapers were even more excited a few days later, when they learned that Stanton would use a secret military commission to try the eight conspirators. The *New York Evening Post* declared, "The government is making a prodigious and fearful mistake in the mode of trial it has adopted for the conspirators in the late assassination. It makes a double blunder, in fact, first in resorting to a military tribunal, and secondly, in causing the proceedings to be held in secret. . . . The civil law is everywhere in the ascendant, and the ordinary courts are competent to any criminal inquest or decision." The *New York Commercial Advertiser* commented that the secret military trial would be like the Spanish Inquisition or "the hideous pretensions to justice of despotic medieval rulers." The *New York World* referred in headlines to "Mr. Stanton's Star Chamber." Even the *New York Times* asked whether the American people would "really believe that peace has been restored when a most atrocious crime has to be tried and punished by a military court sitting in secret in the national capital, and in a country in which all secret things, and above all secret trials, have always been held in abhorrence."[52]

Only a few papers supported Stanton on the secrecy issue. The *Washington Morning Chronicle* argued that a closed trial was necessary to protect the witnesses; if the assassins were prepared to murder the president, surely they would murder the witnesses against them. The *Philadelphia Inquirer* reported that Speed had presented to the cabinet "a written opinion upon the subject of military and civil trials." Speed supposedly advised Johnson that Lincoln "was *de facto* as well as *de jure* commander-in-chief of the Army and Navy in time of war," that "the crime was committed at a military post, garrisoned and under the command of a military governor," and that the courtroom "should not be open to spectators, as there is a very large number of witnesses to be examined, and none should know what the others have testified." If these were indeed Speed's views, he had not yet put them in writing. Welles noted in his diary that Stanton was "emphatic" in a cabinet discussion that the trial should be by military commission rather than civil court and that Speed also "advised a military commission," although initially he seemed to Welles "otherwise inclined."[53]

Horace Greeley, in an editorial in the *New York Tribune* titled "Secret Military Trials," described "a curious old document in existence, known as the Constitution of the United States, which formerly had the force and effect of law in that large portion of the country not specially dominated by the Slave Power." This document "seems to have gone out of fashion" and after "Mr. Stanton's accession to the control of the War Department, it has become practically obsolete." Since it seemed there was "no copy extant in the Federal City, we quote from one in our possession, for the instruction and admonition of our magnates." Greeley acknowledged that military commissions were appropriate in some cases but insisted that this was not such a case. "To try a doctor [Mudd] for his life, because he set a stranger's broken bone and gave, or sold, or lent him a pair of crutches, may just do; but to try him in secret allowing no report of the testimony but such as the prosecution sees fit to make, is nothing less than abominable." At the end Greeley was even harsher: "Gentlemen of the Cabinet! The War eastward of the Mississippi is ended; the Rebellion is suppressed; the Union is re-established, and Peace virtually restored: wherefore the People demand of you a speedy and thorough return to the safe and orderly ways of Law and Liberty. Do not compel them to speak in tones you cannot refuse to hear!"[54]

Stanton was outraged, almost deranged by this editorial. He dashed off a telegram to Judge Edwards Pierrepont, informing him that he wanted to prosecute Greeley and the owners of the newspaper. The charge: "Greeley's persistent efforts during the last four weeks to incite assassins to finish their work by murdering me." Both civil and criminal suits were necessary: "I shall not allow them to have me murdered and escape responsibility without a struggle for life on my part." Pierrepont and his friend Francis Cutting, another leading New York lawyer, responded by asking whether Stanton had any proof that Greeley wrote with the "actual malice" the law required for a libel case. Stanton replied, "I have proof of express personal malice against me by Greeley, and believe that I can establish a combination between him and others which may end in accomplishing my death, as it did against Mr. Lincoln." It seems that Pierrepont had to visit Stanton in Washington to calm him down, to persuade him that it would make no sense to start a libel lawsuit against a leading editor.[55]

The first session of the Booth military commission, on May 9, was held behind closed doors, in a heavily guarded courtroom on the third floor of the Old Arsenal Penitentiary. The eight defendants were marched into the room dressed in black, bound by handcuffs and leg shackles, and the seven male defendants were wearing white cloth hoods. One of the military judges, Gen. August Kautz, recalled later that the "scene partook so much of what my imagination pictured the Inquisition to have been, that I was quite impressed with its impropriety." Stanton (or whatever subordinate had ordered the hoods) relented within a few days, ordering the hoods removed so that the prisoners could see and breathe. Stanton also relented on the question of secrecy: the courtroom was opened on May 13 to selected reporters, and thereafter the newspapers were filled day after day with details about the trial.[56]

One of the hundreds of witnesses before the military commission was Lt. Kilburn Knox. He testified that he had been on the steps of Stanton's house a little after ten o'clock on the evening of April 13, watching the fireworks and listening to the music. Stanton, Grant, and others were inside, and Knox testified that one of the defendants, Michael O'Laughlen, had approached Knox and asked after Stanton. O'Laughlen also asked if Knox was the officer on duty, to which he (foolishly) replied, "There is no officer on duty here." O'Laughlen entered the alcove of the house, from where he could see into the parlor; this worried Knox, especially since O'Laughlen seemed "under the influence of liquor." Knox and Stanton's nephew David persuaded O'Laughlen to leave. David Stanton corroborated Knox's testimony and added that O'Laughlen had also asked about General Grant.[57]

The military commission that tried the Booth conspirators. On the right are the three judge advocates: John Bingham, Henry Burnett, and Joseph Holt.

Stanton did not attend the daily sessions of the trial, but he was active behind the scenes. For example, he sent a telegram to Halleck, in Richmond, describing a document that seemed to be a recommendation to Davis "in regard to the destruction of northern boats" with "an endorsement in his own handwriting." Stanton asked Halleck to find in Richmond and send to Washington a government clerk who could testify before the military commission about the standard Confederate office marks and (ideally) about Davis's handwriting. Stanton also sent a telegram to the American consul in Montreal, asking him to send two witnesses to Booth's relations with Confederates there to Washington at once: "Spare no expense or labor to get them here speedily." He wrote Secretary Seward, who was recovering remarkably from his wounds, to share a rumor that Powell, the man who had stabbed Seward, was the son of Sydney Smith Lee, and thus a nephew of Gen. Robert E. Lee.[58]

Stanton learned on May 13 that Union soldiers under Gen. James Wilson had captured Jefferson Davis and several others near Macon, Georgia. Stanton immediately relayed what he learned from Wilson to the press, including an erroneous report that Davis was disguised as a woman when he was captured. The *New York Times* the next day mocked the way Davis "seized the gold of the Richmond banks" and then "sneaked through his own lines, crept away from the brave but deluded men who had upheld his cause through years of blood." Stanton instructed Wilson to take every step necessary to prevent the escape or rescue of Davis, and he instructed Halleck in Richmond to make arrangements to hold Davis captive in Virginia "until trial which will be immediately after his arrival." A few days later, when Stanton learned that Davis, Stephens, and Clay had arrived as prisoners at Fort Monroe, he directed Halleck to go there and arrange personally for secure prison cells. Stanton also sent Dana to Fort Monroe, where he issued orders in Stanton's name on May 22 authorizing Gen. Nelson Miles, the local commander, "to place manacles and fetters upon the hands and feet of Jefferson Davis and Clement C. Clay whenever he may think it advisable in order to render their imprisonment more secure."[59]

Four days later there were reports in several Northern papers that Davis was not only in a prison cell but in manacles and chains. Thurlow Weed, ever alert to political winds, wrote Stanton that he could not at first believe the reports about the manacles: "If the mistake has been made, I am sure it must have been without authority, and I pray that you will immediately correct it." By the time he received Weed's letter, Stanton had already instructed Miles to remove the manacles from Davis. But public opinion was starting to shift on the Davis question, in part because Stanton and Holt had not yet shown a connection between Booth and Davis. Yes, there was evidence that Booth had a Confederate cipher in his trunk, and that Booth had met with Confederate agents in Canada. But this was not proof that Davis and other senior Confederates approved or supported Booth's plan to kill Lincoln. The *Columbian Register* in New Haven, Connecticut, commented in late May that the evidence that Davis had any role in the Lincoln assassination was "of so flimsy a character, that no court in the world except Mr. Stanton's packed commission would give it a moment's consideration."[60]

Washington was busy in late May preparing for the Grand Review, during which first Meade's army and then Sherman's would march down Pennsylvania Avenue before being discharged and heading home. Sherman was still angry at Stanton about the peace terms. In a letter to Grant upon his arrival in Alexandria, where he would camp with his army, he announced that the "Vandal Sherman" had arrived "untamed and unconquered." Both Grant and Sherman appeared at this time before the

Committee on the Conduct of the War. Grant testified that Stanton had performed his duties "admirably," that Stanton had provided the armies with everything they needed to win the war. In contrast, Sherman attacked Stanton, claiming that his truce with Johnston simply followed through on Stanton's suggestion, while they were together in Savannah, that Sherman should consider political as well as military issues. Both Grant's praise and Sherman's attack were soon in the papers.[61]

On May 23 the *New York Tribune* reported that the senior officers of Sherman's army intended "to demand of President Johnson the removal of Secretary Stanton for his warfare upon their commander while in the field." The *Tribune* expected that there would be some "demonstration of the feeling of the rank and file of Sherman's army toward the Secretary of War when it shall march past the official stand in front of the White House." The troops marched in good order, but Sherman himself insulted Stanton. When Sherman reached the reviewing stand, he shook hands with Johnson, Grant, Meade, and the others there, but he refused to shake hands with Stanton. The *Chicago Tribune* reported that when Stanton "rose and extended his [hand] General Sherman turned on his heel and seated himself at the further end of the platform, without even bowing recognition. The slight was no sooner given than it was noticed by the multitude, who in the enthusiasm of the moment loudly applauded the act, and even laughed at the Secretary in his discomfiture." In his memoir, Sherman wrote proudly, "He offered me his hand, but I declined it publicly, and the fact was universally noted."[62]

Grant sympathized with his friend Sherman, but he also worried about keeping the troops under control. He sent a stern letter to Sherman, relating reports that some of Sherman's officers, while drinking in Washington, were threatening violence against Stanton or his aides. Grant did not make any orders but suggested that Sherman keep his men south of the Potomac River: "What we want is to preserve quiet and decorum." Sherman reassured Grant but said that his soldiers regarded Stanton's messages as "a personal insult to" their commander: "I have not yet seen a man, Soldier or Civilian, but takes the same view of it, and I could not maintain my authority over troops if I tamely submitted to personal insult." Sherman told Grant that although he would obey orders, he could never respect Stanton again. If this caused difficulties for Johnson or Grant, Sherman suggested that Grant ask for his resignation, knowing of course that Grant would never do that.[63]

In the midst of his difficulties with Sherman, Stanton received a message from New Orleans that Gen. Edmund Kirby Smith's deputy had signed terms to surrender his forces. Stanton relayed this to Dix in what would prove the last of his many press reports by that means. The *New York Times* printed Stanton's message under the headline "Peace at Last." Stanton was somewhat more cautious, writing to a friend that "with the surrender of the last of the rebel forces under Kirby Smith the path of peace seems to be opening. I share with you in the abiding faith that whoever may be taken or spared, the nation will be saved."[64]

Johnson and Stanton continued to work on reconstruction questions. Stanton's friend Chase, touring the conquered South, wrote from North Carolina to urge Stanton to issue a formal order prohibiting the use of the word "contraband" to describe the recently freed slaves. "Words are things," Chase wrote, "& terms implying degradation help to degrade." Stanton did not issue any order, but he agreed with Chase's sentiment and worked hard for the freedmen. It seems that Stanton's first choice to head the new Freedmen's Bureau was Gen. James Yeatman, who declined the position. Reverend Henry Ward Beecher urged Stanton to appoint instead Gen. Oliver Howard: "He is, of all men, the one who should command entire confidence of the *Christian public* in the post, and I do not know of anyone who would also, to such a degree, unite the secular public." Stanton, who had met and liked Howard, did not need much persuasion. Howard recalled that Stanton summoned him to Washington, handed him a basket full of letters, and said with a smile, "Here's your Bureau." On the day after Howard's appointment, Stanton asked Halleck to examine the list of confiscated lands around Norfolk: "Let me know what should be secured for the freedmen and refugees." Stanton was serious about implementing the promise of the legislation, to provide freedmen with land confiscated from the rebels.[65]

After a cabinet discussion about reconstruction in early May, Welles recorded that there was "no great difference of opinion" within the cabinet "except on the matter of suffrage." Stanton and two other cabinet members favored giving Southern blacks the right to vote; Welles and two others opposed the measure. Welles complained in his diary that Stanton had changed his mind on this issue and accused him of playing politics. The *Pittsburgh Daily Commercial* reported that the cabinet had debated reconstruction, especially "negro suffrage," for several hours. Without identifying those in favor and those against, the *Commercial* stated that some in the administration wanted "all the loyal elements in the South [to] have an opportunity to participate in rehabilitation of state governments in the states recently in insurrection." The *New York Herald* reported a few days later, "Stanton is understood to differ very decidedly from the President and some of his colleagues in regard to the proper course to be pursued in restoring the rebellious states to their status in the Union." The "question of negro suffrage is the great stumbling block in the way of harmony. There is reason to believe that the President is disinclined to take the responsibility of extending the suffrage to the colored citizens until he has had an opportunity of ascertaining the sentiment of Congress upon the subject." It would seem, based on these reports, that Stanton and Johnson were arguing this issue not only within the cabinet but through the press.[66]

At the end of the month, Johnson issued two major proclamations. In one he granted almost all Southerners amnesty and the return of their property (except slaves) if they would swear allegiance to the United States. Fourteen categories of rebels, however, were excluded from this general amnesty, including those who had held senior posts in the Confederate government, those who had served in the Confederate Army with the rank of colonel or above, and those with property estimated to be worth $20,000 or more. Rebels in these categories would have to apply to the president personally for a pardon, though newspapers predicted that Johnson would be generous in granting such pardons. In the second proclamation Johnson appointed a provisional governor for North Carolina who would organize a convention to draw up a new state constitution. Only those who were eligible to vote under the terms of the prior state constitution, and who had taken the new loyalty oath, would be allowed to vote in this election of convention delegates. In other words, blacks would not be eligible to vote in the election for the convention and (unless the white delegates at the convention gave them the vote) would not be able to vote in state elections thereafter. Stanton later testified that

Johnson's views on black voting were "fixed" and that Stanton and the rest of the cabinet "assented to the arrangement as it was specified in the proclamation relating to North Carolina."[67]

Northern papers generally praised these two proclamations. "The grand feature of the President's plan is its simplicity," the *New York Times* commented. "He imposes no conditions but those of simple obedience to the laws and support of the proclamations of the national government." Many Southern papers agreed. "The war is over," declared the *Daily Phoenix* of Columbia, South Carolina. "The authority of the Government is complete. The Union of the States as one and indivisible has been established for all time." The duty of each Southern citizen was to "renew his allegiance and fealty to our common country, and cheerfully to co-operate with and aid the Government in the re-establishment of law and order."[68]

As the Booth military commission heard final witnesses and closing arguments, Stanton watched its progress but worked on other issues. He relayed to Halleck, still in Richmond in early June, a disturbing report that the city government had reinstated the "old school negro whippers" as the local police. "If there be any truth in the allegations," Stanton wrote, "you will please correct them at once and punish or reverse the officers by whose neglect or abuse of authority they are being practiced." Stanton defended Halleck when Johnson relayed complaints from Richmond leaders about Halleck's ban on the sale of hard liquor: "The small gains that would accrue to one or more liquor dealers, on the profits they might realize from this traffic, can be no consideration for a riot, a mob, or a military tumult, endangering arsenals, depots, and millions of public property." Although Seward recovered, and returned soon to his place at the cabinet table, his wife, Frances, never strong, was overwhelmed with the horror of the assassination attempt and died in late June. Stanton made the train arrangements for Seward to return to upstate New York, for the funeral, and then kept in daily touch with Seward while he was away.[69]

The military commission reached its decision at the end of June, finding all eight prisoners guilty of conspiring to kill Lincoln and Seward. Edman Spangler, the man who held Booth's horse, was sentenced to six years in prison; Arnold, Mudd, and O'Laughlen were sentenced to life in prison at hard labor; and Atzerodt, Herold, Powell, and Mary Surratt were sentenced to death. Five members of the commission drafted a petition to Johnson, recommending that he commute Mary Surratt's sentence to life in prison, on account of her age and sex. The military commission's decision was not announced immediately, because Holt had to review the case and obtain the approval of Johnson, and the president was seriously sick in the first few days of July. Stanton was also sick. The *Baltimore Sun* reported on July 4 that Stanton had not been at the War Department, that he was "too seriously indisposed to leave his room." Speed wrote to Lieber on July 5 that Stanton was "in feeble health."[70]

Mary Surratt, the owner of the board-inghouse where the Booth conspirators met, who was hanged for her role in the conspiracy. After Stanton's death, some papers claimed he had committed suicide out of remorse for his role in her execution.

When Johnson and Holt met on July 5, Johnson approved the sentences, including the death sentence for Mary Surratt, and fixed the time of execution as midday on July 7, only twenty-four hours after the sentences were made public. In later years Holt and Johnson fought bitterly about this meeting, Johnson claiming that Holt did not show him the clemency petition and Holt insisting that they had discussed it. Some of those involved remembered Stanton taking part in the debate. For example, James Harlan, the secretary of the interior at the time, recalled participating in a discussion with Johnson, Stanton, and Seward about whether Johnson should stay the execution of Mary Surratt. Harlan wrote that either Stanton or Seward said, "Surely not, Mr. President, for if the death-penalty should be commuted in so grave a case as the assassination of the head of a great nation on account of the sex of the criminal, it would amount to an invitation to assassins hereafter to employ women as their instruments, under the belief that if arrested and condemned they would be punished less severely than men. An act of executive clemency on such a plea would be disapproved by the government of every civilized nation on earth." Stanton would have agreed with this argument, but the conversation Harlan described almost certainly did not occur, for Johnson, Stanton, and Seward were all sick at the time of this supposed meeting. Stanton's one comment on this issue was a July 6 telegram to Robert Todd Lincoln, in Springfield, simply informing him that the four death sentences would be carried out the next day. In spite of last-minute appeals, the four condemned criminals, including Mary Surratt, were hanged as scheduled at the Washington Arsenal. Stanton received a short formal note from the general in charge, informing him that the orders had been carried out. On the next day, Anna Surratt wrote a letter to Stanton to plead for her mother's body so that she could provide her with a Christian burial. Stanton responded through an aide that Johnson had decided the arsenal grounds were "the proper place for persons found guilty of the crime for which they suffered."[71]

The bodies of George Atzerodt, David Herold, Lewis Powell, and Mary Surratt at the Washington Arsenal, immediately after their execution on July 7, 1865.

Chapter 16

"A Born Tyrant"

—— 1865–1866 ——

T
he War Department and the army were shrinking rapidly during the summer and fall of 1865. The total number of Union soldiers declined from more than 1 million in April, to about 300,000 at the end of June and about 100,000 at the end of the year. Stanton and Grant were mustering men out of the army as rapidly as they could, but they could not work fast enough for the impatient North. Stanton received dozens of letters from governors, members of Congress, and personal friends, pleading for their family members to be discharged. He and Grant were also *changing* the army, transforming it into an army of occupation. To control and occupy the South, the army created about four hundred posts, some in cities, some in small towns, some to hold a railroad line. Gen. Quincy Adams Gillmore, in charge of South Carolina and Georgia, directed his subordinates to "station troops at all important towns" so they could "keep the whole country under military surveillance." The number of posts in South Carolina increased from only eight in May to thirty-nine by the end of the year, and there were similar increases in other states. Commanders on the ground wanted troops, including expensive cavalry troops, to keep control over the still rebellious South. Gillmore wrote to Stanton that he would like to have at least 2,000 cavalrymen to "keep up constant communication between scattered posts and be able to reach quickly any point where

disorder may be threatened." He and other generals did not get all they wanted: by year's end there were only a few cavalry troops left in South Carolina.[1]

To the extent that there was any order in the South in the summer and fall of 1865, it was order provided by the Union Army. Former rebel soldiers and others formed outlaw gangs, robbing and raiding. Although Southern whites had feared that the end of slavery would lead to black-on-white violence, as had happened in the Haitian Revolution, this did not happen in the United States. What emerged instead, and continued for years, was white-on-black violence. After a tour of Texas in the fall, a federal officer reported that blacks were "frequently beaten unmercifully, and shot down like wild beasts, without any provocation." To secure more information, more reliable information, Stanton persuaded retired general Carl Schurz to make an extensive tour of the South. Schurz explained to his wife that Stanton said it was "absolutely necessary that I accept the mission; that my report, even if it did not decide the President's course of action, would be of the most vital interest in the discussions of the next Congress."[2]

The Southern state governments at this time were rather rudimentary. There were four states with governments formed under Lincoln: Arkansas, Louisiana, Tennessee, and Virginia. Even in these, however, the effective authority of the state government was limited to the area under control of the Union Army. Starting in late May, with North Carolina, President Johnson appointed provisional governors for the seven other former rebel states. In the summer these provisional governors started to make appointments and to set schedules for constitutional conventions to revise their state constitutions. In these states as well, order was provided by the Union Army under Grant and under Stanton.[3]

Stanton was concerned about the violence in the South, especially against blacks. In July, for example, he directed Gen. Henry Slocum, in charge in Vicksburg, Mississippi, to receive and hold a white prisoner accused of shooting and killing a black man: "Cause him to be tried before a military commission and carry its sentence into effect. If any effort should be made to release him by *habeas corpus* you are directed to disobey the writ and to arrest the person issuing or attempting to execute it." Southern state courts were gradually starting to function again, but they would not try or convict whites accused of attacking blacks, and in some cases, as Stanton's note to Slocum suggests, the Southern courts would interfere with federal military commissions. Later in the month Stanton issued a general order to allow Southern blacks to travel without passes: "To secure equal justice and the same personal liberty to freedmen as to other citizens and inhabitants, all orders issued by past district or other commanders, adopting any system of passes for, or subjecting them to any restraints or punishments not imposed on other classes, are declared void."[4]

Stanton was also worried about the rapid rate at which Johnson was releasing and pardoning the rebels. Johnson's May pardon proclamation allowed any Southerner who was not pardoned by its general terms, such as a senior general, to apply to the president for a personal pardon. By midsummer Johnson was granting more than a hundred such pardons every day. Stanton did not approve of this, writing to Johnson in the case of one prisoner, "If rebellion were any crime his guilt is without apology." Johnson released the man over Stanton's objection. In another case, Stanton himself visited the prisoner, Stephen Mallory, the former Confederate secretary of the navy, and afterward wrote to Seward that all he had learned was that Mallory hoped "to be released without having changed his sentiments." Johnson released Mallory as well.[5]

In the middle of July, Johnson asked his cabinet for advice about Jefferson Davis, the most prominent of the rebel prisoners, still in military prison at Fort Monroe, Virginia. Even Johnson, at least at this point, was not thinking about a pardon for Davis; he was asking the cabinet when and how Davis should be tried. Seward suggested there was no rush, that the first step was to examine the Confederate files. He insisted that Davis should be tried by a military commission rather than a civil court. Stanton agreed, saying it should take only a few weeks to review the relevant records. Welles objected, arguing that Davis should be tried by a civil court and tried for treason, not for his supposed role in the assassination. Welles was annoyed that Stanton and Seward interrupted him, and annoyed that Johnson did not resolve the issues.[6]

Stanton wanted his department to assemble the evidence against Davis and try him before a military commission. He was especially keen to tie Davis to Lincoln's assassination. But he failed, perhaps because (as most but not all scholars today believe) the Confederate leaders had nothing to do with the assassination, or perhaps because the War Department investigation was inadequate. Stanton knew it was essential to gather the Confederate government's papers from Richmond, and he issued the necessary orders as soon as Richmond was in Union hands. In May he asked his Boston friend Horatio Woodman to come to Washington to review the rebel files, estimating that with the aid of clerks it would only "take ten days or two weeks." Woodman was a curious choice for the assignment, being an editor, not a lawyer, and in any case he declined. Stanton then waited weeks before asking Francis Lieber to head up the Bureau of Confederate Records. Lieber was another curious choice, a famous scholar but not a prosecutor who could assemble a criminal case. Lieber accepted and started work in late summer, reviewing with his clerks hundreds of boxes, barrels, and bags of records. This review, which would take months, was necessary but not sufficient. Stanton should also have tasked some of his lawyers to "work backwards" from some specific war crimes, such as the Fort Pillow massacre, to see if they could be traced to the Confederate leaders. But other than some research into Booth and his Canadian connections, the department did not attempt this kind of investigation.[7]

Johnson's eagerness to pardon Southern rebels, to restore their rights to them, soon stopped Stanton and General Howard from distributing land to Southern blacks. The Freedmen's Bureau Act authorized, indeed perhaps required that the government provide to the freedmen the land it was holding, hundreds of thousands of acres seized or abandoned. After obtaining an opinion from the attorney general, Stanton and Howard started to distribute this land to the blacks. Southern whites complained, and on August 16 Johnson issued an order to Howard, specifying that a presidential pardon restored a former rebel "to all his rights of property except as to slaves." Johnson's order was arguably inconsistent with the act, but Stanton and Howard obeyed. Southern whites, not blacks, would receive the lands that were in the federal government's hands.[8]

Radical Republicans, including Chief Justice Chase and Senator

Sumner, were concerned about Johnson's course and believed that Congress should give Southern blacks the right to vote. Chase wrote to Sumner after an August visit with Stanton, "He is unchanged, but does not feel inclined to urge the suffrage views on the President." Johnson himself, at almost this same time, suggested privately to the provisional governor of Mississippi that the state constitutional convention might want to extend the right to vote to a few blacks. Johnson's goal, however, was not to help Southern blacks but to counter his congressional critics. "The Radicals," Johnson wrote, "who are wild upon negro franchise, will be completely foiled in their attempts to keep the Southern States from renewing their relations with the Union by not accepting their Senators and Representatives." Seeing and talking with Johnson every day in a way that Chase and Sumner did not, Stanton knew Johnson's views, which is why he was not inclined to press him on the question of black voting.[9]

Stanton also devoted more time this summer to the Indians. Before the war, keeping peace on the Indian frontier was the main task of the U.S. Army, and many wanted the army to return to this focus as soon as possible. Congress sent Senator James Doolittle to Colorado, and Stanton sent him messages to confirm that Johnson wanted Doolittle to negotiate "such treaties and arrangements subject to his approval as in your judgment may suspend hostilities and establish peace with the Indians and afford security to our citizen settlements and travelers on the frontier." In early August, Stanton was alarmed to hear that an armed expedition of more than 20,000 soldiers was heading into Indian territory. He wrote to Grant several times, explaining that the federal government simply could not afford such a large and expensive expedition, and Grant agreed, writing to Sherman that there was no need for such a force "now that the Indians cannot expect aid from rebels."[10]

***

Stanton's name was often in the papers this summer, often in a negative way. For example, John Ford announced in July that he would reopen his Washington theater, the theater in which Booth had shot Lincoln. But on Johnson's orders, on the day of the planned first performance, Stanton sent troops to close and seize Ford's Theatre. The *New York Tribune* attacked Stanton at length, demanding to know what law authorized him to seize Ford's property. The *Ohio Statesman*, still a staunch Democratic paper, also condemned Stanton for his arbitrary action. George Templeton Strong wrote, "Stanton has done the country great service and will take high place in history. But he is a born tyrant. He likes to use official power to crush and destroy rebels and sympathizers with rebellion and anybody else who may happen to stand inconveniently in his way. And I think he likes this use of his power best when it has the 'game flavor' of illegality." A few weeks later a small item in the *Philadelphia Inquirer* noted that Henry Winter Davis, acting as Ford's lawyer, had spoken with his friend Stanton and reported, "The matter will be amicably settled." But this resolution received almost no press attention.[11]

The *New York Tribune* also denounced Stanton for supposedly preventing a Catholic priest from visiting Mary Surratt just before her execution unless the priest would first promise not to discuss the military trial. The *Philadelphia Inquirer* defended Stanton, publishing a letter from the general who had handled the priest's request for a pass, saying that he acted on his own in suggesting to the priest that he should not talk with the condemned woman about the trial. The *Inquirer* noted that the *Tribune*, although usually an administration paper, had for some reason been shooting "poisoned arrows" at Stanton, and that with each shot Democratic editors "rubbed their hands in glee, and exclaimed 'a hit, a palpable hit.'"[12]

Both Frank Blair (the former general) and his brother Montgomery Blair (Stanton's former cabinet colleague) made speeches against Stanton during the summer of 1865. Montgomery Blair alleged that Stanton had encouraged Albert Brown of Mississippi just after he resigned from the Senate in early 1861, that Stanton "told him he was right, that it was the only route for the South; he must keep his constituents to it." Blair also accused Stanton of working now with the Radical representative Thaddeus Stevens to foment a new and violent revolution. According to Blair, Stevens wanted "a guillotine [and a] butcher to reign on its scaffold and ply its axe." He asked rhetorically, "Can any one doubt that Mr. Stanton would take this part?"[13]

The most popular angle of attack on Stanton during this summer was that he was responsible for the deaths of the Union prisoners at Andersonville. Stanton had refused to exchange prisoners on reasonable terms with the South, the argument went, and because of this refusal, Northern prisoners died. In a widely reprinted letter, a former Andersonville prisoner accused Stanton of being "unquestionably the digger of the unnamed graves that crowd the vicinity of every Southern prison." The *San Francisco Examiner* went a step further: "Mr. Stanton demanded that the Confederates should acknowledge the negro as the equal to the white man, as a condition precedent to an exchange of prisoners. This, of course, could not be done, and hence it was for this insane idea, Union soldiers were suffered to pine and die in Southern prisons. Think of it, you men of Anglo-Saxon descent—think of it, you descendants of those who framed our Constitution for white men!" The *Examiner* was in a sense right, for Stanton *had* insisted that black prisoners be included in any prisoner exchanges, but the racist rhetoric belied the real reason for the attacks on Stanton.[14]

Stanton worked on Andersonville himself this summer, in two different ways. As part of a general effort to find and consecrate the graves of Union solders, he sent a mission to Andersonville, headed by James Moore, a quartermaster officer, and Clara Barton, the famous nurse. Moore and Barton quarreled from the moment they left Washington; she later complained to Stanton that she "had not expected to be systematically ignored during the whole expedition." When they reached Andersonville, Barton wrote Stanton urging him to establish a national cemetery there: "Be assured Mr. Stanton that for this prompt and humane action of yours the American people will bless you long after your willing hands and mind have ceased to toil for them." Relying, it seems, on an obscure provision in an 1862 military statute, which authorized the purchase of burial grounds "to be used as a national cemetery for the soldiers who shall die in the service of the country," Stanton gave the orders to establish a cemetery at Andersonville. By October a Northern correspondent could report that more than 12,000 Union soldiers were buried in the forty-seven acres of the new national cemetery.[15]

Clara Barton, whom Stanton sent to Andersonville to identify and mark the graves of Union prisoners, and who urged him to establish a national cemetery there.

In August, in a courtroom in Washington, a military commission commenced the trial of Henry Wirz, the Swiss-born Confederate officer who had commanded the prison camp at Andersonville. The department's prosecutors, in their initial charges against Wirz, alleged that he was involved in a conspiracy with rebel leaders, including Robert E. Lee, to murder the prisoners. Stanton directed Norton Chipman, the lead prosecutor, to revise the charges so that they would *not* name the Southern leaders. After this change, however, Stanton let Chipman handle the case without much interference. It was a mistake. Chipman presented weak and perhaps perjured evidence against Wirz and then kept the defense lawyers from calling key witnesses. Some Democratic newspapers attacked the military trial, and by implication Stanton. The *New York World* argued, "Important, essential, relevant evidence in Wirz's favor is ruled out with a promptitude only paralleled by that with which irrelevant hearsay testimony against him was before admitted." At the end of the trial, as Stanton expected and hoped, the military commission found Wirz guilty and sentenced him to death.[16]

Perhaps because of the public criticism of Stanton, perhaps to encourage him to remain in office, John Hay, Lincoln's former private secretary, wrote Stanton a long letter:

> I know you generally care very little what people say or think of you, but it cannot but be gratifying even to you to know that confidence in you strengthens the confidence of good people in the government, and stiffens their hopes for the future. And I want you to let me say that in a very long journey this summer, embracing nearly every State in the North and the Border, I was surprised to see the near unanimity in this matter. You know that there were many meddlers whose knuckles you had rapped, many thieves whose hands you had tied, and many liars whose mouths you had shut for a time by your prompt punishments, who had occupied themselves in traducing you, so as to shake the faith of many decent people in you. That is all over now. Very frequently, when I had occasion to speak of you, I found you were understood and appreciated by strangers just as you are by your friends. It is already known, as well as the readers of history a hundred years hence will know, that no honest man has cause of quarrel with you, that your hands have been clean and your heart steady every hour of this fight, and that if any human names are to have the glory of this victory, it belongs to you among the very few who stood by the side of him who has gone to his better reward, and never faltered in your trust in God and the People. Not everyone knows, as I do, how close you stood to our lost leader, how he loved you and trusted you, and how vain were all efforts to shake that trust and confidence, not lightly given and never withdrawn.

Knowing that Stanton would find all this too much, Hay closed by saying, "It is not my habit to say this sort of thing, nor yours to listen to it. I wanted to tell you this when I saw you last, and now say it, and have done."[17]

Stanton and his wife Ellen left Washington in August for a month, the first long leave he took since he joined the government in early 1862. It was not altogether a vacation: Stanton visited army installations at West Point and elsewhere, and he took along a young telegraph clerk, David Bates, to keep in communication with the War Department. But by and large the Stantons stayed with friends and relaxed. They visited the financier Isaac Bell Jr. and his wife in Tarrytown, New York; the merchant Robert Minturn and his wife in Highlands, New Jersey; the banker Charles H. Russell and his wife in Newport, Rhode Island; Representative Samuel Hooper and his wife in Boston; and Senator Edwin D. Morgan and his wife at their mansion on Fifth Avenue in New York City.[18]

There was not much press coverage of Stanton's trip, probably because he did not want much. In early September the *National Republican* reported, "Secretary Stanton has been the guest of Mr. Minturn, at the Highlands . . . and at his residence on the North River. The Secretary has been yachting in the Bay and in the North and East Rivers. His health has been greatly improved by a little fishing." A week later a report in the *Daily News* in Newport criticized Stanton for traveling in a four-hundred-ton government steamer, "which has been kept lying here at his disposal during his stay." The next day the editor of the *Daily News* published an abject apology, acknowledging that the prior report was "false," that the steamer would have come to Newport with or without Stanton. A week later the *New York Times* reported on its front page that Morgan had hosted a large party for Stanton and listed the many prominent preachers, generals, and politicians who greeted the secretary. The *Times* claimed that Stanton "came quietly, had a good time socially, and has gone about his business."[19]

The Stantons returned to Washington in late September 1865, in the midst of the fall election campaign. This was, in part, an election about Stanton, whom some Northern Democrats denounced as a leader of the "Radical party" or the "Abolition party." In Bedford, Pennsylvania, for example, the *Gazette* warned those who voted for Republicans, "You give your endorsement to Stanton and declare to the world that you approve of the policy by which thousands of the brave soldiers of the Union were doomed to fearful privation, horrible suffering and untimely death." Stanton's friend and colleague Seward defended and praised him in a late October speech, declaring that because of Stanton the United States had achieved "the greatest military results," indeed "results which the whole world regarded as impossible. There is not one of those results that is not more or less directly due to the fertile invention, sagacious preparation and indomitable perseverance and energy of the Secretary of War." Seward was speaking as a moderate Union Party man, arguing that Johnson and Stanton were pursuing the same reconstruction policies as Lincoln and urging votes for the Union candidates, as Republicans still styled themselves.[20]

Issues about blacks, however, were even more important in this election than questions about Stanton. In the North, three states, Connecticut, Minnesota, and Wisconsin, voted against proposals to allow blacks the right to vote. In the South, the question was not whether blacks should vote but what limited rights, if any, they should have. In Mississippi, for example, where a few candidates advocated that blacks be allowed to testify in civil courts, Northern papers reported that those opposed to black testimony had prevailed. Mississippians elected as their governor the former Confederate general Benjamin Humphreys, even though he was technically not eligible to hold the office, not having received a presidential pardon. (Johnson provided the pardon soon after the election.) Louisiana Democrats declared in their platform, "This government was made and is to be perpetuated for the exclusive political benefit of the white race." Southern voters generally elected to Congress men who had served in senior positions in the Confederate government and army. And the new Southern legislatures, as they gathered in late 1865, started work on what we now call the Black Codes, a set of laws to limit and deny rights to blacks: prohibiting blacks from traveling without passes, from owning guns, from working where and as they wanted. Republicans reacted to these statutes with understandable anger. The *Chicago Tribune* declared, "The men of the North will convert the State of Mississippi into a frog pond before they will allow such a law to disgrace one foot of soil in which the bones of our soldiers sleep."[21]

Stanton's views on the Southern situation at this time are suggested by his support for the provisional governor of Alabama, Lewis Parsons. By Southern standards, Parsons was a moderate man. He urged his state to ratify the constitutional amendment to end slavery, and he denounced the proposed Alabama Black Code, telling the state legislators that to require a freedman to carry a pass at all times or to prohibit him from having even "a *light* in his dwelling after any given hour, is not only inconsistent with our American notions of freedom, it is utterly at war with them." But when Parsons visited Washington, he urged Johnson to close the Freedmen's Bureau, claiming it had "caused much trouble in the southern states." As Parsons headed north in early November, Stanton sent letters to several friends, including Beecher and Sumner, introducing Parsons as a "loyal and patriotic man entitled to respect and confidence." After meeting with Parsons in Boston, Sumner wrote Stanton that Parsons had told him "that rather than allow negroes to vote he would emigrate." For this alone Sumner viewed Parsons as a "bad example." He reported to Stanton, "At the club this evening Gov. P. made an address which seemed to me and many others true Pecksniffism." Sumner was telling Stanton that in his view Parsons was as bad as the selfish, hypocritical, indeed evil character Pecksniff in the Dickens novel *Martin Chuzzlewit.*[22]

Stanton's views are also suggested by the November speech of his friend Speaker of the House Schuyler Colfax. Stanton sent at least three friendly letters to Colfax this year, including one in October in which he said that he wanted to see Colfax as soon as he returned to Washington. In his speech, Colfax approved of the president's decision to form provisional state governments before Congress gathered and the president's insistence that the Southern states should ratify the antislavery amendment. Colfax wanted to ensure that the rights of Southern blacks were protected, that they were guaranteed equal civil rights, before the Southern states were restored their full political rights. He also wanted to see the Southern people ratify the changes to their state constitutions that had been made (often under intense federal pressure) over the summer. "Let us make haste rather slowly," Colfax said, before treating the Southern states as equal members of the Union.[23]

As Colfax and other members of Congress gathered, the Republican majority faced the question of whether to seat the Southern representatives in Congress. One problem was the so-called ironclad oath, a federal statute requiring all federal officers, including members of Congress, to swear that they had not supported the Confederacy. Many of those elected to Congress from the Southern states could not take this oath, and although Congress could change the law, few Republicans favored such a change. Far more serious was the question of the basis of Southern representation. Under the Constitution, states could count each slave as three-fifths of a white person for purposes of representation in Congress. Northerners had long resented this compromise, necessary to persuade the South to accept the Constitution, because it increased the power of the slave states both in Congress and in the Electoral College. Now the Constitution was about to be amended, as the necessary number of states ratified the amendment to end slavery. This would mean the Southern states could count each former slave not merely as three-fifths of a person but as a whole person, even though those states would not allow blacks to vote. At a single stroke this change would dramatically increase the power of the South in Congress. Almost no Republicans were prepared to allow this; if blacks could not vote, they should not count in the representation calculation. The only disagreement among Republicans on this subject was on how best to accomplish this end. Finally, there were serious questions about how the Southern states were treating blacks. Sumner and other Radical Republicans wanted to insist that the South allow blacks to vote, but this was a minority view; after all, three Northern states had just voted against allowing black voting. But as Colfax indicated, almost all Republicans were troubled by the Black Codes and wanted to do something to ensure that blacks had civil rights.[24]

Because of these concerns, Republican legislators agreed among themselves before the first day of the session that they would not seat the Southern representatives immediately. Instead they would form a Joint Committee of Reconstruction to look at the question of representation and to study the Southern situation more generally. The chairman of the new committee was Stanton's friend and former cabinet colleague, the moderate senator from Maine, William Fessenden. Stanton probably approved of this approach, as did the *New York Times*, which concluded that the new committee would allow Congress to decide the issues "without being complicated or embarrassed by questions of regularity or returns in the case of individual members." Even Johnson did not oppose this approach, at least not in public, at least not yet.[25]

Johnson was still popular in both North and South with both Republicans and Democrats, and he sought to maintain this popularity with a carefully worded annual message. To appeal to Democrats and Southerners, he called upon Congress to seat the Southern representatives as soon as possible. To appeal to Republicans, he endorsed protection for Southern blacks, asserting that the nation owed them basic rights. Newspapers from all sides praised the message. The *New York World* claimed that Johnson endorsed Democratic principles, and the *New York Tribune* declared that the message would "be generally and justly approved."[26]

Stanton spent a week in late December visiting his mother and sister in Ohio. Pamphila later described this as a pleasant, peaceful time: "He loved to throw himself down on our old-fashioned sofa, stretched at full length, with a volume of Dickens, mother sitting beside holding one of his hands." When she asked him which of the author's novels he liked most, Stanton replied that "he liked *David Copperfield* very much, but on the whole he liked *Little Dorrit* the best." Stanton returned to Washington in time for Christmas, writing to his sister, "Our children are rejoicing over a Christmas tree as vigorously as if the wax-tapers and trinkets that had made it so glorious to behold, were not the same that have done duty the past three years."[27]

On the second day of the new year, 1866, the Stantons went to Baltimore to attend the funeral of Henry Winter Davis. On the way back Stanton and Ellen shared a railroad car with Salmon Chase. The two friends had a long and frank talk. Chase noted in his diary that Stanton strongly supported giving blacks the right to vote in local elections in Washington, but "in the states he did not think it so important to ensure suffrage to the colored people as to ensure them lands." Chase "agreed as to the District but as to the states thought it easier to reach farms through suffrage than suffrage through farms." In other words, Chase was urging a reluctant Stanton to press for black suffrage in the South. Chase added, "Mrs. Stanton, who is one of the best women as well as the loveliest, I know expressed great horror of having negroes at her table! though anxious that they should have their rights."[28]

Stanton was not a sociable man; he preferred to spend his evenings at his office or at home with his family, not at receptions. But this January the papers announced, "Mrs. Secretary Stanton will receive every Saturday evening," and after one such reception the *Washington Evening Star* reported that the "magnificent parlors were thronged with the fashion and elite of Washington society." It was an extravagance that Stanton, on his government salary of $6,000 a year, could not well afford. A few nights later the *Star* mentioned that Stanton and his wife were among the guests at a party held by Surgeon General Barnes and his wife.[29]

There were again reports that Stanton would resign and that he should resign. The *New York Herald* tried a new argument: "The man who was a good war minister during a war cannot be expected to be a good peace minister during a peace. The enmities, hatreds, and jealousies, and the martinet practice inseparable from the position of Minister of War, render the same man an unfit, however conscientious, counselor for the Executive." The *Herald* claimed that Stanton had already offered his resignation and that Johnson would send Stanton overseas as a diplomat, perhaps even as the minister to England. Connecticut's *Hartford Courant* called the report "bosh" and insisted, "Stanton will remain Secretary of War."[30]

There were also reports of tension between Stanton and Grant, and these had some foundation. In late January, Grant sent a long letter to Stanton, expressing concern about their respective roles. He understood that, during the crises of the war, it had sometimes been necessary for Lincoln and Stanton to communicate directly with generals in the field. Now Grant requested that *all* communications with generals and others in the army should pass through his office. Stanton did not respond in writing to Grant's letter, but Sherman later wrote that Stanton "had promptly assured [Grant] in conversation that [Stanton] approved of his views as expressed in this letter." Stanton also continued to communicate with generals directly, however, at least from time to time, no doubt annoying Grant.[31]

One of the bills working its way through Congress in the first few weeks of 1866 was intended to expand the powers and extend the life of the Freedmen's Bureau. Stanton supported the bill. The bureau was part of his department and was doing what he viewed as essential work in feeding, housing, and protecting the former slaves of the South. He received at this time a letter from one of Grant's wartime aides, the Seneca Indian Ely Parker. After visiting several Southern states, Parker wrote that he feared Southern whites were throwing obstacles in the way "of the successful operation of the Freedmen's Bureau." Given the situation, Parker believed it was necessary "to retain troops in the late slave holding states in order to protect the negro in his life, freedom and the few rights he has acquired by becoming a freedman." Stanton agreed and forwarded a copy of Parker's letter to Johnson.[32]

By the middle of February, both houses had passed the bill to extend and strengthen the bureau and the bill had reached Johnson's desk. The *New York Tribune* admitted that Johnson had "doubts as to the wisdom of some provisions of the bill" but urged him to sign it nevertheless, since "more than two-thirds of the Congress have passed the bill after the most careful consideration." On Friday, February 16, at what one paper termed a "very animated" cabinet meeting, Johnson indicated he would veto the measure even though Stanton and Seward pressed him to approve. On Sunday, Stanton was "so anxious over the political situation" that he left church early to find Fessenden, who, as it happened, was meeting with Johnson to discuss the bureau bill. Fessenden left the White House convinced that "the President would act with Congress"; when he heard this news from Fessenden, Stanton "expressed great relief at the prospect of harmonious action."[33]

On Monday, however, when Johnson presented his veto message to the cabinet, Stanton knew there would be no harmony. Johnson rejected the Freedmen's Bureau bill in its entirety. A freedmen's bureau, in his view, was unnecessary, intrusive, expensive, and unconstitutional. He objected in particular to the use of military courts in time of peace, and he questioned the very right of Congress to pass the bureau bill while eleven Southern states, the states "mainly affected by its provisions," did not have any congressional representatives. In essence, Johnson was threatening to veto not only this particular bill but any future reconstruction bill unless and until Congress complied with his demand that it seat the Southern members. Stanton, Seward, and Interior Secretary James Harlan all objected to the draft message, but Johnson issued his veto that same afternoon.[34]

Thomas Nast shows Johnson vetoing the freedmen's bill, kicking a bureau down the stairs.

The Senate considered Johnson's veto message on Tuesday, February 19. Senator Lyman Trumbull of Illinois, a friend of Lincoln and of Stanton, gave a long speech that probably reflected Stanton's views as well. The president "believes [the bill] will involve great expense; I believe it will save expense. He believes that the freedman will be protected without it; I believe he will be tyrannized over, abused and virtually re-enslaved without some legislation by the nation for his protection." At the end of the debate, when the votes were counted, Trumbull's motion received only thirty votes, with eighteen votes against, including from a few moderate Republicans. Since the motion did not receive the required two-thirds majority, Johnson's veto was sustained, and the freedmen's bill would not become law.[35]

Johnson rejoiced. Speaking from the White House steps to a crowd of supporters on February 22, he declared that the present leaders of Congress were just as bad as the former rebel leaders. When a voice from the crowd called for names, Johnson obliged, naming Thaddeus Stevens, Charles Sumner, and others. Johnson even accused his enemies of plotting to assassinate him. "Are the opponents of the government not yet satisfied? Are those who want to destroy our institutions, and to change the character of the government, not yet satisfied with the quantity of blood that has been shed? Are they not satisfied with one martyr in this place? Does not the blood of Lincoln appease their vengeance and their wrath?" For moderates like Stanton, Johnson's veto message was bad, but this speech was worse: the president seemed utterly unhinged.[36]

Some papers now reported that Stanton had disagreed with Johnson about the freedmen veto and would resign. Other papers denied these rumors: the *New York Times* even asserted, "There is high authority for stating that Mr. Stanton fully approves the President's action." Stanton, commenting on these conflicting news reports, told Lieber, still working in Washington on the rebel records, that he would not resign, but rather force Johnson to remove him. "They must muster me out."[37]

In March, Congress passed a different bill to protect Southern blacks: the Civil Rights bill. Designed to overturn the Black Codes, this bill declared that all citizens would have the right to make and enforce contracts, to sue and be witnesses in courts, and to enjoy the equal protection of the laws. The bill gave federal courts jurisdiction over claims for violation of these rights, if and to the extent that blacks could not enforce their rights in the state courts. Welles wrote that when Johnson asked the cabinet for their views, "Stanton made a long speech, showing he had devoted much time to the bill," and saying that although the bill "was not such a one as he would have drawn or recommended," he advised Johnson "that under the circumstances it should be approved." Sumner wrote that Stanton reviewed the bill "section by section" at the cabinet meeting and "pronounced it an excellent and safe bill every way from beginning to end. But the veto message was already prepared and an hour later was sent to Congress."[38]

Johnson's veto of the Civil Rights bill insisted that the federal government had no role in civil rights; these were questions for the states alone. He pointed out that many states, Northern and Southern, had laws that treated whites and blacks differently, such as the laws prohibiting blacks from marrying whites. If this bill became law, Johnson argued, Congress could next sanction the "revolting" practice of marriage between whites and blacks. Indeed, alluding to the recent votes on black suffrage, he warned that Congress was heading toward a national law requiring that states allow blacks the right to vote. The bill, in Johnson's view, was "another step, or rather stride, toward centralization and the concentration of all legislative powers in the national government." Two of Stanton's friends, Senators Fessenden and Morgan, visited the White House to see if there was some possible compromise, but Johnson would not budge. Fessenden, Morgan, and other moderates then joined the Radicals to override the veto; Welles noted bitterly that "all of Stanton's pets were active in opposing the veto." The bill passed into law, the first major legislation to become law over a president's veto in U.S. history.[39]

In early April 1866, without consulting with his cabinet, Johnson issued a proclamation declaring that the rebellion had ended in all the states but Texas. If consulted, Stanton would surely have objected, especially to the part of the preamble stating that "standing armies, military occupation, martial law, [and] military tribunals . . . are in time of peace dangerous to public liberty, incompatible with the individual rights of the citizen, contrary to the genius and spirit of . . . free institutions, and exhaustive of the national resources." Stanton favored the continued military occupation of the South, and the continued use of military tribunals there, both to protect Southern blacks (effectively not protected by Southern courts) and to protect the military itself (when whites attacked federal officers). When Gen. C. R. Woods asked Stanton by telegram whether the proclamation meant he could no longer use military tribunals, Stanton responded that the proclamation did not "limit the jurisdiction or authority of such tribunals," but meant only that the president wanted "to dispense with [military] tribunals to the utmost extent possible consistent with the public peace and welfare." Through this and other instructions, Stanton and Grant allowed the commanders on the ground to continue using military commissions, and Johnson did not attempt to overrule them.[40]

Congress, in parallel with its work on the Civil Rights and Freedmen's Bureau bills, was working on an even more important measure: a constitutional amendment. Sumner proposed a sweeping guarantee of equal rights, including equal voting rights, but most Republicans realized this was not politically possible: a constitutional amendment would have to be ratified by three-quarters of the states, and the Southern states would not accept Sumner's language. So moderate Republicans focused on civil rights, such as the right to make contracts and appear in court, as distinct from political rights, such as the right to vote. Section 2 of the draft amendment would limit the representation in Congress of states that denied or abridged black voting rights, and section 3 would deny voting rights for several years to former rebels. Stanton's friends kept him posted on their progress; indeed the Stanton papers at the Library of Congress include a printed draft of the amendment with his marginal notes.[41]

On May 1, when Johnson asked his cabinet for their views on this evolving draft amendment, there was long and heated debate. Stanton said that although he could not approve the amendment in its current form because of the provision denying voting rights, he favored it in general and hoped that Johnson and the Congress could reach a compromise. Welles declared himself "unequivocally opposed" to the amendment. Stanton said that Welles "was opposed to any terms with Congress. That I was ironclad on the subject of Reconstruction, and had not only fifteen-inch guns leveled against Congress, but was for running my prow into them." The next day some papers reported that the whole cabinet agreed with Johnson and opposed the amendment. The *New York Tribune* dissented, believing that Stanton "has made no speech in material antagonism to the congressional policy of Reconstruction or in especial support of the President, and that the anonymous rumor is set afloat to induce him to say or do something that would afford an excuse for his summary removal from the Cabinet." The *New York World* laughed at the *Tribune* and other "radical organs" and insisted that Stanton "came out squarely and unequivocally in favor of the President's policy."[42]

These articles regarding Stanton ran side by side with articles about a three-day race riot in Memphis. One, dated midnight on May 1 from Memphis, reported that "negroes are being pursued and shot down in the streets" and that, so far, ten blacks and three whites had been killed. Grant, summarizing for Stanton, listed "murder, arson, rape, and robbery, in which the victims were all helpless and unresisting negroes." Southerners and some Democrats blamed the Republicans for the riots; the *Memphis Avalanche* declared, "The bloody appetite of the Radicals in and out of Congress has begun its bloody satiation." Republicans viewed the Memphis riots as proof that the Southern states were not yet ready to govern themselves.[43]

The National Union Club of Washington, a group of ardent Johnson supporters, wanted to pin Stanton down: Did he or did he not support the president's policy? On May 17 the group announced that it would "serenade" Stanton, that is, come to his house and demand a speech. Stanton declined the honor. On May 23, however, when about a thousand men showed up at his house in the evening, along with a military band, Stanton was ready.[44]

Standing on his front steps, with men on either side of him to hold candles, Stanton read his prepared speech. He started by recalling the chaotic conditions when Johnson took office: the collapse of the Confederacy, the assassination of Lincoln. Quoting at length from Johnson's first annual message, he approved of how the president had appointed provisional governors and encouraged the formation of new state governments. Stanton also quoted a part of the message the president perhaps now regretted, in which he had said that "good faith" required securing "the freedmen in their liberty and their property, their right to labor, and their right to claim the just return of their labor." These views on the nation's obligations to the freedmen, Stanton said, "received and continue to receive my hearty concurrence." He admitted that he and Johnson had disagreed in February about the Freedmen's Bureau bill, that he had advised Johnson to sign the bill into law, but the question was now moot because the bill was "no longer a living measure." Turning to the new constitutional amendment under discussion, Stanton called it a "measure or series of measures of prime importance." He could not support the amendment in its current form, because of the section denying former rebels the right to vote until July 1870. With the rapid changes in the South, Stanton said, this might tie the hands of Congress unnecessarily and improperly. By mentioning only this one section, out of the five sections of the amendment, Stanton implied that he would support the amendment if this section was changed.[45]

The *Chicago Tribune* praised Stanton's speech, saying it would "commend the Secretary of War anew to the confidence of the Republican party." Connecticut's *Hartford Daily Courant*, from the opposite side of the political divide, claimed Stanton had "heartily approved the policy of

President Johnson." When questioned by Samuel Shellabarger, a worried Republican representative, Stanton explained that he supported "the Johnson whom we nominated and elected, not that apostate who is now in sympathy with the traitors." The *Philadelphia Daily Age* mocked Stanton, saying that he "expressed the warmest affection for everybody, and the highest respect for everybody's principles and prejudices. It is plain that his deep devotion to Mr. Johnson is equaled only by his romantic affection for Mr. Sumner." The *New York Herald* sneered, "Stanton sustains both the President and Congress, although the Bible assures us that no man can serve two masters."[46]

Stanton probably knew the Bible better than did the editors of the *New York Herald*. He revealed his religious side in a letter in late May to Moses Odell, a former member of the Joint Committee on the Conduct of the War, now dying of cancer at his home in Brooklyn. "To a devoted and professing Christian like yourself," Stanton wrote,

> it is not for me to offer consolation of a spiritual nature; for, to you, disease, and even death, can have no terrors, and can only be regarded as a passage, more or less rough, from this to a better world. Of late, my own mind has experienced strange sensations—present things are losing their hold; and dwelling on past events, especially of the last few years, my heart yearns toward those who have been, as it were, soldiers by my side, and are gone, or are going, forward to the front as an advanced guard. They will soon meet, or have already joined, Mr. Lincoln and others of that glorious army of martyrs, many of whom we have known here on earth.

Stanton closed by writing that it was his prayer that God would sustain his friend "while your march continues, and receive you into that bliss designed for those who have faithfully done their part in this world."[47]

———————

After much debate and many revisions, Congress approved and submitted to the states a civil rights constitutional amendment, what we now know as the Fourteenth Amendment. The first section provided that all persons born or naturalized in the United States and subject to its jurisdiction would be citizens of the United States and of the state in which they resided. No state could "deprive any person of life, liberty, or property, without the due process of law; nor deny to any person within its jurisdiction the equal protection of the laws." Under the second section, states would have representatives in the House in proportion to their adult male population, reduced if and to the extent that a state denied or abridged the right to vote to any of its adult male inhabitants. The third section no longer had the language to which Stanton had objected, denying the right to vote to all former rebels until 1870. Instead the provision would affect a much smaller group, basically former Southern officeholders, and would not deny them the right to vote but only the right to hold office, unless and until Congress removed this condition. Fourth, neither the federal government nor any state government could pay or assume any of the debt incurred in aid of the rebellion. (Most of the rebel debt was owed to former rebels, but the Union government was adamant that it would not even pay foreigners who had loaned to the Confederates.) The fifth and final section authorized Congress to pass laws to implement the amendment.[48]

This amendment was largely drafted and passed by moderate Republicans. One of these, Stanton's friend John Bingham from Ohio, was the principal author of the vital first section. Another friend, William Fessenden, played a major role in the Senate debate. Fessenden and other moderates thought of the amendment as a compromise between the Republican Congress and the Southern states; if the Southern states would ratify the amendment, make it part of the Constitution, Republicans would allow their representatives back into Congress. To underscore this, when Tennessee ratified the amendment, Congress promptly voted to admit its representatives. The amendment was also the Republicans' campaign platform for the fall 1866 congressional elections. Republicans contrasted their approach (protecting Southern blacks and limiting for a time the political power of Southern whites) with the approach of Johnson (exposing Southern blacks to white violence and giving immediate political power to Southern whites).[49]

Johnson opposed the amendment, both as a policy and as politics. He did not want to see Republicans (whom he thought of as almost all

Radicals) elected in 1866; he favored Democrats, although he hoped to entice conservative Republicans to join his National Union movement. Johnson issued a message opposing the amendment, saying that it was wrong for Congress to pass such a measure without Southern representatives. In late June the papers printed another message, effectively from Johnson although nominally from Senator James Doolittle: a call for a National Union convention, composed of representatives from all thirty-six states, to meet at Philadelphia in August. The convention was in part about the 1866 congressional election but also in part about the 1868 presidential election, since Johnson believed he could win that election if the Southern states were allowed to vote. Indeed "National Johnson Convention" was the headline used in some papers to describe the proposed Philadelphia meeting.[50]

Johnson's allies wanted him to remove from the cabinet all those who did not support the National Union movement. George Morgan, a leading Ohio Democrat, wrote to Johnson, "Constant complaints are made at the retention in your cabinet of men who are known to be hostile to you and your policy." Stanton was "justly more detested than any man in America" and should be removed and replaced. Doolittle, probably at Johnson's request, wrote to ask each member of the cabinet to declare whether he supported the National Union Convention. Seward, Welles, and Treasury Secretary Hugh McCulloch complied with Doolittle's request, writing letters to support the convention. Speed, Harlan, and Postmaster General William Dennison refused and resigned. Stanton drafted but did not send a letter to Doolittle supporting the constitutional amendment and opposing the Philadelphia convention, which would consist in his view of Southern rebels and their Northern supporters.[51]

Why didn't Stanton send this letter? Why didn't he resign from the cabinet of a president whom he viewed as an "apostate"? In part the answer is that Republicans now viewed Stanton, and he viewed himself, as a critical check on Johnson. Representative Shellabarger, writing to another Republican, asserted that Stanton "loathes the present Johnson movement as much as you do and if there is any ambiguity in his position it is owing to the fact that good men demand him to stay in the Cabinet." Newspapers reported the same: that Republican members of Congress insisted Stanton remain in office. Stanton and other Republicans did not see this as disloyal or improper; after all, Republicans had elected Lincoln and Johnson in 1864, and Stanton was simply adhering to the Republican policies of Lincoln. Stanton was convinced, in particular, that if he resigned, Johnson would withdraw the army from the South, with the result that the Southern slaves whom Lincoln had freed would be attacked and in some cases killed. Stanton also had personal reasons for staying in office. His salary of $6,000 a year was not much by the standards of a successful private lawyer, but if he resigned, he would have to start work as a lawyer once again, which was far more difficult in those days, when there were no large Washington law firms filled with former government officials. Stanton also was the defendant in *Smithson v. Stanton*, in which the plaintiff was seeking $35,000 in damages for an alleged wrongful imprisonment during the war. As secretary of war, Stanton could have the government pay his defense costs and could perhaps obtain legislation to stop such suits altogether. He would have far less power as a former government official. So he remained.[52]

"Mars as Stanton." Thomas Nast mocks Stanton as a Roman military figure.

On Sunday morning, July 29, Stanton received a telegram from Gen. Absalom Baird, in command in New Orleans in the absence of Gen. Philip Sheridan: "A convention has been called, with the sanction of Governor [James Madison] Wells, to meet here on Monday. The lieutenant governor and city authorities think it unlawful, and propose to break it up by arresting the delegates. I have given no orders on the subject, but have warned the parties that I could not countenance or permit such action without instructions to that effect from the President. Please instruct me at once by telegraph." Stanton must have been somewhat mystified. The Northern press had not paid much attention to the plan of some Louisiana Radicals to reassemble the state constitutional convention of 1864, to rewrite the state constitution, perhaps to give blacks the right to vote. Nor had the press reported much on the racial tension in New Orleans. Stanton did not have a copy of the message Johnson had received Saturday from Albert Voorhies, the lieutenant governor, reporting that a "radical mass meeting" the previous evening had ended in a riot, and asking Johnson whether the army would support the local judges who planned to order the arrest of the convention delegates. Nor did Stanton have Johnson's response to Voorhies: "The military will be expected to sustain and not obstruct and interfere with the proceedings of the courts." If Johnson intended to issue an order to Baird, the army officer on the ground, the way to do so would have been through Stanton.[53]

We know what Stanton did not do: he did not share Baird's telegram with Johnson, nor did he answer Baird himself. But we do not know why Stanton chose this course. When questioned later by a congressional committee, Stanton explained that he thought Baird's existing instructions were sufficient, that Baird knew he was supposed to prevent race riots. This is a partial but not full answer. Baird's message placed Stanton in a difficult position. If the issue were up to him, Stanton would probably have directed Baird to protect the convention delegates, black and white, from street violence and questionable arrests. But Baird's message asked for instructions from Johnson, and Stanton knew that if he consulted Johnson, the president would give the opposite instructions. Indeed the president already had issued such instructions, although Stanton did not know that.[54]

On Monday morning the *New York Tribune* printed a report from

New Orleans, dated Sunday, describing "great excitement in the city and loud threats . . . made by the rebels to break up" the constitutional convention planned for Monday. The *Tribune* even printed a garbled version of the Saturday messages between Johnson and Voorhies. Stanton probably saw this report at some point on Monday, but he did not learn of the New Orleans riot itself until Tuesday, when Johnson showed him a message from Voorhies, reporting that there had been a riot, that several people were dead. Details arrived over the next few days: a white mob, aided by the police, attacked first a black parade, and then the constitutional convention itself. More than thirty people were dead, almost all of them black. In the words of General Sheridan, reporting from New Orleans to Grant and soon quoted in the Northern newspapers, "It was an absolute massacre."[55]

Republicans blamed Johnson for the New Orleans riot. The *New York Tribune* regretted the "direct personal sympathy between the President and rioters" and insisted that Johnson bore the "most fearful personal responsibility." Stanton would surely have agreed. Democrats blamed the Radical Republicans, calling it madness to attempt to revise the state constitution. Southern papers praised the New Orleans authorities for suppressing what they saw as an illegitimate, Radical, black convention. One paper declared that Southerners would "never submit to be ruled and made strangers in their homes by Northern emissaries, a few mischievous Southern men and their negro allies."[56]

Preparations were under way for another convention, the National Union convention in Philadelphia. In early August, while they waited for a cabinet meeting to start, Stanton mentioned to Welles that he had refused a request from the Philadelphia organizers for bunting to decorate their hall. Welles teased Stanton a bit, urging him to "show your flag." Stanton said that if Welles was asking for his view, he was against the convention. Welles claimed that he had not known this because Stanton had not answered Doolittle, like the rest of the cabinet. Stanton replied that he "did not choose to have Doolittle and any other little fellow draw an answer from me." The delegates in Philadelphia cheered as former rebel generals entered the hall arm in arm with former Union leaders. Stanton was not impressed. When Johnson and all the other cabinet members gathered at the White House to receive a formal report after the convention, Stanton skipped the event.[57]

Stanton was also not part of the group that left Washington with Johnson in late August for a two-week political tour. The Johnson entourage included Seward, Welles, and Grant. Johnson's stated purpose was to go to Chicago to dedicate a memorial to the late Stephen Douglas, but his real goal was to rally the voters to support Democrats in the fall elections. They traveled slowly, making many stops where Johnson gave speeches and responded to hecklers. In St. Louis, for example, he accused the Radicals in Congress of causing the New Orleans riot: "Every drop of blood that was shed is upon their skirts." He claimed that he had been "traduced" and "slandered" and "called Judas—Judas Iscariot." He accused the Republican leaders of comparing "themselves with the Savior of men, and everybody that differs with them in opinion, and try and stay and arrest their diabolical and nefarious policy, is to be denounced as a Judas."[58]

In a long letter to his friend James Ashley, a Republican representative from Ohio, Stanton criticized Johnson and his "Swing Round the Circle." He was especially worried that Johnson might pull Grant to his side, for the general "goes daily, almost hourly, to the White House, in full view of the populace, and at this moment is gyrating through the country on a deplorable jaunt with Mr. Johnson." Stanton admitted that he longed to resign. "These new and augmenting dangers increase my longings to be free—to return to my family, friends, and profession; to rest; to have peace." He was also troubled that Seward, on this political tour, was giving speeches to support Johnson. He hoped that Congress would "tie the hands of Johnson and Seward so that they will not be able to wreck the country and throw us into another revolution, although they have gone so far already that no statutes can prevent their acts from bringing on a reign of chaos and bloodshed in the South that will horrify the civilized world."[59]

Soon after writing this letter, Stanton learned that Seward was sick, near death, and that his children were bringing him back by special train to Washington. Stanton alerted Seward's housekeeper, arranged an ambulance and stretcher crew to meet Seward at the train, and met the family himself with "kind words" for each of the children. Was Stanton a hypocrite, to criticize Seward one day and greet him the next? Or was he a friend, who, even though they now disagreed on politics, still cared for Seward as a person? Later that day Stanton was part of the much larger crowd that gathered at the rail station to greet Johnson as he returned from his tour. The *New York Herald*, still trying to paint Johnson as popular, claimed that Stanton saluted the president "with a cordiality that left no room for doubt as to the feelings of gratification that he experienced on the occasion."[60]

Stanton and the War Department still held Jefferson Davis prisoner at Fort Monroe. The Northern as well as Southern press was increasingly critical. The *New York Tribune* in late September declared that the government was "disgracing itself by its treatment of this prisoner—that it ought to have brought him to trial long since, and let him know his fate—that it is playing a shabby, shuffling, cowardly part with regard to him—that it should either retract its charge of assassination or have him indicted and tried thereon according to law." At an early October cabinet meeting the new attorney general, Henry Stanbery, raised the question of Davis: "Stanton very excitedly declared that Davis had forfeited all his rights—that he had no right to demand anything—we could hold him as long as we pleased—we ought to hold him, and he was opposed to any action in the case at present." A few days later Stanton presented to the cabinet a short paper, arguing that since the government lawyers were not yet prepared to present a treason case in civil court, Davis should remain where he was, in an isolated military prison, under Stanton's control. Stanton also suggested that Stanbery himself should handle the trial of Davis, with whatever assistants he wanted. Stanbery responded that "his place was here as the legal adviser to the President and cabinet—that he was not required to attend any Court but the Supreme Court, and that it would be improper for him to do so." There was no resolution of these issues, although the cabinet did agree that the military guards should "extend to Mr. Davis all the liberty, day and night, compatible with his safe keeping."[61]

In October several papers speculated that Stanton would resign, that he would be sent abroad, that Sherman would take his place as the head of the War Department. Seeing these reports, Sherman wrote to Grant, "This cannot be"; he did not want to join the cabinet, to leave the army, where he was "commissioned for life." Friends of Stanton, seeing the same papers, urged him to stay. Ohio District Judge Humphrey Leavitt wrote, "So far as I know the views and wishes of your friends in Ohio, they desire you may remain where you are, and if the President desires your position to be vacated, that you will throw upon him the responsibility of your removal." Fessenden wrote, "I trust, at all events, that you will not leave before the Congress assembles." Stanton replied to Fessenden that it seemed Johnson had decided to appoint Sherman: "The Copperheads think it indispensable to get me out of the War Department, and I think the arrangement has been made. Sherman is to be here today. No earthly power could induce me to go to Spain or any foreign country or accept any appointment whatever. My removal from this Department will gratify no one so much as myself. But it is only the forerunner of efforts to get Grant out of the way." Indeed Johnson was trying to persuade Grant to go to Mexico on a diplomatic assignment, but Grant (in the words of one his biographers) "smelled the rat." Grant rejected the Mexican assignment, Sherman rejected the War Department, and Stanton remained in his position.[62]

On the Friday before the November elections, Grant reported to the cabinet that it seemed to him, based on a visit to Baltimore the prior day, that there would be election riots in that city. Stanton and the others agreed that Johnson should issue public instructions to Grant to stand ready in case there was a proper call for federal aid from Maryland's governor. Governor Thomas Swann traveled back and forth between Washington and Baltimore over the weekend, meeting several times with Johnson and Stanton. In the end, election day passed quietly in Maryland, one of only two states where Democrats won. Everywhere else, Republicans prevailed. The *Philadelphia Evening Telegraph* declared that, in the quarrel between Johnson and Congress, "the people of the United States have determined to sustain Congress."[63]

Chapter 17

"Wily Old Minister"

— 1866–1867 —

After the election defeats of October and November 1866, a more prudent president would have considered compromise with the other party. But Andrew Johnson was not a statesman of the compromising kind. He prepared a draft of his annual message to Congress in which he insisted on his positions. The message urged that Congress, as its first priority, admit representatives and senators from the South. There was "no measure more imperatively demanded by every consideration of national interest, sound policy, and equal justice than the admission of loyal members from the now unrepresented states." Johnson did not mention the ongoing armed attacks against Southern blacks and federal soldiers. Nor did he refer to the pending constitutional amendment to protect black civil rights. When Johnson presented the message in draft form to the cabinet, Stanton said he would have been pleased to see the president support the amendment. Perhaps this was Stanton's way of suggesting that he hoped Johnson would extend an olive branch to moderate Republicans in and outside of Congress. Johnson ignored the suggestion.[1]

Although Stanton did not say so in this cabinet meeting, he believed the most pressing issue facing the nation was how to stem Southern violence. He knew the details because he saw the reports from army officers stationed in the South of the frequent attacks, rapes, and murders.

A long summary prepared for him of "outrages committed in Southern states" included a report from an officer in Alabama of a fourteen-year-old black girl, "ravished and both ears cut off," and a report from Texas of two federal soldiers "found murdered on the road." Stanton wrote in early December to Horace Greeley that he feared for those "exposed to persecutions in rebel communities. Reports from military commanders press this [issue] as urgent and represent that in some places no spirit of forbearance or forgiveness exists, and that loyal persons for loyal acts during the war, are pursued with relentless hate."[2]

Stanton's concern only increased a few weeks later when the Supreme Court issued its final decision in *Ex parte Milligan*. The case started in Indiana in early 1864, when the army arrested Lambdin Milligan and several others, accused them of plotting to seize the state arsenal and overthrow the state government, tried them before a military commission, and sentenced them to death. The majority of the Supreme Court, in an opinion by Justice David Davis, sided with Milligan, ruling that since there was no actual warfare in Indiana at the time of the trial and since the civil courts were open in Indiana, the military commission was not constitutional. Stanton denounced the *Milligan* decision, testifying before a congressional committee that the Court's opinion was not "justified by any principle of law" and was "wholly inconsistent with the protection of persons in the military service, or with the preservation of peace and safety in any of the states in insurrection." Stanton was not alone in his concerns: Thaddeus Stevens warned that the *Milligan* decision had "taken away every protection in every one of these rebel states from every loyal man, black or white."[3]

There was not much that Stanton could do about the *Milligan* decision other than to disregard it and continue to authorize military commissions in the South, which he generally did. He also tried to protect the army in other ways. Representative George Boutwell recalled Stanton telling him in December 1866 that he was "more concerned for the fate of the country than he was at any time during the war." This recollection is buttressed by contemporary news reports, including one quoting Stanton telling Representative John Covode that "the country was in a worse condition, and one of more danger, than at any period of the war." Stanton was troubled, Boutwell wrote, by reports that Johnson had issued orders to the army "of which neither he nor General Grant had any knowledge." He was even more worried by rumors that Johnson intended to "reorganize the government by the assembling of a Congress in which the members from the seceding states and the Democratic members from the North might obtain control." Stanton dictated to Boutwell language to limit Johnson's authority: to require that all orders from Johnson to the army pass through the general in chief (Grant) and to prohibit Johnson from transferring the general in chief to any place other than Washington. Boutwell forwarded Stanton's draft to Stevens, who was chairman of the relevant committee, and the language was soon part of the pending army appropriation bill.[4]

Stanton's disagreements with Johnson became more visible, first in the cabinet and then in the newspapers. In early January the cabinet discussed whether Johnson should veto a bill giving blacks the right to vote in local elections in the District of Columbia. Every cabinet member other than Stanton advised Johnson to veto the bill; in a brief memorandum, Stanton urged Johnson to sign the bill, saying that the Constitution gave Congress complete authority over the District of Columbia. Johnson, as he had probably intended all along, vetoed the bill, arguing in his message that blacks were not yet ready to vote. Congress passed the bill into law over the veto.[5]

A few days later Johnson asked the cabinet for their comments on a bill introduced by Stevens to abolish the present Southern state governments, strip many former rebels of their voting rights, and give voting rights to some Southern blacks. Stanton used this as a chance to agree with the president, saying that he had "approved and advised the reconstruction policy of both President Lincoln and President Johnson—that what had been done was right—that it was the President's duty to reconstruct the states as he did—that in no other way could he have saved them from anarchy—that the existing governments were lawful, and that he was opposed to the congressional scheme of reducing the states to territories." As to the Stevens bill, Stanton claimed he had not read it and would not bother to do so, since "it was one of those schemes which would end in noise and smoke."[6]

But a week later, when Johnson asked for the cabinet's view on bills to admit Colorado and Nebraska as states, Stanton was again a minority of one. He recommended that the president sign both bills, but all the other cabinet members objected. Johnson and his cabinet (except Stanton) believed that the population of the territories was too small to warrant statehood, and they objected to the clause in the bills that required the states, as a condition of statehood, to allow blacks to vote. In his veto messages Johnson attacked this as an unconstitutional interference in each state's right to determine who should vote in state elections. Perhaps he also had another, unstated objection. The House Judiciary Committee had started to investigate whether the House should impeach Johnson on various grounds; if impeached, he would be tried by the Senate; if they were states, Colorado and Nebraska would each have two senators, almost certainly Republicans, likely votes against Johnson. Riding with Welles in the carriage back to their adjoining departments, Stanton said he "wished this matter of vetoes might be over." Welles replied that vetoes were "unavoidable whilst Congress passed unconstitutional legislation." Congress passed the Nebraska bill into law over the veto, but not the Colorado bill, for even some Republicans agreed that its population was too small to justify statehood.[7]

Congress in early 1867 was also considering a measure that would play a central role in the life of Stanton and indeed the nation, the Tenure of Office bill. The bill would prohibit the president from removing, without Senate consent, any federal officer whose initial appointment had required Senate consent. One key question for Congress was whether this restriction should apply to cabinet officers, and in particular to Stanton. In early February, Representative Thomas Williams, a Republican from Pittsburgh, offered an amendment to extend the bill's protections to cabinet officers. After the amendment failed on a close vote, the *New York Times* commented that many members wanted to reconsider because "in no other way could Mr. Stanton be retained in his present position. No one advanced this argument publicly, but it was whispered around among the Republican members, and resulted in placing the bill in a position for further amendments tomorrow." Two days later the House approved the Williams amendment so that cabinet members could not be removed without Senate consent.[8]

This was not the end of the question, for the Senate version of the bill did not apply to cabinet officers. The two houses appointed a conference committee that devised an ambiguous compromise. Cabinet officers would "hold their offices respectively for and during the term of the President by whom they may have been appointed, and for one month thereafter, subject to removal by and with the advice and consent of the Senate." Did this protect Stanton from removal without Senate consent? Senators disagreed even before the bill was passed. During the debate on the conference report, Senator George Williams suggested that cabinet members were protected from removal unless and until there was a change of president. Senator James Doolittle argued that, because Stanton was appointed by Lincoln, nothing in the bill would prevent Johnson from removing him "tomorrow." The senators agreed, however, that it was unlikely any cabinet officer would remain if a president wanted him to resign. Williams said that no cabinet officer with "a particle of self-respect" would remain in the cabinet "after the President had signified to him that his presence was no longer needed." Senator John Sherman added that "no gentleman" would stay in the cabinet "after his chief desired his removal." Both houses passed the bill with the compromise language and sent it to Johnson.[9]

Congress was not only passing bills to limit the president's authority; it was considering whether to impeach and remove him. Four times, in the course of the spring of 1867, Stanton testified before the House Judiciary Committee as it deliberated whether to impeach Johnson. The committee's first questions for Stanton related to whether Johnson had directed that government railroads be transferred for nominal sums to his political friends. Stanton testified that transferring the railroads was not Johnson's idea; Stanton and Meigs believed that, once the war ended, the government should transfer the railroads "as speedily as possible" to their prior owners so they could once again be "channels of commerce and trade between the states." Stanton explained that the federal government had seized the railroads for use only during the war; it had not acquired title, so once the war was over, the railroads rightfully belonged to their private owners. Some members were so anti-Johnson they thought he might have been involved in the assassination of Lincoln; they pointed to pages ripped out of John Wilkes Booth's diary that may have detailed

Johnson's role. So Stanton was called back and testified that the pages were missing when he first received the captured diary. In general, Stanton's testimony did not help the impeachment effort; rather the reverse.[10]

Johnson and his cabinet allies did not give Stanton much credit for this; they viewed him as working with and for the Radical Republicans. An incident involving a report by Oliver Howard intensified Johnson's anger against Stanton. Early in the year Congress had requested information about violations of the Civil Rights Act. Stanton relayed the request to Howard, as head of the Freedmen's Bureau, who responded with a long report regarding attacks on and murders of Southern blacks. Grant forwarded Howard's report to Stanton, who forwarded it to Johnson and recommended at a cabinet meeting that Johnson release the report. All the other cabinet members objected; Welles termed the Howard report a mere "*omnium gatherum* of newspaper gossip and rumors of negro murders and troubles." Secretary of the Interior Orville Browning was outraged, writing that Stanton "manifestly wanted to do the President an injury," and adding, "I have no faith in him. He has no sincerity of character, but is hypocritical and malicious." Johnson, it seemed to Welles, was finally starting to think about removing Stanton.[11]

On February 22 the cabinet debated the most important bill of the year, the most sweeping statute of the decade, the First Military Reconstruction bill. This law divided ten former rebel states (Tennessee was excepted) into five military districts, each district under the command of an army general appointed by the president. The principal duty of these military commanders was "to protect all persons in their person and property, to suppress insurrection, disorder, and violence, and to punish, or cause to be punished, all disturbers of the public peace and criminals." The military commanders could rely upon state courts to try alleged criminals, if they wished, but they could also "organize military commissions or tribunals for that purpose." The act also set out the long path that the covered Southern states would have to follow if they wanted to be represented in Congress again, starting with elections for constitutional conventions, elections in which blacks could vote but many whites, because of their Confederate service, could not. The new state constitutions would have to allow for black voting, and the new states would have to ratify the pending constitutional amendment.[12]

Johnson had no intention of signing this bill into law; indeed he told his private secretary he would rather have his right arm "severed from [his] body with a cleaver." But he asked his cabinet for their views, perhaps in order to put Stanton on the record in favor of what Johnson considered an utterly unconstitutional outrage. Welles recorded Stanton saying that "though he should have framed the bill differently, and altered it in some respects, he should give it his sanction, and advised the President to give it his approval." The other cabinet members denounced the bill, and Johnson enlisted Stanton's former friend Jeremiah Black to help him draft the veto message.[13]

A few days later, on February 26, Johnson asked his cabinet for their views on the Tenure of Office bill. Johnson was perhaps surprised to find that, on this issue at least, Stanton shared his position. Indeed, according to Browning's diary, "Stanton was more earnest and emphatic in the expression of his objections than any other member of the cabinet." Stanton viewed the measure as an unconstitutional restriction of the president's power to appoint and remove executive officers. Welles later recalled that during this discussion Stanton said, "Any man who would retain his seat in the cabinet as an adviser when his advice was not wanted was unfit for the place." Johnson asked Stanton to draft the veto message, but Stanton "declined on account of the rheumatism in his arm." When pressed, he agreed to help Seward prepare the message.[14]

Johnson published his two veto messages on March 2. Congress, on the same day, passed into law over the vetoes both the Tenure of Office Act and the Military Reconstruction Act. Modern legal scholars would generally agree with Johnson on the legal issues: the Tenure of Office Act unduly limited the president's authority over the executive branch; the Military Reconstruction Act violated the Constitution as interpreted by the Supreme Court in *Ex parte Milligan*. But Johnson did not have the votes, for many moderate Republicans joined their Radical colleagues in voting to override Johnson's vetoes and turn these bills into law.[15]

Two days later Johnson and his cabinet gathered in the president's room in the Capitol to consider the last few bills passed in the session. One of these was the Army Appropriation bill, which included the language Stanton had secretly provided to Boutwell limiting the president's authority over the army. Most of the cabinet urged Johnson to veto this bill, viewing the Stanton language as unconstitutional, but Seward and Stanton urged the president to sign the measure, so as not to deprive the army of funding. Johnson decided to sign, but with a protest, and then asked each cabinet member whether he approved of the draft protest. Stanton ducked, saying, "I make no objection to it." Johnson persisted: "I wish to know whether you approve of a protest." Stanton ducked again: "I approve your taking whatever course you may think best."[16]

———

At noon on March 4, 1867, the Thirty-ninth Congress ended. Under normal nineteenth-century practices, the Fortieth Congress would not have started its work until December. But these were not normal times, and the new Congress started work on the same day, within the hour. One reason Republicans wanted to remain in session was that they feared Johnson would refuse to appoint the five commanders under the Military Reconstruction Act. At the cabinet meeting on March 8, Treasury Secretary McCulloch urged Johnson to appoint the district commanders soon because it "would tend to prevent impeachment. The President got very angry, and swore vehemently, and said they might impeach and be damned, he was tired of being threatened—that he would not be influenced by any such considerations, but would go forward in the conscientious discharge of his duty without reference to Congress." But Johnson quietly conferred with Grant, who suggested five names, and just after the next cabinet meeting the president informed Stanton that he would accept Grant's five generals. Stanton was "unusually jubilant, had a joke or two with McCulloch, and could not suppress his feelings."[17]

Johnson appointed Gen. John Schofield to command in the first district (Virginia), Gen. Daniel Sickles in the second (the Carolinas), Gen. John Pope in the third (Georgia, Florida, and Alabama), Gen. Edward Ord in the fourth (Arkansas and Mississippi), and Gen. Philip Sheridan in the fifth (Louisiana and Texas). Welles was especially troubled by the appointment of Sickles, whom Stanton had defended in his murder trial, and he feared that all five generals would answer to Stanton. "The slime of the serpent is over them all," Welles wrote. But the newspapers generally approved of the appointments; for instance, the *New York Times* commented, "Probably no fitter choice of military commandants for the five southern districts was easily possible."[18]

Even before Johnson named the five commanders, Congress was fixing a gap in the Reconstruction Act, specifying who could vote in the elections for state constitutional conventions. The Second Military Reconstruction Act, passed over Johnson's veto on March 23, denied the vote to any person who was an "executive or judicial officer of any state" before the Civil War and "engaged in insurrection or rebellion against the United States." This would not affect black voters, for none of them held state offices before the war. It would disenfranchise only whites, but how many would depend upon how one interpreted the act. Would every man who had ever held any office under the state government, even a minor municipal office, and then served in the Confederate Army, even if drafted and forced to serve, lose the right to vote? Several district commanders asked Washington for guidance, and Attorney General Stanbery started work on a legal opinion. But as the weeks passed, the district commanders had to register voters, and they did so using their own interpretations. Grant encouraged the commanders in this approach, assuring them that the statute gave each commander authority to interpret the law in his own district. Sheridan, for one, issued orders directing that registrars should "exclude from registration any person about whose right to vote there may be a doubt." In practice this meant that about half of the white citizens in his district were denied the right.[19]

As March ended and April began, the members of Congress considered whether they should adjourn and for how long. Radical members wanted to remain in session or to adjourn for only a short time because they wanted to ensure that Johnson implemented the reconstruction laws. Welles wrote in his diary that the Constitution "makes it the duty of the President to see that the laws are executed, but the Radical majority openly usurps this power and proposes a perpetual session in order to cripple the Executive and concentrate all power in the Congress." The Washington correspondent of a South Carolina paper reported that Stanton himself went to the Senate on March 27, where the "wily old minister moved from the ear of one senator to that of another," urging them to stay in session. Why? According to the reporter, Stanton knew that if there was a long recess, Johnson would remove him from office, relying on the provision for suspensions during a congressional recess. The *National Republican* predicted that Congress would adjourn for the summer because members wanted to "go on a buffalo hunt." Whether to hunt buffalo or for other reasons, the House adjourned at the end of March and the Senate in mid-April after a short session to consider appointments and the treaty with Russia to acquire Alaska.[20]

When Seward first described for the cabinet his proposed purchase of Alaska for $7 million, Stanton did not object. Browning wrote, "We all approved the purchase but made some criticism on the draft of the treaty, which is to be modified." Not long thereafter, however, Stanton reportedly told Johnson "that it was a country of ice and rock. A territorial government, with the necessary military force, would create an annual expenditure of more than a million; and . . . during a war it were better that it should be in the hands of a friendly power than in our possession, as we must take the means for its defense." Whatever Stanton said to Johnson (and the source is somewhat suspect), he did not work against the Alaska treaty. Indeed Stanton's closest friend in the Senate, Charles Sumner, was the treaty's main champion. The Senate voted in favor of the Alaska acquisition by a substantial margin, a rare instance of cooperation in this era of conflict between President Johnson and the Republican Congress.[21]

Stanbery presented and the cabinet discussed his detailed legal opinion on the Second Reconstruction Act at three successive cabinet meetings in the middle of May. The attorney general's opinion would increase the number of Southerners allowed to vote by finding that municipal officers were not "state officers" under the law, nor were road commissioners and similar single-function state officials. Stanbery also believed that district commanders and registration boards could not "look behind" a man's oath and inquire whether he was really qualified to vote; Stanton disagreed, commenting that this would open the door for voting by false oaths. Welles wrote, "Stanton criticized [the opinion] closely, controverted some of the points, is friendly to the bill and probably had much to do in its preparation if he did not originate the measure. He defended it with all the tenacity of an author, and took ground such as would suit the strongest Radicals." The Stanbery opinion appeared in the papers in late May, but Johnson did not require Grant to relay it as an order to the district commanders. Perhaps Johnson was concerned that the House

Judiciary Committee, still in Washington and still working on its impeachment investigation, would consider this an impeachable offense.[22]

In early June, General Sheridan removed Louisiana governor Madison Wells from office, telling Stanton that Wells was a "political trickster, and a dishonest man"; the official reason for removal was that he was obstructing implementation of the reconstruction laws. Republican papers praised Sheridan; Democratic papers denounced him. Over several long, hot days, the cabinet debated point by point a second legal opinion from Stanbery, denying that district commanders had any authority to remove state officials and reiterating Stanbery's position on the voting issues. Stanton disagreed with Stanbery on almost every issue; he took detailed notes of the discussions; he even prepared and read his own legal opinion, arguing that Congress had given the district commanders "absolute military command in their respective districts" and that they could remove from office "any person who may hinder, obstruct, or oppose the execution of the specified acts." The press reported on the cabinet debate daily, probably because Johnson wanted to show that Stanton was alone. The *New York World* stated that the entire cabinet, except for Stanton, agreed with Stanbery on the removal question. The *Albany Evening Journal* noted that Stanton was the only one who "dissented from the revolutionary opinion annulling the military bill." But the editors were not surprised: if "Johnson should decide to re-establish slavery, Seward, McCulloch and Welles would probably agree."[23]

In late June, at the conclusion of this long debate, Stanbery's legal opinion was sent to the five district commanders and published in the newspapers, with a preamble largely drafted by Stanton. The preamble stated that Johnson accepted Stanbery's opinion and directed that it be transmitted to the district commanders, but did not require that the commanders follow the opinion. Sheridan wrote to Grant, asking whether Johnson's message was an order and deriding Stanbery's opinion as a "broad macadamized road for perjury and fraud." (Sheridan was referring, in particular, to Stanbery's assertion that a commander could not look behind a man's claim that he was entitled to vote.) Sheridan's letter appeared in the papers almost immediately, and there was another outcry. Even the *New York Times* criticized him for insubordination and suggested he should resign.[24]

Many papers again reported that Stanton would resign. The *New York Herald* reported that Stanton "has prepared his letter of resignation to be sent to the President, and is arranging matters with a view to an early departure." The *New York World* claimed that in fact Stanton had already resigned "because of the decision of the cabinet touching the restoration of the southern officials." The *New York Tribune* mocked these reports: "Mr. Stanton belongs to the class that rarely die, and never resign. As to his political sympathies, they may be expressed by saying that there are three parties in the country now—the Democrats, the Republicans, and Mr. Stanton."[25]

Congress returned to Washington for a brief session in July 1867, mainly to pass legislation to overturn the Stanbery legal opinion. With Stanton's help—there are drafts of the bill among his papers—Republicans drafted the Third Military Reconstruction bill, to clarify that district commanders did indeed have authority to remove and replace state officials and also to interpret voting requirements. Johnson vetoed the measure, complaining that Congress was denying the "sacred guaranties" of the Constitution to twelve million Southerners. Congress promptly passed the bill over Johnson's veto, and Stanton and Grant, who were cooperating closely, ensured that the district commanders received copies.[26]

Radical Republicans by this time believed that Johnson was acting as a dictator, but some Democrats feared that Stanton and Grant wanted to set up as dictators. Frank Blair, former Union general and member of Congress, wrote in August to his father, complaining that the five commanding generals were working to Stanton's instructions. Blair called Stanton the "evil genius of our country who has corrupted the mind of Grant and whispered to him the prospect of absolute and permanent power." Blair did not elaborate on how Grant and Stanton would achieve "absolute and permanent power," but presumably he had in mind perpetual military control of the South, including the electoral votes of the Southern states. Stanton would be Bismarck, Blair wrote, under Grant as King Wilhelm. It was a remarkable accusation against Grant, now the leading Republican candidate for president, and Stanton, whose name also appeared in some papers as a possible president.[27]

By early August there was no doubt that Johnson wanted Stanton out of his cabinet. As the *New York Herald* explained, "They differ on questions of national policy as widely as it is possible for two men to differ, and recently this difference seems to have ripened into a mutual distaste for each other's society." But the *Herald*, like most other papers, doubted that Stanton would resign. On August 1 Johnson drafted a letter asking Stanton to step aside, and Johnson asked Grant whether he would be willing to serve as secretary of war in Stanton's stead. Grant urged Johnson by letter that day not to attempt to oust Stanton, pointing out that the Tenure of Office Act prevented him from removing Stanton without Senate consent: "The meaning of the law may be explained away by an astute lawyer but common sense, and the mass of loyal people, will give to it the effect intended by its framers."[28]

Johnson might have allowed Stanton to remain but for what he viewed as a final outrage. In federal court on August 3, during closing arguments in the civil trial of John Surratt for conspiracy to assassinate Lincoln, one of the prosecution lawyers, Stanton's friend Edwards Pierrepont, remarked that Johnson had condemned Mary Surratt in spite of a petition to spare her life. When Johnson read this in the newspapers, he told his private secretary that he had never seen or heard of any such petition. But Johnson knew who had presented the papers for the executions: Stanton's friend and colleague Joseph Holt. On August 5 Johnson sent two letters to Stanton. One demanded that Stanton provide him at once with the original documents regarding the Surratt execution; the other informed Stanton, "Public considerations of a high character constrain me to say, that your resignation as Secretary of War will be accepted."[29]

Stanton refused to resign. "Public considerations of a high character," he replied, "which alone have induced me to remain at the head of this Department, constrain me not to resign the office of Secretary of War before the next meeting of Congress." His refusal is hard to square with his reported statement during the cabinet discussion of the Tenure of Office bill, that "any man who would retain his seat in the cabinet as an adviser when his advice was not wanted was unfit for the place." But Stanton now believed, as did many Republicans, that he should remain as secretary to serve as a check upon Johnson. "It would doubtless be gratifying to his own feelings," commented one Republican paper, "to retire from his burdensome post of duty to private life, but the country demands that he should stay where he is. Not until Andrew Johnson has ceased to be president, either by impeachment and removal, or by the expiration of his term, will the people consent that Edwin M. Stanton shall leave his post."[30]

Stanton's letter suggested another reason he refused to resign at this time: the Senate was in recess. When a federal position requiring Senate confirmation becomes vacant during a recess, the Constitution allows the president to make a recess appointment, and the person so appointed may serve until the end of the next session of Congress. The next session would not start until November or December and would probably last until at least March. Stanton was unwilling to allow Johnson to appoint anyone he chose to serve for so long. There were also personal factors as well. Stanton had been secretary of war for more than five years; he might claim to be tired, but he liked the power and the work. He did not have a law practice to which he could return, and there were no law firms eager to hire former senior federal officials. In short, Stanton was not going to give up his post without a fight.[31]

The newspapers printed Johnson's demand and Stanton's refusal on August 7, leading to more comments, both public and private. "The whole loyal North," Woodman wrote from Boston, "will justly feel that you have deserted them if any pressure or any diminution of your powers induces you to give up your hold of the machinery of the War Department." George Templeton Strong liked the brief, pointed language Stanton used. "War to the knife has seldom been declared with such distinctness and such brevity." The *New York Herald* urged Johnson to suspend not only Stanton but the five military reconstruction commanders: "The honors of martyrdom, in being thus divided among half a dozen martyrs, will be neutralized."[32]

Johnson summoned Grant to the White House on Sunday, August 11, and informed him he would suspend Stanton from office and appoint Grant interim secretary of war. Suspension and interim appointment were clearly allowed under the Tenure of Office Act during a recess of Congress. Grant said he would accept the interim appointment; it seems that he and Stanton had agreed it was better that Grant rather than a stranger take the position. Later that day Grant warned Stanton of Johnson's decision.[33]

So Stanton was not surprised to receive a letter from Johnson the next day suspending him immediately from all his duties and rights as secretary of war. Stanton also received a letter from Grant, saying that Johnson had named Grant interim secretary of war and that he would accept the position. "I cannot," Grant wrote to Stanton, "let the opportunity pass without expressing to you my appreciation of the zeal, patriotism, firmness and ability with which you have ever discharged your duties." Stanton wrote back to both that he "had no alternative but to submit, under protest, to the superior force." With this he left his office and went to his home on K Street. There he wrote to his wife, who was with the children at the Soldiers' Home, "I congratulate you. I am out of office and Grant is in. We can now make such arrangements for our northern trip as you may desire. I have applied for a special car to take us to New York starting tomorrow at noon or next day as suits you best."[34]

———

Even before he was suspended, Stanton had been planning to visit Samuel Hooper, a member of Congress from Boston, and Horatio Woodman, an editor in the same city. Now the Stantons could take a long and leisurely vacation. Leaving their son Eddie behind in Washington, where he remained an officer in the War Department, and leaving the three younger children as well, Stanton and his wife arrived in Boston on the morning of August 16. Charles Sumner reported to a friend the next day that Stanton seemed "worn and indifferent to newspapers" and that "his wife does not wish him to see a newspaper." Stanton complained to Sumner that the "adjournment of Congress [was] a simple betrayal of the country to the President." The sooner Congress returned to work, the sooner the Senate could vote to overturn his suspension.[35]

Some of Stanton's friends thought that he should aim higher than the War Department, that he should aim at the White House. Francis Lieber wrote to a friend, "If Stanton were not so alarmingly void of ambition he could easily turn his semi-dismissal into a very proper lever to be lifted into the place where now the incorrigible trickster sits. . . . What a President he would make! And then the southerners hate him so delightfully. It makes one's mouth water." A western Republican agreed, writing in a public letter, "The magnificent fight [Stanton] is now making, single-handed and alone, against the President in behalf of the Union men of the South, is every day strengthening the hold he has upon the affections of the people." But most observers thought that Stanton had made too many enemies; they expected Grant to win the nomination and the election.[36]

Stanton probably did not hear these rumors, for he was with the Hoopers at their isolated beach house on Cape Cod. He wrote from there to Eddie, "Every day increases my satisfaction at being out of Johnson's administration and the mode of leaving it could not have been approved more highly." He even claimed that he would "probably pursue my professional designs and leave public cares to others." Nothing suggests, however, that he tried to resume his legal work during his suspension; it seems that he intended and expected the Senate to return him to his place in the War Department. A few days later Hooper wrote a friend in Boston to say that both Stantons were regaining their health and to ask whether he had a bottle of Murdock's cayenne pepper sauce, "the only thing [Stanton] needs here and now."[37]

Samuel Hooper, member of Congress from Massachusetts, perhaps Stanton's best friend in the last years of his life.

The Stantons and Hoopers traveled by boat one fine day to Naushon Island, visiting there with John Clifford, a former governor of Massachusetts. A few days later they took the ferry to Nantucket, where Stanton met some of his distant Macy cousins, relatives through his grandmother Abigail Macy Stanton. "We drove over to Siasconset and looked about the town," Hooper wrote, "so that we felt, at nine o'clock the next morning, when the steamer left, as if we knew as much about Nantucket as if we had been a month there." On their return, Hooper read to Stanton a letter from Sumner expressing doubts about Grant as a presidential candidate. Sumner "thought the cause could only be trusted to one who by life and profession was committed to our principles." Stanton "playfully remarked" to Hooper, "How verdant Sumner seems," in other words, how politically green. Sumner was quoted in the papers at this time calling the suspension of Stanton "a national calamity."[38]

The Stantons left Cape Cod on September 3 and spent a night or two in Boston with Woodman. A few days later Representative Elihu Washburne wrote his friend Grant that he was "astonished and pained" to learn from Sumner that Stanton had criticized Grant. Washburne reported that Stanton said that "there was no understanding or communication between you and him in regard to his removal and your assuming the Dept.—that the first he knew of anything in regard to the matter was your letter to him telling him you had been appointed &c—that he only yielded to you as the head of the army and that he would not have yielded to anyone else. He gave the impression that you were in collusion with the President to get him out." Stanton's comments, if Washburne relayed them rightly, suggest that he was annoyed with Grant; it is likely he assumed that Grant would communicate with him on department matters, would seek his advice. Stanton was probably especially puzzled that Grant did not consult with him before he yielded to Johnson's demands that he remove Sheridan as district commander. For whatever reason, Grant did not communicate with Stanton; the published Grant papers contain not one letter or telegram between the two men during the five months of Stanton's suspension.[39]

From Boston the Stantons traveled by train to St. Albans, Vermont, where they stayed with former governor Gregory Smith and his wife. Ann Smith later recalled that Stanton "ran across the garden like a boy, exclaiming 'how delightful the air is! I can breathe! See, I can breathe!'" While he stayed with the Smiths, Stanton "joked and laughed with the children, rode often with [their] young daughter in a single carriage, walked alone in the grove and garden." The local paper reported on September 13 that the governor and his wife opened their "handsome residence" one evening to "all who desired to call upon Mr. Stanton," who spoke "in very cautious terms of our national difficulties."[40]

The Stantons left St. Albans in mid-September and traveled to Burlington, Vermont, where they were greeted by Senator George Edmunds. Introducing Stanton to the crowd that had assembled, Edmunds said that he was "faithful to his country when faithless and treacherous men were all around him" and that he would "soon be restored" to his office. At the end of September, when the Stantons were visiting friends in Hoboken, New Jersey, Ellen opened a letter from Eddie, presumably reporting on politics, for he was still at the War Department. Ellen wrote back to Eddie that she had not shown the letter to his father, for "the least thing upsets him; and I do not see any use in troubling him about matters which he cannot attend to until he returns home. I think one interview with General Grant would do more to set matters right than all the letters that could be written."[41]

The Stantons spent the first week of October with Edwards Pierrepont at his magnificent mansion, Garrison, overlooking the Hudson River. Hooper reported to Sumner on October 8 that Stanton was back in Washington, "well and in good spirits—and says his health is much improved." A few days later, in the October elections, Ohio Republicans elected as governor Rutherford Hayes, but they lost control of the legislature and fell short in an effort to extend the right to vote to blacks. Senator John Sherman thought the black suffrage question was the "chief trouble" for Republicans. Senator Benjamin Wade, who would lose his seat because Republicans no longer controlled the legislature, was more blunt: "The nigger whipped us." In Pennsylvania, Democrats gained control of both houses of the legislature. Stanton, however, according to one Ohio paper did "not regard the recent elections as any serious disaster to the Union party."[42]

Stanton was soon in Ohio himself, traveling there to attend the wedding on October 16 of Lizzie Dennison, daughter of former governor William Dennison, with James Forsyth, chief of staff for General Sheridan. The wedding was held in Trinity Church, Columbus, where Stanton had met his first wife through Reverend William Preston, one of the ministers officiating at the Dennison-Forsyth wedding. Sheridan was among those present, and Stanton almost certainly talked with him privately about his time in the South and his current duties on the western frontier. Senator Sherman, seeing from the newspapers that Stanton was in Columbus, invited him to visit his home in nearby Mansfield. But it seems that Stanton went instead to Gambier to visit his mother and sister and see his alma mater Kenyon College. Eddie was with him on this visit, and "they enjoyed greatly roaming around the place connected with so many delightful recollections incidental to the college life of each."[43]

By early November, Stanton was visiting friends in Pittsburgh. (One hostile paper described him "vegetating" there without attracting any attention.) Democrats prevailed in the November elections in several states, including New York. As the results arrived, Democrats rejoiced and Republicans tried to look ahead to the next year. The *Nashville Union & Dispatch* opined that the elections were "a sweeping condemnation of every principle and every measure which the party in the majority in Congress . . . upheld or adopted." The *New York Times* argued that the elections made it clear Republicans should opt for Grant as their presidential nominee in the next year, for he was a moderate who could appeal to moderate Democrats. As one Republican put it in a letter to Schuyler Colfax, moderates would have to tell Radicals, "Thus far we have gone with you, but we cannot go any further. . . . You see the disasters which have happened to our cause in the fall elections, from adopting your views."[44]

Stanton arrived back in Washington just after the November elections, and within a few days he called at the War Department and "had a long interview with General Grant." Newspapers were already reporting that one of the first questions the Senate would have to consider when it returned to work in early December was whether to reinstate Stanton. The *Georgia Weekly Telegraph* commented bitterly that Stanton was "arranging with his friends for a conflict with President Johnson. He is determined, if possible, to force himself back into the position whence he was kicked out."[45]

Chapter 18

"Stand Firm!"

—— 1867–1868 ——

A s Republican leaders returned to Washington in November 1867 to prepare for the next session of Congress, Stanton talked with his congressional friends about his situation. The *New York Tribune* reported that he told several senators "he had no desire whatever to resume his position in the War Department, but he thought that Congress should take some action in the matter, and make his case a test one under the Tenure-of-Office bill, with a view to rebuke Mr. Johnson for his unwarrantable assumption of power." According to the *Washington Evening Star*, "Stanton has intimated to his friends that if reinstated by a vote of the Senate he should immediately resign, as he has no desire to again enter upon the duties of the War Office." Other papers had similar reports.[1]

The first order of business for Congress, however, was whether to impeach the president. Under the Constitution, impeachment is a two-stage process: the House of Representatives may charge, or "impeach," a federal official for "treason, bribery, or other high crimes and misdemeanors," but it is then up to the Senate to decide whether to convict and remove the official. Conviction requires a two-thirds vote of those present and voting in the Senate. In late November the House Judiciary Committee recommended that the full House impeach Johnson, citing as his crimes such actions as suspending Stanton and opposing the constitutional amendment on civil rights. After two days of intense debate, the first time the full House had ever considered impeaching a president, the House voted on December 7 against impeachment. More than sixty moderate Republicans joined forty Democrats in voting no. At least for the time being, the Radical crusade to impeach and remove Johnson had failed.[2]

Stanton did not have much time to consider these events because he learned on December 8 that his nephew David Stanton, the only son of his late brother Darwin, had died that day in Steubenville. Stanton immediately boarded a train and headed west. A brief obituary in the *Washington Evening Star*, almost certainly prepared by Stanton, stated that David, only twenty-seven when he died of tuberculosis, "met death with the calmness and hope of a Christian." Stanton stayed in Steubenville several days, doing what he could to allay "the deep affliction of Nancy Stanton and her daughters." While there he received a telegram from his son, reporting that Senator Jacob Howard, a senior Republican on the Military Affairs Committee, wanted Stanton back in Washington to help respond to Johnson's arguments as to why the Senate should not reinstate Stanton to his position. At least initially, Stanton was not inclined to help Howard in this process, writing back to his son, that the "question concerns the Senate and Country more than it does me." Stanton also thought that, if he returned to Washington, "Johnson's pensioned liars of the press" would "invent all manner of calumnies." Moreover his mother's health seemed "to be failing fast," and he would go to Gambier to see her. He added detailed directions on how his son should telegraph him without the message becoming part of the department's files.[3]

After visiting his mother and sister for a few days Stanton was back in Washington on December 22. By that time he had read Johnson's message about him, submitted to the Senate on December 12 and soon printed in full in the Ohio papers. Johnson explained that he and Stanton disagreed about reconstruction policy, notably the military reconstruction laws. Johnson admitted that a cabinet member could have different opinions than the president. "What I do claim," he continued, "is that the President is the responsible head of the Administration, and when the opinions of a head of Department are irreconcilably opposed to those of the President in grave matters of policy and administration, there is but one result which can solve the difficulty, and that is a severance of the official relation." Johnson criticized Stanton's "effrontery" in remaining in office even after he had demanded his resignation. Johnson claimed to be stunned that Stanton was now relying upon the Tenure of Office Act, because Stanton had insisted that the law was unconstitutional. And Johnson chastised Stanton for failing to give him the urgent telegram Stanton had received from Baird on the eve of the New Orleans riot, the telegram asking for immediate presidential instructions. This alone, Johnson argued, was sufficient reason why Stanton should not be his secretary of war.[4]

Reaction to Johnson's message divided on party lines, with Republicans opposing and Democrats supporting Johnson. The *New York World* argued that Stanton, by withholding the Baird message from Johnson, and then suggesting that Johnson was responsible for the New Orleans riot, had acted like a snake: "Stanton lay like a coiled reptile among the papers of the War Department, stealthily watching the swelling caused by his fangs. The serpent, having bitten in secret, slunk to his den. He had poisoned the public mind against Mr. Johnson, and if he also applied the antidote he would cancel his merit with the President's enemies."[5]

After Johnson's message, Stanton's fate was up to the Senate. If the Senate voted to concur with Johnson, the Tenure of Office Act provided that the president could remove Stanton and appoint a new secretary of war in his place. But if the Senate refused, the law provided that Stanton would "forthwith resume the functions of his office." Apparently, when he returned to Washington, Stanton changed his mind about helping Howard, for he drafted a long, point-by-point answer to Johnson's message. He did not claim in this document, he could not really claim, that he and Johnson worked well together, but Stanton said that he had always treated the president with proper respect. He admitted that he had opposed the Tenure of Office bill while it was under consideration in the cabinet, but the bill was now the law, and both Johnson and he were bound to follow the law. As to the charge that he had improperly failed to share Baird's telegram, Stanton insisted (not very persuasively) that there was nothing about the message that suggested he needed to show it to Johnson immediately. The real reason Johnson wanted to remove him, Stanton asserted, was that they disagreed about reconstruction. Here Stanton minced no words. After putting "a million men into the field" during the war, he was "unwilling to abandon the victory they had won, or to see the 'Lost Cause' restored over the graves of nearly four hundred thousand loyal soldiers, or to witness four million of freedmen subjected, for want of legal protection, to outrages upon their lives, persons, and property, and their race in danger of being returned to some newly invented bondage."[6]

It seems likely that Stanton shared this document with Howard, for parts of the draft were in the third person, as if he were drafting it as Howard. In any case, Howard's own long committee report, vindicating Stanton and attacking Johnson, appeared in newspapers on the evening of January 8. Welles complained to his diary that Howard had released the report to the press before getting his committee's approval or the Senate's permission. The Howard report denounced Johnson for his "open, violent antagonism to the will of the nation, as expressed by the two Houses of Congress, evincing at times a disposition . . . to disregard their legislation, and even to disperse them, and seize, if possible, the reins of absolute power." Stanton, on the other hand, "favored a faithful execution" of the congressional reconstruction laws. The Howard committee recommended that the Senate should not concur in the suspension of Stanton, in other words, that the Senate should restore Stanton at once to his post.[7]

After reading the Howard report and counting the substantial Republican majority in the Senate, even Johnson must have realized that the Senate would vote soon to reinstate Stanton. But Johnson had a plan. On January 11 he asked Grant to stay in office as interim secretary of war for a while after the Senate vote. This would give Johnson time to appoint a different interim secretary, or perhaps simply to prevent Stanton from entering the department and thus exercising his functions as secretary. Johnson later claimed that Grant agreed to this plan. Grant, however, insisted that he told Johnson he would not remain in office for even one hour after the Senate vote, for that would be a criminal violation of the

Tenure of Office Act. Some suspected it was Stanton himself who advised Grant of this legal risk.[8]

On this same day, the Senate started to debate behind closed doors whether it should return Stanton to the War Office. Fessenden warned Stanton that some senators believed that he had not done enough to free the Northern soldiers from Southern prisons. Stanton again took up his pen to defend himself, again writing in the third person, perhaps to make it easier for Fessenden to read aloud what Stanton wrote. "The official documents prove that from the first hour Mr. Stanton entered the War Department until the end of the war he was earnest, zealous, and unceasing in his efforts to provide for, relieve, and liberate our prisoners . . . and that the starvation and exposure of our prisoners in rebel mews was a deliberate, barbarous policy adopted to secure the overthrow of the United States government."[9]

The Senate spent six hours on January 13 debating whether to reinstate Stanton. Sadly, because this was an executive session, we do not have a record of the remarks. Stanton himself was perhaps present for part of the debate; one hostile newspaper reported that "Stanton was allowed in the Senate during the executive session, where he made any statement he chose, however false and scandalous." That evening the Senate voted in Stanton's favor: thirty-five senators supported him and only six Democratic senators sided with Johnson. Stanton was at his home when he received the official message from the Senate. He apparently spoke with Grant soon thereafter. There was still some question that night as to whether Stanton would be able to resume his duties; one reporter speculated that Johnson would try the next day to relieve Grant, appoint another officer as acting secretary, and thus force Stanton to go to federal court "to establish his claims."[10]

The handover the next day from Grant to Stanton was seamless. Grant went to the secretary's office in the morning, locked the door, then walked across the street to his other office, the office of the commanding general of the army. From there Grant sent a letter to Johnson, saying that his duties as interim secretary "ceased from the moment" he had received official notice of the Senate's vote. Not long after Grant left the War Department, Stanton and his son arrived. Finding the door locked, Stanton sent an aide across the street to retrieve the key, meanwhile chatting with some members of Congress who were present. One paper said Stanton "appeared to be in unusually fine spirits." Returning with the key, the aide "in a sort of 'present arms' style, delivered it up to Secretary Stanton." Some sources (notably a letter from Sherman) suggest that Grant was annoyed at the abrupt way Stanton resumed office, but there was no hint of this in the news reports. When Grant arrived at the secretary's office later that morning, presumably to discuss some of the issues Stanton would have to handle now that Grant was no longer interim secretary, Stanton "shook the General warmly by the hand." Another paper said "their intercourse was as pleasant and cordial as it always has been" and that at day's end Stanton "sent for General Grant and they rode home together."[11]

Stanton was back in his usual office, doing his usual work, but there were questions about whether he should stay. The *New York Times*, although a Republican paper, suggested he should resign. "Is it worth Mr. Stanton's while," the editors asked, "to insist upon a right which brings with it no lasting honor, and in the present circumstances is not likely to afford much room for official usefulness?" Stanton wrote to Pamphila that it had been his firm plan to resign, and that his wife was "vehement against [his] remaining," but that Republican members of Congress insisted he stay. Radical senators may well have insisted that Stanton stay in office, but moderate senators might have been annoyed, believing he had essentially promised that he would resign as soon as the Senate asserted its rights by putting him back in the War Department.[12]

Why, then, did Stanton remain in office in January 1868? He did not have many friends in Washington, but to the extent that he had any, they were Radical Republicans such as Sumner. Stanton now agreed with Sumner that Johnson's reconstruction policies would result in the loss of freedom for Southern blacks, indeed in some cases in the loss of their lives in white-on-black violence. The only way to prevent this was with the continued presence of the army, under the War Department, under Stanton. Sumner put this view well in a letter to a British friend: "Stanton will continue in his office, if the Senate desire. Thus far the opinion is strong that he should stay. His presence there will prevent the employment of the influence and opportunities of this office on the side of the Rebellion. [Andrew Johnson] is now a full-blown rebel, except that he does not risk his neck by overt acts; but in spirit he is as bad as [Jefferson Davis]." Some Radicals may have hoped that, by keeping Stanton in office, they might tempt Johnson to violate the Tenure of Office Act by removing him and thereby gain a way to impeach and remove Johnson. Stanton may have shared these hopes.[13]

As Stanton settled back into his office, Johnson and Grant engaged in a public quarrel. One issue in this tussle was whether Grant had really agreed, as the president insisted, that he would remain in office for a period even after the Senate voted to reinstate Stanton. Another question was whether Grant should, as Johnson requested, ignore Stanton's orders. Grant asked Johnson to put this unusual request in writing, and Johnson did so, instructing Grant "not to obey any order from the War Department, assumed to be issued by the direction of the President, unless such order is known, by the General, to have been authorized by the Executive." Grant shared this letter with Stanton and replied to Johnson the next day. "I am informed by the Secretary of War that he has not received from the Executive any order or instructions limiting or impairing his authority to issue orders to the Army as has heretofore been his practice under the law, and the customs of the Department." Unless Johnson issued such an order, Grant would continue to honor Stanton's orders. By the end of January, Stanton was secure in his position: he did not attend Johnson's cabinet meetings, knowing that he would be unwelcome, but the army and his cabinet colleagues were treating him as secretary of war, and that was what mattered most to him.[14]

—————

Almost every evening, however long the day, Stanton found a few minutes to read Dickens. He had first read Dickens as a young man, when the early novels appeared in serial form in the newspapers, and he was still reading and rereading him thirty years later. The famous author himself was in the United States during the winter of 1867 and 1868, reading aloud from his books to packed houses in Boston, New York, Philadelphia, and Baltimore. This was not a modern book tour, in which the author makes money through book sales; this was a lecture series, with thousands of tickets sold in each city, and Dickens taking a substantial share. Dickens arrived in Washington on February 1, and on the next day he broke his usual rule against dining with Americans in order to dine with Sumner, whom he knew from the senator's days in London. Knowing of Stanton's love of Dickens's work, Sumner invited him to the dinner. In a letter Dickens described Stanton as "a man of a very remarkable memory, and famous for his acquaintance with the minutest details of my books. Give him any passage anywhere, and he will instantly cap it and go on with the context. He was commander-in-chief of all the northern forces concentrated here, and never went to sleep at night without first reading something from my books, which were always with him. I put him through a pretty severe examination, but he was better up than I was." Always looking for material, Dickens asked Stanton and Sumner about the night that Lincoln died. Stanton described how Lincoln's breathing in his last hours "sounded like an Aeolian harp, now rising, now falling and almost dying," and "reminded him of what he had noticed in the case of one of his children, who had died in his arms shortly before." Stanton also told Dickens that, at the last Lincoln cabinet meeting, the president said he had had a dream similar to that which he had had before major battles, a dream in which he was in a small boat drifting, just drifting, on a huge river. On this, the last day of his life, Stanton told the somewhat dubious Dickens, the late president told his cabinet that "something very extraordinary is going to happen."[15]

Stanton continued through the first weeks of February to handle the routine work of the War Department. Then, on February 21, at about noon, Adjt. Gen. Lorenzo Thomas arrived at Stanton's office. Thomas, a decade older than Stanton, tall and thin, was a career army officer, with more experience behind a desk than out in the field. When Stanton had first arrived in the department in early 1862, Thomas as adjutant general was responsible for all the paperwork regarding appointments, promotions, and transfers. Stanton disliked Thomas, perhaps because he was a lifelong bureaucrat, perhaps because he had a drinking problem. A friend later recalled Stanton saying that he would "pick Lorenzo Thomas up with a pair of tongs and drop him from the nearest window." Another source quoted Stanton as saying that Thomas was "only fit for presiding over a crypt of Egyptian mummies like himself." Stanton, as we have seen, sent Thomas to the Mississippi Valley to recruit black soldiers, effectively making the capable, dutiful Edward Townsend his adjutant general. More recently Stanton had sent Thomas out on a tour to inspect the new national cemeteries. So relations between the two men were not good, and they were about to get much worse.[16]

After preliminary greetings, Thomas handed Stanton a letter from Johnson: the president removed Stanton from office immediately and directed him to turn over all official papers and property to Thomas, who would be the interim secretary of war. Stanton asked Thomas if he could have some time to remove his personal property from his office. Thomas, politely if imprudently, told him, "Act your pleasure." Then Thomas handed Stanton a second letter from the president, addressed to Thomas, appointing him interim secretary. Stanton asked for a copy of this letter and Thomas went out to have a clerk make the copy. When Thomas returned, Stanton told him that he did not "know whether I will obey your instructions or resist them."[17]

But it seems that Stanton had already decided to resist. When Thomas went into the next room to tell two other officers that he was now the interim secretary, Stanton followed him and "directed them not to obey any orders coming from [Thomas] as Secretary of War." Stanton soon followed up with a letter, warning Thomas that his purported orders as secretary were "illegal." He also sent messengers to Congress to inform his friends there of Johnson's attempt to dismiss him. The *New York Times* reported the next day that Johnson's bold action, in plain violation of the Tenure of Office Act, struck Congress "like a thunderbolt." Both houses of Congress dropped their other work and started to debate how to respond; the House worked on an impeachment resolution, while the Senate drafted a resolution expressing its views. As the afternoon turned into evening, Stanton received a stream of visitors and messages from Capitol Hill. The most famous was a single syllable from Sumner: "Stick!" Representative Boutwell hoped Stanton would "hold the office yielding only to force actual and present." Senator Howard wrote, "If force is employed against you, . . . repel it. Stand firm!"[18]

Stanton knew he needed support not only from Congress but also from the army. He probably heard the rumors, reported in the papers, that Johnson would order Grant to remove him by force. Stanton asked Grant for troops to guard the department, troops that would report to Stanton and would remain "until relieved by my order." He added, "I would be glad to see you at the War Department at as early an hour as convenient this evening." Grant may or may not have visited Stanton (it was not reported in the papers), but he did send the troops as requested.[19]

At about eight that evening, Stanton heard that Thomas was "boasting at the hotels that he intends to take possession of the War Department at 9 o'clock" the following day. Stanton immediately wrote to Senators Howard and Fessenden, pleading, "If the Senate does not declare their opinion of the law how am I to hold possession?" An hour later he had the opinion he wanted: the Senate resolved that the president "has no power to remove the Secretary of War and designate any other officer to perform the duties of that office." Stanton now had the official as well as the unofficial support of Congress.[20]

Stanton loads Congress, in the form of a cannon, against Andrew Johnson and Lorenzo Thomas. The rammer in Stanton's hands is the "Tenure of Office Bill."

Stanton's office was crowded that night with generals and congressmen, as well as his friend Bishop Matthew Simpson, who was in Washington midway through a rail journey. Stanton likely heard from one or more of his visitors that Thomas was at a masked ball, drinking and celebrating, bragging about how he would take control of the department in the morning. Stanton was not drinking; he was working, drafting an affidavit to charge Thomas with violating the law by falsely asserting that he was secretary of war. Stanton signed the affidavit at about one in the morning and handed it to his friend David Cartter, the chief judge of the local courts, who was in Stanton's office and immediately issued a warrant for Thomas's arrest. Others went home, but Senator John Thayer of Nebraska, a former Union general, stayed through the night. Thayer later wrote that, as soon as they were alone, Stanton asked him to go out and visit with Gen. Eugene Carr, commanding the troops. Stanton wanted to know whose authority Carr would recognize. Carr told Thayer "that he regarded Mr. Stanton as the lawful Secretary of War." Reassured, Thayer settled on a sofa to sleep for a few hours, but Stanton himself did not sleep at all on that tense night.[21]

Some of Stanton's friends returned the next morning and joined him while he ate a modest breakfast sent from his home. He heard reports of how marshals arrested Thomas at his home at about eight in the morning and escorted him to Cartter's courtroom, where the judge released him on bail of $5,000. Not long thereafter Thomas, tired and hungry and hungover, arrived at Stanton's office. Stanton was meeting with several members of Congress, one of whom jotted down the conversation:

Thomas: I am the Secretary of War *ad interim*, and am ordered by the President of the United States to take charge of this office.

Stanton: I order you to repair to your room, and exercise your office as adjutant-general.

Thomas: I am the Secretary of War *ad interim*, and I shall not obey your orders; but I shall obey the order of the President to take charge of this office.

Stanton: As Secretary of War, I order you to repair to your office as adjutant-general.

Thomas: I shall not do so.

Stanton: Then you may stand there, if you please, but you will attempt to act as Secretary of War at your peril.

Thomas: I *shall* act as Secretary of War.[22]

Thomas walked across the hall and into the office of Edmund Schriver, one of the assistant adjutant generals. Stanton followed and closed the door. Thomas later testified that he said to Stanton, "The next time you have me arrested, please do not do it before I get something to eat. I said I had had nothing to eat or drink that day. He put his hand around my neck, as he sometimes does, and ran his hand through my hair, and turned around to General Schriver and said 'Schriver, you have got a bottle here, bring it out.'" When this bottle proved to be almost empty, Stanton sent for another. Pouring a glass of whiskey for each of them, Stanton said to Thomas, "Now this, at least, is neutral ground." The two men drank and talked and relaxed. Stanton asked Thomas when he would have his report about the national cemeteries, as he was anxious for it to be printed and distributed. Townsend later wrote that this seemed to him to be "a lawyer's ruse to make Thomas acknowledge Stanton's authority." Thomas soon left the department, for the moment at least, thwarted.[23]

Stanton knew of course that his real adversary was not Lorenzo Thomas but Andrew Johnson. And Stanton was aware of the possibility of violent clashes. The nation, after all, was filled with thousands of veterans, some loyal to Johnson, some loyal to Congress and Stanton. The *New York Herald* reported that if Johnson tried to use force to eject Stanton from the War Department, "100,000 men [were] ready to come to Washington and put him back." Townsend recalled that Stanton gave a secret order to yield the department building if necessary; "he would not have blood shed on his account, and if an assault on the building were attempted, he would not try to repel it." This was a *secret* order, because Stanton did not want to encourage Johnson to seize the building and evict him from his office.[24]

At some point over this tense weekend, Stanton sent his aide Louis Koerth to the Stanton home for blankets and pillows. Ellen Stanton refused to provide any help. Koerth recalled that she told him bluntly that

Stanton should just come home himself. When Koerth reported back, Stanton sent him instead to the Koerth house to gather up what they would need to "camp out" at the War Department. Koerth remembered that Stanton was not a very good cook; he tried and failed to prepare on a small stove an Irish stew for the two of them to share.[25]

On Monday, February 24 the House of Representatives resumed its debate on the impeachment resolution; by the end of the day it had voted, by an overwhelming margin, to impeach the president. On Tuesday, in a packed Senate chamber, Representatives John Bingham and Thaddeus Stevens presented the impeachment resolution to the Senate. They did not yet present the details, for the House had not yet drafted or voted on charges, but they promised the specifics "in due time." Stanton instructed his lawyers to drop the criminal charges against Thomas, explaining that it would be "needless" to prosecute the subordinate when the principal would face charges in the Senate. Stanton did not want to give Johnson a chance to fight these issues through the case against Thomas in the usual court system; Stanton wanted to force Johnson to defend himself in the Senate impeachment trial.[26]

———

In one sense Stanton was at the center of the impeachment process, for the key question was whether Johnson's attempt to remove him from office was a crime, a "high crime or misdemeanor" sufficient to justify the Senate in removing the president from office. Stanton's name was thus in every newspaper almost every day. Yet in another sense Stanton was isolated from the impeachment process, ensconced in the War Department while the House lawyers prepared their charges and Johnson's lawyers prepared their defenses. Welles wrote to his son Edgar, "This ridiculous conduct makes Stanton a laughing stock. He eats, sleeps, and stays cooped in his entrenched and fortified establishment—scarcely daring to look out the window. . . . Radical senators & representatives go, and sleep & eat with him in the War Department, all his meals being sent there." But that was Johnson and Welles's view of Stanton; the Republican view was that Stanton was defending the fort against an out-of-control president. "God bless you," wrote one of Stanton's many supporters.[27]

The Senate during the impeachment trial of Johnson. Stanton never saw this scene, for he remained in the War Department, even though the attempted removal of Stanton was the central charge against Johnson.

Of course Stanton was not neutral in the impeachment battle; he wanted the Senate to convict and remove Johnson from office. The New Hampshire spring election, just after the House impeached the president, was viewed as a referendum on impeachment. When the Republicans defeated the Democrats, Stanton's former client Dan Sickles wrote from Concord, "New Hampshire sustains you by a decided majority." Stanton wrote warmly to Sickles and to another friend in New Hampshire that the voters there had shown the "precious lives of their brethren were not sacrificed in vain and that enough are left to resist usurpation and prevent the restoration of the rebellion." When retired general Benjamin Butler, one of the House members responsible for presenting the case against Johnson in the Senate, needed help compiling a list of all the federal officers subject to removal by the president, he turned to Stanton. "We would make it up but have not the clerical force at our disposal," Butler explained. Stanton, apparently not troubled by using federal employees to help convict the president, had his staff work over the weekend to compile the information for Butler.[28]

During the first weeks of his isolation in the War Department, Stanton's relations with his wife were strained. He wrote to her in early March, "I have longed much to see you during the past week, but knowing your aversion to the War Office, I have not asked you to come while hoping that love might draw you hither. If in a moment of disappointment and suffering I said anything to occasion you pain, or do you injustice, I humbly crave your forgiveness." When he learned of the death of Bishop Simpson's son, Stanton wrote him a kind note: "To you I will not presume to offer consolation, for you know better than I whence it can come; but I hope it will not be regarded as intrusive for me to ask to share your sorrow." As the weeks passed and it became clear that Johnson and Thomas were not going to attempt to seize the department building by force, Stanton began to venture outside, even spending a few evenings at home. On the first of May he wrote from home to his mother-in-law in Pittsburgh. "The impeachment case has not advanced much," adding that she was lucky to leave Washington when she did for she would have "been talked to death or choked with disgust." Stanton could not of course resign now; his presence in the War Department was the basis of the impeachment charges against Johnson. But Stanton also did not have much work to do as war secretary since the only war was in Washington, over whether the Senate should convict and remove Johnson from office.[29]

While Stanton stayed night after night in the department, political friends talked about other possible positions for him. Francis Lieber wrote to a friend that Grant would receive the Republican presidential nomination, but it was really Stanton who deserved it: "As for Stanton he is simply a brick, but we cannot get him for president, though he is by far the fittest of them all." Edwards Pierrepont wrote to Stanton from New York, "Important negotiations are to be carried on in England which need an able lawyer as minister from the United States. Now I write to know whether *you* will take that place? I think you would like it, and the change of climate and all would put the secretary in good health." At almost this same time, a group of Pennsylvania Republicans wrote to Senator Simon Cameron, saying, "The demoralized condition of the Treasury Department, resulting from the mal-administration of Andrew Johnson, requires for its purification some of the high characteristics exhibited by Mr. Stanton, in the suppression of the rebellion." Stanton responded through Cameron, "Enough of my life has been devoted to public duties. No consideration can induce me to assume those of the Treasury Department, or continue in the War Department longer than may be required for the appointment of my successor." Both letters soon made their way into the newspapers.[30]

There was at least one public duty Stanton would have gladly accepted: justice of the Supreme Court. There was already one vacancy on the Court, and Stanton's old friend Justice Robert Grier had suffered several small strokes and had likely talked with Stanton about taking his place. The only way Stanton could receive *any* of these appointments was from a Republican president, but there would probably be such a president soon. Since there was no vice president, Republican Benjamin Wade, as president pro tem of the Senate, would become the next president if the Senate removed Johnson. Even if Johnson was not removed, it seemed more and more likely that Grant would be elected in November and take office in early 1869.[31]

Everyone understood from the outset that President Johnson, to avoid conviction and removal from office, would have to recruit several Republican senators to his side. Fessenden, though Stanton's friend and former cabinet colleague, was one of the senators often mentioned as likely to vote with Johnson, and Stanton, it seemed, joined the effort to persuade him to vote against the president. In late March, Stanton sent Fessenden a warm thank-you letter for some Senate remarks. A few days later he sent another letter, this time to Fessenden's son Frank, offering him a choice position on a claims commission. In late April, however, Stanton was "furious" to learn that Fessenden and others planned to vote for Johnson, "declaring that such men as Fessenden, Trumbull, Grimes and Sherman had gone back on him." John Russell Young, an editor of the *New York Tribune*, after visiting with Stanton in Washington, wrote an article saying that any Republican senator who voted with Johnson would "be guilty of a treason only equaled by that of Benedict Arnold." Young sent a copy of this article to Stanton, explaining in his cover letter that it would "help prepare the minds of our party for the sentence we must pronounce upon any senator who proves recreant." Stanton agreed, writing back, "The hour of judgment is nigh at hand and should the great criminal be condemned the national deliverance will be due to you more than to anyone else." Stanton had not heard "that Fessenden and Trumbull have shown any improvement, but it is believed there will be enough to convict without them."[32]

One way Johnson reached out to moderate Republican senators was through the nomination in late April of John Schofield as secretary of war. Schofield, a West Point graduate, had a long if not great record in the Civil War, and after the war went to France on a special diplomatic mission for Seward. Neither Johnson nor the Radicals especially liked Schofield, but that was perhaps what made him a good compromise candidate. And if the Senate acquitted Johnson and confirmed Schofield, it would end the absurdity of having two secretaries of war: Stanton in the War Department, with no contact with the president, and Lorenzo Thomas from time to time at the White House, with no contact with the army. The Senate would not take up the Schofield nomination while it was debating whether to convict and remove Johnson, but many papers saw the nomination as a signal that if acquitted Johnson would work with moderates in a sensible way.[33]

Starting in late April, the Senate heard closing arguments for and against Johnson. Thaddeus Stevens, within weeks of his death and visibly weak, praised Stanton's work: "None ever organized an army of a million of men and provided for its subsistence and efficient action more rapidly than Mr. Stanton. . . . When victory crowned his efforts, he disbanded that immense army as quietly and peacefully as if it had been a summer parade." William Groesbeck, one of Johnson's lawyers, argued that Johnson had only tried to "pluck a thorn out of his very heart," the thorn of Stanton. "You fastened it there," Groesbeck reminded the senators, "and you are now asked to punish him for attempting to extract it." As the arguments continued day after day into early May, the future president James Garfield commented that Washington was "wading knee deep in words, words, words."[34]

The Senate scheduled its first vote on impeachment for May 12. On that day, however, Senator Jacob Howard was too sick to attend, and rather than vote without one of their key members, the Republicans delayed for a few days. Stanton wrote to John Russell Young, "Those who are well advised think the success of the impeachment certain. I have no reason for a different opinion as matters now stand." Browning wrote in his diary that he feared the delay would lead to conviction: "Enough may be bought or dragooned into obedience to secure conviction." Stanton drafted and signed a resignation letter, which he intended to deliver if Johnson was acquitted. On Saturday, May 16, a warm spring afternoon in Washington, Stanton was in his office in the War Department while the Senate, at the other end of Pennsylvania Avenue, voted on the article the Republicans thought most likely to pass, the eleventh, the catch-all article of impeachment. Stanton received the news by telegraph: thirty-five senators had voted "guilty" and nineteen had voted "not guilty." Because there was not a two-thirds majority, Johnson had escaped, for now. Among the Republicans who voted for Johnson were Stanton's friends Fessenden and Trumbull. Stanton wrote to Young that he was "sad and disappointed but not disheartened or discouraged and feel like continuing the fight to the bitter end." It seemed likely that the bitter end would come in about ten days, for the Senate had adjourned until May 26. This was, in part, to allow time for the Republicans to attend their national convention in Chicago, set for the intervening week, and in part to allow time for Butler and his committee to investigate charges of corruption in the Senate vote. Perhaps Butler could find enough evidence in ten days to persuade some senator, fearful of exposure, to change his vote. If so, if Johnson was removed from office, Stanton would presumably have the right to remain as secretary under President Wade. Whether Stanton *would* remain in office under Wade—that was a question for another day.[35]

On May 21 Stanton learned by telegram that the Republican convention had nominated Grant for president. One of Grant's aides recalled that Stanton raced across Seventeenth Street to Grant's office, "panting for breath lest someone should precede him." The papers of the day did not report this, however, mentioning only that Stanton was among those who relayed the news to the general, who "received the intelligence very quietly." Stanton's Indiana friend Schuyler Colfax had received the vice presidential nomination, and later in the day, in his own office, Stanton "expressed his warm approval of both nominations." He hoped that Grant would be elected both because he was now a committed Republican and because he thought, given their long and close relationship, that

Grant would either keep him as war secretary or find another suitable position for him, perhaps on the Supreme Court.[36]

Butler published a preliminary report on his investigation on Monday, May 25, suggesting but by no means proving that some senators had received bribes in return for their votes for Johnson. That night and the next morning, it was unclear whether the Senate would vote on impeachment on Tuesday or would delay yet longer. Some Radicals wanted further delay, for perhaps another four weeks, but many moderates wanted to finish the process one way or the other. In the end, the Senate voted Tuesday afternoon on two different impeachment articles. Not a single senator changed his vote, so Johnson was acquitted on both counts. The House lawyers then abandoned their effort, and the Senate adjourned the impeachment court. When he heard the news, Stanton drafted a new letter to Johnson. He did not resign but instead informed Johnson, "I have relinquished charge of the Department," leaving it in the care of Townsend. Stanton assumed the senators would now confirm Schofield as secretary of war, as they did within a few days. Stanton walked out of his office, down the steps, out the front door, and headed home.[37]

Townsend visited the Stanton home that evening and recalled that Stanton, exhausted, said he "could not be expected to make any further sacrifice for the possession of the office." It would appear that, during the few remaining months of his life, Stanton never again visited the War Department, where he had spent almost every day and many nights for six long years.[38]

Chapter 19

"Final Charge"

— 1868–1869 —

S tanton's enemies rejoiced to see him finally out of the War Department. The *New York Herald* reported from Washington that Stanton was "arranging his affairs with a view to an early departure from the scene of his inglorious defeat." Welles claimed that Stanton left office "without respect except on the part of ignorant and knavish partisans." Welles had never liked Stanton, and now, after six years together in the cabinet, he hated him, describing him in his diary as "imperious to inferiors and abject to superiors, given to duplicity, with a taste for intrigue." Stanton's "administration of the War Department cost the country unnecessarily untold millions of money and the loss of thousands of lives." Others disagreed. On the day after Stanton left office, Senator George Edmunds proposed a resolution to thank him for his great service. During the Senate debate on this resolution, Simon Cameron, Stanton's predecessor in the War Department, claimed credit for Stanton's appointment, asserting that it was he who had persuaded Lincoln to appoint Stanton. Senator Oliver Morton, the wartime governor of Indiana, declared that Stanton had worked eighteen hours out of every twenty-four. Senator William Fessenden said he was glad to vote for the resolution because some might have misinterpreted his vote against impeachment as a vote against his friend Stanton. The Senate approved the resolution by a vote of 35 to 11, and the House joined with a similarly strong vote.[1]

Stanton left the department in the midst of the 1868 election, one of the most vicious and violent in American history. Democrats attacked Republican reconstruction policies, arguing that the army should be withdrawn from the Southern states so that Southerners could once again govern themselves—meaning Southern *whites* should govern Southern *blacks*. Frank Blair, the Democratic candidate for vice president, declared that Republicans had "put under foot all the people of our race in ten of the Southern States, they have bound a million of people to the earth with their bayonets, and they have put on top of them this hideous black barbarism." Democrats, in the words of the *Ohio Statesman*, were against "the retention of the standing army in the South, to enforce Negro Suffrage" and "in favor of sending the army to the frontiers to defend the settlers, white men, white women, and white children now being scalped by the merciless savages." The need for a stronger frontier defense was a common theme in this campaign. In Texas the *Galveston News* declared that any president or secretary of war or general "who fails to know all about the wants of the frontier and to do all in his power for its safety, is more unfit for his position than if he could neither read nor write." Democrats did not limit their attacks to speeches and articles. In Georgia a white mob, headed by the local sheriff, broke up a black Republican election rally, then hunted down the attendees, killing about a dozen people. In Louisiana a similar mob destroyed the offices of a Republican newspaper and attacked blacks throughout the parish, killing perhaps two hundred. In South Carolina white men shot and killed several black state legislators, one of them while he was standing just outside the county courthouse.[2]

Stanton did not especially want to get involved in this campaign. When some newspapers speculated that he might become the next senator from Pennsylvania, he wrote his friend John Russell Young that he would not be a candidate "under any circumstances," that no "public or official station presents any temptation—I covet only rest, and the restoration of health to pursue my profession." But he shared the view of other Republicans that if the Democrats prevailed and attempted to reverse reconstruction, they would start another civil war. And he was concerned that the Democrats *might* prevail through a combination of violence in the South and persuasion in the North. In early August newspapers reported that Stanton would campaign in the Midwest for Grant and other Republican candidates. One paper observed, "His friends are sure that he will occupy a place in Grant's cabinet." Stanton probably considered this possibility; he was perhaps encouraged by an early September letter from Senator Roscoe Conkling of New York, writing that Grant had spoken to him about Stanton with a "strong feeling of friendship." But the main reason Stanton campaigned was that he believed in the Republican cause.[3]

THE RADICAL PARTY ON A HEAVY GRADE.

"The Radical Party on a Heavy Grade." An anti-Grant cartoon from 1868 shows Grant struggling to carry the party. Stanton, Butler, and Sumner are among the Radicals whom Grant cannot lift up the slope.

Stanton's first priority was his home state of Ohio, where congressional elections were set for October 13 and several Republican members of Congress were in close contests with their Democratic challengers. As Stanton packed his bags to head for Ohio he wrote another letter to Young. He was pleased to learn that the *New York Tribune* was sending a reporter to cover his speeches, but he hoped it would be someone "reliable," explaining, "There will be great disposition to pervert and misrepresent what I may say." Stanton was not yet sure of his itinerary—that would "depend upon my health when I reach the West"—but he planned to speak in at least Pittsburgh, Steubenville, Dayton, and Cleveland. He claimed that he had not yet prepared any speeches, that he would "talk to the occasion and audience as may appear proper at the time."[4]

Stanton reached his hometown of Steubenville in ill health, for the train trip had aggravated his asthma. He spent some time at the Union Cemetery, visiting the grave of his first wife, Mary, and told friends that he wanted to be buried there himself, next to her. The weather was wet, so he had to speak indoors, at Kilgore Hall, which was packed with people in the early afternoon of September 25. One of those in the audience later recalled being shocked by Stanton's appearance: "Was that feeble tottering man the giant who had borne on his shoulders the weight of the greatest rebellion the world had ever known?" Stanton did not even have the strength to stand to deliver his speech; he spoke mainly from a chair, although he did rise from time to time to make key points.[5]

Stanton started his speech by describing this as a vital election, upon which could turn the "choice of peace or of war, of domestic tranquility or civil discord, freedom or slavery, in short of all the blessings that can follow good government, or the evils that bad government can inflict upon the human race." This year was much like 1864, when just as "Sherman and his army were forcing their way over the fortifications and entrenchments at Atlanta, the [Democratic] convention at Chicago declared the war to be a failure, and demanded the cessation of hostilities." The voters in 1864 had rallied around the American flag and supported President Lincoln, and they should now rally around the flag again and support General Grant. Stanton reminded the audience that Frank Blair had been nominated at the recent Democratic convention by William Preston, a former rebel general, and seconded by Nathan Bedford Forrest, another rebel general, infamous for the Fort Pillow massacre. "If there is any man among you that would compel the armies of the Potomac, of the James, of the Ohio, of the Cumberland, of the Tennessee and of the Gulf to be again gathered at the tap of the drum and surrendered as prisoners of war to Lee and Johnston, Beauregard and Forrest and Preston, let him vote against General Grant."[6]

Stanton emphasized the financial aspects of the war and the election: "When the rebellion broke out the treasury was empty, its arms and magazines had been plundered, and there was no means to carry on the war."

But the Union government and the Northern people "were equal to the emergency. By the purchase of bonds and current notes enough money was raised to meet the emergencies of the war." The government borrowed from the people to pay for the war: for salaries of the soldiers and sailors, for their arms and ammunition, for their food and clothing and shelter, for their transportation, and for all the other necessary expenses. Now, Stanton argued, the Democrats wanted to repudiate the war debt incurred to save the Union. Why? "Mindful of the uncertainty of war and that the public credit and public faith was a cornerstone that upheld the country against rebellion, it is deemed proper to destroy the public debt by repudiation, to smooth the way for the restoration of the Lost Cause."[7]

As Stanton hoped, this Steubenville speech was printed in many major newspapers, including the *Chicago Tribune*, the *Cincinnati Enquirer*, the *New York Herald*, the *New York Times*, the *New York Tribune*, the *Philadelphia Evening Telegraph*, and the *Pittsburgh Commercial*. On September 27 he wrote to his wife from Steubenville that because of his poor health his "political labors [were] over." Although he had "scores of invitations," he assured her that he would "make no more speeches." A few days later, however, on October 1, he wrote Senator Zachariah Chandler that during the next week, he would speak in four different Ohio congressional districts: those of John Bingham, Robert Schenck, Columbus Delano, and William Lawrence. "On the eighth I expect to be at Cleveland," he added, and he could then decide upon dates to speak in Michigan, as Chandler hoped he would. Why the change of plans? Perhaps there was no change; Stanton may have written his wife what he knew she would want to hear, as many men have over the years. Perhaps with his health a bit better and the congressional races too close to call, Stanton believed that his duty was to continue the campaign.[8]

On October 2 he addressed twenty thousand people at Carlisle, Ohio, supporting the Republican candidate Robert Schenck, the general who had been so involved in the Maryland election. Schenck's opponent was Clement Vallandigham, the former member of Congress whom Burnside had arrested and Lincoln had exiled. Stanton did not mention Vallandigham by name, but he contrasted opponents of the war with Schenck's unwavering support for it. "Were you not in favor of the war?" he asked his audience. "Were not the people of this district in its favor?

Were not the people of this country in its favor? Why, if you were not, did you send forth from eight to ten thousand of your sons or fathers, of the best blood of this district, to the field of battle?" Schenck was also in favor of paying the war debt. "Is there any man, opposed to paying the war debt, that didn't oppose the war debt in the beginning? And why did they oppose the war debt? Because without money the war could not go on." Addressing the Irish and German immigrants in the audience, Stanton argued that Schenck supported programs that would help immigrants, such as the homestead legislation to open up western lands.[9]

Stanton spoke at Cleveland on October 8 to an audience estimated at more than 50,000. According to one report he started by saying that "ill health" would prevent him from saying more than a few words as to why they all "should rally around the flag held this day by Grant and Colfax." Stanton quoted from Lincoln's speech at Gettysburg: "We are engaged in a great civil war to see if a nation dedicated to the proposition that all men are free, can endure." Stanton asked whether the Union soldiers who died at Gettysburg had died in vain. "No, no," voices cried from the crowd. "Let us here," he continued, "every one of us, with uplifted hands declare before God that the gift of this great heritage consecrated in the blood of our soldiers shall never perish from the earth." He raised his hand and said "I swear," and many members of the audience did the same.[10]

Stanton gave at least one more speech in Ohio on the eve of the state election, at Circleville, and it is possible that there were others that were not covered in the newspapers. The congressional elections in Ohio in October 1868 were very close. Republican candidates generally prevailed, but by narrow margins. Robert Schenck, for example, beat Vallandigham by only 475 votes out of more than 30,000 cast in the third district. John Bingham, one of the leaders of the House impeachment team, won his district by just 416 votes out of more than 26,000. So Stanton's time was not wasted; his speeches and his mere presence likely tipped some of these close contests in favor of the Republicans.[11]

It was probably just after the October election that he stopped for a few days to see his mother and sister. Pamphila later recalled that she was "shocked" by her brother's appearance, that she "did not see how one in his condition could make the journey, must less speak on a public platform." A few days later Stanton arrived in Cincinnati, where he argued a federal patent case for two days before a circuit court composed of Justice Noah Swayne, of the U.S. Supreme Court, and Judge Humphrey Leavitt, his old friend from the Ohio District Court. Stanton was thus, to an extent at least, resuming his legal as well as political work. On October 24, somewhat to the surprise of his hometown, he returned to Steubenville. There was another election coming, the presidential election, set for November 3. In a second Steubenville speech Stanton urged his Republican friends to return to the battlefield, to vote for Grant: "Let every man be there to take his part and bear his share to gain the final crushing victory, let no true man be able to look back and say he was absent from the final charge, in which the triumph of our glorious cause, and the election of Grant and Colfax, was assured."[12]

Stanton spoke in Pittsburgh and then in Philadelphia just before the presidential election. In addition to praising Grant, he attacked the Democratic candidate, Horatio Seymour, the wartime governor of New York. In recent speeches Seymour had questioned why the War Department rather than the Navy Department had handled military transport during the war. Stanton mocked Seymour's question: it was the responsibility of the War Department to transport soldiers, whether by land or by sea. "How great is the ignorance of this man in relation to affairs military and naval! And yet this man his party would elect as the next Commander-in-Chief." Seymour and his supporters had also been citing some of the telegrams that Stanton, in the midst of the Gettysburg crisis, had sent to thank Seymour for raising militia and sending them to Pennsylvania. These telegrams, Stanton now said, "meant nothing." Seymour had been compelled to raise the troops by the crisis. That Seymour was "not in hearty and loyal accord with the government" was proven by his actions during the draft riots, when the governor famously addressed the rioters as "my friends."[13]

Stanton returned to Washington on the eve of the presidential election utterly exhausted. Three million Americans voted for Grant on November 3, 1868, but more than 2.7 million voted for Seymour. The election was especially close in several important states: Grant prevailed by only a few percentage points in Alabama, Connecticut, Indiana, and Pennsylvania. Again Stanton could take some small credit for the victory. His former assistant secretary Charles Dana, now the editor of the *New York Sun*, wrote that Stanton's speeches were the only ones on either side of the campaign that showed "the highest style of oratory." Stanton, according to Dana, "thinks with passion; his imagination is always subordinate to the feeling of his discourse; and his language is strong, compact, and often picturesque." As the election results arrived by telegram, Stanton exulted to his friend Peter Watson that Seymour was "pretty thoroughly skinned from snout to tail."[14]

Two weeks later, not long after his mother's birthday, Stanton wrote to her that he had hoped to be with her in Ohio for the day, but he had "not sufficiently recovered to undertake so long a journey." He wrote her again in December, on his own fifty-fourth birthday, to assure her: "My health is slowly improving." (Stanton did not describe his illness, but he was almost certainly suffering from congestive heart failure as well as his lifelong asthma.) He told her that he intended "to remain out of public life—to accept no office of any kind, and by attending solely to my profession to avoid all public cares and duties." Since Stanton's name was already in the papers as a likely member of the cabinet of President Grant, Stanton's mother probably took this with a grain of salt.[15]

On Christmas Eve 1868, Stanton was so sick that he remained in bed, but he wrote a letter to his three younger children in the voice of Kris Kringle. Of Ellie, now eleven, he wrote that she was "growing too fast for me to make her any more visits, unless she turns out to be an uncommon good girl. She must learn to govern her temper and be patient to her brother and little sister." Lewis, eight years old, "has been a very good boy and minds his mother very well. I hope he will continue to do so, and that when I come again, he will have learned to read very well." Bessie, only five, "has generally been as good as any little girl that I have seen on my journey, but she cries too much when she gets angry; if she quits that, she will be a great favorite of mine." Stanton as Kringle closed by giving each of the children a figurative kiss and saying that he looked forward to seeing them in a year's time. He would not live that long.[16]

A few weeks later, in the middle of January 1869, Stanton and his son Eddie, now training as a young lawyer, traveled by rail to Wheeling, West

Virginia, site of the famous bridge against which Stanton had worked so hard for so many years. Stanton was in Wheeling this time to argue before the new state's highest court in a case involving disputed land titles in the Kanawha Valley. One of the judges later recalled that he was disappointed: "I had conceived [Stanton] to be an immense, burly, rough, and resistless man"; instead the former secretary was a "feeble and exhausted invalid, whose death-like pallor shocked all beholders." Just before leaving Washington for West Virginia, Stanton had taken the difficult step of writing to Watson to ask for a loan. Upon his return, he was pleased to learn that Watson had spoken with Stillman Witt (a Cleveland financier whom Stanton probably knew through the Hutchison family) and that Witt had sent Stanton a check for $5,000. Witt intended this as a gift, but Stanton would not accept it in this form, and he sent Witt a promissory note for the amount, payable with interest in one year's time. Stanton explained to Witt in his cover letter, "If my life is spared and health restored, I hope to find no trouble in making payments out of the gains of my profession. If my time has come, or I am called while the debt is outstanding, my estate will have enough to pay it."[17]

Stanton claimed in his letter to his mother that he was not interested in a post in Grant's cabinet, that he would "remain out of public life." But he was at least interested in seeing some of his friends receive senior positions. In late February a Republican leader wrote that Stanton's close friend Judge Edwards Pierrepont had a good chance of becoming attorney general, "as Stanton especially asks this appointment from Grant, wanting nothing himself." But Stanton could not influence Grant if he did not see Grant, and a few days later Sumner wrote, "Stanton has not seen Grant since the election. [Stanton] has been too ill to call, and Grant called only once, when Stanton was too ill to see him." In early March 1869, when Grant became president and sent his nominations to the Senate, Stanton's name was not among them, nor were the names of any of his protégés. In April, Stanton received a letter from the new secretary of state, Hamilton Fish of New York, asking him to be minister to Mexico. Stanton responded coldly, in a clerk's handwriting, that the post "would not be agreeable."[18]

Stanton was not able to do much legal work in the spring and summer of 1869; Dana noted that Stanton was "obliged to leave several engagements unfulfilled." During a visit with Stanton in Washington in May, Dana urged him to write an article about "a disputed point in the history of the rebellion" for the *New York Sun*. As Dana left the house, Stanton said to him, "If I get well, I will write you an article; and if I don't, you will write me one."[19]

Stanton was encouraged in late June to receive a letter from Pierrepont, reporting on a conversation with the Grants at a dinner in New York City. President Grant "spoke several times of you with *marked* favor—and after dinner Mrs. Grant talked with me for a long time privately, & *kept speaking* of you in the highest terms of praise the *very highest*—saying how much was due to you & that the General had made a mistake in not giving you a place of the highest grade &c & that it ought to be done now." Stanton must have been discouraged after this to hear nothing further from Grant.[20]

Stanton considered the possibility of traveling west in the summer of 1869, to see the Rocky Mountains. General Sherman, hearing of this, wrote him a long and warm letter, outlining how he could travel to the Far West with "as little fatigue as Ohio, by dividing up the country according to your strength." Sherman thought Stanton's breathing would improve in the clear, pure western air. "Say the word and I will call to see you, and elaborate the details." Sherman had not forgotten how Stanton treated him in the summer of 1865—a few years later in writing his memoirs Sherman would attack Stanton unmercifully—but at least for the moment he was prepared to suspend hostilities. Stanton likewise was prepared to suspend hostilities with his old friend and now enemy Jeremiah Black, writing of his worry on reading that Black had suffered serious injuries in a railroad accident, hoping "that surrounded by friends family and familiar objects you may speedily be restored to your wonted vigor."[21]

Instead of going to the distant west Stanton and his wife headed north for a summer vacation, spending time in New Hampshire and on Cape Cod with Samuel Hooper. Even to his mother Stanton now had to admit that his health was weak. He wrote in September 1869, "I have this summer been diligently seeking health on mountains and seashore, hoping to find some place where we could both be free from asthma. But my search has been in vain and tomorrow I start for home scarcely as well as when I set out."[22]

Back in Washington, too ill to work effectively as a private lawyer, Stanton decided to try one more time for an appointment from Grant. In October he wrote Bishop Matthew Simpson to try to persuade Grant to name him to the Supreme Court. "There is a vacancy on the Supreme Bench," Stanton wrote, "for which I have adequate physical power, & so far as I can judge of my intellect, its powers are as acute and vigorous as at any period of my life—and perhaps more so. General Grant in justice to the Country, to himself & to me, ought to give me that appointment. So far as relates to himself not all his friends in the United States, upheld & advanced him as firmly & successfully during the war as I did in my official acts." Moreover there was no man other than Stanton "who would uphold the principles of the war on which his usefulness and fame must rest, with more or equal vigor from the bench." Stanton closed by telling Simpson, "I have communicated to you more fully than ever before to mortal man, and in confidence you will do what seems right."[23]

Simpson spoke with Grant and then reported Grant's concerns to Stanton. The president's friend George Childs, the Philadelphia publisher, had advised Grant that Stanton's health was not up to the demands of serving on the Court. Reading this, Stanton wrote back to Simpson, that Childs was "an active bitter enemy of mine because of my annulling a bargain between him & General Cameron which I disapproved." Stanton viewed his health as "an evasive excuse by Childs for his predetermined purpose, influenced by quite different considerations from that assigned." Stanton tried to sound resigned, but instead sounded bitter.[24]

When Congress returned to Washington in December 1869, some newspapers suggested that Grant would nominate Stanton for the vacant seat on the Supreme Court. Others observed that there would soon be a second vacant seat because Robert Grier was about to resign. In fact a North Carolina paper reported that it was "stated on good authority that Stanton can have the seat on the Supreme Court to be created by the resignation of Justice Grier." The *New York Sun* believed, on the other hand, that Grant would not nominate Stanton because he had "insulted General Sherman," and Grant always listened to his best friend Sherman. The *New York World* mocked the suggestion that Stanton would be appointed: "Now, when a life office is vacant, his health is alright." (Stanton's health was not at all right: Dr. Barnes visited him daily during December and later wrote that his "dropsy of cardiac disease"—what we would call heart failure—was so severe that Stanton "rarely left his bed.") Grier submitted a resignation letter to Grant on December 11, to take effect on February 1, allowing Grier to participate in the Court's current cases. Grant, however, when he finally made his first Supreme Court nomination, on December 14, chose his attorney general, Rockwood Hoar of Massachusetts.[25]

Perhaps prompted by Stanton, perhaps acting on their own, several of his congressional friends now wheeled into action. Matthew Carpenter, a senator from Wisconsin with whom Stanton had worked on a number of legal cases, drafted and circulated a letter in the Senate, urging Grant to nominate Stanton for the second vacant seat on the Court. In less than twenty minutes, Carpenter recalled, he obtained thirty-seven senatorial signatures. In the House, Representative James Blaine drafted and circulated a similar letter, obtaining over one hundred signatures. Before delivering the Senate letter to Grant, Carpenter showed it to Stanton. "As he glanced over it tears started down his cheeks," Carpenter later wrote. "He said not a word." The congressional pressure turned Grant around, and he told Carpenter that he could tell Stanton "his name would be sent in Monday morning." Perhaps Grant calculated that Stanton's health would not allow him to serve long so that he could name another justice to take his place. In any case the *Washington Evening Star* reported on December 17 that there was now "no doubt" that Grant would nominate Stanton to take Grier's place on the Court.[26]

On December 19, a Sunday, Grant and Colfax called upon Stanton at his home to tell him that Grant would nominate him to the Supreme Court. Stanton thanked them warmly. The next day, when Grant submitted Stanton's nomination, to take effect when Grier left, the Senate immediately confirmed him. The vote was 46 in favor and 11 against. The *New York Times* commented that the nomination and confirmation of Stanton "combined to form a tribute alike graceful and well merited to honorable public services and conspicuous ability and worth." George Templeton Strong, who had often censured Stanton during the war, was more measured: "A great war minister is not necessarily able to become even a second-rate judge. Stanton has been a successful advocate, and has industry, pluck, and backbone enough for ten. But neither his mind nor his temper seem in the least judicial. I approve the appointment, however. With all his faults, he has done the country good service." The *New York World* deplored the appointment, saying that even Stanton's friends admitted he had "overbearing manners" and an "imperious nature." The *World* insisted, "No man could be more out of place than such a hasty, violent, imperious zealot on the bench of the Supreme Court."[27]

On December 21 Stanton sat up in his sick bed to write a thank you letter to Grant. The Supreme Court was "the only public office I ever desired," Stanton wrote: "I accept it with great pleasure. The appointment affords me the more pleasure as coming from you with whom for several years I have had personal official relations such as seldom exist among men. It will be my aim so long as health and life permit to perform the solemn duties of the office to which you have appointed me with diligence, impartiality and integrity."[28]

Stanton's health did not permit him to perform the duties of the office for even a single day. A family servant later testified that, although Stanton was too sick to leave his bed in late December, "his mind was clear and tranquil and his temper cheerful and his remarks indicated hope of recovery." At about midnight on December 23, Stanton's distress and coughing increased so much that Dr. Barnes sent for Stanton's minister, Reverend Thomas Starkey of Epiphany Episcopal Church. Not long after Starkey arrived, at about three o'clock on the morning of December 24, 1869, Edwin Stanton died of congestive heart failure. He was fifty-five years old.[29]

Chapter 20

"Strangely Blended"

In the days and weeks after his death, many praised Stanton. In his official order announcing that government offices would close for the full day of the funeral, President Grant described him as "unceasing in his labors, earnest and fearless in the assumption of responsibilities necessary to his country's success, respected by all good men and feared by wrong doers." In a private note to Ellen Stanton, Grant wrote that he was "at a loss to find words expressive of my sympathy for you in your great affliction, and of the estimation I placed upon the ability, integrity, patriotism and services of him whom a nation joins you in mourning the loss of." Lincoln's son Robert wrote a warm note to Stanton's son Eddie: "When I recall the kindness of your father to me, when my father was lying dead and I felt utterly desperate, hardly able to realize the truth, I am as little able to keep my eyes from filling with tears as he was then." Attorney General Rockwood Hoar, in his official speech to the Supreme Court, did not say much about Stanton's legal career, which would have disappointed Stanton, for he prided himself on his legal work, especially the California land and the Wheeling Bridge cases. Hoar focused instead on Stanton's work as war secretary, where he showed "a capacity for labor that seemed inexhaustible; unflinching courage, indomitable will, patience and steady persistence . . . a trust in the people that never faltered, an integrity which corruption never dared approach, and singleness of purpose which nothing could withstand."[1]

In a long obituary in the *New York Sun*, Charles Dana wrote of Stanton as he knew him in the War Department: "Night as well as day found him assiduous at his post. That he was sometimes harsh and imperious amid his heavy cares and constant toil is certain; indeed, he could otherwise hardly have accomplished his work, but none of his enemies has ever questioned the sincerity of his devotion to his duty." Dana noted that Stanton pressed Lincoln to issue an emancipation proclamation and then, after the proclamation was published, "at once took measures to organize negro regiments." There was nobody in the administration who "cared more faithfully than he for those humble defenders of the Union." In the first months of their work together, Lincoln "was somewhat shy at this positive, uncompromising, intractable man, but this feeling soon wore off." By the end of Lincoln's life "none of his advisers had so much weight with him as Mr. Stanton." And Dana described some sides of Stanton that most men never saw: his delight in children, "of whose company he was fond," and the pleasure he took in quiet conversation with his friends. "He liked anecdotes, told a story with effect, and had no objection to a joke." But Stanton "had no patience with levity when serious business was at hand"—and here Dana described Stanton's outrage at Lincoln reading humorous stories on the night of the 1864 election.[2]

Francis Lieber, in a resolution he drafted for the Union League Club of New York City, called Stanton "the greatest War Minister of modern times, to whose energy and lofty patriotism the ultimate success of the national hosts is owing as much as to any other individual man." Stanton "trusted in the people, and called forth and organized victorious armies in an age which was until then unmilitary." He was an "unsullied citizen, through whose hands flowed more millions than ever passed through those of any other man; he entered his high office not rich and left it poor; the stern and sterling man who was sincerely averse to holding public office, however high; who sacrificed his health, his property, his life to it when the salvation of the country was at stake." In a private letter Lieber said that he meant every word of this resolution and added what he called the "greatest praise" of Stanton: "He was throughout and is to this day by far the most hated of all hated by the enemies of the country."[3]

Stanton's legal friend Philip Phillips, speaking in the Washington courtroom in which they had successfully defended Dan Sickles on murder charges, said, "No member of the profession ever impressed me more strongly by the vigor of his intellect and his great resources." Another lawyer, Thomas Marshall, recalling how Stanton mastered the details of a complex church property dispute, wrote that "I have known men more richly endowed with natural gifts; I have known more learned men, more eloquent men, more persuasive men; but I have never met another man who was capable of such prodigious, continuous, and incessant mental labor."[4]

George Templeton Strong wrote in his diary that, if Stanton had lived, he would probably have been only a "mediocre" justice of the Supreme Court, but Stanton's "reputation of honor as Lincoln's right-hand man during nearly the whole period of the war, entitles him to an exalted place in our history, whatever the *New York World* may say." Strong continued: "These three, Lincoln, Stanton and Grant, did more than any other three men to save the country. Good and evil were strangely blended in the character of this great War Minister. He was honest, patriotic, able, indefatigable, warm-hearted, unselfish, incorruptible, arbitrary, capricious, tyrannical, vindictive, hateful, and cruel. Robespierre had certain traits in common with Stanton. I mean no disrespect to Stanton, who was infinitely bigger and better than that miserable Frenchman—but their several failings were not unlike."[5]

The city of Washington was closed on December 27 for the Stanton funeral. A congressional delegation had suggested to Ellen Stanton that the funeral should be held in the Capitol, but she declined, and she also declined the suggestion that the services be at Epiphany Church. So the services were held at the Stanton home on K Street, starting at noon. Those present included Stanton's mother, who arrived by special train from Ohio, President Grant, the cabinet members, the leaders of Congress, the Supreme Court justices, and several generals, including Sherman. Stanton's own minister and two other Episcopal priests led the mourners through the simple service. Presumably at Ellen's request there were no eulogies. Afterward the mourners formed a long procession of about a hundred carriages. Several black leaders asked for and obtained places in the line, including men whom Stanton had commissioned as the nation's first black army officers. The procession passed through packed streets and "cold drizzling rain" to Oak Hill Cemetery in Georgetown, where Stanton's coffin was lowered into the ground, next to that of his late son, Jamie.[6]

In the evening Samuel Hooper convened a meeting of Stanton's friends to discuss the family's financial situation. Somewhat like his father, Stanton left behind a widow, three young children, and almost no assets. Hooper and the others resolved that they would raise a fund of at least $100,000 in order to provide financial support for the Stanton family. The next day Hooper wrote to Woodman in Boston, urging him to form a local committee to raise funds and saying that he already had some commitments, including $1,000 from President Grant and $2,000 from Senator Zachariah Chandler. By April the papers were reporting that the Stanton fund had reached almost $150,000. Stanton's congressional friends also passed legislation to pay Ellen the equivalent of the salary he would have earned in his first year as an associate justice. It was enough that she and the children could live comfortably but not lavishly.[7]

Yet even in the first days after Stanton's death his enemies did not hesitate to attack him. The New York World argued on December 25, 1869, that Stanton had merely reflected the mood of the moment. "At the outbreak of the war he was a secessionist," in line with the "strong pro-southern feeling then prevailing in Washington." When McClellan "became the idol of the hour," Stanton was "the most demonstrative of his flatterers." When the tide turned against McClellan, the new secretary "became the enemy of McClellan and plotted his ruin." Although Stanton worked with Radicals, he was merely "their echo, their creature, their tool." Soon even more scathing stories appeared, including the claim that Stanton committed suicide because he regretted his role in the death of Mary Surratt. The New York Democrat proclaimed in January 1870, "God is just!" for Stanton "died by his own hand rather than longer bear the torture which was his own to bear from the execution of Mary E. Surratt." Papers claimed that he had seized his barber's razor and slit his own throat. "It will be remembered," insinuated the Charleston News from South Carolina, "that no one outside the family were allowed to see the remains, even on the day of the funeral." This was not correct. There was no general public viewing of the corpse, as in the case of Lincoln, but some people saw Stanton's body, for the *Washington Evening Star* reported, "The appearance of the face is perfectly natural, and very placid, there being no discoloration." On the day of his funeral the *Star* noted that just before the services "his family and immediate friends were summoned and took a last look at the features of the illustrious dead."[8]

Still the suicide story persisted. A few years later some papers printed a longer version, in which Stanton's "colored valet" paused in shaving him, stepped across the room, and "turned just in time to see the glistening steel flash by the bared throat, leaving a streak in its wake." To refute such stories Dr. Barnes wrote a long public letter in 1879, and two former Stanton servants gave sworn statements. Barnes explained that he was with Stanton constantly in the hours before his death, and that those who witnessed his death included himself, Reverend Starkey, Stanton's wife, his four children, and several servants. The cause of death was heart failure, not any external injury. One of the former servants swore in an affidavit that after Stanton's death he washed and shaved and dressed the body and "there were no marks of violence upon his head, face, or neck."[9]

Stanton's friend Henry Wilson and his former friend Jeremiah Black had a vigorous public debate about Stanton's role in the last months of the Buchanan administration. The debate started with an article Wilson published in February 1870, just two months after Stanton's death, describing Buchanan's administration as "weak and wicked" and praising Stanton for his "fierce and fiery denunciation" of Secretary of War Floyd's plan to abandon Fort Sumter. According to Wilson, it was largely due to Stanton that the United States survived the perils of the secession winter. Black, who had already begun drafting an essay on Stanton, published a long response in June. He disagreed with Wilson's characterization of Stanton as an abolitionist, saying that Stanton condemned the abolitionists "for their hypocrisy, their corruption, their enmity to the Constitution, and their lawless disregard for the rights of states and individuals." Stanton was not, as Wilson suggested, sympathetic with the Republicans while serving in a Democratic administration; he "was what he seemed to be, a sound and sincere friend, political and personal, of the men who showered their favors upon his head." Black admitted that Stanton later changed his mind and supported Lincoln and the Republicans, but Black insisted that while Stanton was a Democrat he was really a Democrat. He "was in perfect accord with the [Buchanan] administration, before and after he became a part of it, on every question of fundamental principle." If, as Wilson claimed, Stanton was telling Republicans during the secession winter that he was surrounded by treason, then Stanton was "an accomplished imposter."[10]

Wilson responded in October with another long article, supported by letters from other men who had known Stanton over the years. The abolitionist Theodore Dwight Weld, for example, wrote about meeting Stanton after a lecture in Steubenville, when Stanton told him that he now realized "all men hold their rights by the same title deed." Charles Sumner related that he first met Stanton through the antislavery Salmon Chase, that he saw Stanton from time to time at the home of the abolitionist editor Gamaliel Bailey, and that when there were questions about Stanton just after his nomination as secretary of war, Sumner vouched for him with Republicans, asserting, "He was one of us." William Henry Seward described how he communicated during the secession winter with Stanton, sharing their common concern about "the danger of a factious resistance by the rebels at the seat of the government." Black replied in early 1871, defending Buchanan and arguing that if Stanton had indeed sided both with the Democrats and the Republicans on the central issue of abolition, then "he was the most marvelous imposter that ever lived or died."[11]

A similar controversy arose in 1872, during Grant's reelection campaign. Sumner was utterly opposed to a second term for Grant, whom he described (in widely published reports) as "venal, ambitious, vulgar . . . obstinate and unmanly." Sumner tried to enlist the late Stanton in his crusade, claiming that in the weeks before his death Stanton had told him solemnly, "I know General Grant better than any other person in the country can know him [and] *he cannot govern this country*." Senator Chandler responded to Sumner with long quotations from Stanton's 1868 campaign speeches for Grant. Chandler noted that he saw Stanton often, daily during the war years, and visited him just days before his death, when he "expressed the highest opinion of President Grant." Senator Carpenter agreed, describing in detail how Stanton praised Grant at the time Grant nominated him to the Supreme Court. Carpenter said that, if Stanton had really said to Sumner what Sumner claimed, then Stanton was "the most double-faced and dishonest man that ever lived."[12]

Grant did not comment on the Sumner-Chandler-Carpenter debate at the time, but the controversy may have changed his views on Stanton, or at least prompted him to share some of his views. Just before his own death from cancer in 1885, in one of the last sections of his memoir that he was able to write, Grant contrasted Lincoln and Stanton, writing that Lincoln "preferred yielding his own wish to gratify others," while Stanton "cared nothing for the feelings of others." Indeed "it seemed to be pleasanter to him to disappoint than to gratify." Moreover, contrary to the general view that Lincoln was soft and Stanton strong, Grant now asserted that Stanton "was very timid." One could argue that this criticism was not contrary to Grant's earlier praise of Stanton's energy and dedication, but certainly Grant had changed his tone from his praise of Stanton in his congressional testimony in 1865 and his letter to Stanton's widow in 1870.[13]

Stanton's critics were right in many respects. He was duplicitous and even deceitful. Before the Civil War he would speak against slavery in private conversations with abolitionists, and he would mock and attack the abolitionists when he was with his Democratic colleagues. During the secession winter he shared with Seward and other Republicans the inner workings of the Democratic administration of which he was a cabinet member. (A modern politician would describe Stanton's work during this winter as "bipartisan," but that word did not yet exist in the American political vocabulary.) After the Civil War, when Stanton wrote that Lincoln had told him he could not resign, he was simply putting words into Lincoln's mouth. Stanton's memory of his own words was sometimes equally creative, such as when he claimed that he had advised Buchanan on how to deal with secession on the eve of the Lincoln election.[14]

Strong was more or less right when he wrote that Stanton was "arbitrary, capricious, tyrannical, vindictive, hateful, and cruel." Everyone who dealt with him in the war years, including Strong, encountered his legendary anger, saw the way he made hasty and sometimes rash decisions. And as Buchanan and others knew, Stanton could also flatter and fawn when necessary. "To his superiors or those who were his equal in position," Gideon Welles would write after Stanton's death, "he was complacent, sometimes obsequious." Stanton paid little attention to the rights of others, even the most basic rights. He arrested General Stone on slight grounds, and then kept him in a prison cell for months without a court-martial. He arrested or encouraged the arrests of hundreds of civilians during the war, ranging from rebel spies to innocent editors. We must condemn him, and Lincoln, for these arbitrary arrests, but remember that they were struggling to save the Union and save the Constitution. As Lincoln said at Gettysburg, the issue was not only whether this nation, "conceived in Liberty, and dedicated to the proposition that all men are created equal," could survive; the issue was whether "any nation so conceived and so dedicated, can long endure."[15]

Stanton was prone to panic. Even if Welles, writing years later, exaggerated Stanton's reaction to the *Merrimack*, there is no doubt that Stanton was fearful and angry at the news that a Southern ironclad was wreaking havoc upon the North's wooden warships. A few weeks later he panicked again, when he sent his telegram to all the governors, announcing, "The enemy in great force are advancing on Washington." He also sometimes reacted too rapidly to political pressure, such as when he suspended recruiting because some senators were complaining about costs.[16]

Yet Stanton was a great man and a great secretary of war. In an era known for corruption, in a department especially known for corruption, Stanton was incorruptible, and he insisted on *systems* that prevented corruption and ensured economy throughout the War Department. Perhaps his greatest contribution was his ability to create and to operate systems: a central systematic telegraph office, a single national railroad system using both private and public tracks and engineers, a code of military law and a military justice system that were far better than anything that had preceded them. Stanton learned on the job. He learned that warfare had changed since the days of Joshua, and by the end of the war he was a master at bringing both technology and public opinion to bear in modern warfare.

Stanton believed in systems, but he also believed in disregarding the rules when necessary. He was often in direct telegraphic contact with generals in the field, ignoring the chain of command. When the *Merrimack* threatened the troop transports heading south in the spring of 1862, Stanton did not wait for the Navy Department to handle the issue.

No, he contacted Cornelius Vanderbilt in New York and obtained, reinforced, and dispatched the *Vanderbilt* as a ram to destroy the *Merrimack*— all to the intense annoyance of Welles. When raising additional troops required promising them an additional bounty, Stanton promised the bounty, even before he had the legislation from Congress to authorize the payment. He viewed his task as winning the war, and he did not let details get in the way of his determination, his obsession, with that great task.

Stanton worked tirelessly. His friend and cabinet colleague Seward would spend most evenings with friends around the dinner table and then the card table; Stanton spent his evenings and often his nights in the telegraph office, sleeping on the weathered couch. The intense period of work involved in transporting 20,000 troops to Chattanooga in a week's time was merely one of many episodes when he spent night after night at the War Department, sending and receiving messages at all hours. And he was doing this while meeting and talking daily with Lincoln, with members of Congress, with generals, with soldiers, with common citizens. It is no wonder that his health failed from time to time; the wonder is that he managed to work as hard and long as he did.

Lincoln deserves his reputation as the "Great Emancipator," but Stanton should perhaps be known as the "Implementer of Emancipation." He pressed Lincoln to issue the initial emancipation proclamation. Starting even before then, but especially in the months after the proclamation was issued, Stanton worked to recruit and train black soldiers, not only because the Union Army needed them as additional troops but because he realized how service in the armed forces would change the lives of the soldiers and their families. He investigated the conditions in the contraband camps, pressed Congress to pass the freedmen's legislation, and formed the Freedmen's Bureau within the War Department. He was adamant with President Johnson that the army had to remain in the South to protect Southern blacks from the wave of white violence. Johnson was equally adamant that the army should leave the South, should allow Southern whites to govern as they wished. This was the central issue on which Stanton and Johnson disagreed; this was why Johnson wanted to remove Stanton from the War Department; this was why Johnson's attempt to remove Stanton led to his impeachment and nearly led to his removal. Yes, Stanton was stubborn and difficult and even insubordinate with Johnson. But he was on the right side.

One way to capture Stanton's contribution is to consider what would have happened if Lincoln had kept Simon Cameron as secretary of war through the end of the Civil War. The Union would almost surely have won the war over the Confederacy, but it would have taken longer and it would have cost more. The North had great advantages over the South in manpower and materiel and manufacturing, but Stanton helped to *organize* these advantages into military might. Stanton disliked the phrase "organizing victory" because it was McClellan's way of describing his cautious, step-by-step approach; Stanton was far more fond of Grant's bold approach. But organizing the Union victory is a good description of what Stanton did in the War Department, aided by capable colleagues such as Montgomery Meigs, Daniel McCallum, and the great Union generals Grant, Sherman, Sheridan, and others. Stanton also helped to organize one other critical victory, the electoral victory of 1864, for we tend to forget how close that election was and forget that if McClellan had prevailed, the Confederacy might well have survived through some form of compromise or peace agreement. Although Cameron had more years in politics than Stanton, Cameron would not have been nearly as effective as Stanton in the 1864 election campaign, for it required balancing political and military concerns, coordinating troops and trains—the sort of detailed work at which Stanton excelled.[17]

Another way to prove Stanton's contribution is to note that, although some newspaper editors started pressing Lincoln to replace Stanton within weeks of his appointment, Lincoln retained him. In part this was because Grant and others advised Lincoln to keep Stanton in place at the head of the War Department. But the more important reason was that Lincoln himself saw firsthand Stanton's work and knew his virtues. The two men were not close personal friends; they did not swap stories and jokes in the way of Lincoln and Seward. Lincoln and Stanton did not always agree, notably when Lincoln placed McClellan back in charge of the Army of the Potomac just before the Battle of Antietam. But Lincoln and Stanton liked and respected one another. John Hay was right when he wrote that Lincoln "loved" and "trusted" Stanton and that "all efforts to shake that trust and confidence" were efforts in vain.[18]

It is impossible to imagine Stanton with his virtues but without his vices. As the Russian historian and novelist Alexander Solzhenitsyn observed, "The line dividing good and evil cuts through the heart of every human being." This was never more true than in the case of Edwin Stanton. The energy and diligence that enabled him to work so long and hard were matched by the haste and impatience that led him to commit errors. The disregard for personal considerations that allowed him to move generals and troops about like mere pieces on a chessboard was the same impersonal, dictatorial approach that so alienated his colleagues. Stanton's tendency to exaggerate, even to deceive, was linked with his ability to persuade a jury or a judge and his ability to inspire the nation through his press releases. His determination to win the war at all costs was the same determination that enabled him to arrest generals and editors and others whom he believed were hindering the war effort. Stanton's good and evil sides, as Strong observed, were "strangely blended."[19]

So Stanton was not a good man, but he was a great man. He played a central role in winning the central war in American history. He lived and worked with great men, Lincoln and Grant and Sherman. He was one of them. For all his faults, he deserves our praise.

Acknowledgments

The first people I must thank are my agent, Scott Waxman, and my editor, Alice Mayhew. They persuaded me that Edwin McMasters Stanton was my next subject; they kept me on track; they pushed me over the finish line.

Next I need to thank my predecessors, the prior biographers of Stanton, especially Frank Flower, George Gorham, Eugene Drozdowski, Benjamin Thomas, Harold Hyman, and William Marvel. I started my work by reading their books and finding and reading their sources. I have not always agreed with them, but I could not have written this book without theirs. More generally I have built upon the works of hundreds of other scholars, as I have indicated in the notes and bibliography.

Libraries store the raw material of history. One simply cannot write history books without libraries and the good librarians who work there. I have worked in dozens of libraries in my research, ranging from grand institutions like the Library of Congress to small rooms in rural Ohio. My research assistants have visited other libraries, and in some cases librarians have kindly helped from afar. Thanks to the following libraries, their staffs, and their supporters: Allen County Public Library in Indiana, American Antiquarian Society, Amistad Research Center at Tulane University, Boston Public Library, Bowdoin University Library, Brown University Library, Carnegie Library of Pittsburgh, Chicago History

Center, Clements Library at the University of Michigan, Colby College Library, Columbia University Library, Columbus Metropolitan Library, Connecticut Historical Society, Cornell University Library, Dartmouth University Library, Dayton Public Library, Detroit Public Library, Duke University Library, Friedrich-Ebert-Stiftung Library in Bonn, Gilcrease Museum and Library in Tulsa, Hagley Museum and Library in Wilmington, Delaware, Harvard University Libraries, Heinz Historical Center in Pittsburgh, the Historical Society of Pennsylvania, Huntington Library and Gardens in San Marino, California, the Jefferson County Chapter of the Ohio Genealogical Society, Kenyon College Library, Leatherby Libraries at Chapman University, Library of Congress, Louisiana State University Library, Massachusetts Historical Society, Mississippi State University Library, National Archives and Record Administration, New-York Historical Society, New York Public Library, Newport Beach Public Library, Ohio County Public Library, Ohio History Connection, Phillips Exeter Academy Library, Princeton University Library, Public Library of Steubenville and Jefferson County, Rutherford Hayes Library in Fremont, Ohio, Surratt House Museum in Clinton, Maryland, University of California at Irvine Library, University of California at Los Angeles Library, University of Chicago Library, University of Florida Library, University of Maine Library, University of Michigan Library, University of New Hampshire Library, University of Pittsburgh Library, and Yale University Library.

More and more primary sources are available on the Internet. I have used, almost daily, the online Stanton Papers at the Library of Congress, the online Grant Papers at Mississippi State, and the online *Official Records* at Cornell University. I am grateful to those involved in making and keeping these and other such resources available.

My research assistants were invaluable eyes and ears. Thank you to Nora Genster, Drew Goydan, Harry Halem, Ron King, Lauren Krebs, Molly McCarthy, Karen Needles, Rohan Pavuluri, John Reed, Lisa Pasquinelli Rickey, Ryan Shinkel, Kyle Skinner, Yumika Takeshita, and Margaret Zhu. Catherine Stanton Richert kindly shared some Stanton family letters.

Several friends read parts or all of the manuscript and offered insightful comments. Thank you to Frank Borchert, Dan Crofts, Jack Herney,

Andy McCarthy, John McGinnis, and Jonathan Wallenberger. Many scholars aided with questions, comments, or sources. Thank you to Allan Guelzo, Harold Holzer, Tripp Jones, John Marszalek, William Marvel, Elizabeth Monroe, John David Smith, Edward Steers Jr., Craig Symonds, Amy Taylor, and Jonathan White.

I am proud to tell people that my editor is the legendary Alice Mayhew of Simon & Schuster. Jonathan Cox, Stuart Roberts, Elizabeth Gay, Stephen Bedford, and others at Simon & Schuster helped as the book neared publication and promotion.

Like Stanton, I am an Episcopalian, not the best Episcopalian. Since May 2015, when I have not been working on Stanton, I have been working to save our church, St. James the Great, in Newport Beach, from the bishop's plans to sell it to a developer so that it can be torn down to make way for town houses. In late June 2015, the bishop locked the doors of St. James, forcing the congregation to worship in a nearby park and then in a rented space. As I write this in the spring of 2017, I do not know whether the building will be spared from sale, whether the congregation will survive as a congregation. But I am grateful for all the friends I have made in the struggle and all their work to save our church.

My wife, Masami, often feels that she is "last on the list," after my parents, after the church, after Edwin Stanton. But she is, in fact, first on the list—the person without whom I could not do anything else. This book is dedicated to her.

Notes

The Stanton Papers, now available on the website of the Library of Congress, were the main manuscript source for this book. Other Stanton letters are scattered far and wide, and many of the best quotes are from letters about rather than from Stanton. For the war years, the Stanton Papers contain only a small fraction of the correspondence. The *Official Records* (more formally known as *The War of the Rebellion: A Compilation of the Official Records of the Union and Confederate Armies*) contain hundreds of Stanton messages, but there are hundreds more in the National Archives. I found the telegrams sent from the secretary's office, on microfilm M473, especially useful. Printed primary sources were essential, including the collected works of Lincoln, edited by Roy Basler; the diary of Gideon Welles, in the excellent new edition edited by William and Erica Gienapp; and the papers of Ulysses Grant, edited first by John Simon and now by John Marszalek. Newspapers were also vital. I looked at a few papers in original form, chiefly at the American Antiquarian Society, others in microfilm, and yet more in electronic format. I have sometimes expanded newspaper titles for clarity; for example, the *World*, published in New York, is cited as the *New York World*.

I have tried to cite accessible rather than obscure sources. When a message is in the *Official Records* or in the *New York Times*, I have cited these sources rather than M473. I have modernized spelling and punctuation but not changed any words.

I have used the following abbreviations in the notes:

HSP: Historical Society of Pennsylvania

LC: Library of Congress

M473: Records of the Office of the Secretary of War, Telegrams Collected by the Office of the Secretary of War, National Archives, microfilm

MHS: Massachusetts Historical Society

NA: National Archives

OR: *The War of the Rebellion: A Compilation of the Official Records of the Union and Confederate Armies*; Series 1 unless otherwise noted

ORN: *Official Records of the Union and Confederate Navies in the War of Rebellion*; Series 1 unless otherwise noted

RG: Record Group (at National Archives)

Introduction

1 Eckert to Grant, Apr. 15, 1865, *OR*, vol. 46, pt. 3, pp. 744–45; Dana to Grant, Apr. 15, 1862, ibid., 756; Meigs to Augur, Apr. 15, 1862, ibid.

2 Tanner to Welch, Apr. 17, 1865, in Peckham, "James Tanner's Account," 177–81.

3 Stanton to Dix, Apr. 15, 1862, *OR*, vol. 46, pt. 3, pp. 780–81 (four messages).

4 Dana, *Recollections of the Civil War*, 274; Leale, *Lincoln's Last Hours*, 10–11. Dana wrote a similar account in his obituary of Stanton: *New York Sun*, Dec. 25, 1869.

5 Eisenschiml, *Why Was Lincoln Murdered?*; O'Reilly, *Killing Lincoln*, 287; Marvel, *Lincoln's Autocrat*, xiv ("shameful injustices"); Steers, "A Missed Opportunity" ("that Stanton had nothing to do with Lincoln's murder has been proven time and again"); Turner, *Beware the People Weeping*, 1–17 (responds to Eisenschiml).

6 *Boston Advertiser*, May 27, 1862; *New York World*, Aug. 8, 1863; *New York Times*, Sept. 7, 1865; Hay to Stanton, July 26, 1865, in Burlingame, *At Lincoln's Side*, 105–6.

Chapter 1: "Dreams of Future Greatness"

1 *New York Evening Post*, Feb. 6, 1815 (New Orleans); ibid., Feb. 13, 1815 ("Peace"); *Baltimore Sun*, Jan. 9, 1840 (Jackson Day celebrations); *Rochester (N.Y.) Democrat & Chronicle*, Jan. 9, 1936 (FDR's Jackson Day speech); *Joplin (Mo.) Globe*, Jan. 9, 1954 ("annual Jackson Day shindig"); Flower, *Edwin McMasters Stanton*, 22.

2 Cramer, *The Navigator*, 24, 31, 54, 81; Darby, *Emigrant's Guide*, 228–29; Ambler, *A History of Transportation in the Ohio Valley*.

3 Alexis de Tocqueville to father, Dec. 20, 1831, in Zunz, *Tocqueville and Gustave de Beaumont in America*, 191–92; U.S. Census Bureau, *Historical Statistics of the United States, 1789–1945*, 133.

4 Stanton, *Book Called Our Ancestors*, 39–45, 75–80 (includes will); Burke and Bensch, "Mount Pleasant and the Early Quakers of Ohio"; Smith, "The Quaker Migration to the Upper Ohio"; Wolcott, *Edwin M. Stanton*, 10–16; Caldwell, *History of Belmont and Jefferson Counties*, 544 ("while the memory").

5 Jones, *An 18th Century Perspective*, 81–96; Norman, *History of the Culpeper County Normans*, 15–22; Wolcott, *Edwin M. Stanton*, 19–20; *Washington Evening Star*, Apr. 15, 1859 ("proud to say").

6 Ohio County Marriages (FamilySearch database); Hinshaw, *Encyclopedia of American Quaker Genealogy*, 4:279; Forbes to J. M. Grinnan, Jan. 12, 1931, Thomas Forbes Papers (tailor); Wolcott, *Edwin M. Stanton*, 23.

7 Doyle, *In Memoriam*, 12 ("delicate"); Wolcott, *Edwin M. Stanton*, 25 ("somewhat imperious"); Flower, *Edwin McMasters Stanton*, 23 (membership dates); Calvary Methodist Church, Steubenville, Ohio, *Sesquicentennial Program* (1960), 5 (Stanton a member). See Hempton, *Methodism*; Williams, *Religion and Violence in Early American Methodism*, 69–70 (numbers).

8 David Stanton to Benjamin Stanton, Apr. 29, 1821, William Stanton Papers, Huntington; Stanton, *Book Called Our Ancestors*, 568–69 (dates).

9 *Steubenville (Ohio) Republican Ledger*, Jan. 2, 1828; Wolcott, *Edwin M. Stanton*, 27–29 (includes obituary).

10 *Steubenville (Ohio) Republican Ledger*, Apr. 8, 1828 (advertisement); *Baltimore Sun*, Dec. 28, 1869 ("just high enough"); *Steubenville (Ohio) Weekly Herald*, Jan. 21, 1870; Flower, *Edwin McMasters Stanton*, 23; Wolcott, *Edwin M. Stanton*, 31.

11 Caswall, *America and the American Church*, 27, 28, 34; Smythe, *Kenyon College*, 56–73, 79–85, 99 ("patriarchal institution" on 99); Wheeler, "The Antebellum College in the Old Northwest," 70–75; Wheeler, "Philander Chase and College Building in Ohio."

12 Stanton Accounts, 1831, Edwin Stanton Papers, LC, box 1, image 1 (available online at Library of Congress website); Stanton to Alexander Beatty,

July 21, 1832, Kenyon College; Smythe, *Kenyon College*, 95–101; Wheeler, "The Antebellum College," 75–77.

13 Philomathesian Society Minute Book; Parker, "Edwin M. Stanton at Kenyon."

14 Philomathesian Society Minute Book, July 13, 20, 27, Aug. 3, 1832.

15 Stanton, "Our Admiration of Military Characters Unmerited," [1832], Edwin Stanton Papers, LC, box 1, images 3–5.

16 Stanton, "The Duty of a Good Soldier on the Eve of Battle," [1832], Edwin Stanton Papers, LC, box 1, images 6–7.

17 Stanton to Alexander Beatty, July 21, 1832, Kenyon College. Transcripts (with some silent editing) of these letters are in Parker, "Edwin M. Stanton at Kenyon."

18 Stanton to Daniel Collier, Aug. 18, 1832, Kenyon College; Stanton to Andrew McClintock, Oct. 10, 1832, ibid.

19 Cole, *A Fragile Capital*; Lee, *History of the City of Columbus*; *Ohio State Journal*, Dec. 25, 1832 (advertisement); "Largest Urban Places," 1830, 1840, 1850, U.S. Census Bureau website.

20 Stanton to Andrew McClintock, Nov. 2, 1832, Kenyon College; Lisa P. Rickey, "Glancing Backwards: Biographical Sketch of Horton Howard," Rickey website.

21 Klein, *Be It Remembered*, 23–30; Wolcott, *Edwin M. Stanton*, 46, 112–13.

22 Ebenezer Thomas to Samuel Forrer, Aug. 1833 (four letters), Forrer-Pierce-Wood Papers; *Ohio State Journal*, Aug. 17 and Sept. 3, 1833 (re: Ann Howard's death); Cole, *A Fragile Capital*, 24–25.

23 The exhumation story is in Flower, *Edwin McMasters Stanton*, 30; Wolcott, *Edwin M. Stanton*, 112–13; Forman, "The First Cholera Epidemic in Columbus," 419–20; Thomas and Hyman, *Stanton*, 13–14. Marvel, *Lincoln's Autocrat*, 15–16, disputes the story, which is even less plausible in light of the Thomas letters. See Ebenezer Thomas to Samuel Forrer, Aug. 1833 (four letters), Forrer-Pierce-Wood Papers; Stanton to Collier, Sept. 14, 1833, Kenyon College; Stanton to McClintock & Mitchell, Sept. 27, 1833, ibid.

24 Stanton to Collier, Sept. 14, 1833, Kenyon College; Stanton to McClintock and Mitchell, Sept. 27, 1833, ibid.; Stanton to McClintock, Jan. 30, 1834, ibid. For sale of the Stanton house see *Western Herald*, July 31, 1833, and Wolcott, *Edwin M. Stanton*, 40–41.

25 Stanton to McClintock and Mitchell, Sept. 27, 1833, Kenyon College; Stanton to McClintock, Jan. 30, 1834, ibid. For Campbell's death, see Campbell, *Biographical Sketches*, 9–11. For Tappan's appointment, see Alexander, *A Place of Recourse*, 219–20.

26 Stanton to McClintock, Jan. 30, 1834, Kenyon College; Wolcott, *Edwin M. Stanton*, 41–42.

27 Wolcott, *Edwin M. Stanton*, 103–6.

28 Ibid., 47–49.

29 William Boyce to Stanton, June 8, 1836, Edwin Stanton Papers, LC box 1, image 34; Flower, *Edwin McMasters Stanton*, 31; Thomas and Hyman, *Stanton*, 16–17.

30 Flower, *Edwin McMasters Stanton*, 31; see Marvel, *Lincoln's Autocrat*, 21, for another case Stanton handled before admission.

31 Shotwell, *Driftwood*, 72–73; Graves, "The Early Life and Career of Edwin M. Stanton," 30.

32 Mary Lamson to Stanton, Oct. 12, 1836, in Wolcott, *Edwin M. Stanton*, 105–6; Tappan to Tappan Jr., Dec. 28, 1836, Benjamin Tappan Papers, LC; *Ohio State Journal*, Jan. 3, 1837 (reports wedding); Benjamin Tappan Jr. to Stanton, Feb. 26, 1837, Benjamin Tappan Papers, LC; Flower, *Edwin Mc-Masters Stanton*, 32–33. On average age at first marriage, see Hacker, "Economic, Demographic, and Anthropomorphic Correlates."

Chapter 2: "Obstinate Democrat"

1 Stanton to McClintock, Oct. 10, 1832, Kenyon College ("too quietly"); Tappan to Tappan Jr., Mar. 8, 1837, Benjamin Tappan Papers, LC (Stanton and wife with the Tappans); Howard to Tappan, Jan. 12, 1841, ibid. ("obstinate Democrat"); *Steubenville (Ohio) American Union*, May 31, 1837 (notice of partnership); Feller, "A Brother in Arms"; Wolcott, *Edwin M. Stanton*, 50–53 ("second home").

2 Holt, *American Whig Party*, 75–76; Roberts, *America's First Great Depression*, 1–43; Wilentz, *American Democracy*, 507 (origins of term Loco Foco).

3 On national politics, see Holt, *American Whig Party*; Howe, *What Hath God Wrought*; Wilentz, *American Democracy*. On Ohio, see Holt, *Party Politics in Ohio*; Maizlish, *Triumph of Sectionalism*.

4 Johnston, *Trial of Daniel M'Cook*; Whalen and Whalen, *The Fighting McCooks*, 25–26.

5 Wolcott, *Edwin M. Stanton*, 56–61. Wolcott does not give precise dates, and there are no letters in the Stanton papers from this period, but it seems Stanton was in the East when New York banks suspended specie payments on May 10, 1837.

6 Wolcott, *Edwin M. Stanton*, 61–72.

7 *Steubenville (Ohio) American Union*, July 18 and Aug. 23, 1837 (Tappan for state senate); Stanton to Tappan, July 24, 1837, Benjamin Tappan Papers, LC; Stanton to Cowan, Aug. 20, 1837, in Wolcott, *Edwin M. Stanton*, 85–86.

8 *Steubenville (Ohio) American Union*, Oct. 18 and 25, 1837 (election results);

Graves, "Early Life and Career of Stanton," 35 (Stanton's work as prosecutor).

9 *Steubenville (Ohio) American Union*, June 12, 1838 (Oella); Jefferson County Common Pleas Journal, May 1839, vol. I, p. 222 (Pamphila); *Steubenville (Ohio) American Union*, July 9, 1839 (Darwin); Wolcott, *Edwin M. Stanton*, 71–73. On Darwin's medical studies, see Harvard University, *Catalogue of the Officers and Students of Harvard University for the Academical Year 1837–8* (1837) (listing Darwin as a student on p. 12); Marvel, *Lincoln's Autocrat*, 25 (citing University of Pennsylvania Commencement Program); Wolcott, *Edwin M. Stanton*, 53 (saying her brother went to Harvard).

10 *Maumee Express* (Maumee City, Ohio), Oct. 27, 1838 (election results); ibid., Dec. 29, 1838 (Tappan elected).

11 *Daily Ohio Statesman*, Jan. 3, 1840; draft of same article, Edwin Stanton Papers, LC, box, 1 images 65–66; Tappan to Stanton, Jan. 8, 1840, Benjamin Tappan Papers, LC; Stanton to Tappan, Jan. 14, 1840, ibid.; *Daily Ohio Statesman*, Jan. 14, 1840 ("into what hands"); Reuben Wood biography, Ohio State Supreme Court website.

12 *Daily Ohio Statesman*, Jan. 6, 1840; Stanton to "Gentlemen," Feb. 1, 1840, Edwin Stanton Papers, LC, box 1, image 46.

13 Stanton to Tappan, Jan. 14, 1840, Edwin Stanton Papers, LC, box 1, image 36 (misdated by Stanton as 1839); Tappan to Stanton, Feb. 20, 1840, Benjamin Tappan Papers, LC; *Steubenville (Ohio) Log Cabin Farmer*, Apr. 23, 1840 (mocking Van Buren's "presidential palace").

14 *Congressional Globe*, 26th Cong., 1st Sess., pp. 171–72 (Feb. 7, 1840) (Tappan); Tappan to Stanton, Feb. 8, 1840, Benjamin Tappan Papers, LC; Stanton draft editorial, Feb. 1840, Edwin Stanton Papers, LC, box 1, images 93–94 (misdated 1844); Tappan to Stanton, May 12, 1840, Benjamin Tappan Papers, LC.

15 Wolcott, *Edwin M. Stanton*, 73. In one letter Stanton wrote to Tappan, "The boy," apparently the son of Dr. Tappan and Oella, "is growing at a fast rate and is already as big as my girl." Stanton to Tappan, Feb. 22, 1841, Benjamin Tappan Papers, LC.

16 Forester to Stanton, July 21, 1840, Edwin Stanton Papers, LC, box 1, images 63–64; *Steubenville (Ohio) Log Cabin Farmer*, July 23, 1840; Shotwell, *Driftwood*, 81–82 (quoting Bingham); Magliocca, *American Founding Son*, 20–23.

17 Holt, *American Whig Party*, 112 ("one fact above all determined the election; the depression deepened as the year progressed"). Holt destroys the myth that 1840 was an "issue-free" election.

18 Stanton to Tappan, Feb. 6, 1841, Edwin Stanton Papers, LC, box 1, images 67–68; *Steubenville (Ohio) American Union*, Feb. 6, 1841 (twenty or thirty applicants for post office); Stanton and Means to Tappan, Feb. 22, 1841,

Benjamin Tappan Papers, LC; Stanton to Tappan, Feb. 22, 1841, ibid.; Stanton to Tappan, Mar. 7, 1841, Edwin Stanton Papers, LC, box 1, images 71–72.

19 Tappan to Stanton, June 7, 1841, Benjamin Tappan Papers, LC; Stanton to Tappan, June 27, 1841, ibid.

20 Wolcott to Tappan, Aug. 27, 1841, Benjamin Tappan Papers, LC ("death of his only child"); Wolcott, *Edwin M. Stanton*, 74 ("constant in his attendance"); Flower, *Edwin McMasters Stanton*, 38 (quoting Buchanan); Marvel, *Lincoln's Autocrat*, 33.

21 *Steubenville (Ohio) American Union*, Jan. 1, 1842; *Proceedings of the Democratic State Convention . . . January 1842*; Stanton to Tappan, Jan. 30, 1842, Edwin Stanton Papers, LC, box 1, images 73–74; *Daily Ohio Statesman*, Mar. 8, 1842 (court reporter); *Steubenville (Ohio) American Union*, Mar. 12, 1842 (same); Flower, *Edwin McMasters Stanton*, 37 (salary as court reporter).

22 Stanton to Tappan, Apr. 20, 1842, Edwin Stanton Papers, LC, box 1, images 76–77; Tappan to Stanton, May 5, 1842, Benjamin Tappan Papers, LC; *Richmond (Va.) Enquirer*, May 6, 1842 (Darwin Stanton elected as Democrat); *Roanoke (Va.) Advocate*, May 11, 1842 ("Locos will have the majority"); *Richmond (Va.) Enquirer*, Feb. 28, 1843 (Darwin a delegate to state Democratic convention); *Richmond (Va.) Enquirer*, May 5, 1843 (Darwin reelected as Democrat). The sources that err by calling Darwin a Whig include Flower, *Edwin McMasters Stanton*, 37; Marvel, *Lincoln's Autocrat*, 33; Thomas and Hyman, *Stanton*, 28 ("Stanton's zeal").

23 Stanton to Tappan, May 31, 1842, Edwin Stanton Papers, LC, box 1, images 79–81; *Ohio Democrat*, June 30, 1842; *Brooklyn Daily Eagle*, July 11, 1842, quoting *Cincinnati Microscope* ("almost desperate"); Roberts, *America's First Great Depression*, 12–43.

24 Stanton to Tappan, May 31, 1842, Edwin Stanton Papers, LC, box 1, images 79–81 (Mairs case).

25 Stanton to Tappan, Apr. 20, 1842, ibid., 76; Stanton to Tappan, July 17, 1842, Benjamin Tappan Papers, LC; *Georgetown (Ohio) Democratic Standard*, Nov. 8, 1842 ("begged, appealed").

26 Stanton to Pamphila Wolcott, Dec. 25, 1842, in Wolcott, *Edwin M. Stanton*, 77–78; Stanton to Tappan, Dec. 27, 1842, Edwin Stanton Papers, LC, box 1, images 82–83.

27 Mary Lamson to Stanton, Dec. 1842, in Wolcott, *Edwin M. Stanton*, 108; Stanton to Mary Lamson, Dec. 1842, in Thomas and Hyman, *Stanton*, 21.

28 Tappan to Stanton, July 12, 1840, Benjamin Tappan Papers, LC; Stanton to Tappan, Feb. 8, 1843, Edwin Stanton Papers, LC, box 1, images 86–87; *Norwalk Ohio Experiment*, Feb. 8, 1843, quoting *Ohio Statesman* (Cass in Columbus); *Georgetown (Ohio) Democratic Standard*, Feb. 14, 1843 (similar);

Klunder, *Lewis Cass*, 127–29 (Cass in Ohio); Wilentz, *American Democracy*, 533–34 (Calhoun).

29 *Carroll County (Ohio) Free Press*, Apr. 28, 1843 (notice by Stanton); *Daily Ohio Statesman*, June 21, 1843 ("most promising"); Stanton to Emanuel Hooker, July 16, 1843, Hooker Papers; *New York Tribune*, Sept. 5, 1843 (Wilkins candidate); Stanton to William Wilkins, Sept. 25 and Oct. 12, 1843, Wilkins-Hutchison-Wells Family Papers; *New York Tribune*, Oct. 18, 1843 (Wilkins elected); Slick, "William Wilkins."

30 Mary Lamson to Stanton, Dec. 13, 1843, in Wolcott, *Edwin M. Stanton*, 108–9; Stanton to Mary Lamson, Dec. 31, 1843, ibid., 109.

31 Stanton to Tappan, Jan. 8, 1844, Edwin Stanton Papers, LC, box 1, image 84; William Medill to Tappan, Jan. 12, 1844, Benjamin Tappan Papers, LC; *Proceedings and Address of the Democratic State Convention*.

32 Flower, *Edwin McMasters Stanton*, 39 ("could not work"); Marvel, *Lincoln's Autocrat*, 37 (suggests tuberculosis); Wolcott, *Edwin M. Stanton*, 100–101 ("searched the house").

33 Stanton to Lewis Tappan, Mar. 20, 1844, Lewis Tappan Papers, LC; Tappan to Stanton, Mar. 26, 1844, ibid.

34 Stanton to Tappan, Apr. 28, 1844, Edwin Stanton Papers, LC, box 1, image 89; Van Buren to W. H. Hammett, April 20, 1844, in *New York Tribune*, Apr. 30, 1844; S. A. Bronson to Christopher Wolcott, May 12, 1844, in Wolcott, *Edwin M. Stanton*, 158 ("true policy"); *Cadiz (Ohio) Sentinel*, May 15 & 22, 1844 (murder trial); Wilentz, *American Democracy*, 566–69.

35 *Steubenville (Ohio) American Union*, June 5, 1844; *Woodsfield (Ohio) Spirit of Democracy*, Oct. 11, 1844 ("Who is James K. Polk?"); Klunder, *Lewis Cass*, 138–42; Wilentz, *American Democracy*, 569–72.

36 *Cadiz (Ohio) Sentinel*, June 26, Aug. 7, Aug. 28, and Sept. 25, 1844; *Steubenville (Ohio) American Union*, July 25, Sept. 5 ("skinned the coons"), Sept. 12, 1844.

37 *Cadiz (Ohio) Sentinel*, Oct. 16, 1844 (Stanton write-in votes); *Steubenville (Ohio) American Union*, Nov. 14, 1844.

38 *Sunbury (Pa.) American*, Nov. 23, 1844 (predicts Cass in cabinet); Stanton to Tappan, Dec. 5, 1844, Benjamin Tappan Papers, LC; Stanton to Tappan, Dec. 26, 1844, Edwin Stanton Papers, LC, box 1, image 90.

39 *New York Tribune*, Jan. 17, 1845 ($45,000 missing); *Brooklyn Daily Eagle*, Jan. 18, 1845 (McNulty "denies having appropriated one cent of House funds to his own use"); *New York Tribune*, Jan. 20, 1845 (House approves resolution calling for criminal prosecution); *Vermont Phoenix* (Brattleboro), Jan. 24, 1845 (McNulty involved with "degraded prostitutes"); Stanton to Tappan, Jan. 27, 1845, Edwin Stanton Papers, LC, box 1, images 100–101.

40   *Congressional Globe*, 28th Cong., 2d Sess., pp. 131–32 (Jan. 13, 1845) (Brinker-hoff); Stanton to Brinkerhoff, Jan. 19, 1845, in *New York Sun*, Mar. 14, 1892.

41   *Pittsburgh Daily Post*, Feb. 15, 1845 (summary of the pamphlet); Stanton to Sanders, June 18, 1845, Edwin Stanton Papers, LC, box 1, image 106; Sanders, *Memoirs*.

42   Flower, *Edwin McMasters Stanton*, 42–43; Graves, "Early Life and Career of Stanton," 42–43; Howe, *Historical Collections of Ohio*, 1:976 ("travelled all over the country").

43   *Daily Ohio Statesman*, Nov. 26, 1845; *Cadiz (Ohio) Sentinel*, Nov. 26, 1845. At about this time an Ohio Democrat wrote to Senator Allen, asking about Tod's views on banks and saying, "[If Tod is] not sound I am in favor of Stanton." Whitman to Allen, Nov. 23, 1845, Allen Papers.

44   *Baltimore Sun*, Dec. 18–21, 1845 ("severest" in Dec. 18); *National Intelligencer*, Dec. 17–21, 1845 (delay in Dec. 17); *New York Herald*, Dec. 18–21, 1845 ("eloquent appeal" Dec. 20).

45   Darwin Stanton to Pamphila Wolcott, [Dec. 21, 1845,] in Wolcott, *Edwin M. Stanton*, 90–91; *National Intelligencer*, Dec. 22, 1845; *New York Herald*, Dec. 22, 1845.

46   *Baltimore Sun*, Dec. 23, 1845 (closing); ibid., Dec. 25, 1845 (acquittal); *New London (Ct.) News*, Dec. 27, 1845 ("legal quibble"); *Cleveland Herald*, Dec. 27, 1845, quoting *Baltimore Clipper*; *Daily Ohio Statesman*, Dec. 30, 1845 ("fine specimen").

47   *Speech of Hon. William Allen, of Ohio . . . Oregon Notice*; Stanton to Allen, Feb. 20, 1846, Allen Papers; *The Tennessean*, May 11, 1846; *New York Tribune*, May 13, 1846 (Polk's message); *Steubenville (Ohio) American Union*, May 14, 1846 ("from the Rio Grande"); Eisenhower, *So Far from God*, 64–68; Greenburg, *A Wicked War*; Johannsen, *To the Halls of the Montezumas*, 7–20.

48   *Steubenville (Ohio) American Union*, May 28 (war meeting); ibid., June 11, 1846 (departure); Whalen and Whalen, *The Fighting McCooks*, 28–29.

49   George McCook Diary, Jan. 16 and Feb. 27, 1847, McCook Family Papers; Stanton to Margaret Beatty, 1847 and undated, ibid.; Whalen and Whalen, *The Fighting McCooks*, 29–30.

50   *Steubenville (Ohio) American Union*, Sept. 24, 1846; Mary Hooker to Emanuel Hooker, Oct. 7, 1846, Hooker Papers; Nancy Stanton to Hooker, Nov. 22, 1846, ibid.; Flower, *Edwin McMasters Stanton*, 45; Wolcott, *Edwin M. Stanton*, 122.

51   *Carroll County (Ohio) Free Press*, Sept. 25, 1846 (black law issue in election); *Ravenna (Ohio) Portage Sentinel*, Sept. 30, 1846 (same); *Woodsfield (Ohio) Spirit of Democracy*, Oct. 3, 1846 ("complete inundation"); Stanton to Chase, Nov. 30, 1846, in Niven, *Chase Papers*, 2:134–37 ("events of the past summer"); Blue, *Salmon P. Chase*; Ellen Eslinger, "The Evolution of Racial Politics in Early Ohio," in Cayton and Hobbs, *The Center of a Great Empire*, 81–104 (on

Ohio black laws); Holt, *Party Politics in Ohio*, 238–49 (black laws in 1846 campaign); Niven, *Salmon P. Chase*.

52 Stanton to Chase, Jan. 5, 1847, in Niven, *Chase Papers*, 2:138–41 ("game he played"); Stanton to Chase, Mar. 11, 1847, ibid., 142–44 ("work on the circuit"); Stanton to Chase, May 1, 1847, Chase Papers, UPA, reel 6 ("dirty work").

53 *Steubenville (Ohio) American Union*, July 8, 1847 (troops return); McCook to Margaret Beatty, Aug. 1847, in Whalen and Whalen, *The Fighting McCooks*, 30 (McCook-Beatty marriage on Aug. 5, 1847); Stanton to Chase, Dec. 2, 1847, Chase Papers, UPA, reel 6 ("my nature"); Stanton to Sanders, Feb. 21, 1848, Edwin Stanton Papers, LC, box 1, image 116 ("laurels in Mexico"). Greenburg, *A Wicked War* is excellent on the emerging opposition to the war.

Chapter 3: "The Blackest Place"

1 Dickens, *American Notes*, 153; Mackay, *The Western World*, 3:86; Trollope, *North America*, 2:100; Graves, "Early Life and Career of Stanton," 56–63; Nasaw, *Andrew Carnegie*, 30; Reiser, "Pittsburgh."

2 *New York Tribune*, Sept. 5, 1843 (Shaler among Democratic candidates); *Pittsburgh Daily Post*, Oct. 29–30, 1847; *Daily Ohio Statesman*, Nov. 1, 1847; Stanton to Chase, Dec. 2, 1847, Chase Papers, UPA, reel 6; *Pittsburgh Daily Post*, Dec. 9, 1847; Eastman, *Courts and Lawyers of Pennsylvania*, 3:620–21.

3 Stanton to Chase, Dec. 2, 1847, Chase Papers, UPA, reel 6; Chase to Stanton, Jan. 9, 1848, in Niven, *Chase Papers*, 2:163–64; *Woodsfield (Ohio) Spirit of Democracy*, Jan. 14, 1848 (convention); Stanton to Pamphila Wolcott, Jan. 20, 1848, in Wolcott, *Edwin M. Stanton*, 161; *Kalida (Ohio) Venture*, Jan. 25, 1848 (convention); Stanton to Chase, Feb. 16, 1848, Chase Papers, UPA, reel 6.

4 Vallandigham to Stanton, June 26, 1848, Edwin Stanton Papers, LC, box 1, image 121; Chase to John Van Buren, July 19, 1848, in Niven, *Chase Papers*, 2:176; Flower, *Edwin McMasters Stanton*, 54 (Lecky Harper); Earle, *Jacksonian Antislavery*, 144–62.

5 Stanton to Pamphila Wolcott, Nov. 11, 1848, in Wolcott, *Edwin M. Stanton*, 163; Earle, *Jacksonian Antislavery*, 163–80; Holt, *American Whig Party*, 259–382; Wilentz, *American Democracy*, 602–32.

6 *Pittsburgh Daily Post*, Dec. 22, 1848; *Daily Ohio Statesman*, Dec. 26, 1848 ("we know of no one, whose opinions are entitled to more weight and respect"); *Washington Daily Union*, Dec. 28, 1848.

7 Stanton to Chase, Feb. 24 and May 7, 1849, Chase Papers, UPA, reel 7; *Washington Daily Union*, Feb. 27, 1849 ("Free Soil Democrat"); Blue, *Salmon P. Chase*, 68–74; Maizlish, *Triumph of Sectionalism*, 124–42 ("three months of intrigue"); Niven, *Salmon P. Chase*, 114–25.

8   Stanton to Chase, June 28, 1850, Chase Papers, UPA, reel 8; Bordewich, *America's Great Debate*; Stahr, *Seward*, 120–23.

9   Chase to Stanton, Mar. 15 and May 27, 1850, Edwin Stanton Papers, LC, box 1, images 144 and 146; *Pittsburgh Daily Post*, June 20, 1850 (Walker); Stanton to Chase, June 28, 1850, Chase Papers, UPA, reel 8; Chase to Morse, Oct. 30, 1850, in Niven, *Chase Papers*, 2:311 (Stanton for Senate).

10 Stanton to Sanders, June 13 and July 17, 1849, Edwin Stanton Papers, LC, box 1, images 127–28, 132–34; Sanders to Stanton (with endorsement), July 29, 1849, ibid., images 134–35; Maizlish, *Triumph of Sectionalism*, 162–64.

11 Stanton to Tappan, Aug. 4, 1851, Benjamin Tappan Papers, LC, reel 9; *Cadiz (Ohio) Sentinel*, Aug. 9, 1851 (Democratic convention); Stanton to Chase, Sept. 7, 1851, Chase Papers, UPA, reel 9.

12 Stanton to Tappan, Feb. 9, 1852, Benjamin Tappan Papers, LC; Stanton to Lucy Stanton, June 5 and Oct. 25, 1852, in Gorham, *The Life and Public Services*, 1:74; Wilentz, *American Democracy*, 662.

13 *Steubenville (Ohio) True American*, Jan. 4, 1855 ("Americans should rule America"); ibid., Feb. 8, 1855 ("Edwin M. Stanton"); Corry to Holt, May 1, 1856, Holt Papers, LC; Leonard, *Lincoln's Forgotten Ally*, 78.

14 Stanton to Ellen Hutchison, May 11, 1856, Edwin M. Stanton Family Papers (from Washington); *Official Proceedings of the National Democratic Convention*, 8 (McCook); *Proceedings of the First Three Republican National Conventions*, 40 (Wolcott); Pamphila Wolcott, "Was Mr. Stanton a Pro-Slavery Democrat?," *New York Sun*, Mar. 14, 1892; Wilentz, *American Democracy*, 694–706.

15 Stanton to Chase, Dec. 1847, Chase Papers, UPA, reel 6; Stanton to Sanders, June 13, 1849, Edwin Stanton Papers, LC, box 1, image 127.

16 Stanton to [Maria Bates], 1848 and 1849, in Wolcott, *Edwin M. Stanton*, 114–19; Stanton to Maria Bates, July 22, 1848, Vertical File, Ohio History Connection. Wolcott did not name Maria Bates, but the letters fit perfectly with details of the Kelley and Bates family, such as the death of Alfred Kelley in December 1859. See Stanton to [Maria Bates], Feb. 2, 1860, in Wolcott, *Edwin M. Stanton*, 154 (consoling her on the death of her father). See Gold, *Democracy in Session*, 54–55 (Alfred Kelley); Kelley, *A Genealogical History*, 101 (Maria Kelley Bates); Klein, *Be It Remembered*, 25–27, 51 (Kelley and Bates at Trinity); *Weekly Law Bulletin & Ohio Law Journal*, May 5, 1890 (obituary of James Bates).

17 *St. Cloud (Minn.) Democrat*, Jan. 30, 1862 (Swisshelm); Carnegie, *Edwin M. Stanton*, 5; Wolcott, *Edwin M. Stanton*, 124 (Plutarch), 128 (Eyre), 161 (Copperfield); Hoffert, *Jane Grey Swisshelm*.

18 Stanton to Chase, Sept. 7, 1851, Chase Papers, UPA, reel 9; Flower, *Edwin McMasters Stanton*, 51 ("loved his son"); Marvel, *Lincoln's Autocrat*, 65–66 (Oella).

19 *Pittsburgh Daily Post*, Nov. 27, 1849 ("the cap of the knee was badly fractured by the fall. Mr. Stanton was taken back to Steubenville on Saturday morning, in *Messenger No. 2*, where he will remain until his restoration shall be complete"); Stanton to Walker, Nov. 28, 1849, Edwin Stanton Papers, Huntington ("the accident that laid me up with a broken limb"); *Pittsburgh Daily Post*, Dec. 11, 1849 (Stanton's "recovery will be slow and the process painful"); Stanton to Maria Bates, Jan. 14, 1850, in Wolcott, *Edwin M. Stanton*, 141 ("longer than ever before"); Flower, *Edwin McMasters Stanton*, 56 ("while interviewing"); Wolcott, *Edwin M. Stanton*, 139 ("had to cross").

20 James Hutchison to Ellen Hutchison, Nov. 13, 1846, in Richert, *Ellen Hutchison Stanton Letters*, 40–41 (engagement to Wilkins); Ellen Hutchison to Mary Hutchison, Mar. 26, 1849, ibid., 122–23 ("too stupid"); Ellen Hutchison to Mary Hutchison, Nov. 22, 1849, ibid., 138–39 ("our beaux here are about the same"); Federal Census, Pittsburgh, 1850, on University of Pittsburgh website (listed as Lewis Hutchinson); Stanton to Reuben Walworth, Dec. 6, 1851, Edwin Stanton Papers, LC, box 1, image 165 ("young lady"). Marvel, *Lincoln's Autocrat*, 69, suggests that Stanton met Ellen at St. Peter's Episcopal Church. The Hutchisons were founding members of St. Peter's, but the church did not open until late 1852, which seems too late for a first meeting between Stanton and Ellen. *Historical Sketch of St. Peter's Church, 1850–1918*, on film at University of Pittsburgh Archives.

21 Federal Census, Pittsburgh, 1850, on University of Pittsburgh website (listed as Edward Stanton); Stanton to William Stanton, Oct. 26, 1854, William Stanton Papers, Huntington.

22 Stanton to Tappan, Feb. 9, 1852, Benjamin Tappan Papers, LC; Stanton to Ellen Hutchison, Dec. 11, 1854, Edwin M. Stanton Family Papers. There is a photocopy of these letters in the miscellaneous manuscripts at the Huntington, thanks to Harold Hyman.

23 Stanton to Ellen Hutchison, July 1854, in G. T. Stanton, *Edwin M. Stanton*, 1–2 ("wild glen a few miles from town"); Stanton to Ellen Hutchison, Oct. 12 and 28, 1854, Edwin M. Stanton Family Papers; *Logan (Ohio) Democrat & Sentinel*, Oct. 26, 1854 (Black).

24 Stanton to Ellen Hutchison, Feb. 15, 1855, undated (two letters) and Mar. 14, 1856, Edwin M. Stanton Family Papers. The undated letters are HM27118 and 27119 at the Huntington.

25 Stanton to Ellen Hutchison, Jan. 4, Feb. 13, May 11, 1856, Edwin M. Stanton Family Papers; Ashmore, *Dates of Supreme Court Decisions*, 68 (*Dred Scott* case argued Feb. 11–13, 1856) (online at the Supreme Court website).

26 Stanton to Ellen Hutchison, June 25, 1856, Edwin M. Stanton Family Papers; parish register, St. Peter's Episcopal Church, June 25, 1856, on film at

University of Pittsburgh Archives; *Pittsburgh Gazette*, June 27, 1856; James Hutchison to daughter, June 27, 1856, Edwin Stanton Papers, LSU (typescript); *Steubenville (Ohio) True American*, July 2, 1856. We have no letters from the honeymoon period so cannot be sure of the couple's travels.

27 *Woodsfield (Ohio) Spirit of Democracy*, Jan. 6, 1849 (bridge will open in May); *Ravenna (Ohio) Portage Sentinel*, May 16, 1849 (bridge under construction); *Pittsburgh Daily Post*, June 30, 1849 (Shaler chairs meeting); Ellet, *The Wheeling Bridge Suit*. Ellet is a major figure who deserves a proper biography.

28 James Baker to Charles Ellet Jr., Aug. 6, 1849, Ellet Papers (Grier has received telegram from Stanton); Stanton to Chase, Aug. 9, 1849, Chase Papers, UPA, reel 7 (expects to leave for Philadelphia next day); *Pittsburgh Daily Post*, Aug. 11, 1849 (state will apply to Grier for injunction); *State of Pennsylvania v. The Wheeling & Belmont Bridge Co. . . . Motion for Injunction before Mr. Justice Grier* (1849) (pamphlet among Elizabeth Monroe Papers); Monroe, *The Wheeling Bridge Case*, 50–51.

29 *Baltimore Sun*, Aug. 20, 1849; *Pittsburgh Daily Post*, Aug. 23, 1849 (argument "concluded yesterday"); *State of Pennsylvania v. The Wheeling & Belmont Bridge . . . Motion for Injunction before Mr. Justice Grier* (1849); Monroe, *Wheeling Bridge Case*, 50–54.

30 *Motion for Injunction before Mr. Justice Grier*; Stanton to Sanders, [Aug. 26, 1849,] Edwin Stanton Papers, LC, box 1, image 125; *Pittsburgh Daily Post*, Aug. 30, 1849 (Grier issued his opinion on Aug. 29); *Baltimore Sun*, Aug. 31, 1849 (similar); Monroe, *Wheeling Bridge Case*, 54–55.

31 Stanton to Sanders, [Aug. 30, 1849,] Edwin Stanton Papers, LC, box 1, image 138. The letter is dated just "Thursday," but that was Aug. 30 in 1849.

32 *Woodsfield (Ohio) Spirit of Democracy*, Nov. 3, 1849 (bridge now open); Stanton to Sanders, Nov. 4, 1849, Edwin Stanton Papers, LC, box 1, image 108; *Pittsburgh Daily Post*, Nov. 12, 1849 (*Messenger* stopped at bridge); *Pittsburgh Daily Dispatch*, Nov. 13, 1849 (*Hibernia* stopped at bridge); *Daily Wheeling (Va.) Gazette*, Nov. 14, 1849 (accuses Stanton of persuading *Hibernia* captain not to lower stacks); *Pittsburgh Daily Post*, Dec. 21, 1849 (Wheeling papers view Stanton as "diabolical counselor"); Monroe, *Wheeling Bridge Case*, 58–67. Stanton's handwriting is poor, but the reference to the Wheeling Bridge case and Washington show that the proper date for this letter is 1849 and not 1847. Marvel, *Lincoln's Autocrat*, 50–51 errs on this, I believe.

33 Stanton to Walker, Nov. 28, 1849, Edwin Stanton Papers, Huntington; *Pittsburgh Daily Post*, Dec. 21, 1849 ("some of the citizens"); Flower, *Edwin McMasters Stanton*, 56; Wolcott, *Edwin M. Stanton*, 139.

34 *Pittsburgh Daily Post*, Feb. 14, 1850 (Stanton leaving for Washington to attend to the Wheeling Bridge case); *Republic* (Washington), Feb. 26, 1850 (Stanton admitted to the Court); Stanton, *The Wheeling Bridge Case*; Stanton to Ellen

Hutchison, Dec. 6, 1854, in G. T. Stanton, *Edwin M. Stanton*, 2 ("floor hand-somely carpeted").

35 *Pittsburgh Gazette*, Mar. 1, 1850; Stanton to Walker, Mar. 28, 1850, in Monroe, *Wheeling Bridge Case*, 79; Dyer, *Records of an Active Life*, 143–44 ("slight lisp").

36 *Pennsylvania v. Wheeling & Belmont Bridge Co.*, 50 U.S. 647 (1850); Stanton to Sanders, June 28, 1850, Edwin Stanton Papers, LC, box 1, image 147; Monroe, *Wheeling Bridge Case*, 76–77; Walworth, *Order of Reference*, 3–4.

37 Stanton to Walworth, July 29 and Aug. 29, 1850, Edwin Stanton Papers, LC, box 1, images 153–54; *Ebensburg (Pa.) Mountain Sentinel*, Nov. 14, 1850 (Stanton and Walworth in Cincinnati); Monroe, *Wheeling Bridge Case*, 78–87; Walworth, *Order of Reference*, 4 (Wheeling), 380 (Cincinnati).

38 Stanton to Walworth, Jan. 5 and 12, 1851, Edwin Stanton Papers, LC, box 1, images 155–56; *Gallipolis (Ohio) Journal*, Feb. 20, 1851 (quote from Walworth's report); Stanton to Walworth, Feb. 26, 1851, Edwin Stanton Papers, LC, box 1, image 160 (from Washington); *Ravenna (Ohio) Portage Sentinel*, Mar. 3, 1851 (case adjourned); Stanton to J. and J. W. Johnson, Mar. 15, 1851, Gratz Papers; Stanton to [Maria Bates], Mar. 21, 1851, in Wolcott, *Edwin M. Stanton*, 161 (from Washington); Monroe, *Wheeling Bridge Case*, 87, 95–100.

39 *Republic* (Washington), Apr. 1, 1851, quoting *Ohio State Journal*; *American Telegraph* (Washington), Apr. 11, 1851; *New Orleans Daily Crescent*, Apr. 17, 1851; *Philadelphia Public Ledger*, Sept. 30, 1851; *Gallipolis (Ohio) Journal*, Oct. 2, 1851.

40 Stanton to Walworth, Dec. 6, 1851, Edwin Stanton Papers, LC, box 1, images 164–65; Stanton, *Argument for the Complainant* (pamphlet version of Stanton's argument); Monroe, *Wheeling Bridge Case*, 101–14 (summary arguments).

41 *Pennsylvania v. Wheeling & Belmont Bridge Co.*, 54 U.S. 518 (1852); Monroe, *Wheeling Bridge Case*, 123–24 (debate among justices on height). Stanton sent a message on Jan. 25, saying that the Court would decide in favor of Pittsburgh and that McLean would write the opinion. If Stanton knew this, it seems likely he knew at least something of the horsetrading on the height issue. Ibid., 126.

42 Charles Ellet Jr., to Elvira Ellet, Feb. 23 and 26, 1852, Ellet Papers ("flaming speech"); *National Intelligencer*, May 29, 1862 (McLean's opinion); Monroe, *Wheeling Bridge Case*, 126–28.

43 *Congressional Globe*, 32d Cong., 1st Sess., pp. 2439–42 (Aug. 28, 1852); ibid., 2479–80 (Aug. 30, 1852); *Wheeling (Va.) Intelligencer*, Sept. 1, 1852 ("question is settled"); Monroe, *Wheeling Bridge Case*, 131–46, esp. 141–42 re: Stanton's role.

44 Reverdy Johnson to Ellet, Feb. 17, 1853, Ellet Papers; *Pittsburgh Daily Post*, Dec. 13, 1853 (Stanton argues Erie RR case); *Wheeling (Va.) Intelligencer*, Dec. 14, 1853; *Cadiz (Ohio) Telegraph*, Dec. 21, 1853 ("withdrawn her opposition

to that noble structure"); *Meigs County (Ohio) Telegraph*, Dec. 27, 1853 ("yields to the sentiments of the nation"); *Indiana American*, Dec. 30, 1853 ("last of this foolish proceeding"); Monroe, *Wheeling Bridge Case*, 146–48.

45 *Wheeling (Va.) Daily Intelligencer*, May 18, 1854; Monroe, *Wheeling Bridge Case*, 150–54.

46 Stanton to Ellen Hutchison, Dec. 3, 1854, Edwin M. Stanton Family Papers (from Washington); *Pennsylvania v. Wheeling & Belmont Bridge Co.*, 59 U.S. 421 (1856); *Wheeling (Va.) Daily Intelligencer*, Apr. 26, 1856 ("bridge stands"); *Ashland (Ohio) Union*, Apr. 30, 1856 (another report); Monroe, *Wheeling Bridge Case*, 154–56.

47 Population figures from U.S. Census Bureau website.

48 Stanton to Chase, June 5, 1847, in Niven, *Chase Papers*, 2:139–40; Randolph, *Memoir*.

49 Calvert, "The Allegheny City Cotton Mill Riot," pp. 97–114.

50 *Pittsburgh Daily Post*, Dec. 6, 1848; Calvert, "Allegheny City Cotton Mill Riot," 113–24.

51 *Pittsburgh Gazette*, Jan. 18–20, 1849 ("surprised" on Jan. 18); *Pittsburgh Daily Dispatch*, Jan. 18–20, 1849; Calvert, "Allegheny City Cotton Mill Riot," 124–29.

52 *Ravenna (Ohio) Portage Sentinel*, Feb. 21, 1849 (quoting Philadelphia paper); Calvert, "Allegheny City Cotton Mill Riot," 129–30.

53 *Pittsburgh Daily Dispatch*, Apr. 11, 12, 20, 24, 1849; *Pittsburgh Daily Post*, Apr. 11, 12, 13, 17, 18, 1849; *Pittsburgh Gazette*, Apr. 23, 1849; Stanton to Barlow, Nov. 23, 1861, in Flower, *Edwin McMasters Stanton*, 122–23 ("the nigger-arming question").

54 Stanton to Chase, Dec. 2, 1847, Chase Papers, UPA, reel 6 ("impressed me favorably"); Yulee to Stanton, Feb. 23, 1848, Edwin Stanton Papers, LC, box 1, image 117; Rosen, *The Jewish Confederates*, 55–85 (on Yulee).

55 Stanton to Tappan, Feb. 26, 1852, Benjamin Tappan Papers, LC ("will return in March to argue Yulee's case"); *Sumter Banner* (Sumterville, S.C.), Apr. 6, 1852 (Stanton argued Yulee's case in late March); *American Telegraph* (Washington), June 10, 1852 (Stanton argued Yulee's case); Stanton, *Florida Contested Election*.

56 Stanton, *Florida Contested Election*; Sen. Rep. No. 349, 32d Cong., 1st Sess. (Aug. 21, 1852); *Congressional Globe*, 32d Cong., 1st Sess. App. 1070–75 (Aug. 27, 1852).

57 *Pleadings, Exhibits and Evidence, in the Case of Joshua Nachtrieb*. Though lacking the cover page, this 158-page pamphlet is at the Bibliothek Friedrich-Ebert-Stiftung. On the Society in general see Arndt, *George Rapp's Harmony Society*.

58 *Pleadings, Exhibits and Evidence*; *Nachtrieb v. Harmony Settlement*, 17 Fed. Cases 1139 (1855). The opinion published in *Federal Cases* blends both Grier's first

opinion, on Nachtrieb's departure, and second opinion, after the accounting. A copy of the first Grier opinion is with the *Pleadings* pamphlet in the files of the Bibliothek Friedrich-Ebert-Stiftung; both Grier opinions are in the pamphlet of Stanton's Supreme Court argument: *Romelius L. Baker, et al., versus Joshua Nachtrieb . . . Edwin M. Stanton for the Appellee* (1856) (pamphlet at LC).

59 *Pleadings, Exhibits and Evidence.* Irwin's opinion is also with the *Pleadings* pamphlet at the Bibliothek Friedrich-Ebert-Stiftung. See *Richmond (Va.) Dispatch,* Apr. 16, 1852 (summarizing Grier's initial decision); *Meigs County (Ohio) Telegraph,* Aug. 31, 1852 (reporting work of commissioner).

60 *Pleadings, Exhibits and Evidence.* The reported decision is at *Nachtrieb v. Harmony Settlement,* 17 Fed. Cases 1139 (1855) (quote 1145); a newspaper clipping of the decision (including the figure with interest of $3,890) is at Bibliothek Friedrich-Ebert-Stiftung.

61 *Baker v. Nachtrieb,* 60 U.S. 126 (1856); *Washington Evening Star,* Dec. 17, 1856 (reporting decision); *Romelius L. Baker, et al., versus Joshua Nachtrieb . . . Edwin M. Stanton for the Appellee* (1856); Ashmore, *Dates of Supreme Court Decisions,* 67.

62 There are many secondary accounts: Burlingame, *Abraham Lincoln: A Life,* 2:80–83; Donald, *Lincoln,* 185–87; Marvel, *Lincoln's Autocrat,* 71–76; Parkinson, "The Patent Case"; Thomas and Hyman, *Stanton,* 63–66. Burlingame shows that the story first appeared in print in the late nineteenth century.

63 Stanton to Ellen Hutchison, Sept. 25 and 26, 1855, Edwin M. Stanton Family Papers; *Cincinnati Daily Commercial,* Sept. 21, 1855 (Stanton counsel for Manny); ibid., Sept 22, 1855 (Stanton, Harding, Lincoln, and Corwine counsel for Manny); ibid., Sept. 29, 1855 (Stanton's argument).

64 Donald, *Lincoln,* 186; Goodwin, *Team of Rivals,* 174–75; McClellan, *McClellan's Own Story,* 152; Herndon to Weik, Jan. 6, 1887, Herndon-Weik Papers; Dickson to Weik, Apr. 17, 1888, in Wilson and Davis, *Herndon's Informants,* 655 ("never heard nor do I believe Stanton used unseemly language towards Mr. L."). Although dated 1887, McClellan's book was published in December 1886. See *Washington Evening Star,* Dec. 6, 1886 (review). See also Parkinson, "The Patent Case"; Marvel, *Lincoln's Autocrat,* 72–73, 467–69.

65 *McCormick v. Talcott,* 61 U.S. 402 (1857); Parkinson, "The Patent Case."

66 Pamphila Wolcott wrote that her brother and sister-in-law were "boarding at the National Hotel at the time of the sickness which prostrated so many persons in that hotel" (*Edwin M. Stanton,* 132). This seems unlikely. The National Hotel disease affected only Buchanan and one or two others before early March 1857. Walters, *Outbreak in Washington.* Stanton asked his Steubenville servant in February 1857 to send grape vines, an unlikely request for a man living in a hotel. Stanton to Alfred Taylor, Feb. 17, 1857, Edwin

Stanton Papers, LC, box 1, image 170. And Stanton was well settled at his rented residence by mid-March. Stanton to Black, Mar. 12, 1857, Black Papers, reel 1 (with return address).

Chapter 4: "Untiring Industry"

1   Buchanan address, Mar. 4, 1857, in Curtis, *Life of James Buchanan*, 2:189; Stanton to Alfred Taylor, Mar. 5, 1857, Edwin Stanton Papers, LC, box 1, image 171; *Washington Daily Union*, Mar. 12, 1857; Fehrenbacher, *The Dred Scott Case*, 305–16; Paul Finkelman, "James Buchanan, Dred Scott, and the Whisper of a Conspiracy," in Quist and Birkner, *James Buchanan*, 20–45.

2   *Washington Union*, Mar. 7, 1857 (Black nominated and confirmed); *Washington Evening Star*, Mar. 11, 1857 (Black arrived in Washington); Stanton to Black, Mar. 12, 1857, Black Papers, reel 1; Black to Stanton, Mar. 1857, Edwin Stanton Papers, LC, box 1, image 174; Stanton to Black, Mar. 16, 1857, Black Papers, reel 2.

3   Stanton to Black, Apr. 13, 1857, Black Papers, reel 3; Ellen Stanton to Stanton, June 10 and July 1, 1857, in G. T. Stanton, *Edwin M. Stanton*, appendix; Stanton to Black, Aug. 25, 1857, Black Papers, reel 6; Easby-Smith, *The Department of Justice*, 3–18; Langeluttig, *The Department of Justice of the United States*, 1–8.

4   Della Torre to Black, July 4 and Aug. 4, 1857, folder 4, box 7, entry 27, RG60, NA; Black to James Bayard, Apr. 22, 1858, in House Exec. Doc. No. 84, 36th Cong., 1st Sess., pp. 4–6 (1860); Black to R. M. T. Hunter, May 26, 1868, in ibid., 3–4 ("fabricated titles"); Hoffman, *Reports of Land Cases*, 389–99 (Limantour opinion).

5   Stanton to Black, Oct. 26, 1857, Black Papers, reel 7; Black to Stanton, Nov. 20, 1857, folder 1, box 6, entry 27, RG60, NA (asking opinion on Calif. case); John Dimitry to Stanton, Jan. 26, 1858, ibid. (asking opinion on two Calif. cases).

6   Buchanan Annual Message, Dec. 8, 1857, in Moore, *The Works of James Buchanan*, 10:148–51; *Congressional Globe*, 35th Cong., 1st Sess., p. 18 (Dec. 9, 1857) (Douglas); Johannsen, *Stephen A. Douglas*, 576–631; Nevins, *The Emergence of Lincoln*, 1:250–301; Stampp, *America in 1857*, 295–322.

7   Stanton to Douglas, Dec. 11, 1857, Douglas Papers; Black, "Mr. Black to Mr. Wilson," 263 ("always sound").

8   Black to Stanton, Feb. 17, 1858, in House Exec. Doc. No. 84, 36th Cong., 1st Sess. (1860) (instructions); Black to Jacob Thompson, Feb. 17, 1858, ibid. (Stanton starts tomorrow); Black to Stanton, Feb. 17, 1858, Black Papers, reel 8 (fee agreement); Stanton to Black, Feb. 19, 1858, ibid. (regrets that they did not speak "more fully"); Stanton to Black, July 1, 1859, folder

1, box 6, entry 27, RG60, NA ("President advanced to me $250 for his nephew's ticket from New York to San Francisco").

9 *Washington Evening Star*, July 27, 29, and Aug. 3, 1857 (Harrison court of inquiry); Stanton to Eleanor Hutchison, Feb. 20, 1858, Wilkins-Hutchison-Wells Family Papers; Stanton to Ellen Stanton, Feb. 21, 1858, in G. T. Stanton, *Edwin M. Stanton*, 7; Stanton to Watson, Mar. 2, 1858, in Flower, *Edwin McMasters Stanton*, 68; Stanton to Black, July 1, 1859, box 6, entry 27, RG60, NA. The expense report shows payment for passage for Stanton and Harrison but not for Eddie or Buchanan. House Exec. Doc. No. 84, 36th Cong., 1st Sess., p. 10 (1860).

10 Stanton to Ellen Stanton, Feb. 28 and Mar. 3, 1858, in G. T. Stanton, *Edwin M. Stanton*, 11–14.

11 Stanton to Ellen Stanton, Mar. 4–19, 1858, ibid., 14–21; Stanton Diary, Mar. 19, 1858, in Gorham, *The Life and Public Services*, 1:51 (arrived 10 p.m.); Stanton to Watson, Mar. 19, 1858, in Flower, *Edwin McMasters Stanton*, 69; Muscatine, *Old San Francisco*, 136 ("elegant five-story fireproof International Hotel on Jackson Street between Montgomery and Kearny").

12 Stanton to Ellen Stanton, Mar. 21, 1858, in G. T. Stanton, *Edwin M. Stanton*, 39 (already met Della Torre); Hoffman, *Reports of Land Cases*, 390–92 (summarizes documents).

13 *Daily Alta California*, Aug. 13, 1857 (Castañares testimony); ibid., Aug. 22, 1857 (attempt to kill Castañares); ibid., Sept. 11, 1857 (Carrasquedo testimony); Hoffman, *Reports of Land Cases*, 407 ("official position"); Hittell, "Limantour," 158.

14 *Daily Alta California*, Nov. 3, 1857 (Hoffman used commissioners); Stanton to Watson, Apr. 3, 1858, in Flower, *Edwin McMasters Stanton*, 69; Stanton to Ellen Stanton, Apr. 4, 1858, in G. T. Stanton, *Edwin M. Stanton*, 40–41; Stanton to Black, Apr. 16, 1858, Black Papers, reel 9; Gorham, *The Life and Public Services*, 1:53 (quoting R. C. Hopkins); ibid., 1:63 (diary entry for Apr. 27, 1858 re: Benecia documents); Stanton to Buchanan, July 19 and Aug. 4, 1858, Buchanan Papers, LC.

15 Harrison to Black, June 4, 1858, Black Papers, reel 9 ("I have never"); Buchanan Jr. to Black, June 20, 1858, ibid.; Black to Stanton, Apr. 27 and May 15, 1858, in Gorham, *The Life and Public Services*, 1:55–56 (not in Black or Stanton papers); Black to Stanton, July 19, 1858, box 6, entry 27, RG60, NA (quoting Buchanan).

16 Several papers in January 1862 cited Stanton's California work as preparation for his War Department work: *Cincinnati Daily Press*, Jan. 22, 1862 (proved in California his "vigor and ability"); *Philadelphia Inquirer*, Jan. 28, 1862 ("labors in California were Herculean").

17 Stanton Diary, Apr. 27, 1858, in Gorham, *The Life and Public Services*, 1:63 (Benicia boxes); *Sacramento Daily Union*, July 17, 1858 ("rather a clincher");

Stanton to Black, Aug. 2, 1858, in Gorham, *The Life and Public Services*, 1:64 (seals); *Daily Alta California*, Aug. 6, 1858 ("grants to Limantour have peculiar seals"); Stanton to Black, Sept. 5, 1858, in Gorham, *The Life and Public Services*, 1:64–65 (photographs).

18   Black to Stanton, July 19 and Aug. 4, 1858, box 6, entry 27, RG 60, NA; *Daily Alta California*, Sept. 1, 1858 (summary of circuit court complaint); Ascher, "Lincoln's Administration."

19   Circuit Court Complaint, *United States v. Parrot*, Aug. 30, 1858 (copy at University of California–Irvine Library); *Daily Alta California*, Sept. 1, 1858; *Daily Evening Bulletin* (San Francisco), Sept. 1, 1858; Shuck, *History of the Bench and Bar of California*, 261–63.

20   Circuit Court Complaint, *United States v. Parrot*, Aug. 30, 1858 (correspondence 28–73); *Daily Alta California*, Sept. 1, 1858 (order to show cause); Stanton to Watson, Sept. 3, 1858, in Flower, *Edwin McMasters Stanton*, 70. Some have accused Stanton of acting improperly by working for the government on the Castillero case, claiming the New Almaden mine for the government, while he worked against the government in the Fossat case, claiming part of the mine for private parties. The *Sacramento Union* commented, "The Government has been made to interfere and oust parties from the mine, not for its own benefit or the interest of its citizens, but to profit speculators who are shrewd enough to make Uncle Sam pay the expenses while they pocket the gains." *Sacramento Daily Union*, Nov. 23, 1858. A recent biographer argues that Stanton "pursued a case as government counsel in a manner that significantly benefited a private client." Marvel, *Lincoln's Autocrat*, xiii; see also Ascher, "Lincoln's Administration," 39–40. This ignores two key points. First, there is no evidence that Stanton did any work for the Fossat claimants after he left Washington for California. Other lawyers argued the Fossat case in the Supreme Court while Stanton was on the steamship. *Washington Evening Star*, Feb. 27, 1858 (oral argument in Fossat case). Second, although the two cases involved the same mine, the issues were utterly different. The Fossat case was about a vague boundary; the Castillero case was about whether the Castillero claim was based on forged documents. Stanton was not acting on his own in bringing the Castillero case; Black *directed* Stanton to "proceed with all possible diligence & energy in vindicating the rights of the [United] States to the New Almaden quicksilver mine." And it seems almost certain that when Black issued this instruction, he was aware of Stanton's prior work on the Fossat case. Black to Stanton, Aug. 4, 1858, box 6, entry 27, RG60, NA.

21   *Sacramento Daily Union*, July 5 and 7, 1858 (Limantour opposed closing evidence); *Daily Alta California*, Sept. 14, 1858 (government application to set day for final argument); ibid., Sept. 22, 1858 (Limantour lawyers resign);

ibid., Oct. 8, 1858 (Stanton closing in New Almaden); ibid., Oct. 15, 1858 (Stanton closing Limantour); ibid., Oct. 19, 1858 (Limantour lawyer did not argue).

22 *Daily Alta California*, Oct. 30 and 31, 1858; McAllister, *Reports of Cases Argued and Determined*, 272–328 (McAllister opinion); ibid., 328–59 (Hoffman opinion; quote 350).

23 *Daily Alta California*, Nov. 20, 1858; Hoffman, *Reports of Land Cases*, 389–451 (quote 451).

24 Stanton to Ellen Stanton, Mar. 21, 1858, in G. T. Stanton, *Edwin M. Stanton*, 39; Black to Stanton, Apr. 26, 1858, in Gorham, *The Life and Public Services*, 1:55–56.

25 Stanton to Theo Umbstaetter, Apr. 19, 1858, in Flower, *Edwin McMasters Stanton*, 69–70; Clarke, *William Tecumseh Sherman*, 203–27, 317; Ethington, *The Public City*, 86–169; Richards, *The California Gold Rush*, 188–91; Senkewicz, *Vigilantes in Gold Rush San Francisco*; Taniguchi, *Dirty Deeds*. Taniguchi's excellent new book shows that some members of the Executive Committee continued to meet, in secret, while Stanton was in San Francisco. The author's great-great-grandfather Clancey John Dempster was a leader of the Vigilance Committee.

26 Stanton to Ellen Stanton, Apr. 11, 1858, in G. T. Stanton, *Edwin M. Stanton*, 42; Stanton to Theo Umbstaetter, Apr. 19, 1858, in Flower, *Edwin McMasters Stanton*, 69–70; Stanton to Black, Aug. 1, 1858, Black Papers, reel 9.

27 Stanton to Ellen Stanton, Aug. 17 and [Nov. 20], 1858, in G. T. Stanton, *Edwin M. Stanton*, 47, 49. The second letter is dated based on the steamship sailing.

28 *Sacramento Daily Union*, May 1, 1858 ("robbed Stovall of his nigger"); ibid., May 4, 1858 (duel avoided); ibid., Aug. 23, 1858 (Ferguson-Johnston); ibid., Sept. 17, 1858 (Ferguson's death); Stanton to Watson, May 2, 1858, in Flower, *Edwin McMasters Stanton*, 70–71; Stanton to Black, Aug. 1, 1858, Black Papers, reel 9; Ethington, *The Public City*, 80–83; McGrath, "A Violent Birth."

29 Stanton to Watson, Apr. 18, 1858, in Flower, *Edwin McMasters Stanton*, 69; Stanton to Ellen Stanton, Apr. 26, 1858, in G. T. Stanton, *Edwin M. Stanton*, 44 ("greaser"); Robinson, *Life in California*, 73; Moore, "'We Feel the Want of Protection.'"

30 *Sacramento Daily Union*, Sept. 3, 1858 ("Buchanan Democracy achieved a decided triumph"); *Daily Alta California*, Sept. 4, 1858 (similar); Stanton to Black, Sept. 5, 1858, in Gorham, *The Life and Public Services*, 1:77–78; Richards, *The California Gold Rush*, 214.

31 Stanton to Ellen Stanton, Nov. 4, 1858, in G. T. Stanton, *Edwin M. Stanton*, 48–49 ("ready to go but for Eddie's illness"); Stanton to Ellen Stanton,

ca. Nov. 20, 1858, ibid., 49 ("if he continues"); *Daily Alta California*, Jan. 1, 1859 (*Golden Gate* to sail on Jan. 5); Stanton to Ellen Stanton, Jan. 14, 1859, in G. T. Stanton, *Edwin M. Stanton*, 49 (left on Jan. 5; reached Acapulco). Because he was on the boat, and because California papers did not circulate back east, Stanton probably did not see the articles suggesting that the real purpose of his work against Limantour was to help Black and his Philadelphia friends. One paper charged, "[The] Bolton & Barron claim is in the hands of a joint stock company, most of the members of which reside in Philadelphia. The Limantour claim was the only one that stood in the way of this Santillan grant, and it was necessary to dispose of that to ensure the success of the latter. Attorney General Black suddenly turns up as the reputed owner of a large interest in this joint stock company. Mr. Stanton is sent to California to kill off Limantour, and leave a clear road for the Santillan claim." *Daily Alta California*, Jan. 28, 1859. Another paper printed a letter calling Stanton the "friend, counsel and agent of the speculators who own the Santillan claim." *Daily Evening Bulletin* (San Francisco), Feb. 4, 1859. Randolph defended Stanton, saying any Washington lawyer could have done what Stanton had done, consulting on one aspect of the Santillan case, "and it [is] impossible to imagine what ground of censure that fact would furnish against Mr. Black, because he thought [it] proper to employ Mr. Stanton in another case in California, or against Mr. Stanton because he accepted the employment." *Daily Alta California*, Feb. 2, 1859. See also *Daily Evening Bulletin* (San Francisco), May 1, 1858 (Stanton "actually retained by the Bolton & Barron claimants"); Stanton to Watson, May 2, 1858, in Flower, *Edwin McMasters Stanton*, 70–71 (article just a "squib"); Thorne to Buchanan, June 19, 1858, Black Papers, reel 11 (warning Buchanan of rumors that Black and Stanton would dismiss federal case against Bolton and Barron); *Sacramento Daily Union*, Nov. 23, 1858 (government effectively working "to profit speculators").

32 *New York Times*, Feb. 28, 1859; *Washington Evening Star*, Feb. 28 and Mar. 1, 1859 (Stanton, Chilton, and Ratcliffe counsel); *Alexandria (Va.) Gazette*, Mar. 1, 1859 (also names Philadelphia lawyer). For general background on Sickles and the case see Brandt, *The Congressman Who Got Away with Murder*; Keneally, *American Scoundrel*. A clerk in Stanton's office recalled that "the defense tried hard to secure Attorney-General Black but he declined to take any work outside his official duties and referred Sickles to Stanton." King, "My Recollections of the War," 290.

33 *New York Times*, Feb. 28, 1859; *Washington Evening Star*, Feb. 28 and Mar. 1, 1859.

34 *Washington Evening Star*, Mar. 1, 1859; Stanton to Matthew Upton, Mar. 1, 1859, Edwin Stanton Papers, Huntington, HM19272 (Stanton seeing

Buchanan on a patronage question that day); Brandt, *The Congressman Who Got Away with Murder*, 28–31, 188 (Buchanan and Sickles).

35 *Washington Evening Star*, Feb. 28, 1859 ("married when not yet sixteen"); *Baltimore Exchange*, Mar. 1, 1859 (urges arrest of Butterworth); *New York Herald*, Mar. 1, 1859 ("admitted Mr. Key"); *Washington Evening Star*, Mar. 2, 1859 (Butterworth statement); ibid., Mar. 5, 1859, quoting *Albany Evening Statesman*; *Harper's Weekly*, Mar. 12, 1859.

36 *Washington Evening Star*, Mar. 21, 24, 25, 1859; *Trial of the Hon. Daniel E. Sickles*, 6 (indictment).

37 *Washington Evening Star*, Apr. 6–7, 1859; *New York Tribune*, Apr. 7, 1859; *Trial of the Hon. Daniel E. Sickles*, 13–14. I have generally relied on the pamphlet for quotes.

38 *Washington Evening Star*, Apr. 4–6, 1859; *Trial of the Hon. Daniel E. Sickles*, 6–8, 15–16; Brandt, *Congressman Who Got Away with Murder*, 188 ("accused was a fast friend"). Brandt speculates that Ould did not call Butterworth because he would plead self-incrimination; surely Butterworth's public statement waived that privilege (170–71).

39 *Washington Evening Star*, Apr. 11, 1859 (opening); ibid., Apr. 13, 1859 (confession); *Baltimore Exchange*, Apr. 13, 1859 (confession); *Stroudsburg (Pa.) Jeffersonian*, Apr. 14, 1859 ("violent convulsions"); *Trial of the Hon. Daniel E. Sickles*, 25–43.

40 *Washington Evening Star*, Apr. 7, 1859; *Harper's Weekly*, Apr. 16, 1859.

41 *New York Tribune*, Apr. 15, 1859; *Trial of the Hon. Daniel E. Sickles*, 49–52.

42 *Trial of the Hon. Daniel E. Sickles*, 51.

43 *Baltimore Exchange*, Apr. 25, 1859; *Trial of the Hon. Daniel E. Sickles*, 90–93.

44 *Washington Evening Star*, Apr. 26, 1859 ("tearing his clothes"); *Baltimore Exchange*, Apr. 27, 1859 ("deafening shout"); *New York Herald*, Apr. 27, 1859 ("stentorian voice "); *New York Times*, Apr. 27, 1859 ("unable to repress").

45 Stanton to Eben Faxon, June 20, 1859, Gratz Papers ("seven weeks absence in the west").

46 Stanton to Eddie Stanton, Oct. 31, 1859, in G. T. Stanton, *Edwin M. Stanton*, 3; Stanton to [Maria Bates], Mar. 8, 1860, in Wolcott, *Edwin M. Stanton*, 156 ("delighted").

47 Stanton to Lewis Hutchison, Oct. 27, 1859, Lee Kohns Collection, New York Public Library; Stanton to William Addison, Oct. 27, 1859, Wilkins-Hutchison-Wells Papers (Addison, a doctor, apparently reported that Lewis Hutchison would die soon); Marvel, *Lincoln's Autocrat*, 111–12 (home).

48 The California land cases were *United States v. Teschmaker*, 63 U.S. 392 (argued Jan. 26, 1860); *United States v. Bennitz*, 64 U.S. 255 (Feb. 6, 1860); *United States v. Rose*, 64 U.S. 262 (Feb. 6, 1860); *United States v. Noe*, 64 U.S. 312 (Feb. 7, 1860); *United States v. Pico*, 63 U.S. 406 (Feb. 8, 1860); *United*

States v. Garcia, 63 U.S. 274 (Feb. 9, 1860); *United States v. Alviso*, 63 U.S. 318 (Feb. 14, 1860); *United States v. West*, 63 U.S. 315 (Feb. 14, 1860); *United States v. Osio*, 63 U.S. 273 (Feb. 15, 1860); *United States v. Pico*, 64 U.S. 321 (Feb. 16, 1860); *United States v. Galbraith*, 63 U.S. 89 (Feb. 20, 1860); *United States v. Castillero*, 64 U.S. 464 (Feb. 23, 1860); *United States v. Hartnell*, 63 U.S. 286 (Feb. 23, 1860); *United States v. Murphy*, 64 U.S. 476 (Feb. 23, 1860); *Gonzales v. United States*, 63 U.S. 161 (Feb. 24, 1860); *United States v. de Haro*, 63 U.S. 293 (Feb. 24, 1860); *United States v. Vallejo*, 63 U.S. 416 (Feb. 28, 1860); *United States v. Pachecho*, 63 U.S. 225 (Feb. 28, 1860); *Yturbide's Executors v. United States*, 63 U.S. 290 (Feb. 28, 1860); *United States v. Berryesa's Heirs*, 64 U.S. 499 (Feb. 28, 1860); *Yontz v. United States*, 64 U.S. 495 (Mar. 1, 1860); *Castro v. Hendricks*, 64 U.S. 438 (Apr. 25, 1860).

49 The other cases were *Pennock v. Coe*, 64 U.S. 117 (argued Jan. 30–31, 1860); *Bank of Pittsburgh v. Neal*, 63 U.S. 96 (Mar. 1, 1860); *Zabriskie v. Cleveland, Columbus & Cincinnati RR Co.*, 64 U.S. 381 (Mar. 13–14, 1860); *Adams v. Norris*, 64 U.S. 353 (Apr. 12, 16, 17, 1860); *Minturn v. LaRue*, 64 U.S. 435 (Apr. 23–24, 1860).

50 Stanton to Francis Herron, Jan. 25, 1860, Edwin Stanton Papers, New-York Historical Society.

51 *Evansville (Ind.) Daily Journal*, Jan. 24, 1860 (Holt insists Cook resign); Stanton to Buchanan, Feb. 18, 1860, Buchanan Papers, LC (Cook should resign); *Nashville Patriot*, Feb. 20, 1860 ("various kinds of rascality"); *Covode Investigation*, House Rep. No. 648, 36th Cong., 1st Sess., p. 296 (1860). See Nevins, *Emergence of Lincoln*, 2:196–99; Nichols, *Disruption of American Democracy*, 215–19, 247–48; Summers, *The Plundering Generation*, 239–60.

52 Stanton questions, [1860], Buchanan Papers, HSP, box 58; Stanton to Buchanan, June 10, 1860, ibid.; Buchanan to Stanton, June 10, 1860, Edwin Stanton Papers, LC, box 1, image 177; *Nashville Patriot*, June 14, 1860 (Forney testified Buchanan offered diplomatic post "if he would acquiesce in the policy of the administration"); House Rep. No. 648, 36th Cong., 1st Sess., p. 291 (1860) (Forney testimony).

53 *Washington Evening Star*, May 4, 1860; Stanton to Ellen Stanton, May 9, 1860, in G. T. Stanton, *Edwin M. Stanton*, 50; Stanton to Medary, June 4, 1860, Edwin Stanton Papers, Brown University; Stanton to Wolcott, June 28, 1860, in Wolcott, *Edwin M. Stanton*, 165–66; Stanton to Shaler, July 2, 1860, in Flower, *Edwin McMasters Stanton*, 80; Nichols, *Disruption of American Democracy*, 288–320.

54 Black, "To the Public," [Jan. 1870], Black Papers, reel 26; Black to Hoar, Jan. 18, 1870, in *Nashville Union & American*, Feb. 4, 1870; Gorham, *The Life and Public Services*, 1:79 (Ohio friend); *New York Sun*, Feb. 28, 1892 (Sherman); Wolcott, *Edwin M. Stanton*, 165 ("thought for a moment"). Black's "To the

Public" paper was, I believe, written in January 1870, before Wilson's essay appeared in February. See *Wheeling (W. Va.) Daily Intelligencer*, Jan. 24, 1870 (Black "preparing an elaborate paper on the character and career of Edwin M. Stanton"); *Atchison (Kan.) Daily Champion*, Feb. 5, 1870 (noting Wilson's article on Stanton); Wilson, "Edwin M. Stanton."

Chapter 5: "Surrounded by Secessionists"

1 Cooper, *We Have the War Upon Us*, 9–33; Freehling, *The Road to Disunion*, 395–425; Nevins, *Emergence of Lincoln*, 2:318–42. Residents of the District of Columbia did not vote in presidential elections until the Twenty-Third Amendment was adopted in 1961, effectively giving the District three electors in the electoral college.

2 Black to Buchanan, Nov. 20, 1860, in Curtis, *Life of James Buchanan*, 2:319–24; Buchanan message, Dec. 4, 1860, ibid., 337–50; *New York Times*, Dec. 5, 1860; *Cleveland Daily Leader*, Dec. 6, 1860.

3 Wilson, "Edwin M. Stanton," 236; Black, "Senator Wilson and Edwin M. Stanton," 824; John Ropes memo, Feb. 8, 1870, Woodman Papers; Thomas and Hyman, *Stanton*, 88–89.

4 *Wheeling (Va.) Daily Intelligencer*, Dec. 1, 1860 (families packing); *Washington Evening Star*, Dec. 1, 1860 (Cobb likely to leave); *Baltimore Exchange*, Dec. 13, 1860 (Cobb letters); *Washington Evening Star*, Dec. 14–15, 1860; *Baltimore Exchange*, Dec. 15, 1860; *National Republican*, Dec. 15, 1860 ("not a moment to be lost").

5 *Washington Evening Star*, Dec. 15, 1860; *Baltimore Exchange*, Dec. 15, 1860 (Dickinson).

6 *Senate Executive Journal*, Dec. 17, 1860 (Black nomination); *National Republican*, Dec. 18, 1860 (Stanton would succeed Black); *New York Herald*, Dec. 19, 1860 (Buchanan sent telegram to Stanton); *New York Tribune*, Dec. 19, 1860 (similar); *Cincinnati Daily Press*, Dec. 19, 1860 ("some of the ablest"); *Cadiz (Ohio) Democratic Sentinel*, Dec. 19, 1860 ("without doubt"); *Senate Executive Journal*, Dec. 19, 1860 (Stanton nomination); *National Republican*, Dec. 20, 1860 ("yesterday morning"); *Alexandria (Va.) Gazette*, Dec. 21, 1860 (Stanton confirmed); Stanton to Lewis, Dec. 21, 1860, in Konkle, *The Life of Chief Justice Ellis Lewis*, 249–50 ("arrival home this morning after ten days absence").

7 Leavitt to Stanton, Oct. 3, 1865, Edwin Stanton Papers, LC, box 29, images 78–81. Leavitt probably prepared this in response to Blair's claims at this time that Stanton favored secession.

8 *New York Herald*, Dec. 19, 1860; *New York Tribune*, Dec. 19, 1860; *Woodstock (Ill.) Sentinel*, Dec. 19, 1860 ("Old Buck seems to be having a great deal of trouble in his cabinet just now"); Stanton to Lewis, Dec. 21, 1860, in

Konkle, *Life of Chief Justice Ellis Lewis*, 249–50 (had not had any interview); *St. Louis Republican*, Jan. 20, 1862. Ropes wrote that Stanton said, "Towards the end of the month I received a telegram from Judge Black, who was then Secretary of War in place of Lewis Cass, who had resigned because the President would not garrison the forts, summoning me to Washington at once. I went at once and arriving at Washington saw in the morning paper that I had been nominated for Attorney General. While I was eating my breakfast Judge Black came in. He told me of my nomination and said 'of course you will take it.' I said 'I don't know it all depends on what the President is going to do I certainly shall not take it unless the President is going to stand by the Union.' Black said he was and had sent for me to help him. We then went over to the White House and I saw Mr. Buchanan who had just signed my commission. . . . Buchanan asked me about accepting the post much as Judge Black had done, and I made him a similar answer. He replied that he intended to do his best for the country, and had determined to stand by the Union, and had sent for me to help him, to which I replied cheerfully that I would do so." John Ropes memo, Feb. 8, 1870, Woodman Papers.

9   Lewis to Stanton, Dec. 19, 1860, in Konkle, *Life of Chief Justice Ellis Lewis*, 248–49; Stanton to Lewis, Dec. 21, 1860, ibid., 249–50.

10   Buchanan to Stanton, Dec. 24, 1860, in Moore, *Works of James Buchanan*, 11:75; *Washington Evening Star*, Dec. 24–28, 1860; *National Republican*, Dec. 24–28; *New York Times*, Dec. 29, 1860 (demands Floyd impeachment); *Wheeling (Va.) Daily Intelligencer*, Dec. 25, 1860 (reports that Thompson summoned Black, Stanton, and Ould); Nevins, *Emergence of Lincoln*, 2:372–75; Swanberg, "Was the Secretary of War a Traitor?"

11   *New York Tribune*, Dec. 25, 1860 (from Pittsburgh); *Pittsburgh Daily Post*, Dec. 25, 1860 ("plain talk of open resistance"); Gibson to Black, Dec. 25, 1860, Black Papers, reel 17; *Washington Evening Star*, Dec. 26, 1860 ("mob disturbances" in Pittsburgh); *Albany (N.Y.) Evening Journal*, Dec. 28, 1860 ("immense meeting" headed by Robinson); Stanton to Robinson, Dec. 30, 1860, in Flower, *Edwin McMasters Stanton*, 90–91; *Lancaster (Pa.) Gazette*, Jan. 3, 1861 (message from Shaler to Buchanan copied to Stanton); *New York Herald*, Jan. 4, 1861 ("liveliest satisfaction"); *Pittsburgh Daily Post*, Jan. 4–5, 1861; *Pittsburgh Gazette*, Jan. 4–5, 1861. I have not been able to find messages from Pittsburgh to Stanton in either the Stanton papers at the Library of Congress or the attorney general papers at the National Archives. Flower quotes a clerk in Shaler's Pittsburgh office saying that he sent a telegram from Shaler to Stanton (*Edwin McMasters Stanton*, 84).

12   *National Republican*, Dec. 25, 1860 (commissioners coming to Washington; Buchanan likely to yield); *Green Mountain Freeman* (Montpelier, Vt.), Dec. 27, 1860; *National Republican*, Dec. 27, 1860.

13 *Washington Evening Star*, Dec. 27, 1860 ("government forces"); ibid., Dec. 28, 1860 ("impregnable"); *New York Herald*, Dec. 28, 1860; *Philadelphia Public Ledger*, Dec. 31, 1860; Nichols, *Disruption of American Democracy*, 422–23.

14 *National Republican*, Dec. 28, 1860 (Stanton moved admission of Wolcott); Floyd to Buchanan, Dec. 27, 1860, in Crawford, *The Genesis of the Civil War*, 150; *Washington Evening Star*, Dec. 28, 1860 ("until a late hour"); *New York Herald*, Dec. 28–29, 1860 ("shaken to its extremities" is in report dated Dec. 27 in issue of Dec. 29); Stanton to Wolcott, Jan. 14, 1861, in Wolcott, *Edwin M. Stanton*, 170 ("on reaching my office I found a summons to the cabinet council").

15 *New York Tribune*, Dec. 29, 1860; *Washington Evening Star*, Dec. 28–29, 1860; Stanton to Robinson, Dec. 30, 1860, in Flower, *Edwin McMasters Stanton*, 90–91 ("dumbfounded").

16 *New York Tribune*, Dec. 31, 1860; *National Republican*, Dec. 31, 1860. Other papers had similar reports. *New York Herald*, Dec. 30–31, 1860; *New York Times*, Dec. 31, 1860.

17 Black to Holt, Dec. 30, 1860, Holt Papers, LC; Black and Stanton to Buchanan, Dec. 30, 1860, Black Papers, reel 18 (printed copy in Flower, *Edwin McMasters Stanton*, 91–93); Nichols, *Disruption of American Democracy*, 425–26.

18 Black and Stanton to Buchanan, Dec. 30, 1860, Black Papers, reel 18; Stanton to Robinson, Dec. 30, 1860, in Flower, *Edwin McMasters Stanton*, 90–91.

19 Buchanan to Carolina commissioners, Dec. 31, 1860, in Curtis, *Life of James Buchanan*, 2:386–90; *Washington Evening Star*, Jan. 1, 1861 (Holt would serve on interim basis); *New York Tribune*, Jan. 1, 1861 ("great credit"); Leonard, *Lincoln's Avengers*, 14; Nicolay and Hay, *Abraham Lincoln*, 3:89.

20 Stanton to Wolcott, Dec. 29, 1860, in Wolcott, *Edwin M. Stanton*, 169; Wolcott to Pamphila Wolcott, Dec. 30, 1860, ibid., 171; Stanton to Wolcott, Jan. 14, 1861, ibid., 170.

21 *Chicago Tribune*, Jan. 22, 1862. Other papers printed the letter slightly differently. *Philadelphia Inquirer*, Jan. 28, 1862, quoting *St. Louis Republican*.

22 John Nicolay memo, Feb. 17, 1862, in Burlingame, *With Lincoln in the White House*, 69–70. The date, of course, was Dec. 29, not Dec. 19.

23 *Brooklyn Evening Star*, Mar. 4, 1862, quoting *London Star*. There was one obvious error in the Weed article: he wrote that Dix offered his resignation in December, but Dix was not yet secretary of the treasury.

24 Buchanan to Lane, Jan. 16, 1862, in Curtis, *Life of James Buchanan*, 2:522–23; Buchanan to Blake, Apr. 2, 1862, in Moore, *Works of James Buchanan*, 11:265–66; Black to Schell, Aug. 6, 1863, in Curtis, *Life of James Buchanan*, 2:519–20; Schell to Holt, Oct. 3, 1863, Holt Papers, Huntington, box 5. Buchanan's letter to Lane was, I believe, a reaction to the "anti-Buchanan" articles at the time of Stanton's appointment to Lincoln's cabinet. *New York Herald*, Jan. 14, 1862.

25 Stanton to Schell, Oct. 8, 1863, Edwin Stanton Papers, LC, box 17, image 101 (copy in Gorham, *The Life and Public Services*, 1:151–58); Gorham, ibid., 1:158–59 (quoting Holt's comments after Stanton's death on Stanton's draft letter to Schell).

26 Buchanan to Thompson, Jan. 9, 1861, in *Washington Evening Star*, Jan. 11, 1861; Daniel Crofts, "Joseph Holt, James Buchanan, and the Secession Crisis," in Quist and Birkner, *James Buchanan*, 233n34; Klein, *President James Buchanan*, 377–89.

27 Seward to Lincoln, Dec. 29, 1861, Lincoln Papers, LC; Swett to Lincoln, Dec. 31, 1861, ibid.; Stahr, *Seward*, 220–22.

28 Weed to Lincoln, Jan. 12, 1861, Lincoln Papers, LC; *Washington Evening Star*, Feb. 12–13, 1861 (Charlotte Cushman at Washington Theater); Seward to Stanton, Feb. 16, 1861, Edwin Stanton Papers, LC, box 1, image 211; Seward to Stanton, [Feb. 1861], Edwin M. Stanton Family Papers; *Washington Evening Star*, Feb. 20, 1861 (Stanton among managers for Union Inauguration Ball); *New York Times*, Sept. 7, 1865 (Weed); Wilson, "Jeremiah S. Black and Edwin M. Stanton," 465 (Seward writes that "consultations between Mr. Stanton and myself were kept in entire confidence").

29 Stanton to Black, Jan. 10, 1861, Black Papers, reel 17; *National Republican*, Jan. 11, 1861 (first reports); *Alexandria (Va.) Gazette*, Jan. 14, 1861 (more detailed reports); Black to Scott, Jan. 16, 1861, *OR*, 1:140–42. Secondary accounts include Detzer, *Allegiance*, 152–72; Freehling, *Road to Disunion*, 486–97 (*Star of the West* in Southern secession); McClintock, *Lincoln and the Decision for War*, 119–20, 130–31.

30 Thompson to Buchanan, Jan. 8, 1861, in *Washington Evening Star*, Jan. 11, 1861; *National Republican*, Jan. 9, 1861 ("one too many"); *Washington Evening Star*, Jan. 10, 1861 (Dix perhaps for Interior); *New York Tribune*, Jan. 11, 1861 (Dix perhaps for Treasury); *Senate Executive Journal*, Jan. 11, 1861 (Dix nominated and confirmed); *Washington Evening Star*, Jan. 12, 1861 (same); King, *Turning On the Light*, 188–89; Lichterman, "John Adams Dix," 360–64.

31 *Congressional Globe*, 36th Cong., 2d Sess., pp. 294–96 (Jan. 9, 1861); ibid., 572 (Jan. 26, 1861); House Report No. 79, 36th Cong., 2d Sess. (1861), 134; Potter, *Lincoln and His Party*, 261–67; Stahr, *Seward*, 133–37; Wilson, "Jeremiah S. Black and Edwin M. Stanton," 467 (Howard); Winkle, *Lincoln's Citadel*, 84–90.

32 Gienapp and Gienapp, *The Civil War Diary of Gideon Welles*, 234 (July 2, 1863) (quoting Frank Blair); *New York Herald*, Feb. 4, 1865 (reporting Brown speech); *Cadiz (Ohio) Sentinel*, Sept. 20, 1865 (Montgomery Blair speech); Harvey to Black, Oct. 2, 1870, Black Papers, reel 26; Philip Phillips, "Summary of the Principal Events of My Life," 44, Phillips Papers; Marvel, *Lincoln's Autocrat*, 117–18.

33 Stanton to James Hutchison, Jan. 15, 1861, Wilkins-Hutchison-Wells Papers; Stanton to Robinson, Jan. 16, 1861, in *Cadiz (Ohio) Sentinel*, Jan. 22, 1862; Stanton to Brinkerhoff, Jan. 20, 1861, Edwin Stanton Papers, LC, box 1, image 210; Stanton to Oliver, Jan. 21, 1861, in Gorham, *The Life and Public Services*, 1:180.

34 Stanton to Chase, Jan. 23, 1861, Chase Papers, HSP; Sumner to Andrew, Jan. 26, 1861, Andrew Papers; Sumner to Andrew, Jan. 28, 1861, in Palmer, *The Selected Letters of Charles Sumner*, 2:47–48.

35 Clifford and Phillips to Andrew, Jan. 30, 1861, 1861–1865 Collection; Phillips and Clifford to Gray, Jan. 31, 1861, Gray Papers; Philip Phillips, "Account of January 1861 Trip to Washington," Clifford Papers.

36 *Official Opinions of the Attorneys-General*, 10:1–10 (Stanton's opinions); *United States v. Castro*, 65 U.S. 346 (1861) (Calif. land case); *Reddall v. Bryan*, 65 U.S. 420 (1860) (Md. case); *Kentucky v. Dennison*, 65 U.S. 66 (1860); Wolcott to Pamphila Wolcott, Dec. 25, 1860, in Wolcott, *Edwin M. Stanton*, 168–69; *Washington Evening Star*, Feb. 21, 1861 (argument in *Kentucky v. Dennison*); McAllister, "A *Marbury v. Madison* Moment." (*Kentucky v. Dennison*).

37 Stanton to McCook, Feb. 4, 1861, McCook Family Papers; Nichols, *Disruption of American Democracy*, 466–75.

38 Stanton to Clifford, Feb. 11, 1861, Clifford Papers.

39 *Washington Evening Star*, Feb. 23, 1861 (Lincoln arrived early; met cabinet later in the morning); *National Republican*, Feb. 25, 1861 (similar); Crofts, *A Secession Crisis Enigma*, 235 ("crept into Washington"). The memoir is the anonymous *Diary of a Public Man*, which Crofts has proven was written by William Hurlbert in collaboration with Sam Ward.

40 Stanton to Clifford, Mar. 1, 1861, Clifford Papers.

41 Anderson to Cooper, Feb. 28, 1861, Lincoln Papers, LC; Buchanan memo, Mar. 4, 1861, in Moore, *Works of James Buchanan*, 11:156; *Congressional Globe*, 37th Cong., Special Session, p. 1433 (Mar. 4, 1861) ("heads of departments" in procession); Goodwin, *Team of Rivals*, 326–29.

42 Lincoln Inaugural Address, Mar. 4, 1861, Basler, *The Collected Works of Abraham Lincoln*, 4:263–71; Stanton to Della Torre, Mar. 4, 1861, Edwin Stanton Papers, LC, box 1, image 214; Goodwin, *Team of Rivals*, 326–29, 334–35; Nichols, *Disruption of American Democracy*, 486–87.

43 *Senate Executive Journal*, Mar. 5, 1861; *Washington Evening Star*, Mar. 5–6, 1861.

44 Stanton to Lincoln, Mar. 6, 1861, Lincoln Papers, LC (Crittenden nomination papers); Stanton to Holt, Mar. 6, 1861, Holt Papers, Huntington (Stanton on AG letterhead; meeting with Republican delegation); Beale, *The Diary of Edward Bates*, 177 (Stanton presented him at Supreme Court Mar. 6); *National Republican*, Mar. 8, 1861 (Stanton's speech at Supreme Court);

Stanton to Buchanan, Mar. 10, 1861, in Curtis, *Life of James Buchanan*, 2:528–30 (Seward asked him to prepare Crittenden papers).

Chapter 6: "Disgrace & Disaster"

1 Chittenden, *Recollections*, 178.
2 The California Land Commission finished its work in March 1856; appeals were then taken to the district court in California and from there to the Supreme Court. By 1861 most cases had already reached the Supreme Court.
3 Stanton to Buchanan, Mar. 10, 12, 16, 1861, Buchanan Papers, HSP, printed in Curtis, *Life of James Buchanan*, 2:528–30; *New York Herald*, Mar. 11, 1861; *New York Tribune*, Mar. 12, 1861; *National Republican*, Mar. 11, 1861 ("conciliation to the border states").
4 Stanton to Buchanan, Mar. 16, 1861, Buchanan Papers, HSP, printed in Curtis, *Life of James Buchanan*, 2:529–30; Stanton to Dix, Mar. 16 and 19, 1861, Dix Papers (second letter quotes an undated Buchanan to Stanton letter).
5 Stanton to Dix, Mar. 19, 1861, Dix Papers. Chase often complained that Lincoln did not confer with his cabinet. Blue, *Salmon P. Chase*, 189–90; Stahr, *Seward*, 355.
6 Stanton to Dix, Apr. 8, 1861, Dix Papers; Stanton to Buchanan, Apr. 12, 1861, in Curtis, *Life of James Buchanan*, 2:541–42; *National Republican*, Apr. 13, 1861 ("Fort Sumter Attacked"); *Washington Evening Star*, Apr. 13, 1861 (similar). For an excellent general account see McClintock, *Lincoln and the Decision for War*.
7 Stanton to James Hutchison, Apr. 15, 1861, Wilkins-Hutchison-Wells Family Papers; *Chicago Tribune*, Apr. 15, 1861; *New Orleans Times*, Apr. 15, 1861; *New York Times*, Apr. 15, 1861; *Pittsburgh Daily Post*, Apr. 15, 1861; Goodwin, *Team of Rivals*, 347–49. Marvel, *Lincoln's Autocrat*, 141 suggests that Stanton revealed "inside information" to help his brother-in-law, but Lincoln's proclamation was in the papers on the day of Stanton's letter.
8 *New York Herald*, Apr. 21, 1861; *National Republican*, Apr. 22, 1861 ("immense mass meeting was held in New York Saturday"); Stanton to Dix, Apr. 23, 1861, Dix Papers; *National Republican*, Apr. 26, 1861 (N.Y. regiment arrived); Stanton to Eddie Stanton, May 1, 1861, in Thomas and Hyman, *Stanton*, 122; Furgurson, *Freedom Rising*, 74–85.
9 Frederick Seward to Simeon Draper, May 1, 1861, in *Detroit Free Press*, May 2, 1861; *Cleveland Daily Leader*, May 2, 1861; Buchanan to Stanton, May 6, 1861, in Moore, *Works of James Buchanan*, 11:188–89; Stanton to Buchanan, May 13, 1861, ibid., 190–91; *New Orleans Times*, May 18, 1861 (Campbell arrived New Orleans); Saunders, *John Archibald Campbell*, 152–53.

10 *National Republican*, June 7, 1861 (no "evidence of an intention to violate the blockade"); Stanton to Chase, June 10, 1861, Chase Papers, UPA, reel 15; *National Republican*, June 11–12, 1861 (Carrington's argument in the *Tropic Wind* case). The issues raised in the *Tropic Wind* case would ultimately be decided in *The Prize Cases*, 63 U.S. 635 (1862). Stanton may have resented Carrington because he had hoped to become the district attorney himself. Welles recalled that Seward had suggested Stanton for the position, but Blair told Lincoln "a damaging fact which was within his personal knowledge" against Stanton. Blair claimed that Stanton had taken a bribe. Nothing in the 1861 newspapers or letters, however, suggests that Stanton was under consideration as a potential district attorney. *Washington Evening Star*, Mar. 9, 1861 (Carrington urged upon Lincoln); *National Republican*, Apr. 18, 1861 (Lincoln appoints Carrington); Gienapp and Gienapp, *Civil War Diary of Gideon Welles*, 673–74 (retrospective); Blair to Welles, Feb. 25, 1873, Welles Papers, Connecticut Historical Society.

11 *Marshall County Republican* (Plymouth, Ind.), May 9, 1861, quoting *Indianapolis Journal;* Stanton to Dix, June 11, 1861, Dix Papers; *New York Tribune*, June 28, 1861; Stanton to Buchanan, July 16, 1861, Buchanan Papers, HSP, also in Moore, *Works of James Buchanan*, 11:210–11; *National Republican*, July 18, 1861 ("Grand Army Moving Forward!"); McPherson, *Battle Cry of Freedom*, 335–47; Wert, *The Sword of Lincoln*, 16–28.

12 Stanton to Pamphila Wolcott, July [25], 1861, in Gorham, *The Life and Public Services*, 1:222–23; Stanton to Dix, July 25, 1861, Dix Papers; Stanton to Buchanan, July 26, 1861, Buchanan Papers, HSP, also in Moore, *Works of James Buchanan*, 11:213–14; Sears, *George B. McClellan*, 35.

13 McClellan to Barlow, Dec. 27, 1860, in Sears, *The Civil War Papers of George B. McClellan*, 3; *New York Herald*, July 16, 1861; McClellan to Mary Ellen McClellan, July 27, 1861, in Sears, *The Civil War Papers of George B. McClellan*, 70; Sears, *George B. McClellan*, 1–100; Wert, *Sword of Lincoln*, 28–31.

14 Cameron to Butler, Aug. 8, 1861, in *New York Times*, Aug. 12, 1861; Dix to Cameron, Aug. 8, 1861, *OR*, ser. 2, 1:763; Stanton to Dix, Aug. 14, 1861, Dix Papers. For an excellent account of Butler and the contrabands, see Goodheart, *1861*, 295–340.

15 *Washington Evening Star*, Aug. 24 and 26, 1861; *Stillwater (Minn.) Messenger*, Sept. 3 and 10, 1861 (quote from Sept. 10); Moe, *Last Full Measure*, 68–72.

16 Bates to William Sharp, Oct. 11, 1861, Edwin Stanton Papers, LC, box 1, image 243 (draft in Stanton's hand); Stanton notes on Confederate Sequestration Act, [Oct. 1861], ibid., images 288–95; Scott to Stanton, Oct. 15, 1861, ibid., image 256; Cameron order, Nov. 21, 1861, ibid., image 266; William Bond to Black, Nov. 25, 1861, Black Papers, reel 18 (Bond relays Stanton's comment that his "relation to the Government is such as to

preclude his acting, in California land cases, for private claimants"); *National Republican*, Dec. 9, 1861 (Stanton argued Calif. cases); *United States v. Hensley*, 66 U.S. 35 (1861); *United States v. Covilland*, 66 U.S. 349 (1861).

17 Stanton to Dix, Oct. 26, 1861, Dix Papers; Sears, *George B. McClellan*, 95–124; Wert, *Sword of Lincoln*, 32–49.

18 McClellan to Stone, Oct. 20, 1861, *OR*, 5:32 ("slight demonstration"); *New York Tribune*, Oct. 24, 1861; *Cincinnati Daily Commercial*, Oct. 29, 1861; *Frank Leslie's Illustrated Newspaper*, Nov. 16, 1861; Sears, *Controversies and Commanders*, 32–37.

19 Wade to Chandler, Oct. 8, 1861, Chandler Papers; McClellan to Mary Ellen McClellan, Oct. 26, 1861, in Sears, *The Civil War Papers of George B. McClellan*, 112; Tap, *Over Lincoln's Shoulder*, 17–21.

20 McClellan to Mary Ellen McClellan, Aug. 16, Oct. 11 and Nov. 17, 1861, in Sears, *The Civil War Papers of George B. McClellan*, 85, 106–7, 135–36; McClellan, *McClellan's Own Story*, 152.

21 McClellan to Mary Ellen McClellan, Oct. 31, 1861, in Sears, *The Civil War Papers of George B. McClellan*, 113–14; McClellan to Cameron, Oct. 31, 1861, ibid., 114–19 (notes indicate parts in Stanton's hand).

22 Stanton to Dix, Nov. 1, 1861, Dix Papers; Burlingame and Ettlinger, *Inside Lincoln's White House*, 30 (Nov. 1, 1861); Goodwin, *Team of Rivals*, 382–83; Sears, *George B. McClellan*, 122–26.

23 *Findlay (Ohio) Jeffersonian*, Nov. 15, 1861 ("his confidential friend"); *Washington Evening Star*, Nov. 16, 1861 (second edition); Stanton to Dix, Nov. 17, 1861, Dix Papers; McClellan to Mary Ellen McClellan, Nov. 17, 1861, in Sears, *The Civil War Papers of George B. McClellan*, 135; Stahr, *Seward*, 307–23.

24 McClellan to Barlow, Nov. 8, 1861, in Sears, *The Civil War Papers of George B. McClellan*, 128; *National Republican*, Nov. 14, 1861 (Cochrane, Cameron quotes); *New York Tribune*, Nov. 14, 1861 (similar); *New York Times*, Nov. 17, 1861 (prints Dix proclamation); Stanton to Dix, Nov. 17, 1861, Dix Papers.

25 *Chicago Tribune*, Nov. 21, 1861 (Cameron and Smith); Barlow to Stanton, Nov. 21, 1861, Barlow Papers, reel 6; Stanton to Barlow, Nov. 23, 1861, in Flower, *Edwin McMasters Stanton*, 122–23; *New York Tribune*, Nov. 25, 1861; *Detroit Free Press*, Nov. 26, 1861; *New York Herald*, Dec. 2, 1861. Lincoln biographers often suggest that Cameron surprised Lincoln with this section of his report; if so, Lincoln was not reading the newspapers. Goodwin, *Team of Rivals*, 405.

26 *Baltimore Sun*, Dec. 4, 1861 (first version of Cameron's report); *New York Tribune*, Dec. 4, 1861 (both versions); *Boston Daily Advertiser*, Dec. 5, 1861 (first version); *Detroit Free Press*, Dec. 5, 1861 (first version); *Philadelphia Inquirer*, Dec. 5, 1861 (Lincoln tells Cameron he should not dictate to

Congress); *Chicago Tribune*, Dec. 5, 1861 ("brightest page"); *New York Times*, Dec. 6, 1861 (reports "grossly unjust to the President"); *Chicago Tribune*, Dec. 7, 1861 ("emasculation" of Cameron's report); Wilson, "Jeremiah S. Black and Edwin M. Stanton," 470 (quoting Cameron); Flower, *Edwin Mc-Masters Stanton*, 116 (Stanton "wrote this additional paragraph").

27 *Congressional Globe*, 37th Cong., 1st Sess., p. 31 (Dec. 9, 1861) (Fessenden); Tap, *Over Lincoln's Shoulder*, 21–24.

28 *Cincinnati Daily Commercial*, Oct. 29, 1861; *Chicago Tribune*, Nov. 1, 1861 ("death warrant"); *Jeffersonian Democrat* (Chardon, Ohio), Dec. 6, 1861 (Stone "in high favor with Maryland secessionists"); *Chicago Tribune*, Dec. 19, 1861 (Stone's "chief distinction" is "nigger catching"); *Congressional Globe*, 37th Cong., 1st Sess., p. 130 (Dec. 18, 1861) (Sumner); Stone to Sumner, Dec. 23, 1861, Sumner Papers (microfilm).

29 Stanton to Dix, Oct. 26, 1861, Dix Papers; Ellen Stanton to Catherine Hutchison, Jan. 4, 1862, in Richert, *Ellen Hutchison Stanton Letters*, 162–63; Baptism record, Mar. 17, 1862, Epiphany Church, Washington (baptized at home "*in extremis*"); Stanton to Oella Wright, Mar. 24, 1862, in Wolcott, *Edwin M. Stanton*, 179–80 (vaccinated at "the age of two weeks" and soon had "a dreadful eruption").

30 Stanton to Barlow, Jan. 7, 1862, in Flower, *Edwin McMasters Stanton*, 123–24.

31 *Detroit Free Press*, Jan. 1, 1862 ("Cameron is the Jonah of the administration"); *Star of the North* (Bloomsburg, Pa.), Jan. 2, 1862 (similar); *Janesville (Wisc.) Gazette*, Jan. 7, 1862 (Cameron "believes in attacking the traitors at their weakest point").

Chapter 7: "Put Forth Every Energy"

1 Beale, *The Diary of Edward Bates*, 226 (Jan. 11, 1862); Niven, *Chase Papers*, 1:324–25 (Jan. 11–12, 1862); Fessenden to Samuel Fessenden, Jan. 20, 1862, Fessenden Papers; Murray and Hsieh, *A Savage War*, 117 ("it was not necessarily that the secretary was corrupt, but rather that his political machinations, coupled with incompetence, created scandal in his department"). For a more sympathetic view, see Kahan, *Amiable Scoundrel*.

2 Lincoln to Cameron, Jan. 11, 1862, in Basler, *The Collected Works of Abraham Lincoln*, 5:96; Niven, *Chase Papers*, 1:325–26 (Jan. 12, 1862). Although Lincoln's letter to Cameron is dated January 11, Chase's diary makes it clear that Cameron did not receive the letter until late on January 12.

3 Lincoln to Cameron, Jan. 11, 1862, in Basler, *The Collected Works of Abraham Lincoln*, 5:96–97 (revised backdated letter); *Senate Executive Journal*, Jan. 13, 1862 (Cameron and Stanton nominations); *Washington Evening Star*, Jan. 14, 1862; Ives to Bennett, Jan. 15, 1862, Bennett Papers; Fessenden to Elizabeth

Warriner, Jan. 19, 1862, Fessenden Papers; *New York Times*, July 16, 1865 (Cameron's version of suggesting Stanton); Cameron to Frank Flower, Mar. 6, 1887, Cameron Papers (similar). There is some evidence that Lincoln did *not* speak with Stanton before sending his name to the Senate: an article quoting Lincoln saying that "he had not even conversed previously with Mr. Stanton about" the nomination. *Philadelphia Inquirer*, Jan. 20, 1862.

4   Hay Report, Jan. 15, 1862, in Burlingame, *Lincoln's Journalist*, 195–96; Taliaferro, *All the Great Prizes*.

5   *New York World*, Jan. 14, 1862; *Chicago Times*, Jan. 14, 1862; *New York Tribune*, Jan. 14, 1862; *Chicago Tribune*, Jan. 15, 1862.

6   *New York Herald*, Jan. 14, 1862; *Washington Evening Star*, Jan. 14, 1862; Buchanan to Harriet Lane, Jan. 16, 1862, in Curtis, *Life of James Buchanan*, 2:522.

7   Ives to Bennett, Jan. 15 and 27, 1862, Bennett Papers.

8   Sam Ward to Frederick Seward, Jan. 14, 1862, Seward Papers, reel 68; Halleck to Elizabeth Halleck, Jan. 15, 1862, in "Letters of General Henry W. Halleck," 29; Nevins, *A Diary of Battle*, 9–10 (Jan. 19, 1862); Stanton to Halleck, Feb. 8, 1862, *OR*, 8:547.

9   Sumner to Richard Cobden, Jan. 13, 1862, in Palmer, *The Selected Letters of Charles Sumner*, 2:97; Chase to Fessenden, Jan. 15, 1862, Fessenden Papers; Fessenden note, Jan. 15, 1862, ibid. ("we agreed perfectly on all points"); *Senate Executive Journal*, Jan. 15, 1862; *New York Tribune*, Jan. 16, 1862; Fessenden to Elizabeth Warriner, Jan. 19, 1862, Fessenden Papers; Fessenden to Samuel Fessenden, Jan. 20, 1862, ibid.; Francis Fessenden notes, Edwin Stanton Papers, LC, box 2, image 258 ("warm and intimate friendship between Mr. Stanton and Mr. Fessenden").

10 *New York Tribune*, Jan. 16, 1862; *Chicago Tribune*, Jan. 16, 1862; Medill to Stanton, Jan. 21, 1862, Edwin Stanton Papers, LC, box 2, images 146–48. The timing and wording of the *New York Tribune* article suggest that it was based on conversations with Fessenden.

11 Grier to Stanton, Jan. 13, 1862, Edwin Stanton Papers, LC, box 1, image 303; Medary to Stanton, Jan. 14, 1862, ibid., box 2, image 39; Dix to Stanton, Jan. 14, 1862, in Gorham, *The Life and Public Services*, 1:242; Holt to Lincoln, Jan. 15, 1862, Lincoln Papers, LC; Stanton to Clifford, Jan. 21, 1862, Clifford Papers; Stanton to Holt, Jan. 25, 1862, Holt Papers, Huntington.

12 Ingersoll, *A History of the War Department*; McPherson, *Tried by War*; Meneely, *The War Department in 1861*; Perret, *Lincoln's War*.

13 Senator Henry Wilson observed, "The legislation requisite for raising, equipping, and governing the armies, and the twenty-five thousand nominations of officers, from the second lieutenants up to the General-in-Chief; which passed through my committee while he was in the War Department, were often the subject of conference and consideration between us. His office was

open to me at all times by day and night I saw him in every circumstance and condition of the war, in the glow of victory and in the gloom of defeat" ("Edwin M. Stanton," 235). Senator Zachariah Chandler commented that as a senior member of the Joint Committee he saw Stanton "on an average once a day during the whole war." *Congressional Globe*, 42d Cong., 2d Sess., p. 4282 (June 6, 1872).

14 Early letters from Stanton to governors include Stanton to Morgan, Feb. 7, 1862, M473; Stanton to Tod, Feb. 7, 1862, ibid.; Stanton to Curtin, Feb. 9, 1862, OR, ser. 3, 1:884; Stanton to Andrew, Feb. 19, 1862, ibid., 897. There are more than a hundred citations to Stanton in the index to Engle's excellent new book on the Union governors, *Gathering to Save a Nation*.

15 See *infra* especially chapter 13.

16 For an analysis of Stanton's press releases, see David Mindich, "The Inverted Pyramid: Edwin M. Stanton and Information Control," in Mindich, *Just the Facts*, 64–94. The best book on Stanton and military justice is Witt, *Lincoln's Code*.

17 Gienapp and Gienapp, *Civil War Diary of Gideon Welles*, 683 (retrospective).

18 See *infra* and Murray and Hsieh, *Savage War*; Pickenpaugh, *Rescue by Rail*; Wheeler, *Mr. Lincoln's T-mails*.

19 *New York Tribune*, Jan. 21, 1862; *Philadelphia Inquirer*, Jan. 21, 1862 ("as the officers"); U.S. Congress, *Report of the Joint Committee on the Conduct of the War*, 1:74–75 (includes letter of Jan. 21); Flower, *Edwin McMasters Stanton*, 119 ("we must strike hands").

20 *Chicago Tribune*, Jan. 23, 1862 (Mill Springs order); Stanton to Dana, Jan. 24, 1862, Dana Papers; Lincoln Order, Jan. 27, 1862, in Basler, *The Collected Works of Abraham Lincoln*, 5:111–12; Stanton to Dana, Feb. 2, 1862, Beinecke Library, Yale.

21 *Congressional Globe*, 37th Cong., 2d Sess., p. 386 (Jan. 20, 1862) (Stanton "extremely desirous that authority should be given him for two additional assistant secretaries"); Assistant Secretaries of War Act, Jan. 22, 1862, in *Statutes at Large* 12:332; Clerical Force Act, Jan. 27, 1862, ibid., 333; Railroad and Telegraph Act, Jan. 31, 1862, ibid., 334–35; Stanton to William Stanton, Mar. 4, 1862, William Stanton Papers ("I prepared that bill & its amendments"); Miles, "The Origin and Meaning of Miles' Law" ("where you stand depends on where you sit").

22 Stanton to Lincoln, Jan. 23, 1862, Lincoln Papers, LC (suggesting Tucker and Watson); Scott to Stanton, Jan. 23, 1862, OR, ser. 3, 1:807–8 (rail and telegraph); Stanton to Hamlin, Jan. 27, 1862, Edwin Stanton Papers, LC, box 2, image 188 (defending Tucker nomination); Stanton to Scott, Jan. 29, 1862, in Sipes, *The Pennsylvania Railroad*, 15–16 ("Kentucky and Tennessee"); Scott to Stanton, Feb. 1, 1862, Edwin Stanton Papers, LC, box 2,

images 285–87 (details re: rail movement from Washington to West). Scott's 1862 reports to Stanton fill hundreds of pages in the Stanton Papers at the Library of Congress.

23 Stanton to Scott, Feb. 6, 1862, Edwin Stanton Papers, LC, box 45, image 48 ("give no orders"); Scott to Stanton, Feb. 7, 1862, ibid., box 3, image 76 ("I have your message of censure"); Kamm, *The Civil War Career of Thomas Scott*, 87–97.

24 Scott to Stanton, Feb. 12, 1862, Edwin Stanton Papers, LC, box 3, image 193 ("as bad"); Scott to Stanton, May 10, 1862, ibid., box 6, images 131–33 (includes Stanton's note "resignation accepted"); Stanton to Scott, June 1, 1862, ibid., box 7, image 108 ("my entire satisfaction"); Kamm, *The Civil War Career of Thomas Scott*, 130–33.

25 Stanton to Scott, Jan. 31, 1862, M473 (resolve transport issues); Stanton to Scott, Feb. 7, 1862, ibid. (investigate at Cairo); Kountz to Stanton, Feb. 10, 1862, in Simon, *The Papers of Ulysses Grant*, 4:110–11 (complains of arrest, no charges yet); Scott to Stanton, Feb. 12, 1862, Edwin Stanton Papers, LC, box 3, image 211 ("not to be exactly").

26 Thomas to Cameron, Feb. 10, 1862, Cameron Papers; *New York Times*, Feb. 11, 1862; Wilkeson to Cameron, Feb. 12, 1862, Cameron Papers; *New York Times*, Feb. 14, 1862 (Stanton back at work); Burlingame, *Dispatches from Lincoln's White House*, 62 (Feb. 17, 1862); *New York Tribune*, Feb. 19, 1862 (Stanton sometimes stays at his desk through the night).

27 Ives to Bennett, Jan. 27, 1862, Bennett Papers; Stanton to McClellan, Jan. 28, 1862, *OR*, 5:341; Beale, *The Diary of Edward Bates*, 228–29 (Feb. 3, 1862); McClellan to Porter, Feb. 8, 1862, *OR*, 5:341; Joseph Bradley to Stanton, Feb. 16, 1862, and Watson to Bradley, Feb. 20, 1862, both in *Congressional Globe*, 37th Cong., 2d Sess., p. 1663 (Apr. 15, 1862); Sears, *Controversies and Commanders*, 27–50.

28 Ives to Bennett, Jan. 15 and 27, 1862, Bennett Papers; *New York Times*, Feb. 11, 1862 (has Stanton order for Ives arrest); *Philadelphia Inquirer*, Feb. 11, 1862 ("had a perfect right").

29 *Chicago Times*, Feb. 11, 1862 (charges against Stone); *Cleveland Daily Leader*, Feb. 11, 1862 ("fit disposition"); Hay Report, Feb. 11, 1862, in Burlingame, *Lincoln's Journalist*, 215; *New York World*, Feb. 11, 1862 ("every loyal journal"); *New York Herald*, Feb. 11, 1862; *New York Times*, Feb. 12, 1862; *Boston Daily Advertiser*, May 22, 1862 (Ives released); *Baltimore Sun*, Aug. 28, 1862 (Stone released); Stone to Lossing, Nov. 5, 1866, Schoff Collection (account of his arrest and imprisonment).

30 Lincoln Order, Feb. 14, 1862, *OR*, ser. 2, 2:221–23; *New York Herald*, Feb. 19, 1862 ("President's Amnesty"); Stanton order, Feb. 27, 1862, in Gorham, *The Life and Public Services*, 1:267; *New York Herald*, Mar. 21, 1862 (praises

release of political prisoners); Dix to Goldsborough, May 23, 1862, *OR*, ser. 2, 2:576–77; *Brooklyn Evening Star*, May 28, 1862 (describes how federal officers, supported by troops, arrested Carmichael); *Baltimore Sun*, Oct. 23, 1862 (Carmichael released on parole).

31 Scott to Stanton, Feb. 12, 1862, Edwin Stanton Papers, LC, box 3, image 211; *New York World*, Feb. 18, 1862 ("threw up his hat"); *Detroit Free Press*, Feb. 18, 1862 ("no terms except"); *Cleveland Daily Leader*, Feb. 19, 1862 (Grant nominated; "will be confirmed at once").

32 *Washington Evening Star*, Feb. 18, 1862 ("remarkable military combinations"); *New York Tribune*, Feb. 18, 1862 ("to Edwin M. Stanton").

33 Grant to Buckner, Feb. 16, 1862, in Simon, *The Papers of Ulysses Grant*, 4:218; Stanton to Dana, Feb. 19, 1862, Edwin Stanton Papers, LC, box 4, image 2 ("days of Joshua"); *New York Tribune*, Feb. 20, 1862 (printed version).

34 Nevins and Thomas, *Diary of George Templeton Strong*, 3:208 (Feb. 20, 1862) ("next President"); Stanton to Dana, Feb. 23, 1862, Dana Papers ("certain military hero"). Stanton's somewhat naïve approach was common at the time; Mark Neely notes that "the press brought to the war a medieval understanding of combat, with its images of the duel, the spear, the open field, the test of physical heroism" (*The Union Divided*, 70). See also Murray and Hsieh, *A Savage War*, 51 ("almost everything above the level of regimental operations, including operational and logistical planning, deploying large forces in combat, and the complex staff work required to run large armies, had to be learned from the ground up on the battlefield").

35 Halleck to McClellan, Feb. 17, 1862, *OR*, 7:627–28; Scott to Stanton, Feb. 17, 1862, Edwin Stanton Papers, LC, box 3, image 285 ("with this organization as set forth there can be no such thing as fail"); Stanton to Scott, Feb. 21, 1862, ibid., box 4, images 18–24; Halleck to McClellan, Feb. 21, 1862, *OR*, 7:641; Stanton to Halleck, Feb. 21 and 22, 1862, ibid., 648, 652; Halleck to McClellan, Mar. 2, 1862, ibid., 679–80; McClellan to Halleck, Mar. 3, 1862, ibid., 680; Halleck to Thomas, Mar. 15, 1862, ibid., 683–84; White, *American Ulysses*, 203–8. Stanton's endorsement on McClellan's arrest message is in M473 reel 50.

36 Speed to Holt, Feb. 4, 1862, Holt Papers, LC, box 32.

37 Bellows to Eliza Bellows, Jan. 23 and 25, 1862, Bellows Papers; Nevins and Thomas, *Diary of George Templeton Strong*, 3:203 (Jan. 29, 1862); Ingersoll, *A History of the War Department*; Maxwell, *Lincoln's Fifth Wheel*; Meneely, *The War Department in 1861*; O'Harrow, *The Quartermaster*.

38 War Board minutes, March 14 and 21, 1862, Edwin Stanton Papers, LC, box 37, images 51 and 121–24; Kelley, "Fossildom, Old Fogeyism, and Red Tape" (on War Board); Hoogenboom, *Gustavus Vasa Fox*.

39 Hitchcock Journal, Jan. 30 and Mar. 15, 1862, Hitchcock Papers, Gilcrease

Museum; Hitchcock to Stanton, Mar. 19, 1862, Hitchcock Papers, LC ("organic nature").

40 Railroad and Telegraph Act, Jan. 31, 1862, *Statutes at Large*, 12:334–35; *Indianapolis Star*, Feb. 18, 1862 (Stanton summons railroad officials); *Detroit Free Press*, Feb. 21, 1862 ("grand railroad conference called by Secretary Stanton assembled yesterday"); *New York Tribune*, Feb. 21, 1862 (object of conference was "to establish a uniform and satisfactory rate of compensation"); Clark, *Railroads in the Civil War*, 43–44, 62–65; Koistinen, *Beating Plowshares into Swords*, 150; Wilson, *The Business of Civil War*, 76, 135.

41 Ives to Bennett, Jan. 27, 1862, Bennett Papers; Railroad and Telegraph Act, Jan. 31, 1862, *Statutes at Large*, 12:334–35; Lincoln order, Feb. 25, 1862, in *National Republican*, Feb. 26, 1862; *Chicago Tribune*, Feb. 27, 1862; *New York Herald*, Feb. 27, 1862.

42 Bates, *Lincoln in the Telegraph Office*, 38–42; Johnson, "Reminiscences of the Hon. Edwin M. Stanton," 72–73 (Stanton wanted "to preserve a complete telegraphic record of the war"). We do not have a precise date for when Stanton moved the telegraph hub, but it would seem to be after February 18, when McClellan was the first person to learn of Grant's victory, and before March 9, when Stanton was the first person to learn of the *Merrimack* attacks.

43 Tucker to Stanton, Mar. 5, 1862, Edwin Stanton Papers, LC, box 4, image 122 ("everything required is engaged"); Tucker to Stanton, Apr. 5, 1862, *OR*, 5:46 (summary of transport operation); Sears, *To the Gates of Richmond*, 23–24 (description of transport operation).

44 Stanton to Halleck, Mar. 25, 1862, *OR*, 8:643; Stanton to Ellet, Mar. 27, 1862, *ORN*, 27:680 ("proceed immediately to Pittsburgh"); Stanton to Ellet, Mar. 28, 1862, ibid., 22:680; Stanton to Ellet, Mar. 29, 1862, M473 ("spare nothing"); Stanton to Ellet, Mar. 31, 1862, *ORN*, 22:685 ("successful courage"); Hearn, *Ellet's Brigade*, 11–25; Mangrum, "Edwin M. Stanton's Special Military Units," 92–98. Most of the messages from Stanton to Ellet in M473 are in his own hand.

45 Andrew to Stanton, Jan. 25, 1862, *OR*, ser. 2, 1:810–65; Stanton to Morgan, Feb. 7, 1862, M473 (no funds); Stanton to Tod, Feb. 7 and 14, 1862, ibid.; Stanton to Andrew, Feb. 19, 1862, ibid.

46 Stanton to Johnson, Mar. 3, 1862, in Graf, *The Papers of Andrew Johnson*, 5:177 (appointment); *New York Times*, Mar. 4, 1862 (Johnson "will repair at once to Nashville"); Johnson to Stanton, Mar. 13, 14, 21, 27, 1862, in Graf, *The Papers of Andrew Johnson*, 5:201, 205, 220, 250; Bergeron, *Andrew Johnson's Civil War*; Trefousse, *Andrew Johnson*.

47 Lincoln to McClellan, Feb. 4, 1862, in Basler, *The Collected Works of Abraham Lincoln*, 5:118 (original in Edwin Stanton Papers, LC, box 3, images 4-5); Sears, *To the Gates of Richmond*, 3–9; Wert, *Sword of Lincoln*, 52–62.

48   U.S. Congress, *Report of the Joint Committee on the Conduct of the War*, 1:85; De-
     troit Post & Tribune, *Zachariah Chandler*, 226–27; Sears, *George B. McClellan*,
     155–56; Tap, *Over Lincoln's Shoulder*, 112–13. For more on the close relations
     between Stanton and Wade, see Stanton to William Stanton, Feb. 18, 1862,
     William Stanton Papers (he would view it as a "national calamity" if Wade
     not reelected); Wade to William Stanton, Mar. 22, 1862, ibid. (Stanton "has
     the confidence of Congress and the whole country").

49   Stanton to Lander, Feb. 17, 1862, in *New York Herald*, Feb. 20, 1862; *New
     York Tribune*, Feb. 21 and 22, 1862 (Stanton's purported praise of McClel-
     lan); Stanton to Dana, Feb. 23, 1862, Dana Papers; *New York World*, Feb. 24,
     1862 (prints retraction of report); *New York Times*, Feb. 24, 1862 (similar);
     John Meigs to Louisa Meigs, Feb. 24, 1862, in Giunta, *A Civil War Soldier of
     Christ and Country*, 141–42 (sorry to see that Stanton did not praise McClel-
     lan as per original reports).

50   McClellan to Stanton, Feb. 26 and 27, 1862, in Sears, *The Civil War Pa-
     pers of George B. McClellan*, 191–92; Burlingame, *At Lincoln's Side*, 72 (Feb.
     27, 1862) ("damned fizzle"); Nicolay notes, Feb. 27, 1862, ibid., 217–18;
     Horace White to Joseph Medill, Mar. 3, 1862, Ray Papers; Sears, *George B.
     McClellan*, 156–58.

51   Stanton to Holt, Mar. 4, 1862, Holt Papers, Huntington, box 5; McClel-
     lan, *McClellan's Own Story*, 195–96 ("traitorous intent"); Burlingame and
     Ettlinger, *Inside Lincoln's White House*, 35; Sears, *To the Gates of Richmond*, 3–9.

52   Heintzelman Diary, Mar. 8, 1862, Heintzelman Papers; Lincoln General
     War Order No. 2, Mar. 8, 1862, *OR*, 5:18.

53   Wool to Stanton, Mar. 8, 1862, *ORN*, 7:4–5; Burlingame, *With Lincoln in the
     White House*, 74–75 ("very much excited"); Randall, *Diary of Orville Hickman
     Browning*, 1:532–33 (Mar. 9, 1862); Burlingame and Ettlinger, *Inside Lincoln's
     White House*, 35 (Mar. 9, 1862; "fearfully stampeded"); Hay Report, Mar. 9,
     1862, in Burlingame, *Lincoln's Journalist*, 232 ("The evening dispatches made
     people as jolly as those of the morning had made them glum"); Stanton to
     Morgan et al., Mar. 9, 1862, *ORN*, 7:80; Dahlgren to Lincoln, ibid., 78 (tour
     with Stanton); Dahlgren, *Memoir*, 359; Gienapp and Gienapp, *Civil War
     Diary of Gideon Welles*, 678 (retrospective section; "most frightened man");
     Symonds, *Lincoln and His Admirals*, 138–40.

54   Tucker to Vanderbilt, Mar. 15, 1862, *ORN*, 7:129; Randall, *The Diary of Or-
     ville Hickman Browning*, 1:535 (Mar. 19, 1862); Stanton to Vanderbilt, Mar.
     20, 1862, *ORN*, 7:148–49 (accepts gift; gives orders); Stanton to Wool, Mar.
     27, 1862, ibid., 173 ("belongs to the War Department"); Stiles, *The First Ty-
     coon*, 344–48 (Vanderbilt's role).

55   McClellan to Lincoln and Stanton, Mar. 9, 1862, in Sears, *The Civil War
     Papers of George B. McClellan*, 200 ("push the retreat"); McClellan to Stanton,

Mar. 9, 1862, *OR*, 5:739 (requests suspension of order for the formation of army corps); Stanton to McClellan, Mar. 9, 1862, ibid. ("duty of every officer"); McClellan to Stanton, Mar. 10, 1862, ibid., 740–41 ("countermand all"); Stanton to McClellan, Mar. 10, 1862, ibid., 741 ("by divisions"); McClellan to Stanton, Mar. 10, 1862, ibid. These messages to McClellan are in Stanton's hand in M473.

56 Beale, *The Diary of Edward Bates*, 239 (Mar. 11, 1862); Bayard Taylor to Marie Taylor, Mar. 12, 1862, in Hansen, *On Two Continents*, 117.

57 Stanton draft order, Mar. 11, 1862, Edwin Stanton Papers, LC, box 4, images 167–68; Lincoln order, Mar. 11, 1862, in Basler, *The Collected Works of Abraham Lincoln*, 5:155; Burlingame and Ettlinger, *Inside Lincoln's White House*, 36 (Mar. 11, 1862); Beale, *The Diary of Edward Bates*, 239 (Mar. 11, 1862).

58 McClellan memo, Mar. 13, 1862, *OR*, 5:55–56; Stanton to McClellan, Mar. 13, 1862, ibid., 56 ("entirely secure"); Stanton to McClellan, Mar. 13, 1862, ibid., 750 ("all the forces"); McClellan to Stanton, Mar. 13, 1862, in Sears, *The Civil War Papers of George B. McClellan*, 207; Tucker to Stanton, Apr. 5, 1862, *OR*, 5:46 (without a parallel").

59 McClellan Address, Mar. 14, 1862, in Sears, *The Civil War Papers of George B. McClellan*, 211; *New York Herald*, Mar. 16, 1862 ("brilliant address").

60 Stanton order, Mar. 17, 1862, Edwin Stanton Papers, LC, box 4, images 207–8 (his hand); *Philadelphia Inquirer*, Mar. 18, 1862; *Pittsburgh Gazette*, Mar. 18, 1862; *Springfield (Mass.) Republican*, Mar. 22, 1862.

61 Hitchcock Journal, Mar. 17, 1862, Hitchcock Papers, Gilcrease Museum ("most astounding"); Dahlgren, *Memoir*, 361 ("that is for you"); Barnard to McClellan, Mar. 19, 1862, in McClellan, *McClellan's Own Story*, 246; Randall, *Diary of Orville Hickman Browning*, 1:538–39 (Apr. 2, 1862).

Chapter 8: "The Vilest Man I Ever Knew"

1 McClellan to Mary Ellen McClellan, Apr. 1, 1861, in Sears, *The Civil War Papers of George B. McClellan*, 223 ("sink of iniquity"); McClellan to Thomas, Apr. 1, 1862, ibid., 222–23 (troop numbers); Wadsworth to Stanton, Apr. 2, 1862, *OR*, vol. 11, pt. 3, pp. 60–61; Thomas and Hitchcock to Stanton, Apr. 2, 1862, ibid., 62; Lincoln to Stanton, Apr. 3, 1862, ibid., 65–66; Thomas to McClellan, Apr. 4, 1862, ibid., 66; McClellan to Lincoln, Apr. 5, 1862, in Sears, *The Civil War Papers of George B. McClellan*, 228 ("now of the opinion"); Franklin to McClellan, Apr. 7, 1862, ibid., 231 ("blow at you"); Sumner to Andrew, May 18, 1862, in Palmer, *Selected Letters of Charles Sumner*, 2:114–15 ("justly indignant"); Winkle, *Lincoln's Citadel*, 282–83 (Wadsworth).

2 *Congressional Globe*, 37th Cong., 2d Sess., p. 1417 (Mar. 28, 1862); General

War Order No. 33, Apr. 3, 1862, *OR*, ser. 3, 2:2–3; *New York World*, Apr. 4, 1862; *New York Times*, Apr. 5, 1862; *New York Commercial Advertiser*, Apr. 5, 1862; Halleck to Stanton, Apr. 5, 1862, *OR*, vol. 10, pt. 2, p. 93 ("want every man we can get"); Koistinen, *Beating Plowshares into Swords*, 171 ("worst blunder of his tenure in office"); Murray and Hsieh, *Savage War*, 164 (suspension "seemed a reasonable decision at the time," but "events in the summer underlined how overoptimistic this had been"); Thomas and Hyman, *Stanton*, 201 ("what has properly been called one of the colossal blunders of the war"). For Fessenden, see Cook, *Civil War Senator*.

3 Halleck General Orders No. 1, Jan. 1, 1862, *OR*, 8:476–78; Ellis charges and trial transcript, Feb. 25, 1862, ibid., ser. 2, 1:453–57; Hart, "Military Commissions and the Lieber Code," 12–22, 28–30; McPherson, *Battle Cry of Freedom*, 292 ("matched the bushwhackers"); Witt, *Lincoln's Code*, 122–26. Military commissions remain controversial. See *Hamdan v. Rumsfeld*, 548 U.S. 556 (2006); *Boumediene v. Bush*, 553 U.S. 723 (2008).

4 Stanton to Halleck, Apr. 5, 1862, *OR*, ser. 2, 1:276; *Brooklyn Evening Star*, Apr. 7, 1862; *New York World*, Apr. 7, 1862; *Detroit Free Press*, Apr. 8, 1862; Thomas (at Stanton's request) to Frémont, Apr. 9, 1862, *OR*, ser. 2, 2:283; Witt, *Lincoln's Code*, 267 (estimating four thousand military commissions in the North during the Civil War).

5 McClellan to Stanton, Apr. 7, 1862, in Sears, *The Civil War Papers of George B. McClellan*, 232; Stanton to Nimick, Apr. 8, 1862, M473 ("we have glorious news from the West"); Stanton to Wool, Apr. 8, 1862, ibid. ("Island Number Ten has been captured"); Stanton to McClellan, Apr. 8, 1862, ibid. ("after a hard battle"); Hay to Nicolay, Apr. 9, 1862, in Burlingame, *At Lincoln's Side*, 20; Lincoln to McClellan, Apr. 9, 1862, in Basler, *The Collected Works of Abraham Lincoln*, 5:184–85.

6 *New York World*, Apr. 12 and 15, 1862; *New York Commercial Advertiser*, Apr. 15 and 17, 1862; *National Republican*, Apr. 19, 1862; *New York Herald*, May 3, 1862. On McClellan's role in the press attacks on Stanton, see Pierrepont to Stanton, Apr. 16–17, 1862, in Gorham, *The Life and Public Services*, 1:418–21; Porter to Marble, Mar. 17, Apr. 26, June 20, Aug. 3, 1862, Marble Papers.

7 *Congressional Globe*, 37th Cong., 2d Sess., pp. 1662–63, 1735, 1738 (Apr. 15 and 21, 1862); *Detroit Free Press*, Apr. 20, 1862.

8 Stanton to Bonner, Apr. 30, 1862, Dix Papers.

9 Dyer to Stanton, May 16, 1862, Edwin Stanton Papers, LC, box 6, image 167; Stanton to Dyer, May 18, 1862, ibid., images 209–24; Dyer, *Records of an Active Life*, 451–58 (Stanton's letter); Flower, *Edwin McMasters Stanton*, 157–61 (copy of Stanton's letter).

10 Stanton to Dyer, May 18, 1862, Edwin Stanton Papers, LC, box 6, images

209–24. Stanton asked Dyer to keep the letter confidential, and he did so, not printing it until after both Stanton and McClellan were dead.

11 McClellan to Stanton, Apr. 11, 1862, *OR*, vol. 11, pt. 3, p. 86 ("indispensable"); Stanton to McClellan, Apr. 11, 1862, ibid., 90 ("safety of this city"); Tucker to Stanton, Apr. 16, 1862, Edwin Stanton Papers, LC, box 5, image 139 ("abundant means to send supplies"); Tucker to Stanton, Apr. 19, 1862, ibid., image 171 ("roads are now in quite good order"); Stanton to Hitchcock, Apr. 19, 1862, Hitchcock Papers, LC (asking what McClellan needs); Hitchcock to Stanton, Apr. 19, 1862, Edwin Stanton Papers, LC, box 5, image 163 ("large as he can conveniently handle"); Sears, *To the Gates of Richmond*, 61 (Franklin's troops on transport ships); Sears, *George B. McClellan*, 199–200 (troop numbers).

12 Stanton to Frémont, May 1, 1862, *OR*, vol. 12, pt. 3, p. 122; Stanton to Banks, May 1, 1862, ibid.; Stanton to McDowell, ibid., 121; Stanton to Shields, May 1, 1862, M473; Stanton to Wool, May 1, 1862, ibid.; Lincoln to McClellan, May 1, 1862, in Basler, *The Collected Works of Abraham Lincoln*, 5:203; McClellan to Lincoln, May 1, 1862, in Sears, *The Civil War Papers of George B. McClellan*, 251.

13 Stanton to Halleck, May 1, 1862, *OR*, ser. 3, 2:29; Stanton to Halleck, May 1, 1862, *OR*, vol. 52, pt. 1, p. 245; Stanton to Halleck, May 1, 1862, M473; Stanton to Canby, May 1, 1862, ibid.; Stanton to Mitchel, May 1, 1862, *OR*, vol. 10, pt. 2, p. 156.

14 Stanton to Gurowski, May 1, 1862, Gurowski Papers; Stanton to Bradford, May 1, 1862, M473; Stanton to Dix and Pierrepont, May 1, 1862, ibid.; Gienapp and Gienapp, *Civil War Diary of Gideon Welles*, 93 (Dec. 4, 1862); Fischer, *Lincoln's Gadfly*.

15 Stanton to Oella Wright, Mar. 24, 1862, in Wolcott, *Edwin M. Stanton*, 179–80; Stanton to Ellen Stanton, Mar. 28 and 31, 1862, M473 (marked private); Stanton to James Hutchison, Apr. 30, 1862, Wilkins-Hutchison-Wells Family Papers.

16 McClellan to Stanton, May 4 and 5, 1862, in Sears, *The Civil War Papers of George B. McClellan*, 253–56; *New York World*, May 5, 1862; *Detroit Free Press*, May 7, 1862; Sears, *To the Gates of Richmond*, 65–82.

17 Chase to Janet Chase, May 7, 1862, in Niven, *Chase Papers*, 1:336; Chase to Greeley, Sept. 15, 1862, ibid., 3:267–68 (credits Stanton with suggesting the trip to Norfolk); Viele, "A Trip with Lincoln, Chase, and Stanton," 814; Goodwin, *Team of Rivals*, 436–39; Symonds, *Lincoln and His Admirals*, 136–37.

18 Chase to Janet Chase, May 7, 1862, in Niven, *Chase Papers*, 1:336–37 ("plates slipped").

19 Ibid. ("narrow steps"); Stanton to McClellan, May 6, 1862, *OR*, vol. 11, pt. 3, p. 145; McClellan to Stanton, May 7, 1862, ibid., 149 ("vast importance").

20 Chase to Janet Chase, May 7, 1862, in Niven, *Chase Papers*, 1:337–39; Mc-
    Clellan to Stanton, May 7, 1862, *OR*, vol. 11, pt. 3, p. 146; Stanton to Mc-
    Clellan, May 7, 1862, ibid., 147; Lincoln to Goldsborough, May 7, 1862,
    ORN, 7:326 (draft in Stanton's hand in Edwin Stanton Papers, LC, box 6,
    image 41); Stanton to Watson, May 8, 1862, *OR*, vol. 11, pt. 3, p. 153; Baird,
    "Narrative of Rear Admiral Goldsborough," 1028 ("impatient and imperi-
    ous"); Daly, *Aboard the USS* Monitor, 106–7 ("well acquainted"); Symonds,
    Lincoln and His Admirals, 150–51.
21 Chase to Janet Chase, May 8, 1862, in Niven, *Chase Papers*, 1:337–39; Sy-
    monds, *Lincoln and His Admirals*, 151–52.
22 Chase to Janet Chase, May 11, 1862, in Niven, *Chase Papers*, 1:341–42 ("re-
    plied negatively"); Symonds, *Lincoln and His Admirals*, 152–53.
23 Stanton to Watson, May 10, 1862, *OR*, vol. 11, pt. 3, p. 162; Stanton to Mc-
    Clellan, May 10, 1862, M473 (noon "great volumes of smoke"); Stanton to
    Watson, May 10, 1862, in Flower, *Edwin McMasters Stanton*, 155 (midnight);
    McClellan to Stanton, May 11, 1862, in Sears, *The Civil War Papers of George
    B. McClellan*, 263; Chase to Janet Chase, May 11, 1862, in Niven, *Chase Pa-
    pers*, 1:344 ("fairly hugged"); *Cincinnati Gazette*, May 12, 1862 (Lincoln and
    Stanton went ashore at about six on May 10); *Springfield (Mass.) Republican*,
    May 17, 1862 ("not yet recovered"); Viele, "A Trip with Lincoln, Chase, and
    Stanton," 814.
24 Stanton to Watson, May 11, 1862, *OR*, vol. 11, pt. 3, pp. 163–64; Stanton
    to McClellan, May 11, 1862, Edwin Stanton Papers, New-York Historical
    Society; McClellan to Stanton, May 11, 1862, in Sears, *The Civil War Papers
    of George B. McClellan*, 263; Goldsborough to Elizabeth Goldsborough, June
    16, 1862, Goldsborough Papers; Symonds, *Lincoln and His Admirals*, 155.
25 Stanton to Elizabeth Goldsborough, May 12, 1862, Goldsborough Papers
    ("inflamed eye"); *Philadelphia Inquirer*, May 13, 1862 (Stanton "conveyed
    home seriously ill"); Bellows to Van Buren, May 13, 1862, Bellows Papers;
    Nevins and Thomas, *Diary of George Templeton Strong*, 3:226 (May 15, 1862)
    ("Bellows thinks he has some cerebral disease"); Stanton to Wool, May 15,
    1862, Edwin Stanton Papers, LC, box 6, image 165 ("nearly blind"); Stanton
    to McClellan, May 17, 1862, *OR*, vol. 11, pt. 3, p. 176 ("ophthalmia").
26 McClellan to Lincoln, May 14, 1862, in Sears, *The Civil War Papers of George
    B. McClellan*, 264; Stanton to McDowell, May 17, 1862, *OR*, vol. 12, pt. 1, p.
    97; Stanton to McClellan, May 17, 1862, ibid., 97–98; McClellan to Lincoln,
    May 17, 1862, in Sears, *The Civil War Papers of George B. McClellan*, 271; Mc-
    Clellan to Mary Ellen McClellan, May 18, 1862, ibid., 269.
27 Hunter to Stanton, Jan. 29, 1862, Edwin Stanton Papers, LC, box 2, image
    217 ("let me have my way"); Hunter to Stanton, Apr. 3, 1862, *OR*, 6:263–
    64 ("arm such loyal men"); *New York Times*, Apr. 9, 1862 ("using negro

28 Stanton to Saxton, Apr. 29, 1862, *OR*, ser. 3, vol. 2, pp. 27–28 ("take charge");
Niven, *Chase Papers*, 1:334 (May 1, 1862) ("authorized him to procure");
Pittsburgh Gazette, July 14, 1862 (quoting Stanton to Saxton).

29 Mitchel to Stanton, May 4, 1862, *OR*, vol. 10, pt. 2, p. 163; Stanton to
Mitchel, May 5, 1862, ibid., 165 ("assistance of slaves"); Butler to Stanton,
May 25, 1862, ibid., 15:439–42 ("unless all"); Stanton to Butler, June 29,
1862, ibid., 515–16 ("strongly impressed").

30 Hunter proclamation, May 9, 1862, *OR*, 14:341; *New York Times*, May 16,
1862; *New York Tribune*, May 16, 1862; *New York Herald*, May 17, 1862
("there is indeed some reason to believe that Secretary Stanton dictated this
order to General Hunter"); Lincoln proclamation, May 19, 1862, in Basler,
The Collected Works of Abraham Lincoln, 5:219–23; *New York Herald*, May 20,
1862 (praises Lincoln for overruling Stanton); Lincoln to Bennett, May 21,
1862, in Basler, *The Collected Works of Abraham Lincoln*, 5:225; Sumner to
Phillips, May 22, 1862, in Palmer, *Selected Letters of Charles Sumner*, 2:113;
Sumner to Andrew, May 28, 1862, ibid., 115 ("told me this morning"); Atkinson to Philbrick, June 10, 1862, Atkinson Papers ("damn him").

31 *Congressional Globe*, 37th Cong., 2d Sess., p. 3121 (June 9, 1862); Stanton to
Grow, June 14, 1862, *OR*, ser. 3, 2:147–48.

32 *Congressional Globe*, 37th Cong., 2d Sess., p. 3125 (July 5, 1862) (Wickliffe,
Mallory, Stevens).

33 Stanton to McDowell, May 22, 1862, M473 (two messages); Stanton to
Dahlgren, May 22, 1862, ibid.; Dahlgren, *Memoir*, 368–69; Goodwin, *Team
of Rivals*, 441; Haupt, *Reminiscences*, 49 ("nothing in it").

34 Dahlgren, *Memoir*, 369–70 ("fine order" and "did not think much"); *Washington Evening Star*, May 27, 1862 ("afforded a view of their boss").

35 Stanton to Dix, May 24, 1862, *OR*, vol. 12, pt. 3, p. 222; Stanton to Frémont,
May 24, 1862, ibid., pt. 1, p. 642; Stanton to McDowell, May 24, 1862, ibid.,
vol. 12, pt. 3, p. 219; Frémont to Stanton, May 24, 1862, ibid., pt. 1, pp.
642–43; Lincoln to Frémont, May 24, 1862, ibid., 643. For the context, see
Cozzens, *Shenandoah 1862*; Gallagher, *The Shenandoah Valley Campaign of
1862*.

36 Lincoln to McDowell, May 24, 1862, in Basler, *The Collected Works of Abraham Lincoln*, 5:232–33; Stanton to Frémont, May 24, 1862, M473 ("last importance"); Banks to Lincoln, *OR*, vol. 12, pt. 1, p. 527 (in Winchester);
Stanton to Geary, ibid., pt. 3, p. 224 (Banks "probably safe at Winchester";
sent 8:40 p.m.); Stanton to Banks, May 24, 1862, ibid., pt. 1, p. 527 ("more
detailed information").

37 Stanton to McDowell, May 25, 1862, *OR*, vol. 12, pt. 3, p. 231; Stanton to

McDowell, May 25, 1862, ibid., 234; Stanton to governors, May 25, 1862, *OR*, ser. 3, 2:70; Stanton to Andrew, Curtin, and Morgan, May 25, 1862, ibid.; Andrew proclamation, May 25, 1862, in *New York Times*, May 26, 1862.

38 Stanton to Duryee, May 26, 1862, M473 (6:20 a.m.); Stanton to Tod, May 26, 1862, *OR*, ser. 3, 2:78; Stanton to Washburn, May 26, 1862, ibid., 76; Thomas to Washburn, May 26, 1862, ibid., 77 (no more three-month men); Stanton to Andrew, May 27, 1862, ibid., 85; Pearson, *The Life John of Andrew*, 2:18–19 (Andrew had to inform the four thousand men who had gathered in Boston).

39 *Boston Daily Advertiser*, May 27–28, 1862; *New York World*, May 28, 1862.

40 Andrew to Hooper, May 28, 1862, in Thomas and Hyman, *Stanton*, 200 (not in Andrew or Hooper papers at MHS); Hooper to Andrew, May 28, 1862, Andrew Papers (telegram and letter); Sumner to Andrew, May 28, 1862, in Palmer, *Selected Letters of Charles Sumner*, 2:114–15; Pearson, *Life of John Andrew*, 2:19–21.

41 *Boston Evening Transcript*, June 2, 1862; Woodman to Stanton, June 2, 1862, Edwin Stanton Papers, LC, box 7, images 116–17; Hooper to Woodman, June 5, 1862, Woodman Papers; Woodman to Stanton, June 20, 1862, Edwin Stanton Papers, LC, box 8, images 18–20.

42 Stanton to Ellet, Apr. 27, 1862, *ORN*, 23:78; Ellet to Stanton, May 19, 1862, Lincoln Papers, LC; Ellet to Stanton, May 26, 1862, *OR*, vol. 10, pt. 2, p. 215; Ellet to Stanton, May 30, 1862, ibid., 231; Stanton to Halleck, June 5, 1862, ibid., 262; Ellet to Stanton, June 5, 1862, in *New York Times*, June 9, 1862 (upset that "enemy evacuated Fort Pillow last night"); Ellet to Stanton, June 11, 1862, *OR*, vol. 10, pt. 1, pp. 925–27.

43 *New York Times*, June 9, 1862; Ellet to Stanton, June 11, 1862, *OR*, vol. 10, pt. 1, pp. 925–27; Stanton to Ellet, June 13, 1862, *ORN*, 23:154; Brooks to Stanton, June 21, 1862, *OR*, vol. 52, pt. 1, p. 258; Foote, *The Civil War*, 1:386–89; Hearn, *Ellet's Brigade*, 29–42.

44 Autry to Lee, May 18, 1862, *ORN*, 18:492; Halleck to Farragut, July 3, 1862, ibid., 593; Joiner, *Mr. Lincoln's Brown Water Navy*, 81–87; McPherson, *War on the Waters*, 89–95.

45 McClellan to Stanton, June 10, 1862, in Sears, *The Civil War Papers of George B. McClellan*, 295; Wolcott to Pamphila Wolcott, June 11, 1862, in Wolcott, *Edwin M. Stanton*, 182; Stanton to McClellan, June 11, 1862, *OR*, vol. 11, pt. 1, p. 47 (his hand M473); McClellan to Stanton, June 15, 1862, in Sears, *The Civil War Papers of George B. McClellan*, 300.

46 Stanton to Pope, June 19, 1862, M473; *Alexandria (Va.) Gazette*, June 24, 1862 (evening edition reports Pope's arrival); Draft order, June 26, 1862, Edwin Stanton Papers, LC, box 8, images 45–46; Lincoln to Pope, June

26, 1862, in Basler, *The Collected Works of Abraham Lincoln*, 5:287; *New York Times*, June 27, 1862 (Pope appointed); Cozzens and Girardi, *The Military Memoirs of General John Pope*, 115–22; Cozzens, *General John Pope*, 71–75; Tap, *Over Lincoln's Shoulder*, 126–27.

47 *Brooklyn Daily Eagle*, June 24–26, 1862; Lincoln, remarks at Jersey City, June 24, 1862, in Basler, *The Collected Works of Abraham Lincoln*, 5:284; *New York Times*, June 26, 1862.

48 Dyer, *Records of an Active Life*, 251–52; Sears, *To the Gates of Richmond*, 205 ("first of the Seven Days' battles").

49 McClellan to Stanton, June 25–27, 1862, in Sears, *The Civil War Papers of George B. McClellan*, 309–10, 317–18, 321; Stanton to McClellan, June 26, 1862, *OR*, vol. 11, pt. 1, p. 52; Lincoln to McClellan, June 26, 1862, in Basler, *The Collected Works of Abraham Lincoln*, 5:286; Sears, *To the Gates of Richmond*, 205–42.

50 McClellan to Stanton, June 28, 1862, in Sears, *The Civil War Papers of George B. McClellan*, 322–23. For the decision on the night of June 27 to retreat to the James River, see Sears, *To the Gates of Richmond*, 250.

51 U.S. Congress, *Report of the Joint Committee on the Conduct of the War*, 1:310 (omits final sentence); *Pittsburgh Daily Post*, Jan. 19, 1864 (has final sentence); *Urbana (Ohio) Union*, Jan. 20, 1864 (same); *OR*, vol. 11, pt. 1, p. 61 (has final sentence); McClellan, *McClellan's Own Story*, 10–11 (Prime's introduction); Flower, *Edwin McMasters Stanton*, 166–68 (quoting A. E. H. Johnson); Bates, *Lincoln in the Telegraph Office*, 109–11 (similar); Goodwin, *Team of Rivals*, 443 (accepts Johnson version); Marvel, *Lincoln's Autocrat*, 208–9 (rejects Johnson version). Eckert was working for McClellan on the Peninsula at this time; he did not arrive in Washington and start working for Stanton until September 1862.

52 Lincoln to McClellan, June 28, 1862, in Basler, *The Collected Works of Abraham Lincoln*, 5:289–90; Stanton to Halleck, June 28, 1862, *OR*, vol. 17, pt. 2, p. 42; Stanton to Burnside, June 28, 1862, M473 (send McClellan all the troops "that you safely can do"); Lincoln to Dix, June 28, 1862, *OR*, vol. 11, pt. 3, p. 270 ("strain every nerve to open communication" with McClellan); Randall, *Diary of Orville Hickman Browning*, 1:558 (July 14, 1862) ("very harsh").

53 Fulton to Stanton, June 29, 1862, Lincoln Papers, LC (from Baltimore); Stanton to Seward, June 29, 1862, *OR*, vol. 11, pt. 3, p. 274 (Fulton "now with us"); Stanton to Wool, June 30, 1862, M473 (arrest Fulton); Sanford to Fulton, June 30, 1862, in *New York Times*, July 2, 1862 ("obtained facts in confidence"); Stanton to Wool, July 1, 1862, M473 (release Fulton); *Daily Milwaukee News*, July 13, 1862 (Fulton's account); Andrews, *The North Reports the Civil War*, 212–13; Holzer, *Lincoln and the Power of the Press*, 365.

54 Stanton to Seward, June 29 and 30, 1862, *OR*, ser. 3, 2:181–82.

55 Stanton to Seward, June 29–July 1, 1862, M473; Seward to Stanton, June 29–July 1, 1862, Seward Papers, reel 70; *OR*, ser. 3, 2:181–82, 186–88 (printed version of part of the Stanton-Seward correspondence); Andrew to Stanton, July 2, 1862, ibid., 199; Andrew to Francis Blair Sr., July 5, 1862, in Pearson, *Life of John Andrew*, 2:35; *Pittsburgh Gazette*, July 7, 1862, quoting *Boston Chronicle* (why Andrew's name not on the list); Engle, *Gathering to Save a Nation*, 183–88.

56 Lincoln to governors, July 1, 1862, in Basler, *The Collected Works of Abraham Lincoln*, 5:296–97; *New York Times*, July 2, 1862 (printed copy of the correspondence).

Chapter 9: "Hours Are Precious"

1 *Detroit Free Press*, July 3, 1862; *New York Herald*, July 6, 1862; ibid., July 10, 1862, quoting *St. Joseph (Mo.) Democrat*; *New York Times*, July 10, 1862.

2 Chandler to Letitia Chandler, July 6, 1862, Chandler Papers; *Congressional Globe*, 37th Cong., 2d Sess., pp. 3136, 3149–50 (July 7, 1862).

3 *Congressional Globe*, 37th Cong., 2d Sess., pp. 3219–26 (July 10, 1862); Chandler to Letitia Chandler, July 11, 1862, Chandler Papers.

4 Stanton to McClellan, July 5, 1862, in Sears, *The Civil War Papers of George B. McClellan*, 348; Wolcott to Pamphila Wolcott, July 6, 1862, in Wolcott, *Edwin M. Stanton*, 184; McClellan to Lincoln, July 7, 1862, in Sears, *The Civil War Papers of George B. McClellan*, 344–45; McClellan to Stanton, July 8, 1862, ibid., 346–47; Marcy to McClellan, ca. 1880, McClellan Papers, box 107.

5 Stanton to Lincoln, June 29, 1862, Lincoln Papers, LC ("if my child is not dying I will be in town as soon as possible"); Wolcott to Pamphila Wolcott, July 6, 1862, in Wolcott, *Edwin M. Stanton*, 184; Stanton to James Hutchison, July 11, 1862, M473 ("Jamie died last night about one o'clock will be buried Sunday"); Stanton to David Stanton, July 12, 1862, ibid. ("Jamie died Thursday night & will be buried tomorrow morning"); Welles to Mary Welles, July 13, 1862, Welles Papers, LC; *Pittsburgh Gazette*, July 17, 1862, quoting *New York World* ("corpse of his child"). This is the carriage ride in which Lincoln supposedly discussed with Seward and Welles the emancipation proclamation; for the reasons I do not believe there was such a discussion, see Stahr, *Seward*, 339–40.

6 Stanton to Francis Wright, Aug. 2, 1862, M473 (his hand); Stanton to Pamphila Wolcott, Aug. 2, 1862, ibid.; Wolcott to Nancy Stanton, Aug. 2, 1862, ibid.; Wolcott to Pamphila Wolcott, Aug. 2, 1862, ibid.; Wolcott to Anne Dennison, Aug. 2, 1862, ibid.; Stanton to David Tappan, Aug. 19, 1864, courtesy of Mary Langsdorf.

7   McClellan to Mary Ellen McClellan, July 13, 1862, in Sears, *The Civil War Papers of George B. McClellan*, 354–55.

8   Stanton to Halleck, July 11, 1862, M473 ("your early presence is required"); Lincoln to Halleck, July 11, 1862, in Basler, *The Collected Works of Abraham Lincoln*, 5:312–13; *Chicago Times*, July 7, 1862 ("inclined to credit"); McClellan to Mary Ellen McClellan, July 20, 1862, in Sears, *The Civil War Papers of George B. McClellan*, 367; *New York Times*, July 24, 1862 (reports Halleck appointment).

9   Pope Proclamation, July 14, 1862, *OR*, vol. 12, pt. 3, pp. 473–74; Pope General Order No. 5, July 18, 1862, *OR*, vol. 12, pt. 2, p. 50; Pope General Order No. 11, July 23, 1862, ibid., 52; Halleck to Grant, Aug. 2, 1862, *OR*, vol. 17, pt. 2, p. 150; Cox, *Military Reminiscences*, 1:222–23; Hennessy, *Return to Bull Run*, 12–18; Cozzens, *General John Pope*, 83–89 (proclamation "written in longhand by Pope himself"); Murray and Hsieh, *Savage War*, 190 ("such hubris proved a terrible mistake").

10 Porter to J. C. G. Kennedy, July 17, 1862, Porter Papers, MHS; McClellan to Mary Ellen McClellan, July 22, 1862, in Sears, *The Civil War Papers of George B. McClellan*, 368; Sears, *Controversies and Commanders*, 53–59.

11 Second Confiscation Act, July 17, 1862, *Statutes at Large*, 12:589–92; *Chicago Tribune*, July 18, 1862; Masur, *Lincoln's Hundred Days*, 58–76; John Smith, "Let Us All Be Grateful That We Have Colored Troops That Will Fight," in Smith, *Black Soldiers in Blue*, 14 (Confiscation Act had "serious limitations as an instrument of emancipation"); Syrett, *The Civil War Confiscation Acts*, 35–44.

12 *Congressional Globe*, 37th Cong., 2d Sess., p. 3226 (July 10, 1862) (Wilson at War Office "nearly every day of this session"); Militia Act, July 17, 1862, *Statutes at Large*, 12:597–600; *Brooklyn Evening Star*, July 17, 1862; Geary, *We Need Men*, 22–31. I do not see the support for Geary's view that "Wilson may not have been on the best of terms with Edwin Stanton in early July 1862" (30).

13 Hunter to Stanton, July 11, 1862, *OR*, 14:363 ("military necessity" to enlist "all loyal men to be found in my department"); Niven, *Chase Papers*, 1:349 (July 21, 1862) ("not prepared to decide").

14 Lincoln draft, July 22, 1862, in Basler, *The Collected Works of Abraham Lincoln*, 5:336–37; Niven, *Chase Papers*, 1:351–52 (July 22, 1862).

15 Stanton notes, July 22, 1862, Edwin Stanton Papers, LC, box 8, images 149–51; Niven, *Chase Papers*, 1:351–52 (July 22, 1862).

16 Wolcott to Pamphila Wolcott, July 27, 1862, in Wolcott, *Edwin M. Stanton*, 186; Gurowski, *Diary, from March 4, 1861*, 245; Goodwin, *Team of Rivals*, 164–68; Stahr, *Seward*, 341–45.

17 Francis Cutting to Stanton, Feb. 20, 1867, Edwin Stanton Papers, LC, box 32, images 18–22.

18 Stanton order, Aug. 4, 1862, *OR*, ser. 3, 2:291–92; Washburne to Stanton, Aug. 7, 1862, ibid., 318 (question about what information to register); Malmros to Stanton, Aug. 7, 1862, ibid., 319 ("all hands are needed" for the harvest); General Orders No. 99, Aug. 9, 1862, ibid., 333–35 (rules for drafting); Buckingham to Holbrook, Aug. 9, 1862, ibid., 344 (sample of quota); Engle, *Gathering to Save a Nation*, 203–7; Geary, *We Need Men*, 32–38; Hesseltine, *Lincoln and the War Governors*, 273–90; McPherson, *Battle Cry of Freedom*, 492–94.

19 Niven, *Chase Papers*, 1:360 (Aug. 6, 1862); *National Republican*, Aug. 7, 1862 (Lincoln's speech and reaction); Cole and McDonough, *Witness to the Young Republic*, 405 (Aug. 10, 1862).

20 *New York Times*, Jan. 13 and 19, 1862 (reporting Lieber's lectures on law of war); *New York Evening Post*, June 17, 1862 (Lieber's opinion that "slaves escaping during war from one belligerent to another for protection become thereby free"); Lieber to Halleck, Aug. 2, 7, 9, 10, 1862, Lieber Papers, Huntington, box 27; Lieber to Stanton, Aug. 9, 1862, "Memoir on the Military Use of Colored Persons," ibid.; Freidel, *Francis Lieber*; Witt, *Lincoln's Code*, 173–88, 226–29.

21 Stanton to Saxton, Aug. 25, 1862, *OR*, 14:377–78; Mansfield French to Reverend Whipple, Aug. 28, 1862, Amistad Center, Tulane University (French and Smalls met with Stanton in Washington; received copy of order); Watson to Wolcott, Sept. 14, 1862, in Wolcott, *Edwin M. Stanton*, 187; Cornish, *The Sable Arm*, 50–55; Miller, *Gullah Statesman*; Westwood, "Generals David Hunter and Rufus Saxton."

22 Ramsey to Stanton, Aug. 21, 1862, *OR*, 13:590; *New York Tribune*, Aug. 23, 1862; Ramsey to Lincoln, Aug. 27, 1862, *OR*, 13:597; Lincoln to Ramsey, Aug. 27, 1862, in Basler, *The Collected Works of Abraham Lincoln*, 5:396; Nichols, *Lincoln and the Indians*, 76–83.

23 Stanton to Pope, Sept. 6, 1862, *OR*, 13:617; Pope to Sibley, Sept. 17, 1862, ibid., 648–49; Nichols, *Lincoln and the Indians*, 84–88.

24 Yates to Stanton, Aug. 7, 1862, *OR*, ser. 3, 2:316; Stanton order, Aug. 8, 1862, ibid., 370; *New York Times*, Aug. 9, 1862 (prints Stanton's order); Stanton explanation, Aug. 9, 1862, M473 (his hand); *New York Times*, Aug. 10, 1862 (prints explanation without identifying it as official).

25 *New York Times*, Aug. 10, 1862; *Detroit Free Press*, Aug. 12, 1862; *Brooklyn Evening Star*, Aug. 13, 1862; Nevins and Thomas, *Diary of George Templeton Strong*, 3:246–47 (Aug. 16, 1862); Geary, *We Need Men*, 196n48 ("bipartisan editorial opinion in support of restricting skedaddlers").

26 Stanton order, Aug. 8, 1862, *OR*, ser. 3, 2:321–22; *New York Times*, Aug. 9, 1862 (prints order); Neely, *The Fate of Liberty*, 51–54.

27 *Cedar Falls (Iowa) Gazette*, Aug. 15, 1862 (Mahoney arrested); Hoxie to Stanton, Aug. 22, 1862, Turner-Baker Papers, case 413 (Hoxie has delivered

Mahoney to military prison pursuant to Stanton's order); Hughes to Seward, Aug. 27, 1862, ibid.; *Cedar Falls (Iowa) Gazette*, Sept. 12, 1862 (candidate for Congress); *Davenport (Iowa) Daily Gazette*, Nov. 14, 1862 (Mahoney released); Marvel, *Lincoln's Autocrat*, 221–22; Neely, *Fate of Liberty*, 58; Weber, *Copperheads*, 53 (Mahoney "the state's most prominent Copperhead").

28   *Eaton (Ohio) Democratic Press*, June 12, 1862, quoting *Harrisburg Patriot*; [illegible] to Alex Cummings, Aug. 5, 1862, Edwin Stanton Papers, LC, box 8, image 203 (names of the publishers and editors); [Halleck?] to Wadsworth, Aug. 5, 1862, ibid., images 204–6 (order to arrest); *Cleveland Daily Leader*, Aug. 7, 1862; *Janesville (Wisc.) Gazette*, Aug. 9, 1862; Stanton to William Meredith, Aug. 22, 1862, M473 (his hand); *Daily Ohio Statesman*, Aug. 28, 1862, quoting *Harrisburg Patriot*. Stanton's personal interest in the case is shown by the presence of the arrest papers among his papers.

29   *New York Times*, Aug. 28, 1862 (arrest); *Philadelphia Public Ledger*, Aug. 28, 1862 (lists counsel); Millward to Stanton, Aug. 28, 1862, Turner-Baker Papers, case 14; Cadwalader, *Cadwalader's Cases*, 1:587–88; Greenberg, "Charles Ingersoll."

30   Turner order, Sept. 8, 1862, *OR*, ser. 3, 2:521–22; Neely, *Fate of Liberty*, 51–65; Weber, *Copperheads*, 52–58.

31   *New York Times*, July 24, 1862 (Halleck met with Lincoln, Stanton, Pope, and Burnside); Halleck to Stanton, July 27, 1862, *OR*, vol. 11, pt. 3, pp. 337–38 ("finally agreed" and "good chance of success"); Marszalek, *Commander of All Lincoln's Armies*, 132–38; Sears, *George B. McClellan*, 239–41.

32   Halleck to McClellan, Aug. 3, 1862, *OR*, vol. 11, pt. 1, pp. 80–81; McClellan to Halleck, Aug. 4, 1862, in Sears, *The Civil War Papers of George B. McClellan*, 383–85.

33   Lincoln to McClellan, Aug. 29, 1862, in Basler, *The Collected Works of Abraham Lincoln*, 5:399; McClellan to Lincoln, Aug. 29, 1862, in Sears, *The Civil War Papers of George B. McClellan*, 416; Lincoln to McClellan, Aug. 29, 1862, ibid.; Burlingame and Ettlinger, *Inside Lincoln's White House*, 37 (Sept. 1, 1862); Sears, *Controversies and Commanders*, 77–80.

34   Stanton to Halleck, Aug. 28, 1862, *OR*, vol. 12, pt. 3, p. 706; Halleck to Stanton, Aug. 30, 1862, ibid., 739; Stanton, Chase, and Smith to Lincoln, Aug. 30, 1862, in Flower, *Edwin McMasters Stanton*, 181–82 (facsimile); Gienapp and Gienapp, *Civil War Diary of Gideon Welles*, 17–18 (Aug. 31, 1862).

35   Montgomery Meigs to John Meigs, Aug. 30, 1862, in Giunta, *Civil War Soldier of Christ and Country*, 162 (8000 wounded); Stanton to Scott, Aug. 30, 1862, *OR*, vol. 12, pt. 3, p. 766 ("volunteer surgeons are needed); Burlingame and Ettlinger, *Inside Lincoln's White House*, 37–38 (Sept 1, 1862) ("pleasant little dinner"); Stanton to Harrisburg, Sept. 1, 1862, M473 ("do not forward any more surgeons"); Sears, *Landscape Turned Red*, 10 ("volunteer surgeons");

Winkle, *Lincoln's Citadel*, 290–91 (Stanton's "well-meaning gesture back-fired").

36 Gienapp and Gienapp, *Civil War Diary of Gideon Welles*, 18–21 (Aug. 31, 1862).

37 Burlingame and Ettlinger, *Inside Lincoln's White House*, 38 (Sept 1, 1862) ("whipped again"); *New York World*, Sept. 1, 1862 ("little if any fighting today"); Bates et al. to Lincoln, Sept. 1, 1862, Edwin Stanton Papers, LC, box 10, image 66; Gienapp and Gienapp, *Civil War Diary of Gideon Welles*, 24–25 (Sept. 1, 1862) ("this method"); McClellan to Mary Ellen McClellan, Sept. 2, 1862, in Sears, *The Civil War Papers of George B. McClellan*, 428 ("hope I shall succeed").

38 Pope to Halleck, Sept. 2, 1862, *OR*, vol. 12, pt. 3, p. 797; Halleck to Pope, Sept. 2, 1862, ibid.; Sears, *Landscape Turned Red*, 15 (Pope's message was a "confession of final failure").

39 Gienapp and Gienapp, *Civil War Diary of Gideon Welles*, 26–27 (Sept. 2, 1862); Niven, *Chase Papers*, 1:368–69 (Sept. 2, 1862); Bates memo, Sept. 2, 1862, in Basler, *The Collected Works of Abraham Lincoln*, 5:486.

40 Agnew to Marble, Sept. 2, 1862, Marble Papers; *Washington Evening Star*, Sept. 3, 1862 (rumor of resignation); *New York World*, Sept. 4, 1862 ("wasting the millions"); Nevins and Thomas, *Diary of George Templeton Strong*, 3:252 ("reason to hope that Stanton is trembling to his fall") (Sept. 4, 1862); *Boston Daily Advertiser*, Sept. 5, 1862 (Stanton would resign); *New York World*, Sept. 6, 1862 (Stanton *had* resigned).

41 McClellan to Halleck, Sept. 2, 1862, *OR*, vol. 12, pt. 3, p. 802 (arsenal); Halleck to McClellan, Sept. 2, 1862, ibid., 805 (arsenal); McClellan to Lincoln, Sept. 2, 1862, in Sears, *The Civil War Papers of George B. McClellan*, 430–31; Stanton to Butler, Sept. 2, 1862, in Marshall, *Private and Official Correspondence of Benjamin Butler*, 2:250. The key memoirs are McClellan, *McClellan's Own Story*, 535–36 (section drafted by William Prime); William Irwin, "Washington under Banks," in Johnson and Buel, *Battles and Leaders*, 2:542; and Flower, *Edwin McMasters Stanton*, 179 (quoting E. D. Townsend). Secondary accounts include Leech, *Reveille in Washington*, 240 ("could be carried"); Thomas and Hyman, *Stanton*, 219; Hennessy, *Return to Bull Run*, 451 ("steamer be anchored"). Newspapers include *Washington Evening Star*, Sept. 2, 1862; *New York Tribune*, Sept. 3, 1862 ("Washington wears a very busy look today and tonight, and reminds one of its appearance last year").

42 Halleck to McClellan, Sept. 3, 1862, *OR*, vol. 19, pt. 2, p. 169; Stanton to Halleck, Sept. 3, 1862, ibid., 169; Marszalek, *Commander of All Lincoln's Armies*, 146–48; Murray and Hsieh, *Savage War*, 207 ("It would take Lincoln and Stanton until 1863 to divine [Halleck's] actual abilities. By summer 1863, they were largely using him as a clerk."); Sears, *Landscape Turned Red*, 49–69.

43 Townsend order, Sept. 5, 1862, *OR*, vol. 19, pt. 2, p. 188; Halleck to Pope, Sept. 5, 1862, M473 (report to Stanton); Pope to Stanton, Sept. 5, 1862, Edwin Stanton Papers, LC, box 9, image 9 ("because of the treachery"); McClellan to Halleck, Sept. 6, 1862, in Sears, *The Civil War Papers of George B. McClellan*, 436; Gabler, "The Fitz John Porter Case," 178 ("September 5, 1862, was a bad day for generals").

44 Gienapp and Gienapp, *Civil War Diary of Gideon Welles*, 31 (Sept. 6, 1862); McClellan to Halleck, Sept. 10, 1862, in Sears, *The Civil War Papers of George B. McClellan*, 444–45; Curtin to Stanton, Sept. 7–9, 1862, *OR*, vol. 19, pt. 2, pp. 203, 216, 229 (multiple messages); Niven, *Chase Papers*, 1:380 (Sept. 11, 1862).

45 *New York Herald*, Sept. 11, 1862 (Lincoln should remove radicals from cabinet); *New York World*, Sept. 13, 1862 ("mercurial"); *New York Tribune*, Sept. 14, 1862 (Stanton "drilled from every direction"); *National Republican*, Sept. 15, 1862 ("wisdom"); Chase to Greeley, Sept. 15, 1862, in Niven, *Chase Papers*, 3:267–68 ("Stanton's voice").

46 Gienapp and Gienapp, *Civil War Diary of Gideon Welles*, 42–44 (Sept. 12, 1862).

47 Belmont to Lincoln, Sept. 4, 1862, Lincoln Papers, LC; Lincoln to Stanton, Sept. 11, 1862, in Basler, *The Collected Works of Abraham Lincoln*, 5:416 ("yours as ever").

48 McClellan to Halleck, Sept. 17, 1862, in Sears, *The Civil War Papers of George B. McClellan*, 467–68; Stanton to railroad officials, Sept. 17, 1862, *OR*, vol. 19, pt. 2, pp. 313–14; Sears, *Landscape Turned Red*.

49 McClellan to Halleck, Sept. 19, 1862, *OR*, vol. 19, pt. 2, p. 330 (two messages); Sears, *Landscape Turned Red*, 298–309.

50 McClellan to Mary Ellen McClellan, Sept. 20, 1862, in Sears, *The Civil War Papers of George B. McClellan*, 473, 476 (two letters).

51 Niven, *Chase Papers*, 1:393–95 (Sept. 22, 1862); Gienapp and Gienapp, *Civil War Diary of Gideon Welles*, 53–55 (Sept. 22, 1862); Welles, "The History of Emancipation," 846 ("emphatic speech"); Masur, *Lincoln's Hundred Days*, 1–7; Goodwin, *Team of Rivals*, 481–82.

52 *New York Tribune*, Sept. 23, 1862; *New York Times*, Sept. 23, 1862; *Albany (N.Y.) Evening Journal*, Sept. 23, 1862; *Daily Ohio Statesman*, Sept. 26, 1862, quoting *Louisville (Ky.) Journal*; *Pittsburgh Gazette*, Sept. 29, 1862, quoting *Harrisburg Weekly Patriot*; *Nashville Daily Union*, Oct. 17, 1862 ("conflict has ceased"); Masur, *Lincoln's Hundred Days*, 101–15.

53 Lincoln proclamation, Sept. 24, 1862, in Basler, *The Collected Works of Abraham Lincoln*, 5:436–37; Guelzo, *Redeeming the Great Emancipator*; Neely, *Fate of Liberty*, 64–65. Lincoln interpreted the Constitution as authorizing him to suspend the writ; he disagreed with and did not follow Chief Justice Taney's opinion on this issue. Lincoln message, July 4, 1861, in Basler, *The Collected*

Works of Abraham Lincoln, 4:430–31; Burlingame, *Abraham Lincoln: A Life*, 2:152.

54 *New York World*, Sept. 8, 1862; *Daily Ohio Statesman*, Oct. 12, 1862; Neely, *The Union Divided*, 7–34; Weber, *Copperheads*, 2–3, 43–71.

55 Tuttle to Stanton, Sept. 18, 1862, *OR*, ser. 3, 2:569; Stanton to Tuttle, Sept. 18, 1862, ibid.; Stanton to Tuttle, Oct. 13, 1862, ibid., 663; Davis to Lincoln, Oct. 14, 1862, Lincoln Papers, LC; *Chicago Times*, Oct. 16, 1862 ("flood-gates"); Smith, *No Party Now*, 55–56 ("timing that was appalling for the administration"); Tap, "Race, Rhetoric, and Emancipation"; Voegeli, *Free but Not Equal*, 60–62 (Stanton's order "a blunder").

56 Nevins and Thomas, *Diary of George Templeton Strong*, 3:272 (Nov. 5, 1862).

57 *New York Herald*, Oct. 23, 1862; *New York Tribune*, Oct. 24, 1862; Garfield to Burke, Oct. 13, 1862, in Williams, *The Wild Life of the Army*, 160–61; Chase to Hiram Barney, Oct. 26, 1862, in Niven, *Chase Papers*, 3:306; Stanton to Halleck, Oct. 27, 1862, *OR*, vol. 19, pt. 1, p. 7; Halleck to Stanton, Oct. 27, 1862, ibid., 7–9 (published *New York Times*, Nov. 10, 1862).

58 General Orders No. 82, Nov. 5, 1862, *OR*, 21:82 (relieving McClellan and appointing Burnside); McClellan to Mary Ellen McClellan, Nov. 7–8, 1862, in Sears, *The Civil War Papers of George B. McClellan*, 519–20 (Burnside and Buckingham arrived about 11:30 p.m. on Nov. 7); *New York Herald*, Nov. 9, 1862 (McClellan removed); Paris, *History of the Civil War*, 2:555–57 (quoting Buckingham).

59 *Brooklyn Daily Eagle*, Nov. 18, 1862; *Richmond (Va.) Dispatch*, Nov. 18, 1862 (Burnside approaching Fredericksburg); Hooker to Stanton, Nov. 19, 1862, *OR*, 21:773–74; Parke to Hooker, Nov. 20, 1862, ibid., 104–105 (Burnside's response to Hooker); Marvel, *Burnside*, 159–74.

60 Fessenden to Warriner, Dec. 14, 1862, Fessenden Papers; Burnside to Halleck, Dec. 16, 1862, *OR*, 21:65 ("necessary to withdraw the army to this side of the river"); *Daily Ohio Statesman*, Dec. 18, 1862, quoting *Cincinnati Commercial*; Rable, *Fredericksburg!*, 255–87.

61 *New York Herald*, Dec. 16, 1862; *New York World*, Dec. 17, 1862; *Chicago Times*, Dec. 18, 1862; Nevins and Thomas, *Diary of George Templeton Strong*, 3:281 (Dec. 18, 1862); Rable, *Fredericksburg!*, 347–48 (attacks on Stanton).

62 *New York Herald*, Dec. 18, 1862; Raphel to Stanton, Dec. 18, 1862, Edwin Stanton Papers, LC, box 10, image 258; Dana to Stanton, Dec. 19, 1862, ibid., images 260–62.

63 Fessenden notes, Dec. 1862, Fessenden Papers. A printed copy of the notes is in Fessenden, *Life and Public Services*, 1:231–36. Secondary accounts include Marvel, *Lincoln's Autocrat*, 263–66; Stahr, *Seward*, 353–60.

64 Fessenden notes, Dec. 1862, Fessenden Papers; Gienapp and Gienapp, *Civil War Diary of Gideon Welles*, 98–100 (Dec. 19, 1862).

65 Fessenden notes, Dec. 1862, Fessenden Papers; Gienapp and Gienapp, *Civil War Diary of Gideon Welles*, 100–105 (Dec. 20, 1862); *New York Herald*, Dec. 23, 1862 ("evidently aimed").

66 *New York Herald*, Dec. 19, 1862 (meeting at Cooper Union); Gienapp and Gienapp, *Civil War Diary of Gideon Welles*, 102–4 (Dec. 20, 1862); Fessenden notes, Dec. 1862, Fessenden Papers.

67 Gienapp and Gienapp, *Civil War Diary of Gideon Welles*, 104–5 (Dec. 20, 1862).

68 Ibid., 105; Lincoln to Seward and Chase, Dec. 20, 1862, in Basler, *The Collected Works of Abraham Lincoln*, 6:12; *New York Herald*, Dec. 20, 1862; Stahr, *Seward*, 359.

69 Burnside to Halleck, Dec. 19, 1862, in *New York Tribune*, Dec. 23, 1862; Draft Burnside letter, Dec. 19, 1862, Edwin Stanton Papers, LC, box 9, images 263–68; Raymond, "Extracts from the Journal," 424; Thomas and Hyman, *Stanton*, 253 ("The hostile press, however, asserted that Stanton forced Burnside to take the blame"). This is one of several places where Thomas and Hyman refer to the press without citing a newspaper.

70 Stanton opinion, Dec. 26, 1862, Lincoln Papers, LC; Burlingame, *Abraham Lincoln: A Life*, 2:459–62.

71 *Congressional Globe*, 37th Cong., 2d Sess., p. 3125 (July 5, 1862) (Mallory, Stevens); Stanton to McClellan, July 5, 1862, in Sears, *The Civil War Papers of George B. McClellan*, 348; Gienapp and Gienapp, *Civil War Diary of Gideon Welles*, 105 (Dec. 20, 1862) ("ready to tender").

72 Halleck to Stanton, Oct. 28, 1862, *OR*, vol. 19, pt. 1, p. 8 ("no armies"); Nicolay and Hay, "Plans of Campaign," 925 ("if he had a million men"); Murray and Hsieh, *Savage War*, 173 ("no matter how many soldiers McClellan received, nothing would have changed his unwillingness to engage the enemy").

73 *New York Tribune*, Feb. 20, 1862 ("days of Joshua"); Lincoln to Halleck, June 10, 1863, in Basler, *The Collected Works of Abraham Lincoln*, 6:257.

74 Stanton annual report, Dec. 1, 1862, *OR*, ser. 3, 2:903.

75 Nevins and Thomas, *Diary of George Templeton Strong*, 3:203 (Jan. 29, 1862).

Chapter 10: "Indomitable Energy"

1 Burnside to Lincoln, Jan. 1 and 5, 1863, *OR*, 21:941–42, 944–45; Burnside testimony, U.S. Congress, *Report of the Joint Committee on the Conduct of the War* 1:717–19; Sears, *Controversies and Commanders*, 146–47.

2 Lincoln to Halleck, Jan. 1, 1863, in Basler, *The Collected Works of Abraham Lincoln*, 6:31; Sears, *Controversies and Commanders*, 148 (Halleck's "concept of the job was so restrictive that he had become little more than a glorified chief clerk for the army").

3 *Sacramento Daily Union*, Jan. 29, 1863 (Brooks letter from Washington); Brooks, *Washington in Lincoln's Time* (1896), 41 ("unfestive day"); Goodwin, *Team of Rivals*, 497–99.

4 Foote, *Civil War*, 2:107 (New Year's was "dead center" of Lincoln's "period of deepest gloom and perplexity of spirit" for "commanders had failed him utterly"); Marszalek, *Sherman*, 202–14; Masur, *Lincoln's Hundred Days*, 205–18; McPherson, *Battle Cry of Freedom*, 577–79 (Grant, Sherman).

5 Stanton to Rosecrans, Mar. 22, 1862, Rosecrans Papers (handwritten letter to support Rosecrans); Rosecrans to Anna Rosecrans, Apr. 11, 1862, ibid. (pleasant meeting with Stanton; "good luck"); *New York Times*, Jan. 1, 1863 ("preparations for a great battle"); Rosecrans to Stanton, Jan. 5, 1863, *OR*, vol. 20, pt. 1, pp. 185–86; Stanton to Rosecrans, Jan. 5, 1863, ibid., 299–300 ("country is filled with admiration of the gallantry and heroic achievement of yourself and the officers and troops under your command"); Hartsuff to Rosecrans, Jan. 8, 1863, Rosecrans Papers (Stanton has a "senseless but strong prejudice against you," but "he has yielded it up now"); McPherson, *Battle Cry of Freedom*, 583 ("Rosecrans felt unable to renew the offensive for several months"); Murray and Hsieh, *Savage War*, 328 ("instead of acting [Rosecrans] besieged Washington with requests for ever more men, horses, and equipment, as well as excuses as to why he could not yet attack"). For a more sympathetic view, see Lamers, *The Edge of Glory*, 246–73.

6 Grant General Orders No. 11, Dec. 17, 1862, in Simon, *The Papers of Ulysses Grant*, 7:50; Wolff to Lincoln, Dec. 29, 1862, ibid., 54n; *Cincinnati Enquirer*, Jan. 2, 1863 (has copy of Grant's order); Halleck to Grant, Jan. 4, 1863, *OR*, vol. 17, pt. 2, p. 530 (revoke order); Isaac Wise to Stanton, Jan. 5, 1863, in Simon, *The Papers of Ulysses Grant*, 7:55; *Daily Ohio Statesman*, Jan. 6, 1863 (Jews protesting Grant's order); *Milwaukee News*, Jan. 7, 1863 (Halleck has issued an order revoking that of Grant); Sarna and Shapell, *Lincoln and the Jews*, 112–18. Although Halleck's order to Grant is dated Jan. 4 in the *Official Records*, the absence of press reports before Jan. 7 suggests it may have been sent later.

7 Yates to Lincoln, Sept. 26, 1862, Lincoln Papers, LC; Stanton to McClernand, Oct. 21, 1862, *OR*, vol. 17, pt. 2, p. 282 ("when a sufficient force"); McClernand to Stanton, Oct. 28, 1862, ibid., 300; Stanton to McClernand, Oct. 28, 1862, ibid. ("everything here is favorable for your expedition"); Stanton to McClernand, Oct. 29, 1862, ibid., 302; Stanton to McClernand, Oct. 30, 1862, ibid., 308; Stanton to McClernand, Oct. 31, 1862, ibid., 310; Stanton to McClernand, Nov. 5, 1862, M473; Stanton to McClernand, Nov. 15, 1862, *OR*, vol. 17, pt. 2, pp. 348–49 ("your expedition"); Stanton to McClernand, Nov. 16, 1862, ibid., 349 ("your expedition"); Stanton to McClernand, Nov. 18, 1862, M473 ("your expedition"); Browning

to McClernand, Dec. 2, 1862, in Simon, *The Papers of Ulysses Grant*, 6:289 ("very anxious for you"); McClernand to Stanton, Jan. 3, 1863, *OR*, vol. 17, pt. 2, pp. 528–30 ("I have been deprived of a command"); Foote, *Civil War*, 2:60–65; Kiper, *Major General John Alexander McClernand*, 148–52; McPherson, *Battle Cry of Freedom*, 577–78; Work, *Lincoln's Political Generals*, 2 (McClernand failed as a general).

8 *Detroit Free Press*, Dec. 27, 1862 (Butler ordered to Washington); Strong Diary, Dec. 30, 1862 ("today's story is that Secy Stanton goes out & Butler succeeds him"); *Detroit Free Press*, Jan. 3, 1863 (Butler would be secretary of war); *New York Herald*, Jan. 7, 1863 (Butler "closeted" with Stanton); Sumner to Butler, Jan. 8, 1863, in Marshall, *Private and Official Correspondence of Benjamin Butler*, 2:570–71; Lincoln to Stanton, Jan. 23, 1863, in Basler, *The Collected Works of Abraham Lincoln*, 6:76–77 ("Butler should go to New Orleans again"); Draft order, Feb. 17, 1863, Lincoln Papers, LC (partly in Stanton's hand); Chase to Butler, Feb. 24, 1863, in Marshall, *Private and Official Correspondence of Benjamin Butler*, 3:15; Butler to Chase, Feb. 28, 1863, ibid., 21–27; Butler to Stanton, Mar. 23, 1863, ibid., 40 (asking permission to give speeches); Stanton to Butler, Mar. 26, 1863, ibid., 40 (granting permission).

9 Pierrepont to Seymour, Feb. 22, 1863, in Eisenschiml, "An Intriguing Letter," 13–14; Barnes, *Memoir of Thurlow Weed*, 428. The letter, at the time Eisenschiml printed it, was in private hands. Thomas and Hyman, *Stanton*, 259.

10 Burnside draft order, Jan. 23, 1863, *OR*, 21:998–99; Williams to daughter, Jan. 24, 1863, in Quaife, *From the Cannon's Mouth*, 159 (mules); Raymond, "Extracts from the Journal," 422 (Hooker quotes); Rable, *Fredericksburg!*, 408–23; Sears, *Chancellorsville*, 1–25.

11 Lincoln to Hooker, Jan. 26, 1863, in Basler, *The Collected Works of Abraham Lincoln*, 6:78–79; Charles Benjamin, "Hooker's Appointment and Removal," in Johnson and Buel, *Battles and Leaders*, 3:240 ("first conclusion"); Wert, *The Sword of Lincoln*, 216–18.

12 *Congressional Globe*, 37th Cong., 3d Sess., App. 55 (Jan. 14, 1862) (Vallandigham).

13 Stanton annual report, Dec. 1, 1862, *OR*, ser. 3, 2:904 ("serious defects"); Senate Bill 511, Feb. 9, 1863 (available on LC website); *Congressional Globe*, 37th Cong., 3d Sess., p. 978 (Feb. 16, 1863) (Wilson worked with "most experienced military men" in drafting his bill); Gienapp and Gienapp, *Civil War Diary of Gideon Welles*, 268 (Aug. 10, 1863); Geary, *We Need Men*, 47–57.

14 Senate Bill 511, Feb. 9, 1863 (LC website); *Congressional Globe*, 37th Cong., 3d Sess., p. 1443 (Mar. 2, 1863) (Sherman: commutation "fixes the price of the substitute at the standard price"); Stanton to Morgan, July 17, 1863, in Gorham, *The Life and Public Services*, 2:109 ("$300 exemption clause was

always in my judgment a highly objectionable feature of the bill, but it was enacted by Congress"); McPherson, *Battle Cry of Freedom*, 603 ("Republican architects of the draft law inserted commutation as a means of putting a cap on the price of substitutes").

15 *Congressional Globe*, 37th Cong., 3d Sess., App. 174 (Feb. 23, 1863) (Vallandigham); *Luzerne Union* (Wilkes-Barre, Pa.), Feb. 25, 1863 (bill passed Senate; includes foreigners).

16 *Congressional Globe*, 37th Cong, 3d Sess., p. 1291 (Feb. 25, 1863) (amendment to delete "treasonable practices" language); Conscription Act, Mar. 3, 1863, *Statutes at Large*, 12:731–37; Geary, *We Need Men*, 57–64.

17 Habeas Corpus Suspension Act, Mar. 3, 1863, *Statutes at Large*, 12:755–58; Gienapp and Gienapp, *Civil War Diary of Gideon Welles*, 556 (Dec. 23, 1864); Randall, "The Indemnity Act of 1863."

18 *Congressional Globe*, 37th Cong, 3d Sess., pp. 1097, 1119 (Feb. 19–20, 1863) (conference committee appointed); ibid., 1435–77 (Mar. 2–3, 1863) (Senate debate; quoted passage 1477); Randall, "Indemnity Act of 1863," 592–94 (legislative history).

19 Habeas Corpus Suspension Act, Mar. 3, 1863, *Statutes at Large*, 12:755–58.

20 *Dayton Daily Empire*, Nov. 26, 1862 (Democratic nomination); *Detroit Free Press*, Feb. 22, 1863 (Harriman nomination); *Cleveland Daily Leader*, Mar. 11, 1863 (preliminary results); Engle, *Gathering to Save a Nation*, 280–81; Hadley, *Life of Walter Harriman*, 143–52.

21 Edward Rollins to Lincoln, July 14, 1863, Lincoln Papers, LC; Nehemiah Ordway to Lincoln, July 23 and 24, 1863, ibid. (N.H. Republicans want Harriman promoted); Lincoln to Stanton, July 27, 1863, in Basler, *The Collected Works of Abraham Lincoln*, 6:352 ("please see and hear Mr. Ordway of New Hampshire"); Lyford, *Life of Edward H. Rollins*, 152–57.

22 *Cincinnati Enquirer*, Feb. 6, 1863 ("Let the Soldiers Vote"); *Cecil (Md.) Whig*, Feb. 28, 1863 (Fourteenth Regiment address); *Green Mountain Freeman* (Montpelier, Vt.), Mar. 7, 1863 (supports address); White, *Emancipation*, 18 ("Following the Democratic victories of 1862, Republicans almost unanimously decided that soldiers ought to have the right to vote").

23 *Chicago Tribune*, Mar. 11, 1863 (legislature is Republican so "election of Gov. Gilmore is certain"); *New York Herald*, Mar. 12, 1863 (Eastman would have been elected but for "party trick"); Special Orders No. 119, Mar. 13, 1863, in *Milwaukee News*, Apr. 3, 1863 (dismissing Edgerly); *Detroit Free Press*, Apr. 29, 1863 (criticizing Stanton for dismissing Edgerly); Marvel, *Lincoln's Autocrat*, 280–81.

24 Stanton to Buckingham, Mar. 21, 1863, Edwin Stanton Papers, LC, box 39, image 30; *New York Tribune*, Apr. 7, 1863; *Daily Ohio Statesman*, Apr. 10, 1863 (furloughs for Republicans); *Ohio Democrat*, Apr. 17, 1863, quoting

New York Express ("give their names to me"); Cowden, *"Heaven Will Frown,"* 25–44; Weber, *Copperheads*, 2–3, 93.

25   Buckingham to Stanton, Apr. 8, 1863, Edwin Stanton Papers, LC, box 11, image 160 ("thank you for your cordial congratulations by telegram"); Stanton to Isabella Beecher Hooker, May 6, 1863, in Wolcott, *Edwin M. Stanton*, 192 (most important election).

26   *St. Cloud (Minn.) Democrat*, Feb. 26, 1863 ("radical idea"); *Semi-Weekly Wisconsin*, Apr. 17, 1863, quoting *Hartford (Ct.) Press* ("masterly sketch"); Stanton to Isabella Beecher Hooker, May 6, 1863, in Wolcott, *Edwin M. Stanton*, 192; Gallman, *America's Joan of Arc*, 24–30; Warshauer, *Connecticut*, 106–15; White, *The Beecher Sisters*.

27   Morton to Stanton, Feb. 9, 1863, Edwin Stanton Papers, LC, box 10, images 232–39; Morton to Stanton, Mar. 6, 1863, ibid., box 11, image 60; Morton to Stanton, Apr. 21, 1863, ibid., images 188–89 (sending messenger for the money); Engle, *Gathering to Save a Nation*, 307–8; Hesseltine, *Lincoln and the War Governors*, 310–15; Stampp, *Indiana Politics*, 176–85; Towne, "Killing the Serpent Speedily"; Wilson, "Edwin M. Stanton," 242 ("if the cause fails"). Although one might question the quote—Wilson does not suggest that he was present at the meeting between Stanton and Morton—there is no question Stanton provided Morton with federal funds. See Morton to Stanton, Dec. 26, 1864, Edwin Stanton Papers, LC, box 24, images 111–12; Stanton to Morton, Dec. 26, 1864, ibid., image 113 (discussing repayment).

28   Militia Act, July 17, 1862, *Statutes at Large*, 12:596–97 (sections 5 and 6); Leonard, *Lincoln's Forgotten Ally*, 158–59; Magliocca, *American Founding Son* (Bingham); Moran, *John Chipman Gray*; Witt, *Lincoln's Code*, 263–66 ("Holt's Bright Young Men").

29   Hartigan, *Lieber's Code*, 1–29; Witt, *Lincoln's Code*, 199–229.

30   Special Orders No. 399, Dec. 17, 1862, *OR*, ser. 3, 2:951 ("code of regulations"); General Orders No. 100, Apr. 24, 1863, ibid., 3:156 (articles 75–76).

31   Garfield to Rhodes, Dec. 14, 1862, in Williams, *Wild Life of the Army*, 195; Gabler, "The Fitz John Porter Case"; Leonard, *Lincoln's Forgotten Ally*, 166–72; Sears, *Controversies and Commanders*, 53–67.

32   Porter to Marble, Apr. 26 and June 20, 1862, Marble Papers; Stanton to Lincoln, Jan. 1863, in Thomas and Hyman, *Stanton*, 262. Thomas and Hyman state that at the time of their research the memo was in the possession of Stanton's descendant, Mrs. E. K. Van Swearingen. Although most of the letters they cite to Van Swearingen are now at the National Archives, in the Edwin M. Stanton Family Papers, I did not see this memo among them.

33   Stanton to Hunter, Jan. 6, 1863, *OR*, vol. 12, pt. 2, supp. 1041; Porter to [unidentified], Jan. 23, 1863, Porter Papers, MHS; *Woodstock (Ill.) Sentinel*, Jan. 28, 1863 ("tool of McClellan"); *Detroit Free Press*, Jan. 30, 1863

("extraordinary and infamous verdict in the case of the gallant Fitz John Porter"). For Porter's struggle to clear his name, see Sears, *Controversies and Commanders*, 67–71; Gabler, "The Fitz John Porter Case," 331–475.

34 Hart, "Military Commissions and the Lieber Code," 37–38 (Halleck's editing); Witt, *Lincoln's Code*, 270 (officers "carried with them the pocket-sized pamphlet code of rules issued by Lincoln and written by Francis Lieber").

35 General Orders No. 100, Apr. 24, 1863, *OR*, ser. 3, 3:149, 157–58 (articles 13, 82, 84, 88).

36 *Brooklyn Daily Eagle*, Apr. 14, 1863 (Vallandigham for president); *New York Tribune*, May 6, 1863 (arrest); *Detroit Free Press*, May 8, 1863 (arrest); Stanton to Burnside, May 8, 1863, *OR*, vol. 23, pt. 2, p. 316 ("in your determination"); *Cleveland Daily Leader*, May 20, 1863 (quoting Vallandigham after arrest); Cowden, *"Heaven Will Frown,"* 155–80; Curtis, "Lincoln, Vallandigham."

37 *Ex parte Vallandigham*, 28 Federal Cases 874 (May 16, 1863); *Janesville (Wisc.) Gazette*, May 19, 1863 ("eminently sound").

38 *New York Tribune*, May 15, 1863; Stanton to Burnside, May 19, 1863, *OR*, ser. 2, 5:656 (his hand in M473); Stanton to Burnside, May 19, 1863, ibid., 657 (send prisoner to Rosecrans); Klement, "Clement L. Vallandigham's Exile."

39 Arnold and Trumbull to Lincoln, June 3, 1863, Lincoln Papers, LC; Lincoln to Stanton, June 4, 1863, in Basler, *The Collected Works of Abraham Lincoln*, 6:248; Stanton to Burnside, June 4, 1863, *OR*, ser. 3, 3:252; Stanton to Burnside, June 4, 1863, M473 ("if you have not acted"); Stanton to Burnside, June 1863, *OR*, ser. 2, 5:724 ("take an early occasion"); *New York Tribune*, June 4, 1863; *Chicago Times*, June 5, 1863; Tenney, "To Suppress or Not to Suppress."

40 Lincoln to Corning et al., June 12, 1863, in Basler, *The Collected Works of Abraham Lincoln*, 6:260–69; *New York Tribune*, June 15, 1863.

41 Lincoln to Birchard et al., June 29, 1863, in Basler, *The Collected Works of Abraham Lincoln*, 6:300–06. Opinion on Lincoln's letters is still divided. Compare Goodwin, *Team of Rivals*, 525 ("as the American people absorbed the logic of Lincoln's argument, popular sentiment began to shift") with Curtis, "Lincoln, Vallandigham," 191 ("Lincoln was wrong in his justification of Vallandigham's arrest").

42 Hart, "Military Commissions and the Lieber Code," 41–44; Lowry, *Merciful Lincoln*, 119–36 ("potpourri of military commissions"); Winthrop, *Digest of Opinions*, 225 ("using disloyal language"); Witt, *Lincoln's Code*, 267–70.

43 Holt to Stanton, June 9, 1863, *OR*, ser. 2, 5:765–66; White, *Abraham Lincoln and Treason*, 150 (Holt's lists partial); Witt, *Lincoln's Code*, 266–67 ("Holt ingeniously reasoned away the act's constraint on executive power").

44 Manning, *Troubled Refuge*; Rose, *Rehearsal for Reconstruction*.

45 Russell to Stanton, Dec. 25, 1862, American Freedmen's Inquiry Commission Papers. The full title of Russell's report is "Report on the Condition, Necessities, and Capacity of the Colored Refugees from the Enemy in Fortress Monroe and the Vicinity, in regard to the Unpaid Wages of Their Labor for the Government."

46 Stanton to Commissioners, Mar. 16, 1863, *OR*, ser. 3, 3:73–74; Stanton to Robert Dale Owen, Mar. 19, 1863, Edwin Stanton Papers, LC, box 39, image 21 (secretary); Preliminary Report, American Freedmen's Inquiry Commission, June 30, 1863, *OR*, ser. 3, 3:430–54; Manning, *Troubled Refuge*, 22–23 (Commission gathered "thousands of pages" of testimony from army officers, former slaves, missionaries); Sproat, "Blueprint for Radical Reconstruction," 33–35 (background of the Commission).

47 Sumner to Forbes, Dec. 28, 1862, in Palmer, *Selected Letters of Charles Sumner*, 2:135–36; Lincoln proclamation, Jan. 1, 1863, in Basler, *The Collected Works of Abraham Lincoln*, 6:30; Lincoln to Johnson, Mar. 26, 1863, ibid., 6:149–50; Lincoln to Conkling, Aug. 26, 1863, ibid., 6:410.

48 Stanton to Andrew, Jan. 20, 1863, *OR*, ser. 3, 3:20–21; Stanton to Thomas, Mar. 25, 1863, ibid., 100–101; General Orders No. 143, May 22, 1863, ibid., 215–16 (establishing Bureau); Berlin, *Freedom*, 76; Shannon, *The Organization and Administration of the Union Army*, 2:145 ("slow, uncertain"). In addition to Thomas, Stanton relied on Daniel Ullman, a New York political general, to recruit black regiments. See Stanton to Ullman, Jan. 13, 1863, *OR*, ser. 3, 3:14; Stanton to Ullman, Mar. 13 and 19, 1863, M473; Stanton to Taylor, Mar. 24, 1863, Edwin Stanton Papers, LC, box 39, image 40 ("to raise 4,500 colored troops"); Stanton to Ullman, Mar. 25, 1863, *OR*, ser. 3, 3:101–102; Lincoln to Banks, Mar. 29, 1863, in Basler, *The Collected Works of Abraham Lincoln*, 6:154; Stanton to Ullman, Apr. 1, 1863, M473 ("the president is impatient"); Ullman to Thomas, May 19, 1863, in Berlin, *Freedom*, 144–46.

49 Stanton to Thomas, Mar. 25, 1863, *OR*, ser. 3, 3:100–101 (initial orders); Halleck to Grant, Mar. 30, 1863, in Simon, *The Papers of Ulysses Grant*, 8:93–94; *Berlin City (Wisc.) Courant*, June 18, 1863, quoting *New York Evening Post* ("nigger on the brain"); Michael Meier, "Lorenzo Thomas and the Recruitment of Blacks in the Mississippi Valley, 1863–1865," in Smith, *Black Soldiers in Blue*, 256–61.

50 Thomas to Stanton, Apr. 4, 1863, *OR*, ser. 3, 3:116; Thomas to Stanton, Oct. 5, 1865, ibid., 5:118 (conditions at Cairo).

51 Thomas to Stanton, Apr. 6, 1863, *OR*, ser. 3, 2:117; Thomas to Stanton, Apr. 9, 1863, ibid., 121; Sherman to John Sherman, Apr. 26, 1863, in Simpson and Berlin, *Sherman's Civil War*, 461; Meier, "Lorenzo Thomas and the Recruitment of Blacks," 247–55.

52   Thomas to Stanton, Apr. 12, 1863, *OR*, ser. 3, 2:121; Thomas to Stanton, May 18, 1863, ibid., 212.

53   Banks to Halleck, May 30, 1863, *OR*, vol. 26, pt. 1, p. 45; *New York Times*, June 11, 1863; Richard Lowe, "An Ironic Route to Glory: Louisiana's Native Guards at Port Hudson," in Smith, *Black Soldiers in Blue*, 107–35; Trudeau, *Like Men of War*, 34–44 (Port Hudson).

54   *Cleveland Daily Leader*, June 13, 1863; Dana to Stanton, June 21 and 22, 1863, *OR*, vol. 24, pt. 1, pp. 105–7; *Harper's Weekly*, July 4, 1863; Richard Lowe, "Battle on the Levee: The Fight at Milliken's Bend," in Smith, *Black Soldiers in Blue*, 107–35.

55   Jefferson Davis proclamation, Dec. 23, 1862, *OR*, 15:906–8; *Journal of the Congress of the Confederate States of America*, 6:487 (May 1, 1863); Trudeau, *Like Men of War*, 59–60 (Milliken's Bend).

56   General Orders No. 100, Apr. 24, 1863, *OR*, ser. 3, 3:155 (arts. 57, 58, and 61); Witt, *Lincoln's Code*, 240–49.

57   General Orders No. 100, Apr. 24, 1863, *OR*, ser. 3, 3:151 (arts. 27 and 28); Witt, *Lincoln's Code*, 231.

58   Stanton to Saxton, Aug. 25, 1862, *OR*, 14:377–78; Militia Act, July 17, 1863, *Statutes at Large*, 12:599 (section 15); Whiting to Stanton, *OR*, ser. 3, Apr. 25, 1863, 5:632–63; Stanton to Tod, June 27, 1863, in Berlin, *Freedom*, 370–71.

59   Berlin, *Freedom*, 12 (table).

60   Stanton to Pamphila Wolcott, Jan 27. 1863, M473 (arrangements for getting Wolcott home to Akron); Stanton to Upson, Apr. 4, 1863, ibid. ("will attend the funeral if the President returns in time"); Stanton to Lincoln, Apr. 7, 1863, Lincoln Papers, LC; Lincoln to Watson, Apr. 7, 1863, in Basler, *The Collected Works of Abraham Lincoln*, 6:165; *Steubenville (Ohio) Daily Herald*, Apr. 7, 1863; Watson to Lincoln, Apr. 9, 1863, Lincoln Papers, LC; Stanton to Lucy Stanton, Apr. 12, 1863, M473; *New York Times*, Apr. 14, 1863 (Stanton's special train); Goodwin, *Team of Rivals*, 513–17 (Lincoln's visit with Hooker); Wolcott, *Edwin M. Stanton*, 187–90 (illness and death of Wolcott).

61   Stanton to Dana, May 5, 1863, *OR*, vol. 24, pt. 1, p. 84 (his hand in M473); Dana, *Recollections of the Civil War*, 30; Mahaifer, "Mr. Grant and Mr. Dana"; White, *American Ulysses*, 259 (Grant, "sensing his visitor's mission from the start, welcomed him").

62   Brooks report, Apr. 12 , 1863, in Burlingame, *Lincoln Observed*, 37 (Aquia Creek); Bellows to Eliza Bellows, Apr. 19, 1863, Bellows Papers ("spoke slightingly"); Sedgwick to sister, Apr. 20, 1863, in Stoeckel, *Correspondence of John Sedgwick*, 2:90–91; Nicolay to Hay, Apr. 20, 1863, in Burlingame, *With Lincoln in the White House*, 109 ("President and the Secretary of War went off on a reconnaissance . . . returned in the evening"); *Sacramento*

Daily Union, May 18, 1863 (Lincoln left "before daylight" returned same night).

63 Bellows to Eliza Bellows, Apr. 23, 1863, Bellows Papers; Nevins and Thomas, *Diary of George Templeton Strong*, 3:314 (Apr. 25, 1863).

64 Brooks report, May 2, 1863, in Burlingame, *Lincoln Observed*, 46–47.

65 Fanny Seward Diary, Apr. 5, 1862, Seward Papers, reel 198; Stanton to Harriet Beecher Stowe, Mar. 19, 1863, Edwin Stanton Papers, LC, box 39, image 18; Stanton to Isabella Beecher Hooker, May 6, 1863, in Wolcott, *Edwin M. Stanton*, 192; Dana, *Recollections of the Civil War*, 158–59; Hedrick, *Harriet Beecher Stowe*, 307 (Stanton helped secure leave for Stowe's son Frederick).

66 Dana, *Recollections of the Civil War*, 158–59.

67 Gienapp and Gienapp, *Civil War Diary of Gideon Welles*, 178, 180 (May 4 & 6, 1863); Butterfield to Lincoln, May 6, 1863, *OR*, vol. 25, pt. 2, p. 434; Stanton to Hooker, May 6, 1863, ibid., 435 (Lincoln and Halleck on way to see Hooker); Burlingame, *Lincoln Observed*, 241–42 ("my God"); Burlingame, *Lincoln's White House Secretary*, 306 ("darkest day").

68 Stanton to Hooker, May 7, 1863, *OR*, vol. 25, pt. 2, p. 439; Stanton to governors, May 7, 1863, ibid., 437–38; *New York Herald*, May 9, 1863; Brooks report, May 30, 1863, in *Sacramento Daily Union*, June 12, 1863; Engle, *Gathering to Save a Nation*, 295 ("Stanton's masterful spin" in the message to the governors).

69 Hooker to Lincoln, June 10, 1863, *OR*, vol. 27, pt. 1, pp. 34–35; Lincoln to Hooker, June 10, 1863, in Basler, *The Collected Works of Abraham Lincoln*, 6:257; Stanton to Whipple, June 10, 1863, M473 (Couch on his way to Harrisburg); Stanton to Thomas Scott, June 10, 1863, ibid.; Couch report, July 15, 1863, *OR*, vol. 27, pt. 2, pp. 211–12 (left Washington on June 11 to take charge of Department of the Susquehanna); Guelzo, *Gettysburg*, 32–34; Sears, *Gettysburg*, 1–17.

70 Scott to Curtin, June 15, 1863, M473 ("on arrival here at 1 am"); Stanton to Tod, June 15, 1863, ibid. (sent 2 a.m.); Lincoln proclamation, June 15, 1863, in Basler, *The Collected Works of Abraham Lincoln*, 6:277–28; Cameron to Lincoln, June 15, 1863, *OR*, vol. 27, pt. 3, p. 141; Stanton to Cameron, June 15, 1863, ibid., 141–42; Stanton to Seymour and vice versa, June 15, 1863, ibid., 138–40 (multiple messages); Stanton to Seymour, June 21, 1863, in *Daily Ohio Statesman*, Oct. 29, 1868 ("cannot forbear"); Couch to Stanton, June 22, 1863, *OR*, vol. 27, pt. 3, p. 264; Couch to Stanton, June 29, 1863, ibid., 407. On the militia, see Sears, *Gettysburg*, 90–92.

71 Stanton to Halleck in Baltimore, June 23, 1863, M473 ("Hooker is here. When will you return?"); Hooker to Halleck, June 27, 1863, *OR*, vol. 27, pt. 1, p. 60 ("request that I may be at once relieved"); Halleck to Hooker, June

27, 1863, ibid. ("dispatch has been duly referred for Executive action"); John Ropes memo, Feb. 8, 1870, Woodman Papers; Guelzo, *Gettysburg*, 84–85; Sears, *Gettysburg*, 86–89, 119–21.

72 Halleck to Meade, June 27, 1863, *OR*, vol. 27, pt. 1, p. 61; James Hardie note, June 28, 1863, Hardie Papers (time and date of delivery by Hardie to Meade); Gienapp and Gienapp, *Civil War Diary of Gideon Welles*, 228–29 (June 28, 1863); Browne, *The Every-Day Life of Lincoln*, 596 ("like lead"); Rice, *Reminiscences of Abraham Lincoln*, 128 ("canvassed the merits").

73 Dana to Stanton, June 14, 1863, *OR*, vol. 24, pt. 1, pp. 98–99; Dana to Stanton, June 29, 1863, ibid., 112 (sent June 29 received July 3); Foote, *Civil War*, 2:405–27 (siege of Vicksburg).

74 Halleck to Rosecrans, June 16, 1863, *OR*, vol. 23, pt. 1, p. 10; Rosecrans to Halleck, June 16, 1863, ibid.; Rosecrans to Halleck, June 24, 1863, ibid.; Foote, *Civil War*, 2:663–64 (Rosecrans "would not budge").

75 Stanton to Lincoln, June 30, 1863, Edwin Stanton Papers, LC, box 40, image 34; Gienapp and Gienapp, *Civil War Diary of Gideon Welles*, 231 (June 30, 1863); Bates, *Lincoln in the Telegraph Office*, 7.

76 Lincoln endorsement, Mar. 7, 1863, Lincoln Papers, LC ("submitted to Mars & Neptune"); Lincoln to Couch and Couch to Lincoln, June 24, 1863, in Basler, *The Collected Works of Abraham Lincoln*, 6:293; Cameron to Lincoln, June 27, 1863, *OR*, vol. 27, pt. 3, p. 364; Lincoln endorsement, June 27, 1863, in Basler, *The Collected Works of Abraham Lincoln*, 6:298; Stanton to Cameron, June 27, 1863, *OR*, vol. 27, pt. 3, p. 365. The March 7 letter is the one solid case I could find of Lincoln referring to Stanton as Mars. See also Bates, *Lincoln in the Telegraph Office*, 400 ("sometimes he addressed Stanton as 'Mars'"); Flower, *Edwin McMasters Stanton*, 145 (Lincoln sometimes visited "Old Mars"); Gurowski, *Diary from Nov. 18, 1862*, 197 ("Mars Stanton, Neptune Welles, are good and reliable"); Charles Tinker, "A Telegrapher's Reminiscence," in Ward, *Abraham Lincoln*, 164 (Lincoln "often called Mr. Stanton 'Mars' and appeared to enjoy his discomfort at the fitting title").

77 Benjamin, "Recollections of Secretary Edwin M. Stanton," 768; A. E. H. Johnson interview, *Chicago Tribune*, July 16, 1891; Thomas and Hyman, *Stanton*, 381–91.

78 Couch to Halleck, June 30, 1863, *OR*, vol. 27, pt. 3, p. 434; Stanton to Meade, June 30, 1863, ibid., pt. 1, p. 69 (relays report from Haupt); Haupt to Stanton, July 2, 1863, ibid., pt. 3, p. 494; Turner, *Victory Rode the Rails*, 275–81 (Haupt's role).

79 Meade to Halleck, July 2, 1863, *OR*, vol. 27, pt. 1, p. 72; Meade to Halleck, July 3, 1863, ibid., 74–75 (three messages); Stanton to Burnside, July 4, 1863, Schoff Collection ("prospect of complete victory"); Lincoln to press,

July 4, 1863, in Basler, *The Collected Works of Abraham Lincoln*, 6:314; Stanton to Dix, July 4, 1863, *OR*, vol. 27, pt. 3, p. 529.

80 *National Republican*, July 8, 1863. Slightly different versions of Stanton's speech appeared in the *New York Herald*, July 8, 1863; *New York Times*, July 8, 1863; *New York Tribune*, July 8, 1863.

Chapter 11: "Too Serious for Jokes"

1 Halleck to Kelley, July 4, 1863, *OR*, vol. 27, pt. 3, p. 528; Kelley to Townsend, July 5, 1863, ibid., 549–50; Stanton to Kelley, July 5, 1863, ibid., 550 ("minutes are precious"); Lincoln to French, July 5, 1863, in Basler, *The Collected Works of Abraham Lincoln*, 6:317 ("cannot the enemy ford the river?"); French to Halleck, July 6, 1863, *OR*, vol. 27, pt. 3, p. 564; Lincoln to Halleck, July 6, 1863, in Basler, *The Collected Works of Abraham Lincoln*, 6:318.

2 Halleck to Meade, July 7, 1863, *OR*, vol. 27, pt. 1, p. 83; Meade to Halleck, July 8, 1863, ibid., pt. 3, pp. 605–6; Meade to Halleck, July 10, 1863, ibid., pt. 1, p. 89; Meade to Halleck, July 12, 1863, ibid., 91; Halleck to Meade, July 13, 1863, ibid., 92 (sent 9:30 p.m.); Sears, *Gettysburg*, 473–92.

3 Sanford to Stanton, July 13, 1863, *OR*, vol. 27, pt. 2, pp. 886–87 (three messages); Stanton to Sanford, July 14, 1863, ibid., 887; Schecter, *The Devil's Own Work*, 125–70.

4 Meade to Halleck, July 14, 1863, *OR*, vol. 27, pt. 1, p. 92; Burlingame and Ettlinger, *Inside Lincoln's White House*, 62–63 (July 14, 1863); Gienapp and Gienapp, *Civil War Diary of Gideon Welles*, 246–48 (July 14, 1863); Stanton to McClure, July 22, 1863, Edwin Stanton Papers, LC, box 40, image 47. Debate about what Meade could and should have done continues: Guelzo, *Gettysburg*, 432–40; Sears, *Gettysburg*, 475–90; Wittenberg, *One Continuous Fight*.

5 Stanton to Opdyke, July 14, 1863, *OR*, vol. 27, pt. 2, p. 916; Opdyke to Stanton, July 14, 1863, ibid.; Sanford to Stanton, July 14, 1863, ibid., 887–89; Stanton to Sanford, July 14, 1863, ibid., 889 (his hand M473); Stanton to Schenck, July 14, 1863, M473; Jay to Stanton, July 14, 1863, Edwin Stanton Papers, LC, box 13, image 169; Stanton to Field, July 14, 1863, in Gorham, *The Life and Public Services*, 2:108; Halleck to Dix, July 15, 1863, *OR*, vol. 27, pt. 2, pp. 919–20.

6 Seymour speech, July 4, 1863, in Cook and Knox, *Public Record*, 120; Seymour speech, July 14, 1863, ibid., 127; *National Republican*, July 15, 1863; Gurowski, *Diary from Nov. 18, 1862*, 361; Schecter, *Devil's Own Work*, 113–24, 185–87.

7 Stanton to Lewis, July 17, 1863, Edwin Stanton Papers, LC, box 40, image 42; Stanton to Brady, July 23, 1863, in Gorham, *The Life and Public Services*, 2:109–12; Seymour to Lincoln, Aug. 3, 1863, *OR*, ser. 3, 3:612–19; Lincoln

to Seymour, Aug. 4, 1863, in Basler, *The Collected Works of Abraham Lincoln*, 6:369–70; Gienapp and Gienapp, *Civil War Diary of Gideon Welles*, 267 (Aug. 4, 1863) (Lincoln's answer "vigorous and decisive"). The leading scholar notes that the official total of 105 dead "is almost certainly low" and that the actual number "probably lies somewhere between the documented figure and the sober contemporary estimate of 500." Schecter, *Devil's Own Work*, 152.

8 Stanton to Dix, Aug. 15, 1863, in Gorham, *The Life and Public Services*, 2:111–12 (originals in Dix Papers); *New York Times*, Aug. 22, 1863.

9 Preliminary report, Freedmen's Commission, June 30, 1863, *OR*, ser. 3, 3:430–54; *Pittsburgh Gazette*, Aug. 10, 1863; *Liberator* (Boston), Aug. 14, 1863; Owen to Butler, Dec. 10, 1863, in Marshall, *Private and Official Correspondence of Benjamin Butler*, 3:196–97 (Stanton has not "authorized us to carry it out").

10 Lincoln to Stanton, July 21, 1863, in Basler, *The Collected Works of Abraham Lincoln*, 6:342 (send Thomas back to Mississippi); *Cleveland Daily Leader*, Aug. 4, 1863 (Thomas heading back to West); Stanton to Seward, Aug. 5, 1863, Edwin Stanton Papers, LC, box 40, images 68–69 (progress report); Stanton to Garfield, Aug. 26, 1863, ibid., image 98 (introduces Stearns as "the General Recruiting Commissioner of this Department for organizing colored troops"); Stanton to Rosecrans, Aug. 26, 1863, Rosecrans Papers ("desire of the President that every commander should aid to the utmost in this work"); Stanton to Lawrence, Aug. 31, 1863, Edwin Stanton Papers, LC, box 40, images 111–12 ("never supposed"); Stanton to Forbes, Aug. 31, 1863, ibid., image 113 ("along the line"); Johnson to Stanton, Sept. 17, 1863, in Graf, *The Papers of Andrew Johnson*, 6:376; Stanton to Stearns, Sept. 19, 1863, M473 ("all dissension"); Stearns to Stanton, Sept. 19, 1863, in Berlin, *Freedom*, 173–74; Stearns to Stanton, Oct. 24, 1863, in ibid., 177–80.

11 Lincoln proclamation, July 30, 1863, in Basler, *The Collected Works of Abraham Lincoln*, 6:357; Douglass to Stearns, Aug. 1, 1863, in Simpson, *The Civil War*, 428–29; *New York Times*, Aug. 3, 1863 (prints proclamation); Kendrick and Kendrick, *Douglass and Lincoln*, 150–55.

12 Douglass to Stearns, Aug. 12, 1863, in Simpson, *The Civil War*, 457–59; *Cleveland Daily Leader*, Aug. 15, 1863 (reporting Douglass met Stanton and would join Thomas).

13 Foster to Douglass, Aug. 13, 1863, Douglass Papers; Douglass to Webster, Aug. 19, 1863, in Foner, *The Life and Writings of Frederick Douglass*, 3:377; Foster to Douglass, Aug. 21, 1863, Douglass Papers (summarizes Douglass to Stanton); Gates, *Frederick Douglass*, 788 ("have no doubt"); Stauffer, *Giants*, 21–23.

14 Stanton Report, Dec. 5, 1863, *OR*, ser. 3, 3:1132.

15 Ibid., 3:1132–33.

16 *Cleveland Daily Leader*, Jan. 28, 1862 (Stanton appoints Hamilton Fish and Bishop Ames to go to Richmond); *New York Times*, Feb. 3, 1862 (demands general prisoner exchange); Stanton and Wolcott to Dix, July 14, 1862, *OR*, ser. 2, 4:209 (instructions); Dix-Hill Cartel, July 22, 1862, ibid., 266–67; Hesseltine, *Civil War Prisons*, 1–31.

17 *Detroit Free Press*, Nov. 20, 1863; Hesseltine, *Civil War Prisons*, 69–113; Witt, *Lincoln's Code*, 258 ("Lincoln, Stanton, Halleck and Hitchcock decided the Union would not take part in any system of exchange so long as the South persisted in its treatment of black soldiers as criminals").

18 Stanton to Hitchcock, Nov. 25, 1863, Edwin Stanton Papers, LC, box 19, image 165 ("I had better see it before publication that it may conform with my report"); Hitchcock to *New York Times*, Nov. 28, 1863, *OR*, ser. 2, 6:594–600; *New York Times*, Dec. 2, 1863; Witt, *Lincoln's Code*, 258–60.

19 Stanton report, Dec. 5, 1863, *OR*, ser. 3, 3:1129–31; Stanton to Butler, Dec. 21, 1863, Edwin Stanton Papers, LC, box 41, image 80 (asks him to make immediate personal inspection of Point Lookout); Butler to Stanton, Dec. 27, 1863, *OR*, ser. 2, 6:763–64 (reports prisoners "well fed, perfectly well covered as far as tents"); *Pittsburgh Commercial*, Dec. 29, 1863 (Lincoln and Stanton returned from Point Lookout; "not less than a thousand" would enlist).

20 Stanton to Ellen Stanton, Aug. 25, 1863, in G. T. Stanton, *Edwin M. Stanton*, 52–53; Stanton to Garrett, Sept. 4, 1863, M473 (approves rail arrangements); Stanton to Scott, Sept. 4, 1863, ibid. ("greatly obliged"); Watson to Stanton, Sept. 5, 1863, ibid. ("no news"); Lincoln to Stanton, Sept. 6, 1863, in Basler, *The Collected Works of Abraham Lincoln*, 6:436 (Stanton at Bedford); Stanton to Nelson, Sept. 8, 1863, M473 (returned to Washington); *Bedford (Pa.) Gazette*, Sept. 11, 1863.

21 Lincoln to Halleck, July 29, 1863, in Basler, *The Collected Works of Abraham Lincoln*, 6:354; Gienapp and Gienapp, *Civil War Diary of Gideon Welles*, 295 (Sept. 21, 1863); Stanton to Meigs, Oct. 4, 1863, *OR*, vol. 30, pt. 4, p. 78 ("All quiet on the Potomac. Nothing to disturb autumnal slumbers."); Wert, *Sword of Lincoln*, 310–15.

22 Stanton to Rosecrans, July 7, 1863, *OR*, vol. 23, pt. 2, p. 518; Rosecrans to Stanton, July 7, 1863, ibid.; Halleck to Rosecrans, July 24, 1863, ibid., 552; Halleck to Rosecrans, Aug. 9, 1863, ibid., 601–2; Chase to Garfield, Aug. 17, 1863, in Niven, *Chase Papers*, 4:103; Foote, *Civil War*, 2:675–77.

23 Stanton to Rosecrans, Aug. 30, 1863, *OR*, vol. 30, pt. 3, p. 229; Stanton to Dana, Aug. 30, 1863, Edwin Stanton Papers, LC, box 40, image 109; Rosecrans to Halleck, Sept. 9, 1863, *OR*, vol. 30, pt. 3, p. 479 ("Chattanooga is ours without a struggle"); Dana to Stanton, Sept. 12, 1863, ibid., pt. 1, p. 185 ("arriving here yesterday").

24 *Janesville (Wisc.) Gazette*, Sept. 14, 1863 (Longstreet moving to West); *Brooklyn Daily Eagle*, Sept. 19, 1863 (Longstreet or Hill or both with Bragg); Dana to Stanton, Sept. 20, 1863, *OR*, vol. 30, pt. 1, pp. 192–93 ("deplorable importance"); Clark, *Railroads in the Civil War*, 88–118 (Southern rail movement); Cozzens, *This Terrible Sound*; McPherson, *Battle Cry of Freedom*, 670–75; Pickenpaugh, *Rescue by Rail*.

25 Halleck to Hurlbut, Sept. 15, 1863, *OR*, vol. 30, pt. 1, p. 161; Lincoln to Burnside, Sept. 21, 1863, in Basler, *The Collected Works of Abraham Lincoln*, 6:469–70 (two messages); Grant to Halleck, Sept. 22, 1863, *OR*, vol. 30, pt. 1, p. 162 (received Sept. 29); Rosecrans to Lincoln, Sept. 22, 1863, ibid., 161; Marvel, *Burnside*, 286.

26 Dana to Stanton, Sept. 23, 1863, *OR*, vol. 30, pt. 1, p. 197 (received 9:45 p.m.); Garfield to Chase, Sept. 23, 1863, ibid., pt. 3, p. 792 (received 10 p.m.); Rosecrans to Lincoln, Sept. 23, 1863, ibid., pt. 1, p. 168 (received 10:40 p.m.). Chase noted in his diary that Stanton handed him Garfield's message when he arrived at the War Department about midnight. Niven, *Chase Papers*, 1:453 (Sept. 23, 1863).

27 Burlingame and Ettlinger, *Inside Lincoln's White House*, 85–86 (Sept. 23, 1863); Niven, *Chase Papers*, 1:450 (Sept. 23, 1863); Stanton to Seward, Sept. 23, 1863, Seward Papers, reel 80; Stanton to Garrett, Felton, and Scott, Sept. 23, 1863, *OR*, vol. 29, pt. 1, pp. 146–47.

28 Burlingame and Ettlinger, *Inside Lincoln's White House*, 85–86 (Sept. 23, 1863); Niven, *Chase Papers*, 1:450–53 (Sept. 23, 1863) (two entries).

29 Niven, *Chase Papers*, 1:450–53 (Sept. 23, 1863). Years later one of McCallum's aides related that Lincoln asked McCallum to estimate how long the process would take and that McCallum swore the transfer could be done in seven days. Flower, *Edwin McMasters Stanton*, 204. There is no trace of this in Chase's diary or other sources, however, and "if McCallum actually made such a dramatic statement, someone would have remembered it." Clark, *Railroads in the Civil War*, 148.

30 Niven, *Chase Papers*, 1:452 (Sept. 23, 1863); Garrett to Stanton, Sept. 24, 1863, Edwin Stanton Papers, LC, box 15, image 109; Stanton to Garrett, Sept. 24, 1863, M473; Halleck to Meade, Sept. 24, 1863, *OR*, vol. 29, pt. 1, p. 147 (2:30 a.m.); Meade to Halleck, Sept. 24, 1863, ibid.; Stanton to Dana, Sept. 24, 1863, ibid., 155 (3:30 a.m.).

31 Stanton to Scott, Jan. 29, 1862, in Sipes, *Pennsylvania Railroad*, 15–16 ("Kentucky and Tennessee"); Garrett to Stanton, Sept. 24, 1863, Edwin Stanton Papers, LC, box 15, image 123 ("full information"). Clark, *Railroads in the Civil War* is especially good on the organizational challenges.

32 Garrett to Stanton, Sept. 24, 1863, Edwin Stanton Papers, LC, box 15, image 123 (arriving about 10 a.m.); Scott to Stanton, Sept. 24, 1863, ibid., image

124 (arriving about noon); Stanton to Bowler, Sept. 24, 1863, *OR*, vol. 29, pt. 1, p. 153 (11:20 a.m.); Bowler to Stanton, Sept. 24, 1863, ibid. (received 2:40 p.m.); Hecker to War Department, Sept. 24, 1863, in Clark, *Railroads in the Civil War*, 153.

33 Garrett to Jewett, Sept. 24, 1863, Edwin Stanton Papers, LC, box 15, images 139–40; similar messages to other railroads in same box; Pickenpaugh, *Rescue by Rail*, 84, 101, 121 (maps).

34 Stanton to Boyle, Sept. 24, 1863, *OR*, vol. 29, pt. 1, p. 149; McCallum to Stanton, Sept. 24, 1863, ibid., 154; Stanton to McCallum, Sept. 24, 1863, M473 (cautions not to disclose destination); Meade to Halleck, Sept. 24, 1863, Edwin Stanton Papers, LC, box 15, image 102; Stanton to Meade, Sept. 24, 1863, ibid., image 103 ("General Halleck having gone home I answer your telegram").

35 Garrett to Hooker, Sept. 25, 1863, *OR*, vol. 29, pt. 1, p. 158; Stanton to McCallum, Sept. 25, 1863, M473 (his hand); Clark, *Railroads in the Civil War*, 151–61; Pickenpaugh, *Rescue by Rail*, 82–83 ("track that had been put down only a few months earlier through the streets").

36 Smith to Stanton, Sept. 26, 1863, *OR*, vol. 29, pt. 1, p. 161; Halleck to Meade, Sept. 26, 1863, Edwin Stanton Papers, LC, box 16, image 4; Stanton to Buford, Sept. 26, 1863, ibid., image 1 (send railroad cars "with utmost speed and report"); Clark, *Railroads in the Civil War*, 171 (movement "hit full stride Saturday September 26").

37 Stanton to McCallum, Sept. 27, 1863, Edwin Stanton Papers, LC, box 16, image 76 ("nothing from you later than ten o'clock last night"); McCallum to Stanton, ibid., image 77 (first division loaded); Smith to Stanton, Sept. 27, 1863, *OR*, vol. 29, pt. 1, p. 167 ("scows and barges"); Stanton to Koontz, Edwin Stanton Papers, LC, box 16, image 50 ("please report to me the arrival of each train from the front"); Stanton to Scott, ibid., image 75 ("whole force").

38 Smith to Stanton and vice versa, Sept. 27, 1863, *OR*, vol. 29, pt. 1, pp. 167–69 (multiple messages); Stanton to Schurz, Sept. 27, 1863, ibid., 169 (draft in M473 in Stanton's hand); Schurz to Stanton, Sept. 28, 1863, ibid., 172 (from Benwood); Stanton to Schurz, Sept. 28, 1863, ibid.; Trefousse, *Carl Schurz*.

39 *New York Evening Post*, Sept. 26, 1863; *Boston Daily Advertiser*, Sept. 28, 1863; *Reading (Pa.) Daily Times*, Sept. 28, 1863; Brooks report, Oct. 2, 1863, in Burlingame, *Lincoln Observed*, 64–66.

40 Koontz to Stanton, Sept. 27, 1863, Edwin Stanton Papers, LC, box 16, image 53 (10:20 p.m.); Koontz to Stanton, Sept. 28, 1863, ibid., image 86 (1:45 a.m.); McCallum to Stanton, Sept. 28, 1863, ibid., image 94 ("all troops gone"); Stanton to Smith, Sept. 28, 1863, ibid., image 105 ("I have no report west of the Ohio"); Smith to Stanton, Sept. 28, 1863, *OR*, vol. 29, pt. 1, pp.

172–73 (three messages including report from Jewett); Stanton to Smith, Sept. 28, 1863, ibid., 173 (go to Indianapolis); Smith to Stanton, Sept. 28, 1863, ibid., 174 (cannot go); Scott to Stanton, Sept. 28, 1863, ibid., 174 (change gauge?); Stanton to Scott, Sept. 28, 1863, ibid. ("whatever work in your judgment").

41 Niven, *Chase Papers*, 1:456–57 (Sept. 28, 1863).

42 Scott to Stanton, Sept. 29, 1863, Edwin Stanton Papers, LC, box 16, image 131 (first train arrived at Louisville); Stanton to Scott, Sept. 29, 1863, ibid., image 132 ("thousand thanks"); Smith to Stanton, Sept. 29, 1863, *OR*, vol. 29, pt. 1, p. 178 ("upon a track three times redeemed"); Scott to Stanton, Sept. 29, 1863, Edwin Stanton Papers, LC, box 16, image 133 (first train should reach Bridgeport by 6 a.m.); Scott to Stanton, Sept. 30, 1863, *OR*, vol. 29, pt. 1, p. 180 (first trains reached Bridgeport); Pickenpaugh, *Rescue by Rail*, 130–40.

43 Hooker to Stanton, Oct. 11, 1863, *OR*, vol. 29, pt. 4, p. 291; McPherson, *Battle Cry of Freedom*, 675; Nevins, *War for the Union*, 3:202.

44 Stanton to Dana, Sept. 30, 1863, *OR*, vol. 30, pt. 3, p. 946; Burlingame and Ettlinger, *Inside Lincoln's White House*, 98–99 (Oct. 24, 1863) ("stunned duck"); Sword, *Mountains Touched with Fire*, 36–50.

45 Dana to Stanton, Oct. 3, 1863, *OR*, vol. 30, pt. 1, pp. 205–6; Meigs to Stanton, Oct. 5, 1863, ibid., pt. 4, pp. 101–2; Meigs to Scott, Oct. 10, 1863, ibid., 245; Dana to Stanton, Oct. 16, 1863, ibid., pt. 1, pp. 218–19; Halleck to Grant, Oct. 16, 1863, ibid., pt. 4, p. 404; Stanton to Scott, Oct. 16, 1863, M473 ("Mr. Stager leaves here tomorrow morning for Louisville expecting to reach there with instructions for you by Sunday night or Monday morning. Please meet him at the Galt House."); Stanton to Meigs, Oct. 16, 1863, M473 (similar). For some reason, in sending a message to Dana, Stanton revealed that he was the messenger. Stanton to Dana, Oct. 17, 1863, M473 ("meet me at Galt House").

46 *Cleveland Daily Leader*, Oct. 21, 1863 (Stanton arrived Sunday evening); *New York Herald*, Oct. 23, 1863 (Stanton arrived Sunday afternoon); Grant, *Personal Memoirs*, 2:17–18. The *Herald*'s story seems more reliable, based on sources in Grant's staff.

47 Wilson, *The Life of Charles A. Dana*, 276 ("somewhat impulsively"); Grant, *Personal Memoirs*, 2:118 ("I had never met Mr. Stanton up to that time, though we had held frequent conversations over the wires the year before"); Dana, *Recollections of the Civil War*, 129–31; Badeau, *Military History*, 1:422. See Simpson, *Ulysses S. Grant*, 226–27 ("the man he greeted so vigorously was not Grant but his medical director, Dr. Edward Kittoe"); White, *American Ulysses*, 295 (Stanton "shook hands with Grant's personal physician, Dr. Edward Kittoe of Galena, saying he recognized him as General Grant from his pictures").

48 Halleck to Grant, Oct. 16, 1863, in Simon, *The Papers of Ulysses Grant*, 9:297; Stanton to Halleck, Oct. 19, 1863, ibid., 298; Grant, *Personal Memoirs*, 2:26.

49 *New York Herald*, Oct. 23, 1863; Grant, *Personal Memoirs*, 2:17–18; Simon, *The Personal Memoirs of Julia Dent Grant*, 123.

50 Grant General Orders No. 1, Oct. 18, 1863, in Simon, *The Papers of Ulysses Grant*, 9:296–97; Rosecrans to Grant, Oct. 19, 1863, *OR*, vol. 30, pt. 4, p. 478 (received orders; will execute); Grant to Thomas, Oct. 19, 1863, ibid., 479; Grant, *Personal Memoirs*, 2:26.

51 There is a report that Stanton visited Nashville and stayed there with Judge Catron (*Hartford [Ct.] Courant*, Oct. 22, 1863), but it seems to be in error. I do not see any mention of Stanton's visit in Nashville papers. And George Stearns, in charge of recruiting blacks in Tennessee, reported to Stanton from Nashville a few days later in a way he would not have if he had just seen Stanton. Stearns to Stanton, Oct. 24, 1863, in Berlin, *Freedom*, 177–80.

52 *Daily Ohio Statesman*, Aug. 8, 1863 (letter from Vallandigham); Nevins, *War for the Union*, 3:155; Shankman, "Soldier Votes," 97–104; Weber, *Copperheads*, 118–24.

53 Stanton to Fessenden, Aug. 3, 1863, Fessenden Papers; Stanton to Hamlin, Aug. 20, 1863, Edwin Stanton Papers, LC, box 40, images 88-89 (leave granted to Howard); *National Republican*, Aug. 25, 1863 (General Howard in Maine); Stanton to Blaine, Sept. 9, 1863, M473 ("furloughs you ask will be ordered"); Stanton to Blaine, Sept. 14, 1863, ibid. ("nine cheers for Maine!"); *Brooklyn Daily Eagle*, Sept. 15, 1863 (criticizes Republicans for calling themselves Union Party); *New York Times*, Sept. 16, 1863 ("gallant soldiers").

54 Stanton to Dennison, Oct. 7, 1863, M473 ("if there be"); Stanton to Mason, Oct. 7, 1863, ibid. ("giving them transportation"); Stanton to Cox, Oct. 7, 1863, ibid. ("you may also adopt"); Shankman, "Soldier Votes"; Weber, *Copperheads*, 118–20.

55 Clark, *Railroads in the Civil War*, 178–81; Pickenpaugh, *Rescue by Rail*, 104.

56 Stanton to John McCook, Oct. 13, 1863, M473; Stanton to Brough, Oct. 13, 1863, ibid.; Stanton to Forney, Oct. 14, 1863, ibid. (1:00 a.m.); Shankman, "Soldier Votes," 103–4 (table showing votes).

57 Randall, *Diary of Orville Hickman Browning*, 1:605 (Dec. 24, 1862) (Blair called Stanton and Halleck "heartless scoundrels"); Beale, *The Diary of Edward Bates*, 490–91 (May 10, 1863) (Blair called Stanton an "unprincipled liar"); Gienapp and Gienapp, *Civil War Diary of Gideon Welles*, 269 (Stanton complained that Blair fomented press attacks against him); Blair, *Speech*, 4 ("make manumission"); Burlingame and Ettlinger, *Inside Lincoln's White House*, 97 (Oct. 22, 1863) (Lincoln on Blair and Davis); Harris, *Lincoln and the Border States*, 268–80.

58 Prince George's County (Md.) Petition, [Oct. 21,] 1863, Lincoln Papers, LC; Lincoln to Schenck, Oct. 21, 1863, in Basler, *The Collected Works of*

Abraham Lincoln, 6:530; Schenck to Lincoln, Oct. 21, 1863, Lincoln Papers, LC; Burlingame and Ettlinger, *Inside Lincoln's White House*, 97 and notes (Oct. 22, 1863).

59 Schenck General Order No. 53, Oct. 27, 1863, *OR*, vol. 29, pt. 2, pp. 394–95; Bradford to Lincoln, Oct. 31, 1863, *OR*, ser. 3, 3:967–68; Stanton to Schenck, Nov. 1, 1863, ibid., 968; Schenck to Stanton, Nov. 1, 1863, ibid.

60 Lincoln to Bradford, Nov. 2, 1863, in Basler, *The Collected Works of Abraham Lincoln*, 6:556–57; Garfield to Rosecrans, Nov. 2, 1863, Rosecrans Papers (emancipation supporters "are about certain of success"); Davis to Du Pont, Nov. 4, 1863, Du Pont Papers; Marvel, *Lincoln's Autocrat*, 337.

61 Burlingame and Ettlinger, *Inside Lincoln's White House*, 108–9 (Nov. 3–5, 1863); Stanton to Sanford, Nov. 4, 1863, M473 (thanks for sending election returns); *New York Times*, Nov. 6, 1863; *Detroit Free Press*, Nov. 10, 1863; Harris, *Lincoln and the Border States*, 277–83.

62 Stanton to Chase, Mar. 7, 1863, in Goodwin, *Team of Rivals*, 563; Burlingame and Ettlinger, *Inside Lincoln's White House*, 88 (Sept. 28, 1863); Chase to Stanton, Nov. 12, 1863, Chase Papers, UPA, reel 29 (blockade dispute); Stanton to Chase, Dec. 30, 1863, ibid., reel 30; Baptism record, Jan. 21, 1864, Epiphany Church, Washington (Bessie); see Marvel, *Lincoln's Autocrat*, 312–13.

63 Lincoln proclamation, Oct. 3, 1863, in Basler, *The Collected Works of Abraham Lincoln*, 6:496; Lincoln to Watson, Nov. 25, 1863, ibid., 7:30; Watson to Stanton, Nov. 25, 1863, M473; Watson to Stanton, Nov. 27, 1863, ibid.; Wolcott, *Edwin M. Stanton*, 193.

64 Stanton Report, Dec. 5, 1863, *OR*, ser. 3, 3:1128; Lincoln proclamation, Dec. 8, 1863, in Basler, *The Collected Works of Abraham Lincoln*, 7:53–56; *New York Herald*, Dec. 27, 1863; *New York Times*, Dec. 29, 1863 ("this war will be ended"); Harris, *With Charity for All*, 123–47.

Chapter 12: "You Cannot Die Better"

1 Joint Resolution, Dec. 23, 1863, *Statutes at Large*, 13:400; Stanton to Lincoln, Jan. 5, 1864, *OR*, ser. 3, 4:5; Lincoln to Congress, Jan. 5, 1864, in Basler, *The Collected Works of Abraham Lincoln*, 7:106; Chase to Stanton, Jan. 7, 1864, Chase Papers, UPA, reel 30; Stanton to Chase, Jan. 8, 1864, ibid.; *New York Tribune*, Jan. 8, 1864 (senators concerned about "heavy drain upon the Treasury"); Chase to Fessenden, Jan. 11, 1864, Edwin Stanton Papers, LC, box 20, images 117–19; Chase to Stanton, Jan. 11, 1864, in Niven, *Chase Papers*, 4:249–50; Fry to Stanton, Jan. 29, 1864, *OR*, ser. 3, 4:57–58 (increasing call to 500,000); McPherson, *Battle Cry of Freedom*, 719–20.

2 Stanton to Andrew, Dec. 26, 1863, M473; Stanton to Morton, Jan. 11, 1864, *OR*, ser. 3, 4:24; Stanton to Butler, Jan. 18, 1864, in Basler, *The Collected*

Works of Abraham Lincoln, 7:135–36; Stanton to Yates, Jan. 26, 1864, *OR*, ser. 3, 4:54.

3   Thomas to Stanton, Feb. 1, 1864, *OR*, ser. 3, 4:59–60; Bramlette to Lincoln, Feb. 1, 1864, Lincoln Papers, LC; Stanton to Lincoln, Feb. 8, 1864, ibid. ("until lately"); Thomas to Stanton, Feb. 10, 1864, *OR*, ser. 3, 4:91 (from Tennessee); Lincoln to Stanton, Mar. 8, 1864, in Basler, *The Collected Works of Abraham Lincoln*, 7:272; Engle, *Gathering to Save a Nation*, 399–400; Smith, "Recruitment of Negro Soldiers in Kentucky."

4   [Hammond,] *Statement of the Causes*; Nevins and Thomas, *Diary of George Templeton Strong*, 3:385 (Dec. 23, 1863); Blustein, *Preserve Your Love for Science*; Pat Leonard, "William Hammond and the End of the Medical Middle Ages," *New York Times*, Apr. 27, 2012.

5   Circular letter, Jan. 1, 1864, Edwin Stanton Papers, LC, box 20, images 106–7 (with Agassiz and Peirce comments); Hooper to Warren, Jan. 8, 1864, Warren Papers (also on MHS website); *Washington Evening Star*, Jan. 9, 1864 (reports that Agassiz and Peirce repudiate the letter); Warren to Hooper, Jan. 12, 1864, Edwin Stanton Papers, LC, box 20, images 126–27.

6   *New York Tribune*, Jan. 8, 1864 (Seward reception); Nevins and Thomas, *Diary of George Templeton Strong*, 3:394 (Jan. 16, 1864).

7   Order Confirming Dismissal of William Hammond, Aug. 18, 1864, in Basler, *The Collected Works of Abraham Lincoln*, 7:503; Nevins and Thomas, *Diary of George Templeton Strong*, 3:476 (Aug. 23, 1864); *Baltimore Sun*, Aug. 24, 1864 (government will prosecute Hammond for fraud); *Medical and Surgical Reporter*, Sept. 3, 1864 ("inferior quality") (available through Hathi-Trust).

8   *New York Times*, Jan. 5, 1864 (summary of report); *Philadelphia Daily Age*, Jan. 18, 1864 (copy of McClellan's message); *Constitutional Union* (Washington, D.C.), Jan. 22, 1864; *Chicago Tribune*, Feb. 25, 1864 (prints additional messages); Waugh, *Reelecting Lincoln*, 23–31 ("McClellan clearly the front-runner").

9   Blue, *Salmon P. Chase*, 207–23; Flood, *1864*, 33–37.

10   *Sacramento Daily Union*, Feb. 22, 1864 (Brooks); Gallman, *America's Joan of Arc*, 35–38.

11   *National Republican*, Jan. 18, 1864.

12   *Pittsburgh Commercial*, Feb. 22, 1864 (Pomeroy circular); Gienapp and Gienapp, *Civil War Diary of Gideon Welles*, 356, 363–64 (Feb. 3 and 22, 1864); Blue, *Salmon P. Chase*, 221–23.

13   Stanton to Benjamin Loan, Feb. 22, 1864, Edwin Stanton Papers, LC, box 20, images 241–42; Blue, *Salmon P. Chase*, 226.

14   Gienapp and Gienapp, *Civil War Diary of Gideon Welles*, 371 (Mar. 4, 1864); *New York Tribune*, Mar. 11, 1864 (Chase letter dated Mar. 5); Beale, *The*

Diary of Edward Bates, 343, 345 (Mar. 9 and 13, 1864); *New York Herald*, Mar. 12, 1864; Blue, *Salmon P. Chase*, 223–27; Waugh, *Reelecting Lincoln*, 116–20.

15   Grant to Burns, Dec. 17, 1863, in Simon, *The Papers of Ulysses Grant*, 9:541; *New York Herald*, Dec. 22, 1863; Rawlins to Washburne, Jan. 20, 1864, in Simon, *The Papers of Ulysses Grant*, 9:543; Waugh, *Reelecting Lincoln*, 121–25.

16   Lincoln to Hooker, May 8, 1863, in Basler, *The Collected Works of Abraham Lincoln*, 6:202–203; Butler to Wistar, Feb. 4, 1864, in Marshall, *Private and Official Correspondence of Benjamin Butler*, 3:373–74; Butler to Stanton, Feb. 5, 1864, ibid., 380–81; Stanton to Butler, Feb. 8, 1864, ibid., 400; Butler to Stanton, Feb. 8, 1864, *OR*, 33:144. Gurowski described the raid as "concocted between Kilpatrick and Lincoln" (*Diary: 1863–'64–'65*, 132 [Mar. 8, 1864]). Secondary sources for this section include George, "'Black Flag Warfare'"; Long, "Lincoln, Davis, and the Dahlgren Raid"; Sears, "The Dahlgren Papers Revisited"; Steers, "Why Was Lincoln Murdered?"; Wittenberg, *Like a Meteor*.

17   Kilpatrick to Parsons, Feb. 16, 1864, *OR*, 33:172–73; *Richmond (Va.) Examiner*, Mar. 5, 1864 (quoting Dahlgren papers).

18   Stanton to Dahlgren, July 24, 1863, Dahlgren Papers, box 38; Wittenberg, *Like a Meteor*, 43, 128–29, 145–56.

19   Kilpatrick to Parsons, Feb. 16, 1864, *OR*, 33:172–73; *Richmond (Va.) Examiner*, Mar. 5, 1864.

20   *Richmond (Va.) Examiner*, Mar. 5, 1864; *New York Times*, Mar. 15, 1864.

21   Sears, "Dahlgren Papers Revisited"; Steers, "Why Was Lincoln Murdered?"; Tidwell et al., *Come Retribution*.

22   Garfield to Rosecrans, Dec. 9, 1863, Rosecrans Papers (Stanton "disgusted" by inactivity of Army of the Potomac); Gurowski, *Diary: 1863–'64–'65*, 118 (Feb. 27, 1864); William Fessenden to Samuel Fessenden, Mar. 7, 1864, Fessenden Papers; Fessenden to William Fessenden Jr., Mar. 12, 1864, ibid.; Gurowski to Andrew, Mar. 27, 1864, Andrew Papers.

23   Lincoln nomination, Feb. 29, 1864, in Simon, *The Papers of Ulysses Grant*, 10:188; Stanton to Grant, Feb. 29, 1864, ibid.; Nicolay memorandum, Mar. 8, 1864, in Burlingame, *With Lincoln in the White House*, 129–30; Nicolay to Bache, Apr. 19, 1897, ibid., 239–40; Simpson, *Ulysses S. Grant*, 260.

24   Grant speech, Mar. 9, 1864, in Simon, *The Papers of Ulysses Grant*, 10:195; Matthew Brady interviewed by James Kelly, ca. 1884, in Styple, *Generals in Bronze*, 102.

25   Grant to Sherman, Apr. 4, 1864, *OR*, vol. 32, pt. 2, pp. 245–46; McPherson, *Battle Cry of Freedom*, 722.

26   Stanton to Grant, Apr. 7, 1864, in Simon, *The Papers of Ulysses Grant*, 10:555; Badeau to Stanton, Apr. 7, 1864, ibid.; Stanton to Grant, Apr. 21, 1864, ibid., 335; Grant to Stanton, Apr. 21, 1864, ibid.; Stanton to Lincoln, Apr. 22,

1864, in Basler, *The Collected Works of Abraham Lincoln*, 7:312–13; Stanton to Grant, Apr. 26, 1864, Edwin Stanton Papers, LC, box 41, images 128–29; Grant to Stanton, Apr. 27, 1864, in Simon, *The Papers of Ulysses Grant*, 10:358 (Meigs); Stanton to Meigs, Apr. 28, 1864, Edwin Stanton Papers, LC, box 41, image 131.

27 Stanton to Grant, Apr. 15, 1864, *OR*, vol. 32, pt. 3, pp. 366–67; Stanton to Sherman, Apr. 16, 1864, ibid., 85; Sherman to Stanton, Apr. 23, 1864, ibid., 464; Gienapp and Gienapp, *Civil War Diary of Gideon Welles*, 401 (May 3, 1864); Lincoln to cabinet, May 3, 1864, in Basler, *The Collected Works of Abraham Lincoln*, 7:328; Stanton to Lincoln, May 5, 1864, Lincoln Papers, LC; McPherson, *Battle Cry of Freedom*, 794–95; Tap, *Over Lincoln's Shoulder*, 195–200.

28 *New York Herald*, Apr. 21, 1864; Halleck to Sherman, Apr. 29, 1864, *OR*, ser. 3, 4:332–33; Grant to Lincoln, May 1, 1864, in Simon, *The Papers of Ulysses Grant*, 10:380; *Daily Ohio Statesman*, Sept. 23, 1864 (prints Lincoln-Grant correspondence); *Detroit Free Press*, Sept. 23, 1864 (same).

29 Nevins and Thomas, *Diary of George Templeton Strong*, 3:438–42 (May 4–6, 1864); Stanton to Governors, May 4, 1864, M473; Dana to Eckert, May 7, 1864, *OR*, vol. 36, pt. 1, p. 63; Ethan Allen Hitchcock Diary, May 8, 1864, Croffut Papers; Stanton to Ellen Grant, May 8, 1864, in Simon, *The Papers of Ulysses Grant*, 10:444n; Dana, *Recollections of the Civil War*, 188, 194.

30 Stanton to Butler, May 6, 1864, M473 (sent at 11 p.m. and based on "a dispatch of the *New York Tribune* reporter just received"); *New York Tribune*, May 7, 1864 (report dated Union Mills, Virginia, 9 p.m.; ends "I am on my way to Washington with more complete reports that I will send tomorrow"); Dana to Eckert, May 7, 1864, *OR*, vol. 36, pt. 1, p. 63 (just arrived on Rappahannock); Bates, *Lincoln in the Telegraph Office*, 244–46; Dana, *Recollections of the Civil War*, 187–89 (Dana sent by Lincoln and Stanton to Grant); Wing, *When Lincoln Kissed Me*. Wing's account is somewhat fanciful, but Stanton's message to Butler, and Wing's report in the *Tribune*, prove the basic point: that Wing's report reached the paper through the department.

31 Stanton to Dix, May 8, 1864, *OR*, ser. 3, 4:277–78; *New York Times*, May 9, 1864.

32 Grant to Stanton, May 11, 1864, in Simon, *The Papers of Ulysses Grant*, 10:422; Grant to Halleck, May 11, 1864, ibid., 422–23; Stanton to Dix, May 11, 1864, M473 (his hand); *Albany (N.Y.) Evening Journal*, May 12, 1864 (all caps); *New York Times*, May 12, 1864; *Nashville Union*, May 18, 1864 (Grant's words "positively sublime"); *Philadelphia Inquirer*, May 12, 1864 (all caps); *Washington Evening Star*, May 13, 1864.

33 *New York Times*, May 12, 1864; *Chicago Tribune*, May 17, 1864; *New York Times*, May 29, 1864 (praising War Department's "unvarnished" reports);

Smart, *A Radical View*, 1:201–4 (criticizing errors in Stanton's reports but finding that they were overall "clear, concise, satisfactory").

34 Dix to Seward, Seward to the public, and Stanton to Dix, all May 18, 1864, *OR*, ser. 3, 4:387–88. Stanton's aide Eckert received the full text of the purported proclamation from New York at about 10 a.m. but for some reason did not show it to Stanton until Dix's message arrived. Roberts to Eckert, May 18, 1864, *OR*, ser. 3, 4:386–87.

35 Lincoln to Dix, May 18, 1864, in Basler, *The Collected Works of Abraham Lincoln*, 7:347–48; Stanton to Dix, May 18, 1864, *OR*, ser. 3, 4:388–89; Stanton to Cadwalader et al., May 18–19, 1864, M473. Secondary sources: Blondheim, "Public Sentiment," 889–99; Holzer, *Lincoln and the Power of the Press*, 487–97; Thomas and Hyman, *Stanton*, 301–2.

36 Lincoln's draft proclamation, with Stanton's editing, is in Blondheim, "Public Sentiment," 894. For the Associated Press role, see *Chicago Tribune*, May 21 and 23, 1864; *Cleveland Leader*, May 21, 1864; *Hartford (Ct.) Courant*, May 21, 1864.

37 Dix to Stanton, May 18, 1864, *OR*, ser. 3, 4:389 (4 p.m.).

38 Stanton to Dix, Mar. 16 and 19, 1861, Dix Papers; Stanton to Dix and Dix to Stanton, May 18, 1864, *OR*, ser. 3, 4:389–90.

39 Sydney Gay et al. to Lincoln, May 19, 1864, Lincoln Papers, LC; *New York Evening Post*, May 19, 1864; Bates, *Lincoln in the Telegraph Office*, 242–43 (arrest of Villard, questioning of White).

40 Stanton to Dix, May 20, 1864, *OR*, ser. 3, 4:395; *Daily Ohio Statesman*, May 21, 1864 (arrest of Medary); *New York World*, May 23, 1864 (resumes publication). Medary was arrested on a warrant issued by the federal district court; there is nothing in Stanton's files to suggest that he ordered the arrest, but many assumed a connection. Smith, *Samuel Medary and the Crisis*, 136–41.

41 Harper, *Lincoln and the Press*, 289–99; Bates, *Lincoln in the Telegraph Office*, 243; *Bridgeport (Ct.) Republican Farmer*, May 27, 1864, quoting *Rochester (N.Y.) Democrat*.

42 Rosecrans to Lincoln, June 2, 1864, Lincoln Papers, LC; Burlingame and Ettlinger, *Inside Lincoln's White House*, 203 (June 17, 1864; describing events on June 9); Stanton to Rosecrans, June 13, 1864, *OR*, vol. 34, pt. 4, p. 337; Rosecrans to Stanton, June 13, 1864, ibid., 338; Grant to Stanton, June 25, 1864, in Simon, *The Papers of Ulysses Grant*, 11:128–29; Hardie to Rosecrans, June 26, 1864, *OR*, ser. 2, 7:417 (release Barrett); Klement, *Dark Lanterns*, 79–87.

43 *New York Times*, May 30, 1864; Murray and Hsieh, *Savage War*, 367 ("the troops had abundant clothing, good equipment, plentiful rations, and an efficient logistical system from which the North's economic bounty flowed").

44 Stanton to Halleck, June 17, 1864, Edwin Stanton Papers, LC, box 42, image 101; *Washington Evening Star*, June 17, 1864; *National Intelligencer*, June 18, 1864; *New York Tribune*, June 18, 1864; Brooks report, June 20, 1864, in Burlingame, *Lincoln Observed*, 115–16; Swanson, *Bloody Crimes*, 177–80; Wilson, *The Business of Civil War*, 72–84.

45 Grant to Halleck, June 3, 1864, *OR*, vol. 36, pt. 1, p. 11; Stanton to Dix, June 4, 1864, M473; *New York Times*, June 6, 1864; Furgurson, *Not War but Murder*; McPherson, *Battle Cry of Freedom*, 733–37.

46 Grant to Halleck, June 14, 1864, *OR*, vol. 40, pt. 1, p. 12; Stanton to Dix, June 15, 1864, M473; *New York Times*, June 16, 1864; Sherman to Halleck, July 7, 1864, *OR*, vol. 38, pt. 5, p. 73 ("ask Mr. Stanton"); Stanton to Dix, Aug. 11, 1864, M473; *New York Times*, Aug. 12, 1864 ("Sherman knocking Atlanta"). Sherman viewed newspaper correspondents as spies. Sherman to Ewing, Feb. 17, 1863, in Simpson, *The Civil War*, 47.

47 Grant to Halleck, May 7, 1864, *OR*, vol. 36, pt. 2, p. 480; Stanton to Meade, May 12, 1864, ibid., 654; Meade to Lee, May 17, 1864, ibid., 841; *Cleveland Daily Leader*, May 18–19, 1864 (Wadsworth's body); Sherman to Halleck, June 27, 1864, *OR*, vol. 38, pt. 4, p. 607; Stanton to George McCook, June 28, 1864, M473; Stanton to Alexander McCook, June 28, 1864, ibid.; *New York Times*, June 29, 1864 (has Stanton-to-Dix message that mentions McCook); Stanton to Alexander McCook, July 16, 1864, M473 (offers leave to go home); Stanton to John McCook, July 16, 1864, ibid. (Alexander on way home with commission); Stanton to George McCook, July 18, 1863, ibid. ("sincere condolences"); Whalen and Whalen, *The Fighting McCooks*, 273–87.

48 Meigs to Stanton and Stanton to Meigs, June 15, 1864, in Poole, *On Hallowed Ground*, 61.

49 Stanton to Brough, July 14, 1864, M473 ("Sherman objects"); Sherman to Halleck, July 14, 1864, *OR*, vol. 38, pt. 5, p. 138; Lincoln to Sherman, July 18, 1864, in Basler, *The Collected Works of Abraham Lincoln*, 7:449–50; Sherman to Lincoln, July 21, 1864, *OR*, vol. 38, pt. 5, p. 210 ("I have the highest veneration for the law"). Fellman, *Citizen Sherman*, 157, 161 is especially good on Sherman's persistent opposition to the administration, which he terms "insubordination."

50 Sherman to Spooner, July 30, 1864, *OR*, vol. 38, pt. 5, pp. 305–6.

51 *New York Times*, Aug. 16, 1864 (prints Sherman's Spooner letter); *Brooklyn Daily Eagle*, Aug. 18, 1864; *New York Tribune*, Aug. 18, 1864; Sherman to Halleck, Sept. 4, 1864, *OR*, vol. 38, pt. 5, pp. 791–95; Sherman to McPherson, [Sept.] 1864, in Simpson and Berlin, *Sherman's Civil War*, 727.

52 Stanton to Dana, June 7, 1864, M473; Stanton to Butler, June 8, 1864, ibid. For Johnson as military governor, see Bergeron, *Andrew Johnson's Civil War*.

Thomas and Hyman believed that Stanton "was displeased" by the Johnson nomination, but I do not see this in Stanton's letters (*Stanton*, 312).

53 Chase to Lincoln, June 29, 1864, in Basler, *The Collected Works of Abraham Lincoln*, 7:414n; Lincoln to Chase, June 30, 1864, ibid., 7:419; Chase to Stanton, June 30, 1864, Edwin Stanton Papers, LC, box 22, image 25. For more on Chase's resignation and Fessenden's appointment, see Blue, *Salmon P. Chase*, 233–37; Donald, *Lincoln*, 507–9; Goodwin, *Team of Rivals*, 631–39.

54 Stanton to Dana, July 1, 1864, Edwin Stanton Papers, LC, box 22, image 42 (reporting that Tod declined and Fessenden would serve); Fessenden to Elizabeth Warriner, July 3, 1864, Fessenden Papers.

Chapter 13: "Tower of Strength"

1 Garrett to Stanton, June 29, 1864, *OR*, vol. 37, pt. 1, pp. 694–95; Sigel to Townsend, July 2, 1864, ibid., 174–75; Garrett to Stanton, July 3, 1864, ibid., pt. 2, p. 17; Stanton to Garrett, July 3, 1864, ibid.; Stanton to Brough, July 5, 1864, ibid., 70; Stanton to Hunter, July 6, 1864, ibid., 85; Feis, "A Union Military Intelligence Failure"; Cooling, *Jubal Early's Raid on Washington*.

2 Garrett to Stanton, July 7, 1864, *OR*, vol. 37, pt. 2, pp. 100–101 (multiple messages); Cohen, *Supreme Command*, 27 ("predecessor of the modern Situation Room").

3 Couch to Stanton, July 7, 1864, *OR*, vol. 37, pt. 2, p. 117 (muster in by companies?); Stanton to Couch, July 8, 1864, ibid., 130 (muster by regiments); Halleck to Grant, July 8, 1864, ibid., 119 ("considerable alarm"); Halleck to Grant, July 8, 1864, ibid., 119–20 ("considerable reinforcements"); Cooling, *Monocacy*, 82–84.

4 Lincoln to Garrett, *OR*, vol. 37, pt. 2, p. 138; Garrett to Stanton, July 9, 1864, ibid., 139 (two messages); Wallace to Halleck, July 9, 1864, ibid., 145; Stanton to Dix, July 10, 1864, ibid., 190 (press report); *New York Times*, July 11, 1864 (prints press report); Cooling, *Monocacy*; Stahr, *Seward*, 402–3.

5 Stanton to Barnes, July 11, 1864, M473; Stanton to Garrett, July 11, 1864, ibid.; Stanton to Wallace, July 11, 1864, *OR*, vol. 37, pt. 2, p. 214; Burlingame and Ettlinger, *Inside Lincoln's White House*, 203 (July 11, 1864); Gienapp and Gienapp, *Civil War Diary of Gideon Welles*, 444 (July 11, 1864); Randall, *Diary of Orville Hickman Browning*, 1:676 (July 12, 1864) (Stanton "felt no apprehension whatever for the safety of the city"); *Washington Evening Star*, Oct. 12, 1895 (A. E. H. Johnson). Some secondary sources place Stanton at Fort Stevens (e.g., Winkle, *Lincoln's Citadel*, 393), but I do not see this in the primary sources.

6 Stanton to Wright, July 13, 1864, *OR*, vol. 37, pt. 2, pp. 284–85 (4:30 p.m.); Wright to Stanton, July 13, 1864, ibid., 285 (from Fort Reno); Wright to

Halleck, July 13, 1864, ibid., 285; Cooling, *Jubal Early's Raid*, 177–89; Foote, *Civil War*, 3:460–61 (Early's force reached White's Ferry by midnight on July 13).

7 Halleck to Stanton, July 13, 1864, Lincoln Papers, LC; Lincoln to Stanton, July 14, 1864, in Basler, *The Collected Works of Abraham Lincoln*, 7:439–40; Lincoln to Blair, Sept. 23, 1864, ibid., 8:18 (requests resignation); Herbert to Butler, Sept. 26, 1864, in Marshall, *Private and Official Correspondence of Benjamin Butler*, 5:318 ("good drunk"); Goodwin, *Team of Rivals*, 658–61.

8 Pass, July 13, 1864, Edwin M. Stanton Family Papers; Carpenter, *The Inner Life of Abraham Lincoln*, 302; Pinsker, *Lincoln's Sanctuary*.

9 Bates, *Lincoln in the Telegraph Office*, 397–98.

10 Thomas and Hyman, *Stanton*, 384–85 (quoting memoir owned by Gideon Townsend Stanton).

11 Army Appropriation, June 15, 1862, *Statutes at Large*, 13:129; Trudeau, *Like Men at War*, 252–55. Brooks wrote a fine description of the flurry as the session closed: Brooks report, July 5, 1864, in Burlingame, *Lincoln Observed*, 121–24.

12 *Congressional Globe*, 38th Cong., 1st Sess., p. 895 (Mar. 1, 1864) (House passes bill); ibid., 3332 (June 28, 1864) (Wilson's argument); ibid., 3350 (June 28, 1864) (Senate passes bill); Donald, *Sumner and the Rights of Man*, 173–78.

13 Lincoln proclamation, Dec. 8, 1863, in Basler, *The Collected Works of Abraham Lincoln*, 7:53–56 (10 percent plan); Wade-Davis bill, July 2, 1864, in Hyman, *The Radical Republicans and Reconstruction*, 128–34; Harris, *With Charity for All*, 186–90.

14 Burlingame and Ettlinger, *Inside Lincoln's White House*, 217–19 (July 4, 1864); Lincoln proclamation, July 8, 1864, in Basler, *The Collected Works of Abraham Lincoln*, 7:433–34. Hay mentions Stanton in this diary entry but not in the section dealing with the Wade-Davis discussion.

15 *New York Tribune*, Aug. 5. 1864.

16 Grant to Halleck, Aug. 1, 1864, *OR*, vol. 40, pt. 1, p. 17; *Cleveland Daily Leader*, Aug. 1, 1864 (Chambersburg); *New York Herald*, Aug. 3, 1864 ("why do we get no more war bulletins from Secretary Stanton?"); Castel, *Decision in the West*, 442–45; Goodwin, *Team of Rivals*, 645–50.

17 J. K. Herbert to Butler, Aug. 11, 1864, in Marshall, *Private and Official Correspondence of Benjamin Butler*, 5:35–36; Waugh, *Reelecting Lincoln*, 270–75.

18 Raymond to Lincoln, Aug. 20, 1864, in Basler, *The Collected Works of Abraham Lincoln*, 7:517–18; Lincoln memo re: reelection, Aug. 23, 1864, ibid., 514; Lincoln to Raymond, Aug. 24, 1864, ibid. (draft); Nicolay to Hay, Aug. 28, 1864, in Burlingame, *With Lincoln in the White House*, 154; Stahr, *Seward*, 404–7.

19 *New York Herald*, Aug. 19 and 22, 1864; Black to Stanton, Aug. 24, 1864, Black Papers, reel 21; Stanton to Black, Aug. 31, 1864, ibid. Black's visit came on the heels of a similar visit to Canada by Greeley and Hay. McPherson, *Battle Cry of Freedom*, 762–68; Taliaferro, *All the Great Prizes*, 85–89.

20 Democratic platform, Aug. 30, 1864, in Simpson, *The Civil War*, 336–37; *Janesville (Wisc.) Gazette*, Aug. 31, 1864 ("miserable, cowardly"); McClellan draft, Sept. 4, 1864, in Sears, *The Civil War Papers of George B. McClellan*, 590–92 (second of six drafts); Waugh, *Reelecting Lincoln*, 276–302.

21 Stanton to Dix, Sept. 2, 1864, M473 (8 p.m.); Stanton to Dix, Sept. 2, 1864, ibid. (10:45 p.m.); *New York Times*, Sept. 3, 1864 (prints both messages); Nevins and Thomas, *Diary of George Templeton Strong*, 3:480–81 (Sept. 3, 1864); Stanton to Dix, Sept. 4, 1864, M473 (includes "Atlanta is ours"); *New York Times*, Sept. 5, 1864 ("Atlanta is ours"); *Bloomington (Ill.) Pantagraph*, Sept. 6, 1864 ("Atlanta Ours, Fairly Won"); *Pittsburgh Commercial*, Sept. 6, 1864 ("Atlanta Fairly Ours"); Castel, *Decision in the West*, 533–34.

22 Stanton to Cony, July 18, 1864, M473; Cony to Stanton, July 22, 1864, *OR*, ser. 3, 4:538; Stanton to Cony, July 22, 1864, ibid., 538; Cony to Stanton, July 25, 1865, ibid., 544–45.

23 Stanton to Cony, Aug. 11, 1864, *OR*, ser. 3, 4:609.

24 Stanton to Grant, Sept. 11, 1864, *OR*, ser. 3, 4:709–10 ("would be glad"); Grant to Stanton, Sept. 12, 1864, ibid., 712–13 ("ought to have"); Sherman to Stanton, Sept. 13, 1864, *OR*, vol. 39, pt. 1, p. 390; Cony to Stanton, Sept. 13, 1864, *OR*, ser. 3, 4:714 ("little more time"); Stanton to Cony, Sept. 13, 1864, ibid. ("urgent appeals"); *Cleveland Daily Leader*, Sept. 14, 1864 ("glorious news from Maine"); *New York Times*, Sept. 15, 1864 (both Grant and Sherman messages).

25 Benton, *Voting in the Field*, 434–35; Waugh, *Reelecting Lincoln*; White, *Emancipation*.

26 *National Republican*, Aug. 10, 1864 (Stanton would resign); *New York Times*, Aug. 11, 1864 (editorial); Henry C. Wilson to Stanton, Aug. 12, 1864, Edwin Stanton Papers, LC, box 22, images 183–84; Stanton to William Dickson, Oct. 13, 1864, Dickson Papers.

27 Morton et al. to Stanton, Sept. 12, 1864, in Foulke, *The Life of Oliver P. Morton*, 1:367–69; Stanton to Morton, Sept. 18, 1864, *OR*, ser. 3, 4:732; Lincoln to Sherman, Sept. 19, 1864, in Basler, *The Collected Works of Abraham Lincoln*, 8:11.

28 Stanton to Allen, Oct. 2, 1864, M473; Stanton to Morton, Oct. 3, 1864, ibid. (relays message from Allen); Stanton to Meigs et al., Oct. 4, 1864, M421, reel 2, NA.

29 Stevenson to Stanton, Sept. 20, 1864, *OR*, vol. 43, pt. 2, p. 124; Stanton to Dix, Sept. 20, 1864, M473 (three messages); *New York Times*, Sept. 21, 1864 (prints Stanton's messages to Dix); Burlingame, *Inside the White House in War Times*, 132–33 (Stoddard article published 1866).

30 Burlingame and Ettlinger, *Inside Lincoln's White House*, 238–39 (Oct. 11, 1864); Dana, *Recollections of the Civil War*, 261–62. Dana misdates these events; they were in October, not November. Thomas and Hyman, *Stanton*, 330n9.

31 Burlingame and Ettlinger, *Inside Lincoln's White House*, 240–41 (Oct. 11, 1864). Burlingame identifies some of those mentioned in his notes; the only Quartermaster McKim I can find is William W. McKim, based in Boston. *OR*, ser. 3, 5:453.

32 Lincoln to Grant, Oct. 12, 1864, in Basler, *The Collected Works of Abraham Lincoln*, 8:45 (summarizes vote); Stanton to Sherrand, Oct. 12, 1864, M473 ("ten Union to one Copperhead"); Stanton to Wright, Oct. 12, 1864, ibid. ("army vote so far heard stands ten Union for one Copperhead").

33 Grant to Sherman, Oct. 11, 1864, *OR*, vol. 46, pt. 1, p. 37; Sherman to Grant, Oct. 11, 1864, ibid.; Stanton to Grant, Oct. 12, 1864, *OR*, vol. 39, pt. 3, p. 222 ("maturely considered"); Grant to Stanton, Oct. 12, 1864, ibid., 239; Stanton to Sherman, Oct. 13, 1864, ibid., 240 ("whatever results"); White, *American Ulysses*, 389.

34 Sherman to Grant, Oct. 9, 1864, *OR*, vol. 39, pt. 3, p. 162 ("make Georgia howl"); Sherman to Stanton, Oct. 25, 1864, ibid., 428–29; Fellman, *Citizen Sherman*, 162 ("any black troops organized to his rear would not join him on his march . . . his army would remain racially pure").

35 Stanton to Chase, Oct. 13, 1864, M473 (7 a.m.); Stanton to Grier, Oct. 13, 1864, ibid.; Grier to Stanton, Oct. 13, 1864, in Gorham, *The Life and Public Services*, 2:469–70 (facsimile); Chase to Stanton, Oct. 13, 1864, in Niven, *Chase Papers*, 4:435–35.

36 Burlingame and Ettlinger, *Inside Lincoln's White House*, 241 (Oct. 13, 1864) (Lincoln tells Hay he will not discuss appointment for a while); Randall, *Diary of Orville Hickman Browning*, 1:687–88 (Oct. 15–17, 1864) (conversation with Ellen); Stanton to Lincoln, Oct. 16, 1864, *OR*, vol. 41, pt. 4, p. 3 (from Fort Monroe); Pierrepont to Stanton, Oct. 18, 1864, Edwin Stanton Papers, LC, box 23, image 233 (urges Stanton to seek chief justice position).

37 Grant to Butler, Oct. 16, 1864, in Simon, *The Papers of Ulysses Grant*, 12:310; *Detroit Free Press*, Oct. 17, 1864; *Chicago Tribune*, Oct. 17, 1864; Porter, *Campaigning with Grant*, 304–6.

38 Lyman to Elizabeth Lyman, Oct. 17, 1864, in Agassiz, *Meade's Headquarters*, 249–50; Lowe, *Meade's Army*, 281 (Oct. 17, 1864); Stanton to Smith, Oct. 19, 1864, M473 (9:30 p.m.); Francis Fessenden to Elizabeth Fox, Oct. 23, 1864, Fessenden Papers, (describing trip with Stanton).

39 Lincoln, "Estimated Electoral Vote," Oct. 13, 1864, in Basler, *The Collected Works of Abraham Lincoln*, 8:46; Prime to McClellan, Oct. 20, 1864, in Sears, *George B. McClellan*, 384.

40 Morton to Lincoln, Oct. 13, 1864, Lincoln Papers, LC; Lincoln to Stanton, Oct. 13, 1864, in Basler, *The Collected Works of Abraham Lincoln*, 8:46; Stanton to Morton, Oct. 13, 1864, M473 (seeks number of furlough soldiers and "where they were furloughed from"); Stanton to Morton, Oct. 14, ibid. (leaves extended for sick and wounded).

41 *Milwaukee Daily Patriot*, Oct. 26, 1864 ("dismissed twenty clerks"); *Daily Ohio Statesman*, Oct. 27, 1864 (similar); *New Orleans Daily True Delta*, Nov. 2, 1864 (similar); *Springfield (Mass.) Republican*, Nov. 12, 1864; *Chicago Tribune*, Dec. 13, 1864; Thomas and Hyman, *Stanton*, 328; White, *Emancipation*, 211–12.

42 Stanton to Wallace, Oct. 26, 1864, M473 (furlough Delaware cavalry); Cannon to Stanton, Oct. 27, 1864, Edwin Stanton Papers, LC, box 23, image 261 ("without the vote of our troops"); Stanton to Grant, Oct. 27, 1864, in Simon, *The Papers of Ulysses Grant*, 12:353; Grant to Stanton, Oct. 27, 1864, ibid.; Stanton to Augur, Oct. 27, 1864, Edwin Stanton Papers, LC, box 43, image 50 (furlough Delaware cavalry); Grant to Stanton, Nov. 1, 1864, *OR*, vol. 43, pt. 3, p. 471.

43 Stanton to Sperry, Oct. 29, 1864, M473; Thomas to Steedman, Nov. 2, 1864, *OR*, vol. 39, pt. 3, p. 603 (instructions from Stanton); *Pittsburgh Daily Post*, Nov. 8, 1864; Thomas and Hyman, *Stanton*, 333 ("troops jammed trains from the Mississippi to the Atlantic").

44 *New York Times*, Oct. 28, 1864; *Washington Morning Chronicle*, Oct. 28, 1864 ("New York Election Frauds"); Stanton to Stevenson, Oct. 28, 1864, M473 (arrest William Turman); *New York Tribune*, Oct. 29, 1864 ("Democratic Balloting among the Dead Soldiers"); Dana to Patrick, Oct. 30, 1864, M473; Marsena Patrick Diary, Oct. 30, 1864, Patrick Papers; White, "Canvassing the Troops."

45 Stanton to Grant, Nov. 1, 1864, *OR*, vol. 42, pt. 3, p. 470; Grant to Butler, Nov. 1, 1864, in Simon, *The Papers of Ulysses Grant*, 12:370; Stanton to Butler, Nov. 2, 1864, in Marshall, *Private and Official Correspondence of Benjamin Butler*, 5:307 (orders); Dix to Stanton, Nov. 3, 1864, *OR*, vol. 43, pt. 2, p. 535 ("not the weak point"); Stanton to Dix, Nov. 3, 1864, ibid., 535–36 ("not designed"); Butler to Stanton, Nov. 3, 1864, ibid., 536; Stanton to Butler, Nov. 3, 1864, in Marshall, *Private and Official Correspondence of Benjamin Butler*, 5:310; Butler, *Butler's Book*, 753–54 (conversation with Stanton).

46 Butler to Stanton, Nov. 5, 1864, *OR*, vol. 43, pt. 2, pp. 549–50; Lincoln to Stanton, Nov. 5, 1864, in Basler, *The Collected Works of Abraham Lincoln*, 8:91–92; Butler to Stanton, Nov. 7, 1864, in Marshall, *Private and Official Correspondence of Benjamin Butler*, 5:326–29; Stanton to Butler, Nov. 7, 1864, *OR*, vol. 43, pt. 2, p. 568; Waugh, *Reelecting Lincoln*, 350–51.

47 *New York Tribune*, Oct. 26, 1864 ("quite ill"); Brooks report, Nov. 11, 1864, in Burlingame, *Lincoln Observed*, 142 ("sick abed"); Goodwin, *Team of Rivals*, 665–66; Waugh, *Reelecting Lincoln*, 350–55.

48 John Brobst to Mary Engelsby, Sept. 27, 1864, in Roth, *Well, Mary*, 92; Castel, *Decision in the West*, 480 ("all that the South need do to achieve [victory] is to hold out a while longer—just six more weeks—until the Northern elections get under way"); McMurry, *Atlanta 1864*, 190 (fall of Atlanta "assured Lincoln's reelection, and in so doing it assured the eventual failure of the Southern bid for independence"); Sears, *George B. McClellan*, 385 ("impossible to imagine").

49 Grant to Stanton, Nov. 9, 1864, in Simon, *The Papers of Ulysses Grant*, 12:395–96; Grant to Stanton, Nov. 10, 1864, ibid., 398; *National Republican*, Oct. 11, 1864; Winther, "The Soldier Vote in the Election of 1864"; White, *Emancipation*, 125. White is excellent on the political pressures on Union soldiers, but also stresses that "the policy of enfranchising soldiers is a crucial component of Lincoln's legacy in civil liberties matters, for it laid the groundwork for the Fourteenth and Fifteenth Amendments by affirming that the right to vote was at the core of what it meant to be a U.S. citizen" (155).

50 *New York Times*, Nov. 16, 1864; *New York Herald*, Nov. 17, 1864; *New York World*, Nov. 18, 1864; *New York Tribune*, Nov. 18, 1864; *Cincinnati Gazette*, Nov. 23, 1864; Silver, *Lincoln's Supreme Court*, 193–94.

51 Stanton to Chase, Nov. 19, 1864, Dreer Collection; Goodwin, *Team of Rivals*, 672–76 (Bates resignation; Speed appointment).

Chapter 14: "Gratitude to Almighty God"

1 *New York Herald*, Nov. 23, 1864; *Cincinnati Daily Gazette*, Nov. 23, 1864 ("persistent clatter" about appointment of Stanton as chief justice); Pierrepont to Lincoln, Nov. 24, 1864, Lincoln Papers, LC; *Janesville (Wisc.) Gazette*, Dec. 1, 1864; *New York World*, Dec. 5, 1864 ("Chase Ruled Out for Chief Justiceship").

2 Meade to Margaretta Meade, Nov. 7, 1864, in Meade, *The Life and Letters*, 2:239 (Meade would regret Stanton's "leaving the war department, for I do not know who there is to take his place, who would be so satisfactory"); Marsena Patrick Diary, Nov. 16, 1864, Patrick Papers (Grant "off to Washington with a view to head off Butler as Secretary of War"); Grant to Stanton, Nov. 23, 1864, in Simon, *The Papers of Ulysses Grant*, 13:16 (in Washington); Grant to Badeau, Dec. 27, 1879, ibid., 29:342; Badeau, *Military History*, 3:199.

3 Beecher to Stanton, Nov. 30, 1864, in Wolcott, *Edwin M. Stanton*, 197–98; Stanton to Beecher, Dec. 4, 1864, ibid., 199–200; Applegate, *The Most Famous Man in America*.

4 *National Republican*, Dec. 6, 1864 (nomination; confirmation); Dana to Pike, Dec. 12, 1864, Pike Papers; *National Republican*, Dec. 15, 1864; *Baltimore Sun*, Dec. 16, 1864; *Cincinnati Daily Gazette*, Dec. 19, 1864: *Cleveland Daily Leader*, Dec. 23, 1864 ("brilliant assemblage").

5 Stanton to Grant, Dec. 2, 1864, in Simon, *The Papers of Ulysses Grant*, 13:50; Stanton to Grant, Dec. 7, 1864, *OR*, vol. 45, pt. 2, p. 84; Grant to Stanton, Dec. 7, 1864, ibid.; Grant to Thomas, Dec. 11, 1864, ibid., 143; Thomas to Grant, Dec. 11, 1864, ibid. ("perfect sheet"); Thomas to Halleck, Dec. 15, 1864, ibid., 194 (received 11:25 p.m.); Stanton to Dix, Dec. 15, 1864, M473 (sent 11:30 p.m.); Stanton to Thomas, Dec. 16, 1864, *OR*, vol. 45, pt. 2, p. 195 (congratulations; sent just after midnight); *New York Times*, Dec. 16, 1864 (summarizes Stanton message). Bates, *Lincoln in the Telegraph Office*, 316–18, describes Eckert bringing the message to the Stanton home, but if the message really arrived at the War Department at 11:25 and Stanton relayed it to Dix at 11:30, Stanton must have been in the office. See Foote, *Civil War*, 3:705–10; White, *American Ulysses*, 390–92.

6 Sherman to Stanton, Dec. 13, 1864, *OR*, vol. 44, pp. 700–701; Sherman to Halleck, Dec. 13, 1864, ibid., 701–2; *Washington Evening Star*, Dec. 19, 1864 (Stanton to Dix). The *Official Records* states that these messages were received on Dec. 15, but Stanton, in his message to Dix, printed in the papers, stated that they arrived Dec. 18.

7 Sherman to Halleck, Dec. 13, 1864, *OR*, vol. 47, p. 702 ("whole army"); Grant to Sherman, Dec. 18, 1864, ibid., 740–41 ("wipe out Lee"); Halleck to Sherman, Dec. 18, 1864, ibid., 741 ("salt"). Halleck was probably alluding to the way the Romans supposedly salted the fields around Carthage, but it now seems that there was no such salt. See Ripley and Dana, *The American Cyclopedia*, 4:39; Ridley, "To Be Taken with a Pinch of Salt."

8 Sherman to Halleck, Dec. 24, 1864, *OR*, vol. 44, pp. 798–800; Grant to Sherman, Dec. 27, 1864, in Simon, *The Papers of Ulysses Grant*, 13:169.

9 Sherman to Lincoln, Dec. 22, 1864, in Basler, *The Collected Works of Abraham Lincoln*, 8:182; Stanton to Dix, Dec. 25, 1864, M473 (quotes Sherman); Stanton to Henry Stanbery, Dec. 26, 1864, ibid.; *New York Times*, Dec. 26, 1864; *Chicago Tribune*, Dec. 26, 1864; *Cleveland Daily Leader*, Dec. 28, 1864; *Western Reserve Chronicle* (Warren, Ohio), Dec. 28, 1864.

10 Grant to Lincoln, Dec. 28, 1864, in Simon, *The Papers of Ulysses Grant*, 13:177–78; Grant to Stanton, Dec. 30, 1864, ibid., 183–84; Stanton to Grant, Dec. 30, 1864, *OR*, vol. 42, pt. 3, p. 1099; Grant to Porter, Dec. 30, 1864, in Simon, *The Papers of Ulysses Grant*, 13:190; Grant to Stanton, Jan. 4, 1865, ibid., 223; Grant to Lincoln, Jan. 6, 1865, ibid.; Foote, *Civil War*, 3:715–21. It is not clear whether Grant had received Stanton's message when he sent his message to Porter on Dec. 30.

11 Lincoln to Blair, Dec. 28, 1864, in Basler, *The Collected Works of Abraham Lincoln*, 8:188; Blair to Davis, Dec. 30, 1864, ibid., 188–89; *New York Tribune*, Jan. 2, 1865; Grant to Butler, Jan. 2, 1865, in Simon, *The Papers of Ulysses Grant*, 13:209 (Blair "left here yesterday to return home thinking no reply would be made to his letter"); *Brooklyn Daily Eagle*, Jan. 3, 1865; *New York Tribune*, Jan. 4, 1865; Gienapp and Gienapp, *Civil War Diary of Gideon Welles*, 571 (Jan. 5, 1865) (Blair received no answer to his letter to Davis until back in Washington; Blair about to return to Richmond); Harris, *Lincoln's Last Months*, 111–13.

12 Chase to Sherman, Jan. 2, 1865, Sherman Papers; Meigs Diary, Jan. 2, 1865, Meigs Papers; *New York Times*, Jan. 8, 1865; *Liberator* (Boston), Jan. 27, 1865 (prints Connolly's Ebenezer Creek letter); *Washington Evening Star*, Jan. 27, 1865 (Senator Wilson demands investigation of Ebenezer Creek); Townsend, *Anecdotes of the Civil War*, 114 (Barnes). For sources that say Stanton had Connolly's letter, or a summary, see Connolly to Mary Connolly, Jan. 18, 1865, in Angle, *Three Years in the Army of the Cumberland*, 373; Royster, *Memoirs of General W. T. Sherman*, 724; Rubin, *Through the Heart of Dixie*, 23.

13 Stanton to Grant, Jan. 5, 1865, *OR*, vol. 47, pt. 2, p. 16; Stanton to Tucker, Jan. 5, 1865, M473; Stanton to Associated Press, Jan. 5, 1865, in *Detroit Free Press*, Jan. 6, 1865.

14 Stanton to Dana, Jan. 6, 1865, *OR*, vol. 46, pt. 2, p. 52; Stanton to Grant, Jan. 6, 1865, in Simon, *The Papers of Ulysses Grant*, 13:240; Grant to Stanton, Jan. 6, 1865, ibid., 237–38; Grant to Stanton, Jan. 7, 1865, ibid., 241.

15 Willard Saxton Diary, Jan. 10, 1865, Saxton Papers; McFeely, *Yankee Stepfather*, 45–46 (Howard's arrival in the Sea Islands); Manning, *Troubled Refuge*, 78–95; Rose, *Rehearsal for Reconstruction*.

16 Sherman to Chase, Jan. 11, 1865, in Niven, *Chase Papers*, 5:6–7.

17 Sherman to Halleck, Jan. 12, 1865, *OR*, vol. 47, pt. 2, pp. 36–37. On Sherman and Halleck, see Marszalek, *Sherman*, 23, 54–57.

18 Sherman to Halleck, Jan. 12, 1865, *OR*, vol. 47, pt. 2, pp. 36–37; *Liberator* (Boston), Jan. 27, 1865; *Washington Evening Star*, Jan. 27, 1865; Royster, *Memoirs of General W. T. Sherman*, 724; Foote, *Civil War*, 3:649–50; Trudeau, *Southern Storm*, 380–84.

19 Transcript, Jan. 12, 1865, meeting, *OR*, vol. 47, pt. 2, pp. 37–41; Niven, *Chase Papers*, 1:521 (Feb. 1, 1865) ("truly eloquent"); Stanton to Sumner, Feb. 12, 1865, Sumner Papers, reel 79; *New York Tribune*, Feb. 13, 1865 (prints minutes).

20 Transcript, Jan. 12, 1865, *OR*, vol. 47, pt. 2, p. 41; Royster, *Memoirs of General W. T. Sherman*, 727.

21 Sherman Special Field Order No. 15, Jan. 16, 1865, *OR*, vol. 47, pt. 2, pp. 60–62.

22 Sherman to Johnson, Feb. 2, 1866, in Graf, *The Papers of Andrew Johnson*, 10:20–21 ("I made the rough draft, and we went over it very carefully, Mr. Stanton making many changes, and the present orders No. 15 resulted, and were made public").

23 Stanton to Grant, Dec. 26, 1864, *OR*, 44:809 ("all sorts of schemes will be got up to hold [cotton] under sham titles of British and other private claimants"); Sherman to Stanton, Jan. 2, 1865, *OR*, vol. 47, pt. 2, pp. 5–6 ("my invariable answer"); Sherman to Stanton, Jan. 19, 1865, ibid., 87–88 (more on cotton); Gienapp and Gienapp, *Civil War Diary of Gideon Welles*, 578 (Jan. 21, 1865) ("much of the cotton was claimed as British property").

24 *Washington Evening Star*, Jan. 9, 1865; Willard Saxton Diary, Jan. 14–15, 1865, Saxton Papers; *Milwaukee Daily Sentinel*, Jan. 30, 1865; *Sacramento Daily Union*, Feb. 20, 1865; Mathilda Saxton to Flower, ca. 1900, in Flower, *Edwin McMasters Stanton*, 420. Saxton did not name Minturn, describing him just as a friend of Draper, but several newspapers did, although it is not possible to determine whether this was Robert Minturn (1805–1866) or Robert Minturn Jr. (1836–1889). Flower (420) erroneously placed the Saxtons in North Carolina rather than in South Carolina.

25 Botume, *First Days among the Contrabands*, 114–15; Mathilda Saxton to Flower, ca. 1900, in Flower, *Edwin McMasters Stanton*, 420.

26 Stanton to Terry and Porter, Jan. 16, 1865, Schoff Collection (thanks for rebel flag; congratulates on "great achievement"; clerk's hand Stanton's signature); Stanton to Lincoln, Jan. 17, 1865, *OR*, vol. 46, pt. 2, pp. 155–57; Stanton to Grant, Jan. 17, 1865, ibid., 157; Grant to Stanton, Jan. 18, 1865, in Simon, *The Papers of Ulysses Grant*, 13:270 ("run to Washington"); Stanton to Grant, Jan. 18, 1865, ibid. ("urgent necessity for me to be in Washington"); Townsend, *Anecdotes of the Civil War*, 118–19.

27 Davis to Blair, Jan. 12, 1865, in Basler, *The Collected Works of Abraham Lincoln*, 8:275; Lincoln to Blair, Jan. 18, 1865, ibid., 8:220–21; *Washington Evening Star*, Jan. 20, 1865 (Blair left on second trip to Richmond); Gienapp and Gienapp, *Civil War Diary of Gideon Welles*, 579 (Jan. 21, 1865).

28 Ord to Stanton, Jan. 29, 1865, *OR*, vol. 46, pt. 2, p. 290; Stanton to Ord, Jan. 29, 1865, ibid., 292; Eckert to commissioners, Jan. 30, 1865, in Basler, *The Collected Works of Abraham Lincoln*, 8:248 (drafted by Lincoln); Stahr, *Seward*, 420–26.

29 Dana to Ashley, Jan. 31, 1865, M473 (asking for telegraphic notice of passage of amendment); Niven, *Chase Papers*, 1:520–21 (Jan. 31–Feb. 1, 1865); *Washington Evening Star*, Feb. 1, 1865; *Baltimore Sun*, Feb. 1, 1865; *New York Times*, Feb. 1, 1865; *New York Tribune*, Feb. 1–2, 1865 ("malefactors" in Feb. 2).

30 Eckert to Lincoln, Feb. 1, 1865, in Basler, *The Collected Works of Abraham Lincoln*, 8:281; Grant to Stanton, Feb. 1, 1865; ibid., 285; Stanton to Garrett, Feb. 3, 1865, M473; Harris, *Lincoln's Last Months*, 113–21.

31 Stanton to Grant, Feb. 4, 1865, in Simon, *The Papers of Ulysses Grant*, 13:362; Grant to Stanton, Feb. 4, 1865, ibid.; Gienapp and Gienapp, *Civil War Diary of Gideon Welles*, 583–84 (Feb. 4, 1865); *Washington Evening Star*, Feb. 4, 1865. If the cabinet met punctually at noon, as Welles stated, Lincoln's message to Grant, sent at 12:20 p.m., must have been drafted before the meeting.

32 Sumner to Bright, Feb. 13, 1865, in Palmer, *Selected Letters of Charles Sumner*, 2:268; Stanton to Dix, Feb. 18, 1865, M473 (Sherman in Columbia); *New York Times*, Feb. 19, 1865 (same); Pierrepont to Stanton, Feb. 22, 1865, Edwin Stanton Papers, LC, box 25, image 6.

33 Lee to Grant, Mar. 2, 1865, in Basler, *The Collected Works of Abraham Lincoln*, 8:331; Grant to Stanton, Mar. 2, 1865, ibid.; Stanton to Grant, Mar. 3, 1865, ibid., 330–31. Basler's notes indicate that the message is in Lincoln's hand except for the "top and tail," in Stanton's hand. Sherman later insisted that he never saw Lincoln's message, although Grant could well have shared the message, or the substance, when the two men were together in late March.

34 Stanton to Sumner, Feb. 12, 1865, Sumner Papers, reel 79; *Congressional Globe*, 38th Cong., 2d Sess., p. 984 (Feb. 22, 1865) (Hale); ibid., 1182 (Feb. 28, 1865) (new version of bill); Freedmen's Bureau Act, Mar. 3, 1865, *Statutes at Large*, 13:507–9; Donald, *Sumner and the Rights of Man*, 194–95.

35 Clifford to Sarah Clifford, Mar. 4, 1865, Clifford Papers; Gienapp and Gienapp, *Civil War Diary of Gideon Welles*, 597–98 (Mar. 4, 1865); Lincoln Inaugural Address, Mar. 4, 1865, in Basler, *The Collected Works of Abraham Lincoln*, 8:332–33; Halleck to Lieber, Mar. 5, 1865, Lieber Papers, Huntington, box 5; *Sacramento Daily Union*, Apr. 10, 1865 (Brooks); Goodwin, *Team of Rivals*, 697–99.

36 Edward Bates to John C. Bates, Dec. 25, 1864, Edward Bates Papers, Virginia Historical Society; Goodwin, *Team of Rivals*, 673–76; Harris, *Lincoln's Last Months*, 87–91.

37 Randall, *Diary of Orville Hickman Browning*, 2:1–12 (Jan. 5 and 30, Feb. 16 and 17, Mar. 11–12, 1865); *Pittsburgh Gazette*, Jan. 18, 1865; Stanton to Grant, Mar. 8, 1865, in Simon, *The Papers of Ulysses Grant*, 14:113; *Washington Evening Star*, Mar. 10, 1865; *National Republican*, Mar. 11, 1865; Harris, *Lincoln's Last Months*, 107–11.

38 *Washington Evening Star*, Mar. 15, 1865 (Stanton left in afternoon); Rawlins to Ord, Mar. 16, 1865, *OR*, vol. 46, pt. 3, p. 10 ("Stanton is here"); *Washington Evening Star*, Mar. 18, 1865; *New York Herald*, Mar. 19, 1865 (lists group); Lowe, *Meade's Army*, 345 (Lyman); Simon, *Memoirs of Julia Dent Grant*, 139–40.

39 *New York Tribune*, Mar. 18, 1865; *Daily Ohio Statesman*, Mar. 25, 1865.

40 Stanton to Lincoln, Mar. 23, 1865, *OR*, vol. 46, pt. 3, p. 87; Stanton to Lincoln, Mar. 24, 1865, ibid., 96–97; Lincoln to Stanton, Mar. 25, 1865, ibid., 109; Stanton to Lincoln, Mar. 25, 1865, ibid.; Porter, *Campaigning with Grant*, 409–10.

41 Clifford to Sarah Clifford, Mar. 4, 1865, Clifford Papers (Stanton sending Anderson to Charleston); Stanton to Lincoln, Mar. 25, 1865, *OR*, vol. 47, pt. 3, p. 18; Stanton to Lincoln, Mar. 27, 1865, ibid., 31; Lincoln to Stanton, Mar. 27, 1865, in Basler, *The Collected Works of Abraham Lincoln*, 8:375; Stanton to Lincoln, Mar. 27, 1865, ibid., 376; Lincoln to Stanton, Mar. 28, 1865, ibid. ("little or no difference").

42 Sherman to Stanton, Mar. 27, 1865, *OR*, vol. 47, pt. 3, pp. 32–33; Stanton to Sherman, Mar. 27, 1865, ibid., 42; Sherman to Stanton, Mar. 28, 1865, ibid.; Stanton to Sherman, Mar. 28, 1865, ibid. ("God speed you"); Porter, *Incidents and Anecdotes of the Civil War*, 313–15; Foote, *Civil War*, 3:854–57.

43 Lincoln to Stanton, Mar. 28, 1865, in Basler, *The Collected Works of Abraham Lincoln*, 8:377; Stanton to Lincoln, Mar. 31, 1865, *OR*, vol. 46, pt. 3, p. 332 ("strong faith"); Lincoln to Stanton, Apr. 2, 1865, in Basler, *The Collected Works of Abraham Lincoln*, 8:383–84 ("all seems well"); Stanton to Dix, Apr. 2, 1865, M473 (four messages); *New York Times*, Apr. 3, 1865 (prints Stanton-to-Dix messages).

44 Lincoln to Stanton, Apr. 3, 1865, *OR*, vol. 46, pt. 3, p. 508; Stanton to Lincoln, Apr. 3, 1865, ibid., 509; Stanton to Dix, Apr. 3, 1865, ibid., 543 ("forces under his command are in Richmond"); *Washington Evening Star*, Apr. 3, 1865; Winslow to Grandfather, Apr. 4, 1865, Griswold Flagg Papers; *Sacramento Daily Union*, May 8, 1865 (Brooks).

45 *Washington Evening Star*, Apr. 3, 1865; *New York Times*, Apr. 4, 1865; *Sacramento Daily Union*, May 8, 1865; Brooks, *Washington in Lincoln's Time* (1958), 220 ("for once in his life"). The different papers have slightly different versions of Stanton's speech; I have used the *Star*.

46 Stanton to White, Apr. 3, 1865, M473 ("conflagration"); Stanton to Tilden, Apr. 3, 1865, ibid. (passes); Lincoln to Stanton, Apr. 3, 1865, *OR*, vol. 46, pt. 3, p. 509; Brooks, *Washington in Lincoln's Time* (1958), 219.

47 Lincoln to Stanton, Apr. 4, 1865, *OR*, vol. 46, pt. 3, p. 544; Stanton to Dana, Apr. 4, 1865, M473; Stanton to Dix, Apr. 4, 1865, ibid. (11 p.m.); *Washington Evening Star*, Apr. 5, 1865 (illumination); Townsend, *Anecdotes of the Civil War*, 122–23.

48 Stanton to Colfax et al., Apr. 4, 1865, M473; Stanton to Beecher, Apr. 5, 1865, ibid.; Stanton to Garrison, Apr. 5, 1865, ibid.; Stanton to Anderson, Apr. 5, 1865, Anderson Papers; Stanton to Anderson, Apr. 6, 1865, ibid. (delay); Stanton to Anderson, Apr. 8, 1865, ibid. ("deeply regret"). On the Charleston trip, see Applegate, *The Most Famous Man in America*, 1–17.

49 Stanton to Lincoln, Apr. 5, 1865, Lincoln Papers, LC (three messages); Stanton to Lincoln, Apr. 6, 1865, ibid. (two messages); Fanny Seward Diary, Apr. 5 and 9, 1865, Seward Papers, reel 198; Stahr, *Seward*, 431–32.

50 Dana to Stanton, Apr. 5, 1865, *OR*, vol. 46, pt. 3, p. 575; Dana to Stanton, Apr. 7, 1865, ibid., 619; Grant, *Personal Memoirs*, 2:506 (Stanton "took the

liberty of countermanding the order authorizing any meeting of the legislature").

51 Stanton to Dix, Apr. 7, 1865, M473; *New York Times*, Apr. 8, 1865; Stanton to Dix, Apr. 8, 1865, M473; Dana to Stanton, Apr. 8, 1865, *OR*, vol. 46, pt. 3, pp. 657–58; *New York Times*, Apr. 9, 1865.

52 Grant to Stanton, Apr. 9, 1865, *OR*, vol. 46, pt. 3, p. 633; Stanton to Grant, Apr. 9, 1865, ibid.; Dana to Stanton, Apr. 9, 1865, ibid., 677; Stanton to Weitzel, Apr. 9, 1865, ibid., 678; Grant to Stanton, Apr. 9, 1865, ibid., 663–64; Stanton to Dix, Apr. 9, 1865, M473 (9:30 p.m.); *New York Times*, Apr. 10, 1865; Conn, *Washington's Epiphany*, 39–40; Flower, *Edwin McMasters Stanton*, 374 ("invited me to pray"); Hall, *A Discourse Preached by Request*, 26–28 ("wall of strength"). On Stanton's relation with Epiphany, see also Brooks report, May 2, 1863, in Burlingame, *Lincoln Observed*, 47 ("goes to an Episcopal church—if at all"); Charles Dana, "Edwin Stanton," *New York Sun*, Dec. 25, 1869 ("Although not a member of any church—unless he may have recently joined one").

53 Dana to Stanton, Apr. 10, 1865, *OR*, vol. 46, pt. 3, p. 684; Weitzel to Stanton, Apr. 10, 1865, ibid., 696–97; Stanton testimony, May 18, 1867, House Report No. 7, 40th Cong., 1st Sess., p. 400 (1867); Brooks, *Washington in Lincoln's Time* (1958), 223 ("most people were sleeping").

54 *St. Cloud (Minn.) Democrat*, May 25, 1865, quoting *New York Independent*; Stanton to Ashley, Sept. 14, 1866, Tarbell Papers. Tarbell noted on her copy that the original was in the possession of Flower, who later published it in *Edwin McMasters Stanton*, 311. The Fehrenbachers assign Stanton's quote of Lincoln a grade of D, saying, "This recollection was self-serving, politically motivated, and chronologically erroneous, but there seems to be no evidence controverting the central assertion, that at some point during those final days Stanton sought to resign and was persuaded otherwise by Lincoln" (*Recollected Words*, 417).

55 Lincoln speech, Apr. 11, 1865, in Basler, *The Collected Works of Abraham Lincoln*, 8:399–405; Masur, *Lincoln's Last Speech*.

56 Sumner to Chase, Apr. 12, 1865, Chase Papers, LC, box 24, images 112–14; Chase to Lincoln, Apr. 11 and 12, 1865, Lincoln Papers, LC; *New York Commercial Advertiser*, Apr. 13, 1865; Masur, *Lincoln's Last Speech*, 166–70 (press reaction).

57 Lincoln to Weitzel, Apr. 12, 1865, in Basler, *The Collected Works of Abraham Lincoln*, 8:405–406; Weitzel to Lincoln, Apr. 12, 1865, *OR*, vol. 46, pt. 3, p. 724; Dana to Stanton, Apr. 12, 1865, Edwin Stanton Papers, LC, box 25, image 200 (quotes *Richmond [Va.] Whig*; received 5:30 p.m.); Lincoln to Weitzel, Apr. 12, 1865, in Basler, *The Collected Works of Abraham Lincoln*, 8:406–7 (starts "I have just seen" and sent 6 p.m.); Dana to Stanton, Apr.

12, 1865, Edwin Stanton Papers, LC, box 25, image 208 (Weitzel ordered out of Richmond); Stanton testimony, May 18, 1867, House Report No. 7, 40th Cong., 1st Sess., p. 400 (1867). The chronology suggests that Dana's message prompted Lincoln's message.

58 *Washington Evening Star*, Apr. 10, 1865 (Raleigh captured by Sherman); Stanton to Grant, Apr. 12, 1865, *OR*, vol. 46, pt. 3, p. 718 ("I desire very much to consult with you"); Grant to Stanton, Apr. 12, 1865, ibid. ("leave here for Washington"); Stanton to Dix, Apr. 13, 1865, ibid., 744 (four points); *New York Times*, Apr. 14, 1865; *Washington Evening Star*, Apr. 14, 1865 (Grant arrived prior afternoon).

59 *Washington Evening Star*, Apr. 14, 1865; Testimony of David Stanton, Kilburn Knox, and John Hatter, May 16, 1865, in Steers, *The Trial*, 226–27.

60 Stanton to Dix, Apr. 15, 1865, *OR*, vol. 46, pt. 3, p. 780; Stanton to Adams, Apr. 15, 1865, ibid., 785.

61 Gienapp and Gienapp, *Civil War Diary of Gideon Welles*, 623 (Apr. 14, 1865). Secondary accounts include Donald, *Lincoln*, 590–92; Goodwin, *Team of Rivals*, 731–33; Harris, *Lincoln's Last Months*, 220–21.

62 Stanton testimony, May 18, 1867, House Report No. 7, 40th Cong., 1st Sess., p. 401 (1867); Dickens to Forster, Feb. 4, 1868, in House and Storey, *The Letters of Charles Dickens*, 12:34–35.

63 Welles, "Lincoln and Johnson," 525–27.

64 Seward, *Seward at Washington*, 274–75.

65 Stanton to Palmer, Apr. 14, 1865, Edwin Stanton Papers, LC, box 25, image 217 (arrest Magoffin); Randall, *Diary of Orville Hickman Browning*, 2:20 (Apr. 15, 1865) (Stanton said he was "at home last night—quite a number of the Military had assembled at his house, and had been making them a speech"); Welles, notes re: Lincoln assassination, ca. 1870, Welles Papers, Huntington, box 7 ("colored procession went with shouts and cheers"); *Cincinnati Enquirer*, Apr. 14, 1918 ("employees of the arsenal" marched through town, stopped at Stanton's).

Chapter 15: "The Stain of Innocent Blood"

1 *Cincinnati Enquirer*, Apr. 14, 1918 (Sterling's account). The *New York Times* reported on April 16, 1865, "Two gentlemen who went to the Secretary of War to apprise him of the attack on Mr. Lincoln, met at the residence of the former a man muffled in a cloak who, when accosted by them, hastened away." Thomas and Hyman, citing the "manuscript diary of an anonymous War Department clerk," now apparently lost at the Library of Congress, give a somewhat similar account, saying that the messenger told Stanton, "[I] saw a man behind the tree-box, but he ran away, and I did not follow him" (*Stanton*, 396).

2 Gienapp and Gienapp, *Civil War Diary of Gideon Welles*, 625 (Apr. 1865); Fanny Seward diary, Apr. 14, 1865, Seward Papers, reel 198; Welles, notes re: Lincoln assassination, ca. 1870, Welles Papers, Huntington, box 7. Welles revised and extended his 1865 diary entry in the 1870 notes. Secondary accounts include Stahr, *Seward*, 1–3; Swanson, *Manhunt*, 99–102; Thomas and Hyman, *Stanton*, 396–97.

3 Gienapp and Gienapp, *Civil War Diary of Gideon Welles*, 625–26 (Apr. 1865); Welles, notes re: Lincoln assassination, ca. 1870, Welles Papers, Huntington, box 7.

4 Gienapp and Gienapp, *Civil War Diary of Gideon Welles*, 626–27 (Apr. 1865). Robert Redford's 2010 movie *The Conspirator*, with Kevin Kline as Stanton, has an excellent version of Stanton's first few minutes at the Petersen House.

5 Stanton to Kennedy, Apr. 15, 1865, *OR*, vol. 46, pt. 3, p. 783; Tanner to Welch, Apr. 17, 1865, in Peckham, "James Tanner's Account," 179–80; Steers, *Blood on the Moon*, 128–29; Swanson, *Manhunt*, 114–18.

6 Stanton to Dix, Apr. 15, 1865, *OR*, vol. 46, pt. 3, pp. 780–81 (three messages); McPhail to War Department, Apr. 15, 1865, in Steers, *Blood on the Moon*, 171.

7 Steers, *Lincoln's Assassination*, 85–86; Steers, *Blood on the Moon*, 173–74; Swanson, *Manhunt*, 119–21.

8 *New York Herald*, Apr. 17, 1865, quoting *Cincinnati Enquirer*; *New York Times*, Apr. 17, 1865; Stanton order, Apr. 28, 1865, *OR*, vol. 46, pt. 3, p. 1002.

9 Leale, *Lincoln's Last Hours*, 10–11; Swanson, *Manhunt*, 106–10, 121.

10 *Washington Evening Star*, Apr. 15, 1865; *New York Herald*, Apr. 16, 1865; *New York Times*, Apr. 17, 1865 (account by Maunsell Field); Tanner to Welch, Apr. 17, 1865, in Peckham, "James Tanner's Account," 179–80; Gienapp and Gienapp, *Civil War Diary of Gideon Welles*, 628 (Apr. 1865).

11 Nicolay and Hay, "The Fourteenth of April," 436; Taft, "Lincoln's Last Hours," 635; James Tanner, "Tanner Also Present," *Washington Post*, Apr. 16, 1905; Tanner to Frear, May 7, 1926, in *Congressional Record*, 69th Cong., 1st Sess., p. 10420 (June 1, 1926). Sources that claim Stanton referred to "angels" include Swanson, *Manhunt*, 138, and Winik, *April 1865*, 258. Discussions include Cannon, "Lincoln"; Eisenschiml, *Why Was Lincoln Murdered?*, 482–85; Fox, "A Phrase for the Ages"; Gopnik, "Angels and Ages"; Guelzo, "Does Lincoln Still Belong to the Ages?"

12 Cabinet to Johnson, Apr. 15, 1865, in Graf, *The Papers of Andrew Johnson*, 7:553; Stanton to Dix, Apr. 15, 1865, *OR*, vol. 46, pt. 3, p. 781; Roger Catlin, "Newseum Exhibition Follows the Day of Lincoln's Death, Edition by Edition," *Washington Post*, Feb. 13, 2015 (notes that 8:45 a.m. edition had Stanton's message).

13 Steers, *Blood on the Moon*, 268–70; Swanson, *Manhunt*, 140–41. Swanson is

my source for Stanton's gift to Mary Jane Welles; Swanson saw the lock of hair and envelope "in a private collection" (426).

14 Gienapp and Gienapp, *Civil War Diary of Gideon Welles*, 628 (Apr. 1865); *Baltimore Sun*, Apr. 17, 1865 ("wrapped in an American flag"); Steers, *Blood on the Moon*, 268–70; Swanson, *Manhunt*, 140–41.

15 Stanton to Adams, Apr. 15, 1865, *OR*, vol. 46, pt. 3, pp. 785–86; Stanton to Sherman, Apr. 15, 1865, *OR*, vol. 47, pt. 3, pp. 220–21; Sherman to Halleck, Apr. 18, 1865, ibid., 425 ("news of Mr. Lincoln's death"); Hodes, *Mourning Lincoln*, 92–93 (reaction in London).

16 Gienapp and Gienapp, *Civil War Diary of Gideon Welles*, 629 (Apr. 15, 1865); Stanton to Dix, Apr. 15, 1865, in *New York Times*, Apr. 16, 1865.

17 Grant to Ord, Apr. 15, 1865, *OR*, vol. 46, pt. 3, p. 762; Ord to Grant, Apr. 15, 1865, ibid.; Grant to Ord, Apr. 15, 1865, ibid.; Stanton to Olcott, Apr. 15, 1865, ibid., 784; Olcott to Stanton, Apr. 15, 1865, ibid.; Stanton to Baker, Apr. 15, 1865, ibid., 783.

18 Hall, *A Mournful Easter*; Hodes, *Mourning Lincoln*, 97–114.

19 *Detroit Free Press*, Apr. 16, 1865 (Davis at Danville in early April); Swanson, *Bloody Crimes*, 82–84 (Davis left Danville on April 10).

20 Grant to Julia Grant, Apr. 16, 1865, in Simon, *The Papers of Ulysses Grant*, 14:396 ("Halleck will go to Richmond"); Halleck to Lieber, Apr. 18, 1865, Lieber Papers, Huntington, box 10; Marszalek, *Commander of All Lincoln's Armies*, 222.

21 Gienapp and Gienapp, *Civil War Diary of Gideon Welles*, 630 (Apr. 16, 1865); Welles to Johnson, July 27, 1869, in Graf, *The Papers of Andrew Johnson*, 16:74–77; Welles, "Lincoln and Johnson," 528. The quotes are from Welles's article. Thomas and Hyman, *Stanton*, 404, say they saw notes by Stanton showing that "there was no pre-arrangement between him and the legislators as Welles always insisted."

22 *New York Tribune*, Apr. 19, 1865 (Arnold confesses to "plot to kidnap the President and deliver him to Richmond"); *Washington Evening Star*, Apr. 20, 1865 ("all parties"); Chamlee, *Lincoln's Assassins*, 79–81; Steers, *Blood on the Moon*, 170–71, 174–78.

23 *Cleveland Daily Leader*, Apr. 13, 1865 ("What Will Kirby Smith Do?"); *Burlington (Iowa) Hawk-Eye*, Apr. 15, 1865 ("best authority" for saying Kirby Smith will surrender); Sherman to Stanton, Apr. 15, 1865, *OR*, vol. 47, pt. 3, p. 221 (received Apr. 17); *Cincinnati Enquirer*, Apr. 18, 1865 ("give the same terms as Grant gave to Lee"); *Cleveland Daily Leader*, Apr. 18, 1865 ("Sherman has offered Johnston the same terms which Grant held out to Lee"); *New York Times*, Apr. 18, 1865 (similar); *New York World*, Apr. 18, 1865 (similar).

24 Moorhead to Stanton, Apr. 20, 1865, *OR*, vol. 46, pt. 3, p. 874; Stanton to Moorhead, Apr. 20, 1865, ibid. (no stop in Pittsburgh); Dix to Stanton, Apr.

20, 1865, ibid., 875; Stanton to Dix, Apr. 20, 1865, ibid. Swanson, *Bloody Crimes* covers the funeral train in detail.

25 Davis to Du Pont, Apr. 19, 1865, Du Pont Papers; *Washington Evening Star*, Apr. 20, 1865.

26 Stanton draft, Apr. 20, 1865, Edwin Stanton Papers, New-York Historical Society; *New York Times*, Apr. 21, 1865 (text of the poster).

27 Stanton note, Apr. 1865, Lincoln Assassination Papers, NA, M599, reel 2 (Mudd); Stanton notes, Apr. 26, 1865, ibid. (interview); Steers, *Blood on the Moon*, 144–54, 166–70.

28 Jones to Stanton, Apr. 20, 1865, NA, M599, reel 2 (Booth in Chicago); Burnett to Sweet, Apr. 22, 1865, ibid. (search in Chicago); Turner, *Beware the People Weeping*, 101–11, is especially good on the confused information facing Stanton.

29 *Cincinnati Enquirer*, Apr. 18, 1865, quoting *New York World*; *Detroit Free Press*, Apr. 23, 1865 (Davis headed for Kirby Smith); *Cleveland Daily Leader*, May 1, 1865 (Smith's "powerful, well-organized" army); Winik, *April 1865*, 147–63 (guerrilla warfare).

30 Sherman to Stanton, Apr. 15, 1865, OR, vol. 47, pt. 3, p. 221; Hitchcock to Grant, Apr. 20, 1865, ibid., 257 ("important dispatches"); Grant to Julia Grant, Apr. 20, 1865, in Simon, *The Papers of Ulysses Grant*, 14:422 ("important dispatches").

31 Gienapp and Gienapp, *Civil War Diary of Gideon Welles*, 632–33 (Apr. 21, 1865); *Washington Evening Star*, Apr. 21, 1865.

32 Grant to Stanton, Apr. 21, 1865, in Simon, *The Papers of Ulysses Grant*, 14:423.

33 Sherman to Grant or Halleck, Apr. 18, 1865, OR, vol. 47, pt. 3, pp. 243–45 (includes terms); White, *American Ulysses*, 415 (Grant "surprised" by Sherman's terms).

34 Secondary sources on the Sherman-Johnston terms include Marszalek, "The Stanton-Sherman Controversy"; Naroll, "Lincoln and the Sherman Peace Fiasco."

35 Stanton to [cabinet member, Apr. 21, 1865,] Edwin Stanton Papers, New-York Historical Society ("a meeting of the Cabinet will be held this evening 8 o'clock at the President's residence corner of H and 18th Street"); Gienapp and Gienapp, *Civil War Diary of Gideon Welles*, 633–34 (Apr. 21, 1865); Grant to Sherman, Apr. 21, 1865, in Simon, *The Papers of Ulysses Grant*, 14:424–25; Stanton to Dix, Apr. 22, 1865, in *New York Times*, Apr. 23, 1865 (prints Stanton's nine points). For Sherman's order in the papers, see *Wilmington (N.C.) Herald*, Apr. 20, 1865; *Detroit Free Press*, Apr. 24, 1865. A few weeks later Stanton tried to explain to Sherman, through Howard, why he had issued the nine points. "[Stanton] said in reply that you [Sherman] put the government entirely on the defensive by announcing in orders that the terms

had been agreed upon which would give peace from the Potomac to the Rio Grande, etc. This order appeared in the morning papers, and on account of it, in order to show the people why the government broke the peace established, he deemed it proper to publish some of the reasons for disapproving the terms." Howard to Sherman, May 12, 1865, *OR*, vol. 47, pt. 3, p. 476. Stanton was wrong in recalling that Sherman's order was in the Northern papers *before* his points but right that concern about being "entirely on the defensive" was the reason he drafted and published his "points."

36 Stanton to Grant, Mar. 3, 1865, in Simon, *The Papers of Ulysses Grant*, 14: 91 (drafted by Lincoln); *New York Herald*, Apr. 17, 1865 (threat to Stanton); *New York Times*, Apr. 17, 1865 (same); Stanton to Dickson, May 28, 1865, Dickson Papers ("severe trial").

37 Gienapp and Gienapp, *Civil War Diary of Gideon Welles*, 633–34 (Apr. 21, 1865); Grant to Sherman, Apr. 21, 1865, in Simon, *The Papers of Ulysses Grant*, 14:424–25; Stanton to Grant, Apr. 21, 1865, ibid., 423–24 (instructions); Stanton to Dix, Apr. 22, 1865, in *New York Times*, Apr. 23, 1865 (Stanton's nine points).

38 Stanton to Grant, Apr. 21, 1865, in Simon, *The Papers of Ulysses Grant*, 14:423–24; Grant to Julia Grant, Apr. 21, 1865, ibid., 428–29; Stanton to Halleck, Apr. 21, 1865, *OR*, vol. 47, pt. 3, p. 264 (sent 10 p.m.).

39 Sherman to Stoneman, Apr. 18, 1865, *OR*, vol. 47, pt. 3, p. 249 ("cease hostilities" and "come to me near Raleigh"); Halleck to Stanton, Apr. 22, 1865, ibid., 477; Stanton to Halleck, Apr. 22, 1865, *OR*, vol. 46, pt. 3, p. 877.

40 Stanton to Dix, Apr. 22, 1865, *OR*, vol. 46, pt. 3, pp. 285–86.

41 Stanton to Dix, Apr. 22, 1865, in *New York Times*, Apr. 23, 1865. Some papers omitted the nine points or printed them separately, which displeased Stanton so much that he had Dana chastise the editors. Dana to Craig, Apr. 24, 1865, M473; Dana to *Baltimore American*, Apr. 25, 1865, ibid.

42 Grant to Stanton, Apr. 24, 1865, *OR*, vol. 47, pt. 3, p. 293 (sent 9 a.m. from Raleigh); Gienapp and Gienapp, *Civil War Diary of Gideon Welles*, 634–35 (Apr. 25, 1865); Stanton to Dix, Apr. 25, 1865, in *New York Times*, Apr. 26, 1865 (sent 10:25 p.m.; reports that dispatch just arrived from Grant in Raleigh; quotes parts of Grant's message).

43 Baker, *The Secret Service in the Late War*, 540–41; Swanson, *Manhunt*, 348–50.

44 Stanton to Dix, Apr. 27, 1865, in *New York Times*, Apr. 28, 1865; Stanton and Welles to Navy Yard, Apr. 27, 1865, Edwin Stanton Papers, LC, box 43, image 101 (allow Barnes, Holt, and others to board *Montauk*; examine Booth's body); Barnes to Stanton, Apr. 27, 1865, in Steers, *Blood on the Moon*, 262–63; Stanton testimony, May 18, 1867, House Report No. 7, 40th Cong., 1st Sess., p. 409 (1867) ("under lock and key"); Alford, *Fortune's Fool*, 316–22 (inspection on *Montauk* and burial at arsenal).

45   Grant to Stanton, Apr. 26, 1865, *OR*, vol. 47, pt. 3, p. 311; Stanton to Thomas, Apr. 27, 1865, *OR*, vol. 49, pt. 1, p. 546; Dana (for Stanton) to Dix, Apr. 28, 1865, M473; Stanton to Dix, Apr. 28, 1865, in *New York Times*, Apr. 29, 1865 (relays news from Grant of Johnston surrender).

46   Speed to Johnson, Apr. 28, 1865, in Graf, *The Papers of Andrew Johnson*, 7:651 (one-sentence opinion); Johnson order, May 1, 1865, ibid., 8:12–13 (forms military commission); Stanton to Townsend, May 1, 1865, M473 (summons Hunter for military commission); Grant to Halleck, May 1, 1865, in Simon, *The Papers of Ulysses Grant*, 14:439 (summoning officers for military commission); Leonard, *Lincoln's Avengers*, 63–68; Witt, *Lincoln's Code*, 285–98. In early July, after the trial and on the eve of the executions, Speed wrote to Lieber, "[I am] preparing my opinion upon the question of the jurisdiction of a military court to try the assassins. My purpose was to have sent you a rough draft and obtained a full and free criticism upon it. Could you make it convenient to visit Washington, a personal interview would be very much more pleasant to me." Speed to Lieber, July 5, 1865, Lieber Papers, Huntington, box 62. The final opinion is dated just "July 1865," suggesting it may well have been finished after the executions. Speed to Johnson, July 1865, in *Official Opinions of the Attorneys-General*, 11:297–317.

47   Stanton draft procedures, [May 2, 1865,] Edwin Stanton Papers, New-York Historical Society; Williams, "Military Justice, Right or Wrong."

48   Leonard, *Lincoln's Avengers*, 67 (Bingham and Burnett); Magliocca, *American Founding Son*, 92 (Bingham).

49   Cyrus Comstock Diary, May 8, 1865, Comstock Papers; Townsend to Comstock and Porter, May 9, 1865, Edwin Stanton Papers, LC, box 27, image 1; *Philadelphia Inquirer*, May 13, 1865 (notes that Tompkins replaced Comstock and Porter); Porter, *Campaigning with Grant*, 501 (defense counsel claimed Comstock and Porter biased because they were on Grant's staff and "he was one of the high officials who was an intended victim of the assassins"); Turner, *Beware the People Weeping*, 150–51.

50   Stanton to Holt, May 2, 1865, Edwin Stanton Papers, LC, box 26, image 223; Beale, *Diary of Gideon Welles*, 2:299–300 (May 2, 1865) (Stanton presented to cabinet a paper from Holt naming Davis and others "in the conspiracy to assassinate President Lincoln"); Johnson proclamation, May 2, 1865, in Graf, *The Papers of Andrew Johnson*, 8:15–16; Leonard, *Lincoln's Avengers*, 63–65 (naming Davis was a "bold and irrevocable step").

51   *Cincinnati Enquirer*, May 5, 1865; *New York Times*, May 5, 1865; *New York Tribune*, May 5, 1865.

52   *New York Evening Post*, May 10, 1865; *Albany (N.Y.) Evening Journal*, May 11, 1865; *New York Commercial Advertiser*, May 11, 1865; *New York Times*, May 11, 1865; *New York World*, May 13, 1865.

53 Beale, *The Diary of Gideon Welles*, 2:303 (May 9, 1865) ("emphatic"); *Philadelphia Inquirer*, May 10, 1865; *Washington Morning Chronicle*, May 12, 1865.

54 *New York Tribune*, May 11, 1865.

55 Stanton to Pierrepont, May 12, 1865, *OR*, vol. 46, pt. 3, pp. 1141–42; Stanton to Pierrepont and Cutting, May 13, 1865, ibid., 1149; Stanton to Pierrepont, May 18, 1865, M473 ("you are right in taking no action until I can consult you personally").

56 *New York Herald*, May 10, 1865 (trial behind closed doors); *New York Commercial Advertiser*, May 15, 1865 (trial opened Saturday); *New York World*, May 15, 1865 (similar); Kautz, "Memoir," vol. 2, Kautz Papers; Leonard, *Lincoln's Avengers*, 67–71.

57 *Pittsburgh Gazette*, May 17, 1865 (Knox testimony); Steers, *The Trial*, 226–27.

58 Stanton to Halleck, May 18, 1865, M473; Stanton to Wilson, May 19, 1865, *OR*, vol. 49, pt. 2, p. 839; Stanton to Potter, May 22, 1865, M473; Stanton to Seward, June 1, 1865, Seward Papers, reel 89.

59 Dana to Miles, May 22, 1865, *OR*, ser. 2, 8:565.

60 *Philadelphia Inquirer*, May 26, 1865; *Washington Evening Star*, May 26, 1865; *Brooklyn Daily Eagle*, May 26, 1865; *New York Tribune*, May 27, 1865; *Columbian Register* (New Haven, Ct.), May 27, 1865; Weed to Stanton, May 27, 1865, Edwin Stanton Papers, LC, box 27, images 139–40; Stanton to Miles, May 28, 1865, *OR*, ser. 2, 2:577.

61 Grant testimony, May 18, 1865, in *New York Tribune*, May 20, 1865; Sherman to Rawlins, May 19, 1865, *OR*, vol. 47, pt. 3, p. 531 ("vandal Sherman"); Grant to Sherman, May 19, 1865, ibid. ("want to talk to you upon matters about which you feel sore"); Sherman testimony, May 22, 1865, in *New York Times*, June 1, 1865; Tap, *Over Lincoln's Shoulder*, 248–51.

62 *New York Tribune*, May 23, 1865; *Chicago Tribune*, May 25, 1865; Royster, *Memoirs of General W. T. Sherman*, 866; Grant, *Personal Memoirs*, 2:534 (Sherman "showed his resentment for the cruel and harsh treatment that had unnecessarily been inflicted on him by the Secretary of War by refusing to take his extended hand").

63 Grant to Sherman, May 27, 1865, *OR*, vol. 47, pt. 3, p. 576; Sherman to Grant, May 28, 1865, ibid., 581–82; Sherman to Grant, May 28, 1865, ibid., 582–83.

64 Stanton to Dix, May 27, 1865, in *New York Times*, May 28, 1865.

65 Stanton to Lincoln, Mar. 24, 1865, *OR*, vol. 46, pt. 3, p. 96 (please ask Grant about Yeatman); Lincoln to Stanton, Mar. 25, 1865, ibid., 109 ("Grant does not seem to know very much about Yeatman"); Beecher to Stanton, May 3, 1865, Howard Papers (recommends Howard); Chase to Stanton, May 5, 1865, in Niven, *Chase Papers* 5:40; Stanton to Beecher, May 12, 1865, M473 (thanks for recommendation; Howard "arrived this morning, accepts and will go to work at once"); Stanton to Halleck, May 13, 1865, ibid. (Howard

appointed; consider confiscated lands); *Washington Evening Star*, May 13, 1865 (Howard will head Bureau); Howard, *Autobiography*, 2:208 ("here's your Bureau").

66 Beale, *The Diary of Gideon Welles*, 2:301 (May 9, 1865) ("no great difference"); *Cincinnati Daily Gazette*, May 10, 1865; *Pittsburgh Commercial*, May 10, 1865; *New York Herald*, May 19, 1865; *Detroit Free Press*, June 13, 1865 (Johnson's views "not at all in harmony with the views of the false philanthropists").

67 Johnson amnesty proclamation, May 29, 1865, in Graf, *The Papers of Andrew Johnson*, 8:128–30; Johnson North Carolina proclamation, May 29, 1865, ibid.; Stanton testimony, May 18, 1867, House Report No. 7, 40th Cong., 1st Sess., p. 401 (1867).

68 *Brooklyn Daily Eagle*, May 30, 1865; *New York Times*, May 30, 1865; *Philadelphia Inquirer*, May 30, 1865 ("prefers to leave the North Carolinians to their own judgment"); *Columbia (S.C.) Phoenix*, June 6, 1865.

69 Stanton to Halleck, June 7, 1865, M473; Stanton to Johnson, June 14, 1865, in Graf, *The Papers of Andrew Johnson*, 8:243–44; Stanton to Garrett, June 21, 1865, M473 (two messages); Stanton to Seward, June 22 and 23, 1865, ibid.; Stanton to Meigs, June 30, 1865, Edwin Stanton Papers, LC, box 43, image 141 (government transportation and help for Barton); Oates, *A Woman of Valor*.

70 *Baltimore Sun*, July 4, 1865; Speed to Lieber, July 5, 1865, Lieber Papers, Huntington; Castel, *The Presidency of Andrew Johnson*, 34–35; Leonard, *Lincoln's Avengers*, 129–33.

71 Anna Surratt to Stanton, July 8, 1865, Edwin Stanton Papers, LC, box 28, image 23 ("she lived a Christian life, died a Christian death"); Townsend to Anna Surratt, July 20, 1865, ibid., box 44, image 16; Harlan to Holt, May 27, 1873, in Holt, *Vindication*, 6. For the debate about whether Holt did or did not show Johnson the petition, see Leonard, *Lincoln's Forgotten Ally*, 216–18, 274–77, 309–12; Marvel, *Lincoln's Autocrat*, 382–86; Turner, *Beware the People Weeping*, 173–80. William Wood claimed years later, and not very persuasively, that Johnson "strongly expressed his detestation of what he termed the 'infamous conduct of Stanton' in keeping these facts from him." *Baltimore Sun*, Mar. 9, 1885.

Chapter 16: "A Born Tyrant"

1 Gillmore to Stanton, May 29, 1865, *OR*, vol. 47, pt. 3, p. 594; Gillmore to Hatch, June 5, 1865, ibid., 627; *New Orleans Times*, July 13, 1865 (letters to Stanton); Downs, *After Appomattox*, 11–39, 89–91.

2 William Strong to Howard, Jan. 1866, in Sen. Exec. Doc. No. 27, 39th Cong. 1st Sess., p. 83; Carter, *When the War Was Over*, 6–23; Foner, *Reconstruction*, 119–23.

3 Carter, *When the War Was Over*, 6–23; Perman, *Reunion without Compromise*, 57–63.

4 Stanton to Slocum, July 13, 1865, M473; General Order No. 129, in *Philadelphia Inquirer*, July 25, 1865; Lieber to Stanton, July 30, 1865, Edwin Stanton Papers, LC, box 28, image 83 (praises use of military commissions).

5 Johnson Amnesty, May 29, 1865, in Graf, *The Papers of Andrew Johnson*, 8:128–30; Grant to Stanton, June 16, 1865, in Simon, *The Papers of Ulysses Grant*, 15:149 (Robert E. Lee); Stanton to Johnson, June 18, 1865, Johnson Papers, reel 15; Lamar to Johnson, June 18 and July 17, 1865, in Graf, *The Papers of Andrew Johnson*, 8:255, 422; *Philadelphia Inquirer*, July 24, 1865 (pardons); Stanton to Seward, Sept. 5, 1865, Edwin Stanton Papers, LC, box 28, image 179; *Cleveland Daily Leader*, Sept. 25, 1865 (Stanton saw Mallory); Foner, *Reconstruction*, 190–92.

6 Beale, *The Diary of Gideon Welles*, 2:365–66 (July 18, 1865); Leonard, *Lincoln's Avengers*, 147–52.

7 Halleck to Cutts, Apr. 22, 1865, *OR*, vol. 46, pt. 3 p. 889; Stanton to Woodman, May 18, 1865, Woodman Papers; Woodman to Stanton, May 18, 1865, ibid.; Stanton to Halleck, May 18, 1865, M473 (seeking clerk familiar with Confederate records); General Order No. 127, July 21, 1865, *OR*, ser. 3, 5:95 (forming Bureau of Confederate Records); Alford, *Fortune's Fool*, 189 ("nothing is definitively known of other arrangements [Booth] may have made or understandings he reached with Confederate officials"); Irvine, "Archive Office of the War Department"; Leonard, *Lincoln's Avengers*, 160–62, 190–98; Tidwell et al., *Come Retribution* (suggesting Confederate role in Lincoln assassination); Robert Wolfe, "Francis Lieber's Role as Archivist of the Confederate Records," in Mack and Lesesne, *Francis Lieber and the Culture of the Mind*, 42–48.

8 Speed to Stanton, June 22, 1865, in *Official Opinions of the Attorneys-General*, 11:255–58; Moore to Johnson, Aug. 3, 1865, in Graf, *The Papers of Andrew Johnson*, 8:536–37; Johnson to Howard, Aug. 16, 1865, ibid., 8:603; Egerton, *The Wars of Reconstruction*, 106–7; McFeely, *Yankee Stepfather*, 126–35. The statute referred to "such tracts of land within the insurrectionary states as shall have been abandoned, or to which the United States shall have acquired title by confiscation or sale, or otherwise." Johnson's position, in essence, was that even those Southern whites who left their farms for months or years never "abandoned" them and that the United States never "acquired title."

9 Johnson to Sharkey, Aug. 15, 1865, in Graf, *The Papers of Andrew Johnson*, 8:599–600; Chase to Sumner, Aug. 20, 1865, in Niven, *Chase Papers* 5:65; *New York Times*, Sept. 15, 1865 (Sumner's speech); Benedict, *Compromise of Principle*, 100–16; Donald, *Sumner and the Rights of Man*, 223–29. Sumner

told Welles that Stanton approved "every word" of Sumner's speech, but this seems inconsistent with Stanton's comments to Chase. Beale, *The Diary of Gideon Welles*, 2:394 (Dec. 8, 1865).

10 Stanton to Doolittle, June 15, 1865, M473; Stanton to Grant, July 28, 1865, in Simon, *The Papers of Ulysses Grant*, 15:287–88; Stanton to Grant, Aug. 12, 1865, ibid., 296; Grant to Sherman, Aug. 21, 1865, *OR*, vol. 48, pt. 2, p. 1199.

11 *Washington Evening Star*, July 10, 1865 (advertisement for Ford's); ibid., July 11, 1865 ("closed by order of the War Department"); *Philadelphia Inquirer*, July 11, 1865; Randall, *Diary of Orville Hickman Browning*, 2:37–38 (July 13, 1865); *New York Times*, July 14, 1865; *New York Tribune*, July 15, 1865; *Daily Ohio Statesman*, July 15, 1865; Nevins and Thomas, *The Diary of George Templeton Strong*, 4:21–22 (July 15, 1865); Schley and Davis to Stanton, July 18, 1865, Edwin Stanton Papers, LC, box 28, images 53–54; Johnson endorsement, July 19, 1865, in Graf, *The Papers of Andrew Johnson*, 8:434; Stanton to Schley and Davis, July 19, 1865, Edwin Stanton Papers, LC, box 44, image 16; *Daily Ohio Statesman*, July 21, 1865; *Philadelphia Inquirer*, July 25, 1865.

12 *New York Tribune*, July 17, 1865; *Philadelphia Inquirer*, July 21, 1865.

13 *New York Herald*, July 16, 1865 ("Blair Family down upon the Cabinet"); Montgomery Blair speech, Aug. 26, 1865, in *Rock Island (Ill.) Evening Argus*, Sept. 6, 1865; *National Republican*, Aug. 28, 1865 (defending Stanton against Blairs); *New York Times*, Aug. 31, 1865 (same).

14 *Bedford (Pa.) Gazette*, Aug. 18, 1865 (letter from Junius Browne); *Daily Ohio Statesman*, Aug. 21, 1865 (same); *State Rights Democrat* (Albany, Oregon), Aug. 21, 1865, quoting *San Francisco Examiner*; *Wheeling (W. Va.) Daily Intelligencer*, Aug. 23, 1865 (Hitchcock letter defending Stanton against Browne); *Cadiz (Ohio) Daily Sentinel*, Aug. 23, 1865 (Browne letter).

15 Act to Define Pay of Certain Officers and for Other Purposes, section 18, July 17, 1862, *Statutes at Large*, 12:596; Barton to Stanton, July 26, 1865, Barton Papers, Andersonville subject file; Barton to Stanton, [July 1865?], ibid.; *New York Times*, Nov. 4, 1865 ("Forty-Seven Acres of Consecrated Graves"); Faust, *This Republic of Suffering*, 212–19; Pryor, *Clara Barton*, 137–43.

16 *National Republican*, Aug. 21, 1865 (original charges against Wirz); ibid., Aug. 23, 1865 (revised charges); *Urbana (Ohio) Union*, Sept. 20, 1865; *Daily Ohio Statesman*, Oct. 12, 1865; Chipman, *Tragedy of Andersonville*, 28 (Stanton directed him to change charges); Leonard, *Lincoln's Avengers*, 158–63; Marvel, *Lincoln's Autocrat*, 387–90; Witt, *Lincoln's Code*, 298–301.

17 Hay to Stanton, July 26, 1865, Edwin Stanton Papers, LC, box 28, images 74–75 (copy in Burlingame, *At Lincoln's Side*, 105–6).

18 Bates, *Lincoln in the Telegraph Office*, 401–3; *Newport (R.I.) Daily News*, Sept. 14, 1865 (Stanton visiting Charles Russell); Hooper to Clifford, Sept. 14,

1865, Clifford Papers (expects Stanton for dinner); Stanton to Simeon Draper, Sept. 15, 1865, Edwin Stanton Papers, LC, box 28, image 220; Russell, *Memoir of Charles Russell*, 96 (relationship between Russell and Stanton).

19 *National Republican*, Sept. 7, 1865; *Newport (R.I.) Daily News*, Sept. 14 and 15, 1865; George Hammond to Stanton, Sept. 15, 1865, Edwin Stanton Papers, LC, box 28, image 216; *New York Times*, Sept. 23, 1865.

20 *Bedford (Pa.) Gazette*, Sept. 15, 1865; *Western Democrat* (Charlotte, N.C.), Sept. 26, 1865; *Cadiz (Ohio) Sentinel*, Sept. 27, 1865; *National Republican*, Oct. 23, 1865 (Seward speech); Stahr, *Seward*, 448–49.

21 *Baltimore Daily Commercial*, Oct. 6, 1865 ("admission of negro testimony"); *New York Times*, Oct. 3, 1865 ("exclusive political benefit"); *Chicago Tribune*, Dec. 1, 1865 ("frog pond"); Carter, *When the War Was Over*, 176–231; Perman, *Reunion without Compromise*, 77–81, 130–31; Foner, *Reconstruction*, 197–207.

22 *Washington Evening Star*, Nov. 2, 1865 (Parsons in Washington); Stanton to Morgan et al., Nov. 3, 1865, Edwin Stanton Papers, LC, box 44, image 33 (eleven addressees); Stanton to Beecher, Nov. 3, 1865, Beecher Family Papers; Stanton to Woodman, Nov. 6, 1865, Woodman Papers; Stanton to Sumner, Nov. 6, 1865, Sumner Papers, reel 34; Sumner to Stanton, Nov. 8, 1865, in Palmer, *The Selected Letters of Charles Sumner*, 2:344; *New York Times*, Nov. 10, 1865 (Parsons in Boston); Carter, *When the War Was Over*, 190–91 (quotes Parsons speech); Donald, *Sumner and the Rights of Man*, 235–36.

23 Stanton to Colfax, May 22, 1865, NA, M473; Stanton to Colfax, June 21, 1865, ibid.; Stanton to Colfax, Oct. 15, 1865, in Hollister, *Life of Schuyler Colfax*, 265; Colfax speech, Nov. 18, 1865, ibid., 270–71.

24 Benedict, *A Compromise of Principle*, 115–33; Foner, *Reconstruction*, 239–53; Summers, *The Ordeal of the Reunion*, 80–91.

25 *New York Times*, Dec. 5, 1865; Benedict, *Compromise of Principle*, 115–33; Castel, *Presidency of Andrew Johnson*, 55–65.

26 Johnson annual message, Dec. 4, 1865, in Graf, *The Papers of Andrew Johnson*, 9:466–85; *New York Tribune*, Dec. 6, 1865; *New York World*, Dec. 6, 1865; Castel, *Presidency of Andrew Johnson*, 55–57.

27 Wolcott, *Edwin M. Stanton*, 206–7 (includes Stanton to Pamphila Wolcott, Dec. 23, 1865).

28 Chase Diary, Jan. 2, 1866, in Niven, *Chase Papers* 1:606; *New York Times*, Jan. 3, 1866 (Stanton and Chase among pallbearers for Davis).

29 *Washington Evening Star*, Jan. 22, 1866; *National Republican*, Jan. 22, 1866; *Washington Evening Star*, Jan. 25, 1866.

30 *New York Herald*, Jan. 12, 1866; *Hartford (Ct.) Courant*, Jan. 17, 1866.

31 Grant to Stanton, Jan. 29, 1866, in Simon, *The Papers of Ulysses Grant*, 16:36–37; Stanton to Sheridan, Mar. 2, 1866, Johnson Papers, reel 21; Sherman to Belknap, Aug. 17, 1870, in Sherman, *Memoirs*, 2:467–68.

32 *Detroit Free Press*, Jan. 21, 1866 (Senate debate on Freedmen's Bureau bill); Parker to Bowers, Jan. 27, 1866, Johnson Papers, reel 20 (forwarded by Stanton to Johnson on Feb. 15, 1866).

33 *New York Tribune*, Feb. 15, 1866; *Columbian Register* (New Haven, Ct.), Feb. 16, 1866 ("very animated"); Fessenden, *Life and Public Services*, 2:34–35 ("so anxious"). Welles did not describe the Friday cabinet meeting but noted that he and Johnson discussed the veto after the cabinet meeting. Beale, *The Diary of Gideon Welles*, 2:433 (Feb. 16, 1866).

34 Beale, *The Diary of Gideon Welles*, 2:434–35 (Feb. 19, 1866); Johnson veto message, Feb. 19, 1866, in Graf, *The Papers of Andrew Johnson*, 10:398–405.

35 *Congressional Globe*, 39th Cong., 1st Sess., pp. 933–43 (Feb. 20, 1866); Castel, *Presidency of Andrew Johnson*, 67–68.

36 Johnson speech, Feb. 22, 1866, in Graf, *The Papers of Andrew Johnson*, 10:145–57; Castel, *Presidency of Andrew Johnson*, 68–70; Trefousse, *Andrew Johnson*, 243–45.

37 *New York Herald*, Feb. 20 and 23, 1866 (rumors of Stanton's resignation); Lieber to Matilda Lieber, Feb. 24, 1866, Lieber Papers, Huntington, box 36 ("muster me out"); *New York Times*, Mar. 1, 1866.

38 Beale, *The Diary of Gideon Welles*, 2:463–65 (Mar. 26, 1866); Sumner to the Duchess of Argyll, Apr. 3, 1866, in Palmer, *Selected Letters of Charles Sumner*, 2:359; Benedict, *Compromise of Principle*, 145–61; Castel, *Presidency of Andrew Johnson*, 70–73.

39 Johnson veto message, Mar. 27, 1866, in Graf, *The Papers of Andrew Johnson*, 10:312–20; Morgan to Weed, Apr. 8, 1866, Weed Papers; Beale, *The Diary of Gideon Welles*, 2:479 (Apr. 10, 1866); Riddleberger, *1866*, 97–104. It would take another hundred years before the Supreme Court ruled that laws against interracial marriage were "invidious racial discrimination." *Loving v. Virginia*, 388 U.S. 1 (1967).

40 Johnson proclamation, Apr. 2, 1866, in Graf, *The Papers of Andrew Johnson*, 10:349–52; Woods to Holt, Apr. 4, 1868, *OR*, ser. 3, 5:933; Stanton endorsement, Apr. 5, ibid.; Downs, *After Appomattox*, 146–48; Leonard, *Lincoln's Avengers*, 208–10.

41 Donald, *Sumner and the Rights of Man*, 236–67; Foner, *Reconstruction*, 251–61; Draft amendment, Apr. 30, 1866, Edwin Stanton Papers, LC, box 30, images 45–47.

42 Beale, *The Diary of Gideon Welles*, 2:495–97 (May 1, 1866); *New York Times*, May 2, 1866; *Boston Daily Advertiser*, May 2, 1866; *New York Tribune*, May 3, 1866; *New York World*, May 4, 1866; *New York Herald*, May 4, 1866 (Radicals "alarmed" because Stanton "unreservedly on the President's side").

43 *Daily Ohio Statesman*, May 3, 1866; *Philadelphia Evening Telegraph*, May 8, 1866; *Ashland (Ohio) Union*, May 9, 1866, quoting *Memphis Daily Avalanche*; Grant to Stanton, July 7, 1866, in Simon, *The Papers of Ulysses Grant*, 16:233–34; Riddleberger, *1866*, 177–82.

44 National Union Committee to Stanton, and Stanton response, both May 17, 1866, Edwin Stanton Papers, LC, box 30, images 79–82; *Boston Daily Advertiser*, May 28, 1866 (pin Stanton down).

45 Stanton speech, May 23, 1866, in Gorham, *The Life and Public Services*, 2:302–10; Beale, *The Diary of Gideon Welles*, 2:513 (May 23, 1866); *New York Times*, May 24, 1866; *Washington Evening Star*, May 24, 1866; *Boston Daily Advertiser*, May 28, 1866.

46 *Chicago Tribune*, May 25, 1866; *Hartford (Ct.) Courant*, May 25, 1866; *New York Herald*, May 25, 1866; *New York Tribune*, May 25, 1866; *Philadelphia Daily Age*, May 25, 1866; *Trenton (N.J.) State Gazette*, May 26, 1866 ("speech indicates the true ground to be taken by the Union party").

47 Stanton to Moses Odell, May 25, 1866, in *Cincinnati Daily Gazette*, Jan. 18, 1870.

48 U.S. Constitution, Fourteenth Amendment.

49 Benedict, *Compromise of Principle*, 150–87; Castel, *Presidency of Andrew Johnson*, 73–76; Magliocca, *American Founding Son*, 108–27; Summers, *Ordeal of the Reunion*, 93–99.

50 Johnson message, June 22, 1866, in Graf, *The Papers of Andrew Johnson*, 10:614–15; *New York Tribune*, June 23, 1866; *Philadelphia Evening Telegraph*, June 26, 1866 ("National Johnson Convention"); *National Republican*, June 27, 1866.

51 Morgan to Johnson, July 7, 1866, in Graf, *The Papers of Andrew Johnson*, 10:654; Dennison to Johnson, July 11, 1866, ibid., 668–69 (resignation); Welles to Doolittle, July 11, 1866, in *New Orleans Times*, July 19, 1866; *New York Herald*, July 13, 1866 (cabinet division); Stanton to Doolittle, July 16, 1866, Edwin Stanton Papers, LC, box 30, images 119–21 (draft); Harlan to Johnson, July 27, 1866, in Graf, *The Papers of Andrew Johnson*, 10:741 (resignation); Castel, *Presidency of Andrew Johnson*, 80–81; Stahr, *Seward*, 469–70.

52 Shellabarger to Comly, May 28, 1866, Comly Papers; *New York Herald*, Aug. 30, 1866 (Smithson case); *Washington Evening Star*, Feb. 14, 1867 (Smithson case).

53 *Wheeling (W. Va.) Daily Intelligencer*, July 26, 1866 (brief report of plan to arrest convention delegates); *Washington Evening Star*, July 26, 1866 (similar); Voorhies and Herron to Johnson, July 28, 1866, in Graf, *The Papers of Andrew Johnson*, 11:750; Johnson to Voorhies, July 28, 1866, ibid., 751; Baird to Stanton, July 28, 1866, in House Exec. Doc. No. 68, 39th Cong., 2d Sess., pp. 4–5 (1867). The Baird message was received in the War Department at

10:20 p.m. Saturday; Stanton later testified that he first received it on Sunday morning.

54 For the debate on Stanton's handling of Baird's message, see Castel, *Presidency of Andrew Johnson*, 82–84; Marvel, *Lincoln's Autocrat*, 405–6; Riddleberger, *1866*, 191–94; Sefton, *The United States Army and Reconstruction*, 85–87; Thomas and Hyman, *Stanton*, 495–97.

55 *New York Tribune*, July 30, 1866; Voorhies to Johnson, July 30, 1866, Johnson Papers, reel 23; Stanton to Johnson, July 31, 1866, in Graf, *The Papers of Andrew Johnson*, 10:772 (noting that Johnson had already shown him Voorhies message); Sheridan to Grant, Aug. 1, 1866, in Simon, *The Papers of Ulysses Grant*, 16:288; Sheridan to Grant, Aug. 2, 1866, ibid., 289 ("absolute massacre"); *Evansville (Ind.) Daily Journal*, Aug. 29, 1866 (quotes Sheridan); Hollandsworth, *An Absolute Massacre*.

56 *New York Tribune*, Aug. 2, 1866; *Brooklyn Daily Eagle*, Aug. 4, 1866; Carter, *When the War Was Over*, 248–54 ("never submit" on 252); Castel, *Presidency of Andrew Johnson*, 84; Foner, *Reconstruction*, 262–64.

57 Beale, *The Diary of Gideon Welles*, 2:573 (Aug. 7, 1866) ("show your flag"); *Washington Evening Star*, Aug. 18, 1866 (Stanton not among those at White House); Dewitt, *The Impeachment and Trial of Andrew Johnson*, 112–13; Riddleberger, *1866*, 201–14; Wagstaff, "The Arm-in-Arm Convention."

58 Johnson speech, Sept. 8, 1866, in Graf, *The Papers of Andrew Johnson*, 11:175–76; Castel, *Presidency of Andrew Johnson*, 89–95; Riddleberger, *1866*, 218–23; Stahr, *Seward*, 471–73.

59 Stanton to Ashley, Sept. 14, 1866, in Flower, *Edwin McMasters Stanton*, 310–12 (corrected "joust" to "jaunt").

60 Stanton to Johnson, Sept. 15, 1866, Johnson Papers, reel 24; Fanny Seward diary, Sept. 15, 1866, Seward Papers, reel 198; *National Republican*, Sept. 15, 1866; *New York Herald*, Sept. 16, 1866 (Stanton greets Johnson); *National Republican*, Sept. 17, 1866 (Seward recovering from cholera); Marvel, *Lincoln's Autocrat*, 408; Stahr, *Seward*, 474–75.

61 *New York Tribune*, Sept. 21, 1866; Randall, *Diary of Orville Hickman Browning*, 2:96–99, 105 (Oct. 2, 9, 30, 1866); Stanton notes re: Davis, Oct. 5, 1866, Edwin Stanton Papers, LC, box 31, images 36–37; Beale, *The Diary of Gideon Welles*, 2:614 (Oct. 9, 1866); *Philadelphia Evening Telegraph*, Oct. 15, 1866; *Columbia (S.C.) Phoenix*, Oct. 17, 1866 ("delay in the trial is denial of justice").

62 *Philadelphia Inquirer*, Oct. 18, 1866 (Sherman will replace Stanton); *New York Tribune*, Oct. 19, 1866; Leavitt to Stanton, Oct. 19, 1866, Edwin Stanton Papers, LC, box 31, images 70–71; Sherman to Grant, Oct. 19, 1866, in Simon, *The Papers of Ulysses Grant*, 16:339; Fessenden to Stanton, Oct. 20, 1866, Edwin Stanton Papers, LC, box 31 images 74–75; Grant to Johnson, Oct.

21, 1866, in Simon, *The Papers of Ulysses Grant*, 16:346–47; *Memphis Public Ledger*, Oct. 25, 1866; Stanton to Fessenden, Oct. 25, 1866, Edwin Stanton Papers, Huntington HM4642; *Washington Evening Star*, Oct. 26, 1866 (Sherman arrived); Randall, *Diary of Orville Hickman Browning*, 2:104 (Oct. 26, 1866); Grant to Stanton, Oct. 27, 1866, in Simon, *The Papers of Ulysses Grant*, 16:357–58 (refusing Mexico); McFeely, *Grant*, 257 ("smelled a rat"); White, *American Ulysses*, 436–37.

63 Randall, *Diary of Orville Hickman Browning*, 2:106–7 (Nov. 2, 1866); *New York Tribune*, Nov. 2, 1866 ("The Trouble in Maryland"); *Boston Daily Advertiser*, Nov. 5, 1866 (Swann visiting D.C. again); *Philadelphia Evening Telegraph*, Nov. 7, 1866 ("the people"); Castel, *Presidency of Andrew Johnson*, 96–98.

Chapter 17: "Wily Old Minister"

1 Beale, *The Diary of Gideon Welles*, 2:628 (Dec. 3, 1866); Johnson message, Dec. 3, 1866, in Graf, *The Papers of Andrew Johnson*, 11:503–17; Castel, *Presidency of Andrew Johnson*, 99–105; Stahr, *Seward*, 476–77; Trefousse, *Andrew Johnson*, 271–73.

2 Stanton to Greeley, Dec. 5, 1866, Edwin Stanton Papers, LC, box 31, image 124; Grant to Stanton, Feb. 8, 1867, in Simon, *The Papers of Ulysses Grant*, 17:50; "Partial list of outrages committed in Southern States," [Feb. 8, 1867], Edwin Stanton Papers, LC, box 31, images 225–28 (enclosed in Grant to Stanton).

3 *Ex parte Milligan*, 71 U.S. 2 (1866); *Congressional Globe*, 39th Cong., 2d Sess., p. 251 (Jan. 3, 1867); Stanton testimony, Jan. 30, 1867, Edwin Stanton Papers, LC, box 31, images 192–98; *New York Tribune*, Feb. 23, 1867 (summarizes Stanton testimony); Coleman, "Call It Peace or Call It Treason"; Fairman, *Reconstruction and Reunion*, 1:214–22; Klaus, *The Milligan Case*.

4 Boutwell, *Reminiscences*, 2:107–8; Boutwell, "Johnson's Plots and Motives," 572–74; *New York Tribune*, Sept. 21, 1866; *Bedford (Pa.) Inquirer*, Feb. 1, 1867; *Maryland Free Press*, Feb. 7, 1867; *Congressional Globe*, 39th Cong. 2d Sess., pp. 1352, 1404 (Feb. 19–20, 1867) (House debate on Stanton language).

5 Beale, *The Diary of Gideon Welles*, 3:3–5 (Jan. 4, 1867); Randall, *Diary of Orville Hickman Browning*, 2:122 (Jan. 4, 1867); Stanton to Johnson, Jan. 4, 1867, in Graf, *The Papers of Andrew Johnson*, 11:576; Johnson veto message, Jan. 5, 1867, ibid., 577–88.

6 *New York Tribune*, Dec. 22, 1866 (Stevens bill); *New York Sun*, Jan. 4, 1867 (Stevens); Beale, *The Diary of Gideon Welles*, 3:3–5 (Jan. 4, 1867); Randall, *Diary of Orville Hickman Browning*, 2:122 (Jan. 4, 1867).

7 *Congressional Globe*, 39th Cong., 2d Sess., pp. 320–21 (Jan. 7, 1867) (impeachment); Beale, *The Diary of Gideon Welles*, 3:22–23 (Jan. 18, 1867);

Johnson Colorado veto, Jan. 28, 1867, in Graf, *The Papers of Andrew Johnson*, 11:634–39; Johnson Nebraska veto, Jan. 29, 1867, ibid., 641–44; Stewart, *Impeached*, 75 (two new states would "add more Radicals in Congress").

8 *Congressional Globe*, 39th Cong., 2d Sess., pp. 943, 969–70 (Feb. 1–2, 1867); *New York Times*, Feb. 2, 1867; *Boston Journal*, Feb. 2, 1867 (similar); *New York Herald*, Feb. 4, 1867.

9 *Congressional Globe*, 39th Cong., 2d Sess., pp. 1515–18 (Feb. 18, 1867) (Senate debate on conference report).

10 "Impeachment Investigation," H. Rep. No. 7, 40th Cong., 1st Sess., pp. 183–86 (1867) (Stanton testimony on Mar. 3, 1867); ibid., 186–94 (Mar. 2, 1867); ibid., 276–82 (Apr. 1, 1867; Booth diary); ibid., 395–410 (May 18, 1867); Stewart, *Impeached*, 81–83.

11 Beale, *The Diary of Gideon Welles*, 3:42–46 (Feb. 15, 1867); Randall, *Diary of Orville Hickman Browning*, 2:130 (Feb. 15, 1867); Niven, *Gideon Welles*, 538.

12 Military Reconstruction Act, Mar. 2, 1867, *Statutes at Large*, 14:428–29; Ackerman, *We the People*, 189–209; Castel, *Presidency of Andrew Johnson*, 106–10; Summers, *Ordeal of the Reunion*, 102–6.

13 Beale, *The Diary of Gideon Welles*, 3:49 (Feb. 22, 1867) ("framed the bill differently"); Moore Diary, Mar. 10, 1867, Johnson Papers, reel 40. It is not clear from Moore's diary to which law Johnson was referring.

14 Randall, *Diary of Orville Hickman Browning*, 2:132, 190 (Feb. 26, 1867, and Mar. 31, 1868); Beale, *The Diary of Gideon Welles*, 3:50–51, 158 (Feb. 26 and Aug. 5, 1867); Stahr, *Seward*, 479–80.

15 *Washington Evening Star*, Mar. 2, 1867; Castel, *Presidency of Andrew Johnson*, 111.

16 Randall, *Diary of Orville Hickman Browning*, 2:134–35 (Mar. 4, 1867); Beale, *The Diary of Gideon Welles*, 3:58 (Mar. 4, 1867); "Notes of Colonel W. G. Moore," 106.

17 Randall, *Diary of Orville Hickman Browning*, 2:135 (Mar. 8, 1867); Beale, *The Diary of Gideon Welles*, 3:64 (Mar. 8, 1867).

18 Grant order, Mar. 11, 1867, in Simon, *The Papers of Ulysses Grant*, 17:80–81; Beale, *The Diary of Gideon Welles*, 3:64–65 (Mar. 12 and 13, 1867); *Wheeling (W. Va.) Daily Intelligencer*, Mar. 14, 1867; *New York Times*, Mar. 15, 1867.

19 Second Military Reconstruction Act, Mar. 23, 1867, *Statutes at Large*, 15:2–5; Grant to Sheridan, Apr. 5, 1867, in Simon, *The Papers of Ulysses Grant*, 17:95–96 ("district commanders shall be their own judges of the meaning of its provisions"); Sheridan orders, Apr. 10 and 20, 1867, in House Exec. Doc. No. 342, 40th Cong., 2d Sess., pp. 163–64 (1868); Sefton, *United States Army and Reconstruction*, 128–31.

20 *Evansville (Ind.) Daily Journal*, Mar. 27, 1867 (Stanton concerned that long adjournment "might be injurious to the progress of reconstruction"); *Wheeling (W. Va.) Daily Intelligencer*, Mar. 27, 1867; *Washington Evening Star*, Mar.

28, 1867; Beale, *The Diary of Gideon Welles*, 3:73 (Mar. 29, 1867) ("makes it the duty"); *National Republican*, Mar. 29, 1867 ("buffalo hunt"); *Charleston (S.C.) Daily News*, Mar. 30, 1867 ("wily old minister").

21 Randall, *Diary of Orville Hickman Browning*, 2:137 (Mar. 15, 1867); Beale, *The Diary of Gideon Welles*, 3:66 (Mar. 15, 1867); "Notes of Colonel W. G. Moore," 106; Stahr, *Seward*, 482–91; Donald, *Sumner and the Rights of Man*, 303–10.

22 Beale, *The Diary of Gideon Welles*, 3:96 (May 21, 1867) ("controverted some of the points"); Stanbery to Johnson, May 24, 1867, in *Official Opinions of the Attorneys-General*, 12:141–68; *Washington Evening Star*, May 27, 1867 (opinion); *Daily Ohio Statesman*, May 28, 1867; Castel, *Presidency of Andrew Johnson*, 126–27; Sefton, *United States Army and Reconstruction*, 131–34.

23 Sheridan to Stanton, June 3, 1867, in Graf, *The Papers of Andrew Johnson*, 12:308; *New York Times*, June 5, 1867; *Sunbury (Pa.) American*, June 8, 1867; Stanbery to Johnson, June 12, 1867, in *Official Opinions of the Attorneys-General*, 12:182–205; *New York World*, June 12, 1867; *Albany (N.Y.) Evening Journal*, June 15, 1867; Stanton opinion, June 19, 1867, in Gorham, *The Life and Public Services*, 2:363–65; *Philadelphia Inquirer*, June 19, 1867; *New York Times*, June 20, 1867.

24 Adjutant general to district commanders, June 20, 1867, in Simon, *The Papers of Ulysses Grant*, 17:200; Sheridan to Grant, June 22, 1867, ibid., 198; *Washington Evening Star*, June 24, 1867 (copy of AG letter); *New York Times*, June 24, 1867 (copy of Sheridan letter); Beale, *The Diary of Gideon Welles*, 3:117 (June 24, 1867) ("impudent and disrespectful"); Castel, *Presidency of Andrew Johnson*, 130–31; Ficklen, *History of Reconstruction in Louisiana*, 187.

25 *New York Herald*, June 21, 1867; *New York World*, June 25, 1867; *Philadelphia Evening Telegraph*, June 25, 1867; *Bloomsburg (Pa.) Democrat*, June 26, 1867; *Gallipolis (Ohio) Journal*, June 27, 1867; *New York Tribune*, June 29, 1867. Thomas and Hyman write that Stanton "collapsed" in late June 1867, but there is nothing in the news reports suggesting this (*Stanton*, 545).

26 *Washington Evening Star*, July 2 and 3, 1867; draft bill, July 1867, Edwin Stanton Papers, LC, box 33, images 178–88; Third Military Reconstruction Act, July 19, 1867, *Statutes at Large*, 15:14–16; Johnson veto message, July 19, 1867, in Graf, *The Papers of Andrew Johnson*, 12:415–23; *Washington Evening Star*, July 20, 1867 (veto override; adjournment); Grant to Stanton, July 20, 1867, in Simon, *The Papers of Ulysses Grant*, 17:235; White, *American Ulysses*, 443–44.

27 Frank Blair to Francis Blair, Aug. 2, 1867, Blair-Lee Papers; *New York World*, Aug. 2, 1867 (unnamed Philadelphia paper favors Stanton); *Flake's Bulletin* (Galveston, Tex.), Aug. 24, 1867 (Cincinnati paper favors Stanton); *New Orleans Times*, Aug. 30, 1867 (Stanton among list of candidates).

28 *New York Herald,* July 30, 1867; *Albany (N.Y.) Evening Journal,* July 30, 1867; "Notes of Colonel W. G. Moore," 107; Grant to Johnson, Aug. 1, 1867, in Simon, *The Papers of Ulysses Grant,* 17:251; *Lowell (Mass.) Daily Citizen,* Sept. 16, 1867 (Grant and Stanton cooperated on letters).

29 *Washington Evening Star,* Aug. 3, 1867 (Surratt trial report); "Notes of Colonel W. G. Moore," 108; Castel, *Presidency of Andrew Johnson,* 132–35; Johnson to Stanton, Aug. 5, 1867, Edwin Stanton Papers, LC, box 33, image 194 (requesting Booth records); Johnson to Stanton, Aug. 5, 1867, in Graf, *The Papers of Andrew Johnson,* 12:461 (requesting resignation).

30 Stanton to Johnson, Aug. 5, 1867, in Graf, *The Papers of Andrew Johnson,* 12:461; Beale, *The Diary of Gideon Welles,* 3:158 (Aug. 5, 1867); *Washington Evening Star,* Aug. 8, 1867, quoting *Philadelphia Evening Telegraph; Cincinnati Daily Gazette,* Aug. 9, 1867 (similar).

31 U.S. Constitution, art. II, sec. 2; see *National Labor Relations Board v. Canning,* 573 U.S. (2014) (recess appointments).

32 *Boston Daily Advertiser,* Aug. 7, 1867 (prints correspondence); *New York Times,* Aug. 7, 1867 (same); Woodman to Stanton, Aug. 8, 1867, Edwin Stanton Papers, LC, box 33, image 235; Nevins and Thomas, *Diary of George Templeton Strong,* 4:148 (Aug. 8, 1867); *New York Herald,* Aug. 8, 1867; *National Intelligencer,* Aug. 9, 1867 (similar).

33 Beale, *The Diary of Gideon Welles,* 3:167 (Aug. 11, 1867); Badeau, *Grant in Peace,* 90; Smith, *Grant,* 439–40; McFeely, *Grant,* 263.

34 Hooper to Woodman, July 28, 1867, Woodman Papers (Stanton in town; Ellen and children at Soldiers' Home); Johnson to Stanton, Aug. 12, 1867, in Graf, *The Papers of Andrew Johnson,* 12:476–77; Stanton to Johnson, Aug. 12, 1867, ibid., 477; Grant to Stanton, Aug. 12, 1867, in Simon, *The Papers of Ulysses Grant,* 17:268; Stanton to Grant, Aug. 12, 1867, ibid., 268–69; Stanton to Ellen Stanton, Aug. 12, 1867, in G. T. Stanton, *Edwin M. Stanton,* 54.

35 *Washington Evening Star,* July 11, 1867 (debate on return date); Stanton to Woodman, Aug. 4, 1867, Woodman Papers (expects to see him at Cotuit soon); Hooper to Clifford, Aug. 5, 1867, Clifford Papers (expects Stanton in Boston on Saturday); *Boston Daily Advertiser,* Aug. 15, 1867 (Stanton and wife will come to Boston); Hooper to Clifford, Aug. 16, 1867, Clifford Papers; Sumner to Chandler, Aug. 17, 1867, in Palmer, *Selected Letters of Charles Sumner,* 2:401. The absence of references to the younger children in the letters from August through October suggests they were not with Stanton.

36 *Semi-Weekly Wisconsin,* Aug. 17, 1867 (Stanton for president); Lieber to Thayer, Aug. 19, 1867, Lieber Papers, Huntington, box 50 ("alarmingly void of ambition"); Lieber to Thayer, Aug. 28, 1867, ibid. ("Grant is quite safe"); Lieber to Thayer, Oct. 12, 1867, ibid. ("Republicans must take up Grant").

37 Hooper to Clifford, Aug. 19, 1867, Clifford Papers; Stanton to Eddie Stanton, Aug. 22, 1867, in G. T. Stanton, *Edwin M. Stanton*, 54; Hooper to Woodman, Aug. 23, 1867, Woodman Papers; *Boston Journal*, Aug. 27, 1867 (Stanton declines public reception in Boston).

38 Stanton to Clifford, Aug. 28, 1867, Clifford Papers; Hooper to Woodman, Aug. 29, 1867, Woodman Papers; *Philadelphia Inquirer*, Aug. 30, 1867 (visit to Naushon); Hooper to Clifford, Sept. 1, 1867, Clifford Papers (visit to Nantucket); Hooper to Sumner, Sept. 1, 1867, Sumner Papers, reel 39 ("how verdant"); *New York Times*, Sept. 5, 1867 (long interview with Sumner).

39 Hooper to Sumner, Sept. 2, 1867, Sumner Papers, reel 39 ("leave here for Boston tomorrow afternoon"); Washburne to Grant, Sept. 9, 1867, in Simon, *The Papers of Ulysses Grant*, 17:292–93; *Lowell (Mass.) Daily Citizen*, Sept. 16, 1867 (Washburne re: coordination between Grant and Stanton).

40 *Vermont Transcript* (St. Albans), Sept. 13, 1867; Stanton to Ann Smith, Aug. 31, 1868, in Flower, *Edwin McMasters Stanton*, 324; Ann Smith to Flower, ca. 1900, ibid., 324–25.

41 *Vermont Transcript* (St. Albans), Sept. 20, 1867; *Burlington (Vt.) Free Press*, Sept. 20, 1867; Ellen Stanton to Eddie Stanton, Sept. 29, 1867, in Gorham, *The Life and Public Services*, 2:410.

42 Hooper to Sumner, Oct. 8, 1867, Sumner Papers, reel 39; *Cincinnati Daily Gazette*, Oct. 9, 1867 (Stanton in Washington); *Daily Ohio Statesman*, Oct. 11, 1867 (election results); *Gallipolis (Ohio) Journal*, Oct. 17, 1867 (Stanton's comments on results); John Sherman to Schuyler Colfax, Oct. 20, 1867, Colfax Papers, Rochester University; *New York Times*, Nov. 8, 1867 (Wade's comments); Castel, *Presidency of Andrew Johnson*, 146–47 (election results).

43 *New York Times*, Oct. 12, 1867 (Stanton leaving to attend wedding); John Sherman to Stanton, Oct. 16, 1867, Edwin Stanton Papers, LC, box 34, images 55–56 (invitation); *Washington Evening Star*, Oct. 18, 1867 (wedding); *Wheeling (W. Va.) Daily Intelligencer*, Oct. 18, 1867 (wedding); *Cincinnati Daily Gazette*, Oct. 19, 1867 (Stanton left Columbus for Gambier); Wolcott, *Edwin M. Stanton*, 207–8 (visit to Gambier).

44 Binney to Colfax, Nov. 2, 1867, in Foner, *Reconstruction*, 315; *New York Times*, Nov. 8, 1867; *Nashville Union & Dispatch*, Nov. 9, 1867; *Memphis Daily Avalanche*, Nov. 10, 1867 (Stanton in Pittsburgh); *Clearfield (Pa.) Republican*, Nov. 21, 1867 ("vegetating" in Pittsburgh).

45 *Philadelphia Evening Telegraph*, Nov. 11, 1867 (Stanton returned Saturday); *Washington Evening Star*, Nov. 11, 1867 (Stanton returned Friday); *Boston Daily Journal*, Nov. 13, 1867 (Senate will consider Stanton); ibid., Nov. 14, 1867 (Stanton called on Grant); *Georgia Weekly Telegraph* (Macon, Ga.), Nov. 22, 1867 ("busily arranging").

Chapter 18: "Stand Firm!"

1 *Boston Daily Journal*, Nov. 13, 1867; *Georgia Weekly Telegraph* (Macon, Ga.), Nov. 22, 1867; *New York Tribune*, Nov. 23, 1867; *Albany (N.Y.) Evening Journal*, Nov. 25, 1867; *Washington Evening Star*, Nov. 29, 1867.

2 *Washington Evening Star*, Nov. 26, 1867 (summary of impeachment report); *Charles Town (W. Va.) Spirit of Jefferson*, Dec. 3, 1867 (impeachment delays all other business); *Washington Evening Star*, Dec 7, 1867; Stewart, *Impeached*, 101–13.

3 *Washington Evening Star*, Dec. 16, 1867 (obituary); Stanton to James Hutchison, Dec. 16, 1867, Wilkins-Hutchison-Wells Family Papers; Stanton to Eddie Stanton, Dec. 17, 1867, courtesy Catherine Stanton Richert; Stanton to Lucy Stanton, Dec. 20, 1867, in Wolcott, *Edwin M. Stanton*, 209; *Washington Evening Star*, Dec. 23, 1867 (Stanton back in Washington). Most authors, following Wolcott, assert that Stanton was in Gambier on his birthday, Dec. 14, but the letters show that he had not yet gone to Gambier, that he visited his mother on about Dec. 18 or 19.

4 Johnson message, Dec. 12, 1867, in Graf, *The Papers of Andrew Johnson*, 13:328–41; *Detroit Free Press*, Dec. 17, 1867.

5 *Philadelphia Evening Telegraph*, Dec. 13, 1867 (defending Stanton); *New York World*, Dec. 18, 1867.

6 Tenure of Office Act, Mar. 2, 1867, *Statutes at Large*, 14:430–32; Gorham, *The Life and Public Services*, 2:413–26 (Stanton draft for Howard).

7 *Washington Evening Star*, Jan. 8, 1868; *New York Times*, Jan. 9, 1868. Welles complained that Howard gave the papers his report before "either the Senate or his committee has seen it." Beale, *The Diary of Gideon Welles*, 3:255 (Jan. 10, 1868).

8 Castel, *Presidency of Andrew Johnson*, 156–58, 163–64; Stewart, *Impeached*, 118–20; White, *American Ulysses*, 453–55.

9 Gorham, *The Life and Public Services*, 2:426–28 (Stanton's statement); Stanton to Fessenden, Jan. 13, 1868, Edwin Stanton Papers, Huntington (cover letter); *Evansville (Ind.) Daily Journal*, Jan. 15, 1868 (summarizing debate).

10 *Senate Executive Journal*, Jan. 13, 1868; *Nashville Union & Dispatch*, Jan. 15, 1868 ("Stanton was allowed"); *Daily Ohio Statesman*, Jan. 15, 1868 (Stanton and Grant conferred); *New York Times*, Jan. 14, 1868 ("establish his claims").

11 Grant to Johnson, Jan. 14, 1868, in Simon, *The Papers of Ulysses Grant*, 18:102–3; *Washington Evening Star*, Jan. 14, 1868; *New York Times*, Jan. 15, 1868; *New York World*, Jan. 15, 1868; *Wheeling (W. Va.) Daily Intelligencer*, Jan. 15, 1868. On Grant's supposed annoyance with Stanton, see Sherman to Grant, Jan. 27, 1868, in Simon, *The Papers of Ulysses Grant*, 18:107–9;

Badeau, *Grant in Peace*, 126 (Grant "disliked extremely the behavior of Stanton").

12 *New York Times*, Jan. 15, 1868; Stanton to Pamphila Wolcott, Jan. 18, 1868, in Wolcott, *Edwin M. Stanton*, 210; Badeau, *Grant in Peace*, 139 (Pierrepont advised Stanton to resign).

13 Sumner to John Bright, Jan. 18, 1868, in Palmer, *Selected Letters of Charles Sumner*, 2:415–16. See also Stanton to Pamphila Wolcott, Jan. 28, 1868, in Wolcott, *Edwin M. Stanton*, 210 ("I do not want to remain a day in the Department but do not feel at liberty to give up immediately").

14 Grant to Johnson, Jan. 24, 1868, in Simon, *The Papers of Ulysses Grant*, 18:121; Grant to Johnson, Jan. 28, 1868, ibid., 116–18; Johnson to Grant, Jan. 29, 1868, ibid., 121–22; Grant to Johnson, Jan. 30, 1868, ibid., 122–23; Randall, *Diary of Orville Hickman Browning*, 2:176, 178 (Jan. 17, 21, 31, 1868) (Stanton not at cabinet meetings).

15 Sumner to Stanton, [Feb. 2, 1868,] Edwin Stanton Papers, LC, box 34, image 65; Moorfield Storey memo, Feb. 2, 1868, in Storey, "Dickens, Stanton, Sumner, and Storey"; *Washington Evening Star*, Feb. 3, 1868; Dickens to J. T. Fields, Feb. 3, 1868, in House and Storey, *Letters of Charles Dickens*, 12:33–34; Dickens to Mary Dickens, Feb. 4, 1868, ibid., 34–36; Dickens to John Forster, Feb. 4 and 7, 1868, ibid., 38–40; Tomalin, *Charles Dickens*, 362–70; Wolcott, *Edwin M. Stanton*, 206.

16 Eggleston, *Lincoln's Recruiter*, 99 ("befuddled old drunk"); Piatt, "Edwin M. Stanton," 470 ("pick Lorenzo Thomas up"); Thomas and Hyman, *Stanton*, 163 ("fit for presiding"); Townsend, *Anecdotes of the Civil War*, 78–80, 125. Given the way Stanton trusted Thomas with black recruiting, I think prior authors have overstated his dislike of Thomas.

17 *Congressional Globe*, 40th Cong., 2d Sess., Supp. 137–41 (Apr. 10, 1868) (Thomas testimony); Johnson to Stanton, Feb. 21, 1868, in Graf, *The Papers of Andrew Johnson*, 13:577; Johnson to Thomas, Feb. 21, 1868, ibid., 577–78; Stewart, *Impeached*, 133–35; Thomas and Hyman, *Stanton*, 583–84.

18 Stanton to Thomas, Feb. 21, 1868, Edwin Stanton Papers, LC, box 34, image 202; Sumner to Stanton, Feb. 21, 1868, ibid., image 221; Boutwell to Stanton, Feb. 21, 1868, ibid., image 204; Howard to Stanton, Feb. 21, 1868, ibid., image 213; Wilson to Stanton, Feb. 21, 1868, ibid., image 208; *New York Times*, Feb. 22, 1868 ("like a thunderbolt"); *Congressional Globe*, 40th Cong., 2d Sess., Supp. 137 (Apr. 10, 1868) (Thomas testimony).

19 Stanton to Grant, Feb. 22, 1868, in Simon, *The Papers of Ulysses Grant*, 18:190; *Washington Evening Star*, Feb. 23, 1868.

20 Stanton to Edmunds, Feb. 21, 1868, in Flower, *Edwin McMasters Stanton*, 311; *Senate Executive Journal*, Feb. 21, 1868 (resolution); *Washington Evening Star*, Feb. 22, 1868 (summarizes Senate debate; quotes resolution).

21 Thayer, "A Night with Stanton in the War Office"; *Washington Evening Star*, Feb. 22, 1868 (includes Stanton affidavit against Thomas); *New York Times*, Feb. 23, 1868.

22 *Congressional Globe*, 40th Cong., 2d Sess., Supp. 137–41 (Apr. 10, 1868) (Thomas testimony); Stewart, *Impeached*, 138–40; Townsend, *Anecdotes of the Civil War*, 126–28.

23 *Congressional Globe*, 40th Cong., 2d Sess., Supp. 137–41 (Apr. 10, 1868) (Thomas testimony); Stewart, *Impeached*, 138–40; Townsend, *Anecdotes of the Civil War*, 126–28.

24 *New York Herald*, Feb. 24, 1868; Townsend, *Anecdotes of the Civil War*, 129; Stewart, *Impeached*, 141–42.

25 *Washington Post*, Feb. 15, 1903; *New York Commercial Advertiser*, Mar. 24, 1903.

26 Pile to Stanton, Feb. 26, 1868, Edwin Stanton Papers, LC, box 35, images 3–5; counsel's notes re: Stanton's instructions, [Feb. 26, 1868,] ibid., image 31; *New York Times*, Feb. 27, 1868 (reporting Stanton's lawyers dropped the Thomas case).

27 Clifford [Stone?] to Stanton, Feb. 24, 1868, Edwin Stanton Papers, LC, box 34, image 255; Welles to John Welles, Mar. 1, 1868, Welles Papers, LC.

28 Sickles to Stanton, Mar. 10, 1868, Edwin Stanton Papers, LC, box 35, image 46; Stanton to Sickles, Mar. 10, 1868, ibid., image 44; Stanton to Smythe, Mar. 11, 1868, ibid., image 52; Butler to Stanton, Apr. 17, 1868, ibid., image 128; Stanton to Butler, Apr. 20, 1868, ibid., image 130.

29 Stanton to Ellen Stanton, Mar. 2, 1868, in Thomas and Hyman, *Stanton*, 596; Stanton to Simpson, Mar. 26, 1868, in Flower, *Edwin McMasters Stanton*, 374; Stanton to Eddie Stanton, Apr. 17, 1868, Edwin Stanton Papers, LC, box 35, image 127 ("I shall probably stay at home this evening"); Stanton to Eleanor Hutchison, May 1, 1868, Wilkins-Hutchison-Wells Family Papers.

30 Lieber to Thayer, Mar. 2, 1868, Lieber Papers, Huntington, box 51; Stanton to Cameron, Apr. 14, 1868, Edwin Stanton Papers, LC, box 35, image 117; Pierrepont to Stanton, Apr. 15, 1868, ibid., image 123; *Indiana American*, Apr. 17, 1868; *Waynesburg (Pa.) Republican*, Apr. 22, 1868 (Stanton-Cameron correspondence).

31 Stewart, *Impeached*, 232–36; White, *American Ulysses*, 455–59.

32 Stanton to Fessenden, Mar. 28, 1868, Fessenden Papers; Stanton to Frank Fessenden, Apr. 1, 1868, Edwin Stanton Papers, LC, box 35, image 88; Moore Diary, Apr. 23, 1868, Johnson Papers, reel 50; *New York Tribune*, May 6 and 8, 1868; Young to Stanton, May 6, 1868, Edwin Stanton Papers, LC, box 35, image 150; Stanton to Young, May 10, 1868, Young Papers.

33 *Washington Evening Star*, Apr. 25, 1868; *Charleston (S.C.) Daily News*, Apr. 28, 1868; Stewart, *Impeached*, 225–27.

34 *Congressional Globe*, 40th Cong., 2d Sess., Supp. 324 (Apr. 27, 1868) (Stevens); ibid., 319 (Groesbeck); Garfield to James Rhodes, Apr. 28, 1868, in Smith, *The Life and Letters of James Abram Garfield*, 1:424.

35 Stanton to Johnson, May, 1868, Edwin Stanton Papers, LC, box 35, image 152; Stanton to Young, May 13, 1868, Young Papers; Randall, *Diary of Orville Hickman Browning*, 2:196–97 (May 12, 1868).

36 Badeau, *Grant in Peace*, 144; *New York Times*, May 22, 1868 ("very quietly").

37 *New York Times*, May 25 and 26, 1868; *Washington Evening Star*, May 25 and 26, 1868; Stanton to Johnson, May 26, 1868, in Graf, *The Papers of Andrew Johnson*, 14:117; Stewart, *Impeached*, 284–87.

38 Townsend, *Anecdotes of the Civil War*, 133.

Chapter 19: "Final Charge"

1 Beale, *The Diary of Gideon Welles*, 3:370–71 (May 27, 1868); *Washington Evening Star*, May 27, 1868 (Edmunds introduces resolution); *New York Herald*, June 1, 1868; *Congressional Globe*, 40th Cong., 2d Sess., pp. 2727–36 (June 1, 1868) (Senate debate and passage); *Wheeling (W. Va.) Daily Intelligencer*, June 20, 1868 (House).

2 *Stark County (Ohio) Democrat*, July 29, 1868 (Blair speech); *Galveston (Texas) Daily News*, Sept. 11, 1868; *Daily Ohio Statesman*, Oct. 12, 1868 ("retention"); Foner, *Reconstruction*, 340–43; Rable, *But There Was No Peace*, 59–80; Summers, *Ordeal of the Reunion*, 141–52; Zuczak, *State of Rebellion*, 50–61.

3 *New York Herald*, June 10, 1868 (Stanton as senator); *Baltimore Sun*, June 13, 1868 (same); Stanton to Young, June 24, 1868, in Thomas and Hyman, *Stanton*, 615 (not a candidate); *Cincinnati Daily Gazette*, Aug. 7, 1868 ("his friends are sure"); *North Carolina Standard*, July 29, 1868 (predicts second civil war); *National Republican*, Aug. 17, 1868 (Stanton will speak in Michigan); Stanton to Robert Schenck, Aug. 27, 1868, Edwin Stanton Papers, LC, box 35, image 201 (intends to go to Ohio); Conkling to Stanton, Sept. 6, 1868, in Gorham, *The Life and Public Services*, 2:468; *Iowa State Register*, Sept. 11, 1868 (Stanton will speak in Iowa); *Vermont Transcript* (St. Albans), Sept. 15, 1868 (Stanton will speak in Ohio and Pennsylvania).

4 Stanton to Young, Sept. 19, 1868, Young Papers.

5 Stanton to Isaac Bell, Sept. 29, 1868, Edwin Stanton Papers, LC, box 35, image 203; Doyle, *In Memoriam*, 294, 308; Flower, *Edwin McMasters Stanton*, 410.

6 Doyle, *In Memoriam*, 295–301.

7 Ibid., 302–7.

8 *Chicago Tribune*, Sept. 26, 1868; *Cincinnati Enquirer*, Sept. 26, 1868; *New York Herald*, Sept. 26, 1868; *New York Times*, Sept. 26, 1868; *New York Tribune*, Sept.

26, 1868; *Philadelphia Evening Telegraph*, Sept. 26, 1868; *Pittsburgh Commercial*, Sept. 26, 1868; Stanton to Ellen Stanton, Sept. 27, 1868, in Thomas and Hyman, *Stanton*, 618; Stanton to Chandler, Oct. 1, 1868, Chandler Papers.

9 *Cincinnati Daily Gazette*, Oct. 3, 1868.

10 *Cincinnati Daily Gazette*, Oct. 9, 1868; *New York Times*, Oct. 9, 1868; *Summit County Beacon*, Oct. 15, 1868.

11 *Cincinnati Daily Gazette*, Oct. 12, 1868; *Western Reserve Chronicle* (Warren, Ohio), Oct. 21, 1868; Smith, *History of the Republican Party in Ohio*, 1:258–59 (election results); Wolcott, *Edwin M. Stanton*, 212.

12 *Cincinnati Daily Gazette*, Oct. 21–22, 1868; *Steubenville (Ohio) Herald*, Oct. 30, 1868; *New York Times*, Oct. 30, 1868; Wolcott, *Edwin M. Stanton*, 213–15.

13 *New York Herald*, Nov. 1–2, 1868; *Philadelphia Enquirer*, Nov. 2, 1868; *New York Sun*, Nov. 2, 1868; *St. Paul (Minn.) Daily Press*, Nov. 4, 1868; McClure, *Abraham Lincoln and Men of War-Times*, 187.

14 *Washington Evening Star*, Nov. 4, 1868 (preliminary returns); *New York Sun*, Nov. 6, 1868; Stanton to Watson, Nov. 8, 1868, in Flower, *Edwin McMasters Stanton*, 399; Stanton to Louis Walker, Nov. 16, 1868, in Wolcott, *Edwin M. Stanton*, 217.

15 *New York Herald*, Nov. 16, 1868 (Stanton in cabinet); *Wheeling (W. Va.) Daily Intelligencer*, Nov. 21 and 25, 1868 (same); Stanton to Lucy Stanton, Nov. 27, 1868, in Wolcott, *Edwin M. Stanton*, 218.

16 Stanton to Stanton children, Dec. 24, 1868, Edwin M. Stanton Family Papers. Grandson Gideon Townsend Stanton gives the dates of birth of the three children as Eleanor, May 9, 1857; Lewis, Jan. 12, 1860; and Bessie, June 28, 1863. G. T. Stanton, *Edwin M. Stanton*, Notes.

17 Stanton to Watson, Jan. 10, 1869, in Flower, *Edwin McMasters Stanton*, 400; Watson to Stanton, Jan. 15, 1869, Edwin Stanton Papers, LC, box 35, images 212–14; *Wheeling (W. Va.) Daily Intelligencer*, Jan. 16, 20, 21, 1869; Stanton to Witt, Jan. 29, 1869, Edwin Stanton Papers, LC, box 35, images 218–20; Flower, *Edwin McMasters Stanton*, 374; Gorham, *The Life and Public Services*, 2:469; Wolcott, *Edwin M. Stanton*, 135–37.

18 Stanton to Lucy Stanton, Nov. 27, 1868, in Wolcott, *Edwin M. Stanton*, 218; Blatchford to Weed, Feb. 23, 1869, in Barnes, *Memoir of Thurlow Weed*, 462; Sumner to Whittier, Feb. 26, 1869, in Pierce, *Memoir and Letters of Charles Sumner*, 4:369; Stanton to Fish, Apr. 15, 1869, Fish Papers.

19 *New York Sun*, Dec. 25, 1869.

20 Pierrepont to Stanton, June 23, 1869, in Simon, *The Papers of Ulysses Grant*, 20:78.

21 *Harrisburg Telegraph*, May 28, 1869 (Black's accident); Stanton to Black, July 17, 1869, Black Papers, reel 5; Sherman to Stanton, July 28, 1869, in G. T. Stanton, *Edwin M. Stanton*, 55.

22 Stanton to Lucy Stanton, Sept. 18, 1869, in Wolcott, *Edwin M. Stanton*, 222; Marvel, *Lincoln's Autocrat*, 458–59.

23 Stanton to Simpson, Oct. 26, 1869, Simpson Papers.

24 Stanton to Simpson, Nov. 3, 1869, Simpson Papers.

25 *Wilmington (N.C.) Journal*, Dec. 3, 1869; *Wheeling (W. Va.) Daily Intelligencer*, Dec. 9, 1869; *Rock Island (Ill.) Evening Argus*, Dec. 13, 1869 (Grier's resignation "creates something of a sensation"); *New York Sun*, Dec. 13, 1869; *Wheeling (W. Va.) Daily Intelligencer*, Dec. 14, 1869; *New York World*, Dec. 14, 1869; Grant to Grier, Dec. 15, 1869, in Simon, *The Papers of Ulysses Grant*, 20:52 (accepts Grier resignation of Dec. 11). Grant's nomination of Hoar was dated December 14 but not delivered until December 15 because of the eulogies for Fessenden. *Washington Evening Star*, Dec. 15, 1869.

26 Colfax et al. to Grant, Dec. 16, 1869, in Simon, *The Papers of Ulysses Grant*, 20:79; *Washington Evening Star*, Dec. 17, 1869; James Blaine et al. to Grant, Dec. 18, 1869, in Simon, *The Papers of Ulysses Grant*, 20:79; *Congressional Globe*, 42d Cong, 2d Sess., App. 560 (June 3, 1872) (Carpenter).

27 *Senate Executive Journal*, Dec. 20, 1869 (Senate vote); Eddie Stanton to Lucy Stanton, Dec. 21, 1869, in Wolcott, *Edwin M. Stanton*, 224 (visit of Grant and Colfax); *New York Times*, Dec. 21, 1869; Nevins and Thomas, *Diary of George Templeton Strong*, 4:265–66 (Dec. 21, 1869); *Philadelphia Evening Telegraph*, Dec. 23, 1869, quoting *New York World* ("overbearing manners"); *New York World*, Dec. 24, 1869.

28 Stanton to Grant, Dec. 21, 1869, in Simon, *The Papers of Ulysses Grant*, 20:79–80; White, *American Ulysses*, 494.

29 *New York Times*, Dec. 25, 1869, Apr. 20, 1879; William Dupee affidavit, Apr. 21, 1879, Pratt Papers.

Chapter 20: "Strangely Blended"

 1 Grant order, Dec. 24, 1869, in Simon, *The Papers of Ulysses Grant*, 20:80; Robert Lincoln to Eddie Stanton, Dec. 24, 1869, in G. T. Stanton, *Edwin M. Stanton*, 56; Grant to Ellen Stanton, Jan. 3, 1870, in Simon, *The Papers of Ulysses Grant*, 20:77–78; Rockwood Hoar remarks, in *Proceedings in the Supreme Court*, 3–9.

 2 *New York Sun*, Dec. 25, 1869.

 3 *Philadelphia Inquirer*, Dec. 27, 1869 (printed copy); Lieber to Sumner, Dec. 28, 1869, Lieber Papers, Huntington (encloses clipping); Lieber to Woodman, Jan. 6, 1870, Woodman Papers.

 4 *National Republican*, Dec. 28, 1869 (Phillips); Gorham, *The Life and Public Services*, 1:35 (Marshall). Stanton and Marshall worked together in a dispute between two Presbyterian factions over a Pittsburgh church. See

Pittsburgh Gazette, Jan. 24–26, 1855; Graves, "Early Life and Career of Stanton," 73–76.

5 Nevins and Thomas, *Diary of George Templeton Strong*, 4:266 (Dec. 24, 1869).

6 *Washington Evening Star*, Dec. 27, 1869; *Baltimore Sun*, Dec. 28, 1869 ("no remarks being made by any of the clergymen"); *New York Herald*, Dec. 28, 1869 ("statesmen"); *Philadelphia Inquirer*, Dec. 28, 1869 ("cold drizzling rain"). The *Washington Evening Star* reported on Dec. 29 that, a few days before his death, Stanton had sent for Reverend William Sparrow of the Alexandria Theological Seminary "and was baptized by him." Flower claimed that Stanton was baptized by Sparrow in March 1869. Flower, *Edwin McMasters Stanton*, 374. It seems more likely that Stanton was received into the Episcopal Church, having been baptized as a boy in the Methodist Church. There is no record of Stanton's baptism in the files of Epiphany Church, although those files do show the home baptisms of two of his children, Jamie and Bessie.

7 Hooper to Woodman, Dec. 28, 1869, Woodman Papers; Hooper to Woodman, Dec. 29, 1869, ibid.; *Philadelphia Evening Telegraph*, Mar. 18, 1870 (one-year salary); *Harrisburg Telegraph*, Apr. 12, 1870 ($146,000). The Hooper and Woodman papers at MHS detail the fundraising.

8 *Washington Evening Star*, Dec. 24, 1869; *New York World*, Dec. 25, 1869; *Philadelphia Inquirer*, Dec. 27, 1869 ("rarely has there been a corpse so lifelike as in this instance"); *Washington Evening Star*, Dec. 28, 1869; *Anderson (S.C.) Intelligencer*, Jan. 27, 1870, quoting *Charleston (S.C.) News* ("no one outside of the family were allowed to see the remains"); *Cairo (Ill.) Bulletin*, Jan. 29, 1870, quoting *New York Democrat* ("God is just!").

9 *Cambridge (Mass.) Chronicle*, Dec. 5, 1874, quoting *Hartford (Ct.) Times* ("colored valet"); Barnes to McPherson, Apr. 16, 1879, in *New York Times*, Apr. 20, 1879; William Dupee affidavit, Apr. 21, 1879, Pratt Papers; David Jones affidavit, Apr. 21, 1879, ibid.

10 Black, "To the Public," [Jan. 1870], Black Papers, reel 26; Wilson, "Edwin M. Stanton"; Black, "Senator Wilson and Edwin M. Stanton."

11 Wilson, "Jeremiah S. Black and Edwin M. Stanton"; Black, "Mr. Black to Mr. Wilson."

12 *Memphis Daily Appeal*, Feb. 25, 1872 ("venal, ambitious"); *Indiana (Pa.) Democrat*, Feb. 29, 1872 (same); *Congressional Globe*, 42d Cong., 2d Sess., pp. 4112–13 (May 31, 1872) (Sumner); ibid., 4282–83 (June 6, 1872) (Chandler); ibid., App. 559–61 (June 3, 1872) (Carpenter); Donald, *Charles Sumner and the Rights of Man*, 529–51.

13 Grant, *Personal Memoirs*, 2:536–37; White, *American Ulysses*, 647 ("wrote a new chapter assessing Lincoln, Stanton, and the major commanders").

14 Stanton to Ashley, Sept. 14, 1866, in Flower, *Edwin McMasters Stanton*, 310–12; Ropes memo, Feb. 8, 1870, Woodman Papers.

15 Lincoln, Gettysburg Address, Nov. 19, 1863, in Basler, *The Collected Works of Abraham Lincoln*, 7:23; Nevins and Thomas, *Diary of George Templeton Strong*, 4:266 (Dec. 24, 1869) ("arbitrary, capricious"); Gienapp and Gienapp, *Civil War Diary of Gideon Welles*, 682 (retrospective).

16 Stanton to governors, May 25, 1862, *OR*, ser. 3, 2:70 ("great force"); Stanton general order, Apr. 3, 1862, ibid., 2–3 (suspends recruiting).

17 Stanton to Dana, Feb. 19, 1862 in *New York Tribune*, Feb. 20, 1862.

18 Hay to Stanton, July 26, 1865, in Burlingame, *At Lincoln's Side*, 105–6.

19 Solzhenitsyn, *The Gulag Archipelago*, 75; Nevins and Thomas, *Diary of George Templeton Strong*, 4:266 (Dec. 24, 1869) ("strangely blended").

Bibliography

Manuscript Collections

Allen, William, Papers. Library of Congress.
American Freedmen's Inquiry Commission Papers. Houghton Library, Harvard University.
Anderson, Robert, Papers. Library of Congress.
Andrew, John Albion, Papers. Massachusetts Historical Society, Boston.
Atkinson, Edward, Papers. Massachusetts Historical Society, Boston.
Banks, Nathaniel, Papers. Library of Congress.
Barlow, S. L. M., Papers. Huntington Library, San Marino, Calif.
Barton, Clara, Papers. Library of Congress.
Beecher Family Papers. Yale University.
Bellows, Henry, Papers. Massachusetts Historical Society, Boston.
Bennett, James Gordon, Papers. Library of Congress.
Bingham, John, Papers. Ohio History Connection, Columbus.
Black, Jeremiah, Papers. Library of Congress.
Blair and Lee Family Papers. Princeton University.
Blair Family Papers. Library of Congress.
Buchanan, James, Papers. Historical Society of Pennsylvania, Philadelphia.
Buchanan, James, Papers. Library of Congress.
Butler, Benjamin, Papers. Library of Congress.
Cameron, Simon, Papers. Library of Congress.
Chandler, Zachariah, Papers. Library of Congress.
Chase, Salmon, Papers. Historical Society of Pennsylvania, Philadelphia.

Chase, Salmon, Papers. Library of Congress.

Chase, Salmon, Papers. Microfilm edition, edited by John Niven, published by University Publications of America (UPA) in 1987.

Clifford, John, Papers. Massachusetts Historical Society, Boston.

Colfax, Schuyler, Papers. Rochester University.

Comly, J. M., Papers. Ohio History Connection, Columbus.

Comstock, Cyrus, Papers. Library of Congress.

Corwin, Edward, Papers. Princeton University.

Croffut, William, Papers. Library of Congress.

Dahlgren, Ulric, Papers. Library of Congress.

Dana, Charles, Papers. Library of Congress.

Department of Justice Papers. Record Group 60. National Archives, Washington, D.C.

Dickson, William, Papers. Clements Library, University of Michigan, Ann Arbor.

Dix, John Adams, Papers. Columbia University.

Douglas, Stephen, Papers. University of Chicago.

Douglass, Frederick, Papers. Library of Congress.

Dreer, Ferdinand J., Collection. Historical Society of Pennsylvania, Philadelphia.

Du Pont, Samuel Francis, Papers. Hagley Museum, Wilmington, Del.

Eckert, Thomas, Papers. Huntington Library, San Marino, Calif.

Edwin M. Stanton Family Papers. National Archives, Washington, D.C.

1861–1865 Collection, New-York Historical Society, New York City.

Ellet, Charles, Papers. University of Michigan, Ann Arbor.

Fessenden, William, Papers. Bowdoin College.

Fish, Hamilton, Papers. Library of Congress.

Flagg, S. Griswold, Papers. Yale University.

Forbes, Thomas, Papers. Library of Congress.

Forrer-Pierce-Woods Papers. Dayton, Ohio, Public Library.

Garfield, James, Papers. Library of Congress.

Gay, Sydney Howard, Papers. Columbia University.

Goldsborough, Louis, Papers. Duke University.

Grant, Ulysses, Papers. Library of Congress.

Grant, Ulysses, Papers. Mississippi State University.

Gratz, Simon, Papers. Historical Society of Pennsylvania, Philadelphia.

Gray, Horace, Papers. Library of Congress.

Gurowski, Adam, Papers. Library of Congress.

Halleck, Henry, Papers. Library of Congress.

Hardie, James, Papers. Library of Congress.

Hay, John, Papers. Library of Congress.

Heintzelman, Samuel, Papers. Library of Congress.

Herndon-Weik Papers. Library of Congress.

Hitchcock, Ethan Allen, Papers. Gilcrease Museum, Tulsa, Okla.

Hitchcock, Ethan Allen, Papers. Library of Congress.

Holt, Joseph, Papers. Huntington Library, San Marino, Calif.

Holt, Joseph, Papers. Library of Congress.

Hooker, Emanuel, Papers. Ohio History Connection, Columbus.

Hooper, Samuel, Papers. Massachusetts Historical Society, Boston.

Howard, Oliver Otis, Papers. Bowdoin College.

Jefferson County Common Pleas Journal. Jefferson County Chapter of the Ohio Genealogical Society, Wintersville.

Johnson, Andrew, Papers. Library of Congress.

Kautz, August, Papers. Library of Congress.

King, Horatio, Papers. Library of Congress.

Lamon, Ward Hill, Papers. Huntington Library, San Marino, Calif.

Lawrence, Amos, Papers. Massachusetts Historical Society, Boston.

Lieber, Francis, Papers. Huntington Library, San Marino, Calif.

Lieber, Francis, Papers. Library of Congress.

Lincoln, Abraham, Papers. Brown University.

Lincoln, Abraham, Papers. Library of Congress.

Lincoln, Abraham, Papers. Yale University.

Manypenny, George, Papers. Library of Congress.

Marble, Manton, Papers. Library of Congress.

McClellan, George, Papers. Library of Congress.

McCook Family Papers. Library of Congress.

McPherson, Edward, Papers. Library of Congress.

Meigs, Montgomery, Papers. Library of Congress.

Monroe, Elizabeth, Papers. Ohio County Public Library, Wheeling, W. Va.

Nicolay, John, Papers. Library of Congress.

Patrick, Marsena, Papers. Library of Congress.

Phillips, Philip, Papers. Library of Congress.

Philomathesian Society Minute Book. Kenyon College.

Pierrepont, Edwards, Papers. New York Public Library.

Pike, James, Papers. University of Maine, Orono.

Porter, Fitz-John, Papers. Library of Congress.

Porter, Fitz-John, Papers. Massachusetts Historical Society, Boston.

Pratt, Fletcher, Papers. Columbia University.

Ray, Charles, Papers. Huntington Library, San Marino, Calif.

Rosecrans, William, Papers. University of California at Los Angeles.

Saxton, Rufus and Willard, Papers. Yale University.

Schoff Collection. Clements Library, University of Michigan, Ann Arbor.

Schuckers, Jacob, Papers. Library of Congress.

Secretary of War Papers. Record Group 107. National Archives, Washington, D.C.

Seward, William Henry, Papers. University of Rochester.

Sherman, William Tecumseh, Papers. Library of Congress.

Simpson, Matthew, Papers. Fort Wayne Public Library, Indiana.

Smith, William, Papers. Ohio History Connection, Columbus.

Stanton, Edwin, Papers. Brown University.

Stanton, Edwin, Papers. Chicago Historical Society.

Stanton, Edwin, Papers. Huntington Library, San Marino, Calif.

Stanton, Edwin, Papers. Kenyon College.

Stanton, Edwin, Papers. Library of Congress.

Stanton, Edwin, Papers. Louisiana State University, Baton Rouge.

Stanton, Edwin, Papers. New-York Historical Society, New York City.

Stanton, Edwin, Papers. University of Chicago.

Stanton, William, Papers. Huntington Library, San Marino, Calif.

Strong, George Templeton. Diary. New-York Historical Society, New York City.

Sumner, Charles, Papers. Harvard University.

Tappan, Benjamin, Papers. Library of Congress.

Tappan, Benjamin, Papers. Ohio History Connection, Columbus. (Copy at Library of Congress.)

Tappan, Lewis, Papers. Library of Congress.

Tarbell, Ida, Papers. Allegheny College.

Turner-Baker Papers. Microfilm M797. National Archives, Washington, D.C.

Warren, Joseph, Papers. Massachusetts Historical Society, Boston.

Weed, Thurlow, Papers. University of Rochester.

Welles, Gideon, Papers. Connecticut Historical Society, Hartford.

Welles, Gideon, Papers. Huntington Library, San Marino, Calif.

Welles, Gideon, Papers. Library of Congress.

Wilkins-Hutchison-Wells Family Papers. Heinz History Center, Pittsburgh.

Woodman, Horatio, Papers. Massachusetts Historical Society, Boston.

Young, John Russell, Papers. Library of Congress.

Newspapers

Albany (N.Y.) Evening Journal

Alexandria (Va.) Gazette

American Telegraph (Washington, D.C.)

Anderson (S.C.) Intelligencer

Ashland (Ohio) Union

Atchison (Kansas) Daily Champion

Baltimore Daily Commercial

Baltimore Exchange

Baltimore Sun

Bedford (Pa.) Gazette

Bloomington (Ill.) Pantagraph

Bloomsburg (Pa.) Democrat

Boston Daily Advertiser

Boston Daily Journal

Boston Evening Transcript

Bridgeport (Ct.) Republican Farmer

Brooklyn Daily Eagle

Brooklyn Evening Star

Burlington (Iowa) Hawk-Eye
Burlington (Vt.) Free-Press
Cadiz (Ohio) Sentinel
Cadiz (Ohio) Telegraph
Cairo (Ill.) Bulletin
Cambridge (Mass.) Chronicle
Carroll County (Ohio) Free Press
Cecil (Md.) Whig
Cedar Falls (Iowa) Gazette
Chicago Times
Chicago Tribune
Cincinnati Daily Commercial
Cincinnati Daily Gazette
Cincinnati Enquirer
Clearfield (Pa.) Republican
Charles Town (W. Va.) Spirit of Jefferson
Charleston (S.C.) Daily News
Cleveland Daily Leader
Cleveland Herald
Columbia (S.C.) Phoenix
Columbian Register (New Haven, Ct.)
Constitutional Union (Washington, D.C.)
Daily Alta California
Daily Evening Bulletin (San Francisco)
Daily Ohio Statesman
Daily Wheeling (Va.) Gazette
Davenport (Iowa) Daily Gazette
Dayton Daily Empire
Detroit Free Press
Ebensburg (Pa.) Mountain Sentinel
Evansville (In.) Daily Journal
Findlay (Ohio) Jeffersonian
Flake's Bulletin (Galveston, Tex.)
Frank Leslie's Illustrated Newspaper
Gallipolis (Ohio) Journal
Galveston (Tex.) Daily News
Georgetown (Ohio) Democratic Standard
Georgia Weekly Telegraph (Macon, Ga.)
Green Mountain Freeman (Montpelier, Vt.)
Harrisburg Telegraph

Hartford (Ct.) Courant
Indiana American (Brookville, Ind.)
Indiana (Pa.) Democrat
Indianapolis Star
Iowa State Register
Janesville (Wisc.) Gazette
Jeffersonian Democrat (Chardon, Ohio)
Joplin (Mo.) Globe
Kalida (Ohio) Venture
Lancaster (Pa.) Gazette
Liberator (Boston)
Logan (Ohio) Democratic Sentinel
Lowell (Mass.) Daily Citizen
Luzerne Union (Wilkes-Barre, Pa.)
Marshall County Republican (Plymouth, Ind.)
Maumee (Ohio) Express
Meigs County (Ohio) Telegraph
Memphis Daily Appeal
Milwaukee Daily Patriot
Milwaukee Daily Sentinel
Milwaukee News
Nashville Daily Union
Nashville Patriot
Nashville Union & American
Nashville Union & Dispatch
National Intelligencer
National Republican
New London (Ct.) News
New Orleans Daily Crescent
New Orleans Daily True Delta
New Orleans Times
Newport (R.I.) Daily News
New York Commercial Advertiser
New York Evening Post
New York Herald
New York Sun
New York Times
New York Tribune
New York World
North Carolina Standard

Norwalk (Ohio) Experiment
Ohio State Journal
Philadelphia Age
Philadelphia Evening Telegraph
Philadelphia Inquirer
Philadelphia Public Ledger
Pittsburgh Commercial
Pittsburgh Daily Dispatch
Pittsburgh Daily Post
Pittsburgh Gazette
Ravenna (Ohio) Portage Sentinel
Reading (Pa.) Daily Times
Republic (Washington, D.C.)
Richmond (Va.) Dispatch
Richmond (Va.) Enquirer
Rock Island (Ill.) Evening Argus
Roanoke (Va.) Advocate
Sacramento Daily Union
St. Cloud (Minn.) Democrat
St. Paul (Minn.) Daily Press
Semi-Weekly Wisconsin
Springfield (Mass.) Republican
Star of the North (Bloomsburg, Pa.)
Stark County (Ohio) Democrat
Steubenville (Ohio) American Union
Steubenville (Ohio) Herald

Steubenville (Ohio) Log Cabin Farmer
Steubenville (Ohio) Republican Ledger
Steubenville (Ohio) True American
Stillwater (Minn.) Messenger
Stroudsburg (Pa.) Jeffersonian
Sumter Banner (Sumterville, S.C.)
Sunbury (Pa.) American
The Tennessean (Nashville)
Trenton (N.J.) State Gazette
Urbana (Ohio) Union
Vermont Phoenix (Brattleboro)
Vermont Transcript (St. Albans)
Washington Daily Union
Washington Evening Star
Washington Morning Chronicle
Waynesburg (Pa.) Republican
Western Democrat (Charlotte, N.C.)
Western Herald & Steubenville (Ohio) Gazette
Western Reserve Chronicle (Warren, Ohio)
Wheeling (Va.) Daily Intelligencer
Wilmington (N.C.) Herald
Wilmington (N.C.) Journal
Woodsfield (Ohio) Spirit of Democracy
Woodstock (Ill.) Sentinel

U.S. Congressional Documents

Congressional Globe, various issues.
House of Representatives. *Expenditures on Account of Private Land Claims in California*. 36th Cong., 1st Sess., 1860, Ex. Doc. 84.
House of Representatives. *General Orders—Reconstruction*. 40th Cong., 2d Sess., 1868, H. Exec. Doc. 342.
House of Representatives. *New Orleans Riots*. 39th Cong., 2d Sess., 1867, H. Exec. Doc. 68.
House of Representatives. Judiciary Committee. *Impeachment Investigation*. 40th Cong., 1st Sess., 1867, H. Rept. 7.
House of Representatives. Select Committee of Five. *Alleged Hostile Organization against the Government within the District of Columbia*. 36th Cong., 2d Sess., 1861, H Rept. 79.

House of Representatives. Select Committee on Alleged Corruptions in Government. *The Covode Investigation*. 36th Cong., 1st Sess., 1860, H. Rept. 648.

Senate. *Message from the President . . . Reports of the Assistant Commissioners of the Freedmen's Bureau*. 39th Cong., 1st Sess., 1866, S. Exec. Doc. 27.

Senate Executive Journal, various issues.

Senate. Select Committee on Memorial of David Yulee. 32d Cong., 1st Sess., 1852, S. Rept. 349.

Statutes at Large, various statutes.

U.S. Congress. *Report of the Joint Committee on the Conduct of the War*. 3 vols. Washington, D.C.: Government Printing Office, 1863.

Other Printed Primary Sources

Agassiz, George, ed. *Meade's Headquarters 1863–1865: Letters of Colonel Theodore Lyman from the Wilderness to Appomattox*. Boston: Atlantic Monthly Press, 1922.

Angle, Paul, ed. *Three Years in the Army of the Cumberland: The Letters and Diary of Major James A. Connolly*. Bloomington: Indiana University Press, 1959.

Baird, Henry C. "Narrative of Rear Admiral Goldsborough, U.S. Navy." *U.S. Naval Institute Proceedings 59* (July 1933): 1023–31.

Barnes, Thurlow, ed. *Memoir of Thurlow Weed*. Boston: Houghton Mifflin, 1884.

Basler, Roy, ed. *The Collected Works of Abraham Lincoln*. 8 vols. New Brunswick, N.J.: Rutgers University Press, 1953–55.

Beale, Howard, ed. *The Diary of Edward Bates*. Washington, D.C.: Government Printing Office, 1933.

———, ed. *The Diary of Gideon Welles, Secretary of Navy under Lincoln and Johnson*. 3 vols. New York: Norton, 1960.

Berlin, Ira, ed. *Freedom: A Documentary History of Emancipation*. Series 2. Vol. 1: *The Black Military Experience*. Cambridge: Cambridge University Press, 1982.

Blair, Montgomery. *Speech of the Hon. Montgomery Blair (Postmaster General) on the Revolutionary Schemes of the Ultra Abolitionists . . . October 3, 1863*, 1863.

———. *Reminiscences of Sixty Years of Public Affairs*. 2 vols. New York: McClure, Phillips, 1902.

Burlingame, Michael, ed. *Abraham Lincoln: Observations of John G. Nicolay and John Hay*. Carbondale: Southern Illinois University Press, 2007.

———. *At Lincoln's Side: John Hay's Civil War Correspondence and Selected Writings*. Carbondale: Southern Illinois University Press, 2000.

———. *Dispatches from Lincoln's White House: The Anonymous Civil War Journalism of Presidential Secretary William Stoddard*. Lincoln: University of Nebraska Press, 2002.

———. *Inside the White House in War Times: Memoirs and Reports of Lincoln's Secretary William O. Stoddard*. Lincoln: University of Nebraska Press, 2000.

———. *Lincoln Observed: Civil War Dispatches of Noah Brooks.* Baltimore: Johns Hopkins University Press, 1998.

———. *Lincoln's Journalist: John Hay's Anonymous Writings for the Press, 1860–1864.* Carbondale: Southern Illinois University Press, 1998.

———. *With Lincoln in the White House: Letters, Memoranda, and Other Writings of John G. Nicolay, 1860–1865.* Carbondale: Southern Illinois University Press, 2000.

Burlingame, Michael, and John Ettlinger, eds. *Inside Lincoln's White House: The Complete Civil War Diary of John Hay.* Carbondale: Southern Illinois University Press, 1997.

Butler, Benjamin. *Butler's Book: A Review of His Legal, Political and Military Career.* Boston: A. M. Thayer, 1892.

Cole, Donald, and John McDonough, eds. *Witness to the Young Republic: A Yankee's Journal, 1828–1870.* Hanover, N.H.: University Press of New England, 1989.

Cook, Thomas, and Thomas Knox, eds. *Public Record: Including Speeches, Messages, Proclamations, Official Correspondence, and Other Public Utterances of Horatio Seymour.* New York: I. W. England, 1868.

Cox, Jacob. *Military Reminiscences of the Civil War.* 2 vols. New York: Charles Scribner's Sons, 1900.

Cozzens, Peter, and Robert Girardi, eds. *The Military Memoirs of General John Pope.* Chapel Hill: University of North Carolina Press, 1998.

Dahlgren, Madeline, ed. *Memoir of John A. Dahlgren.* Boston: J. R. Osgood, 1882.

Daly, Robert, ed. *Aboard the USS* Monitor: *1862. The Letters of Acting Paymaster William Frederick Keeler.* Annapolis, Md.: U.S. Naval Institute Press, 1964.

Dana, Charles A. *Recollections of the Civil War.* New York: D. Appleton, 1902.

Dyer, Heman. *Records of an Active Life.* New York: Thomas Whittaker, 1886.

Eulogies Delivered on the Occasion of the Announcement of the Death of the Hon. Edwin M. Stanton, Associate Justice, Supreme Court of the United States. Washington, D.C.: Judd & Detweiler, 1870.

Fehrenbacher, Don. *The Dred Scott Case: Its Significance in American Law and Politics.* New York: Oxford University Press, 1978.

Fehrenbacher, Don, and Virginia Fehrenbacher, eds. *Recollected Words of Abraham Lincoln.* Stanford: Stanford University Press, 1996.

Foner, Philip, ed. *The Life and Writings of Frederick Douglass.* 5 vols. New York: International, 1950.

Gates, Henry, ed. *Frederick Douglass: Autobiographies.* New York: Library of America, 1994.

Gienapp, William, and Erica Gienapp, eds. *The Civil War Diary of Gideon Welles: Lincoln's Secretary of the Navy.* Baltimore: Johns Hopkins University Press, 2014.

Giunta, Mary, ed. *A Civil War Soldier of Christ and Country: The Selected Correspondence of John Rodgers Meigs, 1859–64.* Urbana: University of Illinois Press, 2006.

Graf, LeRoy, ed. *The Papers of Andrew Johnson.* 16 vols. Knoxville: University of Tennessee Press, 1967–2000.

Grant, Ulysses. *The Personal Memoirs of U.S. Grant.* 2 vols. New York: Charles Webster, 1885.

Gurowski, Adam. *Diary, from March 4, 1861, to November 12, 1862.* Boston: Lee & Shepard, 1862.

———. *Diary from Nov. 18, 1862, to Oct. 18, 1863.* New York: Carleton, 1864.

———. *Diary: 1863–'64–'65.* Washington: W. H. & O. H. Morrison, 1866.

Hall, Charles. *A Discourse Preached by Request in the Church of the Epiphany on January 5, 1873.* Cambridge: Riverside Press, 1873.

———. *A Mournful Easter: A Discourse Delivered in the Church of the Epiphany . . . of Good Friday.* Washington: Gideon & Pearson, 1865.

[Hammond, William.] *Statement of the Causes Which Led to the Dismissal of Surgeon-General William A. Hammond from the Army,* 1864.

Hansen, Marie, ed. *On Two Continents: Memories of Half a Century.* New York: Doubleday, Page, 1905.

Haupt, Herman. *Reminiscences of General Herman Haupt.* Milwaukee: Wright & Joys, 1901.

Hoffman, Ogden. *Reports of Land Cases Determined in the United States District Court for the Northern District of California.* San Francisco: Numa Hubert, 1862.

Holt, Joseph. *Vindication of Hon. Joseph Holt Judge Advocate General of the United States Army.* Washington, D.C.: Chronicle, 1873.

Holzer, Harold, ed. *Lincoln's White House Secretary: The Adventurous Life of William O. Stoddard.* Carbondale: Southern Illinois University Press, 2007.

House, Madeline, and Graham Storey, eds. *The Letters of Charles Dickens.* 12 vols. Oxford: Clarendon Press, 1965–2002.

Howard, Oliver O. *Autobiography of Oliver Otis Howard.* 2 vols. New York: Baker & Taylor, 1908.

Journal of the Congress of the Confederate States of America. 7 vols. Washington: Government Printing Office, 1904–5.

"Letters of General Henry W. Halleck, 1861–62." *The Collector* 21 (1908): 29, 39–40, 52–53.

Lowe, David, ed. *Meade's Army: The Private Notebooks of Lt. Col. Theodore L. Lyman.* Kent, Ohio: Kent State University Press, 2007.

Marshall, Jessie Ames, ed. *Private and Official Correspondence of Benjamin Butler.* 5 vols. Norwood, Mass.: Plimpton Press, 1917.

McAllister, Cutler, ed. *Reports of Cases Argued and Determined in the Circuit Court of the United States for the Districts of California.* New York: John Voorhies, 1859.

McClellan, George B. *McClellan's Own Story*. New York: Charles Webster, 1887.

Meade, George, ed. *The Life and Letters of George Gordon Meade*. 2 vols. New York: Charles Scribner's Sons, 1913.

Moore, John, ed. *The Works of James Buchanan*. 12 vols. Philadelphia, J. B. Lippincott, 1908.

Nevins, Allan, ed. *A Diary of Battle: The Personal Journals of Colonel Charles S. Wainwright, 1861–1865*. New York: Harcourt, Brace & World, 1962.

Nevins, Allan, and Milton Thomas, eds. *The Diary of George Templeton Strong*. 4 vols. New York: Macmillan, 1952.

Niven, John, ed. *The Salmon P. Chase Papers*. 5 vols. Kent, Ohio: Kent State University Press, 1993–98.

"Notes of Colonel W. G. Moore, Private Secretary to President Johnson, 1866–1868." *American Historical Review* 19 (1913): 98–132.

Official Opinions of the Attorneys-General of the United States. 12 vols. Washington, D.C.: R. Farnham, 1852–70.

Official Proceedings of the National Democratic Convention, held in Cincinnati, June 2–6, 1856. Cincinnati: Enquirer Company, 1856.

Official Records of the Union and Confederate Navies in the War of Rebellion. 30 vols. Washington, D.C.: Government Printing Office, 1894–1922.

Palmer, Beverly, ed. *The Selected Letters of Charles Sumner*. 2 vols. Boston: Northeastern University Press, 1990.

Pierce, Edward, ed. *Memoir and Letters of Charles Sumner*. 4 vols. London: Sampson Low, Marston. 1878–93.

Pleadings, Exhibits and Evidence, in the Case of Joshua Nachtrieb. Pittsburgh: Harper & Layton, 1854.

Proceedings and Address of the Democratic State Convention of the State of Ohio, Held in the City of Columbus on the Eighth and Ninth Days of January, 1844. Columbus: S. Medary, 1844.

Proceedings in the Supreme Court of the United States at Their Session Held Monday, January 17, 1870, in Relation to the Death of Hon. Edwin M. Stanton. Washington, D.C.: Government Printing Office, 1870.

Proceedings of the Democratic State Convention, Held in Columbus, Ohio, Seventh and Eighth Days of January 1842. Columbus: S. Medary, 1842.

Proceedings of the Democratic State Convention, Held in Columbus, on the Eighth of January 1840. Columbus: S. & M. H. Medary, 1840.

Proceedings of the First Three Republican National Conventions of 1856, 1860 and 1864. Minneapolis: Charles W. Johnson, 1893.

Quaife, Milo, ed. *From the Cannon's Mouth: The Civil War Letters of General Alpheus S. Williams*. Detroit: Wayne State University Press, 1959.

Randall, James, ed. *The Diary of Orville Hickman Browning*. 2 vols. Springfield: Illinois State Historical Library, 1925, 1933.

Randolph, Thomas Jefferson, ed. *Memoirs, Correspondence and Miscellanies from the Papers of Thomas Jefferson.* 4 vols. London: Henry Colborn & Richard Bentley, 1829.

Raymond, Henry. "Extracts from the Journal of Henry Raymond." *Scribner's Monthly* 19 (Jan. 1880): 419–24.

Richert, Catherine, ed. *Ellen Hutchison Stanton Letters, 1845–1869.* Privately printed, 2014.

Roth, Margaret, ed. *Well, Mary: Civil War Letters of a Wisconsin Volunteer.* Madison: University of Wisconsin Press, 1960.

Royster, Charles, ed. *Memoirs of General W. T. Sherman.* New York: Library of America, 1990.

Russell, Charles. *Memoir of Charles H. Russell, 1776–1884.* New York: 1908.

Sanders, John. *Memoirs on the Military Resources of the Valley of the Ohio.* Washington, D.C.: C. Alexander, 1845.

Sears, Stephen ed. *The Civil War Papers of George B. McClellan.* New York: Ticknor & Fields, 1989.

Seward, Frederick. *Seward at Washington as Senator and Secretary of State: A Memoir of His Life with Selections from His Letters. 1861–1872.* New York: Derby & Miller, 1891.

Sherman, William. *Memoirs of General W. T. Sherman.* 2 vols. New York: Charles Webster, 1890.

Simon, John, ed. *The Personal Memoirs of Julia Dent Grant.* New York: G. P. Putnam's Sons, 1975.

Simon, John, ed. *The Papers of Ulysses Grant.* 32 vols. Carbondale: Southern Illinois University Press, 1967–2012.

Simpson, Brooks, ed. *The Civil War: The Third Year.* New York: Library of America, 2013.

Simpson, Brooks, and Jean Berlin, eds. *Sherman's Civil War: Selected Correspondence of William T. Sherman, 1860–1865.* Chapel Hill: University of North Carolina Press, 1999.

Smart, James, ed. *A Radical View: The "Agate" Dispatches of Whitelaw Reid, 1861–1865.* 2 vols. Memphis, Tenn.: Memphis State University Press, 1976.

Smith, Theodore, ed. *The Life and Letters of James Abram Garfield.* 2 vols. New Haven: Yale University Press, 1925.

Speech of Hon. William Allen, of Ohio, Delivered in the Senate of the United States, February 10 and 11, 1846, on our Relations with England—Being the Opening Speech Pending the Oregon Notice, 1846.

Stanton, Edwin. *Argument for the Complainant, in the Case of the State of Pennsylvania, vs. the Wheeling & Belmont Bridge . . . in the Supreme Court of the United States.* Philadelphia: Brown's, 1852.

———. *Florida Contested Election of the United States Senator: Argument before the Select Committee of the U.S. Senate.* Washington, D.C.: Gibson, 1852.

————. *The Wheeling Bridge Case, Mr. Stanton's Argument.* [1850].

Stanton, Gideon Townsend, ed. *Edwin M. Stanton: A Personal Portrait.* ca. 1950. Typescript available at Louisiana State University, Baton Rouge.

Stoeckel, Carl, ed. *Correspondence of John Sedgwick, Major General.* 2 vols. New York: De Vinne Press, 1902.

Styple, William, ed. *Generals in Bronze: Interviewing the Commanders of the Civil War.* Kearny, N.J.: Belle Grove, 2005.

Trial of the Hon. Daniel E. Sickles for Shooting Philip Barton, Key, Esq., U.S. District Attorney, of Washington, D.C. New York: R. M. De Witt, 1859.

Walworth, Reuben. *Order of Reference of the Supreme Court of the United States in the Case of the State of Pennsylvania, Complainant, against The Wheeling & Belmont Bridge Company and Others, Defendants.* Saratoga Springs, N.Y.: George White, 1851.

The War of the Rebellion: A Compilation of the Official Records of the Union and Confederate Armies. 128 vols. Washington, D.C.: Government Printing Office, 1880–1901.

Ward, William, ed. *Abraham Lincoln: Tributes from His Associates.* New York: Clarke Sales, 1895.

Williams, Frederick, ed. *The Wild Life of the Army: Civil War Letters of James A. Garfield.* East Lansing: Michigan State University Press, 1964.

Wilson, Douglas, and Rodney Davis, eds. *Herndon's Informants: Letters, Interviews and Statements about Abraham Lincoln.* Urbana: University of Illinois Press, 1998.

Winthrop, William. *Digest of Opinions of the Judge Advocate General of the Army.* Washington, D.C.: Government Printing Office, 1868.

Wolcott, Pamphila. *Edwin M. Stanton: A Biographical Sketch by His Sister.* ca. 1895. Typescript available at Ohio History Connection, Columbus.

Zunz, Olivier ed. *Tocqueville and Gustave de Beaumont in America: Their Friendship and Their Travels.* Charlottesville: University of Virginia Press, 2010.

Secondary Sources

Ackerman, Bruce. *We the People*, Vol. 2, *Transformations.* Cambridge, Mass.: Harvard University Press, 1993.

Alexander, Roberta. *A Place of Recourse: A History of the U.S. District Court for the Southern District of Ohio, 1803–2003.* Athens: Ohio University Press, 2005.

Alford, Terry. *Fortune's Fool: The Life of John Wilkes Booth.* New York: Oxford University Press, 2015.

Ambler, Charles. *A History of Transportation in the Ohio Valley.* Glendale, Calif.: Arthur Clark, 1932.

Andrews, J. Cutler. *The North Reports the Civil War*. Pittsburgh: University of Pittsburgh Press, 1955.

Applegate, Debby. *The Most Famous Man in America: The Biography of Henry Ward Beecher*. New York: Doubleday, 2006.

Arndt, Karl. *George Rapp's Harmony Society, 1785–1847*. Philadelphia: University of Pennsylvania Press, 1965.

Ascher, Leonard. "Lincoln's Administration and the New Almaden Mine Scandal." *Pacific Historical Review* 5 (1936): 38–51.

Ashmore, Anne. *Dates of Supreme Court Decisions and Arguments*. 2006. Typescript on Supreme Court website.

Badeau, Adam. *Grant in Peace: From Appomattox to Mount McGregor*. Hartford: S. S. Scranton & Co., 1887.

———. *Military History of Ulysses S. Grant, from April, 1861, to April, 1865*. 3 vols. New York: D. Appleton, 1868–81.

Baker, Lafayette. *The United States Secret Service in the Late War*. Philadelphia: J. E. Potter, 1869.

Bates, David Homer. *Lincoln in the Telegraph Office: Recollections of the United States Military Telegraph Corps During the Civil War*. New York: Century, 1907.

Benedict, Michael. *A Compromise of Principle: Congressional Republicans and Reconstruction, 1863–1869*. New York: Norton, 1974.

Benjamin, Charles. "Recollections of Secretary Stanton." *Century Magazine* 33 (1887): 758–68.

Benton, Joseph. *Voting in the Field: A Forgotten Chapter of the Civil War*. Boston: Privately printed, 1915.

Bergeron, Paul. *Andrew Johnson's Civil War and Reconstruction*. Knoxville: University of Tennessee Press, 2011.

Black, Jeremiah. "Mr. Black to Mr. Wilson." *Galaxy* 11 (Feb. 1871): 257–76.

———. "Senator Wilson and Edwin M. Stanton." *Galaxy* 9 (June 1870): 817–31.

Blondheim, Menahem. *News over the Wires: The Telegraph and the Flow of Public Information in America, 1844–1897*. Cambridge, Mass.: Harvard University Press, 1997.

———. "'Public Sentiment Is Everything': The Union's Public Communications Strategy and the Bogus Proclamation of 1864." *Journal of American History* 89 (2002): 869–99.

Blue, Frederick. *Salmon P. Chase: A Life in Politics*. Kent, Ohio: Kent State University Press, 1987.

Blustein, Bonnie. *Preserve Your Love for Science: Life of William A. Hammond, American Neurologist*. Cambridge, U.K.: Cambridge University Press, 1991.

Bordewich, Fergus. *America's Great Debate: Henry Clay, Stephen A. Douglas, and the Compromise That Preserved the Union*. New York: Simon & Schuster, 2012.

Botume, Elizabeth. *First Days among the Contrabands.* Boston: Lee & Shepard, 1893.

Boutwell, George. "Johnson's Plot and Motives." *North American Review* 141 (Dec. 1885): 572–84.

Brandt, Nat. *The Congressman Who Got Away with Murder.* Syracuse, N.Y.: Syracuse University Press, 1991.

Brigance, William. *Jeremiah Black: A Defender of the Constitution and the Ten Commandments.* Philadelphia: University of Pennsylvania Press, 1934.

Brinton, John. *Personal Memoirs of John H. Brinton.* New York: Neale, 1914.

Brooks, Noah. *Washington D.C. in Lincoln's Time.* Ed. Herbert Mitgang. Athens: University of Georgia Press, 1958.

———. *Washington in Lincoln's Time.* New York: Century, 1895.

Browne, Francis. *The Every-Day Life of Abraham Lincoln.* Washington, D.C.: National Tribune, 1886.

Burke, James, and Donald Bensch. "Mount Pleasant and the Early Quakers of Ohio." *Ohio History* 83 (1974): 220–55.

Burlingame, Michael. *Abraham Lincoln: A Life.* 2 vols. Baltimore: Johns Hopkins University Press, 2008.

Cadwalader, John. *Cadwalader's Cases.* 2 vols. Philadelphia, R. Welsh & Co., 1907.

Caldwell, J. A. *History of Belmont and Jefferson Counties, Ohio.* Wheeling, W. Va.: Historical Publishing, 1880.

Calvert, Monte. "The Allegheny City Cotton Mill Riot of 1848." *Western Pennsylvania Historical Magazine* 46 (1963): 97–133.

Campbell, John. *Biographical Sketches: With Other Literary Remains of the Late John W. Campbell.* Columbus: Scott & Gallagher, 1838.

Cannon, Carl. "Lincoln: Does He Belong to 'the Ages' or 'the Angels'?" *Real Clear Politics*, Apr. 15, 2015.

Carnegie, Andrew. *Edwin M. Stanton: An Address on Stanton Memorial Day at Kenyon College.* New York: Doubleday, Page, 1906.

Carpenter, Francis B. *The Inner Life of Abraham Lincoln: Six Months at the White House with Abraham Lincoln.* New York: Hurd & Houghton, 1868.

Carter, Dan. *When the War Was Over: The Failure of Self-Reconstruction in the South, 1867–1867.* Baton Rouge: Louisiana State University Press, 1985.

Castel, Albert. *Decision in the West: The Atlanta Campaign of 1864.* Lawrence: University of Kansas Press, 1992.

———. *The Presidency of Andrew Johnson.* Lawrence: University of Kansas Press, 1979.

Caswall, Henry. *America and the American Church.* London: J. G. & F. Rivington, 1839.

Cayton, Andrew, and Stuart Hobbs, eds. *The Center of a Great Empire: The Ohio Country in the Early American Republic.* Columbus: Ohio University Press, 2005.

Chamlee, Roy Z. *Lincoln's Assassins: A Complete Account of Their Capture, Trial and Punishment*. Jefferson, N.C.: McFarland, 1990.

Chipman, N. P. *The Tragedy of Andersonville: Trial of Captain Henry Wirz, The Prison Keeper*. San Francisco: Blair Murdock Co., 1911.

Chittenden, Lucius E. *Recollections of President Lincoln and His Administration*. New York: Harper & Brothers, 1891.

Clark, John. *Railroads in the Civil War: The Impact of Management on Victory and Defeat*. Baton Rouge: Louisiana State University Press, 2001.

Clarke, Dwight. *William Tecumseh Sherman: Gold Rush Banker*. San Francisco: California Historical Society, 1969.

Cohen, Eliot. *Supreme Command: Soldiers, Statesmen, and Leadership in Wartime*. New York: Simon & Schuster, 2002.

Cole, Charles. *A Fragile Capital: Identity and the Early Years of Columbus, Ohio*. Columbus: Ohio State University Press, 2000.

Coleman, Elisheva. "Call It Peace or Call It Treason: The Milligan Case and the Meaning of Loyalty in the Civil War." BA thesis, Princeton University, 2005.

Conn, Stetson. *Washington's Epiphany, Church and Parish*. Washington, D.C.: Church of the Epiphany, 1976.

Cook, Robert. *Civil War Senator: William Pitt Fessenden and the Fight to Save the American Republic*. Baton Rouge: Louisiana State University Press, 2011.

Cooling, Benjamin Franklin. *Jubal Early's Raid on Washington: 1864*. Baltimore: Nautical & Aviation Pub. Co. of America, 1989.

———. *Monocacy: The Battle That Saved Washington*. Shippensburg, Pa.: White Mane, 1997.

Cooper, William. *We Have the War upon Us: The Onset of the Civil War, November 1860–April 1861*. New York: Knopf, 2012.

Cornish, Dudley. *The Sable Arm: Black Troops in the Union Army, 1861–1865*. Lawrence: University of Kansas Press, 1957.

Cowden, Joanna. *"Heaven Will Frown on Such a Cause as This": Six Democrats Who Opposed Lincoln's War*. Lanham, Md.: University Press of America, 2001.

Cozzens, Peter. *General John Pope: A Life for the Nation*. Urbana: University of Illinois Press, 2000.

———. *Shenandoah 1862: Stonewall Jackson's Valley Campaign*. Chapel Hill: University of North Carolina Press, 2003.

———. *This Terrible Sound: The Battle of Chickamauga*. Urbana: University of Illinois Press, 1992.

Cramer, Zadok. *The Navigator: Containing Directions for Navigating the Monongahela, Allegheny, Ohio and Mississippi Rivers*. Pittsburgh: Cramer, Spear & Eichbaum, 1814.

Crawford, Samuel. *The Genesis of the Civil War: The Story of Sumter, 1860–1861*. New York: Charles Webster, 1887.

Crofts, Daniel. *A Secession Crisis Enigma: William Henry Hurlbert and "The Diary of a Public Man."* Baton Rouge: Louisiana State University Press, 2010.

Curtis, George. *Life of James Buchanan.* 2 vols. New York: Harper & Brothers, 1883.

Curtis, Michael. "Lincoln, Vallandigham, and Anti-War Speech in the Civil War." *William & Mary Bill of Rights Journal* 7 (1998): 105–92.

Darby, William. *An Emigrant's Guide to the Western and Southwestern States and Territories.* New York: Kirk & Mercein, 1818.

Detroit Post & Tribune. *Zachariah Chandler: An Outline Sketch of His Life and Public Service.* Detroit: Detroit Post & Tribune, 1880.

Detzer, David. *Allegiance: Fort Sumter, Charleston, and the Beginning of the Civil War.* New York: Harcourt, 2002.

Dewitt, David. *The Impeachment and Trial of Andrew Johnson.* New York: Macmillan, 1903.

Dickens, Charles. *American Notes for General Circulation.* London: Chapman & Hall, 1842.

Donald, David Herbert. *Charles Sumner and the Rights of Man.* New York: Knopf, 1970.

———. *Lincoln.* New York: Simon & Schuster, 1995.

Downs, Gregory. *After Appomattox: Military Occupation and the Ends of War.* Cambridge, Mass.: Harvard University Press, 2015.

Doyle, Joseph B. *In Memoriam: Edwin McMasters Stanton, His Life and Work.* Steubenville, Ohio: Herald Printing, 1911.

Drozdowski, Eugene C. "Edwin M. Stanton: Lincoln's Secretary of War." Ph.D. diss., Duke University, 1954.

Earle, Jonathan. *Jacksonian Antislavery and the Politics of Free Soil, 1824–1854.* Chapel Hill: University of North Carolina Press, 2004.

Easby-Smith, James. *The Department of Justice: Its History and Functions.* Washington, D.C.: W. H. Lowdermilk & Co., 1904.

Eastman, Frank. *Courts and Lawyers of Pennsylvania.* 3 vols. New York: American Historical Society, 1922.

Egerton, Douglas. *The Wars of Reconstruction: The Brief, Violent History of America's Most Progressive Era.* New York: Bloomsbury Press, 2014.

Eggleston, Michael. *Lincoln's Recruiter: General Lorenzo Thomas and the United States Colored Troops in the Civil War.* Jefferson, N.C.: McFarland, 2013.

Eisenhower, John. *So Far from God: The U.S. War with Mexico, 1846–1848.* New York: Random House, 1989.

Eisenschiml, Otto. "An Intriguing Letter." *Autograph Collector's Journal* 1 (1948): 13–14.

———. *Why Was Lincoln Murdered?* Boston: Little, Brown, 1937.

Ellet, Charles, Jr. *The Wheeling Bridge Suit: A Notice of Its History and Objects*. Philadelphia: John C. Clark, 1852.

Engle, Stephen. *Gathering to Save a Nation: Lincoln and the Union's War Governors*. Chapel Hill: University of North Carolina Press, 2016.

Ethington, Philip. *The Public City: The Political Construction of Urban Life in San Francisco*. New York: Cambridge University Press, 1994.

Fairman, Charles. *Reconstruction and Reunion, 1864–88*. 2 vols. New York: Macmillan, 1971.

Faust, Drew Gilpin. *This Republic of Suffering: Death and the American Civil War*. New York: Knopf, 2008.

Feis, William. "A Union Military Intelligence Failure: Jubal Early's Raid, June 12–July 14, 1864." *Civil War History* 36 (1990): 209–25.

Feller, Daniel. "A Brother in Arms: Benjamin Tappan and the Antislavery Democracy." *Journal of American History* 88 (June 2001): 48–74.

Fellman, Michael. *Citizen Sherman: A Life of William Tecumseh Sherman*. Lawrence: University Press of Kansas, 1995.

Fessenden, Francis. *Life and Public Services of William Pitt Fessenden*. 2 vols. Boston: Houghton Mifflin, 1907.

Ficklen, John. *History of Reconstruction in Louisiana (through 1868)*. Baltimore: Johns Hopkins University Press, 1910.

Field, Alston. "Attorney-General Black and the California Land Claims." *Pacific Historical Review* 4 (1935): 235–45.

Fischer, LeRoy. *Lincoln's Gadfly: Adam Gurowski*. Norman: University of Oklahoma Press, 1964.

Flood, Charles. *1864: Lincoln at the Gates of History*. New York: Simon & Schuster, 2009.

Flower, Frank. *Edwin McMasters Stanton: The Autocrat of Rebellion, Emancipation, and Reconstruction*. Akron, Ohio: Saalfield, 1905.

Foner, Eric. *Reconstruction: America's Unfinished Revolution*. New York: Harper & Row, 1988.

Forman, Jonathan. "The First Cholera Epidemic in Columbus, Ohio, 1833." *Annals of Medical History* 6 (1934): 410–23.

Foulke, William. *The Life of Oliver P. Morton*. 2 vols. Indianapolis: Bowen-Merrill, 1899.

Fox, Richard. "A Phrase for the Ages." *From the Top Hat: Abraham Lincoln Presidential Library and Museum Blog*, Aug. 10, 2010.

Freehling, William. *The Road to Disunion*. Vol. 2: *Secessionists Triumphant*. New York: Oxford University Press, 2007.

Foote, Shelby. *The Civil War: A Narrative*. 3 vols. New York: Random House, 1958–74.

Freidel, Frank. *Francis Lieber: Nineteenth-Century Liberal.* Baton Rouge: Louisiana State University Press, 1947.

Furgurson, Ernest B. *Freedom Rising: Washington in the Civil War.* New York: Knopf, 2004.

———. *Not War but Murder: Cold Harbor 1864.* New York: Knopf, 2000.

Gabler, Henry. "The Fitz John Porter Case: Politics and Military Justice." Ph.D. diss., City University of New York, 1979.

Gallagher, Gary, ed. *The Shenandoah Valley Campaign of 1862.* Chapel Hill: University of North Carolina Press, 2003.

Gallman, Matthew. *America's Joan of Arc: The Life of Anna Elizabeth Dickinson.* New York: Oxford University Press, 2006.

Geary, James W. *We Need Men: The Union Draft in the Civil War.* DeKalb: Northern Illinois University Press, 1991.

George, Joseph. "'Black Flag Warfare': Lincoln and the Raids against Richmond and Jefferson Davis." *Pennsylvania Magazine of History & Biography* 115 (1991): 291–318.

Glatthaar, Joseph. *The March to the Sea and Beyond: Sherman's Troops in the Savannah and Carolinas Campaign.* New York: New York University Press, 1985.

Goodwin, Doris Kearns. *Team of Rivals: The Political Genius of Abraham Lincoln.* New York: Simon & Schuster, 2005.

Gold, David. *Democracy in Session: A History of the Ohio General Assembly.* Athens: Ohio University Press, 2009.

Goodheart, Adam. *1861: The Civil War Awakening.* New York: Knopf, 2011.

Gopnik, Adam. "Angels and Ages: Lincoln's Language and Its Legacy." *New Yorker*, May 28, 2007.

Gorham, George. *The Life and Public Services of Edwin M. Stanton.* 2 vols. Boston: Houghton Mifflin, 1899.

Graves, Frederick. "The Early Life and Career of Edwin M. Stanton." Ph.D. diss., University of Kentucky, 1956.

Greenberg, Irwin. "Charles Ingersoll: The Aristocrat as Copperhead." *Pennsylvania Magazine of History & Biography* 93 (1969): 190–217.

Greenburg, Amy. *A Wicked War: Polk, Clay, Lincoln, and the 1846 U.S. Invasion of Mexico.* New York: Knopf, 2012.

Guelzo, Allen. "Does Lincoln Still Belong to the Ages?" *Journal of the Abraham Lincoln Association* 33 (2012): 1–13.

———. *Gettysburg: The Last Invasion.* New York: Knopf, 2013.

———. *Redeeming the Great Emancipator.* Cambridge, Mass.: Harvard University Press, 2016.

Hacker, David. "Economic, Demographic, and Anthropomorphic Correlates of First Marriage in Mid-Nineteenth Century America." *Social Science History* 32 (Fall 2008): 307–45.

Hadley, Amos. *Life of Walter Harriman: With Selections from His Speeches and Writings*. Boston: Houghton Mifflin & Co., 1888.

Hall, James. "The Dahlgren Papers." *Civil War Times Illustrated* 22 (1983): 30–39.

Hanchett, William. "The Eisenschiml Thesis." *Civil War History* 25 (1979): 197–217.

———. "The Historian as Gamesman: Otto Eisenschiml, 1880–1963." *Civil War History* 36 (1990): 5–16.

Harper, Robert S. *Lincoln and the Press*. New York: McGraw Hill, 1951.

Harris, William C. *Lincoln and the Border States: Preserving the Union*. Lawrence: University Press of Kansas, 2011.

———. *Lincoln's Last Months*. Cambridge, Mass.: Belknap Press, 2004.

———. *With Charity for All: Lincoln and the Restoration of the Union*. Lexington: University of Kentucky Press, 1997.

Hart, Gideon. "Military Commissions and the Lieber Code: Toward a New Understanding of the Jurisdictional Foundations of Military Commissions." *Military Law Review* 203 (2010): 1–77.

Hartigan, Richard. *Lieber's Code and the Laws of War*. Chicago: Precedent, 1983.

Hattaway, Herman, and Archer Jones. *How the North Won: A Military History of the Civil War*. Urbana: University of Illinois Press, 1983.

Havighurst, Walter. *Ohio: A History*. Urbana: University of Illinois Press, 2001.

Hearn, Chester. *Ellet's Brigade: The Strangest Outfit of All*. Baton Rouge: Louisiana State University Press, 2000.

Hedrick, Joan. *Harriet Beecher Stowe: A Life*. New York: Oxford University Press, 1994.

Hempton, David. *Methodism: Empire of the Spirit*. New Haven: Yale University Press, 2005.

Hennessy, John J. *Return to Bull Run: The Campaign and Battle of Second Manassas*. New York: Simon & Schuster, 1993.

Hesseltine, William. *Civil War Prisons: A Study in War Psychology*. Columbus: Ohio State University Press, 1930.

———. *Lincoln and the War Governors*. New York: Knopf, 1948.

Hinshaw, William. *Encyclopedia of American Quaker Genealogy*. 5 vols. Ann Arbor, Mich.: Edwards Brothers, 1936–46.

Historical Sketch of St. Peter's Church, 1850–1918. Typescript at University of Pittsburgh Archives Center.

Hittell, Theodore. "Limantour." *Overland Monthly* 2 (1869): 154–60.

Hodes, Martha. *Mourning Lincoln*. New Haven: Yale University Press, 2015.

Hoffert, Sylvia. *Jane Grey Swisshelm: An Unconventional Life, 1815–1884*. Chapel Hill: University of North Carolina Press, 2004.

Hollister, O. J. *Life of Schuyler Colfax*. New York: Funk & Wagnalls, 1886.

Hollandsworth, James. *An Absolute Massacre: The New Orleans Race Riot of July 30, 1866*. Baton Rouge: Louisiana State University Press, 2001.

Holt, Edgar. *Party Politics in Ohio, 1840–1850*. Columbus, Ohio: F. J. Heer, 1931.

Holt, Michael. *The Rise and Fall of the American Whig Party: Jacksonian Politics and the Onset of the Civil War*. New York: Oxford University Press, 1999.

Holzer, Harold. *Lincoln and the Power of the Press: The War for Public Opinion*. New York: Simon & Schuster, 2014.

Holzer, Harold, and Sara Gabbard, eds. *1865: America Makes War and Peace in Lincoln's Final Year*. Carbondale: Southern Illinois University Press, 2015.

Hoogenboom, Ari. *Gustavus Vasa Fox of the Union Navy: A Biography*. Baltimore: Johns Hopkins University Press, 2008.

Howe, Daniel Walker. *What Hath God Wrought: The Transformation of America, 1815–1848*. New York: Oxford University Press, 2007.

Howe, Henry. *Historical Collections of Ohio*. 2 vols. Cincinnati: C. J. Kreihbel & Co., 1907.

Hyman, Harold. "Johnson, Stanton, and Grant: A Reconsideration of the Army's Role in the Events Leading to the Impeachment." *American Historical Review* 66 (1960): 85–96.

———, ed. *The Radical Republicans and Reconstruction, 1861–1870*. Indianapolis: Bobbs-Merrill, 1967.

Ingersoll, Lurton D. *A History of the War Department of the United States with Biographical Sketches of the Secretaries*. Washington, D.C.: Francis Mohun, 1879.

Irvine, Dallas. "The Archive Office of the War Department: Repository of Captured Confederate Archives, 1865–1881." *Military Affairs* 10 (1946): 93–111.

Jellison, Charles. *Fessenden of Maine: Civil War Senator*. Syracuse, N.Y.: Syracuse University Press, 1962.

Johannsen, Robert. *Stephen A. Douglas*. New York: Oxford University Press, 1973.

———. *To the Halls of the Montezumas: The Mexican War in the American Imagination*. New York: Oxford University Press, 1985.

Johnson, A. E. H. "Reminiscences of the Hon. Edwin M. Stanton." *Records of the Columbia Historical Society* 13 (1910): 69–97.

Johnson, Robert, and Clarence Buel, eds. *Battles and Leaders of the Civil War*. 4 vols. New York: Century, 1884.

Johnston, William, ed. *Trial of Daniel M'Cook, Esq.* Cincinnati: Hefley, Hubbell & Co., 1839.

Joiner, Gary. *Mr. Lincoln's Brown Water Navy: The Mississippi Squadron*. Lanham, Md.: Rowman & Littlefield, 2007.

Jones, Mary, ed. *An 18th Century Perspective: Culpeper County*. Culpeper, Va.: Culpeper Historical Society, 1976.

Kahan, Paul. *Amiable Scoundrel: Simon Cameron, Lincoln's Scandalous Secretary of War*. Lincoln, Neb.: Potomac Books, 2016.

Kamm, Samuel. *The Civil War Career of Thomas A. Scott*. Philadelphia: University of Pennsylvania Press, 1940.

Kelley, Brooks. "Fossildom, Old Fogeyism, and Red Tape." *Pennsylvania Magazine of History and Biography* 90 (1966): 93–114.

Kelley, Harrison. *A Genealogical History of the Kelley Family*. Cleveland, Ohio: Privately printed, 1897.

Kendrick, Paul, and Stephen Kendrick. *Douglass and Lincoln: How a Revolutionary Black Leader and a Reluctant Liberator Struggled to End Slavery and Save the Union*. New York: Walker Books, 2008.

Keneally, Thomas. *American Scoundrel: The Life of the Notorious Civil War General Dan Sickles*. New York: Nan A. Talese, 2002.

King, Horatio. "My Recollections of the War." *Blue & Gray* (Oct. 1893): 289–91.

———. *Turning On the Light*. Philadelphia: J. B. Lippincott, 1895.

Kiper, Richard L. *Major General John Alexander McClernand: Politician in Uniform*. Kent, Ohio: Kent State University Press, 1999.

Klaus, Samuel, ed. *The Milligan Case*. New York: Knopf, 1929.

Klein, Lisa. *Be It Remembered: The Story of Trinity Episcopal Church in Capitol Square*. Wilmington, Ohio: Orange Frazer Press, 2003.

Klein, Philip. *President James Buchanan: A Biography*. University Park: Pennsylvania State University Press, 1962.

Klement, Frank. "Clement L. Vallandigham's Exile in the Confederacy, May 25–June 17, 1863." *Journal of Southern History* 31 (1965): 149–63.

———. *Dark Lanterns: Secret Political Societies, Conspiracies, and Treason Trials in the Civil War*. Baton Rouge: Louisiana State University Press, 1989.

Klunder, Willard. *Lewis Cass and the Politics of Moderation*. Kent, Ohio: Kent State University Press, 1996.

Koistinen, Paul. *Beating Plowshares into Swords: The Political Economy of American Warfare, 1606–1865*. Lawrence: University Press of Kansas, 1996.

Konkle, Burton. *The Life of Chief Justice Ellis Lewis, 1798–1871*. Philadelphia: Campion, 1907.

Lamers, William M. *The Edge of Glory: A Biography of General William S. Rosecrans, U.S.A*. Baton Rouge: Louisiana State University Press, 1961.

Langeluttig, Albert. *The Department of Justice of the United States*. Baltimore: Lord Baltimore Press, 1927.

Leale, Charles. *Lincoln's Last Hours*. New York: Privately printed, 1909.

Lee, Alfred. *History of the City of Columbus, Ohio*. 2 vols. New York: W. W. Munsell & Co., 1892.

Leech, Margaret. *Reveille in Washington, 1860–1865*. New York: Harper & Brothers, 1941.

Leonard, Elizabeth. *Lincoln's Avengers: Justice, Revenge, and Reunion after the Civil War*. New York: Norton, 2004.

———. *Lincoln's Forgotten Ally: Judge Advocate General Holt of Kentucky*. Chapel Hill: University of North Carolina Press, 2011.

Lichterman, Martin. "John Adams Dix, 1798–1879." Ph.D. diss., Columbia University, 1952.

Long, David. "Lincoln, Davis, and the Dahlgren Raid." *North & South* 9 (Oct. 2006): 70–83.

Lowry, Thomas. *Merciful Lincoln: The President and Military Justice*. Privately printed, 2009.

Lyford, James. *Life of Edward H. Rollins*. Boston: Dana Estes & Co., 1906.

Mack, Charles, and Henry Lesesne, eds. *Francis Lieber and the Culture of the Mind*. Columbia: University of South Carolina Press, 2005.

Mackay, Alex. *The Western World, or, Travels in the United States in 1846–47*. 3 vols. London: Richard Bentley, 1849.

Magliocca, Gerard. *American Founding Son: John Bingham and the Fourteenth Amendment*. New York: New York University Press, 2013.

Mahaifer, Harry. "Mr. Grant and Mr. Dana." *American History* 35 (2000): 24–32.

Maizlish, Stephen. *Triumph of Sectionalism: The Transformation of Ohio Politics, 1844–1856*. Kent, Ohio: Kent State University Press, 1983.

Majeske, Penelope K. "Johnson, Stanton, and Grant: A Reconsideration of the Events Leading to the First Reconstruction Act." *Southern Studies* 22 (1983): 340–50.

Mangrum, Robert G. "Edwin M. Stanton's Special Military Units and the Prosecution of the War, 1862–1865." Ph.D. diss., University of North Texas, 1978.

Manning, Chandra. *Troubled Refuge: Struggling for Freedom in the Civil War*. New York: Knopf, 2016.

Marszalek, John. *Commander of All Lincoln's Armies: A Life of General Henry Halleck*. Cambridge, Mass.: Harvard University Press: 2004.

———. *Sherman: A Soldier's Passion for Order*. New York: Free Press, 1993.

———. "The Stanton-Sherman Controversy." *Civil War Times Illustrated* 9 (Oct. 1970): 4–12.

Marvel, William. *Burnside*. Chapel Hill: University of North Carolina Press, 1991.

———. *Lincoln's Autocrat: The Life of Edwin Stanton*. Chapel Hill: University of North Carolina Press, 2015.

Masur, Louis. *Lincoln's Hundred Days: The Emancipation Proclamation and the War for the Union*. Cambridge, Mass.: Belknap Press, 2012.

———. *Lincoln's Last Speech*. New York: Oxford University Press, 2015.

Maxwell, William Q. *Lincoln's Fifth Wheel: The Political History of the United States Sanitary Commission*. New York: Longmans, Green, 1956.

McAllister, Stephen. "A *Marbury v. Madison* Moment on the Eve of the Civil War." *Green Bag* 14 (2011): 405–21.

McClintock, Russell. *Lincoln and the Decision for War: The Northern Response to Secession*. Chapel Hill: University of North Carolina Press, 2008.

McClure, Alexander. *Abraham Lincoln and Men of War-Times*. Philadelphia: Times Publishing, 1892.

McFeely, William S. *Grant: A Biography*. New York: Norton, 1981.

———. *Yankee Stepfather: General O. O. Howard and the Freedmen*. New Haven: Yale University Press, 1968.

McGrath, Roger. "A Violent Birth: Disorder, Crime, and Law Enforcement." *California History* 81 (2003): 39–44.

McMurry, Richard. *Atlanta 1864: Last Chance for the Confederacy*. Lincoln: University of Nebraska Press, 2000.

McPherson, James M. *Battle Cry of Freedom: The Civil War Era*. New York: Oxford University Press, 1988.

———. *Tried by War: Abraham Lincoln as Commander-in-Chief*. New York: Penguin Press, 2008.

———. *War on the Waters: The Union and Confederate Navies, 1861–1865*. Chapel Hill: University of North Carolina Press, 2012.

Meneely, A. Howard. *The War Department in 1861: A Study in Mobilization and Administration*. New York: Columbia University Press, 1928.

Miles, Rufus. "The Origin and Meaning of Miles' Law." *Public Administration Review* 38 (1978): 399–403.

Miller, Edward. *Gullah Statesman: Robert Smalls from Slavery to Congress, 1839–1915*. Columbia: University of South Carolina Press, 1995.

———. *Lincoln's Abolitionist General: The Biography of David Hunter*. Columbia: University of South Carolina Press, 1997.

Mindich, David. *Just the Facts: How "Objectivity" Came to Define American Journalism*. New York: New York University Press, 1998.

Moe, Richard. *The Last Full Measure: The Life and Death of the First Minnesota Volunteers*. New York: Henry Holt, 1993.

Monroe, Elizabeth. *The Wheeling Bridge Case: Its Significance in American Law and Technology*. Boston: Northeastern University Press, 1992.

Moore, Shirley. " 'We Feel the Want of Protection': The Politics of Law and Race in California, 1848–1878." *California History* 81 (2003): 96–125.

Moran, Gerald. *John Chipman Gray: The Harvard Brahmin of Property Law*. Durham, N.C.: Carolina Academic Press, 2010.

Murray, Williamson, and Wayne Hsieh. *A Savage War: A Military History of the Civil War*. Princeton: Princeton University Press, 2016.

Muscatine, Doris. *Old San Francisco: The Biography of a City from Early Days to the Earthquake*. New York: Putnam, 1975.

Naroll, Raoul. "Lincoln and the Sherman Peace Fiasco—Another Fable?" *Journal of Southern History* 20 (1954): 459–83.

Nasaw, David. *Andrew Carnegie*. New York: Penguin, 2006.

Neely, Mark. *The Fate of Liberty: Abraham Lincoln and Civil Liberties*. New York: Oxford University Press, 1991.

———. *The Union Divided: Party Conflict in the Civil War North*. Cambridge, Mass.: Harvard University Press, 2002.

Nevins, Allan. *The Emergence of Lincoln*. 2 vols. New York: Charles Scribner's Sons, 1950.

———. *The War for the Union*. 4 vols. New York: Charles Scribner's Sons, 1959–71.

Nichols, David. *Lincoln and the Indians: Civil War Policy and Politics*. Columbia: University of Missouri Press, 1978.

Nichols, Roy F. *The Disruption of American Democracy*. New York: Free Press, 1948.

Nicolay, John G., and John Hay. *Abraham Lincoln: A History*. 10 vols. New York: Century, 1890.

Nicolay, John, and John Hay. "Abraham Lincoln: A History, Plans of Campaign." *Century* 36 (Oct. 1888): 912–33.

Nicolay, John, and John Hay. "Abraham Lincoln: A History, The Fourteenth of April." *Century* 39 (Jan. 1890): 428–43.

Niven, John. *Gideon Welles: Lincoln's Secretary of the Navy*. New York: Oxford University Press, 1973.

———. *Salmon P. Chase: A Biography*. New York: Oxford University Press, 1995.

Norman, Nellie. *History of the Culpeper County Normans*. Privately printed, 1972.

Oates, Stephen B. *A Woman of Valor: Clara Barton and the Civil War*. New York: Free Press, 1994.

O'Harrow, Robert. *The Quartermaster: Montgomery C. Meigs, Lincoln's General*. New York: Simon & Schuster, 2016.

O'Reilly, Bill. *Killing Lincoln*. New York: Henry Holt & Co., 2011.

Paris, Louis-Philippe, Comte de. *History of the Civil War in America*. 4 vols. Philadelphia: J. H. Coates, 1875.

Parker, Wyman W. "Edwin M. Stanton at Kenyon." *Ohio Archaeological and Historical Quarterly* 60 (1951): 233–56.

Parkinson, Robert H. "The Patent Case That Lifted Lincoln into a Presidential Candidate." *Abraham Lincoln Quarterly* 4 (1946): 113–15.

Pearson, Henry G. *The Life of John A. Andrew*. 2 vols. Boston: Houghton Mifflin, 1904.

Peckham, Howard. "James Tanner's Account of Lincoln's Death." *Abraham Lincoln Quarterly* 2 (1942): 176–83.

Perman, Michael. *Reunion without Compromise: The South and Reconstruction*. Cambridge, U.K.: Cambridge University Press, 1973.

Perret, Geoffrey. *Lincoln's War: The Untold Story of America's Greatest President as Commander-in-Chief*. New York: Random House, 2004.

Piatt, Donn. "Edwin M. Stanton." *North American Review* 142 (1886): 466–77.

Pickenpaugh, Roger. *Rescue by Rail: Troop Transfer and the Civil War in the West, 1863.* Lincoln: University of Nebraska Press, 1998.

Pinsker, Matthew. *Lincoln's Sanctuary: Abraham Lincoln and the Soldiers' Home.* New York: Oxford University Press, 2003.

Pitman, Benn. *The Assassination of President Lincoln and the Trial of the Conspirators.* Cincinnati, Ohio: Moore, Wilsatch & Baldwin, 1865.

Poole, Robert. *On Hallowed Ground: The Story of Arlington National Cemetery.* New York: Walker, 2009.

Porter, David Dixon. *Incidents and Anecdotes of the Civil War.* New York: D. Appleton, 1885.

Porter, Horace. *Campaigning with Grant.* New York: Century, 1897.

Potter, David. *Lincoln and His Party in the Secession Crisis.* New Haven: Yale University Press, 1942.

Pratt, Fletcher. *Stanton: Lincoln's Secretary of War.* New York: Norton, 1953.

Pryor, Elizabeth. *Clara Barton: Professional Angel.* Philadelphia: University of Pennsylvania Press, 1987.

Quist, John, and Michael Birkner, eds. *James Buchanan and the Coming of the Civil War.* Gainesville: University Press of Florida, 2013.

Rable, George C. *But There Was No Peace: The Role of Violence in the Politics of Reconstruction.* Athens: University of Georgia Press, 1984.

———. *Fredericksburg! Fredericksburg!* Chapel Hill: University of North Carolina Press, 2002.

Randall, J. G. "The Indemnity Act of 1863: A Study in the War-Time Immunity of Governmental Officers." *Michigan Law Review* 20 (1922): 589–613.

Reiser, Catherine. "Pittsburgh: The Hub of Western Commerce, 1800–1850." *Western Pennsylvania Historical Magazine* 25 (1942): 121–34.

Rice, Allen, ed. *Reminiscences of Abraham Lincoln by Distinguished Men of His Time.* New York: North American, 1886.

Richards, Leonard. *The California Gold Rush and the Coming of the Civil War.* New York: Knopf, 2007.

Riddleberger, Patrick W. *1866: The Critical Year Revisited.* Carbondale: Southern Illinois University Press, 1979.

Ridley, R. T. "To Be Taken with a Pinch of Salt: The Destruction of Carthage." *Classical Philology* 81 (Apr. 1986): 140–46.

Ripley, George, and Charles Dana. *The American Cyclopedia.* 17 vols. New York: D. Appleton & Co., 1881.

Roberts, Alasdair. *America's First Great Depression: Economic Crisis and Political Disorder after the Panic of 1837.* Ithaca, N.Y.: Cornell University Press, 2012.

Robinson, Alfred. *Life in California, During a Residence of Several Years in That Territory.* New York: Wiley & Putnam, 1846.

Rose, Willie Lee. *Rehearsal for Reconstruction: The Port Rose Experiment*. Indianapolis: Bobbs, Merrill, 1964.

Rosen, Robert. *The Jewish Confederates*. Columbia: University of South Carolina Press, 2000.

Rubin, Anne. *Through the Heart of Dixie: Sherman's March and American Memory*. Chapel Hill: University of North Carolina Press, 2014.

Sarna, Jonathan, and Benjamin Shapell. *Lincoln and the Jews: A History*. New York: Thomas Dunne Books, 2015.

Saunders, Robert. *John Archibald Campbell: Southern Moderate, 1811–1889*. Tuscaloosa: University of Alabama Press, 1997.

Schecter, Barnet. *The Devil's Own Work: The Civil War Draft Riots and the Fight to Reconstruct America*. New York: Walker Books, 2005.

Sears, Stephen. *Chancellorsville*. Boston: Houghton Mifflin, 1996.

———. *Controversies and Commanders: Dispatches from the Army of the Potomac*. Boston: Houghton Mifflin, 1999.

———. "The Dahlgren Papers Revisited." *Columbiad* 3 (1999): 63–87.

———. *George B. McClellan: The Young Napoleon*. New York: Ticknor & Fields, 1998.

———. *Gettysburg*. Boston: Houghton Mifflin, 2003.

———. *Landscape Turned Red: The Battle of Antietam*. New York: Ticknor & Fields, 1983.

———. *To the Gates of Richmond: The Peninsula Campaign*. New York: Ticknor & Fields, 1992.

Sefton, James. *The United States Army and Reconstruction, 1865–1877*. Baton Rouge: Louisiana State University Press, 1967.

Senkewicz, Robert. *Vigilantes in Gold Rush San Francisco*. Stanford: Stanford University Press, 1985.

Shankman, Arnold. "Soldier Votes and Clement L. Vallandigham in the 1863 Ohio Gubernatorial Election." *Ohio History* 82 (1973): 88–104.

Shannon, Fred. *The Organization and Administration of the Union Army, 1861–1865*. 2 vols. Cleveland, Ohio: Arthur Clark, 1928.

Shotwell, Walter G. *Driftwood: Being Papers on Old-Time American Towns and Some Old People*. London: Longmans, Green, 1927.

Shuck, Oscar ed. *History of the Bench and Bar of California*. Los Angeles: Commercial Printing House, 1901.

Silver, David. *Lincoln's Supreme Court*. Urbana: University of Illinois Press, 1956.

Simpson, Brooks. *Let Us Have Peace: Ulysses S. Grant and the Politics of War and Reconstruction, 1861–1868*. Chapel Hill: University of North Carolina Press, 1991.

———. *Ulysses S. Grant: Triumph over Adversity, 1822–1865*. New York: Houghton Mifflin, 2000.

Sipes, William. *The Pennsylvania Railroad*. Philadelphia, Pennsylvania Railroad Co., 1875.

Slick, Sewell. "William Wilkins: Pittsburgher Extraordinary." *Western Pennsylvania Historical Magazine* 22 (1939): 217–36.

Smith, Adam I. P. *No Party Now: Politics in the Civil War North*. New York: Oxford University Press, 2006.

Smith, H. E. "The Quaker Migration to the Upper Ohio, Their Customs and Discipline." *Ohio Archeological and Historical Society Publications* 37 (1928): 35–85.

Smith, Jean Edward. *Grant*. New York: Simon & Schuster, 2001.

Smith, John, ed. *Black Soldiers in Blue: African American Troops in the Civil War Era*. Chapel Hill: University of North Carolina Press, 2002.

———. "Recruitment of Negro Soldiers in Kentucky, 1863–1865." *Register of the Kentucky Historical Society* 72 (1974): 364–90.

Smith, Joseph, ed. *History of the Republican Party in Ohio*. 2 vols. Chicago: Lewis, 1898.

Smith, Reed. *Samuel Medary and the Crisis: Testing the Limits of Press Freedom*. Columbus: Ohio State University Press, 2007.

Smythe, George F. *Kenyon College: Its First Century*. New Haven: Yale University Press, 1924.

Solzhenitsyn, Alexander. *The Gulag Archipelago, 1918–1956: An Experiment in Literary Investigation*. Abridged edition. New York: Harper & Row, 1985.

Sproat, John. "Blueprint for Radical Reconstruction." *Journal of Southern History* 23 (1957): 25–44.

Stahr, Walter. *Seward: Lincoln's Indispensable Man*. New York: Simon & Schuster, 2012.

Stampp, Kenneth. *America in 1857: A Nation on the Brink*. New York: Oxford University Press, 1990.

———. *Indiana Politics During the Civil War*. Indianapolis: Indiana Historical Research Bureau, 1949.

Stanton, William H. *A Book Called Our Ancestors: The Stantons*. Philadelphia: Privately printed, 1922.

Stauffer, John. *Giants: The Parallel Lives of Frederick Douglass and Abraham Lincoln*. New York: Twelve, 2008.

Steers, Edward, Jr. *Blood on the Moon: The Assassination of Abraham Lincoln*. Lexington: University of Kentucky Press, 2001.

———. *Lincoln's Assassination*. Carbondale: Southern Illinois University Press, 2014.

———. "A Missed Opportunity: Bill O'Reilly's *Killing Lincoln*." *North & South*, Nov. 2011, online.

————, ed. *The Trial: The Assassination of President Lincoln and the Trial of the Conspirators*. Lexington: University of Kentucky Press, 2003.

————. "Why Was Lincoln Murdered?" In Harold Holzer and Sara Gabbard, eds., *1865: America Makes War and Peace in Lincoln's Final Year*. Carbondale: Southern Illinois University Press, 2015, 81–100.

Stewart, David O. *Impeached: The Trial of Andrew Johnson and the Fight for Lincoln's Legacy*. New York: Simon & Schuster, 2009.

Stiles, T. J. *The First Tycoon: The Epic Life of Cornelius Vanderbilt*. New York: Knopf, 2009.

Storey, Moorfield. "Dickens, Stanton, Sumner and Storey." *Atlantic Monthly* 145 (1930): 463–65.

Summers, Mark. *The Ordeal of the Reunion: A New History of Reconstruction*. Chapel Hill: University of North Carolina Press, 2014.

————. *The Plundering Generation: Corruption and the Crisis of the Union, 1849–1861*. New York: Oxford University Press, 1987.

Swanberg, W. A. "Was the Secretary of War a Traitor?" *American Heritage* 14 (Feb. 1963): 34–37, 96–97.

Swanson, James. *Bloody Crimes: The Chase for Jefferson Davis and the Death Pageant for Lincoln's Corpse*. New York: William Morrow, 2010.

————. *Manhunt: The 12-Day Chase for Lincoln's Killer*. New York: William Morrow, 2006.

Sword, Wiley. *Mountains Touched with Fire: Chattanooga Besieged, 1863*. New York: St. Martin's Press, 1995.

Symonds, Craig. *Lincoln and His Admirals: Abraham Lincoln, the U.S. Navy, and the Civil War*. New York: Oxford University Press, 2008.

Syrett, John. *The Civil War Confiscation Acts: Failing to Reconstruct the South*. New York: Fordham University Press, 2011.

Taft, Charles. "Abraham Lincoln's Last Hours." *Century Magazine* 45 (Feb. 1893): 634–36.

Taliaferro, John. *All the Great Prizes: The Life of John Hay, from Lincoln to Roosevelt*. New York: Simon & Schuster, 2013.

Taniguchi, Nancy. *Dirty Deeds: Land, Violence, and the 1856 San Francisco Vigilance Committee*. Norman: University of Oklahoma Press, 2016.

Tanner, James. *While Lincoln Lay Dying*. Philadelphia: Union League of Philadelphia, 1968.

Tap, Bruce. *Over Lincoln's Shoulder: The Committee on the Conduct of the War*. Lawrence: University Press of Kansas, 1998.

————. "Race, Rhetoric, and Emancipation: The Election of 1862 in Illinois." *Civil War History* 39 (1993): 102–25.

Tenney, Craig. "To Suppress or Not to Suppress: Lincoln and the Chicago *Times*." *Civil War History* 27 (1981): 247–59.

Thayer, John. "A Night with Stanton in the War Office." *McClure's Magazine* 8 (Mar. 1897): 438–42.

Thomas, Benjamin, and Harold Hyman. *Stanton: The Life and Times of Lincoln's Secretary of War*. New York: Knopf, 1962.

Tidwell, William A., James O. Hall, and David Gaddy. *Come Retribution: The Confederate Secret Service and the Assassination of Lincoln*. Jackson: University Press of Mississippi, 1988.

Tomalin, Claire. *Charles Dickens: A Life*. New York: Penguin Press, 2011.

Towne, Stephen. "Killing the Serpent Speedily: Governor Morton, General Hascall, and the Suppression of the Democratic Press in Indiana, 1863." *Civil War History* 52 (2006): 41–65.

Townsend, Edward. *Anecdotes of the Civil War in the United States*. New York: D. Appleton, 1884.

Trefousse, Hans L. *Andrew Johnson: A Biography*. New York: Norton, 1989.

———. *Carl Schurz: A Biography*. 2d ed. New York: Fordham University Press, 1998.

Trollope, Anthony. *North America*. 2 vols. Philadelphia: J. B. Lippincott & Co., 1862.

Trudeau, Noah. *Like Men of War: Black Troops in the Civil War, 1862–1865*. Boston: Little, Brown, 1998.

———. *Southern Storm: Sherman's March to the Sea*. New York: Harper, 2008.

Turner, George. *Victory Rode the Rails: The Strategic Place of Railroads in the Civil War*. Indianapolis: Bobbs, Merrill, 1953.

Turner, Thomas R. *Beware the People Weeping: Public Opinion and the Assassination of Abraham Lincoln*. Baton Rouge: Louisiana State University Press, 1982.

U.S. Census Bureau. *Historical Statistics of the United States, 1789–1945*. Washington, D.C.: Government Printing Office, 1949.

Van Tine, Warren, and Michael Pierce, eds. *Builders of Ohio: A Biographical History*. Columbus: Ohio State University Press, 2003.

Viele, Egbert. "A Trip with Lincoln, Chase and Stanton." *Scribner's Monthly* 16 (Oct. 1878): 813–22.

Voegeli, V. Jacques. *Free but Not Equal: The Midwest and the Negro during the Civil War*. Chicago: University of Chicago Press, 1967.

Von Drehle, David. *Rise to Greatness: Abraham Lincoln and America's Most Perilous Year*. New York: Henry Holt, 2012.

Wagstaff, Thomas. "The Arm-in-Arm Convention." *Civil War History* 14 (June 1968): 101–19.

Walters, Kerry. *Outbreak in Washington, D.C.: The Strange Mystery of the National Hotel Disease*. Washington, D.C.: History Press, 2014.

Warshauer, Matthew. *Connecticut in the American Civil War: Slavery, Sacrifice, and Survival*. Middletown, Conn.: Wesleyan University Press, 2011.

Waugh, John. *Lincoln and McClellan: The Troubled Partnership*. New York: Palgrave & Macmillan, 2010.

———. *Reelecting Lincoln: The Battle for the 1864 Presidency*. New York: Crown, 1997.

Weber, Jennifer. *Copperheads: The Rise and Fall of Lincoln's Opponents in the North*. New York: Oxford University Press, 2006.

Weisenburger, Francis. *The Passing of the Frontier, 1825–1850*. Columbus: Ohio Historical Society, 1941.

Welles, Gideon. "The History of Emancipation." *Galaxy* 14 (Dec. 1872): 838–52.

———. "Lincoln and Johnson." *Galaxy* 13 (Apr. 1872): 521–33.

Wert, Jeffry D. *The Sword of Lincoln: The Army of the Potomac*. New York: Simon & Schuster, 2005.

Westwood, Howard C. *Black Troops, White Commanders, and Freedmen During the Civil War*. Carbondale: Southern Illinois University Press, 1992.

———. "Generals David Hunter and Rufus Saxton and Black Soldiers." *South Carolina Historical Magazine* 86 (1985): 165–81.

Whalen, Charles, and Barbara Whalen. *The Fighting McCooks: America's Famous Fighting Family*. Bethesda, Md.: Westmoreland Press, 2006.

Wheelan, Joseph. *Terrible Swift Sword: The Life of General Philip Sheridan*. New York: Da Capo Press, 2012.

Wheeler, Kenneth. "The Antebellum College in the Old Northwest: Higher Education and the Defining of the Midwest." Ph.D. diss., Ohio State University, 1999.

———. "Philander Chase and College Building in Ohio." In Warren Tyne and Michael Pierce, eds., *Builders of Ohio: A Biographical History*. Columbus: Ohio State University Press, 2003, 72–84.

Wheeler, Tom. *Mr. Lincoln's T-mails: The Untold Story of How Abraham Lincoln Used the Telegraph to Win the Civil War*. New York: HarperCollins, 2006.

White, Barbara. *The Beecher Sisters*. New Haven: Yale University Press, 2003.

White, Jonathan. *Abraham Lincoln and Treason in the Civil War: The Trials of John Merryman*. Baton Rouge: Louisiana State University Press, 2011.

———. "Canvassing the Troops: The Federal Government and the Soldiers' Right to Vote." *Civil War History* 50 (2004): 291–317.

———. *Emancipation, the Union Army, and the Reelection of Abraham Lincoln*. Baton Rouge: Louisiana State University Press, 2014.

White, Ronald. *American Ulysses: A Life of Ulysses S. Grant*. New York: Random House, 2016.

Wilentz, Sean. *The Rise of American Democracy: Jefferson to Lincoln*. New York: Norton, 2005.

Williams, Jeffrey. *Religion and Violence in Early American Methodism: Taking the Kingdom by Force*. Bloomington: Indiana University Press, 2010.

Williams, Frank. "Military Justice, Right or Wrong: Judging the Lincoln Conspirators." In Harold Holzer and Sara Gabbard, eds., *1865: America Makes War and Peace in Lincoln's Final Year*. Carbondale: Southern Illinois University Press, 2015, 100–112.

Wilson, Henry. "Edwin M. Stanton." *Atlantic Monthly* 25 (Feb. 1870): 234–46.

———. "Jeremiah S. Black and Edwin M. Stanton." *Atlantic Monthly* 26 (Oct. 1870): 463–76.

Wilson, James H. *The Life of Charles A. Dana*. New York: Harper & Brothers, 1907.

Wilson, Mark. R. *The Business of Civil War: Military Mobilization and the State, 1861–1865*. Baltimore: Johns Hopkins University Press, 2006.

Winik, Jay. *April 1865: The Month That Saved America*. New York: HarperCollins, 2001.

Wing, Henry. *When Lincoln Kissed Me: A Story of the Wilderness Campaign*. New York: Eaton & Mains, 1913.

Winkle, Kenneth J. *Lincoln's Citadel: The Civil War in Washington, D.C.* New York: Norton, 2013.

———. *The Politics of Community: Migration and Politics in Antebellum Ohio*. Cambridge, U.K.: Cambridge University Press, 1988.

Winther, Oscar. "The Soldier Vote in the Election of 1864." *New York History* 25 (1944): 440–58.

Witt, John F. *Lincoln's Code: The Laws of War in American History*. New York: Free Press, 2012.

Wittenberg, Eric. *Like a Meteor Blazing Brightly: The Short but Controversial Life of Colonel Ulric Dahlgren*. Roseville, Minn.: Edinborough Press, 2009.

———. *One Continuous Fight: The Retreat from Gettysburg and the Pursuit of Lee's Army of Northern Virginia*. New York: Savas Beatie, 2008.

Work, David. *Lincoln's Political Generals*. Urbana: University of Illinois Press, 2009.

Zuczak, Richard. *State of Rebellion: Reconstruction in South Carolina*. Columbia: University of South Carolina Press, 1996.

Illustration Credits

All images are from the collection of the Library of Congress except the following:

Page 12: Kenyon College, Greenslade Special Collections and Archives.

Page 15: Columbus Metropolitan Library.

Page 19: Public Library of Steubenville and Jefferson County.

Page 48: Carnegie Library of Pittsburgh.

Page 57: George Gorham, *The Life and Public Services of Edwin Stanton* (Boston: Houghton Mifflin, 1899), 1:34.

Page 61: University of Michigan Special Collections.

Page 62: Wheeling & Belmont Bridge Company's printed argument before the Supreme Court, online.

Page 94: *Harper's Weekly*, March 12, 1859.

Page 98: *Harper's Weekly*, April 9, 1859.

Page 101: George Gorham, *The Life and Public Services of Edwin Stanton* (Boston: Houghton, Mifflin, 1899), 1:188.

Page 161: David Homer Bates, *Lincoln in the Telegraph Office: Recollections of the United States Military Telegraph Corps During the Civil War* (New York: Century, 1907), 147.

Page 163: Railroad Museum of Pennsylvania.

Page 195: Special Collections, Fine Arts Library, Harvard University.

Page 199: *Vanity Fair*, May 31, 1862.

Page 232: The New-York Historical Society.

Page 366: *New York Times*, September 3, 1864.

Page 450: Surratt House Museum.

Page 468: *Harper's Weekly*, April 14, 1866.

Page 476: Special Collections, Fine Arts Library, Harvard University.

Page 497: National Archives and Records Administration.

Index

Page numbers in *italics* refer to illustrations. Page numbers beginning with 549 refer to notes.

About the Author

Walter Stahr is the author of the *New York Times* bestseller *Seward: Lincoln's Indispensable Man* and *John Jay: Founding Father*, a biography of America's first Supreme Court Chief Justice. A graduate of Stanford University and Harvard Law School, he practiced international law for twenty-five years, including seven years in Hong Kong and five years with the Securities & Exchange Commission in Washington. He lives in Newport Beach, California. Visit him at walterstahr.com.